DYSLEXIA
An Appraisal of
Current Knowledge

DYSLEXIA

An Appraisal of
Current Knowledge

EDITED BY

Arthur L. Benton, Ph.D.
UNIVERSITY OF IOWA

David Pearl, Ph.D.
NATIONAL INSTITUTE OF MENTAL HEALTH

New York
OXFORD UNIVERSITY PRESS

First published by Oxford University Press, New York, 1978
First issued as an Oxford University Press paperback, 1979

Printed in the United States of America

LIBRARY OF CONGRESS CATALOGING IN PUBLICATION DATA

National Institute of Mental Health Conference on Dys-
   lexia, Rockville, Md., 1977.
   Dyslexia
   "Volume results from a National Institute of Mental
Health Conference on Dyslexia, March 7 and 8, 1977."
   Bibliography: p.
   Includes index.
   1. Dyslexia—Congresses.   I. Benton, Arthur Lester,
1909–   II. Pearl, David, 1921–   III. United
States. National Institute of Mental Health.   IV. Ti-
tle. [DNLM: 1. Dyslexia—Congresses.   WM475.3 N277d
1977]
RJ496.A5N37   1977   616.8'553   78–3483

ISBN 0–19–502384–6

ISBN 0–19–502710–8 pbk.

Foreword

Severe reading disability is recognized today as a major social, educational, and mental health problem. Beyond the overall academic learning problems engendered for children, reading difficulties loom large as stressful factors which produce emotional distress and many mental health casualties. The school-age experience is vital in the shaping of the child's self-concept and his interpersonal skills. It also affects how he learns to cope with the myriad of situations and problems he encounters. Children unable to read adequately increasingly become subjected to academic failure and are apt to experience frustration, embarrassment, and devaluation by self as well as by others. Many reactively respond with withdrawal or aggressiveness and erratic behaviors, further assuring interpersonal rejection and increasing the child's sense of interpersonal isolation.

Persistence of reading difficulties into late childhood and adolescence thus is likely to result in serious emotional and behavioral problems. Many of the children seen in mental health centers and clinics because of disturbed or disturbing behavior have such a background. Moreover, reading disorders have been reported as being the major single cause of the 700,000 yearly school drop-outs in this country. Over 75 percent of juvenile delinquents also have a prior history of reading failures.

A large number of children are poor readers because of interference with the learning process by adverse environmental factors and because of ineffective teaching. But there are many children of average or better intellectual and physical status who, though they have adequate environmental and educational opportunity, are yet severely disabled readers. These children are referred to as having specific reading disabilities or as being dyslexics. They have especially attracted attention from educators, clinicians, and scientists because no sufficiently convincing explanations of dyslexia have yet emerged which would provide a rational basis for prevention or remediation. Esimates of their number vary considerably and range up to 10–15 percent of all school children. It is this group with which this book is primarily concerned.

The National Institute of Mental Health (NIMH) planned and sponsored the research conference (March 7 and 8, 1977) for which the chapters in this book were written. As Director of NIMH at that time, I strongly supported this project. The Institute's role in the prevention of emotional, personality, and adaptive disorders in children necessarily includes a specific concern with research on the etiology, prevention, and treatment of developmental dyslexia.

The conference was an outgrowth of an earlier advisory workshop which was convened to advise the Institute on the current status of theory and research on dyslexia (including major problems), on next steps in research and development, and the specific role which NIMH should play in these activities. The workshop consensus noted that although dyslexia is a multifaceted, interdisciplinary problem, there has been insufficient interdisciplinary communication and research by investigators from such disciplines as psychology and psychiatry, education, neurology, and genetics. Comparability and cumulativeness of research findings therefore are uncertain and the validity of much presumed knowledge concerning dyslexia and its application to diagnostic procedures and to preventive and remedial interventions is open to question. The Institute was urged to take the initiative in catalyzing and promoting a comprehensive and critical review of the scientific literature relating to the various facets of dyslexia which could serve as a base for future research and for a rational examination of educational and clinical practices with dyslexic children. The chapters of this volume are the results of that recommendation.

Leading investigators were commissioned to examine critically the scientific literature on dyslexia in various research areas and to write comprehensive state-of-art syntheses. To insure comprehensiveness and balance, each of these state-of-knowledge evaluations was independently assessed by two other prominent researchers who were requested to provide needed amplification, addition, or corrective comment in their critical review papers when they viewed these as justified.

I am very pleased with the comprehensiveness and quality of these research overviews on dyslexia and its facets. They provide a balanced consideration of what we know about dyslexia, major issues and needed research, and what are promising directions for future study. I hope and expect that this volume will be broadly useful to researchers and practitioners and in varying degrees will provide helpful information and guidance to the teacher, psychologist, psychiatrist, pediatrician, neurologist, and all others concerned with the dyslexic child.

BERTRAM S. BROWN, M.D.

Acknowledgments

We wish to acknowledge with thanks the permission of the following journals, authors, or publishers for use of excerpts as indicated:

The editors of *Child Development* for use of Figure 4-1 and the editor of *Cortex* for use of Figure 4-2 appearing in chapter "Toward an Understanding of Dyslexia: Psychological Factors in Specific Reading Disability" by Frank R. Vellutino.

R. Beecher and N. Goldfluss, for use of Tables 17-1 and 17-2, appearing in chapter "Prevention" by Archie Silver.

George Allen & Unwin, Ltd., London, for use of Figure 13-1—Waddington's epigenetic landscape from C. H. Waddington, *The Strategy of Genes,* 1957, appearing in chapter "Dyslexia—Genetic Aspects" by Freya W. Owen.

The chapter entitled "Toward an Understanding of Dyslexia: Psychological Factors in Specific Reading Disability" by Frank R. Vellutino is to appear in an expanded version to be published in 1978 by the M.I.T. Press.

The Victoria studies referred to in the chapter "The Dyslexias: A Discussion of Neurobehavioral Research" by Otfried Spreen were supported by grants from the Department of Health and Welfare, Canada, and the Medical Research Council of Canada.

The author's studies referred to in the chapter "Directions of Neurobehavioral Research," by Robert M. Knights, were supported by the Ontario Ministry of Education Grants-in-Aid.

The author's longitudinal study referred to in the chapter "Some Developmental and Predictive Precursors of Reading Disability" by Paul Satz, was supported by a grant from the National Institute of Mental Health (HEW) (MH-19415).

The contributions of Rosa A. Hagin, a collaborator of many years, to the thinking embodied in his chapter "Prevention" is acknowledged by Archie Silver.

Freya W. Owen acknowledges indebtedness to Professors Alberta Siegel and Joshua Lederberg of the Stanford University School of Medicine for advice relating to her chapter "Dyslexia—Genetic Aspects."

The editors are indebted to Muriel F. Smith for her assistance in all phases of the NIMH Conference and in the preparation of this volume. They thank Trudie Pearl for help in the preparation of the bibliography.

A.L.B.
D.P.

Contents

PART VIII.   INTEGRATIVE SUMMARY

Contributors

Arthur L. Benton, Ph.D.
Departments of Neurology and Psychology
University of Iowa
Iowa City, Iowa   52242

Marion Blank, Ph.D.
College of Medicine & Dentistry of New Jersey
Rutgers Medical School
Department of Psychiatry
Piscataway, New Jersey   08854

Barton Childs, M.D.
Department of Pediatrics
Johns Hopkins University School of Medicine and John F. Kennedy Institute
Baltimore, Maryland   21205

C. Keith Connors, Ph.D.
Department of Psychiatry
University of Pittsburgh and Western Psychiatric Institute & Clinic
Pittsburgh, Pennsylvania   15261

Martha Bridge Denckla, M.D.
Learning Disabilities Clinic
Children's Hospital Medical Center
Boston, Massachusetts   02115

Donald G. Doehring, Ph.D.
School of Human Communication Disorders
McGill University
Montreal, Quebec, Canada   H3G 1A8

Leon Eisenberg, M.D.
Department of Psychiatry
Harvard Medical School and Children's Hospital Medical Center
Boston, Massachusetts   02215

John T. Guthrie, Ph.D.
International Reading Association
Newark, Delaware   19711

John R. Hughes, D.M., M.D., Ph.D.
Department of Neurology
Abraham Lincoln School of Medicine
University of Illinois
Chicago, Illinois   60680

Jeannette Jefferson Jansky, Ph.D.
Robinson Reading Clinic
Department of Pediatric Psychiatry
Babies Hospital, Columbia Presbyterian Medical Center
New York, N.Y.   10032

Doris Johnson, Ph.D.
Learning Disabilities Program
Northwestern University
Evanston, Illinois   60201

Robert M. Knights, Ph.D.
Department of Psychology
Carleton University
Ottawa, Canada   K1S 5B6

Steven Mattis, Ph.D.
Department of Neurology
Montefiore Hospital & Medical Center
Bronx, New York   10467

Gerald E. McClearn, Ph.D.
Institute for Behavioral Genetics
University of Colorado
Boulder, Colorado   80302

Freya W. Owen, Ph.D.
Palo Alto Unified School District and Stanford University
Palo Alto, California   94303

Byron P. Rourke, Ph.D.
Department of Psychology
University of Windsor and Windsor Western Hospital Center
Windsor, Ontario, Canada   N9B 3P4

Michael Rutter, M.D.
Department of Child & Adolescent Psychiatry
Institute of Psychiatry, de Crespigny Park
Denmark Hill
London SE5 8AF, England

Paul Satz, Ph.D.
Department of Clinical Psychology
University of Florida
Gainesville, Florida   32610

Archie A. Silver, M.D.
Department of Psychiatry
Learning Disorder Unit
New York University Medical Center
New York, N.Y. 10016

Otfried Spreen, Ph.D.
Department of Psychology
University of Victoria
Victoria, British Columbia V8W 2Y2
Canada

Frank R. Vellutino, Ph.D.
Child Research and Study Center
Albany Medical College and State University of New York at Albany
Albany, New York 12222

Naomi Zigmond, Ph.D.
Department of Special Education
University of Pittsburgh
Pittsburgh, Pennsylvania 15260

DYSLEXIA
An Appraisal of
Current Knowledge

Part I

NATURE AND PREVALENCE

Chapter 1

PREVALENCE AND
TYPES OF DYSLEXIA

MICHAEL RUTTER

The literature on reading difficulties is full of heated exchange about whether or not dyslexia exists (cf. Downing and Brown, 1967; Franklin, 1962). Much of the argumentation has been more emotional than scientific and demarcation disputes between medical people and educationalists have undoubtedly introduced both bias and passion into the controversy (cf. Reid, 1969; Rutter, 1969). We need not concern ourselves with these aspects of the literature. Nevertheless, it is not possible to discuss the prevalence and types of dyslexia without first considering what is meant by the term. To what condition or group of conditions is the diagnosis of "dyslexia" applied? In this connection, some caution is required. Two influential government committees in Britain concluded, on the basis of a consideration of scientific evidence and educational practice, that the term "dyslexia" is not susceptible to precise operational definition and serves little useful purpose (Department of Education and Science, 1972 and 1975). Moreover, Benton's (1975) excellent critical review of the topic has emphasized that dyslexia is essentially a diagnosis by exclusion and that the presumption of a neurological basis is just that—namely a presumption. We should not presuppose either the existence of any particular condition or the scientific value of the concept. Both require critical examination in the light of empirical research findings.

In order to conduct this examination it is necessary to start by asking how and why the term came into existence, and what criteria are currently used to define the hypothesized condition. Critchley (1970) has described how, about the turn of the century, several clinicians noted cases in which severe persistent reading and spelling difficulties occurred in people of normal intelligence. As far as could be determined, the reading problems were not due to psychiatric disorder, social disadvantage, or lack of schooling. It was suggested that the condition had its origin in some form of intrinsic biological defect or deficit. Over the years a variety of terms (word blindness, strepphosymbolia, etc.) have been employed but "dyslexia" or "specific developmental dyslexia" has now replaced the others and is generally accepted.

The existence of children with the problems described by these early workers has been documented so many times both in clinical practice and through systematic research (Benton, 1975; Critchley, 1970; Money, 1962; Naidoo, 1972; Rutter and Yule, 1973) that it is unnecessary to review the evidence here. It is only the concepts which arise from the observations which are controversial. Two main hypotheses form the basis of most current notions of dyslexia. First, there is the view that difficulties in reading have many causes and encompass a variety of syndromes. Second, there is the suggestion that within the broader group of reading disabilities there are disorders due to some form of inherent biological deficit which is constitutional (i.e., intrinsic to the child) and probably usually genetic in origin. A third hypothesis is often added: that this supposed constitutional disorder constitutes a unitary condition or single disease.

DIFFERENT CAUSES OF
READING DIFFICULTY

These hypotheses may be considered in turn. The first hypothesis provides no problem. Reading is a complex skill which involves a number of rather different components and it is not surprising that reading difficulties may arise when any of these components are impaired in one way or another. Thus, reading is a perceptual task in that the reader must be able to make quite fine perceptual discriminations involving closure (e.g., between O and C), line-to-curve transformations (e.g., between U and V), and rotational transformations (e.g., b and d, or M and W). Although the precise skills which underlie these discriminations remain uncertain (Bryant, 1975), the perceptual capacities required for reading follow a regular developmental course (Gibson, 1965). Sequencing abilities are also needed in that it is essential to recognize that "dog" is not the same as "god," nor does "man hit cat" have the same meaning as "cat hit man." Processes of translating information from one sensory modality to another are also involved. Thus, writing to dictation requires auditory input to be translated into visual symbols, and reading aloud from Braille means that tactile impressions are being used to provide a verbal output. However, most of all, reading is a linguistic skill which requires the understanding of a code of visual symbols used to convey meaning. A child who can read mechanically but who does not comprehend what he has read has not yet mastered what reading is all about. Reading, as much as speech, is essentially a language code utilized for communication between people.

Learning to read is also, of course, a specific example of a learning task. As such, success is based in part on general cognitive skills. Thus, reading attainment correlates about +0.6 with IQ (Yule et al., 1974; Weinberg et al., 1974). However, as with other forms of learning, learning to read also requires motivation and task involvement. Learning strategies also may improve or impede the learning process. How quickly a child acquires reading skills will be determined by the learning opportunities open to him. These will be influenced by his family and sociocultural circumstances. Finally, insofar as reading is a taught skill, the quantity and quality of instruction in reading will also be important. Children who lack schooling are impaired in their cognitive development; reading skills also vary with the quality of education provided (Rutter and Madge, 1976).

Because reading is a highly complex activity which utilizes a great number of skills (Maliphant et al., 1974), it has not proved easy to determine the relative importance of each skill in either reading competence or reading difficulties. Nevertheless, there is good evidence that problems in learning to read can arise in a number of different ways. One way of examining this matter is to determine the frequency of reading difficulties in children with different sorts of specific handicap. Thus, the importance of speech and language skills was shown by the Edinburgh follow-up of children with speech delay (Mason, 1976; Ingram, 1970). Two years after starting school a third of the speech-retarded children were backward in reading and spelling compared with about 1 in 20 controls. The reading difficulties occurred both in children with a true delay in spoken language and in those with only an articulation defect.

In contrast, visuospatial skills appear rather less important. Robinson and Schwartz (1973) followed 41 children identified as having defects in visual perception and/or visuomotor coordination at age five to six years. Three years later the children showed no more reading difficulties than did a matched control group without visuospatial difficulties. The same result comes from a consideration of people with Turner's syndrome (Money, 1973). Although they characteristically have severe visuospatial difficulties, these are

7

not accompanied by problems in reading (Alexander and Money, 1965). A variety of other studies have also shown that visual-perceptual difficulties, although associated to some extent with reading difficulties in younger children, are not particularly important correlates of severe and persistent reading difficulties (see Rutter and Yule, 1973). At first sight this seems surprising, as reading so obviously requires perceptual discriminations. Several possible explanations may be suggested. First, the level of visual discrimination required in reading may be below that usually found in older children with visuospatial defects. That is, although they are perceptually impaired compared with their peers, they still have sufficient skills in discrimination to learn to read. If this is so it would be expected that visuospatial defects should be more important causes of reading impairment in very young children. There is limited evidence that this may be so (Rutter and Yule, 1973; Satz, Rardin, and Ross, 1971). Secondly, it is apparent that good readers do not discriminate each individual word when reading. Rather, they scan the text for key words, placing more reliance on context and meaning than on examination of sentences word-by-word by means of a sequential perception of each visual stimulus (Hochberg, 1970; Maliphant, et al., 1974; Willows, 1974).

✳ There is an association between patterns of eye movement and reading skills (Rutter and Yule, 1973; Heiman and Ross, 1974), but the evidence suggests that it is not a simple cause-and-effect relationship. With rare exceptions, an impaired control of eye movements does not interfere substantially with reading. Presumably, the degree of eye movement control needed for reading is not great.

In an epidemiologically based sample of backward readers having IQs of 80 or higher, Birch and Belmont (1964) found that poor readers did less well than controls on a task requiring the matching of an auditory tap pattern to a visual dot pattern. They suggested that a defect in cross-modal integration might be one important factor contributing to reading disability. It was further shown that skills in audiovisual integration were correlated with reading ability in the normal population (Birch and Belmont, 1965; Kahn and Birch, 1968). These findings have been broadly confirmed in a variety of other studies (see reviews by Benton, 1975 and Rutter and Yule, 1973), but there is considerable doubt as to whether cross-modal sensory transfer is the crucial element.

Most of the studies did not differentiate perceptual discriminations *within* sensory modalities from those *across* modalities, nor did they differentiate temporal-spatial integration from cross-modal integration (Bryant,

1975). When appropriate controls are introduced (cf. Blank and Bridger, 1966; Blank et al., 1968; Bryden, 1972) the results suggest that poor reading is associated with a variety of difficulties in perceptual linking (possibly due to a difficulty in verbal coding), rather than being specifically associated with either cross-modal transfer or temporospatial coordination.

Several studies have indicated that poor readers often have difficulties in the perception of temporal- or spatial-order sequences (Bakker, 1967, 1972; Doehring, 1968; Hayes, 1975). However, children can be taught to some extent to improve their sequencing (Cashdan, 1970; Hayes, 1975). Also, the sequencing deficit in poor readers is most marked when the test stimuli approximate closely to letters and words. It appears that the sequencing skills vary according to the ease or difficulty with which the stimuli can be labeled (Hayes, 1975), suggesting again that poor reading is often related to language difficulties.

⭐ It is commonly supposed that left-handedness, left-eyedness, or mixed laterality are important causes or correlates of reading difficulties. However, all epidemiologically based studies have shown this to be a mistaken notion and it may be concluded that reading difficulties are not usually associated with any particular pattern of handedness, eyedness, or footedness (Belmont and Birch, 1965; Malmquist, 1958; Clark, 1970; Rutter, Tizard, and Whitmore, 1970; Douglas et al., 1967; Helveston et al., 1970). On the other hand, *confusion* between right and left is associated with reading difficulties (Rutter, Tizard, and Whitmore, 1970). It is also possible that a *delay* in the acquisition of left-hemisphere dominance may be associated with some cases of reading difficulty, although the evidence on this point remains inconclusive (Benton, 1975).

The importance of general intelligence in learning to read is shown by Butler's (1971) finding (see also Rutter et al., 1976) that an overall IQ score at age five predicted reading at age seven better than a psychological battery designed to identify children with specific disabilities. Similarly, Bax and Whitmore (1973) found that a high frequency of neurodevelopmental difficulties at the time of school entry was associated with a much increased risk of both reading and behavioral difficulties. The relative importance of different types of neurodevelopmental abnormality was not examined.

⭐ Numerous studies have shown that children with cerebral palsy show a high rate of reading problems (Rutter, Graham, and Yule, 1970). Seidel et al. (1975) have recently demonstrated that this is so even in cerebral palsied children of normal intelligence. Brain damage incurred at an early stage

9

of development may markedly impede the acquisition of reading skills even when overall IQ is normal. Chronic physical handicaps which do not involve brain pathology have much less impact on scholastic attainment, although there is some effect (Rutter, Tizard, and Whitmore, 1970; Rutter and Yule, 1973).

Follow-up studies of children of low birthweight have shown that a disproportionate number are intellectually backward (Birch and Gussow, 1970), but the association with reading difficulties appears less strong (Barker and Edwards, 1967; Davie, Butler, and Goldstein, 1972). Overall, the findings suggest a weak, but possibly meaningful, association between low birthweight and reading difficulties (Rutter and Yule, 1973).

Although EEG abnormalities are probably somewhat increased in frequency in children with reading difficulties, perhaps especially so in those with poor attainment in other subjects as well (Ingram et al., 1970), most reading-retarded children have a normal EEG, and electroencephalographic abnormalities provide a very poor guide to a child's reading skills (Benton, 1975; Hughes, 1968, 1971; Rutter and Yule, 1973). On the other hand, preliminary findings using computer analysis of the EEG have shown that poor readers have greater power spectra than good readers in the eye-open condition (Maxwell et al., 1974). This, together with factor analytic findings (Maxwell, 1972) which showed higher loadings on a general factor and a missing verbal factor in poor readers, has been used to argue for less efficient brain functioning in poor readers (Maxwell et al., 1974). The observation has no direct clinical relevance at the moment but should be productive of further research into the links between cognitive functioning and physiological brain activity. The same applies to the evidence suggesting that reading difficulties may be associated with "poor spatial organization" of the EEG (Fenelon et al., 1972) weaker expectancy waves (Fenelon, 1968), or differences in the cortical-visual evoked response (Conners, 1971).

Temperamental attributes have been found to be quite strongly associated with reading difficulties. Epidemiological inquiries in Britain (Rutter, Tizard, and Whitmore, 1970) and Scandinavia (Malmquist, 1958) have shown that children with reading difficulties are much more likely than other children to show poor concentration—even on tasks not involving reading. De Hirsch et al. (1966) found that "hyperactive, distractive, impulsive, and disinhibited" characteristics were associated with poor reading in a predictive study; Kagan (1965) found that six-year-old children who were impulsive and quick to jump to conclusions read less well than reflective, more deliberate children; and Feshbach et al. (1973) noted that teachers' ratings of children's behavior in their first year at school were the strongest predictors of reading skills one year later. These traits are to some extent modifiable, and some studies of training suggest that the learning of reading is impaired in impulsive children not so much by their too rapid responses, as by their poor learning strategies (Egeland, 1974).

Many investigations have shown that low socioeconomic status and large family size tend to be associated with both low verbal intelligence and poor reading attainment (Rutter and Madge, 1976). In fact, apart from IQ, social class and birth order are much the strongest correlates of reading attainment (Davie et al., 1972). A detailed consideration of the evidence suggests that the associations reflect both genetic and environmental influences (Rutter and Madge, 1976).

✗ Finally, it is known that children's reading attainment varies according to the area of the country in which they live, the amount of interest their parents take in academic matters, and the schools that they attend (Rutter and Yule, 1973). Thus, reading standards are significantly higher in Scotland than they are in England in spite of the fact that social disadvantages are more prevalent in the former area. Similarly, specific reading difficulties are more than twice as common in children living in inner London than in those with homes on the Isle of Wight, an area of small towns and countryside just off the south coast of England. Children's reading attainments also vary systematically according to the characteristics of the elementary schools they attend (Rutter et al., 1975). It might be thought that this variation could be an artefact of selective intake, but longitudinal studies indicate that children's reading skills in high school still vary according to school characteristics even after the children's level of reading attainment at the time of entering the school is taken into account (Yule and Rutter, 1976).

It is clear that a very wide range of factors are associated with reading difficulties. However, although the research findings provide valuable information on the causes and correlates of reading difficulty, they are of limited relevance to the concept of dyslexia, in that many of the investigations have been based on the implicit assumption that all reading difficulties, and indeed all learning disabilities, are of the same kind (Applebee, 1971). In short, there is ample evidence and widespread acceptance of the fact that reading difficulties can have many causes. What is more in dispute is whether this also means that there are several distinct and different syndromes of reading disability.

DIAGNOSTIC CRITERIA FOR DYSLEXIA

The second main hypothesis involves the postulate that although there are many causes of reading disability, there is one specific syndrome in which the reading difficulties are due to an intrinsic constitutional deficit, i.e., the condition of dyslexia. Broadly speaking, two research approaches have been followed in this connection. The first approach involves providing an operational definition of dyslexia and then going on to examine the characteristics of the children who fit this definition. The second approach, unlike the first, does not presuppose the existence of dyslexia but rather involves investigations to determine how the broad group of reading disabilities may best be subdivided.

The first approach is that which has been followed by many neurologists. The best example is provided by the World Federation of Neurology definition of "specific developmental dyslexia" which states that it is: "a disorder manifested by difficulty in learning to read despite conventional instruction, adequate intelligence and sociocultural opportunity. It is dependent upon fundamental cognitive disabilities which are frequently of constitutional origin" (Critchley, 1970). As a piece of logic this definition is a nonstarter. First, it merely adds confusion by begging a whole series of further questions. What is "conventional instruction"? Does this mean that dyslexia is undiagnosable in a child taught by i.t.a. (initial teaching alphabet)? What is "adequate intelligence"? Does this mean average intelligence? If it does, it implies that dyslexia cannot occur in children of below-average intelligence. Or does it mean that the IQ must be high enough for reading skills to be acquired? If so, this clause is almost redundant because reading has been taught to children of IQ 50, or occasionally even below that level. What is "sociocultural opportunity"? Is it suggested that dyslexia cannot occur in a child from a deprived background?

A negative definition of this kind not only fails to aid conceptual clarity but also implies that dyslexia cannot be diagnosed in a child from a poor or unconventional background (Reid, 1969). In short, it suggests that if all the known causes of reading disability can be ruled out, the unknown (in the form of dyslexia) should be invoked. A counsel of despair, indeed.

The latter half of the definition is a little more helpful in that it specifies the presence of "fundamental cognitive disabilities." But without further elaboration, it is too vague to be helpful in the individual child. Nevertheless, if the literature on dyslexia is consulted to add further detail to what is meant by "cognitive disabilities," it appears that the following characteristics are usually included: disorders in speech and language, clumsiness and incoordination, difficulties in the perception of space relationships, directional confusion, right–left confusion, disordered temporal orientation, difficulties in naming colors and in recognizing the meaning of pictures, and inadequate, inconsistent, or mixed cerebral dominance (Rutter, 1969). To this list is usually added severe and bizarre spelling errors and a family history of reading difficulties. The evidence on the importance of these features as correlates and causes of specific reading difficulties has been fully considered elsewhere (Benton, 1975; Rutter and Yule, 1973). The findings may be briefly summarized by stating that most of these characteristics have been shown to be important. The one exception is mixed-handedness which all epidemiological studies have shown is not a common feature (Belmont and Birch, 1965; Clark, 1970; Malmquist, 1958; Rutter, Tizard, and Whitmore, 1970). Otherwise, the characteristics supposedly associated with dyslexia have been shown to be important features in children whose reading difficulties are not explicable in terms of low intelligence.

Unfortunately this listing of features does not provide a very useful operational guide to the diagnosis of dyslexia. In the first place, the measurement of these developmental characteristics is much dependent on the child's age. In general, all the features are commoner in younger children. Youngsters who showed quite marked visuospatial problems, speech delay, or sequencing difficulties in early childhood may reveal little evidence of these disabilities by the time they reach adolescence (cf. Satz et al., 1975). The reading or spelling difficulties may continue in spite of the fact that the developmental problems on which they are based do not. In the second place, the presence of these features provides an unsatisfactory subcategorization of reading difficulties in view of the fact that, at least in early and middle childhood, most children with reading difficulties of any kind show at least one or two features. Thirdly, the presence of these features does not mean that family or school influences can be ruled out (Rutter, 1969).

The last part of the World Federation of Neurology definition specifies "frequently of constitutional origin." It is not entirely clear what this is supposed to mean. If it implies that the cognitive disabilities are often due in large part to factors within the child of some kind, then this definition certainly applies to many cases of reading difficulty. While the nature and causation of the cognitive disabilities are not known, the early history of speech and language delay in the absence of environmental deprivation suggests that, at least in a substantial minority of children, the disabilities are "constitutional." But other cases show no evidence of "constitutional" disability. The evidence for a genetic basis for reading difficulties is rather unsatisfactory, but it seems highly likely that there is an important genetic component. There is abundant evidence that reading difficulties run in families (Benton, 1975; Rutter and Yule, 1973) but this observation does not help in the differentiation between biological and social inheritance. Twin studies are more helpful in this connection. The published reports suffer from defects in definition and sampling but they all show that the concordance for reading disability is much greater in monozygotic pairs than in dizygotic pairs (Hallgren, 1950; Hermann, 1959; Bakwin, 1973). These findings suggest a genetic component, although they do not indicate what is inherited (see below for a further discussion on this point).

It must be concluded that this attempt of the World Federation of Neurology to provide an operational definition for dyslexia is unsatisfactory and unworkable. It is not that the basic notions are unsound, but rather that the definition not only falls short on logic (which would not matter very much if it worked in practice), but also fails to provide effective guidance for day-to-day clinical practice.

DIFFERENTIATION OF SYNDROMES

In considering differential diagnosis in a child presenting with low academic achievement, three basic distinctions have to be made (Rutter, 1974). First, a failure to *acquire* educational skills must be differentiated from a later *loss* of these skills which is related to failure to make scholastic progress. Although systematic comparative research is lacking, children who fall behind in their schoolwork after having mastered the basic scholastic skills almost certainly have quite a different set of problems from those of children who have failed to learn to read or to do number work from the very outset (Pearson, 1952). Later educational failure usually concerns a wide range of subjects rather than just one specific skill, and in most cases the problem concerns a lack of *utilization* of skills rather than a lack of general or specific cognitive *capacity*. As the term "dyslexia" is usually only applied to children who have failed to acquire reading skills rather than to those who have lost the skills, there will be no further discussion of the latter group.

The second distinction in differential diagnosis involves classification according to the scholastic skill involved. Most attention in published reports has been paid to reading and spelling, two skills which are very closely associated. There has also been some concern with mathematical disabilities (e.g., Cohn, 1961; Slade and Russell, 1971). Surprisingly little attention has been paid to the similarities and differences between underachievement in different subjects. The very limited available evidence suggests that arithmetical difficulties are more associated with visuospatial and parietal lobe functions (Slade and Russell, 1971; Money, 1973) in contrast to the greater link between reading skills and linguistic functions (Rutter and Yule, 1973). However, this cannot be regarded as more than a hypothesis worth testing in view of the absence of systematic studies of any large groups of children with arithmetical disability. From the point of view of the subclassification of reading disorders, interest focuses on the possibility of a difference between reading retardation which is associated with failure in mathematics or other subjects and reading failure which occurs as an isolated disability. This point is discussed further below.

The third basic distinction is that between *general* backwardness (i.e., low achievement in relation to the average for that age, but without taking IQ into account) and *specific* retardation (i.e., achievement which is low after taking both age and IQ into account). The evidence on this differentiation is discussed below. In addition, two further distinctions may also be made: reading disorders may be categorized according to the particular pattern of cognitive disability shown, or, alternatively, reading disorders may be categorized according to the supposed etiology (for example, the presence or absence of brain damage). The limited evidence on both these other differentiations is discussed below.

General reading backwardness vs. specific reading retardation

General reading backwardness refers to reading which is poor in relation to the average attainment for that age regardless of intelligence. Specific reading retardation is a term used to describe a specific disability in reading—specific in the sense that reading difficulties are not explicable in terms of the child's general intelligence (Rutter, Tizard, and Whitmore, 1970). It follows from these definitions that children backward in reading tend to be of well below average intelligence, whereas children with specific reading retardation will have a mean IQ which is roughly average for the general population. In the past there has been some skepticism about the validity of this distinction, and certainly the differentiation can only be justified if it can be shown to have practical value (Davis and Cashdan, 1963). Recent epidemiological studies in London and on the Isle of Wight have provided that evidence (Rutter and Yule, 1975).

The syndrome of specific reading retardation is defined in terms of a discrepancy between attainment as predicted on the basis of age and IQ and actual attainment as observed (see below for a discussion of measurement). On statistical grounds alone there are bound to be some children with extreme degrees of underachievement in reading, so that specific reading retardation could merely represent the lower end of a normal continuum with nothing else remarkable about the children. In fact, this is *not* the case (Yule et al., 1974). Five population studies have all shown that extreme degrees of specific reading retardation occur much more often than expected on statistical grounds. Children with the disorder form a "hump" at the bottom of the normal curve.

Other evidence from the same studies indicates that the syndrome is medically as well as statistically valid in that there are important differences between children with specific reading retardation and those with general reading backwardness (Rutter and Yule, 1975). The main differences found are as follows: (1) children with specific reading retardation are more likely to be boys (ratio of about 3 or 4 to 1), whereas the sex distribution for general reading backwardness is nearly equal; (2) overt neurological disorder was much more frequent in the generally backward group; (3) children with general reading backwardness tended to have a wide range of developmental difficulties including motor and praxic abnormalities, whereas specific reading retardation was strongly associated only with speech and language impairment; and (4) more of the generally backward children came from socially disadvantaged homes.

These differences imply that the two types of reading disability have a somewhat different origin. Findings from the same investigation showed that they also carry different educational implications (Yule, 1973). As might be expected from their superior general intelligence, the children with specific reading retardation made *more* progress in mathematics between the ages of 10 and 14 years than those with general reading backwardness. However, in spite of their better IQ level, they made significantly *less* progress in both reading and spelling.

The study by Ingram, Mason, and Blackburn (1970) also supports the validity of a distinction between specific reading retardation and backwardness in most school subjects. They found that children with a specific reading disability were *less* likely to have neurological or EEG abnormalities but *more* likely to show primitive spelling errors of audiophonic origin.

It may be concluded that the designation òf specific reading retardation not only picks out a statistically distinctive category within the broader group of poor readers but also that the diagnosis carries with it important clinical and educational implications.

Differentiation according to cognitive pattern

The distinction between specific reading retardation and general reading backwardness carries with it an associated differentiation according to cognitive pattern, as already discussed. The specific disorder is more often associated with developmental delays or deviations only in language and sequencing functions, whereas general backwardness is frequently accompanied by a wide range of deficits in language, praxic, and perceptuomotor functions. Nevertheless, specific reading retardation is not a homogeneous condition and the question arises as to whether any finer subdivision is possible.

This matter has been investigated by several groups of workers using rather different approaches. Satz, Friel, and Goebel (1975) found that psychological deficits identified in kindergarten predicted reading achievement at the end of grade 2, in spite of the fact that the deficits themselves had largely been overcome. A separate study by the same research group also showed that impaired visuomotor and auditory–visual integration was characteristic of younger dyslexic children but not older ones (Satz, Rardin, and Ross, 1971). Conversely, although language skills were somewhat impaired in dyslexic children of all ages, they were most characteristic of older dyslexics. It appears that cognitive patterns are in part a function of age and that any attempt to subdivide dyslexia according to cognitive pattern must control for age.

Naidoo (1972) used a cluster analysis technique to examine the possibility of subtypes within a clinic sample of dyslexic boys. She found some distinction between cases with language impairment and a strong family history of reading and/or speech difficulties and those with neither characteristic who had no single clear cognitive pattern. However, many boys fell in neither group, and in any case the distinction was far from clear-cut. Rutter (1969) in a general population study of 10-year-olds with severe specific reading retardation also found no clear-cut clustering of characteristics, although there was some tendency for constructional difficulties, motor incoordination, and articulation problems to intercorrelate.

The only study indicating that there may be independent psychological syndromes within the dyslexic group is that by Mattis, French, and Rapin (1975). They investigated 113 children aged 8–18 years referred to a neurological clinic for a learning or behavior disorder, with a verbal or performance IQ exceeding 80, with normal vision and hearing, without psychosis, and who had had "adequate academic exposure." Eighty-two of these 113 children were diagnosed dyslexic on the basis of reading two or more grades below age level. Fifty-three dyslexic children were further classified as "brain damaged" on the basis of history and/or examination. However, there were no significant differences between the brain-damaged and the non-brain-damaged dyslexics on any cognitive test. On the other hand, all but 3 of the 29 children in the latter (developmental dyslexic) group could be put into one of three subgroups operationally defined in terms of neuropsychological test findings. Eight children showed a language disorder, 14 showed articulatory and graphomotor dyscoordination, and 4 had a visuospatial perceptual disorder.

The findings are striking and important, but caution is required in accepting the authors' conclusion that there are three independent dyslexic syndromes. First, the results need to be replicated, particularly as other workers have failed to isolate discrete groupings. Secondly, the study was conducted with a highly selected clinic population and it remains uncertain how far this may have biased the findings. Third, the differentiation could be an artefact of age differences. While that possibility was ruled out with respect to the brain-damage vs. non-brain-damage distinction, mean ages were not reported for the three neuropsychological syndromes. The verdict so far must be "nonproven." Numerous investigations have indicated that dyslexic children can be subdivided into three groups: those with mainly language, mainly articulation, or mainly visuospatial problems. On the other hand, there has usually seemed to be appreciable overlap between groups and a sizeable proportion of children who do not fall into a definable category. The matter requires further investigation.

Differentiation according to types of spelling error

Since the very earliest papers on developmental dyslexia, there has been an emphasis on the very strong association between reading difficulties and problems in spelling (Critchley, 1970). This association has been confirmed in many systematic cross-sectional and longitudinal studies (e.g., Naidoo, 1972; Rutter, Tizard, and Whitmore, 1970; Yule, 1973). However, only relatively recently have researchers investigated the possibility of using spelling errors to subclassify within the dyslexia group. Naidoo (1972) systematically compared children with severe reading difficulties and children with severe spelling difficulties but relatively satisfactory reading (both groups were of above

average intelligence). Strikingly, the spelling attainment of the reading retardates was somewhat below their reading attainment, and their spelling was
actually worse than that of the spelling retardates. In short, when there was a
severe reading difficulty, spelling was also almost always very poor. Thus, it
is not possible to subdivide children with specific reading retardation according to the presence or absence of spelling difficulties (since they are almost
never absent).

On the other hand, there were children with marked problems in
spelling but with little or no problems in reading. Naidoo (1972) contrasted
the neuropsychological findings for this group with those for the reading retardates. The pattern was strikingly similar in both cases, although the deficits
tended to be somewhat milder in the "pure" spelling retardation group. It
may be concluded that it is likely that spelling retardation and reading retardation are usually different facets of the same group of disorders.

The satisfactory classification of spelling or reading errors has proved
quite difficult and there have been few attempts to group dyslexic children according to these characteristics. Ingram, Mason, and Blackburn (1970) differentiated between audiophonic difficulties (where there is a confusion of
sounds, as between "bun" and "but") and visuospatial difficulties (involving
confusion of letter shapes or orientation such as between *b, d,* and *p*). The
differentiation proved valid in that audiophonic errors were much more common in children with specific reading or spelling difficulties but adequate attainment in arithmetic and other school subjects, as compared with children
whose attainments were generally poor across the board. Boder's (1971) distinction between dysphonetic and dyseidetic errors is closely similar. Like Ingram, she found that the former types were most characteristic of children
with specific dyslexia. Only 9 percent showed pure dyseidetic errors, but 28
percent showed either a mixed or undetermined pattern. Marshall and Newcombe (1973) suggest distinctions between visual errors, grapheme-phone
errors, and syntactico-semantic errors. These approaches are certainly promising as a possible means of differentiating children with a specific dyslexia
from those with a more generally poor scholastic attainment. Their value as a
means of differentiating *within* the specific group has yet to be determined,
but it clearly warrants systematic study.

Differentiation according to presence or absence of brain damage
Clearly it is important to distinguish cases of dyslexia due to genetic or psychological influences from those caused by perinatal or postnatal damage to
the brain. This differentiation is often difficult in practice because of the lack

of any valid means of detecting brain damage when there is no overt neurological disease or disorder (Rutter, Graham, and Yule, 1970; Rutter, 1976). Nevertheless, the distinction is important and meaningful. Ingram et al. (1970) found that *general* reading difficulties (i.e., those associated with poor attainment in other school subjects) were more often associated with evidence of brain damage/dysfunction as indicated by birth history, developmental milestones, clinical examination, and EEG than was the case with *specific* reading or spelling difficulties. Rutter and Yule (1975) found much the same correspondence. It seems that overt damage to the brain is associated more with general scholastic difficulties than with specific dyslexia. Nevertheless, brain damage, whether resulting from perinatal complication (Rutter, Graham, and Yule, 1970; Seidal et al., 1975) or from postnatal injury (Shaffer et al., 1975), may cause specific reading and spelling difficulties in cases where there is no impairment of general intelligence. The limited available evidence suggests that in these cases the pattern of cognitive deficits is closely similar to that in cases of specific dyslexia without evidence of brain damage (Mattis, French, and Rapin, 1975).

Differentiation according to presence or absence of psychiatric disorder
Many studies of dyslexic children have excluded those with any form of emotional or behavioral disorder on the grounds that the reading problem could be different in such cases. In fact, the evidence suggests that this may not be a particularly useful differentiation. Rutter, Tizard, and Whitmore (1970), in a total population epidemiological study, showed that children with *both* specific reading retardation and antisocial behavior had more in common with children who had a "pure" reading retardation than with those who had a "pure" antisocial disorder. Thus, antisocial disorder in retarded readers was not associated with broken homes but was associated with large family size, a family history of reading difficulties, speech delay, poor right-left differentiation, and very poor concentration. Similarly, in London, Varlaam (1974) found that children with both reading and behavior difficulties tended to come from a large sibship, from an unstimulating environment, or from a West Indian family. These characteristics were associated with reading difficulties but not with behavioral problems per se, although such problems might co-exist with poor reading attainment. (Varlaam examined poor reading attainment without differentiating any subgroup with specific reading retardation or dyslexia.) Sturge's (1972) findings were in partial agreement. However, her analysis was complicated by the fact that the demarcation in her sample between the factors leading to reading retardation and those leading

to antisocial behavior was not as clear. Virkkunen and Nuutila (1976) showed that adolescent delinquents with specific reading retardation did not differ from nondelinquent reading retardates with respect to severity of reading difficulties, clumsiness, poor handwriting, or abnormal childhood conditions. However, the delinquents did differ in behavior characteristics, showing more features indicating hyperactivity and inattention.

There is a strong and well-demonstrated association between specific reading retardation and antisocial behavior. The nature of this association remains ill-understood. But it seems that it is due in part to the same temperamental attributes (impulsivity, poor attention, etc.) predisposing to both conditions; in part to psychosocial disadvantage predisposing to both, and in part to educational failure leading to discouragement, loss of self-esteem, and antagonism which may contribute to the development of delinquent activities. However, whatever the true explanation, it appears that the types of reading retardation associated with psychiatric disorder or delinquency are not basically different in kind from those occurring without the other two disorders.

Differentiation according to presence or absence of social disadvantage
It is well established that reading difficulties are more common in children from socially disadvantaged homes or from families with a large sibship (Rutter and Madge, 1976). In addition, it has been found that specific reading retardation is twice as common in London, a metropolis, as on the Isle of Wight, an area of small towns (Berger, Yule, and Rutter, 1975). Moreover, the rate of reading difficulties varied considerably from school to school in London. Specific reading retardation was considerably more frequent in schools with high rates of teacher turnover, pupil turnover, or a high population of children eligible for school meals (Rutter et al., 1975).

Thus, reading difficulties may be due to poor family circumstances or poor schooling. It would seem reasonable to exclude such cases when studying dyslexia supposedly due to constitutional influences. Nevertheless, this differentiation does not work well in practice. Of course, serious social disadvantage often leads to general backwardness rather than specific reading retardation and, for reasons already discussed, the general–specific differentiation is useful and valid. The problem arises with cases of specific reading retardation (i.e., reading greatly below that expected on the basis of the child's age and IQ) in children from disadvantaged families, schools, or geographical areas. The limited available evidence indicates that the specific reading retardation in these children shows much the same pattern (with respect to sex ratio, developmental anomalies, etc.) as that found in youngsters from middle-class or professional families (Rutter, Tizard, and Whitmore, 1970) or in those living in more prosperous areas (Rutter et al., 1975). Certainly the differentiation has been inadequately studied up to now, but the findings so far indicate that the differentiation will prove useful.

It is necessary to consider why this should be the case. The relevant data are lacking but probably there are three main reasons. First, there are no grounds for supposing that social disadvantage protects children from dyslexia. It is likely that constitutionally determined reading difficulties occur with approximately the same frequency in all social groups. Second, all studies indicate that dyslexia does not prevent children from learning to read— it just makes it more difficult for them to do so. Follow-up studies are inadequate, but it seems that although most dyslexic individuals remain poor spellers and many remain indifferent readers, the majority improve, making slow progress in their reading skills (Robinson and Smith, 1962; Silver and Hagin, 1964; Balow and Bloomquist, 1965; Rawson, 1968; Yule, 1973; Herjanic and Penick, 1972; Kline and Kline, 1975). It is highly probable, although not yet demonstrated, that children with constitutionally determined reading difficulties will make less progress if they come from a disadvantaged family and attend a poor school. Thus, although the constitutionally determined condition may occur equally often in all social groups, its overt manifestations in the form of specific reading retardation may actually be more frequent in underprivileged children. Third, the available evidence suggests that large family size (the psychosocial variable most strongly associated with specific reading retardation) leads to reading difficulties through its retarding effects on verbal and language development. This is relevant because it seems that constitutional varieties of reading difficulty are also frequently a function of impaired language and sequencing skills. It may be that the types of reading retardation due to language difficulties are broadly similar irrespective of whether the language problem is due to constitutional or environmental factors.

Whatever the validity of these suggestions, it remains the case that differentiation within the group of dyslexics according to the presence or absence of social disadvantage is not particularly useful at the present stage of knowledge.

Differentiation according to genetic background
As already indicated, there is evidence suggesting that hereditary influences play a part in the genesis of dyslexia. In itself this statement is neither very surprising nor very helpful. Almost all human attributes have a genetic com-

ponent. Of course, the extent of individual variation attributable to heredity varies considerably according to which attribute or which disorder is being considered. Unfortunately, the genetic evidence regarding dyslexia is inadequate for a judgment regarding the degree of heritability. The three main limitations are (1) selective sampling (for example Bakwin's 1973 sample contains an excess of monozygotic pairs), (2) inadequate assessment of reading or spelling skills in the co-twins or relatives of probands, and (3) the fact that assessments have not been conducted blindly.

However, even an accurate estimate of heritability for a particular population is not very helpful in itself. It is necessary to go on to determine both *what* is inherited and *how* it is inherited (i.e., polygenic, autosomal dominant, sex-linked recessive, etc.). Data are singularly lacking on both issues. It is usually assumed that dyslexia is inherited as a qualitatively distinct condition or disorder which you either have or do not have. On the other hand, it is quite possible that it is inherited as quantitative variations in a polygenically determined trait (like height and intelligence). In order to differentiate these two possibilities it is essential to determine if other family members have reading difficulties of the same or different type. Ideally there should be some kind of biological marker for this purpose, but none is available at the moment. In its absence a behavioral marker is required. Thus at the very least, families need to be studied in terms of *specific* reading or spelling retardation (i.e., reading or spelling which is markedly poor in relation to both age and IQ), and preferably with assessment of the type of cognitive deficit and/or type of reading/spelling errors. Failure to do this opens the way for all sorts of biases and misinterpretations. Thus, Hallgren (1950) came to rather firm conclusions on the mode of inheritance in spite of the fact that his affected relatives did not show the marked preponderance of males which has been typical of all studies of dyslexia—in the general population as well as in clinic groups. It must be concluded that it is highly probable that many of his supposedly affected relatives read poorly for reasons other than dyslexia.

If dyslexia reflects *quantitative* variations in a trait it would not be meaningful to make a *qualitative* differentiation of cases according to whether or not the disorder is genetically determined. If, however, a *condition* is inherited, such a distinction would be highly desirable. A positive family history of reading difficulties has usually been used for this purpose. Unfortunately, use of this criterion is unworkable in both theory and practice. It does not work in theory for two main reasons. First, as already discussed, the other family members may read poorly for reasons other than dyslexia. Second, a positive family history may reflect social inheritance (i.e., shared experiences of disadvantage or learned patterns of family interaction) rather than biological transmission. Thus, Rutter, Tizard, and Whitmore (1970) found that a positive family history was much commoner with reading retarded children from large families than with those from small families (even after taking into account the number of relatives at risk).

It does not work in practice because a positive family history is so common in nondyslexic children with other types of reading disability. For example, Ingram et al. (1970) and Rutter and Yule (1975) both found that a family history of reading difficulties or speech delay was almost as common in children with general backwardness in scholastic attainment as in those with specific reading retardation. Also, both Rutter (1969) and Naidoo (1972) found only a very weak association between a positive family history and neuropsychological dyslexia characteristics.

Further genetic research into dyslexia would be highly worthwhile, but at present the genetic data provide no usable guide to the subdivision of cases of dyslexia.

PREVALENCE

It is clear from the evidence already discussed that it is not yet possible either to define dyslexia in any acceptable way or to identify cases of dyslexia. Rather, the concept of dyslexia constitutes a hypothesis—the hypothesis that within the large overall group of disabled readers there is a subgroup with a distinct constitutionally determined condition. There can be no serious doubt that constitutional influences play an important part in the determination of some (perhaps many) cases of reading difficulty. However, it remains uncertain whether these influences interact with others in some form of multifactorial determination, or whether they lead to some qualitatively distinct condition. Until this issue is settled (by the identification of some valid biological or behavioral marker) it is meaningless to attempt any estimate of the prevalence of dyslexia.

On the other hand, meaningful estimates of the prevalence of specific reading or spelling retardation can be obtained. Such estimates must specify the severity of retardation and the age group under consideration, as both variables will markedly affect prevalence estimates. Furthermore, the assessments must be based on regression equations rather than achievement ratios (see below). The only data that meet these criteria are the British studies in inner London and on the Isle of Wight (Berger, Yule, and Rutter, 1975). They confirm that specific reading retardation (defined in terms of underachievement at least two standard errors below prediction) is much commoner in boys than in girls, with a ratio of about 3.5 to 1. Because reading-retarded children make less progress in reading than other children (Yule, 1973), they tend to fall further behind (relatively speaking) with the result that the prevalence rises somewhat in older children (Rutter and Yule, 1975). However, the most striking finding is the very marked variation in prevalence according to geographical area. Specific reading retardation occurred in about 10 percent of London 10-year-olds but in only about 4 percent of Isle of Wight 10-year-olds. This variation is very unlikely to be caused by genetic factors, and the finding emphasizes the fact that specific reading retardation (defined in statistical terms) cannot be equated with a genetically determined condition.

It is often stated (e.g., Benton, 1975) that dyslexia may be somewhat more frequent in Scandinavia and somewhat less frequent in Italy, Spain, and Japan than it is in the United States and the British Isles. But these estimates are based on noncomparable data and no valid inferences are possible with respect to national variations. Certainly, cases of dyslexia have been reported for many nations and for many languages and it seems most unlikely that any country will be found in which the syndrome does not occur. It would be useful to determine whether dyslexia varies in any systematic way according to the type of written language or according to the methods of instruction in schools, but such data have still not been obtained.

METHOD OF MEASUREMENT

In order to identify children with specific reading (or spelling) retardation it is necessary to have some means of assessing underachievement in reading. Obviously, underachievement is not something that is simply present or absent; it is a matter of degree. Very few children will perform exactly at the level expected on the basis of their chronological age and IQ. Thus, the questions are: what should be the expected level of attainment for any child and how does one decide what is significantly below that level?

The traditional approach has been to use some form of achievement ratio (such as reading age divided by mental age) or the difference between mental age and achievement age. Unfortunately, this attractive and common-sense approach is invalid and seriously misleading because it assumes that IQ and reading run exactly in parallel (which they do not) and because it fails to take account of the "regression effect." The use of statistics such as the achievement ratio will overestimate the number of highly intelligent and underestimate the number of less intelligent children with specific reading retardation. The theoretical basis for this artefact is well explained in Thorndike (1963), and the empirical data that the artefact occurs in practice as well as in theory are provided by Yule et al. (1974).

The appropriate procedure (and the only one that avoids this problem) is the use of some kind of regression equation in which achievement is predicted on the basis of the observed correlations between educational attainment, age, and IQ in the general population (Yule, 1967; Rutter, Tizard, and Whitmore, 1970; Berger et al., 1975; Silberberg, Iversen, and Silberberg, 1969). This approach enables both the calculation of the degree of a child's underachievement in reading and an estimate of the expected frequency of different degrees of underachievement. The decision on what cut-off point to use for a clinically significant degree of specific reading retardation is necessarily somewhat arbitrary. However, follow-up studies show that children whose achievement in reading is more than two standard errors of prediction below expectations tend to have a very persistent disability which constitutes a real handicap (Yule, 1973; Rutter and Yule, 1975; Rutter et al., 1976).

Nevertheless, while this cut-off point provides a useful guide, there are both statistical snares to avoid and other considerations to take into account. First, in obtaining an IQ score for the prediction equation, it is necessary to use a test which does not require the child to read. In practice this means that group tests are inappropriate. Second, although a formula derived from a normal general population sample may be safely applied to other groups (Berger et al., 1975), it is not valid to extend the equation to age groups other than those on which it was based. This is because the age component in the regression equation will be much influenced by the age spread in the population tested. Thirdly, there is uncertainty about the clinical significance of reading levels which are in the average range but which, because of very high IQ, still reflect severe underachievement. Fourth, although the syndrome is called specific reading retardation, it is important to recognize that the spelling disability is often more severe. Many children who were severely retarded in reading but who have now more or less made up lost ground remain severely impaired in their spelling (and often slow in their writing). This means that spelling must always be tested. Fifth, there are many children with severe reading problems whose attainments are nevertheless better than two standard errors below prediction. In short, this cut-off point provides a minimal estimate of the number of children with specific reading retardation.

CONCLUSION

Although the term "dyslexia" has been used repeatedly throughout this paper, it does not refer to any well-defined group of disorders. Rather it constitutes a hypothesis regarding the supposed existence of a nuclear group or groups of disorders of reading and/or spelling caused by constitutional factors, probably genetic in origin. Or, alternatively, it refers to a more heterogeneous group of reading disabilities characterized by the fact that reading/spelling attainment is far below that expected on the basis of the child's age or IQ. If the latter usage is employed it is probably preferable to use the terms specific reading retardation or specific spelling retardation which involve no theoretical assumptions.

In investigating the dyslexia hypothesis further (as already indicated this is a most worthwhile endeavor as the hypothesis is both plausible and important) it is essential to utilize better-defined study populations than those often used in the past. In this connection, the best established and most valid differentiation is between general reading backwardness and specific reading retardation. This differentiation requires individual psychological testing with respect to both reading and intelligence. It also requires the use of appropriate regression techniques rather than the now-discredited achievement ratios. The latter provide a useful rough-and-ready guide but are open to biases which invalidate their use in most quantitative investigations.

Nevertheless, the identification of children with specific reading retardation is not a sufficient basis for the study of dyslexia, although it is an essential starting point. First, it is abundantly clear that, especially in adolescents and adults, the disorder may be evident only in the form of spelling difficulties. These may be identified by the same techniques as those used for reading, but up to now they have been far less studied. Second, it is highly desirable to conduct research with the aim of a finer valid subdivision of cases within the category of specific reading/spelling retardation. The approaches which warrant exploration include the identification of specific cognitive patterns or specific reading/spelling errors, and the investigation of particular neurophysiological characteristics. Genetic studies which focus on possible biological or behavioral markers which characterize the particular disorders of reading which run in individual families are likely to be espec ally informative in this connection. Lastly, in addition to research into the possibility of a qualitatively distinct condition of dyslexia, there should also be research into the possibility that there is no separate condition, but rather multifactorial influences and quantitative variations in biologically determined characteristics.

Chapter 2

DEFINITIONS OF DYSLEXIA: THEIR CONSEQUENCES FOR RESEARCH AND POLICY

There can be no quarrel with the logic of Rutter's (Chap. 1) caustic critique of the World Federation of Neurology definition of dyslexia. As he demonstrates, the key terms, "conventional instruction," "adequate intelligence," and "sociocultural opportunity," are so imprecise and unspecified as to appear meaningless. If anything, the second half of the definition, to which he is unaccountably kind, is even vaguer in its reference to "fundamental cognitive disabilities" and "constitutional origin." In the face of logical analysis, the entire concept collapses so totally that one begins to wonder just how a distinguished group of neurologists came to agree on a non-definition of a non-entity. And yet, as a clinician, I am convinced, no less than my neurological colleagues are, that a disorder (better, a group of disorders) exists which does somehow correspond to the Loch Ness monster the World Federation of Neurology attempted to classify, i.e., a category of patients who fail to learn to read in the absence of any of the ordinary causes for poor reading.

Such situations are not uncommon in the history of medical efforts to separate out from a larger set of patients with common symptoms a subset who differ sufficiently from the others to suggest that a different entity is present. The process begins with the report of a puzzling and hitherto undescribed case or group of cases. Initially, attention is directed at differentiating the new "disease" from superficially similar conditions. Some decades pass during which doctors disagree on the diagnosis and invoke experience as authority. Next, a fundamental pathogenic lesion is discovered and confirmed by other workers to be present in typical cases. As its mechanism is clarified, the disease is redefined in terms of the underlying pathology. Now, new and variant clinical forms can be identified, cases that would not have met the original criteria. A hematological example may serve to illustrate the process.

In 1925, Cooley and Lee separated out from the group of childhood anemias (known as von Jaksch's anemia) five cases with hepatosplenomegaly, skin pigmentation, thick bones, and oddly shaped red cells with decreased osmotic fragility. Cooley's anemia was renamed thalassemia in 1932 by Whipple and Bradford who noted that the children came from families of Mediterranean origin. The genetic basis of thalassemia was established by Wintrobe in 1940 in a paper which distinguished thalassemia minor (the heterozygous state) from thalassemia major (the homozygous state). Fifteen years later, Kunkel discovered the normal minor hemoglobin component, hemoglobin A_2, and found it to be elevated in individuals with thalessemia minor (Weatherall, 1976a). A subsequent explosion of research on the hemoglobin molecule has led to the recognition of some fifty combinations of genetic errors which can produce the clinical picture of thalessemia.

In the transition from clinical to laboratory criteria, the definition of the disease was radically altered. Thus, the first edition of Wintrobe's *Clinical Hematology* (1942), states that: "Mediterranean anemia is characterized by chronic progressive anemia commencing early in life, well-marked erythroblastosis in the peripheral blood, a characteristic facies, splenomegaly, and a familial and racial incidence." But the current edition (1974) states that: "Thalassemia comprises a heterogeneous group of inherited disorders of hemoglobin synthesis. Indeed, it can no longer be said that the presence of hypochromic, microcytic red corpuscles, which are not the result of iron deficiency and whose osmotic fragility is decreased, is the sina qua non of thalassemia. The morphologic picture varies in the different thalassemia syndromes, even to the point of total absence of morphologic features or clinical manifestations in some heterozygotes." Or, to turn to a current review by Weatherall (1976b): "The thalassemias are a group of disorders of hemoglobin synthesis resulting from the reduced rate of production of one or more of the globin chains of hemoglobin. The result of this unbalanced chain synthesis is the production of a relative excess of the partner chains which are synthesized at a normal rate. Most of the clinical features of thalassemia can be related to the deleterious effects on erythropoiesis caused by the precipitation of these unpaired globin chains. The disorder can be classified broadly into alpha and beta thalassemia and each of these can be further subdivided into several distinct subtypes."

The process that began with the abstraction of a Platonic "type" based on clinical features led to the isolation of a group of "classical" cases which provided the basis for laboratory research. In turn, the research enabled the disease to be redefined in terms of its pathogenesis. It became possible by laboratory methods to recognize cases lacking some of the typological clinical features. But the gain in precision also led to a recognition of the molecular heterogeneity of what appeared to be a clinical entity. In our study of reading disorders, we are still trying to characterize the equivalent of Cooley's anemia (dyslexia) in the midst of cases of von Jaksch's anemia (retarded reading). The thalassemia variants lie ahead in the future.

This brief history of research on thalassemia provides one paradigm for untangling the intertwined syndromes of dyslexia, a strategy thus far barely exploited in pedigree studies of the families of children who have been identified as dyslexic. We start with the working hypothesis that reading failure is the final common expression for more than one and probably multiple underlying causal factors. Thus, estimates of "heritability" in such mixed populations are likely to yield little useful information other than what we already know; namely, that reading difficulties show familial associations. It will only be an accident of case aggregation in an otherwise unspecified group of poor readers and their families that will lead to higher or lower coefficients in particular studies. On the other hand, if we can categorize the pattern of reading errors in an index case with some specificity and search his family pedigree for members with similar reading errors (using age-corrected tests), it may prove possible to isolate a specific syndrome that is transmitted by Mendelian inheritance (Finucci et al., 1976). Once such families are identified, the investigator can then search for biological indices (Conners, 1970) in these disabled readers and for linkage with known genetic markers. If successful, the genetic approach would not only permit the isolation of a Mendelian "disease" within the heterogeneous group of reading disabilities, but would also provide us with fundamental information about one biological characteristic necessary, though not sufficient, for normal development. The National Institute of Mental Health would do well to allocate funds to encourage the application of medical genetics as one potentially fruitful strategy in exploring the causes of dyslexia.

But that lies in the future. For now, how are we to separate out from the larger category of backward reading the admittedly heterogeneous category of developmental dyslexia? Rutter has been generous enough to direct his barbs at the definition of the World Federation of Neurology and, by so doing, to omit mention of the rather similar formulation I set forth some years ago. I wrote: "Operationally, specific reading disability may be defined as the failure to learn to read with normal proficiency despite conventional instruction, a culturally adequate home, proper motivation, intact senses, normal intelligence and freedom from gross neurologic defect" (Eisenberg, 1967). All I can say in my defense is that I emphasized that the adjective "specific" referred only to a "species" of disorder and that the term was used in the medical sense of being idiopathic or of unknown cause. Be that as it may, the two definitions are essentially rewordings of the concept advanced by Morgan (1896) in the last decade of the nineteenth century when he reported a case of "congenital word blindness," a label he chose by analogy to acquired alexia in the adult resulting from cortical lesions. In describing additional cases of congenital word blindness, Hinshelwood (1902) expressed precisely the concerns that motivate this conference: "It is a matter of the highest importance to recognize the cause and the true nature of this difficulty in learning to read which is experienced by these children, otherwise they may be harshly treated as imbeciles or incorrigibles, and even neglected or punished for a defect for which they are in no wise responsible."

All that has changed in the subsequent 70 years is (1) the loss of an innocent expectation that a specific brain lesion would readily be identified and (2) some increase in sophistication about the factors that contribute to reading proficiency in the average child. For all of the looseness and circularity in these definitions of dyslexia, I suggest that they nonetheless have utility as a strategy for research, although I acknowledge the problems they create in the clinic. At the cost of too many false negatives (that is, truly dyslexic children who are excluded because they are dull or suffer social disadvantage), these definitions yield a somewhat "purer" group for study by ruling out false positives (that is, children who are retarded readers without being dyslexic). Let me explain.

The definition begins with the characteristic: "failure to learn to read with normal proficiency," which implies an evaluation of the patient's performance against a normal range determined by the use of standardized reading tests. Unspecified is the extent of deficit required for clinical diagnosis. Both issues are laden with important methodological problems. Normative scores differ depending upon the "standard test" applied; moreover, within a given test series, the responses required for the middle school tap different skills from those assessed by the version for the primary grades. Moreover, a decision must be made about whether retardation is to be defined by statistical considerations (e.g., more than so many standard deviations below the norm) or in absolute terms (that is, more than so many grade levels below the norm). With either convention, a quantitative distinction is converted into a qualitative one (that is, mild disability is ignored by a deliberate focus on severe instances). If we recall the example of thalassemia, the recognition of the thalassemia minor form permitted the identification of the genetic basis for thalassemia major but it also had to come at a later stage of knowledge, one that has not been reached in the field of dyslexia.

There are other questions to be faced. Is the retarded reader one who does less well than his *chronological* age-mates or his *mental* age-mates? Furthermore, are the population norms for the entire country the basis for determining cutoffs or the norms for the school the child attends and the social class from which he comes? It should be kept in mind that private school reading scores far exceed those for public schools (Eisenberg, 1967). I found that with retarded children excluded, 28 percent of the sixth grade children in Baltimore public schools were reading two years or more behind the national norm for their grade; this was true for none of those in three private schools surveyed. The median reading level for these urban public school sixth-graders was 5.0 to 5.5 in contrast to 10.0 to 10.5 for those in the private schools. If private school norms were to constitute the appropriate standard, the percentage of retarded readers in the public school system would be doubled. National reading norms underestimate the potential for cognitive achievement in much the same way that hemoglobin levels derived from a population of malnourished children would be an inappropriate measure of good health. We may have little choice at the present, for purely pragmatic reasons, except to take as our first priority the remediation of children who are below the anemic national standards. I hope the day is not far hence when we can turn our attention to the general attainment of levels now reached only by the privileged.

The first term of exclusion in the definition is "despite conventional instruction." It was formulated with a view to both quantitative and qualitative deficits in teaching. No one would label dyslexic a child who had never been taught. There are many children (those in migrant farmworker families, for example) who are absent for considerable parts of the school term. It seems likely that their poor reading achievement might result from too little instruction. Most of us assume that there is some minimum amount of teaching that is necessary for learning to read, although experience suggests that children vary widely in the adroitness with which they pick up reading. A few seem able to learn with remarkably little instruction. As to qualitative defects, when the definition was written a decade ago, there was much debate about phonic versus whole-word teaching. The view was widespread among the public that reliance on whole-word teaching was contributing to an "epidemic" of poor reading. That seems highly dubious. My supposition is that most children are quite capable of learning with either system but that there

35

well may be a significant fraction who prosper more readily with one rather than the other, with a combination of the two, or with i.t.a. (initial teaching alphabet). If we assume that the way children are taught has something to do with the way they learn, it is probable that potentially dyslexic children are at greater risk for reading failure because a lock-step instructional mode, tailored to the needs of school system administrators, fails to provide alternative teaching styles that might serve particular children better. Present data permit only the Scotch verdict of not proven.

The second restriction, "(despite) a culturally adequate home," highlights developmental experiences, both antecedent to and contemporary with schooling, which influence reading achievement. For a child to profit from reading instruction, he must first possess adequate linguistic skills: phonologic, lexical, and syntactic. The design of the standard first-grade curriculum assumes that these skills are the common possession of all entering students. We would not (or at least we should not) try to teach a child to read English if the only language he knows is Spanish, though such practices are regrettably widespread for immigrant children. And if his English is nonstandard, his vocabulary impoverished, and his syntax either restricted or based on a different system (Osser et al., 1967; Frank and Osser, 1970; Dillard, 1972), similar impediments to learning to read exist. Further to the point, schooling, though it should be fun, is also work and requires motivation to sustain the necessary effort. Middle-class cultural values and behaviors, both at home and in the community, reinforce the relevance of schooling to the child's future as well as the acquisition of a "work ethic" for academic success. The most consistent finding in community-wide surveys of school achievement is the direct correlation with social class (Eisenberg and Earls, 1975). The Maudsley studies (Rutter et al., 1970; Yule et al., 1974; Berger et al., 1975) demonstrate an association between reading backwardness and economic disadvantage and they pinpoint particular aspects of the child's social environment related to reading performance (large family size, birth order, teacher turnover, area of residence).

Rutter is certainly correct that low social class, a broken home, and a large sibship not only do not "protect" a child against dyslexia but, in all probability, contribute to its prevalence as evident from the differences in rate by class and place of residence in the Isle of Wight and inner London (Berger, Yule, and Rutter, 1975). From a public policy viewpoint, a definition that excludes socioeconomically disadvantaged children is mischievous in the extreme, in view of the demonstration that they are at higher, not lesser, risk for the disorder. This is a point to which we will return. That error arises in the context of an attempt to identify a relatively "pure" group of cases for research purposes. The middle-class dyslexic has been unable to learn despite what we take to be an advantaged home. We lack reliable criteria to distinguish the lower-class dyslexic from the one who is a backward reader for other reasons. However, at the clinical level, it is entirely unwarranted to limit therapeutic intervention to those defined as dyslexic by restricted research criteria, particularly since there is no reason to anticipate any loss for the backward reader from being instructed as though he were dyslexic.

The reference to "intact senses" excludes children with peripheral sensory defects in order to emphasize the need for special compensatory methods for the hard-of-hearing or visually handicapped child. What is remarkable is how little sensory acuity is required for learning how to read, provided that the handicap is recognized and dealt with appropriately. Central perceptual or processing defects are an entirely different matter and may well play a role in the dyslexic syndromes.

The fifth term of exclusion, "(despite) normal intelligence," is embedded in a similar complex of environmental determinants and circular logic. Operationally, there is a phenomenologic difference between the child who tests well on IQ and poorly on reading, and the one who tests poorly on both. This is not really different from distinguishing a child who reads poorly but succeeds at other academic tasks from the one who fails in all areas. Rutter points out that a severe discrepancy can exist between statistically predicted and observed reading achievement in children with borderline as well as superior IQ. The point is well taken but the problem in defining dyslexia in terms of intelligence is much greater. There is no better reason for assuming that the measured IQ represents intellectual potential than that reading level reflects reading potential. We may safely conclude that the child who tests well on IQ and still cannot read, despite instruction which suffices for his peers, has some special handicap. We are not on equally firm ground if we take borderline and mildly defective IQ scores to explain reading failure without considering the numerous environmental factors that influence IQ (Eisenberg, 1967). As Rutter and Yule (1975, p. 182) point out: "It would be just as valid to predict IQ on the basis of reading as to follow the more usual converse procedure." Both academic achievement and IQ scores are strongly predicted by social class alone (Bowles and Gintis, 1973). It is, however, still legitimate, as a first-order task, to focus on children whose reading scores are below those expected (after appropriate statistical corrections) from their IQ scores, so long as we do not then forego consideration of the learning and educational problems of those who have depressed scores in both areas.

The final term of exclusion, "freedom from gross neurological defect," has its own difficulties. It is noteworthy that the Maudsley studies, employing epidemiological and statistical criteria to identify the "hump" in the distribution curve, have established that neurodevelopmental disorders are less frequent in dyslexics than in children with general reading backwardness (Rutter and Yule, 1975). At the same time, they have shown that some children with cerebral palsy exhibit severe reading disorders even when IQ is unimpaired (Seidel, Chadwick, and Rutter, 1975). Are they dyslexic *and* brain-injured or dyslexic *because* they are brain injured? The question is not answerable with present information. Part of the difficulty stems from the imprecision in the category "brain-injured." What examination reveals are deficits resulting from injury to the sensory and motor systems of the brain. We suppose that the visible signs of injury increase the likelihood of other cerebral lesions; these, however, are not distributed in a predictable fashion. Furthermore, there is strong evidence that the functional consequences of brain impairment are conditional on environmental interactions (Eisenberg, 1977). Separating the poor reader with cerebral palsy from the one without obvious neurological defect is a useful strategy in the effort to isolate the factors that contribute to reading disorder. However, in no way does this imply that the brain-injured child who cannot read should be excluded from remedial instruction.

Whatever the merits of these arguments for clinical research, they present serious hazards for public policy. This is strikingly evident in the terminology of the Education For All Handicapped Children Act, Public Law 94-142. In writing legislation to support remedial education for handicapped children so as to assure that appropriate funds will be used for the purposes described (rather than being diffused throughout the school budget), the U.S. Congress has defined children with specific learning disabilities as:

> those children who have a disorder in one or more of the basic psychological processes involved in understanding or in using language, spoken or written, which disorder may manifest itself in imperfect ability to listen, think, speak, read, write, spell, or do mathematical calculations. Such disorders include such conditions as perceptual handicaps, brain injury, minimal brain dysfunction, dyslexia and developmental aphasia. Such term does not include children who have learning problems which are primarily the result of visual, hearing, or motor handicaps, of mental retardation, of emotional disturbance,

or environmental, cultural, or economic disadvantage (Office of Education, 1976).

This should not be misinterpreted. It is not an attempt by legislative fiat to define a medical condition into (or out of) existence, akin to the absurd exercises in several state legislatures to regulate the value of *pi*. Rather, it represents a response of an informed Congress to well-intentioned lobbying from parents and professionals in behalf of children with learning disabilities, at a time when no satisfactory definition of the disorders to be included emerged from legislative testimony. The Congress was concerned with the potential cost of the services as well as with insuring that they be delivered to the targeted population. Costs are to be contained by establishing a "cap" on the total number of children who can be included by specifying that "children with specific learning disabilities may not constitute more than one-sixth of the children eligible to be counted as handicapped" and by providing that "a state may not count more than 12 percent of the number of children aged 5–17 as handicapped." Targeting is to be guaranteed by requiring the Commissioner of Education to specify (1) the criteria for conditions that may be included, (2) the appropriate diagnostic procedures, and (3) methods to monitor state and local educational agencies.

The preamble to the regulations acknowledges the limitations of the present state of the art with the comment: "The only generally accepted manifestation of a specific learning disability is that there is a major discrepancy between expected achievement and ability which is not the result of other known and generally accepted handicapping conditions or circumstances" (Office of Education, p. 52404). In order to emphasize service for the severely impaired, "the regulations require that a child be achieving at or below 50% of his expected achievement level . . ." (p. 52405). This is to be determined by the use of the following formula:

$$\text{C.A.} \left(\frac{IQ}{300} + 0.17\right) - 2.5 = \text{severe discrepancy level}$$

(Office of Education, p. 52407)

After specifying the composition of an appropriate evaluation team, the regulation states firmly: "The team may not identify a child as having a specific learning disability if the severe academic discrepancy is primarily the result of: (1) a visual, hearing, or motor handicap; (2) mental retardation; (3) emotional disturbance, or (4) environmental, cultural, or economic disadvantage" (Office of Education, p. 52406).

39

The intent of the legislation is unexceptionable. Its complexities arise from the difficulty in writing the rules that will govern the administration of the program. The wording of the regulations virtually guarantees two serious problems. First, disproportionate effort and cost will be consumed by the certification process. Second, the categories of exclusion will deny service to a significant number of children with learning disabilities, particularly those who also suffer from sociocultural disadvantage and emotional disturbance.

In reference to dyslexia, as the legislation is written ("imperfect ability to . . . read, write, spell . . ."), it includes the children encompassed by the two definitions we considered. The addition of such other "diagnostic" terms as "perceptual handicaps," "minimal brain dysfunction," and "developmental aphasia" is of little practical effect since these labels reflect differences in terminology rather than differences in children. However, the specification of "brain injury" includes children with cerebral palsy (if "brain-injured" has any meaning at all) and that is all to the good for service programming. The exclusion of children with "visual, hearing, and motor handicaps" may not be as much of a disservice as it appears if we assume that appropriate compensatory classes are available to them under other administrative rubrics. However, such a limitation does testify to the continuing fragmentation of children's services into multiple special service categories, to the detriment of adequate care for all. What will result from ruling out poor readers who are considered mentally retarded will depend upon the criteria used to define retardation. For example, if the category is limited to children who score less than 67 on IQ tests, it may not pose a practical problem. Such children are likely to need special instruction in all academic subjects. If the definition includes those in the borderline range (IQ 67 to 85), the result will be to doubly penalize the economically disadvantaged who constitute a disproportionate percentage of those who test in this range, a serious error.

The exclusion of the emotionally disturbed is bound to be troublesome. It is based upon the supposition that there is an identifiable group of children whose learning disability results directly from a primary psychiatric disorder. While it is probable that such children do exist (Rabinovitch et al., 1954), they are not easily distinguished from learning-disabled children whose emotional disturbance is secondary to their academic difficulty (Eisenberg, 1975). As Rutter notes, "The types of reading retardation associated with psychiatric disorder or delinquency are not basically different in kind from those occurring in 'pure' form." The assessment team is likely to become bogged down in interminable argument if it accepts the charge to distinguish antecedent from consequent emotional disorder in poor readers. Since a psychiatric diagnosis will result in an absolute disqualification from the special education program, those concerned with securing service for needy pupils are likely to respond by avoiding psychiatric evaluation at all costs. The net result will be a denial of psychiatric care to that significant fraction of disabled readers for whom it is an important component of a total rehabilitation program (Eisenberg, 1975).

The most unfortunate exclusion in the proposed rules is that regarding children who suffer from "environmental, cultural, or economic disadvantage." They are barred from the category of specific learning disability despite the fact that severe reading retardation is more common in just such children. Moreover, the clinical pattern is indistinguishable from that found in middle-class dyslexics (Rutter and Yule, 1975). If there is any justification for identifying the disadvantaged poor reader, it should be in order to provide more, rather than fewer, remedial services (i.e., family income maintenance, home visits by social workers, after-school enrichment programs, and the like *in addition to* reading tutoring). Unhappily, the legislation, as written, abandons those most in need of help in favor of children whose families already command the largest share of available resources.

The Office of Education publication came to hand as I was in the midst of writing this chapter. It reinforces, beyond further argument, Rutter's critique of the social dangers as well as the logical circularities in the existing definitions of dyslexia. I therefore propose that we abandon them. And yet we should not back off from continuing the search for the pathophysiological mechanisms underlying the several syndromes of reading failure. The challenge is to carry out that search in a way that does not hamper the provision of service to children in need. Let me, then, suggest a modified definition for specific reading disability that may meet both needs:

Specific reading disability (or developmental dyslexia) should be diagnosed when individually administered reading and intelligence tests given by competent examiners reveal a severe performance deficit (greater than two standard errors of prediction) between the obtained reading level and that expected on the basis of age and intelligence—in a child who has received reading instruction in his native language in kind and amount ordinarily sufficient for his peers.

This definition makes no assumption of homogeneity in the causes and mechanisms of the reading problems thus identified; indeed, present evidence suggests heterogeneity in the factors underlying the difficulty in learning to read, factors which it will be the task of future research to specify in order to devise more precise methods of remediation. If sensory defect, socio-cultural disadvantage, psychiatric disorder, and/or neurological impairment coexist with the inability to read, programs of remediation should attempt to correct or compensate for these other handicaps. In studying the clinical features of disabled readers and in evaluating the outcome of remedial programs, results should be reported separately for those with and without additional handicaps in order to provide a basis for comparability among investigations and to permit identification of the different syndromes which have reading disability as their common outcome.

Chapter 3

DYSLEXIA SYNDROMES: A WORKING HYPOTHESIS THAT WORKS

STEVEN MATTIS

The organization of Rutter's (Chap. 1) extensive review of the literature and the conclusions which he draws are, in large measure, a function of a basic premise which he makes explicit in his introduction. He does not feel that the findings presented in the literature are themselves particularly debatable but rather it is . . . "only the concepts which arise form the observations which are controversial." While I would agree that the present concepts of dyslexia are controversial, I would not totally agree with Rutter that the observations themselves should not be subject to debate. Research findings, albeit replicable, are determined to a great extent by the hypothetical constructs held by the investigators before studies are conducted. That is, the working hypothesis concerning the nature of dyslexia determines the selection of control groups, the definition of dyslexia itself, the measures to be obtained, and the overall research design and method of data analysis. The degree to which findings are effective in furthering our understanding of the nature of dyslexia is therefore largely a function of the degree to which the explicit or implicit model of dyslexia underlying the research is valid and of heuristic value.

After reviewing current research findings concerning types of dyslexia, Rutter concludes that at present the term "does not refer to any well-defined group of disorders." This is a reasonable but nonetheless disappointing conclusion, given the fact that this group of disorders was first brought to clinical attention at the turn of the century (Hinshelwood, 1895, 1900, 1917; Morgan, 1896) and has been the subject of intensive investigation for the last 40–50 years. I submit that Rutter's conclusion suggests that the underlying hypotheses guiding dyslexia research have not been particularly useful. We might do well therefore either to define existing hypotheses more rigorously, or discard those previously entertained because of their lack of heuristic value, and work toward developing new ones.

I would like therefore to present a working hypothesis derived in part from the adult alexia literature which somewhat redefines the criteria for identifying types of dyslexia. The model will be, I hope, delineated clearly enough so that its major premises and the findings it can generate will be testable and clearly refutable. Moreover the model, if supported over time, gives us a somewhat different perspective with which to view (1) the significance of existing, sometimes seemingly conflicting, findings, and (2) the implications for developing specific treatment approaches as a function of the diagnosis of a specific type of dyslexia.

In the neuropsychological examination of the adult, the finding of an alexia, i.e., the loss of previously acquired reading skill, very significantly raises the index of suspicion of cerebral impairment. But an alexia per se is not pathognomonic of a lesion in a given locus. One must place the alexia in the context of other disorders in higher cortical functions in order to infer a specific locus of lesion. The adult neuropsychology literature implicates at least four separate loci, generally in the dominant hemisphere, which are commonly seen in patients in whom an alexia is a prominent feature (Benson et al., 1971; Benson and Geschwind, 1975). Thus one can diagnose: an alexia without agraphia seen in patients with medial left-hemisphere occipital-lobe lesions impinging upon the corpus collosum; a fluent aphasic alexia; angular gyrus alexia in which sequencing difficulties are prominent; and, frontal or Broca's aphasia alexia. Each locus of lesion is associated with a different deficit or cluster of deficits which, for the patient, are critical impediments to his execution of reading. There is not in adults, therefore, a single causal defect underlying all alexias but rather several independent causal deficits. This clinical reality in adults is the basis of a model of dyslexia in children which I submit is a reasonable one to pursue at this point in our current understanding of the literature on children's dyslexia.

DYSLEXIA SYNDROMES: INDEPENDENT CAUSAL DEFECTS

There are two major assumptions underlying a model of independent causal defects. The first is to take seriously what every investigator states before going on to simplify the problem, namely, that reading is indeed a very complex process requiring the successful integration of moderately complex input, output, and mediating subprocesses. The second assumption is that a defect or distortion of any single one of these necessary subprocesses will impair subsequent integration, resulting in atypical development of reading skill. This model supposes that the population of dyslexic children is composed of several smaller groups, each of which presents differing deficits or clusters of deficits in higher cortical functions. Each separate syndrome reflects a different defect in a critical subprocess, and each syndrome therefore represents the necessary and sufficient conditions to distort the acquisition of the more complex skill of reading.

DYSLEXIA SYNDROMES: SUPPORTING EVIDENCE

If the individual skills probably necessary for normal reading (Maliphant et al., 1974) are analyzed, a large but nonetheless finite number of different processes which, in theory, would be critical appear to be present. However, it seems reasonable to assume that, of all the possible disorders which could occur, only a limited number of different clusters actually do occur clinically with any significant frequency.

Mattis et al. (1975) isolated three independent dyslexia syndromes which accounted for 90 percent of the 82 dyslexic children studied. It became clinically apparent that for one group a language disorder was the most prominent finding, a second group appeared to have few cognitive or perceptual difficulties but had significant speech dysarticulation and gross and fine motor dyscoordination, and for the third group the most prominent finding, on superficial inspection, was significant visual-constructional difficulties with language development well within normal limits. However, there were inconsistent secondary features, even within the three primary groups. Thus there were some aphasic children with and others without gross motor dyscoordination and some with and without hyperkinecity. A matched group of brain-damaged children who were not dyslexic was available in this study. It was assumed that many of the deficiencies reportedly associated with dyslexia and observed in our population were indeed manifestations of central nervous system dysfunction, but that only a few were causally related to dyslexia.

Therefore, by disregarding as causal to dyslexia deficiencies in higher cortical functions found in the brain-damaged readers, the following dyslexia syndromes were isolated and empirically defined.

I. *Language Disorder*
  (A) Anomia (20% or greater proportion of errors on the Naming Test) and one of the following:
  (B) Disorder of comprehension (performance on Token Test at least one standard deviation below the mean) or
  (C) Disorder of imitative speech (performance greater than one standard deviation below the mean on the Sentence Repetition Test) or
  (D) Disorder of speech sound discrimination (10% or greater proportion of errors on discrimination of 'e' rhyming letters).

II. *Articulatory and Graphomotor Dyscoordination*
  (A) Performance on ITPA Sound Blending subtest greater than one standard deviation below the mean; and
  (B) Performance on graphomotor test greater than one standard deviation below the mean; and
  (C) Acoustosensory and receptive language processes within normal limits.

III. *Visuospatial Perceptual Disorder*
  (A) Verbal IQ more than 10 points above performance IQ; and,
  (B) Raven's Coloured Progressive Matrices percentile *less than* equivalent performance IQ; and,
  (C) Benton Visual Retention Test (10-sec exposure, immediate reproduction) score at or below the borderline level.

Observed in the brain-damaged reader group were such findings as hyperkinecity; severe gross and fine motor dyscoordination; sinistrality without a family history of left-handedness; ambidexterity; mixed eye, hand, and foot dominance; severe deficits in drawing, puzzle, and block construction; speech difficulties due to defects in oral peripheral structures and dysarthria; dyscalculia; disorders in lateral awareness; and disturbed awareness of finger order and differentiation. Sometimes the last three disorders were seen in the same patient.

Denckla (1975) has reported a retrospective study of 52 dyslexic children selected from 297 patients between the ages of 7 and 14 seen in consultation consecutively during a 12-month period. Independent of etiology, 28 of the children (54%) presented a language disorder in which an anomia was prominent, 6 (12%) presented the articulatory and graphomotor dyscoordination syndrome, and 2 (4%) presented the visual-perceptual disorder syndrome which was not pure in that both children also demonstrated an anomia. Two other syndromes were suggested but without a brain-damaged reader group for control. Seven children (13%) were reported to have a *dysphonemic sequencing difficulty* . . . "wherein poor repetition scores characterized by phonemic substitutions and missequencings occur despite normal . . . naming . . . comprehension and speech-sound production (articulation). . . ." Five children (10%) presented a *"verbal memorization (learning) disorder* wherein sentence repetition and verbal paired-associate learning are deficient but language skills otherwise are not demonstrably disturbed." The paired-associate learning test (Wechsler Memory Scale) was given only to the 13- and 14-year-olds, an age range beyond the ceiling of the naming tests standardized by Denckla and Rudel (1974). Denckla felt that the poor paired-associate performance reflected anomic difficulty and in her discussion states that had she and Rudel ". . . devised tests sensitive to anomia in older children and adolescents the necessity for operationally designating a 'verbal memorization' subgroup might not have arisen."

We have recently completed a cross-validation study in collaboration with Gerald Erenberg, formerly Director for the Center for Child Development, a Montefiore Affiliate. Demographic, social, financial, academic achievement, medical-neurological, and neuropsychological data were obtained for the first 400 children seen at the Center. The population within the catchment area is black and Hispanic, generally level IV or V on the Hollingshead Scale, with an adult female as head of the household. Despite the clinic's location within a disadvantaged area, the distribution of chief complaints, diagnoses, and academic achievement levels does not appear to differ clinically from that reported from similar developmental disabilities centers whose base population is more affluent (Erenberg et al., 1976). Two hundred ninety-three of the 400 children were of school age. Of the school-age children 163 were diagnosed as dyslexic, 70 as retarded, 24 as borderline intelligence, and 36 as "normal intelligence." The dyslexic population ranged from ages 8 to 14 with a modal age range between 8 to 10, a somewhat younger population than reported by Mattis et al. (1975) in which the mean age for each syndrome was between 11 and 12. In this larger study with younger children

49

more representative of the school population from which they were referred, the three dyslexia syndromes previously isolated were again observed. However, the percentage of children presenting each syndrome and the total number of children accounted for by these syndromes differed from that found in the initial study. Using the criteria established by Mattis, French, and Rapin: 63 percent of the dyslexic children presented the language disorder syndrome, 10 percent the articulatory and graphomotor dyscoordination syndrome, and 5 percent the visual-perceptual disorder syndrome. All syndromes, as in the initial study, were seen in genetic and secondary dyslexic children.

As in Denckla's study, in this young population the largest percentage of dyslexic children presented with the language disorder syndrome and the smallest percentage with the visual-perceptual disorder syndrome. Since in this large sample only 5 percent presented with the visual-perceptual disorder syndrome, it is not surprising that in her sample of only 52 children this syndrome was not observed by Denckla.

Unlike our initial study in which each dyslexic child presented only one syndrome, in the cross-validation study 9 percent presented with two syndromes (although none presented all 3). Four of the children (2.5%) presented with both language and visual-perceptual disorders similar to that observed by Denckla, 10 (6%) presented with both language and articulographomotor disorders, and 1 child (0.6%) with articulatory and visual-perceptual syndromes. In the initial study each child was carefully screened by a pediatric neurologist before being referred on to the Division of Neuropsychology as a child of normal intelligence with a learning disability. This screening was reflected in the fact that within each syndrome either the mean verbal or performance IQ was about 100. Those children in the cross-validation study presenting more than one syndrome reflected their multiple deficits in their IQ scores. Thus the poorer of their two scores fell into the defective range and the other barely maintained itself about 80, which was the interdisciplinary team's criterion for identification of the child as having a specific learning disability rather than being borderline or retarded. Of the 293 school-age children seen, 29 presented multiple syndromes. Of these, 15 were eventually diagnosed as dyslexic and 14 diagnosed as borderline or retarded.

The three syndromes, taken independently, accounted for 77 percent of the dyslexic children, and the multiple syndromes together accounted for an additional 9 percent. Sixteen other children (10%) presented findings which supported Denckla's observation suggesting a "sequencing" disorder syndrome. I am reluctant to affirm, at present, that this new deficit cluster has been isolated. Similar to those of the initial study, the dyslexia syndromes were generally apparent by the nature of the prominent finding each child demonstrated. However, in the initial study it was necessary to discount variable findings associated with central nervous system impairment but irrelevant to dyslexia by disregarding as causal those deficits observed in a contrast group of brain-damaged readers. In the cross-validation study, the number of brain-damaged readers was quite small since most of the school-age children were referred to the Center for Child Development because of severe reading disabilities. At present, we are attempting to accrue a sufficient number of brain-damaged readers—matched for age, IQ, and socioeconomic status—the Pediatric Neurology clinic population at Montefiore which has a different catchment area than the Center for Child Development but whose population shares many of the same cultural and economic features.

While Denckla's additional syndrome has not been empirically isolated for replication, the broad outline of the cluster seems clinically apparent. The children present with defective performance on the WISC Digit Span subtest and Spreen-Benton Sentence Repetition subtest. Most of the children have either defective WISC Picture Arrangement subtest scores or Picture Arrangement is among the lowest subtest scores. There is no anomia. Speech is well articulated. Language comprehension as tested by the Token Test may be deficient, but errors are confined to the latter portion of the test in which the child must comply with requests requiring appreciation of words denoting temporal-spatial events. Indeed, most but not all the children in this group do not have a stable concept of "before and after." They can count rapidly from one to ten and name the days of the week in correct order but cannot answer such questions as "what number comes before four . . . after seven . . . what day comes before Sunday . . . after Tuesday." Some, but not all, have deficient lateral awareness, i.e., do not know their own left and right hand. Some have graphomotor dyscoordination. In brief, psychometric and clinical findings indicate a temporal sequencing deficit. In adults this cluster would be consonant with a left-hemisphere inferior posterior parietal lesion resulting in a conduction aphasia and incidental findings consonant with this locus.

In summary, preliminary results of the cross-validation study reiterate the existence of the three independent dyslexia syndromes initially reported, support the contention that the syndromes are found in both genetic and secondary dyslexia (also reported by Denckla, 1975), and corroborate the observation of Denckla of an additional "sequencing disorder" syndrome. In both Denckla's study and the cross-validation study, the language disorder syndrome was most frequently observed. I would agree with her effort to differentiate children within this syndrome, but, since the major emphasis in children is on cognitive process rather than locus of lesion, I would suggest that differentiation among children with language disorder be explored along psycholinguistic parameters rather than aphasia nosology. Regardless of the number of syndromes to be eventually determined, there appears to be sufficient evidence to date to submit that a dyslexia syndromes model which presumes several independent causal defects is a tenable working hypothesis to guide future research.

TOWARD A DEFINITION OF DYSLEXIA AND CRITERIA FOR DIAGNOSIS

Implicit in the dyslexia syndromes model are several guidelines for redefining or expanding the definition of dyslexia, its etiology, and its clinical diagnosis. The model postulates that there are several moderately complex higher cortical skills necessary for the development of the "hypercomplex" cortical process, reading, and that a defect in any one of these critical processes will result in distorted or impaired integration of these processes and concurrent atypical reading development. Reading is therefore viewed as a dynamic process, changing and developing over time, and dyslexic reading is viewed as an atypical or abnormal development of this process. Rutter and co-workers report that those children whose attained reading level is more than 2 standard deviations below expectation demonstrate a persistent reading problem. Moreover, achievement over time is even poorer than in lower IQ children whose initial reading level was consonant with their expected level (Yule, 1973; Rutter and Yule, 1975; Rutter et al., 1976).

Within the framework of the dyslexia syndromes model, therefore, dyslexia is a clinical diagnosis of atypical reading development which without intervention is expected to persist and is due to a well-defined defect in any one of several specific higher cortical processes.

There appear to be two aspects of this definition which require some elaboration, i.e., the terms "atypical" and "due to." When one is confronted with the word "atypical" it is reasonable to ask, "as compared to what?" It is at this point that, as a clinician, I empathize with the initial statement of the definition of specific developmental dyslexia provided by the World Federation of Neurology as ". . . a disorder manifested by difficulty learning to read despite conventional instruction, adequate intelligence, and socio-cultural opportunity . . ." (Critchley, 1970). While Rutter views this statement as a logical "nonstarter," unfortunately this is exactly where the clinician must start. Dyslexia is only one of several diagnoses that the clinician may decide upon after examining a child for whom the chief complaint is "poor reader." Whether or not it is explicitly stated, the entire examination is focused on the question of how atypical is this child's reading. If he asks the child to read and the child, age eight or nine, can read only one or two words and does not recognize several letters, the clinician quite correctly will conclude, having seen hundreds of nine-year-olds, that this is atypical for age. Before continuing his examination, he might review his interview with the parents. Has the child been in school the last three years? If there have been multiple relocations in the last three years and the child's asthmatic condition kept him home most of the time, the clinician may decide that the child's reading is consonant with his lack of educational opportunity and reschedule an appointment in one year during which time the child would attend the neighborhood school. If the child has been attending school, the clinician might ask where and, if he has had enough experience, conclude that the child's reading is atypical even for a nine-year-old who attends a New York City school. In practice, the environmental factors are often accounted for by the manner in which the child is referred to clinical attention. Most of the time the school has observed that the child, exposed to the instructional approaches used in that school, has demonstrated atypical reading progress as compared with his classmates who share his sociocultural opportunities. The clinician might then check hearing and vision. If visual acuity is defective, the clinician may conclude the examination, having decided that the child's reading is quite typical for those of his age with profound myopia, and he may prescribe corrective lenses. On the other hand he may find a mild to moderate myopia and continue his examination, having concluded that reading is atypical even for a nine-year-old New York City child with moderate myopia.

Having excluded environmental and acuity factors, the clinician then looks into factors more centrally inherent to the child. If the child is not sitting quietly humming to himself, snatching imaginary flies, and intermittently answering questions that the examiner has not asked and, in addition, has cooperated with the examination procedures, then the examiner will exclude profound psychopathology as consonant with the child's reading. He might then administer an IQ test (whatever that is). If he infers clinically that the child's observed reading skill is unusual even given his (at best) low average intelligence, then he has now excluded from diagnostic consideration a significant number of parameters for which the child's reading skill might be typical. At this point the index of suspicion is seriously raised that subsequent examination will confirm a diagnosis of dyslexia.

The definition of dyslexia might therefore be expanded to include a clause modifying the term "atypical." Dyslexia is a diagnosis of atypical reading development as compared to other children of similar age, intelligence, instructional program, and sociocultural opportunity which, without intervention, is expected to persist and is due to a well-defined defect in any one of several specific higher cortical functions.

What is needed, of course, is a good measure of atypical reading development. Isomorphic with the dyslexia syndromes model would be a procedure which would elicit evidence of atypical reading. Perhaps the closest measure is that suggested by Boder (1973) who reports no overlap between dyslexic and normal readers in their proportion of correct spelling of correctly read sight words. However, without obtaining data on brain-damaged readers (many of whom have motor and some spelling difficulty) and data on inner city children, I would be reluctant to rely on this ratio. Moreover a measure of the reading process itself would be more suitable and perhaps in the future a creative analysis of reading errors might produce such a measure. The measure proposed by Rutter in Chapter 1 at present appears most promising. However, if one accepts that the reading difficulty manifested by dyslexic children reflects atypical development of this process, then Dr. Rutter's concern for obtaining some means of assessing *under-achievement* in reading is somewhat misplaced.

The reading tests that we administer are measures in a given moment in time of the product of the integration and development of subprocesses necessary to reading. The fact that a dyslexic ten-year-old obtains a raw score of 26 on this measure and that a similar raw score has been previously obtained by most school age children by mid first grade does not in any way imply that the ten-year-old reads like a normal first grader. He indeed has not integrated these subprocesses so as to achieve the reading developmental level of most seven-year-olds. If our patient were now reading like a normal well-integrated first grader, then we could predict with confidence that next year he would read like a second grader, and the year after like a third grader, etc. just like all normal first graders do. But we know, in fact, that he will not (Yule, 1973; Rutter and Yule, 1975; Rutter et al., 1976).

Rutter's suggested criteria for specific reading disability, although couched in terms of underachievement, is statistically a measure of deviance. Those children whose reading level is 2 or more standard deviations below the level expected on the basis of a multiple regression equation in which age and IQ are the predictor variables, would be considered to evidence dyslexic reading. Since the constants obtained for this equation were derived from the correlations between reading level, age, and IQ in the general population, the effects of severe deviations in educational opportunity and sociocultural factors were minimized by the infrequency of their occurrence in the general population. I would be very surprised if the constants in the equation and concurrent absolute levels constituting a standard deviation were not significantly altered should the statistical procedure be applied to the South Bronx. Conceptually the use of a deviance measure is appealing and empirically the measure is exceedingly useful in detecting children who have persistent handicaps. Perhaps the number of predictor variables can be expanded to account for the social and instructional factors. However, to be more practical: age, IQ, and reading levels for children are obtained by almost all school districts in the United States. Therefore, it would seem feasible to generate the appropriate expectancy levels for each school district, thereby keeping the environmental factors relatively constant for that population.

CAUSAL FACTORS: NEUROPSYCHOLOGICAL AND NEUROLOGICAL ETIOLOGY

The second term in the proposed definition of dyslexia which bears elaboration is "due to," which explicitly refers to causal factors. Within the model, the causal factors are cognitive defects, i.e., deficits in a process or skill critical to the acquisition of reading. What then are some of the characteristics of a defective critical skill?

If one reviews the literature comparing dyslexic children to normals, one finds almost every disorder in higher cortical functions known to occur in children to be more frequently found in poor readers. Within the dyslexic syndromes model, one would expect that many incidental findings, the manifestation of central nervous system dysfunction, would be more frequently observed in dyslexic children than in non-brain-damaged readers and therefore present as correlated with dyslexia. But correlates are not necessarily causal. The main problem in isolating causal factors is to distinguish between those findings which are relevant to limiting the acquisition of reading skills and those that are incidental to reading.

What is critical about a critical defect is that the cluster is confined

55

to dyslexic children. It is difficult to overemphasize the necessity of using a group of brain-damaged children who read in making this determination. A given disorder repeatedly reported in dyslexic children should be viewed as a reliable, replicable, statistical associate of dyslexia but, if it is also observed in brain-damaged readers, it must logically be considered irrelevant as a factor causal to dyslexia. The prevalence of these incidental findings mask those factors which are peculiar to dyslexia. I suggest that the failure of cluster analysis techniques to determine meaningful subtypes within a large group of dyslexic children (Naidoo, 1972; Rutter, 1969) prior to those reported by Mattis et al. (1975) is due primarily to the inadequate use of a brain-damaged reader contrast group.

Determining causal factors from data derived from large groups of specifically poor readers, generally backward students, and normal children also presents an interesting problem in statistical analysis in that critical defects are not linearly related to reading. The presence of a specific disorder in a critical process implies the presence of dyslexia, however the absence of this specific defect does not imply the absence of disordered reading. The child could have a defect in a different critical process and be dyslexic or present no other critical defects and be a normal reader. Moreover, data concerning the frequency with which a given syndrome is observed in the dyslexic population are not easily adapted to correlational analyses. For example, the fact that the visual-perceptual disorder syndrome is not frequently observed in the dyslexic population does not imply a "weak association" with dyslexia. On the contrary, the presence of a visual-perceptual disorder syndrome is as highly predictive of dyslexia as is the presence of the language disorder syndrome.

Within the dyslexia syndromes model the several independent critical clusters of deficiencies in higher cortical function are each viewed as the necessary and sufficient conditions to limit the acquisition of reading skill. Within the framework of neuropsychology it is difficult to see a specific cluster of deficits known to result from a focal lesion and not seriously entertain the hypothesis that this deficit reflects specific morphological-physiological abnormality in brain. As to the neurological-etiological factors which might produce such specific cognitive dysfunctions, one would expect that an early encephalopathic event, i.e., anoxia, trauma, stroke, encephalitis, etc. or a genetically determined agenesis or vulnerability of specific brain structures would be logical to explore. It should be noted that neither the clear indication of an encephalopathic event nor a family history of dyslexia are in themselves directly etiologically related to dyslexia. It would only be in those cases in which such a history is obtained in a child manifesting a dyslexia syndrome that a more molecular etiology could be entertained. My own bias as a clinician is that future research will demonstrate underlying anatomic and neuropsychological disorders specific to each syndrome. This expectation is supported somewhat by the recent report by Hauser et al. (1975) of the pneumoencephalographic study of 18 cases of language disorder in children, 17 of which were diagnosed as infantile autism. The major finding was of temporal-lobe abnormality, the expected finding in a population with a prominent language disorder. While I do not believe that such invasive techniques, with their finite morbidity rate, will see widespread use in the study of dyslexia, I see hope in the eventual utility of second- and third-generation computerized transaxial tomography, a noninvasive radiographic technique having amazingly fine resolution. One would expect that judicious use of CTT scans would enable clinical-pathological correlational studies in children to approach the sophistication of those conducted in adults.

At this point in our current knowledge it is not clear what importance one should attach to a positive or negative history of early brain damage or family history of dyslexia in a group of children presenting the same syndrome.

The neurological-etiological factors might indeed be of significant import if future research should determine that the reading disorder of children within a given syndrome shows different courses and outcomes as a function of genetic and/or encephalopathic factors. I suspect that those factors will be important. In follow-up studies at the Center for Child Development and the Neuropsychology Service at Montefiore, the syndrome that a given patient presents remains relatively constant through adolescence for most patients. Anecdotally, those few children to date who indeed demonstrate reading spurts in adolescence have had a family history in which the father or uncle reports a similar course. Concurrent with the spurt, and in two cases one year prior to this surge in reading, the dyslexia syndrome was no longer present.

SUMMARY

Presented for consideration because of its heuristic value is a model of dyslexia which presumes that a defect in any one of several independent clusters of higher cortical functions will result in atypical development of reading skills. The necessity for inclusion of a brain-damaged reader group in future studies attempting to isolate causal factors was strongly emphasized. At present, while a morphological-physiological abnormality of brain is strongly suspected, the presence or absence of such brain damage, given the inadequacy of brain–behavior correlative studies in children, is not critical to the dyslexia syndromes model. Within the framework of the model, dyslexia is defined as the presence of atypical reading development as compared to that of other children of similar age, intelligence, instructional program, and sociocultural opportunity which, without intervention, is expected to persist and is due to a well-defined defect in any one of several specific higher cortical functions. Therefore, the diagnosis of dyslexia is not based on a single measurement of reading, but, like any other clinical diagnosis, on both positive and negative findings obtained by history and examination.

Part II

PSYCHOLOGICAL FACTORS

Chapter 4

TOWARD AN UNDERSTANDING OF DYSLEXIA: PSYCHOLOGICAL FACTORS IN SPECIFIC READING DISABILITY

FRANK R. VELLUTINO

DEFINITION

Dyslexia is a medical term referring to disorder in reading, presumably due to some form of neurological dysfunction. It is also known as specific reading disability, and the terms are employed interchangeably. The literature dealing with the problem is uniform in its suggestion that dyslexia is an intrinsic developmental anomaly, the etiology of which is qualitatively different from reading difficulties arising because of extrinsic or environmental factors. The fact remains, however, that dyslexia is not a well-defined entity and its characteristics are not easily distinguished from any other form of reading deficiency. Indeed, some believe that there is little point in attempting to differentiate neurologically based reading disorder from reading problems caused by other factors, especially since its remedy lies almost exclusively upon reeducation and other behavioral treatment methods (International Reading Association, 1972).

Yet in spite of this attitude, one that from a practical standpoint is reasonable and justified, those concerned with reading disability are puzzled by children, apparently normal in other respects, who have inordinate difficulty in learning to read. Such children have attracted the attention of researchers as well as practitioners and prompted them to circumscribe their definition of the disorder to exclude probable extrinsic causes, and consider the possibility of basic developmental deficiency in the population so defined. Thus it has

This chapter is a synopsis of a monograph entitled "Theory and Research in Dyslexia" to be published by the Massachusetts Institute of Technology Press in 1978.

been suggested (Rabinovitch, 1959; Johnson and Myklebust, 1967) that the study of dyslexia is best undertaken in children with average or above average intelligence, who have no peripheral sensory deficits, severe brain damage, or other debilitating physical problems, who have not been hampered by serious emotional and social disorders or by cultural disadvantage, and who have had adequate opportunity to learn (Rabinovitch, 1959; Johnson and Myklebust, 1967; Eisenberg, 1966 and this vol. Chap. 2).

The above definition is, of course, one of exclusion, and, thus carries with it all of the weaknesses inherent in such definitions. The most obvious weakness, of course, is the fact that it provides us with little positive information which unequivocally defines specific learning disability. However, given our limited understanding of the nature of this disorder, it would seem that the investigator has little choice but to employ exclusionary criteria in identifying a research population, in order to avoid confounding by secondary or extrinsic variables such as those outlined above. Yet there are certain pitfalls in doing so.

Most researchers studying the etiology of reading disability would agree that the reading problems of children with subnormal intelligence are not primarily due to developmental dyslexia. Because of their conceptual deficits, such children can be expected to have general rather than specific learning disability. Yet there is no general consensus as to how one should evaluate conceptual development in poor readers. The significance of this difficulty will be brought into focus when it is pointed out that the measure of intelligence employed by those interested in conducting research in this area is by no means an arbitrary choice and depends upon their conceptions of both intelligence and reading ability. To be specific, the theorist who postulates that dyslexia is attributable to visuospatial disorder would be ill-advised to employ, for sample selection, a measure of intelligence that is heavily laden with items that require spatial reasoning and visualization. A similar difficulty would obtain for linguistically oriented theorists who select subjects through the use of intelligence tests that contain a large proportion of verbal items. For those who suggest that dyslexia encompasses subgroups of poor readers with *either* verbal *or* nonverbal learning difficulties, selection of intelligence tests that are not balanced with respect to verbal and nonverbal content would create unnecessary problems of interpretation (e.g., Mylkebust and Johnson, 1962; Ingram, Mason, and Blackburn, 1970; Boder, 1971; Mattis, French, and Rapin, 1975).

That commonly employed tests of intelligence may yield differential results in poor and normal readers is provided some support by a large number of studies finding reader group differences on the verbal and performance subscales of the Wechsler Intelligence Scale for Children (e.g., Belmont and

Birch, 1966; Warrington, 1967; Lyle and Goyen, 1969). Thus the researcher would do well to employ intelligence measures in accord with the limitations of the theory he wishes to test, traditional considerations of reliability and validity notwithstanding. Unfortunately not all studies of reading disability currently available in the literature have complied with this standard.

The logic of testing for sensory acuity in sampling for dyslexia would seem to be clear-cut. Nevertheless, some authors suggest that deficiencies in oculomotor functioning can lead to visuoperceptual problems, and thereby to reading difficulties in spite of adequate visual acuity (e.g., Getman, 1962; Flax, 1970; Rosner, 1972). However, as has been pointed out by Lawson (1974) and Benton (1975) there is no convincing evidence to support this view.

The remaining exclusionary criteria are not so clear-cut. For example, to suggest that children with known brain damage be excluded from samples of dyslexics may seem at variance with the suggestion that specific reading disability is a developmental disorder of neurological origin. Yet there is no necessary contradiction in such exclusion because brain damage implies tissue destruction which could result in a number of secondary sequelae. Dyslexia, on the other hand, may involve no apparent tissue damage and yet result from developmental neurological difficulty of a functional nature.

Physical disability may be defended as an exclusion criterion on the strength of the possibility that children so afflicted may be subjected to environmental circumstances that do not provide them with the intellectual and personal experiences that normally facilitate adequate growth and achievement (e.g., Schonell, 1956). The exclusion of culturally and economically disadvantaged children from research samples can be justified on similar grounds (Rabinovitch, 1959, 1968; Eisenberg, 1966, this vol.—Chap. 2; Birch and Gussow, 1970).

It would also seem reasonable to exclude children with significant emotional and adjustment problems from samples of prospective dyslexics, since these deficiencies inevitably lead to difficulties in attention, motivation, and effort. However, attempting to do so is problematic since there are currently no satisfactory measures of emotional and adjustment status in children. Because of this difficulty, the researcher must content himself with the identification and exclusion of children with the more obvious forms of emotional disorder.

And while children who have not been exposed to educational programs of good quality cannot be reasonably studied as possible dyslexics, the development of adequate evaluative criteria has been fraught with difficulty (Worthen and Sanders, 1973). In fact, there are at present no readily available techniques for assessing adequacy of educational programming that have been extensively validated. Consequently, the researcher must rely upon indirect methods for controlling the possibility that some poor readers in his samples may be the victims of inadequate educational opportunity.

With respect to their reading behaviors, dyslexics are described as children who have unusual difficulty in identifying words as wholes, as well as in segmenting them into their component sounds. They also have apparent difficulty in abstracting and generalizing the common constituents of given words, and are inclined to treat those (words) containing redundant elements (*cat* vs. *fat*) as discrete entities. In addition, dyslexics are characterized by a tendency to make orientation and sequencing errors in reading and writing (e.g., b/d or was/saw). Such children also tend to be poor spellers and their written language is markedly deficient in all respects.

There are also a number of other characteristics, not uniformly apparent in dyslexics, which are said to occur often enough to be examined for their possible significance (Bryant, 1965; Critchley, 1970). Among those mentioned in the literature are the following: (1) boys are observed to have reading problems more often than girls; the ratios generally exceed 4 : 1 (Eisenberg, 1966); (2) frequently, there is a significant incidence of reading difficulties in the families of poor readers (Hermann, 1959; Hallgren, 1950; Owen, this vol.—Chap. 13) (3) poor readers have been said to experience apparent difficulty in other forms of representational learning, such as telling time, naming the months and seasons of the year, and discriminating left from right; (4) some have observed in poor readers the occasional appearance of neurological "soft" signs such as abnormal reflexes or minor coordination problems; and (5) poor readers are frequently characterized by a history of developmental deficiencies, particularly in one or more aspects of language (Kawi and Pasamanick, 1958; Lyle, 1970).

It should be apparent from the above that criteria for the nature and origin of developmental dyslexia are not very definitive. Yet for research purposes, there are some useful guidelines which one may employ for operationally defining the "probable" dyslexic, i.e., the impaired reader whose reading difficulties are quite likely attributable to basic developmental disorder rather than extrinsic or environmental factors. As a result of our own study of the problem, my colleagues and I have evolved the following tentative criteria for circumscribing a research population.

First, we would identify as a probable dyslexic, only the child who has extreme difficulty in identifying single words, and who, consequently, has difficulty with all other aspects of reading (Shankweiler and Liberman, 1972). Secondly, the probable dyslexic not only sustains difficulty in his ability to recognize printed words on sight, but finds it equally difficult to analyze their component sounds. Some authors propose that there are subgroups of poor readers characterized by difficulties in *either* sight word learning *or* word analysis, as a result of neurological dysfunction that is qualitatively different in each instance (e.g., Myklebust and Johnson, 1962; Boder, 1970; Ingram, Mason, and Blackburn, 1970; Mattis, French, and Rapin, 1975). However, there is reason to believe (Chall, 1967) that this subdivision of the pattern emerges primarily in children who have had limited exposure to one or the other strategy for word decoding, respectively, and that it would not be very parsimonious to attribute reading problems in such children to disturbed neurology.

Finally, we would apply the term "dyslexia" only to children who have severe decoding problems and not to children with adequate decoding skills but with poor comprehension of what they read. Nor would we employ the term with children who are mildly to moderately impaired in reading. Thus the probable dyslexic might best be selected through the use of individually administered measures of oral reading and word analysis skills, making one's selection criteria stringent enough to identify only the most severely impaired readers. The use of silent reading tests for selecting children of this description is to be avoided since these measures are too easily confounded by poor motivation, inattention, and deficient study skills.

In our own sampling, we have relied initially upon referrals from teachers who were asked to provide us with the names of their most severely impaired readers for possible inclusion in our studies. We then tested all subjects referred and tentatively selected only those children scoring two or more years below their grade placement. This achievement criterion was adopted to be consistent with the standard employed in most of the research literature and to compare our findings with the results of studies evaluating similar hypotheses. The only exception was the use of one or more years below "grade" level as the criterion for second graders. These procedures have consistently yielded samples of poor readers whose reading achievement scores on the oral reading test employed (Gilmore, 1968) have typically fallen between the *fourth* and *tenth* percentile, i.e., between one and two standard deviations below the means of the standardization samples.

Application of the exclusionary criteria outlined above is generally a more formidable undertaking than defining reading achievement. Evaluating children for sensory problems typically causes the least amount of difficulty since most school systems conduct their own screening programs, and information about the adequacy of a child's hearing and vision is usually available to the researcher. Similarly, gross neurological and physical disabilities, as well as the more severe forms of emotional disorder can be ruled out on the basis of information provided by parents and school officials.

Assessing intelligence is more troublesome, since there are few measures that are balanced with respect to verbal and nonverbal content. As indicated above, the failure to employ an intelligence test that minimizes confounding by virtue of differing verbal and nonverbal abilities in poor and normal readers, may well lead to sampling problems that preclude reasonable tests of etiological hypotheses which differentially implicate these abilities as possible areas of difficulty. Thus in sample selection, it is advisable to employ an intelligence test that does not create the risk of excluding the population of interest. Therefore, in order to avoid this difficulty the researcher should employ either one test that specifically balances verbal and nonverbal content or several measures that are factorially homogeneous with respect to their assessment of these general areas. In our own research, we have typically employed the WISC as a selection measure, including only children who achieved an IQ of 90 or above on *either* the verbal or performance subscales. This strategy has allowed us to contrast our subjects' performance on standardized measures of verbal and nonverbal skill with their performance on experimental tasks designed to test specific hypotheses related to these skills.

In order to avoid contamination by sociocultural factors, the researcher may employ objective measures of socioeconomic and cultural status. If such information is unattainable, some control over these variables is afforded by sampling only in schools located in middle- or upper-middle-class neighborhoods, except when reading problems in environmentally disadvantaged youngsters is employed as a contrast variable. Because in our own locale it has been difficult to obtain information of the type in question, we have had to rely upon the latter method for controlling for sociocultural differences in poor and normal readers.

Finally, since there is no adequate control for such factors as more subtle emotional and adjustment problems, attentional and motivation deficiencies, and/or inadequate opportunity for learning, the researcher has no other recourse but to indirectly control for these factors by (1) designing cross-validation studies with independent samples, (2) varying his methods of testing given hypotheses, and (3) employing identical sampling procedures in all such studies. We also suggest that, because of the high probability of encountering problems of the types just mentioned, the researcher would be ill-advised to routinely employ clinic populations in initial study of specific reading disability, except when comparisons of clinic and nonclinic cases is the object of study. Our own investigations have uniformly excluded clinic cases in sample selection.

We should add the important caveat that specific developmental disorders which could lead to reading difficulties in otherwise normal children may theoretically occur in those who would typically be excluded from research study because of one or more of the extrinsic variables discussed above. Thus a child with low intelligence or one who is culturally disadvantaged may also sustain a specific development anomaly that itself could contribute to reading disability. However, it would be difficult in such instances to differentiate primary and secondary contributing factors and the exclusion of such children from research samples would seem to be necessary when the object of study is the isolation of factors that cause specific rather than general learning disabilities.

THEORIES OF DYSLEXIA

In spite of these definitional problems, there is enough evidence from research and clinical practice to warrant further study of reading problems in children who are apparently normal in other respects. Accordingly, the remainder of this chapter will be devoted to a critical review of current conceptualizations of the etiology of specific reading disability. Major theoretical explanations of the disorder will be related to recent empirical findings with the aim of suggesting some alternative avenues for future investigation. Relevant research will be reviewed and integrated with the results of research from our own laboratory. Emphasis will be placed upon *immediate* or behavioral correlates of specific reading disability rather than *ultimate* or neurological correlates. An excellent review of current theorizing with respect to the neurological bases of reading disability has recently been provided by Benton (1975) and the reader is referred to that source for detailed information on the topic.

The literature in the area of reading disability provides us with several possible explanations of the disorder. The theories which have emerged are of two general types: those which emphasize a single underlying cause of reading disability, and those which suggest that there is more than one basic deficiency which leads to reading problems. The *single-factor theories* constitute the largest collection of hypothesized explanations of dyslexia (Vellutino, 1978). These typically have a medical-organic foundation and, with few exceptions, postulate some form of neurological dysfunction as the basis of reading disability. The majority make reference to dysfunction in visuospatial processing as the primary factor contributing to reading disability (e.g., Orton, 1925, 1937; Bender, 1956, 1957, 1975; Hermann, 1959), while a lesser number (e.g., Rabinovitch, 1959; Downing, 1973; Elkonin, 1973; Liberman and Shankweiler, in press) ascribe a significant role to language and speech problems as possible explanations of dyslexia.

Some authors have underscored the importance of maturational factors that lead to various types of disorder affecting cognitive processes (e.g., Orton, 1925, 1937; Eustis, 1947a, b; Olson, 1949; Bender, 1956, 1957; Staz and Sparrow, 1970). Others (e.g., Hermann, 1959) have stressed the importance of hereditary factors in explanation of inferred perceptual deficiencies in dyslexics, and a few have suggested that reading disability is attributable to dysfunction in temporal-order processing (e.g., Zurif and Carson, 1970; Bakker, 1972; Corkin, 1974).

In contrast to single-factor explanations of reading disability, *multifactor theories* generally implicate modality-specific deficits which represent distinctly different underlying causes of the disorder. Thus several authors have made reference to different types of "dyslexia" characterized by children whose primary deficiencies presumably occur either in the auditory or the visual spheres (Myklebust and Johnson, 1962; Johnson and Myklebust, 1967; Boder, 1970, 1971; Ingram, Mason, and Blackburn, 1970; Mattis, French, and Rapin, 1975).

Perhaps the most influential of the multi-factor theorists was Birch (1962), who suggested that there may exist at least three subcategories of dyslexia. These include (1) children whose reading difficulties are attributable to the failure to establish visual hierarchical dominance, resulting in figure-ground problems, (2) poor readers who experience disorder in visual analysis and synthesis, i.e., in learning (visual) part-whole relationships, and (3) poor readers who are primarily deficient in intersensory integration.

However, in spite of the diversity which characterizes both single and multifactor explanations of dyslexia, four basic processes are consistently implicated as possible areas of difficulty: visual perception, intersensory integration, temporal ordering, and verbal processing. The following sections are devoted to a selective review of research relating to each of these areas.

DEFICIENCIES IN VISUAL PERCEPTION

Of all of the theories advanced in explanation of specific reading disability, there is little doubt that the perceptual deficit hypothesis has been the most popular. The most widely held version of this conceptualization is that of Orton (1925, 1937) who suggested that reading disability is caused by visuo-spatial confusion associated with neurological deficiency. Orton rejected earlier suggestions (Morgan, 1896; Hinshelwood, 1900, 1917) that developmental dyslexia is associated with structural damage to portions of the brain support-ing visual memory. He proposed instead that the disorder is caused by a neurological-maturational lag resulting in delayed lateral dominance for language, leading in turn to disturbances in perceptual functioning. Such dis-turbances were thought to be apparent in both spoken and written language, characterized in reading by the failure to develop the normal "habit" of sup-pressing the symmetrical or "mirror engrams" of printed letters and words believed to be situated in each of the hemispheres.

Orton also suggested that such dysfunction was the basic cause of apparent perceptual distortions in reading (i.e., reading *b* as *d*, or *was* as *saw*), as well as the orientation and sequencing errors commonly observed in the writing of dyslexics (e.g., mirror writing). These inaccuracies were con-sidered to be of the utmost importance in understanding the nature and basic cause of reading disability, and, in effect, constituted the primary evidence in support of the theory. Noteworthy here is Orton's belief that errors of the type in question would only be manifested in the processing of symbolic stimuli and not in dealing with events and objects of a concrete nature.

Orton's view stimulated much interest in the problem of reading disability in young children and gave rise to several other theories stressing dysfunction in visual processing as a basic cause of this disorder. Space limita-tions permit only brief mention of a few. For example, Bender (1956, 1957) postulated that reading disability is quite likely associated with a develop-mental delay resulting in poorly established lateral dominance. However, the cardinal disturbance leading to reading difficulties was thought to be dysfunc-tion in figure-ground organization as reflected in deficient graphomotor func-tions and other so-called "perceptual" activities. A similar position was adopted by Drew (1956) and later by Birch (1962), as noted earlier.

Hermann (1959) also suggested that specific reading disability is the result of dysfunction in visuospatial processing, but unlike Orton and Bender, he attributed the disorder to a genetic disposition toward directional confusion. Hermann apparently conceptualized directional set as an inborn entity with absolute characteristics. Noteworthy in this connection is his suggestion that directional confusion should be apparent in the dyslexic's encounters with other symbolic stimuli such as numerals and musical notations, as well as in the learning of spatial relationships encountered in the world of objects.

Finally, several authors have suggested that reading disability may be associated with abnormal motor development which presumably results in deficient integration of "perceptual-motor systems" (e.g., Kephart, 1960; Cruickshank, 1968; Frostig and Maslow, 1973). Still others suggest that reading failure may be attributed to a variety of optical deficiencies leading to perceptual disorder (Getman, 1962; Anapolle, 1967).

It can be seen that the common thread in all of the above theories is the view that developmental reading disability is primarily the result of problems in visual organization and visual memory. However, in our opinion, perceptual deficiencies of the types variously proposed by Orton and others (e.g., Bender, 1956, 1957, 1975; Hermann, 1959) are unlikely sources of reading disability. We believe this to be true for several reasons.

First, it would seem to be both illogical and counterintuitive to suggest that dyslexics are subject to optical reversibility, spatial disorientation, and figure-ground difficulties in the literal sense since such disorders should be apparent in many other functions in daily living (Orton, 1925, 1937; Bender, 1956, 1957, 1975; Hermann, 1959). Yet there is no evidence that dyslexics do show these disorders in diverse activities. Furthermore, Orton's suggestion that perceptual distortions should occur only in symbolic learning seems implausible, particularly since there are more parsimonious explanations of apparent "spatial disorientation" in dyslexics as will be seen below.

It also seems unnecessary to posit that poor readers are inherently deficient in their ability to establish a "dircetional sense" (Hermann, 1959). Orientation in two- or three-dimensional space is a relative rather than an absolute function that emerges largely because of acquired relationships, and not because of inborn capacities. We store information to program proper orientation and such information has functional value in relation to the unique properties of specific environmental and/or representational coordinates, most of which are quite arbitrary in nature. Thus, written English proceeds from left to right while Hebrew and Arabic script proceeds from right to left. Directionality in such instances must be learned. It is not innate as suggested in directional-set theories of reading disability.

Secondly, we concur with the suggestion of a number of authors that reading is primarily a linguistic skill (Goodman, 1965, 1968; Smith, 1971; Mattingly, 1972; Liberman and Shankweiler, in press). This is contrary to traditional views which suggest that vision is the more influential system in acquiring skill in reading (Young and Lindsley, 1971), and it is certainly at variance with the perceptual-deficit theories at issue here. However, if one carefully analyzes the reading process, it will become clear that this function taxes the visual and linguistic systems unequally and, further, that the heavier burden appears to be on the side of language.

In support of this suggestion, we might make the rather elementary point that reading is a process which involves not only recognition or familiarity with the visual constituents of printed words but also recall or reproduction of their verbal constituents. In addition, the orthographic structure of written English, ultimately, allows for a good deal of economy of visual processing, by virtue of the redundancies inherent in an alphabetic symbol system. Such redundancy is reflected in the recursive use of a limited number of alphabetic characters (26 letters in English) and in the high frequency with which certain letter combinations (e.g., *qu, th, tion, ing,* etc.) occur in given words (Smith, 1971). Furthermore, of the five categories of information contained in even a single word (i.e., graphic, orthographic, phonologic, semantic, and syntactic), three have reference to linguistic functions. Thus, it would seem that in reading the demands upon memory are greater in the verbal sphere than in the visual sphere and the acquisition of skill in reading would thereby appear to be especially vulnerable to disorder in one or more aspects of language.

Finally, it is suggested that the positional and directional errors commonly observed in the reading and writing of poor readers (e.g., b/d, was/saw) and long thought to be compelling evidence in favor of a perceptual deficit explanation of reading disability, are in fact linguistic intrusion errors caused by imprecision in verbal mediation, rather than visual distortions caused by dysfunction at the level of the central nervous system, as suggested by Orton (1925, 1937) and others (e.g., Bender, 1956, 1957; Hermann, 1959). In simpler terms, it is our contention that children who called *b d* or *was saw* do not literally "see" these configurations differently than normal readers, but, because of one or more deficiencies in verbal processing, cannot remember which verbal label is associated with which printed symbol.

The more general inference here is that the linguistic attributes inherent in printed letters and words (assuming normal ability to associate these visual symbols with their verbal counterparts), ultimately constitute implicit mnemonics which aid the reader in making critical visual discriminations necessary for accurate decoding. The child who is sensitized to the phonemic and articulatory differences in graphically similar letters and words (e.g., *b d, p q, was saw, loin, lion*) and who, in the case of the words, knows the differences between their meanings and uses in sentences, has a variety of linguistic cues to aid him in programming the correct orientations and sequences characteristic of those configurations. Conversely, the child who has difficulty in acquiring such verbal information is at a distinct disadvantage in making the fine-grained visual discriminations necessary for learning the code and for establishing visual-verbal equivalence generally. Thus, he will continue to make the kinds of positional and directional errors which support the belief that he is "perceptually impaired." Evidence for this contention will be presented in the following sections.

RESEARCH EVIDENCE

In an early review of research issuing from perceptual-deficit theories of reading disability, Benton (1962) made note of methodological weaknesses and conflicting results in studies supporting such theories and concluded that deficient form perception and disturbed directional functioning are not important correlates of reading disability. He also suggested that reading disability in children at the age levels assessed (9 years and above) may be due to dysfunction in verbal mediation. However, he allowed for the possibility that reading disability in children at younger age levels (below 9 years) may be due to perceptual deficiencies.

In a later review, Benton (1975) again found conflicting results in studies evaluating perceptual-deficit theories of dyslexia and concluded that "the importance of visuoperceptive and visuomotor difficulties as determinates of reading failure has been overrated by some authors" (Benton, 1975, p. 15).

We are in essential agreement with Benton, as has been clearly indicated in the point of view outlined in the preceding section. However, more definitive support for the present position will necessitate some explanation of disparate findings which have appeared in the literature. Accordingly, the following sections are devoted to a brief review of a representative sampling of these studies, giving particular emphasis to those which are more recent.

It has long been suggested that specific reading disability may be diagnosed with the aid of "maturation sensitive" tests which presumably measure basic aspects of neuromotor development. This has been a popular notion among both clinicians and researchers, having received initial impetus from the developmental studies of Schilder (1944), Gesell (1952), and Bender (1956, 1957). Thus, a number of investigators have reported significant correlations between performance on figure drawing tests (e.g., Bender-Gestalt Test) administered to kindergartners and reading achievement measures administered after some instruction in reading (de Hirsch, Jansky, and Langford, 1966; Wedell and Horne, 1969; Jansky and de Hirsch, 1972; Satz, Friel, and Rudegeair, 1974, 1976). Several others have reported differences between good and poor readers on like measures administered concurrent with reading achievement tests (Silver and Hagin, 1960, 1971; Lovell, Shapton, and Warren, 1964; Lovell, Gray, and Oliver, 1964).

However, the results of these studies afford at best tenuous support for perceptual-deficit explanations of reading disability. First, it should be pointed out that poor readers in all of these investigations performed below the level of normal readers on a variety of tasks that were both verbal and nonverbal in nature, and not only on measures of visuomotor functions. It may therefore be erroneous to infer that the poor readers in these samples were selectively impaired in visual perception. A more parsimonious interpretation of the results is that these children were hampered by general rather than specific learning difficulties, quite possibly associated with conceptual, experiential, emotional, and/or motivational factors.

The latter possibility would be consonant with the second point we wish to make that, in all but two of these studies (Lovell, Shapton, and Warren, 1964; Lovell, Gray, and Oliver, 1964), there were no adequate controls for possible confounding by socioeconomic factors. Furthermore, in a number of these investigations results were based upon clinical populations, which typically include children with multiple handicaps (Silver and Hagin, 1960, 1971; de Hirsch, Jansky, and Langford, 1966; Jansky and de Hirsch, 1972). It would, therefore, seem to be difficult to defend the inference that reading disability is associated with specific learning disability characterized by visuomotor dysfunction on the basis of results from the studies in question.

In contrast to the above, are the findings of four other studies reporting no substantial differences between poor and normal readers, either on measures of visuomotor skill or on tests of visual retention (Nielsen and Ringe, 1969; Symmes and Rapoport, 1972; Vellutino et al., 1973; Vellutino et al., 1975b). Noteworthy in these studies is the fact that in all instances the samples were carefully screened to exclude children whose reading difficulties may have been caused by the extrinsic variables discussed earlier (e.g., intelligence, emotional and social factors, cultural disadvantage, etc.).

Finally, a general criticism that can be applied to the use of visuomotor tasks to evaluate visual perception is that they incur the risk of confounding motor deficiencies with perceptual processing, which may be particularly problematic among children who have propensities toward disorder in both reading and visuomotor functioning. In such instances a causal relationship may be inferred between these two variables when no such relationship exists.

The perceptual-deficit theory of reading disability has taken a variety of other forms. Thus, it has been suggested that the "perceptual" problems of poor readers will become manifest on tests of visual analysis, high-speed visual processing, spatial orientation, and visual memory. A brief review of selected laboratory studies investigating these possibilities follows.

The suggestion that poor readers may sustain basic deficiencies in visual analysis (Birch, 1962) was tested in two studies comparing dyslexic and normal readers on the ability to educe simple figures embedded in complex visual arrays (Goetzinger, Dirks, and Baer, 1960; Lovell, Gray, and Oliver, 1964). In each of these investigations poor readers performed below the level of normal readers on the measure in question.

However, these findings cannot necessarily be taken as support for the contention that poor readers suffer from basic perceptual deficiency. We might point out initially that both of these investigations yielded inconsistent results in that poor readers performed as well as normals on some measures of visual analysis and not as well on others. Thus, the reliability of the findings is in doubt.

The results of these studies can also be questioned on interpretive grounds. Aside from the possibility that poor readers (or any deficient learner) may be generally less attentive than normal readers in engaging any task that requires effort and concentration, it is conceivable that poor readers have not acquired appropriate "orienting attitudes" that allow one to process patterned (visual) information efficiently, in part *because* of negative learning associated with reading failure. We refer in this instance to the development of a cognitive skill characterized by the ability and disposition to "search" for invariant and distinguishing relationships, as a result of successful experience in processing complex visual material (Gibson, 1969, 1971). It may well be that successful achievement in reading is a very significant factor in developing such "attitudes." On the other hand, failure in reading may lead to inefficiency in processing patterned visual stimuli, partly because of negative affect leading to avoidance, but perhaps, more importantly, because it may impede the development of an implicit "'set" to search for invariant and anchoring relationships that will facilitate discrimination and economy of perceptual processing.

Of interest here is the results of a study by Gottschalk, Bryden, and Rabinovitch (1964) in which it was found that the ability to systematically scan a complex visual array did not emerge until ages five and six. In evaluating these findings, Vernon (1971), speculates that the development of such ability might be a by-product of successful experience in learning to read. Thus, the poor readers in these studies may not have a primary perceptual deficiency, but may have been inefficient in abstracting embedded figures because of reading difficulty.

A logical extension of the perceptual-deficit hypothesis is that poor readers would be differentiated from normal readers in presentations of visual material emphasizing speed and economy of visual processing. Thus, a few studies have reported differences between poor and normal readers on visual search and match to standard tasks under timed conditions (e.g., Doehring, 1968; Katz and Wicklund, 1971, 1972). However, the results of these investigations are equivocal on three counts. First, the reliability of the findings is in doubt because poor and normal readers did not always differ on the visual matching tasks administered. Secondly, in all three studies, reader groups were compared on the high-speed scanning of printed letters and words, with the exception of the study by Doehring (1968) which employed both verbal and nonverbal stimuli. To infer that poor readers suffer from perceptual deficiency on the basis of findings employing letters and words would seem to be somewhat misguided in that learning involving such stimuli is known to be problematic for poor readers.

The third equivocal aspect of the studies in question is that they typically did not control for the possible effects of reader-group differences in verbal coding ability. Since the tasks employed in three studies by definition taxed the upper limits of visual short-term memory (Miller, 1956; Sperling, 1960; Simon, 1972), dysfunction in the recoding and synthesizing of visual stimuli could have resulted in performance deficits. Thus, given the possibility that poor readers are less adequate than normal readers in effecting such recoding (Blank and Bridger, 1966; Blank, Weider, and Bridger, 1968; Kastner and Rickards, 1974), it may be in error to conclude that reader-group differences on visual matching and visual search tasks are attributable to perceptual deficiency in poor readers.

In this connection, Calfee (1977) has criticized the widespread use of visual discrimination tests which typically employ the match-to-standard procedure characterized by presentation of a target stimulus prior to search of a multiple-choice array. He suggests that such tasks are inadvertently confounded by upper limits on short-term visual memory, as a result of (1) the amount of material to be processed, interacting with (2) the limited duration of the visual after-image corresponding with the standard. Thus, he has demonstrated that when the target and the distractor items are laid out horizontally, the probability of error increases as the location of the correct match moves farther to the right. Calfee has contrasted these findings with results derived from match-to-standard tasks employing a single-alternate format. He reports that by comparison, the latter procedure reduces the error rate to negligible proportions even among very young children (kindergartners). These findings indirectly support the contention that the visual matching tasks employed in the studies discussed above may have been confounded by constraints on visual short-term memory, and thus by possible readergroup differences in verbal coding ability.

A similar criticism can be applied to recent studies by Lyle and Goyen, comparing dyslexic and normal readers on tests of visual memory. In five separate investigations poor readers (ages 6 to 9 years) were found to be less accurate than normal readers on short-term memory for both verbal and nonverbal material presented visually (Lyle, 1968; Goyen and Lyle, 1971a, 1971b; Goyen and Lyle, 1973; Lyle and Goyen, 1975). The tasks employed were typically of the match-to-standard type and involved both immediate and delayed recognition.

Noteworthy in these studies is the fact that poor and normal readers were differentiated only on visual processing tasks that were characterized by *brief* exposures of visual material. In contrast, comparably selected reader groups were not found to be different on the WISC Block Design, a measure of spatial ability involving no significant memory factor (Lyle and Goyen, 1969). Furthermore, the latter finding was derived from contrasts of poor and normal readers who were also found to differ on memory for geometric designs (Lyle, 1968), the results from the two data sets being published separately. This disparity provides indirect support for the notion that readergroup differences on the visual memory tasks employed in the above studies were attributable to short-term memory problems possibly associated with verbal coding deficiency rather than perceptual disorder. The results of another study by these investigators (Goyen and Lyle, 1971b) reinforce the latter interpretation: poor and normal readers did not differ on visual-associates learning. It can be inferred that both groups displayed both adequate perception and (long-term) visual memory.

As noted earlier, a basic premise of perceptual-deficit theories of reading disability is that poor readers are inclined toward spatial and directional confusion, as manifested in such anomalies as (1) orientation and sequencing errors in writing and oral reading, (2) inability to establish a left–right directional set, and (3) difficulties in distinguishing the right and left sides of the body and like problems. While the literature is replete with *indirect* tests of this hypothesis (as is reflected in the sampling of studies discussed above), only a few investigations have directly assessed its validity (Benton, 1962, 1975). Prototypical studies include tests of left–right discrimination (e.g., Belmont and Birch, 1965) and evaluation of orientation and directional errors in reading and writing (e.g., Lyle, 1969; Liberman et al., 1971; Shankweiler and Liberman, 1972). A general finding in these studies is that poor readers are differentiated from normal readers in applying the correct verbal labels to items characterized by positional and directional constancy. While some authors ascribed such error patterns to spatial confusion (e.g., Lyle, 1969), others do not.

For example, Liberman et al. (1971) found that orientation (b/d) and sequencing (was/saw) errors accounted for only 25 percent of the total percentage of errors in lists containing words that could be easily confused (e.g., was/saw; top/pot). Furthermore, correlations of these types of errors were low, which is contrary to directional-confusion theories of reading disability. It was thereby concluded that inaccuracies caused by failure to account for directional and positional constancy, as commonly observed in poor readers, are linguistic intrusion (mislabeling) errors rather than perceptual distortions. It seems that this interpretation is also a plausible alternative to the popular notion that inaccuracies in naming the two sides of the body are the result of spatial and directional confusion.

While the most common description of (inferred) perceptual deficiency in poor readers suggests that these individuals sustain difficulties in form perception and spatial orientation, as indicated above, a more recent perceptual deficit theory has emerged which suggests that poor readers are characterized by inadequacies in "perceiving" spatial location and spatial redundancy (Mason, 1975; Mason and Katz, 1976). According to this point of view, poor readers are comparable to normal readers in distinguishing the visual features and general shapes of letters and words, but are inefficient in employing the "spatial redundancies" which inhere in the recurrent appear-

ance of letters in given spatial locations, such redundancy being a characteristic of all orthographies based on an alphabet. The proponents of this viewpoint further suggest that the poor reader's inadequacies in "perceiving"
spatial locations may be generalized to nonalphabetic material and they have
produced evidence which presumably accords with this suggestion. Specifically, poor readers demonstrated longer latencies than normal readers in
searching for spatially redundant IBM characters, although these groups did
not differ in detecting spatial location in nonredundant arrays employing the
same characters. The authors, therefore, conclude that the ability to "perceive" the spatial location of letters is quite distinct from the ability to perceive their shapes, and that these two functions may be "mediated by different
brain regions" (Mason and Katz, 1976, p. 347).

This variation of the perceptual deficit explanation of reading disability is not very compelling. While it is not surprising to find that poor
readers do not "search" spatially redundant letter strings as well as normals,
this difficulty does not necessarily imply a basic deficiency in the central nervous system. A more plausible explanation of these findings is perceptual
inefficiency, which itself may be a by-product of basic coding difficulties in
reading. Dysfunction in abstracting and generalizing the orthographic and
phonemic redundancies characteristic of an alphabet is a predictable correlate
of reading disability and need not be attributed to a primary defect in central
processing. Furthermore, the fact that poor and normal readers differed, even
on nonalphabetic material, does not necessarily support the inference of a primary central processing defect, since differential ability to detect spatial redundancy in letter arrays could generalize to the detection of such redundancy in letter-like strings, particularly when speed rather than accuracy
distinguishes reader groups. Mason and Katz (1976) assumed that employing
IBM characters controlled for confounding by linguistic factors, but the
critical variable in this study was visual search of redundant stimuli which we
presume is an acquired skill that can be implicitly applied to the discrimination of both letter and letter-like strings. Thus, the Mason and Katz (1976)
study provides no clear support for their theory.

Reinforcing the above conclusions is the fact that poor readers did
not differ from normals in the number of errors they made on the search task
employed in this study and differed only in the time taken to detect a standard.
It may also be pointed out that these studies did not control for reader group
differences in intelligence and other exclusionary variables.

In order to avoid the methodological and interpretive problems characteristic of the investigations discussed above, my colleagues and I designed

several studies in which we systematically assessed the influence of verbal mediation on visual processing. Three general strategies were employed. One approach was to compare poor and normal readers on short-term visual recall of letters and words when instructions were varied to facilitate attendance to either the visual or the verbal features of these stimuli. It was predicted that poor readers would perform as well as normal readers on visual encoding (graphic reproduction) of the letters and words but not as well as the normals on verbal encoding (naming). This prediction was derived from Gibson's (1971) theory of word perception, one component of which states that the featural attributes of words are apprehended sequentially and hierarchically, attendance to one attribute (e.g., *graphic* features) momentarily precluding attendance to another (e.g., phonologic features).

A second approach was to compare poor and normal readers on short- and long-term visual memory for letters and words derived from a novel orthography. The performance of these two groups was also contrasted with that of children who were familiar with the orthography. The expectation was that the children (poor and normal readers) who were unfamiliar with the novel-stimulus words would be equivalent on the visual memory tasks but would not perform as well as the children who were acquainted with these words.

A third approach was to compare reader groups on verbal and non-verbal learning tasks involving visual constituents. It was anticipated that the performance of poor readers would generally be comparable to that of normals on the visual-nonverbal learning tasks, but the groups would differ on the visual-verbal learning tasks. This research strategy, as well as those outlined above, was designed to evaluate our contention that the visual processing "deficits" apparent in poor readers are a secondary manifestation of verbal encoding difficulties in such children, and not the result of deficiencies in form perception and/or visual-spatial confusion.

This hypothesis was initially tested in two separate investigations employing the first approach mentioned above (Vellutino, Steger, and Kandel, 1972; Vellutino et al., 1975b). Poor and normal readers between the ages of 7 and 14 were selected in strict accord with the operational criteria outlined earlier and administered brief visual presentations of *three-, four-,* and *five-* item *words, scrambled letters,* and *numbers* as well as *geometric designs* and asked to copy each stimulus from memory (see Fig. 4-1). A second presentation of the verbal stimuli required subjects to pronounce each of the words and then "spell out" their letters in correct order. They were also asked to spell out the scrambled letters and numbers in correct order.

REAL WORDS

Three Letter	Four Letter	Five Letter
fly	loin	blunt
bed	form	drawn
was	calm	chair

SCRAMBLED LETTERS

Three Letter	Four Letter	Five Letter
dnv	jpyc	ztbrc
hbd	gzfs	yfpqg
mcw	qvlt	qldnr

NUMBERS

Three Digit	Four Digit	Five Digit
382	4328	96842
974	3724	31579
296	9156	86314

GEOMETRIC DESIGNS

Two Items   Three Items

Figure 4-1

Stimuli employed in poor and normal reader contrasts on immediate visual recall of verbal and nonverbal stimuli. Reproduced with the permission of the editors of *Child Development.*

A reliable finding in both investigations was that poor readers performed considerably better in the copying of the verbal stimuli than they did in naming those same stimuli. Furthermore, the performance of poor readers was comparable to that of normals on the graphic reproduction of these stimuli except when the number of items in each set (4 and 5) began to tax the limit of visual short-term memory (Miller, 1956; Simon, 1972).

An especially interesting finding in one study (Vellutino et al., 1975b) was the group-by-age (grade) interaction observed on both the copying and letter naming tasks. In this investigation, reader-group samples were stratified at second and sixth grade. It was found that only the second graders faltered in copying and naming (in correct order) the letters in four- and five-letter words, although the poor readers in second grade did not do as well as the second grade normals with these particular items. Yet, in the two reader groups in sixth grade, copying and letter naming errors were negligible. This is an impressive finding because it suggests that poor readers had acquired some knowledge of the orthographic structures of the word stimuli in spite of the fact that they had difficulty in correctly naming these stimuli.

The above results indicate that the visual perception of a given word is not necessarily reflected in the pronunciation or verbal labeling of that word. The poor readers in our samples often copied stimuli such as "was" and "calm" correctly, but nevertheless misread them as "saw" and "clam," respectively. Indeed, even the normal readers manifested this pattern to some extent, as in the case of the stimulus word "loin," on which the reader groups did not differ, either in copying or in naming. Subjects in both groups copied the word correctly, but named it incorrectly ("lion").

Also noteworthy in these studies was the fact that poor and normal readers did not differ with respect to the visual recall of geometric designs. The latter results combined with the above findings raise serious doubts about the validity of perceptual-deficit explanations of reading disability. They are also in accord with the suggestion of Liberman et al. (1971) that the orientation and sequencing inaccuracies which are so often observed in the reading and writing of poor readers are in fact linguistic intrusion errors rather than perceptual distortions.

Additional support for the above conclusions is derived from two other studies conducted in our laboratory (Vellutino et al., 1973; Vellutino et al., 1975e). In order to control for previous experience with letters and words, poor and normal readers (ages 7 to 12) were presented with three-, four-, and five-letter words printed in Hebrew, an unfamiliar orthography (see Fig. 4-2). All stimuli were exposed for substantial durations (one sec-

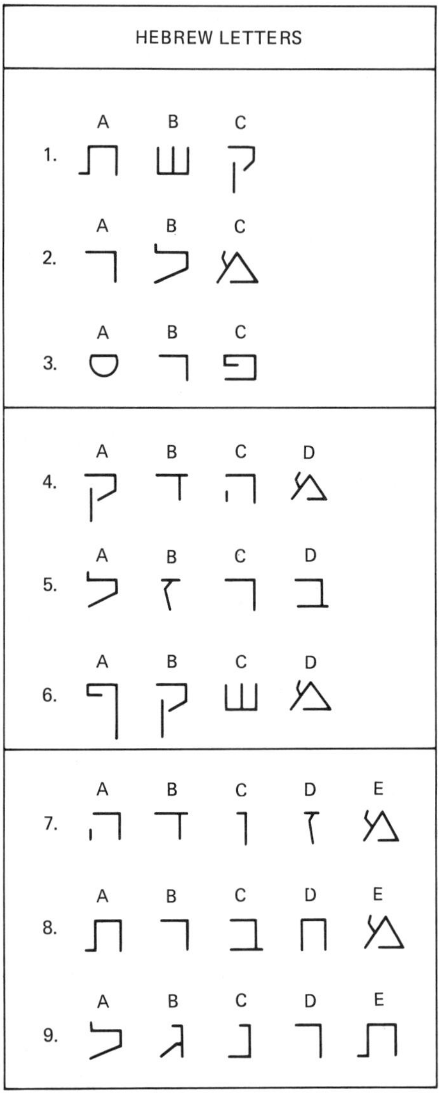

Figure 4-2

Hebrew word stimuli presented to poor and normal readers. Reproduced with permission of the editor of *Cortex*.

ond for each letter in each word) and subjects were asked to reproduce each from memory. Consistent with expectations, poor readers performed as well as normal readers on this task. In contrast, neither group performed as well as children learning to speak, read, and write Hebrew.

Also of interest was the fact that poor and normal readers who were unfamiliar with Hebrew manifested comparable (left–right) scanning tendencies, as evident in the inclination to make almost all of their errors at the right terminal positions of the word stimuli. Not surprisingly, this pattern was reversed in the case of the children who were learning to read Hebrew. These findings are at variance with the suggestion that poor readers cannot establish a left–right directional set in reading because of visuospatial confusion (e.g., Orton, 1925, 1937; Hermann, 1959).

Several of our studies compared dyslexic and normal readers on measures of long-term visual memory. For example, in a modification of those investigations employing the Hebrew letters format mentioned above poor and normal readers were found to be no different on the visual recognition of randomly arranged Hebrew letters presented for immediate and delayed recall (24 hours and 6 months) (Vellutino et al., 1975c). However, these groups did not perform as well as children who were learning Hebrew, except for the six-month delay condition, where there were no differences among any of the groups. An impressive finding in this study was that several children in each of these groups recognized a statistically significant number of items after the six-month delay period and the distributions for recognition of these items was approximately the same in all three reader groups. It can be inferred that the range of individual differences for long-term visual memory is no different among poor readers than among normal readers.

Two other studies compared poor and normal readers (grades four, five, and six) on visual-paired associates learning involving novel stimuli and found no differences between these two groups (Vellutino, Steger, and Pruzek, 1973; Vellutino et al., 1975a). However, in one of these studies the poor readers performed below the level of the normal readers on a measure of visual-verbal learning and transfer (Vellutino et al., 1975a). These data reinforce the above contention that poor readers are comparable to normals with respect to long-term visual memory. They also suggest that the learning difficulties encountered by poor readers in the visual coding of linguistic symbols may be related to dysfunction either in some aspect of verbal learning or in visual-verbal learning per se.

In summary, our review of studies evaluating perceptual-deficit explanations of reading disability suggests that support for such explanations is at best tenuous. The results of most of these investigations are equivocated by methodological and control problems and conclusions drawn from them are therefore open to question. Particularly notable in this regard is the failure to hold constant possible reader-group differences in verbal coding ability. The latter problem was particularly evident in several studies contrasting poor and normal readers on memory for visually presented material. Such difficulty was compounded in many instances by the utilization of letters and words as matching stimuli, a procedure which clearly places the poor reader at a disadvantage. Thus, it would seem in error to suggest on the basis of such findings that poor readers sustain basic deficiency in visual perception.

In contrast, there is a growing body of evidence that reading disability is not associated with dysfunction in visual processing. Strong support for this view is derived from recent research which suggests that the positional and directional inaccuracies commonly observed in the reading and writing of poor readers, and long thought to be classic indicators of perceptual deficiency, may be verbal mediation errors rather than visuospatial distortions. Additional support for this view comes from several other investigations demonstrating that poor and normal readers are comparable with respect to short- and long-term memory for complex visual stimuli. These results conflict with previous findings as reviewed by Benton (1962, 1975). However, many of the studies conducted more recently were characterized by more stringent definitions of the research population, as well as systematic control for possible differences between poor and normal readers in verbal encoding ability. This was especially true of studies issuing from our own laboratory, which included a series of replications with independent samples of comparably selected subjects and the use of varying methodological strategies in tests of similar hypotheses.

DYSFUNCTION IN INTERSENSORY INTEGRATION

A second theory of reading disability that has received widespread consideration in the literature is Birch's (1962) suggestion that some poor readers may have difficulty integrating information taken in through different sense modalities. The latter hypothesis was derived from extensive work which provided some evidence that intersensory integration in normal children increases with chronological age (Birch and Lefford, 1963). Birch believed that the establishment of liaisons among the sense modalities was closely linked to the establishment of "sensory hierarchical dominance," whereby proprioceptive (internal) sensory systems eventually become subordinated to the teleoreceptor (external) systems. The cardinal assumption in this theory is that vision gradually emerges (Birch, 1962) as the superordinate modality. It is also assumed that development within sensory systems takes place prior to the establishment of relationships between systems and that sensory hierarchical dominance is an important determinant of the order in which such relationships emerge.

In extending the conceptualizations to specific reading disability, Birch (1962) suggested that there may exist a subgroup of poor readers who have not developed connections among the senses necessary for success in reading and related skills. According to this theory, poor readers would be differentiated from normal readers on tasks requiring the ability to establish equivalent sensory representations of objects and events. An additional inference was that such difficulty should not be unique to any specific modality. A series of laboratory studies was designed to evaluate this hypothesis and the results stimulated considerable research of the problem. Some of these studies are reviewed below.

RESEARCH EVIDENCE

In an initial test of the intersensory-deficit theory of reading disability, Birch and Belmont (1964) compared selected samples of poor and normal readers (ages nine to ten years) on the ability to establish equivalence between simple rhythmic patterns and their visual matches (dot patterns) presented in multiple-choice arrays. It was found that normal readers as a group performed significantly better on this task than poor readers. However, some poor readers performed adequately, while some normals did not do so. It was therefore concluded that deficiencies in the transfer of cross-modal relationships may characterize only some poor readers.

Similar results were found in a later study in which the same task was administered to children from kindergarten through sixth grade (Birch and Belmont, 1965). However, audiovisual integration was found to be correlated with reading only in the case of children in first and second grades, while intelligence was more highly correlated with reading achievement beyond that level. The authors concluded that cross-modal transfer ability must be influential at the beginning stages of reading, while intellectual factors may be more important later on.

These seminal studies by Birch and Belmont (1964, 1965) precipitated a series of investigations attempting to replicate their findings. Thus, Beery (1967) presented poor and normal readers with visual-auditory as well as auditory-visual matching tasks and found that poor readers (ages 8 to 13 years) performed below the level of normals on both measures. Sterritt and Rudnick (1966) found essentially the same results with a modified matching procedure which involved the delivery of auditory stimuli through the use of a tape recorder.

Muehl and Kremenak (1966) assessed the predictive validity of inter- vs. intramodal matching and found that the intermodal tasks correlated significantly with reading achievement at the end of first grade. In contrast, there were no significant correlations between reading achievement and intramodal matching.

The above studies represent but a sampling of the many investigations that have evaluated the intersensory-deficit theory of reading disability employing the match to standard procedure. Among those that have produced results which are contrary to the theory are the widely quoted studies of Blank and her associates (Blank and Bridger, 1966; Blank, Weider, and Bridger, 1968). These authors found that poor readers (first and fourth graders) generally performed below the level of normal readers on temporal-ordering tasks involving both intra- and intermodal stimuli. However, the poor readers were also less able than the normal readers in employing verbal mnemonics to aid recall. The authors, therefore, suggested that group differences found in previous studies evaluating poor and normal readers on intermodal matching and like measures may have been caused by "verbal concept" deficiencies rather than dysfunction in intersensory integration. Kastner and Rickards (1974) came to a similar conclusion in finding that poor readers did not employ verbal rehearsal strategies as well as normal readers as an aid to temporal-order recall.

These findings suggest that a confounding variable which may have characterized both the original studies of Birch and Belmont (1964, 1965) and many which appeared subsequently was the failure to control for *intra*-modal deficiency. This argument was made rather vigorously by Bryant (1968), who pointed out that most of the studies which had appeared in the literature prior to his critique suffered this deficiency. Additional support for this contention was derived from a study by Zigmond (1966), who found that disabled readers were inferior to normal readers on nine measures of intrasensory (auditory) functioning. Not surprisingly, the poor readers were less able than the normal readers on six out of seven intersensory tasks. She concluded that reader-group differences on intersensory functioning may have been due to intrasensory deficiencies.

A different approach to the evaluation of the theory in question was made in studies conducted by Senf and his associates (Senf, 1969; Senf and Feshbach, 1970; Senf and Freundl, 1971). Deficient and normal readers (ages 8 to 15) were compared on the ability to organize and recall visual and auditory stimuli presented simultaneously. Two conditions of recall were typically employed: *free* and *directed*. Under free recall conditions, subjects were told to remember as many test stimuli as they could, regardless of modality. Under directed recall, subjects were required to remember stimuli either in bisensory pairs or within a modality.

Generally, it was found that the poor readers did not perform as well as the normal readers under both conditions. The groups were also differentiated with respect to the qualitative aspects of performance. Specifically, the poor readers recalled the intermodal stimuli in pairs less often than the normal readers. There was also an age by reader-group by condition interaction: the poor readers at the younger age levels manifested significantly more errors than the normal readers on presentations within a modality, but the groups were not differentiated on the bisensory memory task at these age levels. However, the pattern was reversed in the case of older children, where poor readers performed below the level of the normal readers only with the pair-order stimuli. Noteworthy is the fact that in one study (Senf, 1969), poor readers were less accurate than normal readers on ordered recall, but these groups did not differ on gross memory or item recall. The authors inferred from these results that poor readers may be deficient in the ability to organize and integrate intersensory information. It was also suggested that poor readers may differ from normals with respect to their ability to remember serial-order information.

However, both conclusions are open to question. Initially it might be pointed out that in all three studies poor and normal readers were differentiated on *both* intra- and intermodality recall, thereby suggesting that reader-group disparities were not necessarily attributable to dysfunction in intersensory integration. In fact the age by reader-group by condition interaction observed in these studies would seem to be contrary to Birch and Belmont's (1965) suggestion that intersensory integration would be more influential at the beginning than at the later stages of reading. Thus, there is reason to doubt Senf's (1969) suggestion that reader-group differences on the visual-auditory integration tasks employed in these studies is related to deficient cross-modal transfer.

Two later studies support the above contention (Vande Voort, Senf, and Benton, 1972; Vande Voort and Senf, 1973). In both investigations poor readers did not perform as well as normal readers on intramodal matching tasks, but in only one (Vande Voort, Senf, and Benton, 1972) were the groups differentiated on intermodal matching. The authors suggested that the observed differences between poor and normal readers in the earlier studies (Senf, 1969; Senf and Feshbach, 1970; Senf and Freundl, 1971) may have been due to attentional and/or stimulus encoding problems, possibly associated with "central perceptual deficits" (Vande Voort, Senf, and Benton, 1972), or deficiencies in "memory" (Vande Voort and Senf, 1973). However, they did not expand upon the nature of these inferred disorders, and it is therefore difficult to evaluate the validity of their inferences.

Senf's (1969) suggestion that poor and normal readers may differ only with respect to their ability to recall ordered information is rather tenuous, given the fact that in three later studies these groups differed on measures of both gross (item) and serial-order recall (Senf and Feshbach, 1970; Senf and Freundl, 1971, 1972). Temporal-order deficiency as a possible explanation of specific reading disability is discussed in a later section of this chapter.

Because virtually all the studies investigating this theory employed tasks that relied heavily upon short-term memory and perceptual functioning, they may have been confounded both by attentional deficits and by intramodal disorder. In order to control for such confounding, poor and normal readers were contrasted on measures of long-term memory devoid of linguistic content, specifically, on nonverbal paired-associates learning. Thus, it was found that poor readers did not differ from normal readers in learning to associate visual-visual, auditory-auditory, and visual-auditory tasks involving nonverbal stimuli and responses (Vellutino, Steger, and Pruzek, 1973). Similar results were obtained in three other studies employing like procedures (Steger, Vellutino, and Meshoulam, 1972; Vellutino et al., 1975d; Vellutino et al., 1975a). In contrast, comparably selected reader groups were found to differ on paired-associates learning involving visual-verbal integration tasks simulating sight word learning and phonemic generalization (Vellutino et al., 1975d; Vellutino et al., 1975a). These findings suggest that verbal ability may be the critical factor which differentiates poor and normal readers.

Finally, the intersensory-deficit explanation of reading disability has been criticized on theoretical grounds. In a review of studies dealing with the concept of cross-modal transfer as a developmental phenomenon, Friedes (1974) suggested that Birch's theory of intersensory development (Birch and Lefford, 1963) is highly questionable. He was particularly critical of Birch's (1962) theory of sensory dominance which, in essence, constitutes the basic foundation of intersensory development as Birch conceptualized it. Specifically, it was suggested that sensory hierarchical dominance is not an inherent developmental phenomenon that is ordered invariantly; instead, it changes with the nature and demands of a particular task. Thus, the modality that "dominates" when the individual is performing a given function is purportedly the one that is most "adept" at processing the information that is relevant to that function. Support for this contention is derived from a series of studies conducted by Pick (1970) demonstrating that no specific modality consistently occupied the superordinate position in perceptual judgments based on the interaction of two sources of sensory information. Sensory dominance in such instances was always specific to a given task. Such findings pose significant problems for Birch's theory of sensory dominance and, by extension, his intersensory-deficit theory of dyslexia.

It seems reasonable to conclude from the sampling of studies discussed above that the intersensory-deficit theory of reading disability, as originally articulated by Birch (1962), has questionable validity. While differences between poor and normal readers on cross-modal tasks seem reliable, the derivation of such differences is unclear. As noted earlier, most of the investigations in the literature employed intermodal matching as the dependent variable, and it is likely that the results were confounded by short-term memory factors and/or intramodal deficiencies, specifically reader-group differences in verbal coding ability. It is therefore difficult to infer unequivocally that observed disparities between poor and normal readers in these investigations were attributable to the inability on the part of poor readers to establish intersensory equivalences.

Furthermore, several studies which have attempted to control for short-term memory and intramodal deficiencies, through the use of nonverbal learning tasks, have found no differences between poor and normal readers on tasks involving intersensory integration. These findings, coupled with the tenuous assumptions associated with Birch's conceptualization of intersensory development in normal children, raise serious doubts about the validity of the intersensory-deficit theory of reading disability.

DYSFUNCTION IN TEMPORAL-ORDER RECALL

A third possible explanation of specific reading disability that has recently received considerable attention in the literature is that the disorder is caused by dysfunction in temporal-order recall. This conjecture has long been popular among clinicians and educators, but only in recent years has it been evaluated in laboratory research (Johnson and Myklebust, 1967; Bannatyne, 1971). Bakker (1972) has attempted to formalize such a theory. A description of this theory and research associated with it will be presented below. Empirical findings obtained from other studies evaluating serial-order memory in poor and normal readers will also be presented.

RESEARCH EVIDENCE

Bakker conceived of temporal-order and gross (item) memory as separate entities and suggested that the dyslexic is especially deficient in the former area. This suggestion was based in part upon research by Hirsh demonstrating that the ability to perceive order in a succession of stimuli is centrally derived and requires an interstimulus interval of approximately 20 msec for initial detection (1959; Hirsh and Sherrick, 1961). Bakker (1972) also suggested, in line with previous findings that the left hemisphere supports temporal sequencing for verbal stimuli, while the right hemisphere carries out this function in the case of nonverbal stimuli (Milner, 1962, 1967; Efron, 1963).

He also inferred that poor readers are deficient only in perceiving the temporal order of verbal stimuli, and do not differ from normal readers in the temporal perception of nonverbal stimuli. This inference apparently emerged from the results of two previous studies (Bakker, 1967; Groenendaal and Bakker, 1971). In these investigations, it was found that poor readers made more errors than normal readers on the sequencing of meaningful figures and printed letters, but were not different from normals in correctly ordering nonverbal stimuli. Bakker (1972) also made reference to several cross-modal transfer studies, noting that each found differences between poor and normal readers on tasks which involved temporal order (e.g., Birch and Belmont, 1964, 1965; Blank et al., 1966, 1968). Special mention was made of

Senf's (1969) finding that poor readers did not differ from normal readers on measures of gross memory but were below the level of the normals on order memory. As additional support for his theory, Bakker (1972) cited evidence derived from two other studies from his laboratory, one demonstrating age differences in sequential ordering, and another demonstrating differences between poor and normal readers on measures of serial memory for letters presented visually, auditorily, and haptically.

Bakker's theory of reading disability seems questionable for a variety of reasons. Initially, it might be pointed out that his assumption that order and item information are processed by two separate memories is, itself, a controversial theoretical issue that has not yet been resolved (e.g., Brown, 1958; Conrad, 1964, 1965; Healy, 1974). Since a duplicity theory of memory is central to Bakker's theory of reading disability, his conceptualization is tenuous by virtue of this controversy alone.

A second assumption made by Bakker is that poor and normal readers differ with respect to general threshold for perceiving order. This notion is derived from the cited studies of Hirsh, which suggested an absolute threshold (20 msec) for detecting order in a succession of stimuli. Bakker's theory again rests on a weak foundation, in view of recent evidence (Warren, 1974) which challenges the concept of a general threshold for perception of temporal order. However, even if such a threshold were valid, the fact remains that all of the studies cited by Bakker (1972) in support of reader-group difference in temporal-order perception provided no direct evidence for this theory. To be specific, none of these studies compared poor and normal readers on measures evaluating thresholds for temporal-order perception employing the methodology used in previous research for assessing this phenomenon.

Finally, Bakker's suggestion that poor readers are deficient only in perceiving temporal order in verbal stimuli seems to be at variance with parsimony, given the evidence he cites to support this idea (Bakker, 1967; Groenendaal and Bakker, 1971; Bakker, 1972). The reader is reminded that in all contrasts between poor and normal readers discussed in studies cited by Bakker (1972), poor readers were differentiated from normal readers only on measures involving verbal stimuli. The observed disparities in these instances might be more simply attributed to reader-group differences in verbal encoding and rehearsal. Bakker's initial interpretations of his earliest findings were consistent with this suggestion (Bakker, 1967; Groenendaal and Bakker, 1971).

A number of other investigators have conducted studies which provided additional evidence that poor readers are not as effective as normal readers in processing serial-order information (e.g., Doehring, 1968; Zurif and Carson, 1970, Senf and Freundl, 1971; Corkin, 1974). The implicit assumption in most of these studies seems to have been that memory for item information and memory for order information constitute separate capacities and that poor readers are selectively deficient with respect to the latter. The qualification directed at Bakker's theory would seem to apply to these studies as well. That is, that serial-order and gross recall may not be distinct memory systems, thereby calling for a different interpretation of reader-group differences in ordered recall. Noteworthy in this connection is Conrad's (1964, 1965) finding that order errors on both visually and auditorily presented letters are determined by the degree of acoustic similarity characteristic of stimulus letters. This finding suggests that inaccuracies in serial order may be a function of the specific content of the items themselves. If this is true then temporal-order theories of reading disability would be obviated (but see Healy, 1974).

The tasks employed in all of the above studies required synthesis and rehearsal of a variety of types of information in short-term memory. Thus, the results could be explained by reader-group differences in verbal coding ability. That this interpretation is tenable is suggested in the results of a study by Kastner and Rickards (1974) which specifically evaluated serial-order recall in poor and normal readers. They employed a procedure similar to that used in the mediational studies of Flavell, Beach, and Chinsky (1966), requiring that subjects indicate the precise order in which the examiner touched either novel or familiar stimuli (presented on wooden blocks), after a delay of 15 sec. As anticipated, normal readers performed better on this task than poor readers. However, poor readers were not as inclined to employ a verbal rehearsal strategy to aid recall as often as normal readers, as determined by a self-report procedure following testing. The authors inferred, in line with previous suggestions by Blank et al. (1966, 1968), that poor readers may be more deficient than normal readers in the ability to employ verbal mnemonics to facilitate short-term recall.

The results of the Kastner and Rickards (1974) study should be viewed with caution because of its failure to control for intelligence. In addition, the self-report method employed in this investigation for determining verbal rehearsal strategies is weak and quite possibly unreliable. Nevertheless, the results were consistent with the results of Blank et al. (1966, 1968) in demonstrating verbal rehearsal difficulties in poor readers. Thus, a verbal-coding deficit interpretation of reader-group differences in ordered recall is a reasonable alternative to the suggestion that poor readers are characterized by specific dysfunction in temporal-order processing.

A final point that can be made here is that the studies evaluating serial-order recall in poor and normal readers did not always compare these groups on both gross and serial-order memory. Yet among those that did do so poor readers were often found to be different from normals on gross as well as order memory (Blank et al., 1966, 1968; Senf, 1969; Senf and Feshbach, 1970; Senf and Freundl, 1971); in some instances, the groups were differentiated only on gross memory (e.g., Senf and Freundl, 1972). Thus, to infer that poor readers have a specific deficiency in serial-order recall would seem to overextend available evidence. However, the issue is not yet resolved.

In summary, a number of recent studies have specifically evaluated the popular notion that poor readers do not perform as well as normal readers on short-term memory tasks involving serial-order recall. The general finding in these studies is that poor readers do indeed have more difficulty than normal readers in remembering things in order. This appears to be true regardless of the modality in which stimuli are presented. However, the derivation of reader-group disparities on serial-order tasks is open to question. While some authors suggest that such disparities are associated with disorder in central processes which specifically support ordered recall (e.g., Doehring, 1968; Bakker, 1972), this interpretation can be questioned on both theoretical and empirical grounds. Particularly notable among the contraindications discussed is the fact that the theoretical distinction between item and order information as separate entities is itself a tenuous conceptualization which is currently the center of considerable controversy. It was pointed out, in addition, that there is presently no convincing evidence that poor readers are selectively deficient in serial-order recall as contrasted with normal readers, and, at the same time, comparable to the normals in gross or item recall. The evidence is quite to the contrary, indicating that the groups can be found to differ on both types of recollection when experimental tasks require synthesis and rehearsal of information that taxes the limits of short-term memory. Reader-group differences under such circumstances have been a common theme in the studies discussed thus far, and thereby necessitate an explanation of their results that is more encompassing than those proffered. A viable alternative to the theoretical positions already discussed is the suggestion made throughout this chapter that poor readers may be characterized by significant disorder in one or more aspects of verbal processing.

DYSFUNCTION IN VERBAL PROCESSING

In the critiques of the explanations of reading disability presented above, we have repeatedly suggested that observed differences between poor and normal readers on a variety of measures involving visual and auditory memory could be attributed to reader-group disparities in verbal encoding ability. We inferred that poor readers have difficulty on short-term memory tasks because they lack implicit verbal coding devices which will facilitate efficient storage and retrieval of stimulus input. A corollary to this inference is that the poor reader supports deficiencies at the level of long-term memory characterized either by a limited fund of verbal information and/or inaccessibility of such information. Thus, a child who has significant difficulty in (1) relating the semantic or meaning components of words to their acoustic counterparts, (2) acquiring optimal sensitivity to the phonetic structure of speech, or (3) developing a functional command of syntactic usages required for the understanding and production of both oral and written language, will have difficulty in integrating these complex components of language and will, therefore, lack skill in their application. Specifically, a rich fund of verbal information (when the latter refers to all three components of language) provides a broad variety of implicit mnemonics as well as a variety of contexts that will allow one to readily symbolize or code stimulus input for efficient processing. The child who lacks such devices will be at a distinct disadvantage when presented with short-term memory tasks that require rapid coding of information for effective rehearsal and retrieval. It will be recalled that many of the measures evaluating the theories of dyslexia already discussed were of this type. It is our belief that poor and normal readers were differentiated on such measures because the normal readers were better equipped than the poor readers to employ verbal mnemonics to assist them in remembering.

Verbal-skills deficiencies may also be reflected in various types of reading difficulty, both directly and indirectly. Perhaps the most suggestive manifestations of such difficulty are the numerous word substitution and pronunciation errors characteristic of the dyslexic's efforts at word decoding. Typical examples of word substitution errors would include the words "kitty" and "mouse" as responses to the graphically and phonetically dissimilar word *cat*. Phonetic errors are exemplified in the response "sip," "chip," or "shop" when the stimulus word *ship* is presented. Such inaccuracies may well be reflective of respective malfunction in semantic and phonological processing, although the relative contribution and/or interaction of these two functions as determinants of specific types of reading errors is unclear.

Syntactic deficits that may exist in poor readers would not be as apparent in word recognition errors as semantic and phonological deficits, but may nevertheless constitute a significant impediment to code acquisition. For example, knowledge of a word's use in sentences, comprehension of the meaning it generates when used in relation to other words, familiarity with the morphological generalizations it contains (e.g., *ed, ing*), and like syntactic details would seem to be the type of information that can be employed to good advantage in word decoding as well as sentence comprehension.

Indirect manifestations of linguistic deficiencies may also be observed in reading and writing, primarily in the form of visual discrimination and positional and directional errors. Thus, as suggested earlier, the child who continues to confuse letters and words with common graphic features (e.g., b/d, was/saw, loin/lion), has probably failed to integrate discriminating linguistic cues necessary for accurate decoding. For example, b's and d's are confusable, not only because of their visual similarities, but also as a result of their acoustic similarities. They, nevertheless, have both visual and articulatory features that are distinctive; and until such a time as these are discerned and integrated, that same child will continue to confuse these letters. The same holds true of words like *was* and *saw, loin* and *lion,* and analogous configurations. And if a child lacks information about the meanings and/or grammatic distinctions which characterize these words, he will obviously have fewer associates to aid in discrimination and ultimate recall.

On the other hand, the child who has such information readily available to him will have incorporated a variety of alternative linguistic cues to assist in accurate decoding, such alternatives becoming particularly useful in discriminating minimally contrasted stimuli such as the exemplars above. In incorporating such discriminating cues, he will have encountered these stimuli in a variety of linguistic contexts, encompassing the semantic, syntactic, and phonological aspects of spoken and written language.

RESEARCH EVIDENCE

Thus, we consider the various components of language to be of cardinal importance in learning to read, all other systems being subordinate to language in acquiring this skill. Yet, as pointed out earlier, the possibility that reading disability is caused by dysfunction in verbal processing has until recent years received little attention in the literature. The initial impetus for this point of view was provided by Rabinovitch (1959, 1968), who suggested that children with reading disabilities may be characterized by subtle linguistic defects which could be observed in expressive language disorder, word-finding difficulties, and deficiencies in symbolic learning, as manifested in deficient reading and related disabilities.

While Rabinovitch's observations appeared to be based largely on clinical study of dyslexics, suggestive evidence in support of his conjectures was initially provided by retrospective and post hoc studies comparing poor and normal readers on the incidence of linguistic deficiencies. For example, in two separate accounts (Ingram and Reid, 1956; Ingram, Mason, and Blackburn, 1970), it was reported that a sizeable proportion (approximately half) of children referred to a clinic for reading problems had a history of speech and language difficulties. Lyle (1970) found essentially the same results. Similarly, Owen et al. (1971) found that children with a low verbal, high performance IQ pattern on the Wechsler Intelligence Scale for Children (Wechsler, 1949), were described by relatives and peers as being deficient in verbal ability.

Caution is also indicated in generalizing the above findings, inasmuch as the samples included may not have been representative of the population of interest here. Samples in specific instances included clinic cases and culturally disadvantaged children. Furthermore, these studies carry with them all the weaknesses inherent in retrospective and post hoc studies.

In the following sections, a number of investigations will be reviewed that provide more direct evidence for reader-group differences in verbal processing. Three areas of possible difficulty may be distinguished: deficiencies in semantic processing, syntactic deficiencies, and phonological deficiencies. As will be seen, research evaluating these functions as correlates of reading disability is at a seminal stage and the available results must be considered heuristic rather than conclusive.

DEFICIENCIES IN SEMANTIC PROCESSING

A number of studies have evaluated poor and normal readers on measures of semantic encoding and verbal memory. For example, Perfetti and Goldman

(1976) specifically tested the hypothesis that "children who are not skilled in reading comprehension are relatively unskilled in encoding linguistic information in working memory." It was predicted that poor readers would be comparable to normal readers in short-term recall of nonlinguistic material, but these subjects were expected to be less able than normal readers in short-term memory for linguistic material. The hypothesis was tested in two separate contrasts. Subjects were third and fifth graders selected on the basis of reading comprehension and intelligence scores. All were average or above in intelligence. In the first study, poor and normal readers were compared on a probe digit task employing a procedure similar to that of Waugh and Norman (1965). Subjects were required to recall a particular digit which directly followed given probe digits presented aurally. Poor readers did not differ from normals on this task. However, on an analogue of this procedure employing probe words embedded in meaningful sentences, poor readers performed below the level of normal readers. The hypothesis was thereby supported.

The results of a study by Waller (1976) are in accord with these findings. Its major purpose was to evaluate the degree to which poor and normal readers are differentially sensitive to the meaning and structural attributes of sentences they read. The dependent variable was a sentence recognition task similar to that employed by Paris and Carter (1973). Subjects were specifically contrasted on false recognition errors. All subjects could read the words used in each of the sentences. The important finding in this investigation was that poor readers were able to encode the meanings of sentences they read as well as normal readers. However, they were not as effective as normal readers in retaining verbal details such as grammatical markers and specific word strings. The authors inferred from these results that poor readers have no generalized memory deficiency. It was also suggested that poor readers quite possibly have difficulty in employing a verbal code to store information and may thereby rely more heavily upon a visual code to do so.

The results of both the above studies are consonant with the results of studies discussed earlier (Blank et al., 1966, 1968; Kastner and Rickards, 1974) in which poor readers were found to be less proficient than normal readers in employing verbal mediators to assist recall. They also reinforce previous findings (Liberman et al., 1971; Vellutino et al., 1972) which suggest that the orientation and sequencing errors observed in the reading and writing of poor readers, are verbal mediation inaccuracies rather than visuospatial confusions. Thus, the data from all these studies constitute a rather impressive body of evidence to support the inference that poor readers have verbal coding deficiencies which can be observed in reading as well as other cognitive tasks.

A number of investigations have addressed the possibility that poor readers may experience difficulty in word finding and/or speech motor encoding. To illustrate, Denckla and Rudel (1976a, 1976b) compared dyslexic and normal readers (ages 7 to 12) on amount of time taken to name a variety of items which included common objects, colors, letters, words, and numerals, each presented visually. Poor readers took significantly longer and made more errors in naming these items than did normal readers. In explaining these results, the authors suggested that disabled readers may be characterized by basic dysfunction in word retrieval (see also Denckla, 1972a, 1972b).

The latter suggestion was reinforced by the results of a later study comparing poor and normal readers on time taken to name printed words. Perfetti and Hogaboam (1975) found that children who were poor in reading comprehension had significantly longer vocalization latencies than normal comprehenders on rapid naming of (1) high- and low-frequency English words, (2) pseudowords, and (3) words that were varied so that each child could define some, but not all, of these stimuli. The authors inferred from their results that deficiencies in reading comprehension are in all probability associated with the poor reader's inability to develop automatized decoding skills. Similar results were found by Eakin and Douglas (1971), Spring and Capps (1974), and Spring (1976). Poor readers in these studies were also compared on rapid naming tasks and were generally slower in vocalizing responses than were the normals.

Finally, several investigations have compared reader groups on paired-associates learning involving both meaningful and novel material. In exploring the possibility that reading disability might be specifically associated with dysfunction in verbal learning, Vellutino and his colleagues systematically varied verbal and nonverbal learning tasks in contrasts of poor and normal readers on the association of different combinations of visual, auditory, and haptic stimuli (Steger, Vellutino, and Meshoulam, 1972; Vellutino, Steger, and Pruzek, 1973; Vellutino et al., 1975d; Vellutino et al., 1975a). A reliable finding which characterized these investigations is that poor readers did not perform as well as normal readers on visual-verbal learning tasks but were comparable to the normals on nonverbal learning tasks. Similar findings were obtained in the studies of Brewer (1967), Gascon and Goodglass (1970), and Rudel, Denckla, and Spalten (1976).

In summary, the results support the notion that poor readers are less adequate than normal readers in both short- and long-term memory for verbal material. However, such inadequacies appear to be selective, affecting recall for specific linguistic units (e.g., words and word parts, phrases, etc.) rather than the general meanings conveyed by words and sentences. This suggests that at least some poor readers may have a specific disorder in semantic processing as may be manifested in a variety of linguistic deficiencies such as dysfunction in basic naming and labeling, word finding problems, and expressive language difficulties.

A note of caution is indicated, since some investigations were characterized by methodological weaknesses that affected their findings. For example, in both of the studies conducted by Perfetti, reading comprehension was employed as the measure of achievement, making it difficult to be certain that the poor readers in the sample were representative of the population of interest here (Perfetti and Hogaboam, 1975; Perfetti and Goldman, 1976). The studies by Spring did not control for possible reader-group differences in intelligence and it is possible that the results were confounded by this inadequacy. Nevertheless, the findings are suggestive, and further exploration of semantic processing deficiencies in poor readers is warranted.

SYNTACTIC DEFICIENCIES

The relationship between the syntactic components of language and reading disability has not received much attention. However, a few studies provide some support for the possibility that subtle deficiencies in knowledge of syntax may be intrinsically associated with poor achievement in reading.

In two separate but parallel investigations, Fry (1967) and Schulte (1967) compared samples of second-grade poor and normal readers (age seven) on measures of expressive language; they generally found that the normal readers were linguistically more sophisticated than the poor readers. Specifically, the normal readers were characterized by larger speaking vocabularies and greater verbal fluency than the poor readers. The normal readers also manifested greater use of abstractions, a greater tendency toward substantive rather than descriptive use of words, better organization and integration of verbal concepts, and more appropriate use of grammar and syntax.

In a later review, Fry, Johnson, and Meuhl (1970) suggested that language deficits such as those observed could have an adverse effect not only upon reading comprehension and written expression, but also upon the acquisition of word decoding skills, by limiting the number and variety of "verbal labels and mediators" available for acquiring the (graphic) symbol and sound relationships encountered in learning to read. They also pointed out that observed differences between poor and normal readers could not be the cumulative effect of long-standing reading disorder because children in their samples were only in second grade.

The results of a later study complement the above findings, although the contrasts made between poor and normal readers in this particular investigation were more circumscribed. Wiig, Semel, and Crouse (1973) reported differences between poor and normal readers (age nine years) on Berko's (1958) test of morphological usage. The poor readers made significantly more errors than the normal readers on this measure. In addition, their errors were generally more idiosyncratic and less predictable than those of the normal readers. These findings suggest that poor readers may be significantly delayed in the acquisition of basic morphological generalizations, a linguistic accomplishment which is characteristic of children at younger age levels (i.e., by seven years; Berko, 1958; Brown, 1973). That such deficiency is a possible cause rather than a result of reading disability is suggested in an additional contrast where neurologically impaired four-year-olds performed below the level of normally developing children on the same test of morphological usage employed in the reader-group comparisons discussed above. The authors concluded from these combined findings that syntactic deficiencies may be significant precursors of reading disability. They, therefore, recommended that remediation of such deficiencies be undertaken prior to formal reading instruction (i.e., kindergarten or first grade).

The third and final study to be discussed was conducted by Vogel (1974), who compared dyslexic and normal readers at the second-grade level (age seven years) on a battery of nine measures of oral syntax. The latter included tests of morphological usage, listening comprehension, sentence repetition, "oral cloze" (sentence completion), and ability to detect melodic variations. Dyslexics were found to be inferior on seven of the nine measures. Noteworthy is the fact that one of these measures was a test of morphological usage similar to the one employed by Wiig et al. (1973) discussed above. Vogel's results, therefore, reinforce the findings of those authors. Apparently, knowledge of morphology and deficient reading are significantly related and it is possible that they have a common base. This inference is consistent with the fact that syntactic deficiencies were observed in poor readers at very young age levels (about seven years), a finding which characterized three of the four studies reviewed (Fry, 1967; Schultz, 1967; Vogel, 1974).

In summary, the few studies comparing poor and normal readers on various measures of syntax provide suggestive evidence that grammatic deficiencies are intrinsically related to reading disability. Poor readers were generally less capable than normal readers on tasks evaluating knowledge of words, knowledge of syntax, ability to employ words abstractly, and verbal fluency in general. Since most of these findings were derived from contrasts of poor and normal readers at an early level of development in reading (second grade), it may be reasonably inferred that syntactic deficiencies in poor readers may be of basic origin and not simply a by-product of long-standing reading disorder.

PHONOLOGICAL DEFICIENCIES

Several authors have proposed that reading disability in some children is caused by basic deficiency in phonological processing. This idea has been discussed within the context of two different conceptual frameworks. The more widely held view is that many poor readers are significantly impaired in the "auditory discrimination" of speech sounds and thereby have difficulty in analyzing the internal structure of printed words. This point of view has been especially popular among practitioners, largely as a result of the work of several authors who have concerned themselves with the education of reading-disabled and other exceptional children (e.g., Wepman, 1960, 1961; Johnson and Myklebust, 1967; Bannatyne, 1971).

A more recent conceptualization of phonological deficiencies in poor readers inheres in the suggestion of a number of workers that some children with reading problems have not become sufficiently aware of the phonetic structure of spoken language (e.g., Mattingly, 1972; Savin, 1972; Elkonin, 1973; Downing, 1973; Liberman and Shankweiler, in press). These authors contend that such children may have difficulty in "phonemic segmentation" of both spoken and printed words, which presumably leads to difficulty in mapping alphabetic symbols to their sound counterparts. Such disorder is to be distinguished from auditory discrimination problems as mentioned above. The implicit assumption of those who suggest that deficiencies in auditory discrimination constitute a basic cause of reading disability is that children who sustain this disorder are unable to distinguish between minimally contrasted words (e.g., *pin* and *pen*) when these are paired with no other contextual information available. However, those who postulate that deficiencies in phonemic segmentation are problematic in poor readers reject the notion that such words are not discriminated acoustically (that is as "whole" words). They suggest instead that such auditory problems are characterized by relative insensitivity to the phonemic constituents of given words, resulting in dysfunction in abstracting word components that may be necessary for establishing higher-order relationships in code acquisition. Such individuals may be able to readily distinguish between *pin* and *pen,* as spoken and printed words, but fail, nevertheless, to educe the redundant sounds in those two words, to assist them in learning to decode words they subsequently encounter with like constituents: e.g., *tin* and *ten.* Conversely, the individual who *does* become sensitized to the internal structure of speech has much more information available to him to assist in word analysis, and in code acquisition generally.

Empirical evidence for dysfunction in auditory discrimination as a cause of reading disability is conflicting. Wepman (1960, 1961) was the strongest advocate of this point of view and provided seminal evidence to support the idea. He suggested that auditory discrimination is a perceptual skill partly dependent upon, but not guaranteed by intact acuity. He further suggested that the disorder was attributable to a developmental lag in the "maturation" of auditory perception. In an initial test of his theory, Wepman (1960) employed a match-to-standard task consisting of 40 pairs of highly similar words, *30* pairs of which were identical, and *10* pairs which differed on a single phoneme. Subjects were asked to judge whether the words were the "same" or "different." In a randomly selected sample of first and second graders, he found that many children who did poorly on this task were also low achievers in reading. Similar results were found in a later study (Wepman, 1961). He therefore inferred from these combined findings that many children with reading problems may be hampered by deficiencies in auditory discrimination quite possibly associated with "maturation lag."

Wepman's studies precipitated a great deal of interest and widespread acceptance of his theory as evidenced in the voluminous literature generated by those who subsequently embraced the idea. However, a few studies have since provided evidence that auditory discrimination problems, as conceptualized by Wepman and others, may be an artifact of the means by which the response has been traditionally measured. For example, in two separate investigations comparing poor and normal readers on auditory discrimination of minimally contrasted word pairs, it was found that the groups did not differ when the test response was vocalization of those words (Blank, 1968; Shankweiler and Liberman, 1972). However, these groups were found to differ on same/different judgments (the more traditional procedure), in which instance poor readers did *not* perform as well as normal readers. These authors offered somewhat different interpretations of the observed disparities. It was suggested, on the one hand, that poor and normal readers may have differed with respect to their conceptualization of the match-to-standard (same/different) tasks (Blank, 1968), and, on the other, that the differences were due to phonemic segmentation problems in poor readers (Shankweiler and Liberman, 1972). Regardless of the ultimate validity of either or both of these conjectures, it would seem justifiable to conclude that support for the notion of deficient auditory discriminations, based primarily on results of the Wepman test and/or like measures, is tenuous at best. This conclusion is further supported by the results of another study which suggest that the Wepman Test (Wepman, 1958) and other measures containing an unequal number of same and different responses may be subject to response bias (Vellutino, DeSetto, and Steger, 1972).

While the notion of phonemic segmentation deficiencies in poor readers is a relatively recent suggestion, the evidence accumulated in its favor is increasing. The most definitive work in this area has been done by Liberman and her colleagues.

Liberman et al. (1974) compared nursery school, kindergarten, and first-grade children on the ability to analyze the phonetic structure in spoken words. It was found that the detection of the number of syllables in stimulus words was much easier than the detection of the number of phonemes in those words and that the latter skill increased with age. Furthermore, both cross-sectional and longitudinal study of these same children revealed that deficiency in phonemic segmentation was associated with low achievement in reading (Liberman et al., 1974; Liberman et al., 1976). Similar findings obtained in studies conducted by Helfgott (1976), Zifcak (1976), and Treiman (1976).

Several other investigations were conducted by Liberman and colleagues in assessing the possibility that poor readers are less efficient than normal readers in the phonetic coding of information in short-term memory. In an initial test of this hypothesis, poor readers were found to be less accurate than normal readers in the visual recognition of the same nonsense syllables presented repeatedly (Liberman and Shankweiler, in press). However, the groups did not differ on recognition of recurring novel designs and photographed faces. The authors attributed group differences to the poor readers' difficulties in phonetically recoding the visually presented nonsense syllables.

The results of two other studies support the inference. In both investigations poor readers manifested less disparity than normal readers between tasks involving short-term memory for phonetically confusable (rhyming) and nonconfusable (nonrhyming) letter strings. This was found to be true whether the stimuli were presented visually (Liberman et al., 1976) or auditorily (Shankweiler and Liberman, 1972). While the overall level of performance was higher in normal readers, the different patterns manifested by poor and normal readers with these two types of stimuli suggest that normal readers are more sensitive to the acoustic constituents of words than are poor readers.

In another study, poor readers were found to make more false recognition errors on rhyming as opposed to nonrhyming words (Liberman and Shankweiler, in press). From these and the above findings, the authors concluded that poor readers may be less effective than normal readers in employing a phonetic code for storing information in short term memory.

In summary, a review of available findings indicates that reading disability in some children may be associated with deficiencies in phonological processing. However, there is reason to believe that such deficiencies are not attributable to dysfunction in auditory discrimination. An alternative possibility, one for which there is some supporting evidence, is that many poor readers have not become sensitized to the phonetic structure of spoken words, which in turn impairs their ability to establish the symbol and sound relationships necessary for code acquisition. Such deficiency may characterize only some poor readers, while others may sustain the types of difficulties in semantic and syntactic processing described above. These problems are not, however, mutually exclusive and may exist concomitantly in the same individual.

SUMMARY AND CONCLUSIONS

The present chapter has addressed itself to the psychological variables which must be considered in furthering our understanding of developmental dyslexia, otherwise known as specific reading disability. We initially reviewed problems of definition and concluded that preliminary study of dyslexia should entail stringent operational criteria so as to rule out contamination by a number of variables said to constitute extrinsic rather than intrinsic causes of the disorder. The review of the literature revealed that many studies concerned with this problem have not adopted such criteria and results are thereby equivocal. Benton (1962, 1975) came to a similar conclusion. Therefore, those interested in studying the etiology of dyslexia would do well to consider the difficulties attendant upon the use of inadequate operational criteria, particularly in view of the fact that the very existence of specific reading disability as a unique developmental disorder is a construct, the correlates of which are not well defined.

However, the major purpose of this chapter was to review and evaluate current conceptualizations of dyslexia and existing research relating to those conceptualizations. A brief review of the major theories of dyslexia available in the literature converged upon four areas of basic process dysfunction advanced in explanation of the disorder: deficiencies in *visual perception and visual memory, intersensory integration, temporal order recall,* and *verbal processing.*

We systematically reviewed each of these hypotheses and discussed in some detail relevant findings relating to them. The most commonly cited explanation of specific reading disability was found to be perceptual deficiency, and by extension, deficient visual memory. It was concluded that in spite of conflicting results in the literature (Benton, 1962, 1975; Vernon, 1971), recent findings weigh heavily against perceptual-deficit theories of reading disability, as originally suggested by Orton (1925, 1937) and modified by subsequent investigators (Bender, 1956, 1957, 1975; Hermann, 1959; Birch, 1962).

Our own findings are particularly indicting, for they suggest that apparent perceptual problems in poor readers at both younger (7–8 years) and older (9–14 years) age levels are a secondary manifestation of verbal mediation deficiencies, possibly associated with basic language problems. Noteworthy here is the fact that our studies are distinguished from most in the literature in their systematic variation of verbal and nonverbal stimuli in comparisons of poor and normal readers on measures of short- and long-term visual memory. The findings in all instances were invariant: poor readers were consistently differentiated when verbal factors were introduced in the experimental conditions, but did not differ when the effects of verbal encoding were minimized. Of particular interest in these studies is our finding that instruction for subjects to attend either to the visual or verbal constituents of English words of varying length differentiated poor and normal readers only when instructions drew their attention to the verbal components. We believe that such findings constitute rather strong evidence against the perceptual-deficit explanation of reading disability in the population of poor readers as defined at present. The results of our initial investigations of the perceptual-deficit hypothesis are given additional credibility by the degree of uniformity characteristic of our samples, selected in accord with the operational criteria outlined on pages 66–69.

Finally, it seems that those theories of dyslexia which postulate perceptual deficiency, characterized by visuospatial confusion as the basic etiological factor, suffer on logical grounds, at least in the case of the population in question. As pointed out by Benton (1962, 1975), such deficiencies would seem to be pervasive if they truly exist in poor readers, but there is no evidence that this is so. Furthermore, many of the types of errors said to be classic indicators of reading disability, can be reinterpreted as linguistic intrusion errors (Liberman et al., 1971; Vellutino et al., 1972, 1973). Thus, as suggested earlier, when poor readers call a *b d* or *was saw,* it is not because they perceive these configurations differently from normal readers, but because they have not yet learned their names.

Our contention that specific reading disability is not attributable to visual-perceptual deficiency in the strict sense is obviously countered to multifactor theories which postulate that dyslexia is caused by disorder *either* in visual *or* auditory functioning (e.g., Birch, 1962; Myklebust and Johnson, 1962; Boder, 1970; Mattis, French, and Rapin, 1975). This view is also contrary to recent suggestions in the literature (e.g., Satz, Friel, and Rudegeair, 1974) that dyslexia is associated with "general maturational lag" which results in perceptual difficulties at early stages of development (approximately five to seven years) and language difficulties at older age levels (beyond seven years).

In relation to the intersensory-integration theory advanced by Birch (1962), it will be recalled that the studies reviewed yielded consistent differences between poor and normal readers on various inter- and intrasensory tasks, a large number of which involved matching of auditory and visual equivalents. However, as pointed out by several authors (e.g., Blank et al., 1966, 1968; Vande Voort, Senf, and Benton, 1972; Benton, 1975), the interpretations of these findings are open to question. This is particularly true of the match-to-sample studies that have typically provided no controls for possible response bias. Even more troublesome is the fact that most studies reviewed in relation to the intersensory-deficit theory of reading disability characteristically involved short-term memory for serially presented stimuli, which may be especially taxing for poor readers if, as we infer, they are subject to verbal encoding problems. Such studies may also be confounded by attentional deficits.

In contrast, comparisons of visuoauditory, nonverbal learning (long-term memory) tasks did not differentiate between disabled and normal readers, while comparisons of visual-verbal learning did so repeatedly. It was concluded that deficiency in integrating intersensory information is an unlikely source of reading disability. This conclusion is reinforced by research questioning the theoretical foundations of intersensory integration as conceptualized by Birch (Friedes, 1974). Notable in this connection are studies which failed to confirm the concept of sensory hierarchical dominance, a conceptualization which was basic to Birch's theory of intersensory development.

The suggestion that disabled readers are unable to "perceive" temporal order as well as normal readers seems to be lacking in foundation, in view of the fact that no studies exist which have tested this hypothesis (Bakker, 1972). Research findings advanced in support of this and similar explanations of reading disability are subject to interpretive problems on the same grounds as those testing the intersensory-deficit theory. While in the case of those investigations reviewed, poor readers were almost invariably found to differ from normals on a variety of serial-order tasks, the differences may not be due to basic deficits in temporal-order processing. The possibility of short-term memory problems in poor readers, as a result of inferred deficiencies in verbal encoding was again thought to be a plausible alternative to the temporal-order deficit theories of reading disability reviewed. This appeared especially true in view of the possibility that a distinction between item and order information could be artificial, since both types may be drawn from the same limited capacity system. Some also suggest that order errors are actually item intrusion errors and have provided evidence to support this notion (e.g., Conrad, 1964, 1965). Thus, on both empirical and theoretical grounds, the suggestion that reader disability is caused by deficient temporal-order processing is seriously questioned as a viable explanation of the disorder.

Finally, our review of the literature uncovered a number of studies which more directly assessed the possibility of verbal deficiencies in poor readers, and it was apparent that this hypothesis is receiving considerably greater attention from researchers than it has in years past. In addition to a few studies providing some evidence that many poor readers may be characterized by a history of language delay, there were several which differentiated reader groups on a variety of post hoc measures of verbal skill.

Of greater interest are the results of laboratory studies specifically designed to evaluate diverse types of verbal deficiencies in dyslexics. Largely emphasizing short-term memory tasks, these investigations reported that poor readers performed consistently below the level of normal readers on measures of semantic, syntactic, and phonological functioning, thereby providing strong evidence of verbal processing deficiencies in poor readers. The results were thought to be highly suggestive and are certainly in accord with our own initial speculations as to the role of linguistic deficiencies in learning to read.

That reading problems may be associated with specific language disorder is an especially attractive hypothesis in view of recent research which indicates that, whatever else reading is, it is a decidedly linguistic function. Indeed, several authors (e.g., Goodman, 1968; Smith, 1971) have made an excellent case for conceptualizing reading as an information-gathering skill which leans heavily upon linguistic ability in the general sense. However, given the possibility that reading disability is the result of language disorder, there remains the problem of determining the nature of such disorder and its relationship to the reading process.

Recent research findings have encompassed deficiencies in the semantic, syntactic, and phonological aspects of reading, but there are as yet no definitive data which give any of these functions etiological prominence. Perhaps this is because such aspects are not easily separated, either in the chronically impaired reader, or in the fluent reader. For example, problems in learning whole words may well reflect specific difficulties in verbal labeling and mediation as a result of semantic and/or syntactic deficiencies, as suggested. Conversely, select disorder in phonemic analysis may occur in the absence of semantic and syntactic problems, but difficulties in any one of those areas certainly lead to difficulties in the others, owing to their interdependent nature. Thus, the linguistic skills of chronically impaired readers are typically fragmented and unreliable, and their reading behaviors may appear to be similar, even though their problems may vary as to basic origin. In contrast, proficient readers are able to make efficient and economical use of all of their linguistic abilities, and it is difficult to be certain of those they employ, *or* of the priorities they set in deciphering any bit of printed material (Gibson, 1971). Consequently, greater specificity with respect to the linguistic correlates of reading disability is dependent upon refinement of both our conceptualizations and our measuring instruments, but continued research in the area would appear to be a useful course.

We might add, in this connection, that language deficits of the types proposed could theoretically accrue, either as a result of extrinsic experiential factors, or because of an intrinsic developmental disorder of neurological origin. These causes are not mutually exclusive and could interact to obscure basic etiology. However, it would be counterproductive for researchers to defer from making such distinctions, especially in view of the possibility that the knowledge they may acquire in doing so could lead to significant differences in the remediation of children so impaired.

We began with a bias which is clearly reflected throughout this chapter, namely, that reading may be best viewed as a categorical and synthetic function, certainly necessitating economical and efficient use of all of the child's cognitive skills, but most especially his linguistic abilities. The fluent reader may be described as a verbal gymnast who can employ a variety of linguistic devices for sampling the text selectively, or to use Goodman's (1968) term, for "predicting" and "reconstructing" the information contained therein. The severely impaired reader does not have such an armamentarium available to him, and must be provided with alternative means of deciphering a message when one or more of his decoding skills fail him. Thus, the child who misreads the word *cat* and responds *kitty* may not seriously interrupt the intended meaning of the passage, but if his response is *mouse* or *dog,* he may need some other decoding mechanism that mediates to the correct response, e.g., knowledge of the component sounds of the stimulus words, in addition to knowledge of the meanings of each of these words. In our opinion it is this flexibility in "cross-referencing" the multiform information characteristic of printed words that distinguishes the poor and normal reader. We suggest that the poor reader lacks such flexibility, because of deficiency in verbal processing. Thus, research investigating the correlates of one or more aspects of such deficiency would seem to hold the most promise for an ultimate understanding of the etiology of dyslexia, or specific reading disability.

Chapter 5

REVIEW OF "TOWARD AN UNDERSTANDING OF DYSLEXIA: PSYCHOLOGICAL FACTORS IN SPECIFIC READING DISABILITY"

MARION BLANK

I shall confine my comments to three major areas which are central to Vellutino's presentation. These are:

1. the definition and selection of the dyslexic population;
2. the models to be used in studying dyslexia;
3. the interpretation of reported findings.

Although these areas overlap, each contains its own set of problems.

THE DEFINITION AND SELECTION
OF THE DYSLEXIC POPULATION

As Vellutino emphasizes, there is a major problem as to who is and who is not to be considered dyslexic. In common with other investigators, he chooses to meet this problem by selecting only those retarded readers who are "intellectually, emotionally, and medically normal" (Witelson, 1977). The reasons for using this criterion are clear. For example, it enables one to exclude children whose reading difficulties stem secondarily from some other defect (e.g., deaf children represent one group that can be excluded in this way). While this operational rule is designed to bring simplicity to a complex area, it contains numerous weaknesses. First, as Vellutino points out, there is often considerable overlap between the skills needed for reading and the skills in intelligence tests. Such confounding may well lead dyslexic children of normal intelligence to test below normal and thereby to be excluded from study. Second, the restriction of the population by definition demands the exclusion of numerically large groups of retarded readers. For example, children from low socioeconomic backgrounds who experience reading difficulties are not to be considered dyslexic according to this definition. As a consequence, we have excluded the largest group of retarded readers that exists in our country. Third, the usefulness of the definition rests in large measure on the idea that "dyslexia is a constitutionally based developmental disorder that is qualitatively different from reading problems caused by extrinsic factors." While this view may be widely held, its support is by no means clear. To my knowledge there is no definitive work to indicate that different neurological and/or behavioral mechanisms are responsible for the reading difficulties of middle-class dyslexics and lower-class retarded readers. For example, in the cross-modal paradigm developed by Birch and his colleagues, similar patterns of performance were found for middle-class and lower-class retarded readers. This is not to say that the two groups would behave similarly on other tasks, nor that the same information processing mechanisms are necessarily operative in both groups. But the similar pattern of results provides no support for the assumption that the groups are qualitatively different.

Vellutino recognizes the dangers in the path of exclusion that he has outlined. In particular, he focuses on possible limitations in the "generalizability" of the results. To overcome this problem, he suggests conducting replication studies which employ identical and careful sampling procedures. If the initial sample is carefully selected and tested, there would be little doubt that similar results would be obtained with comparable selected groups of children.* However, what would not be known, and what replication of a similar sample would not reveal is whether the findings are applicable to other groups of retarded readers.

Thus far, my comments have been directed toward the problems stemming from the exclusion of certain groups of children. Problems also arise, however, about the group of children who would be included. Specifically, in

---

* If Vellutino's concern about generalizability stems from the small numbers of children that might be included, then other problems obtain. Specifically, as Tversky and Kahneman (1971) point out, there are great odds against replication involving small samples. Therefore, replication would not provide the desired safeguards against erroneous conclusions. On the other hand, because there are also great odds against obtaining significant results with small samples, there is little reason to doubt the meaningfulness of results that do show significance.

trying to limit the population, the underlying aim seems to be the selection of a uniform population. This goal is not an uncommon one in studies of reading disability. As noted by Mattis, French, and Rapin (1975), "two assumptions are implicit or explicit in many studies seeking the determinants of reading disability: (1) that a clinical entity exists called 'the dyslexic child'; and (2) that reading ability is homogeneous and that one can determine the single causal defect or—in a more sophisticated approach—determine the causal profile of abilities and deficiencies in higher cortical functioning."

Given the complexity of the variables involved in reading skill and given the number of possible areas of malfunctioning (in the subtle brain damage that is assumed to exist in these children), it seems clear that even this narrowly selected population is likely to be composed of a number of different groups (both in terms of causal factors and in terms of current level of functioning). Work such as that of Boder (1973) and Mattis, French, and Rapin (1975) support this view.

In summary, it appears that the reliance on the exclusionary criteria set forth in Vellutino's review entails a number of disadvantages. Specifically, it leads to the assumption of differences when no differences need exist (e.g., the assumed differences between the middle-class dyslexic and the lower-class retarded reader) and, conversely, it leads to the assumption of no differences when differences may well exist (e.g., the differences among middle-class dyslexics). Rather than restrict the sample, the problem of selection might best be met in other ways. First, a broad array of reading difficulties could be studied. In all cases, however, the population studied should be clearly defined so that one knows as precisely as possible which type or types of children were tested. Second, wherever possible, a comparably handicapped group that is not retarded in reading ability should be included in the research (see Chap. 3). For example, if minimally brain-damaged retarded readers are being studied, a group of minimally brain-damaged children who are not having reading problems should also be included. This procedure seems to offer the best safeguard against a common pitfall in studies of children with deficits, namely, drawing conclusions about deficits that may exist but that may well be irrelevant to poor performance on the skill in question.

THE MODEL TO BE USED

The selection of tasks is determined in large measure by the view that one has of the problem. In the studies cited by Vellutino, there seem to have been two major (albeit not totally independent) approaches to this issue. On the one hand, some investigators focus on identifying the skills that may be defective in the dyslexic. They then administer a variety of tests to determine if, in fact, the children lack the hypothesized skills. On the other hand, investigators such as Gibson (1965) and Birch (1964) analyze the demands of the reading task itself. On the basis of this analysis, tasks are created that are designed to mirror the reading process and then the tasks are administered to various groups of defective and normal readers.

Each of these approaches contains potential difficulties. Given our current lack of knowledge and the complexity of the behavior under study, the difficulties cannot be avoided. Nevertheless, it may be helpful for future research if we are more aware of the problems and options of each course. First, let us consider models that focus on what is defective in the dyslexic. A major problem here is not in finding tasks to administer, but in limiting the number of tasks that can and should be administered. The dyslexic does poorly on so many tasks that there is almost no limit to the hypothesized difficulties that may be causing his reading failure. Nowhere is this fact more in evidence than in the study of Doehring (1968) in which poor readers were differentiated from normals on 68 tests. Some order is brought to this range of tasks through the application of factor analysis. Even then, however, we are left with a wide range of skills that seem to differentiate dyslexic and nondyslexic children. Furthermore, there is often no attempt to distinguish between those tasks that represent areas of weakness for the children and are causally related to the reading problem from those tasks that represent areas of weakness but are nonetheless irrelevant to the demands of reading. For example, in my experience, many young retarded readers have difficulties in color naming. Their difficulties in this realm may well be a correlate of the problems that cause reading failure. However, I do not believe that color naming in itself is relevant to reading performance.

A key question therefore is: how is one to distinguish between behaviors that correlate and behaviors that causally relate to reading failure? It is here that the second approach outlined above offers some promise, namely, developing experimental tasks that are designed to mirror the reading situation. Almost by definition, this approach leads to greater selectivity in the tasks that are to be given to the children. The much studied cross-modal task is an illustration of this approach. Birch's view of reading led him to emphasize its cross-modal demands (e.g., the conversion of visual symbols into auditory meanings). He then developed the cross-modal task as a means of experimentally studying these demands. This is not to say that his reasoning was correct. As subsequent studies have shown, the poorer performance of retarded readers does not seem to be dependent upon the cross-modal nature of the demands. If comparable stimuli are given intramodally, the same difficulties obtain. Although the approach may not have been valid, it has nevertheless been productive, for it has led to a well defined and testable set of hypotheses and ultimately to a series of findings that have elucidated the problems of the retarded reader. It is for this reason that I believe a model focused on the precise demands of the reading task is more fruitful than a model focused on what is defective in retarded readers.

THE INTERPRETATION OF THE FINDINGS

The final issue to be considered concerns the interpretations of the findings. In his review, Vellutino repeatedly makes a point with which I largely concur, namely, that the major difficulties of most retarded readers are in the language sphere. As it is presented, however, the emphasis on language may lead to the neglect of several important factors. For example, work on differentiating types of retarded readers, such as that of Boder (1973) and Mattis, French, and Rapin (1975), concludes that the largest group of retarded readers consists of those with language handicaps. Nevertheless, other subgroups have been found, e.g., children with visual-perceptual disturbances. Since the language handicapped represent the largest group, in any overall comparison between dyslexic and nondyslexic youngsters, they may be sufficiently powerful to sway the results toward the finding of a significant language impairment. As a result, the smaller, but nevertheless important, subgroups with deficiencies in other areas may well be overlooked. In other words, a focus on a single area to explain all the findings may leave segments of the dyslexic population undiagnosed.

Vellutino's emphasis on language also leads him to downplay prob-

lems in the visual modality. While simplistic interpretations of visual problems are almost certainly invalid, especially as they have been "sold" to teachers as part of a perceptual-deficits model, vision may nevertheless play a role
in ways that have not been fully explored. For instance, reading seems to require a type of visual information processing that is quite different from the
usual processing of visual information. For fluent reading to occur, many of
the physically salient dimensions of the written word must be disregarded,
e.g., the size, spacing, and color or brightness of the print are basically irrelevant. Moreover, these are precisely the same dimensions that are often the
most important in nonreading visual tasks. As a result, strong, well-established
predispositions in the visual sphere must be suppressed or inhibited if reading is to become a smooth process. My own work (Blank, Berenzweig, and
Bridger, 1975) and that of others (Wilows, 1974) suggest that poor readers experience great difficulty in achieving this suppression. In other words,
they are drawn to the irrelevant but physically salient characteristics of visual
material and hence have difficulty in attending to the more relevant, but less
striking, meaning characteristics of the letters and words.

Another aspect of visual information processing that deserves consideration is the sequential nature of the material. Reading represents one of the
few visual tasks where careful attention must be directed to the sequence and
temporal relationships of the material. Such relationships are always important
in audition; now they must be applied to visual phenomena. Vellutino's interpretation of the work on temporal sequencing leads him to conclude that this
component may not represent a special problem for the dyslexic. My own
experience in working with these children (Blank and Bridger, 1966; Blank,
Weider, and Bridger, 1968) leads me to believe that temporal-sequencing demands play an important role in the children's problems. Admittedly, much
needs to be done to define which of the many temporal and sequencing parameters may be the crucial ones for the retarded reader.* In addition, both components of the visual material discussed here (i.e., suppression of the attrac-
tion to physically salient cues and attention to temporal parameters) could be
a by-product of the development of certain language skills (Slobin, 1964).

---

* The work on temporal perception represents one of the interesting and unexpected
by-products of the cross-modal research. Because of the different parameters that mark
stimuli in the different modalities, experimenters working in this sphere had to attend
to properties that have long been neglected in experimental work on perception (e.g.,
when comparing auditory and visual stimuli, there was a need to control for the temporal nature of the auditory stimuli). In so doing, the potentially significant role of
temporal factors became much more apparent.

Therefore, these difficulties, if they exist, need not be *instead of,* but rather a *corollary* of, the language problems of the dyslexic (see Witelson, 1977 for an extension of this line of reasoning). They are included here not to downplay the role of language but rather to avoid closure on a still undecided issue.

Other aspects of Vellutino's emphasis on language also deserve further consideration. Although there is an increasing consensus on the relationship between language skills and reading ability, we still do not know which aspects of language are central. In line with paradigms adopted from experimental psychology, Vellutino emphasizes such factors as speed of labeling and coding information into language. Overlooked in this perspective is an area of language that may be critical to reading: the realm of language known as metalinguistics, i.e., the use of language to deal with language (see Cazden, 1972). A significant feature of metalinguistic tasks is that they demand a type of reflection that is rarely demanded in other language tasks. For example, in one metalinguistic task—namely rhyming—one has to "pull back" from the usually significant meaning properties of a word and instead pay attention to the generally ignored sound properties. In other words, there must be a conscious effort to refocus our attention to different aspects of the verbal material.

Interestingly, reading seems to require similar sorts of skills. For example, there is much less of a bond between the written word and its referent than there is between the spoken word and its referent. Nevertheless, the child must treat the written word as if it were equivalent to the spoken word. This is the type of achievement that seems to call upon metalinguistic skills. The realm of metalinguistics is far from defined or understood. However, in line with the work of Gleitman and Rozin (1973) and Liberman (1973), we may do well to explore the difficulties of at least some groups of dyslexics from this point of view.

Another area of language functioning that deserves study concerns the language that is used in communication between teacher and child. This area is rarely considered in most experimental studies of children, for the focus of such research is almost always on assessing the child's self-mediated verbal skills (e.g., the common questions are "Does the child invoke verbal aids?", "Does he store the information in verbal form?" etc.). The significance of teacher–child language emerges only when one begins to consider a generally unquestioned observation: namely, that with remediation many dyslexics overcome their reading problems. Of course, improvement does not always occur. Nevertheless, in many cases, the improvement is so great that the reading failure is almost completely resolved.

The change that accompanies special teaching is so well accepted and expected that we frequently do not think about it to any significant extent. Indeed, if this were not to be the outcome, it would be foolish to offer the remediation in the first place. What is significant for our purposes, however, is that the teaching for the dyslexic is different from the teaching offered to other special groups of children such as the deaf or the blind. In these latter syndromes, the children are offered a totally different system (e.g., Braille, sign language, or total communication) or if they are offered the absent system, the success is negligible (e.g., the teaching of spoken language to the deaf). In the case of the dyslexic, however, he is taught precisely the system he is having trouble mastering. In other words, the essential information being offered does not change. When faced with this fact, the question that logically emerges is, "Why do the children fail to learn these skills in the regular classroom setting while they do so in the special teaching setting?" It is this question that leads to a focus on teacher–child language, for clearly what has changed are not the skills being taught, but rather the way in which they are being communicated. Given the lack of attention to this area, we cannot be certain as to which factors are critical. At this point, however, determination of the factors is less important than is the recognition of the importance of this area; that is, recognition of the factors that mediate and facilitate the transmission of information between teacher and child.

This view of the situation is important because it shifts the analysis from an exclusive focus on "what is wrong with the dyslexic?" to "what are the essential components in teaching reading and, in particular, what are these components for children who have difficulty in learning to read?" In the final analysis, the study of the dyslexic will be of little consequence if we fail to pair it to the issue of more effective teaching.

Chapter 6

THE TANGLED WEB
OF BEHAVIORAL RESEARCH
ON DEVELOPMENTAL
DYSLEXIA

DONALD G. DOEHRING

The major part of Vellutino's paper represents a heroic effort to critically appraise the results of studies conducted in an attempt to discover the true behavioral nature of developmental dyslexia. It is clear that he wishes to demonstrate the implausibility of deficits in visual perception, intersensory integration, and temporal-order recall as sole causes of dyslexia and the plausibility of what he terms "verbal-processing deficits" or "verbal-encoding deficiencies" as the sole causes or the most significant factors in dyslexia. In attempting to follow the thread of his argument, the reader must decide whether he agrees with Vellutino's strictures regarding the definition of dyslexia, the nature of the behaviors being measured, and the final interpretation of each of a seemingly endless series of studies. As he labors on, however, the reader becomes aware that Vellutino has provided an invaluable description of the state of the art of behavioral research related to dyslexia. He has not been able to encapsulate the literature because dyslexia and the measured behaviors of dyslexics are not consistently defined. Vellutino's conscientious attempt to rationalize his own theoretical position with a study-by-study analysis of the literature illustrates the chaotic state of the art of behavioral research related to dyslexia.

I wish to carry Vellutino's appraisal further by critically analyzing the research paradigm employed in most of the studies that he has reviewed and by making some suggestions regarding alternative paradigms for further research on developmental dyslexia. The issues to be raised are not new (cf. Wiener and Cromer, 1967; Applebee, 1971; Boder, 1973; Benton, 1975; Mattis, French, and Rapin, 1975; Rourke, this vol.—Chap. 7; Rutter, this vol. Chap. 1) but are intended to provide a useful framework for the critical review of Vellutino's paper. The traditional dyslexia research paradigm, which I will refer to as the single-syndrome paradigm, will be criticized on the basis that no workable definition of dyslexia as a unitary disorder is possible, that reading should not be defined as a unitary process in dyslexics, and that psychological constructs are not sufficiently evolved to justify the use of terms such as attention, perception, memory, cognition, and language as causative factors in dyslexia. The alternative paradigm, which I will term the multiple-syndrome paradigm, treats reading as a complex, multidimensional process and allows for the possibility that there may be a number of different dyslexias, each characterized by a different pattern of reading and associated skills.

The results of research with the single-syndrome paradigm are certainly not without value. These studies have demonstrated that there is no easily discovered cause of dyslexia. Moreover, Vellutino has made a fairly convincing argument that only those behaviors which involve some aspect of language bear an intrinsic relationship to what he defines as dyslexia. Finally, the most recent studies (cf. Perfetti and Hogaboam, 1975; Liberman and Shankweiler, 1976) may lead to important insights about reading, reading acquisition, and reading disability even though they employ a possibly outmoded paradigm.

CRITICAL ANALYSIS OF THE SINGLE-SYNDROME PARADIGM

The basic paradigm compares a group of dyslexic children who are "otherwise normal" except for reading problems to a group of normal readers of the same age, intelligence, and general background. The performances of the two groups are compared on one or a small number of tests that measure certain behaviors designated by terms such as perception, memory, or language. The investigator hopes that a severe deficit in the dyslexics' performance will reveal the cause or one of the causes of dyslexia or he may hope to find no significant difference between groups in order to demonstrate (by accepting the null hypothesis) that this ability is not the cause or one of the causes of dyslexia.

The most frequent objection to this paradigm is that it is too simple. Applebee (1971) has stated the position as follows:

The most sensible approach is to start with the simplest reasonable explanation and only as that proves inadequate to move towards more complex models. Yet . . . research in reading retardation has for too long been methodologically oriented towards the simplest models; . . . this research has been successful only in showing that these simplest models do not fit the problem with which we are dealing; and . . . if we hope in the future to add anything of significance to our understanding of the problem, we must concentrate on new models which correspond more closely to the heterogeneity of the disorder.

The present writer increased the complexity of one aspect of the paradigm, the range of abilities tested, by comparing dyslexics and normal readers on 72 nonreading measures (Doehring, 1968). The dyslexics were significantly deficient on half the measures, a much more extensive deficit than anticipated. This demonstrated the inadvisability of basing inferences about dyslexia on the results of a limited number of tests. Vellutino has interpreted these results as inconsistent and as providing indirect support for his contention that poor readers do not have perceptual deficits. My present thought is that the apparent inconsistency in findings reflects the interaction of the indeterminate construct validity of the tests with the indeterminate heterogeneity of the dyslexic group. These and several other problems of research design are discussed in the following sections.

DEFINITION OF DYSLEXICS AS "OTHERWISE NORMAL"

Vellutino succinctly reviews the usual definitions of dyslexics as otherwise normal in home environment, educational opportunity, personality, sensory status, and intelligence. He states that there appears to be "no satisfactory way to separate subtle emotional and adjustment problems from primary learning disorder for purposes of studying reading disability." He stresses the "importance, in screening for dyslexia, of selecting an appropriate measure of intelligence, particularly one that does not attenuate the chances of mounting a fair test of a given hypothesis by screening out the population of interest." In his own research, Vellutino screens dyslexics for intelligence by requiring an IQ of 90 or above on either the verbal or the performance scale of the WISC, a rather uneasy expedient, and regrets that the researcher is not able to be as precise in operationalizing the remaining exclusionary variables.

Rutter (this vol., Chap. 1) discusses the difficulty of separating dyslexics from backward readers. He concludes that "it is not yet possible either to define dyslexia in an acceptable way or to identify cases of dyslexia," stating that the traditional method of defining dyslexia in terms of the discrepancy between intelligence and reading achievement is invalid. He concludes that the prevalence of specific reading retardation should be assessed by the use of regression equations involving educational attainment, age, and IQ.

Like Vellutino, I was uneasy about equating dyslexics and normal readers on abilities which might themselves be impaired in dyslexics (Doehring, 1968) but decided to proceed with the use of performance IQ (WISC) as an exclusionary criterion. This forced the retarded readers to be no different from normal readers on some skills which might have been associated with their reading problems and may, as a consequence, have "over-matched" them with the normals on other skills. As Rutter has indicated, the idea of using IQ discrepancy scores to define dyslexia, an essential component of the single-syndrome paradigm, should be challenged.

The general problem of exclusionary definitions of dyslexia is well stated by Applebee (1971):

> As presently defined, specific reading disability is a residual disorder, that is, it is part of reading retardation which we have not been able to explain. As new associated defects have been found in one or another subgroup of the population of retarded readers, they have been splintered off and the question has arisen, are these dyslexics? Often the principal investigator says *yes* and those who follow *no*. This curious ambiguity implies that "dyslexia" as such is an artifact of our lack of knowledge, and as a diagnostic category will gradually disappear as our knowledge increases (pp. 93–94).

Applebee's point is well taken. Having accepted Vellutino's demonstration that dyslexia is associated with verbal deficit, why should we not exclude reading problems secondary to verbal deficit in the same manner that we exclude reading problems secondary to personality disorders?

For more than 20 years (cf. Spiker and McCandless, 1954) psychologists have criticized the concept of intelligence, charging that there is no such entity as unitary intelligence or native intelligence, no unequivocal set of measures of the capacity of the intellect. At best, intelligence tests estimate relative proficiencies of behaviors deemed important within a particular culture. More crucial for the issues at hand, there is no clear distinction between measures of intelligence, aptitude, and achievement. "All ability tests—intelligence, aptitude, and achievement—measure what the individual *has* learned—and they often measure with similar content and similar process" (Wesman,

1968, p. 269). The residual abilities that are supposed to vary freely—according to exclusionary definitions of dyslexia—include attention, perception, memory, cognition, and language. How can these behaviors be differentiated from the behaviors sampled by intelligence tests? This confounding of variables is in itself a reason for abandoning the single-syndrome paradigm in its present form.

DEFINITION OF DYSLEXIA
BY A SINGLE MEASURE OF READING

The single-syndrome paradigm uses a single measure of reading achievement to define dyslexia. There is some justification for this, as Vellutino points out, since severely retarded readers will do poorly on all standard measures of reading achievement. However, recent theories (Smith, 1971; LaBerge and Samuels, 1974; and Gibson and Levin, 1975) suggest that reading should not be defined as a unitary process, even for the purpose of defining dyslexia. The investigator of dyslexia should measure more than one aspect of reading achievement. The number and type of measures will depend upon the theories of reading and reading acquisition that he provisionally adopts. The necessity for multiple measures of reading achievement is another reason for giving up the single-syndrome paradigm.

DYSLEXIA AS A UNITARY DISORDER

The single-syndrome paradigm was formally criticized by Wiener and Cromer (1967) and by Applebee (1971) as only one of several possible models of reading disability. The most basic form of the dyslexia research paradigm, as perhaps implicitly accepted by most of the investigators cited by Vellutino, conforms to Model 1 of Wiener and Cromer, a single-antecedent condition (e.g., visual perceptual deficit) with a single consequence (dyslexia). This is also Model 1 of Applebee in which "poor readers represent a homogeneous population deficient in a single ability (i.e., visual perception) essential in learning to read." Although Wiener and Cromer feel that most investigators would reject such a notion and Applebee concludes that no one has produced data which conform to the model, Vellutino's appraisal of the literature suggests that Model 1 has enjoyed a thriving existence. The complex nature of reading suggests the need for more than one syndrome of dyslexia, each of which could involve a different pattern of reading skill deficit, as defined by Models 4 and 5 of Wiener and Cromer and Model 4 of Applebee. Few of the studies reviewed by Vellutino seem to allow for such models, although Vellutino himself suggests the possibility of mutually exclusive deficiencies in phonological and semantic-syntactic aspects of language processing.

INTERPRETATION OF RESEARCH
USING THE SINGLE-SYNDROME PARADIGM

The interpretation of the studies reviewed by Vellutino is worthy of mention, since he has carefully described so many experiments. In addition to the major problem of formulating a general scientific statement, almost any study showing a deficit for the dyslexics can be criticized on the grounds that dyslexia was not properly defined, the reading criterion was inappropriate, or the differences between groups were attributable to abilities other than the one supposedly under consideration. Where no difference was found, the groups could have been "over matched," or very high or very low task difficulty may have attenuated possible differences. Where there was no discernible fault with respect to these factors, the investigator had the dubious honor of accepting the null hypothesis if he wished to claim no effect of the experimental variable. Although many of these problems occur in any comparison of groups, they clearly contribute to the nonadditivity of studies using the single-syndrome paradigm.

VALIDITY OF FUNDAMENTAL CONSTRUCTS

Vellutino assessed evidence that deficits in visual perception, intersensory integration, temporal-order perception, and verbal skills of various kinds might cause dyslexia. The choice of variables was appropriate (Benton, 1975), and it was fitting that Vellutino should relate these constructs to an explicit basic process model. However, there are some troubling questions about the validity of the constructs. The face validity of tests purporting to measure perception, memory, language, and reading can be questioned in terms of variance attributable to extraneous task requirements, as Vellutino has done, and also in terms of a lack of generally accepted theoretical constructs. The latter point is illustrated by the model employed by Vellutino, which includes sensory storage, short-term memory, and long-term memory. This model has been criticized by several writers (cf. Craik and Lockhart, 1972) and may not be as useful as other models (cf. LaBerge and Samuels, 1974). The present writer is inclined to feel that any models which imply the separate identity of perception, short-term memory, and long-term memory may soon be superseded.

PROBLEMS OF CAUSALITY

The single-syndrome paradigm implies a single cause leading to a single effect. Such reasoning makes it easier to impose order on events, but differences between groups or correlations between variables do not prove cause-and-effect relationships. A child's home life, socioeconomic status, and educational opportunity can be considered antecedents rather than consequences of his reading problems; and there is no more reason to classify his intelligence, personality, perception, memory, and language abilities as consequences rather than antecedents of reading difficulty. Oral language skills, for example, are still developing at the time of beginning reading and for several years thereafter. Dyslexia research may become more scientifically acceptable if the numerous variables involved in reading and associated behaviors are studied in terms of their covariance rather than as causes and effects or antecedents and consequences.

AN ALTERNATIVE PARADIGM

I will briefly describe the paradigm that we have adopted, which I will call the multiple-syndrome paradigm; it conforms to the complex models of Wiener and Cromer, and Applebee. We have attempted, with some success, to subdivide reading disabilities on the basis of common patterns of reading skill deficit (Doehring and Hoshko, 1977), and are now investigating the possible nonreading deficits that may be associated with each pattern of reading subskill deficit. The paradigm allows for the possibility of multiple reading disabilities associated with multiple nonreading deficits. Instead of comparing a dyslexic and a normal reader group, we use a factor analytic procedure to classify children with similar reading impairment profiles into subtypes of reading problems. The resulting subtypes do not appear to be statistical artifacts, since they correspond quite well with an independent educational appraisal of the remedial needs of the children.

The multiple-syndrome paradigm may yield different findings for some of the abilities appraised by Vellutino. For example, other investigators who have used this paradigm (Johnson and Myklebust, 1967; Boder, 1973; and Mattis, French, and Rapin, 1975) report a relatively infrequent type of dyslexia characterized by visuoperceptual deficit. Such a deficit might not emerge as a significant correlate of dyslexia with the single-syndrome paradigm, where the rare cases would be overshadowed by other subtypes. One fairly common subtype of reading problem that we have found thus far appears to reflect difficulty in rapid intersensory integration. This does not necessarily conflict with Vellutino's rejection of intersensory integration deficit as a cause of dyslexia, since he allowed for the possibility of "dysfunction specifically associated with the coordination of visual and verbal information, but probably not to cross-modal transfer as defined initially by Birch." Another subtype seems to involve difficulty in temporal ordering, although I suspect we will be able to relate this more directly to a phonemic differentiation problem. Another type that we have identified thus far does appear to involve a linguistic deficit suggestive of difficulty in lexical access.

The multiple-syndrome paradigm should enable us to estimate the incidence of homogeneous subtypes in the dyslexic population, as recommended by Benton (1975). The paradigm can be used with a dyslexia sample defined by the exclusionary definition recommended by Vellutino, but no normal-reading control group is needed. Such a procedure would probably be useful for comparing findings with the new paradigm to previous findings with the single-syndrome paradigm. The results for good and poor readers can be analyzed together, to determine the extent to which normal readers are distinguishable by the pattern as well as the absolute level of their reading skills, and the poor reader sample can include mentally retarded children and other children that Rutter would classify as backward readers. Reading disability subtypes should also be determined at different ages to directly test the hypothesis of Satz and colleagues (Satz et al., this vol.—Chap. 16) that patterns of deficit change with age.

Problems with the face validity of reading and nonreading tests are not avoided by the new paradigm, although it is undoubtedly safer to look at patterns of test scores rather than "levels" of one or a small number of tests (Rourke, this vol.—Chap. 7). In our present state of knowledge, it may be best for different sets of investigators to select tests based on different theories of reading, perception, memory, and language, in the hope of finding the same sets of dyslexia syndromes through converging operations (Garner, Hake, and Eriksen, 1956).

There are at least two problems inherent in the multiple-syndrome paradigm as we use it. The first is statistical. The factor-analytic procedure that we have used thus far is not ideal. Cluster analysis methods have been criticized (Applebee, 1971), but we do hope to find methods of this type that will adequately represent the patterns of deficit. The second problem is that a large number of tests must be given to each child. As Vellutino has pointed out, the reliability of large numbers of tests given in a short time may be questionable. This is a general problem of psychological testing which also adds to the time and expense of research using the multiple-syndrome paradigm. The two problems interact, since the efficacy of the statistical classification procedure depends to some extent on the number and type of tests used.

CONCLUSIONS

It is suggested, largely on the basis of Vellutino's careful appraisal of behavioral research on dyslexia, that alternatives to the single-syndrome paradigm be actively explored. There is some possibility that the linguistic variables reviewed in the latter part of Vellutino's paper might be usefully studied by the single-syndrome paradigm, but reasons may be advanced to the contrary. For example, Perfetti and Hogaboam's (1975) study of the relationship between oral reading and comprehension in poor readers defined poor readers in terms of reading comprehension test scores, whereas Vellutino (p. 67) does not wish to apply the term "dyslexia" to children simply on the basis of their reading comprehension.

Other paradigms should also be developed. There is little chance that final answers to the problem of dyslexia will be found in the near future, considering the continuing uncertainty about the operational definition and the theoretical status of reading, attention, perception, memory, cognition, language, and intelligence. Advances in our knowledge of dyslexia will probably occur not in the form of dramatic discoveries with a simple paradigm, but through a patient working and reworking of complex sets of experimental variables, with clinical validation wherever possible.

If we set aside the exclusionary definitions of dyslexia, as typefied by the description of Critchley (1964), one or more dyslexias may emerge in the total population of good and poor readers of all ages. Such dyslexias would be characterized by specific patterns of reading-skill deficit associated with specific patterns of nonreading deficit. Other reading problems (i.e., backward reading) would be characterized by patterns of reading impairment associated with nonspecic patterns of nonreading impairment. Investigation of reading problems within this larger conceptual framework might produce more substantial contributions to knowledge.

It might be best to broaden the theoretical framework even further and investigate the entire range of behaviors classified as learning problems. Our results thus far and those of others (Boder, 1973; Denckla, 1973; Mattis, French, and Rapin, 1975) lead me to speculate that there are a limited number of relatively frequent patterns of learning deficit, most but not all of which involve reading problems. Such a broad approach would have the disadvantage of increasing the complexity of the task of deriving appropriate tests based on acceptable theoretical constructs. Even the present level of complexity is perhaps too much to grasp. We may need to adopt more comprehensive models of human behavior (cf. Royce and Buss, 1976) and seek the aid of systems analysts (cf. Beer, 1975) in formulating a critical path for research on learning problems. We may finally be able to reapply the term "dyslexia" to certain learning problems, and devote our research efforts to discover their neurological correlates (Benton, 1975) and our remedial efforts to deal with them in proportion to their relative incidence and severity among the total group of childhood learning disorders.

While scientific considerations may dictate a more comprehensive approach to learning problems that eliminates exclusionary definitions, proposed government regulations for diagnosing learning disabilities may continue the traditional approach for purposes of allocating federal funds. Problems of definition similar to those mentioned here are recognized (fledgling status of learning-disabilities field; strong differences of opinion regarding validity of behavioral manifestations as indicators of learning disability; lack of research data to provide reliable statements regarding the characteristics of learning-disabled children; and lack of standardized diagnostic instruments), but there is general agreement among the experts consulted that a specific learning disability is defined as a significant discrepancy between achievement and intellectual ability (Schaar, 1977). Perhaps the government regulations adopted can be modified when the necessary research data become available.

In lieu of further discussion, some of the questions which have occurred to me in thinking about new research paradigms are as follows:

1. Can reading be divided into component skills? If so, how are these skills correlated in normal and retarded readers (Guthrie, 1973)? How do the skills interact during normal and subnormal reading acquisition?

2. Can normal readers be categorized in terms of asymmetries of component reading skills? Do reading problems constitute exaggerations of normal asymmetries or qualitatively different disorders? Is there a continuum of asymmetries of reading skill such that reading disabilities must be defined in terms of arbitrary cutoffs dictated by special education resources?

3. Must component reading skills be overlearned to the point of automaticity to achieve normal reading? How long does this take? Is failure to achieve automaticity the prime factor in reading disability? How important are learning strategies and control processes in reading problems (Calfee, 1975)? How easy is it to define and differentiate such processes?

Are different syndromes of dyslexia associated with failure to achieve automaticity in skills such as visual letter feature extraction, phonemic segmentation of the sound stream, sound-letter association, lexical access, and sentence comprehension?

5. Should intervention focus on nonautomatized reading skills, nonautomatized nonreading skills, or compensatory training based on successfully automatized reading and nonreading skills?

6. Would the determination of response to training in nonautomatized skills constitute a more effective research strategy?

7. Can deficits of reading and associated skills be related to patterns of behavioral deficit observed in brain-damaged adults (Benson and Geschwind, 1969; Hécaen and Kremin, 1976)?

Part III

NEUROBEHAVIORAL RESEARCH

Chapter 7

NEUROPSYCHOLOGICAL RESEARCH IN READING RETARDATION: A REVIEW

BYRON P. ROURKE

INTRODUCTION

This chapter constitutes a selective review and evaluation of the results of investigations in the general area of the neuropsychology of reading retardation. Although neuropsychology is fairly easy to define (i.e., the investigation of the relationships between the brain and behavior), the exact specification of that which constitutes neuropsychological research can be problematic. For example, it is clear that dichotic listening experiments, in which brain-damage and normal persons are used as subjects and where the intent is to demonstrate relationships between the state of the brain and behavior, fall within the realm of neuropsychology. However, some aspects of the investigation of electrophysiological disturbances, sex differences, and the relationship between neurological examination techniques and behavioral variables fall within a type of 'no-man's-land" between neuropsychology and its sister disciplines. Consequently, there is bound to be some overlap between the material discussed in this chapter and the research results reviewed in other chapters of this volume. Although I have attempted to keep this overlap to a minimum, it has been necessary to cite research evidence from some related areas in order to elucidate the implications of research results which fall clearly within the expected scope for this review.

The scope of the neuropsychology of reading retardation is vast. I have attempted to confine the discussion of research results to areas which have clear theoretical and/or clinical significance for the problem at hand. In each section in this review, an attempt is made to highlight the theoretical and/or clinical issues involved, to follow this with a review of representative studies in the field, and to cite some conclusions which can be arrived at on the basis of the evidence accumulated. The final section contains a series of conclusions which appear warranted on the basis of research data presented, with accentuation on methodological problems and judgments regarding fruitful avenues for future research.

In all of this, an attempt has been made to confine the discussion to the most salient issues, and to cite recent or relatively novel work if it appears that these avenues of research are promising. Reviews of this sort must be selective, due to limitations of space. It is hoped that the current review is "selective" in this sense, and not as a function of my predilections regarding the relevance of certain types of research in this field.

As background for the present review, the thorough presentation of Benton (1975) is helpful. In addition, a recent work (Knights and Bakker, 1976) dealing with the neuropsychology of learning disorders contains reviews of research which bear upon many issues discussed in this chapter.

OUTLINE AND METHODOLOGICAL CONSIDERATIONS

The order in which the topics in this chapter have been arranged is the result of compromises worked out among three principles of hierarchical categorization. First, an attempt was made to arrange the topics to reflect the progressive emergence of abilities and occurrence of difficulties throughout the course of ontogenetic development. Secondly, it was intended that "simpler" or "lower" abilities (from the point of view of the brain) would be discussed before more "complex" or "higher" functions. (The interaction of this second principle with the first is obvious.) Finally, an attempt was made to group the studies in order of predominant methodological approaches to the study of brain–behavior relationships. For this reason, among the first topics considered are those having to do with the investigation of pathognomonic signs (e.g., choreiform movements), clinical syndromes (e.g., Gerstmann's syndrome), clinical symptoms (e.g., right–left disorientation), and clinical tests (e.g., the electroencephalogram). These are followed by a discussion of studies which rely heavily upon the "level of performance" approach (e.g., comparisons of the levels of performance of normal and retarded readers on measures of visual-perceptual abilities), the "differential score" approach (e.g., the examination of patterns of Verbal IQ–Performance IQ discrepancies on the Wechsler scales in normal and retarded readers), and comparisons of performance on the two sides of the body (e.g., comparisons of left- and right-ear advantage in normal and retarded readers). It should be noted that some of the areas covered (e.g., neuropsycholinguistics) are more amenable than others (e.g., prenatal factors) to the simultaneous or serial utilization of more than one mode of approach. For a discussion of the relative merits of these modes of approach to neuropsychological research in general, the interested reader is referred to the excellent review by Reitan (1966); an application and modification of these modes of approach to the field of learning disabilities in children is contained in Rourke (1975).

PRENATAL, PERINATAL, AND NEONATAL ABNORMALITIES

If disordered functioning of the brain is thought to be a factor which can interfere with reading acquisition, it would make good sense to investigate the relationship between reading acquisition and those prenatal, perinatal, and neonatal events which are known to pose a risk to the normal development of the brain. There have been several prospective and retrospective studies launched with this aim in mind.

An early study of the relationship between prenatal and perinatal factors and reading disorders in childhood was carried out by Kawi and Pasamanick (1959). In this investigation, the prenatal and perinatal records of 372 white male children with reading disorders were compared with the records of a similar number of matched controls. The results indicated that there were relationships between certain abnormal conditions associated with childbearing and the subsequent development of reading disorders in the offspring. There was a significantly larger proportion of premature births in the group of children who eventually presented with reading disorders than in the control group, and abnormalities of the prenatal and perinatal periods occurred with significantly greater frequency among the children who eventually exhibited reading disorders.

It has also been shown that there are marked sex differences (showing the male to be at a disadvantage) in physical, psychological, and neurological development from birth to 4 years of age (Singer, Westphal, and Niswander, 1968). Males, although they have the advantage of higher birth weight, do less well in these areas than do females from birth through 4 years of age. These data take on potential relevance when we consider that the incidence of reading retardation in males is much higher than in females (usually in the ratio of 6 : 1).

In one investigation it has been shown that, for middle-class boys, the best predictors of reading retardation among the perinatal variables were the symptoms of possible brain injury exhibited by the child (Lyle, 1970). It is interesting to note that, when only middle-class boys were considered, toxemia of pregnancy (preeclampsia) and low birth weight were not related to reading retardation. This would seem to indicate that researchers in this area should attempt to determine the impact of socioeconomic, educational, and related factors in their investigations.

Other retrospective (Galante, Flye, and Stephens, 1972) and prospective (Smith et al., 1972) studies have indicated that long-range prediction of performances in a number of ability areas by using information from prenatal, perinatal, and neonatal developmental periods is feasible, and that an unusual birth history is present to a far greater degree in children who achieve below their apparent level of "intellectual" prowess than in children who achieve up to their "potential." Additionally, Galante et al. (1972) found that an accumulation of minor deficits (unusual birth history, eye muscle imbalance, abnormal EEG, and other signs of neurological dysfunction) appeared in their severe underachievers. In this connection, Silver and Hagin (1964) reported that the 24 children with specific reading disability whom they followed into young adulthood continued to exhibit their specific "perceptual" problems, and evidenced lack of clear-cut cerebral dominance (although in less severe form). Those patients who, as children, had neurological signs in addition to their specific reading disability showed less improvement than did those who did not exhibit such signs.

Conclusions

It is apparent that prenatal, perinatal, and neonatal complications, especially those with presumed neurological significance, are found more frequently and prominently in the histories of retarded readers than in those of children who read well. These data lend support to the view that disordered functioning of the brain can play a role in reading retardation. However, it is also clear that the presence of such complications is neither a necessary nor a sufficient explanation for reading disorders in children. Many children who present with reading retardation do not have a history of such complications and many children who do suffer such complications learn to read quite well. Nevertheless, the data supporting a relationship between such complications and reading retardation are sufficiently compelling to emphasize the need for efforts to minimize such complications. At the same time, on the basis of the data available at present, it would seem inappropriate to adopt a strategy which involves the routine ascribing of etiological significance to early nervous system damage (cf. Gottesman, Belmont, and Kaminer, 1975). Rather it would appear that more could be gained by a thorough, broadly based neuropsychological assessment of the child presenting with reading retardation in an effort to determine the brain-related variables in his ability structure which may be contributing to his particular reading problem. This strategy would seem preferable to one which simply hearkens back to events surrounding the child's birth, the impact of which is, although sometimes clear, seldom specifically contributory to efforts at either current assessment or subsequent remediation (cf. Rourke, 1976b, 1977).

FINGER AGNOSIA AND RIGHT–LEFT DISCRIMINATION DIFFICULTIES

Another approach to the question of brain–behavior relationships in reading retardation is one which has involved the determination of the incidence and type of reading disorder with which the symptoms comprising the so-called Gerstmann syndrome is associated. This syndrome is composed of a tetrad of symptoms: right–left disorientation, finger agnosia, agraphia, and acalculia.

Many of the studies which have been concerned with the investigation of the relationship between finger agnosia and reading retardation have been "clinical" (i.e., intensive analyses of individual cases) in nature (e.g., Benson and Geschwind, 1970; Kinsbourne and Warrington, 1963b). Both of the cited studies were concerned with the implications of the Gerstmann syndrome vis-à-vis reading retardation. Benson and Geschwind analyzed two patients who presented with the "classical" tetrad of Gerstmann symptoms in whom reading ability was preserved. Kinsbourne and Warrington (1963b) reported on seven cases of the developmental Gerstmann syndrome which had been diagnosed in childhood, and demonstrated to their satisfaction that finger agnosia and the other characteristic symptoms of the Gerstmann syndrome are related to reading and writing retardation of a characteristic type.

Croxen and Lytton (1971) also studied finger localization and right–left discrimination in 9- and 10-year-old normal and retarded readers. Both boys and girls in the retarded reading group exhibited significantly greater finger localization and right–left discrimination difficulties than did the control group. The investigators also found a significant correlation between finger localization and right–left discrimination when nonverbal IQ was partialled out. The authors concluded that their results support the view that some children suffering from a reading disability have a "general perceptual deficit."

An investigation focusing on the determination of the relationship between lateralized finger agnosia and reading achievement at ages 6 and 10 was carried out by Reed (1967a). In this study, children at the two age levels were classified in terms of number of finger localization errors on the right hand versus those on the left hand. The results indicated that there was no relationship between reading achievement and finger localization errors at age 6. However, at age 10, the group with a predominance of right-hand errors read significantly less well than did the group with a majority of left-hand errors. Reed concluded that finger localization errors were not related to the acquisition of primary reading skills, but were associated with limitations in the development of proficient reading skills among older children. In addition, he maintained that developmental disturbances in finger localization have behavioral concomitants which are similar to those seen in adults with acquired impairment in finger localization as a result of brain lesions.

Doehring (1968) found some evidence of finger agnosia in his older group of retarded readers; the difference between the groups, favoring the performance of the normal readers, reached conventional levels of statistical significance only for the left hand. Finlayson and Reitan (1976) compared the performances of older (12- to 14-year-old) and younger (6- to 8-year-old) normal boys and girls who had been distributed into two groups on the basis of the number of errors they made on several tests of tactile-perceptual ability. In the older group, children with poor tactile-perceptual skills performed significantly less well on several measures (including reading ability) than did children with few tactile-perceptual errors. There was no significant difference in reading ability between the two groups at the 6- to 8-year-old level.

That disordered development in finger localization may be related to the impaired development of body schemata and to some neuropathological conditions has been hypothesized by Lefford, Birch, and Green (1974). The results of their study, together with those of Satz, Friel, and Rudegeair (1974), would also suggest that finger agnosia has diagnostic potential for preschool children who are at risk for learning disabilities in general, and reading retardation in particular.

146

Conclusions

There is some evidence that (1) finger agnosia and right–left discrimination difficulties can be highly correlated, (2) there is a greater incidence of finger agnosia in retarded readers, especially those at the 10- to 14-year-old level, (3) there is some similarity between the behavioral concomitants of finger agnosia in children and those in adults with acquired impairment in finger localization as a result of brain lesions, and (4) the presence of finger localization errors in children of preschool age would appear to be a "high risk" indicator for reading retardation. The degree of relationship between the Gerstmann syndrome and reading retardation must remain an open question. However, it would seem that there is a relationship between finger agnosia and reading retardation and it may be the case that this relationship, when present, has both diagnostic and prognostic significance as well as theoretical implications with respect to the possible neuropsychological basis for at least some varieties of reading retardation.

THE CHOREIFORM SYNDROME, MINIMAL BRAIN DYSFUNCTION, AND THE NEUROLOGICAL EXAMINATION

Another group of studies has been directed toward the determination of the relationship between reading retardation and the choreiform syndrome, the minimal brain dysfunction (MBD) syndrome, and other "positive" findings of the physical neurological examination.

Although choreiform movements are significantly more prevalent in a learning-disabled population than in a normal population, this syndrome seems to be more directly related to mental age than to specific reading retardation. For example, Rutter, Graham, and Birch (1966) found no relaitonship between reading retardation and the presence of choreiform movements when age and level of psychometric intelligence were held constant.

The cognitive abilities of children with marked reading disorders but without demonstrable neurological dysfunction appear to be very similar to those exhibited by reading-retarded children with well-documented neurological dysfunction (Black, 1973). When subjects are equated for chronological age and level of psychometric intelligence, there appears to be no significant relationship between the nonacademic symptoms of MBD (based on a pediatric neurological evaluation and/or visuomotor impairment as measured by the Bender-Gestalt test) and low academic achievement (Edwards, Alley, and Snider, 1971). More generally, it would appear that the "medical evaluation" (consisting of the history, neurological examination, and EEG) plays a minimal part in the diagnosis and treatment of children with reading problems (Kenny et al., 1972). In a recent paper (Rourke, 1978) it has been suggested that the diagnosis of MBD is no more than marginally necessary for most purposes and may, in fact, be somewhat counterproductive in many contexts.

Conclusions

The significance of the relationships discussed in this section is analogous to that discussed in connection with the prenatal, perinatal, and neonatal factors dealt with above. Although there is some evidence which would support a marginal relationship between the nonacademic symptoms of the MBD syndrome and some of the other "positive" findings of the physical neurological examination on the one hand and reading retardation on the other, the amount of variance in reading retardation which can be accounted for in terms of these factors appears to be rather minimal.

ELECTROENCEPHALOGRAPHIC ABNORMALITIES

Although another chapter in this volume is devoted specifically to a discussion of electrophysiological studies which relate to reading retardation, some mention may be made of electroencephalographic (EEG) research in the present context. The question of interest is as follows: Is there evidence that retarded readers differ from normal readers in their EEG responsivity? If it can be shown that retarded readers exhibit immature or "pathological" EEG patterns, this evidence would lend support to the view that brain dysfunction can play a role in reading retardation.

There is a higher incidence of abnormal EEG patterns in children who exhibit "behavioral" or academic problems than in groups of "normal" children (Benton and Bird, 1963; Torres and Ayers, 1968). Although lateralized dysrhythmia in children is not related to differential Verbal–Performance discrepancies on intelligence test scores (Pennington, Galliani, and Voegele, 1965) and the EEG is not a good predictor of intellectual and academic performance (Hartlage and Green, 1973), there is some evidence that reading disorder (uncomplicated by behavior disorder) is associated with

EEG abnormalities (Muehl, Knott, and Benton, 1965). Nevertheless, the association between EEG abnormality and disordered academic and behavioral functioning is far from clear in the latter study and in one by Tymchuck, Knights, and Hinton (1970).

Hartlage and Green (1973) have suggested that considerably more refined EEG techniques are required in order for EEG findings to be used routinely in predicting types of academic impairment. Studies which have utilized more refined techniques (e.g., visual evoked responses, averaged evoked responses, and responses to semantic and nonsemantic stimuli) have yielded results which suggest that children with reading and other learning disorders can be differentiated from normal readers on the basis of their EEG esponses (Conners, 1970; Fenelon, 1968; Preston, Guthrie, and Childs, 1974; Shields, 1973).

Variations in EEG response (in particular the visual evoked response) seem to be related to chronological age, IQ, reading level, and neurological dysfunction. The only study which has attempted to control for the first three variables (Preston et al., 1974) yielded results which indicated that there is a relationship between visual evoked responses and reading disability. This relationship is reliable but marginal in strength. Finally, the results of one study (Piggot et al., 1972) suggest that the presumed stress involved in work in a deficit area (e.g., reading) may lead to EEG disorganization of brain activity, and that this EEG disorganization may have an effect upon the child's school functioning and behavior.

For a more complete and detailed review of studies in this area, the review of Benton (1975) and Chapters 10-12 in this volume by Hughes, Denckla, and Conners (respectively) may be consulted.

Conclusions

The results of investigations in this area indicate that groups of retarded readers are more likely than normal readers to exhibit indications of brain dysfunction; in this case, immature or otherwise abnormal EEG patterns. However, only a relatively small percentage of retarded readers exhibit such pathological patterns and not all who exhibit such patterns have difficulties in reading acquisition. It would appear that routine clinical EEG tracings cannot be expected to reveal much that is of significance with respect to the causes or correlates of reading disability. However, there would appear to be something of importance to be learned about retarded readers from further investigations which employ "challenges" to the brain (e.g., the visual evoked-response technique).

OCULOMOTOR, VISUOMOTOR, VISUAL-PERCEPTUAL, AND VISUOSPATIAL FACTORS

From time to time, the following have been proposed:

(1) that reading difficulties are, in some cases, due to deficiencies in binocular coordination, faulty scanning, and/or other oculomotor deficiencies;

(2) that poor readers have difficulty in many abilities related to visual perception, including (a) perceiving visuospatial relationships, (b) perceiving the stimulus information necessary for fluent reading, (c) selecting relevant information from the visuospatial field, and (d) visuomotor abilities.

These concerns are germane to a discussion about the neuropsychological aspects of reading retardation because of the direct control exercised by the brain over those activities mentioned in (1), and the well-known relationships which have been demonstrated between brain lesions of various sorts and deficiencies in the abilities cited in (2) (cf. Reitan and Davison, 1974).

With regard to (1), Winters et al (1967) have shown that consistency between eye movements and verbal reports coincides with greater accuracy of recognition in both normal and mentally retarded adolescents. In this study, those retardates who were more consistent in their organization of eye movements and verbal reports gave significantly more correct responses on a reading test than did retardates who were less consistent. Related to this, Goldberg and Arnott (1970) have presented evidence which, in their view, demonstrates that, in reading, it is the degree of comprehension that produces the type of ocular movement, and not vice versa. In other words, it would appear that poor ocular motility is a result rather than a cause of poor reading comprehension. Finally, Fox, Orr, and Rourke (1975) have demonstrated that the standard optometric examination which focuses on ocular motility and similar phenomena, while failing to include an assessment of some "higher-order" perceptual abilities, is not contributory to the diagnosis of even fairly severe reading disabilities in older children.

With regard to (2), Nielsen and Ringe (1969) compared the performances of normal and reading-disabled 9- and 10-year-olds on the Frostig Test of Visual Perception, the Bender Visual-Motor Gestalt Test, and the

Goodenough Draw-a-Person Test. They found more similarities than differences in performance levels between the two groups, and concluded that impaired visual perception and visuomotor dysfunction did not seem to be important correlates of reading disability. Robinson and Schwartz (1973), in a longitudinal study (from approximately the beginning of grade 1 to the end of grade 3) of middle-class children with visual-perception problems, found that, although these children continued to have "perceptual" problems and a lower mean IG at the end of grade 3, their reading scores were not significantly lower than those of the control group. In addition, those authors' findings did not support the view that "perceptual" training will improve reading ability. In contrast, Elkind and Deblinger (1969) demonstrated that disadvantaged children in grade 2 made significantly greater improvement on word form and word recognition following training with nonverbal perceptual exercises than did control groups trained with a commercial reading program.

Doehring (1968) demonstrated that 10- to 14-year-old retarded readers are deficient in a variety of visual-perceptual and visuospatial skills as compared to normals. The results of studies by Reed (1969); Rourke (1976c); and Satz, Friel, and Rudegeair (1974) are in essential agreement with this assertion. Furthermore, the cross-sectional design of Reed's study and the longitudinal designs of the Rourke and Satz et al. investigations allowed them to conclude that visual-perceptual and visuospatial abilities appear to be somewhat less important at advanced stages of the learning-to-read process than they are during the initial stages of reading acquisition.

Finally, Witelson (1976a), in a study of disabled readers, has produced evidence which suggests that a lack of right-hemisphere specialization for visuospatial processing may interfere with left-hemisphere processing of linguistic functioning. In contrast, Symmes and Rapoport (1972) have provided evidence that, among a specific subgroup of retarded readers (which was composed of 53 boys and 1 girl), there is a marked superiority (as compared with normal readers) in certain visual-perceptual skills. However, these findings should be viewed in the context of the results of another study by Witelson (1976b) which suggest that normal girls show evidence of bilateral representation of "spatial" processing until age 13, whereas boys perform in a manner consistent with right-hemisphere specialization for spatial processing as early as age six.

Conclusions
There is little evidence that the abilities mentioned in (1) play a critical role in reading retardation, except in a very limited number of cases. The abilities

mentioned in (2) may be somewhat more important, although the data are ambiguous (Benton, 1975; Doehring, 1968; Vellutino et al., 1975b). At the very least, it would appear that age and sex differences as well as differences in psychometric intelligence and socioeconomic status must be taken into consideration when attempting to interpret these results.

TEMPORAL SEQUENCING AND SERIAL POSITIONING

There is a considerable body of research data which tends to support the view that simultaneous and sequential processing of information are primarily subserved by different systems within the brain (Luria, 1973; Reitan and Davison, 1974). Within the context of this general issue are the more specific problems relating to the accurate processing of temporal sequences and the remembering of serial positions for visual and auditory stimuli. Both of these problems have received substantial attention in research relating to the neuropsychology of reading disorders.

It has been proposed that reading disorders in children may result from general deficit in temporal sequencing. Bakker (1967) has presented evidence to indicate that poor readers make significantly more errors than do good readers in retaining temporal sequences. However, these results were obtained only for meaningful figures and letters. Groenendaal and Bakker (1971) found that above-average readers and below-average readers did not differ significantly in their memory for sequences of meaningless figures. By means of a mediation test, they discovered that "mediators" perceived and retained sequences of meaningful figures better than did "nonmediators." This is important when it is considered that there were approximately the same number of mediators and nonmediators in the two reading groups.

Corkin (1974) found that average readers were significantly better than inferior readers in remembering the correct serial position of visual or auditory stimuli under conditions where demands were made upon immediate memory processes. In a study by Allen (1975), poor readers, as compared to good readers, exhibited a deficiency in the discrimination of temporal and temporal-spatial sequences in those cases where the number of long temporal intervals was changed, or the order of occurrence of the long and short intervals was reversed.

The results of the investigations of Senf (1969) and Bakker (1972) suggest that retarded readers have difficulty in remembering the temporal sequence of digits or figures, especially when auditory and visual stimuli are intermingled. Bakker (1972) found that performance on his "mixed" auditory-visual task was a good predictor of reading achievement.

Young and Rourke (1975) compared the relative efficiency of good and poor readers on auditory and visual sequencing tasks. They employed 32 second-grade and 32 sixth-grade subjects (half of whom were good readers and half of whom were poor readers) who were matched for age and WISC prorated Performance IQ. The subjects were presented with equivalent verbal sequences, which varied in complexity, through the visual and auditory channels. Half of the subjects received the visual task first and the auditory task two days later, while the other half received the auditory task first and the visual task second. The results indicated that all subjects performed faster on the auditory task than on the visual task, regardless of order of presentation or level of complexity. The results also indicated that younger poor readers made more errors than younger good readers on both tasks, but particularly on the auditory task; the performances of older poor and good readers, in general, did not differ.

Conclusions

It appears that retarded readers as a group exhibit deficiencies in temporal sequencing and serial positioning. However, the fact that there are marked individual differences among normal as well as retarded readers on those variables (probably mediational in nature) which appear to affect temporal sequencing ability directly renders the interpretation (and, *a fortiori*, the applications) of these results rather tenuous. Also, there appear to be a number of processes (e.g., immediate and short-term memory, auditory-visual integration) which interact in unspecified ways in a number of experimental paradigms used to investigate these phenomena, thus rendering the interpretation of results in this area difficult. It would seem that, in this as well as in a number of other research areas which have a bearing upon reading retardation in children, there is considerable need, first, for the isolation, and then for the intensive study, of subgroups of retarded readers at different age levels who exhibit or who do not exhibit various patterns of the abilities or deficits in question. If a "level of performance" approach is to yield information which will speak to the neuropsychological significance of the relationships among temporal sequencing, serial positioning, and reading retardation, this type of subgroup analysis would appear to be a *sine qua non*.

AUDITORY-VISUAL INTEGRATION

Luria (1966, 1973) maintains that the integration of sensory-perceptual information received through various sensory modalities is a crucial "step" in the brain's processing of information. He sees this step as especially important for the implementation of complex forms of behaviors (i.e., "higher cortical functions") such as reading.

In a similar vein, Birch and Belmont (1964), working from the notion that the capacity to organize and assimilate multimodal information underlies the higher organism's ability to exhibit behavioral plasticity and to modulate and modify its behavior, have proposed that one of the factors which contributes to reading retardation is a deficiency in the ability to integrate auditory and visual stimuli. They and others have conducted several investigations addressing this issue, the principal results of which can be summarized as follows: (1) the ability to integrate auditory and visual stimuli improves with age (Birch and Belmont, 1965); (2) the ability to treat auditory and visual patterned information as equivalent is one factor which differentiates good from poor readers (Birch and Belmont, 1964); (3) the visual recall of retarded readers is hindered by the presentation of distracting auditory stimuli, which suggests that not only matching, but inadequate "disentangling," of intersensory distractions is an important factor in reading disability (Shipley and Jones, 1969); (4) poor readers have difficulty in matching patterns (i.e., sequences of auditory or visual stimuli), even when auditory-visual transformations are not required (Bryden, 1972); (5) the developmental progression for cross-modal matching tasks is not reliably different from that for within-modal matching tasks in the case of retarded readers (Vande Voort, Senf, and Benton, 1972); (6) the demands of stimulus complexity within the visual modality may be more closely related to reading ability than are the demands of cross-modal shifting (Blank, Berenzweig, and Bridger, 1975); and, (7) there seem to be quite separate and distinct (i.e., uncorrelated) integrative abilities which are correlated with reading ability (Warren, Andoshian, and Widawski, 1975).

Conclusions
Given large enough groups of retarded and normal readers, it can be demonstrated that the retarded readers as a group are deficient in: (a) within-modal (e.g., auditory-auditory) as well as cross-modal (e.g., auditory-visual) inte-

gration, and, (b) a number of quite distinct (i.e., uncorrelated) integrative abilities which are correlated with reading ability. In this area of research, perhaps more than in most others which have a bearing upon reading retardation, the necessity for separating and comparing subgroups of retarded readers who do or do not exhibit these deficiencies is apparent. Until this is done, it is difficult to determine the relative importance of these integrative skills for reading ability. Furthermore, the apparent age differences in the acquisition of at least some of these integrative abilities would suggest that they may be more or less important at different stages in the reading process. In any case, it is clear that these matters must be dealt with more thoroughly before the empirical and theoretical issues involved in the determination of the relationships among auditory-visual integration, reading ability, and the integrity of the brain can be addressed in a meaningful fashion.

CEREBRAL DOMINANCE

Orton (1928) proposed that there is a relationship between cerebral dominance and specific reading disability. He did so on the basis of his analysis of the types of reading errors that reading-disabled children made: these typically involved letter reversals and mirror images of words. He felt that these distortions might be due to confusion between competing images in both cerebral hemispheres which, in turn, may be the result of a lack of development of unilateral cerebral dominance. He coined the term "strephosymbolia" for the reading disorder which he thought resulted therefrom.

One line of investigation related to Orton's theory has involved the examination of the relationship between hand or eye preference and reading disability. Although much research on this topic has been carried out over the past few decades, there has been little unambiguous evidence which would support the hypothesized relationship (Benton, 1975). The results of the majority of reasonably well controlled studies in this area (Belmont and Birch, 1965; Crinella, Beck, and Robinson, 1971; Coleman and Deutsch, 1964; Lyle, 1969; Sabatino and Becker, 1971) have indicated no clearly significant relationships between hand or eye preference and reading ability. Nevertheless, Zangwill (1960, 1962) has suggested that there may be a specific subgroup of retarded readers in whom "incomplete" cerebral dominance is an important etiological feature.

With the advent of more sophisticated procedures (e.g., dichotic listening) for measuring the differential processing capabilities of the two cerebral hemispheres, a fairly direct evaluation of some aspects of Orton's theory has become possible. These techniques have been used in numerous studies designed to determine the relationships between cerebral dominance and reading ability.

STUDIES INVOLVING AUDITION (DICHOTIC LISTENING)

The basic paradigm in dichotic listening studies has involved binaural presentation of verbal material (e.g., multiple-digit lists, single CV syllables, word pairs), with the typical response required of the subject being the recall of the information presented. (Studies involving the presentation of nonverbal material will not be emphasized in this presentation.)

One aim of these studies has been to examine whether and to what extent retarded readers, as compared to normal readers, have delayed, deviant, deficient, or incomplete dominant (usually left) hemispheric speech representation. In view of the results of some sodium amytal studies of patients with lateralized cerebral lesions (e.g., Branch, Milner, and Rasmussen, 1964; Kimura, 1961) and some anatomical and physiological investigations (e.g., Ades, 1959; Rosenzweig, 1954) which have demonstrated that the auditory pathways which cross from one side of the brain to the contralateral primary auditory projection area are "stronger" than those pathways which project to the ipsilateral temporal lobe, it has been assumed that any asymmetries or ear "advantages" which are demonstrated when verbal stimuli are used would reflect the degree of hemispheric lateralization for speech. Satz (1976b) has raised some questions regarding this view, and Bakker (1976) has defended it.

Some investigators (e.g., Witelson and Rabinovitch, 1972; Zurif and Carson, 1970) have reported tendencies toward a right-ear advantage (REA) for normal readers and a left-ear advantage (LEA) for retarded readers. However, Satz (1976a) has pointed out that the results of these two studies can be given very different interpretations than those offered by their authors. What seems clearer are the results of several investigations (Bryden, 1970; Leong, 1976; Yeni-Komshian, Isenberg, and Goldberg, 1975) demonstrating a significant REA for both normal and retarded readers, although there are also some limitations regarding the generalizability of these results (Satz, 1976a).

Another major question involved in these studies has been whether age has a significant effect (e.g., do older normal readers show a greater ear asymmetry relative to older dyslexics than do younger normal readers relative to younger dyslexics?). Witelson (1976a) tested a group of normal and dyslexic children at different ages (ranging between 6 and 14 years of age) and found a significant REA for both younger and older normals and for older dyslexics; the younger dyslexics did not give evidence of a REA. There is a group of studies in which age differences in ear asymmetry between older and younger normal and dyslexic children have been demonstrated. In some of these studies, older normal readers exhibited a greater *degree* of asymmetry (REA) than did older dyslexics, but no significant differences were found between younger normals and dyslexics (Leong, 1976; Satz, Rardin, and Ross, 1971). Darby (1974) reported a significant REA only for older (12-year-old) normal readers, but did not find a significant REA for older dyslexics, younger (5- and 7-year-old) normals, or younger retarded readers; he did, however, report a trend toward a REA in some of these latter groups. These results should be viewed within the context of those of a recent study by Ingram (1975) who produced evidence of a REA as early as three years of age. In this connection, Bakker (1976) has pointed out—and Satz (1976a) seems aware—that the failure of Satz et al. (1971) and others to demonstrate normal or atypical between-ear differences in young dyslexics may be a reflection of the fact that these investigators have used listening tasks which were inappropriate (perhaps, because of insufficient "floors") to disclose some early lateralizing aspects of language. The implications of the results of Berlin et al. (1973)—i.e., that, under certain conditions, the magnitude of the REA does not increase with age (between 5 and 13 years) in normals—would seem to add weight to this contention.

Sex differences in the relationship between cerebral dominance and reading ability have not been studied to any great extent. Kimura (1967) reported a significant REA for younger (5-year-old) normal girls but not for younger boys; both groups demonstrated a significant REA at ages 6 through 8. Taylor (1962), cited in Kimura (1967) reported that "younger" (7- to 11-year-old) dyslexic girls showed a significant REA, but that dyslexic boys at these same ages did not. In both of these studies, "older" (ages not specified) dyslexic boys and girls exhibited a significant REA. However, a subsequent study by Knox and Kimura (1970) produced evidence of a REA for verbal sounds in 5-year-old boys. These findings have led Kimura (1975) to question the reliability of her earlier (1967) results. In a study of children in grades 2, 4, and 6, Bryden (1970) found that boys who were poor readers were more likely to show crossed ear–hand dominance than were boys who were good readers. However, this effect was evident in girls only at the grade-2 level, and the girls showed the adult pattern of ear dominance earlier than did boys. Recently, Bakker (1976) has produced evidence which seems to indicate that between-ear differences (favoring the right ear) increase up to grade 2 for girls and up to grade 3 for boys, after which the magnitude of these differences tends to decline somewhat. Finally, using monaural stimulation with fairly complex sequences of verbal materials, Van Duyne and Bakker (1976) have demonstrated a stronger REA for girls than for boys.

Conclusions

The methodological differences between the studies cited, as well as the possibly unwarranted liberties which have been taken in the interpretation of some results (see Bakker, 1976; Satz, 1976b), render the formulation of generalizations in this area of research a hazardous venture. With these limitations in mind, the following conclusions seem reasonable.

(1) The results of many studies indicate that younger and older normals and older dyslexics exhibit a REA, and that normal readers tend to exhibit a greater *magnitude* of REA than do dyslexics at older age levels. However, given sufficient "floor" for the dichotic tests employed (see Bakker, 1976; Ingram, 1975), it becomes more likely that a REA will be demonstrated in fairly young dyslexics. Under these conditions (i.e., a sufficiently simple test), it may also be possible to demonstrate a greater magnitude of REA for normals at these very tender ages. At the same time, Bakker (1976; Bakker et al., 1976) has produced evidence which may indicate that proficient reading is associated with either LEA or REA (presumably, right- or left-hemisphere dominance, respectively) during the early stages of the learning-to-read process, but only with REA (presumably, left-hemisphere dominance) during the more advanced stages of reading.

(2) If cross-validation studies support the generalizations stated in (1), an interpretation of retarded reading which rests upon either a neuropsychological deficit model or developmental lag model would be supported (see Rourke, 1976a, 1976c).

(3) The issues regarding sex differences in relation to the development of cerebral asymmetries and reading competence appear to merit further attention, especially Bakker's (1976) contention that the exclusive unilateral control of proficient reading is effective in girls earlier than in boys.

(4) The relationship between ear advantage and cerebral asymmetry of function is far from clear (Bakker, 1976; Satz, 1976a). *A fortiori,* the relationship between ear advantage, cerebral asymmetry, and disabilities in reading must, at least for the present, remain something of a mystery. If shown to be sound, the theoretical speculations of Bakker (1976) that early reading is less dependent upon left-hemisphere functioning than is advanced reading would render the situation even more complex, but perhaps more understandable.

(5) Finally, the comparisons of the results of dichotic listening studies which have employed children of different ages, especially if the studies are cross-sectional in nature or the comparisons are made between data from different studies (perhaps employing different dependent variables), must be interpreted with considerable caution. The well-known occurrences of "spurts" and "plateaus" in the course of the development of most abilities render comparisons between groups of children at different age levels in such instances virtually impossible. For a fuller treatment of the latter issue, the reader is referred to the discussion of the developmental lag model "Type 3" in Rourke (1976c).

STUDIES INVOLVING VISION

The most widely used procedure employed in studies in this area has involved the tachistoscopic presentation of verbal material to either the right or left visual field. Comparisons are then made between response latencies and/or the frequency or the percentage of errors—or correct responses within the two visual fields.

Relatively few studies have been designed to determine the relationships between visual field superiority and reading ability. The studies which have been carried out have yielded inconsistent results. For example, a right visual half-field (RVHF) superiority was reported only for retarded readers

(Yeni-Komshian, Isenberg, and Goldberg, 1975), whereas a RVHF superiority for both normal and retarded readers has also been found (Marcel, Katz, and Smith, 1974; McKeever and Huling, 1970). In addition, Marcel and Rajan (1975) have reported that good readers (ages 7–9) show greater RVHF superiority for the recognition of five-letter words than do poor readers. Kershner (1976) found a RVHF superiority in good readers and gifted (high IQ) children, but not in dyslexic children (good and retarded readers were matched on IQ). In this study, he used a procedure similar to that employed in dichotic listening studies: he employed simultaneous, bilateral tachistoscopic presentation, together with a mid-line stimulus. This was done principally to control for the possible influence of "attentional scanning" factors (specifically, a predisposition for scanning to the right) which some investigators claim may account for the RVHF superiority in good readers found under unilateral tachistoscopic presentation conditions (e.g., Heron, 1957; Smith and Ramunas, 1971; White, 1973).

Witelson (1976a) reported a LVHF superiority for normal readers but no significant visual field difference for retarded readers (ages 6–14) on a task involving the recognition of faces. She concluded that these results could be suggestive of a lack of right-hemisphere specialization for spatial processing in dyslexics. Marcel and Rajan (1975) found a LVHF superiority for the recognition of unfamiliar faces by children (ages 7–9), but the extent of this asymmetry was not related to reading ability or to the extent of RVHF superiority in word recognition.

Conclusions

The results of investigations in this area are too inconsistent to allow much confidence to be placed in any generalizations. However, at least theoretically (cf. Bakker, 1976; Gazzaniga, 1970), there is good reason to believe that further research in this area will be fruitful.

STUDIES INVOLVING TACTILE PERCEPTION

The basic paradigm has involved the bilateral, simultaneous presentation of two different nonvisible stimuli (nonsense shapes or letters) which the subject is allowed to palpate for 10 seconds (using the middle and index fingers of each hand). The subject is then required to choose the shapes from a visual display containing similar shapes.

Witelson (1976b) compared the performances of normal males and females (between 6 and 12 years of age) using nonsense shapes. She reported that there was no difference in overall accuracy of performance between the sexes; however, boys demonstrated significantly better recognition for stimuli presented to the left hand relative to the right hand, whereas there was no significant difference in performance between the hands for the girls. On the basis of these results, she argued that the differential performances of the sexes reflected a right-hemisphere superiority for spatial processing in boys and a bilateral hemisphere representation for this type of processing in girls. If the right hemisphere in girls is not specialized "for a particular congitive function," Witelson argued, then language functions may be able to "transfer" more readily to the right hemisphere for girls than for boys following left-hemisphere damage. She concluded that this "sexual dimorphism" could reflect a greater neural plasticity in girls which could, in turn, account for the lower incidence of disorders such as developmental dyslexia or developmental aphasia (Benton, 1975) in females.

In another study, Witelson (1976a) examined the performances of two groups of boys (normal and retarded readers, ages 6 to 14) on two dichaptic tasks, one involving nonsense shapes and the other involving letters. For the nonsense shapes task, she reported the following: (1) the normal boys exhibited significantly superior recognition with the left hand relative to that with the right hand, whereas the retarded readers did not demonstrate a significant difference in performance between the two hands; (2) dyslexics exhibited significantly superior right-hand recognition relative to normals, but there was no difference between the two groups in recognition with the left hand; and, (3) overall recognition accuracy did not differ between the two groups. She concluded that normals show a right-hemisphere superiority for spatial processing, whereas the performance of dyslexics may reflect a lack of right-hemisphere specialization (or bilateral hemispheric representation) for spatial processing. On a dichaptic letters task, normal readers exhibited a significant right-hand superiority relative to the left hand, whereas dyslexics exhibited the reverse pattern (significantly better left-hand recognition relative to that with the right hand). Dyslexics also demonstrated significantly better left-hand recognition relative to the left-hand performance of normals, but there was no difference in right-hand accuracy between the two groups. As with the nonsense shapes task, overall recognition accuracy did not differ between the two groups. Witelson hypothesized that these results may reflect a greater left-hemisphere superiority and the use of a linguistic-analytic approach to this task for normals, whereas there may be greater right-hemisphere involvement and a greater use of a spatial-holistic strategy in the case of dyslexics.

Conclusions

On the basis of these results, Witelson (1976b) has speculated that developmental dyslexia may be associated with two neural abnormalities: (1) a lack of right-hemisphere specialization for spatial processing, and (2) a dysfunction in left-hemisphere processing of linguistic functions.

It seems contradictory that she would associate a lack of right-hemisphere specialization for spatial processing with developmental dyslexia since she concluded (Witelson, 1976a) that a similar pattern (viz., bilateral representation of spatial processing) in normal girls may reflect a greater neural plasticity and, in consequence, a lower incidence of developmental dyslexia in girls. Also, the presumed association between developmental dyslexia and lack of right-hemisphere specialization (based on the results of the dichaptic nonsense shapes test) appears somewhat tenuous since dyslexics exhibited overall recognition accuracy or accuracy with each hand which was at least as good as, and sometimes superior to, that of normals. In order to support the view that a lack of right-hemisphere specialization for spatial processing plays a role in dyslexia, it would seem necessary to demonstrate that dyslexics perform relatively poorly on measures found to be sensitive to the integrity of the right cerebral hemisphere. However, in so doing, it should be borne in mind that there is evidence which is contrary to this formulation (Guyer and Friedman, 1975; Symmes and Rapoport, 1972). For these reasons, the conclusions regarding the relationships between cerebral dominance and reading retardation which Witelson has formulated on the basis of the results of her studies of dichaptic stimulation must remain, for the present time, questionable. A recent paper by Witelson (1975) indicates that she is aware of some of these interpretive problems.

AN EVALUATION OF ORTON'S VIEW OF CEREBRAL DOMINANCE

One way of characterizing Orton's view of the relationships among reading retardation, incomplete cerebral dominance, and brain dysfunction is in terms of the following quasi-syllogism.

(1) Retarded readers exhibit reversals and mirror images.

(2) Reversals and mirror images are the result of incomplete cerebral dominance.

(3) Incomplete cerebral dominance is the result of disordered brain function.

(4) Therefore, retarded readers are suffering from brain dysfunction.

The problems inherent in this particular line of reasoning are numerous. With respect to (1), it should be noted that not all retarded readers exhibit reversals or mirror images (Johnson and Myklebust, 1967). In addition, most normal-for-age beginning readers exhibit reversals and/or mirror images (Johnson and Myklebust, 1967). Point number (2) is simply a statement of a research hypothesis which, in terms of the existing data, would appear to be largely unconfirmed (Benton, 1975; Satz, 1976a). With respect to (3), issues analogous to those mentioned in connection with (1) above are relevant. As in the case of reversals and mirror images, for example, there is evidence that incomplete cerebral dominance (presuming, for the moment, that it is, in fact, a viable construct) is a perfectly normal maturational-developmental phenomenon—i.e., not necessarily a manifestation (symptom or sign) of brain damage (Satz, 1976b). Furthermore, there is evidence that good readers exhibit patterns of right or left cerebral dominance at particular stages of the learning-to-read process, and that left or right cerebral dominance may be more or less important at different times during these stages (Bakker, 1976).

Considering the foregoing, it is clear that the conclusion stated in (4) above is not supported by the results of the studies reviewed in this section. In passing, it should be mentioned that the inverse of (4)—i.e., that children who are suffering from brain dysfunction are also retarded in reading—is also not a supportable generalization (Mattis, French, and Rapin, 1975).

Finally, this review of the investigations of the relationships hypothesized by Orton raises the following concerns.

(1) Lenneberg (1967), on the basis of clinical observations of recovery of function following brain injury in children, has observed a pattern of slower or less functional recovery with increasing age of onset of brain damage. This would suggest that there is increasing unilateral hemispheric participation for particular functions with increasing age (for example, increased left-hemisphere participation in language functions). Many studies which have examined perceptual asymmetries have not considered the influence of known developmental sequelae following cerebral dysfunction in children when attempting to "explain" results that appear contradictory to these developmental effects.

(2) The majority of studies involving the assessment of cerebral dominance and reading have not taken into account the developmental parameters within a normative population. For example, there has been little research to determine what constitutes "normal" performance for average children at different ages on dichotic listening and visual split-field tasks. The one exception to this is the study by Satz et al. (1975) involving dichotic listening.

(3) Although there is evidence to suggest some relative differences in perceptual asymmetry (and, thus, presumed cerebral asymmetry) between normal and retarded readers, these differences have been neither pronounced nor reliable.

(4) Various methodological constraints, such as inadequate "ceilings" and "floors," could have significantly affected the results of many of the studies (see Rourke, 1976c). For example, some of the studies that employed the dichotic listening technique utilized lengths of digit sequences which appeared to be too easy for older subjects, thereby affecting the magnitude of any possible perceptual asymmetries that could have been demonstrated. In one study (Witelson, 1976a), for example, approximately 90 and 96 percent accuracy levels of digit recall for the left and right ears, respectively, were reported for the older normal subjects.

NEUROPSYCHOLINGUISTIC ABILITIES

There is evidence in the adult neuropsychological literature to support the view that a relationship obtains between dysfunction within the left (dominant) cerebral hemisphere and disturbances in language functioning. Reitan and his associates (e.g., Reed and Reitan, 1963; Reitan, 1955) have demonstrated that the Verbal section of the Wechsler scales is particularly sensitive to lesions of the left cerebral hemisphere: typically, adult patients who are suffering from acute lesions confined principally to the left cerebral hemisphere exhibit a pattern of low Verbal IQ relative to Performance IQ on the Wechsler scales. Luria (1973) has observed that, in adults, lesions of the secondary zones of the left (dominant) temporal lobe produce a marked impairment in the ability to differentiate the sounds of speech, and that lesions further removed from the primary projection area of the temporal region of the left cerebral hemisphere eventuate in a profound disturbance in short-term auditory-verbal memory. Luria reports that one of the most apparent effects of such disorders is a pervasive impairment in language abilities.

Psycholinguistic deficiencies similar to those observed in adults with left (dominant) cerebral dysfunction have also been documented in children with dyslexia. For example, Denckla (1972a) has presented results which raise the possibility that a very specific differentiation of function exists within the higher cortical centers thought to subserve verbal language functions, and that discrete malfunction within one or several of these can account for specific subtypes of dyslexia. Mattis, French, and Rapin's (1975) results would lend support to this contention.

With respect to the relationship between a fairly general impairment in language abilities and reading retardation, Belmont and Birch (1966) and Warrington (1967), for example, found a significant association between WISC Verbal IQ–Performance IQ discrepancy (in the direction of lower verbal IQ) and reading retardation. A series of studies in our own laboratory (e.g., Rourke, Dietrich, and Young, 1973a, Rourke and Finlayson, 1975; Rourke et al., 1973b; Rourke, Young, and Flewelling, 1971) have yielded results which are consistent with the latter findings, and with the view that disordered functioning of the left cerebral hemisphere may play a role in the etiology of reading retardation and a number of psycholinguistic disabilities in children. However, the interpretation of these results should be couched in the context of the following: (a) the implications of verbal IQ–performance IQ discrepancies are much clearer in older children (i.e., 10 years of age and above) than in younger children (Reed, 1967b; Rourke, Dietrich, and Young, 1973a); (b) the child with either a verbal IQ or performance IQ in the low-average or dull-normal range appears to be "at risk" with respect to success in middle-class urban schools (Ackerman, Peters, and Dykman,

1971); (c) Black (1974, 1976) has presented data which indicate that verbal IQ–performance IQ discrepancies in either direction are suggestive of cerebral dysfunction in children, but that relatively low performance IQ is more often associated with neurological dysfunction than is low verbal IQ (perhaps because of the nature of the physical neurological examination); (d) there appears to be a specific type of retarded reader who exhibits a lower performance IQ than verbal IQ (see Kinsbourne and Warrington, 1963a; Mattis et al., 1975), for whom the limiting deficiency with respect to reading retardation may be related to sequential ordering (Kinsbourne and Warrington, 1963a).

Johnson and Myklebust (1967) have suggested that some children encounter difficulty in developing reading skills as a consequence of a disorder in discriminating phonemes. This hypothesis is supported by the results of studies which have demonstrated that poor readers do significantly less well on tests for auditory discrimination (Deutsch, 1964; Wepman, 1960) and exhibit significantly more acoustic substitutions (Mohan, 1975) than do normal readers. The findings of McLeod (1965) and Ackerman, Dykman, and Peters (1976) to the effect that dyslexic children perform in a significantly inferior manner as compared to normal readers on the WISC Digit Span, Arithmetic, and Coding subtests suggest that a deficit in short-term memory for verbal information (perhaps due to an inability to formulate or employ mnemonic strategies) may be contributory to dyslexia. The skill(s) tapped by the latter WISC subtests have been referred to as the "sequencing" factor by Ackerman et al. (1976) and Bannatyne (1974). In this connection, Mattis et al. (1975) have described a dyslexic syndrome which is characterized by speech-sound sequencing deficits and anomia.

Deficiencies in word and sentence structure have also been found to be associated with dyslexia. For example, there is evidence that dyslexic children exhibit significantly more morphological errors than do normals (Wiig, Semel, and Crouse, 1973); these errors most frequently involve incorrect inflections for the third-person singular, singular possessives, plural possessives, and adjectives. Utilizing standardized tests of receptive and expressive syntactical ability, Semel and Wiig (1975) demonstrated that (a) dyslexic children exhibit a poor appreciation of syntactical rules, and (b) the degree of syntactical deficiency is similar for younger and older dyslexic children. Finally, Ingram, Mason, and Blackburn (1970) and Fry, Johnson, and Muehl (1970) have demonstrated that oral speech production in retarded readers is inferior to that of normal readers.

Conclusions

Retarded readers as a group have been shown to be deficient in a wide variety of psycholinguistic abilities. The results of such group-wise comparisons with the performance of normal readers would lend support to the view that reading retardation is associated with disordered functioning of the left (dominant) cerebral hemisphere. However, at least three caveats must be mentioned in this connection, viz.: (1) there is fairly clear evidence that there are specific and distinct types or clusters of psycholinguistic deficits (which may reflect the differential integrity of distinct regions within the left cerebral hemisphere) that manifest as specific and distinct types of reading retardation, (2) there is evidence of a small, but significant, group of retarded readers who exhibit fairly intact psycholinguistic abilities and relatively deficient visuospatial and/or visuomotor skills (within the context of the current discussion, this group might be thought of as exhibiting evidence of relatively deficient right cerebral hemisphere integrity); and, (3) there is clear evidence (Boder, 1973; Johnson and Myklebust, 1967) of a "mixed" type of retarded reader, i.e., one who exhibits both psycholinguistic and visuospatial deficits. The latter type may be thought of as one who exhibits impairments in abilities ordinarily thought to be subserved by each of the cerebral hemispheres.

SUMMARY, CRITIQUE, GENERAL CONCLUSIONS

In this section an attempt is made to identify and evaluate the principal research strategies employed in the neuropsychological investigation of reading retardation, to state some general conclusions which seem warranted, and to suggest some directions for future research.

RESEARCH STRATEGIES

There are three principal strategies which have been employed in the neuropsychological investigation of retarded reading in children. One involves comparisons between normal readers and retarded readers on a fairly large number of tests which have shown to be sensitive to the integrity of the cerebral hemispheres (e.g., Doehring, 1968). This approach has the advantage of increasing the likelihood that levels of performance, pathognomonic signs, and specific patterns of brain-related performances associated with impaired reading will emerge. One problem with this approach is that the large number of comparisons employed sometimes makes data analysis quite unwieldy and the emergence of differences due to chance fluctuations almost inevitable. Also, there may be a temptation to "throw anything and everything into the hopper," thus rendering the conclusions arrived at somewhat dubious and the likelihood of cross-validation remote. Nevertheless, the fact remains that studies which are as well designed and as theoretically sound as that of Doehring (1968) can add to our knowledge regarding the neuropsychological correlates of reading retardation.

A second research strategy involves the comparison of normal readers and retarded readers on a specific task, with the intent of demonstrating whether or not the retarded reading group is deficient in the ability or abilities thought to underlie performance on this task. Examples would include the many studies which have attempted to determine if retarded readers exhibit a typical pattern or delayed development of asymmetry of performance on dichotic listening tasks. The principal merit of this approach is that the results are usually fairly unambiguous; the problems with this approach are several. For example, one must take into account how severely retarded in reading the subjects are, because the likelihood of showing any differences between normal readers and retarded readers is dependent upon the degree of severity of the retardation in reading exhibited by the retarded reading group. In addition, because retarded reading per se may not be a sufficient way of "characterizing" a child as far as the brain is concerned, the group-wise analyses of results may serve to obscure important subgroup differences within the retarded reading group. For example, it has become clear that not all retarded readers are retarded in reading for the same brain-related reasons: one may exhibit deficient reading because of a visual-perceptual deficit, whereas another may exhibit reading retardation because of difficulties in phonemic hearing. Unless care is taken to allow for these sorts of differences, the results of this type of experimental research are not as unambiguous as they may appear to be. It should be borne in mind that these criticisms also apply to the exclusive use of the first research strategy mentioned above, although the probability of being able to avoid these particular pitfalls (especially the final one cited) is considerably enhanced when a large number of hypotheses-specific dependent measures which do justice to the complexities involved in brain–behavior relationships are employed.

A third investigative strategy involves the composition of specific disordered reading subgroups. The results of Mattis et al. (1975) in this connection are potentially of considerable importance, as are those of Doehring and Hoshko (1977). In the latter investigation, "types" of retarded readers were identified by means of the Q-technique of factor analysis. Another way of determining subgroups of retarded readers is implicit in some longitudinal descriptive and predictive investigations which have been carried out (e.g., Rourke, 1976c; Rourke and Orr, 1977). In the Rourke and Orr (1977) study, it was possible to specify some characteristics of children initially classified as retarded readers at the age of seven to eight years who improved and those in the group who did not improve in reading ability four years later. If confirmed by cross-validation, it would appear that there are a set of "high-risk characteristics" which can serve as criteria in terms of which retarded readers can be classified (see Satz, Friel, and Rudegeair [1976] for a somewhat similar approach to this issue). The classification scheme of Boder (1973), which involves the formulation of subgroups based on particular approaches to reading and spelling, and that of Knights (1973), which involves a pattern analysis of children with various types of brain lesions, would also appear to have considerable potential with respect to the determination of various subgroups of retarded readers.

The problems of the latter research strategy are few as compared to those faced by the first two approaches mentioned; and the inherent limitations are not nearly as marked as are those of the second research strategy described. The problems with the third research strategy are primarily theoretical and "measuremental." With respect to the former, the excellent analyses provided by Wiener and Cromer (1967), Applebee (1971), Guthrie (1973), Boder (1973), Marshall and Newcombe (1973), LaBerge and Samuels (1974), and Doehring (1976a, 1976b) should be of considerable long-range importance. The problems of measurement will probably be obviated once the relevant types of retarded readers can be distinguished in a reliable fashion.

GENERAL CONCLUSIONS

There are a few generalizations which can be made with respect to the findings of neuropsychological investigations of reading retardation which have been reviewed.

(1) There appears to be a significant, positive correlation between severity of reading retardation and severity of impairment on a large number of brain-related variables.

(2) At the same time, it is abundantly clear that exclusive use of the "level of performance" approach in this field must now be considered to be a "dead" issue. There appears to be nothing to be gained from investigations which simply involve the comparison of the performance of normal and retarded readers in the hope of determining yet another ability in which retarded readers are deficient.

(3) Throughout the elementary school years, some skills (e.g., tactile-perceptual and visuomotor abilities) are less likely to be impaired in retarded readers than are other skills (e.g., auditory-perceptual and neuropsycholinguistic abilities).

(4) However, younger (ages 5–7) retarded readers are likely to exhibit significantly impaired performances in visual-perceptual and visuospatial abilities. Older (ages 9–11) retarded readers are likely to exhibit markedly impaired performance in language-related and higher-order concept formation abilities, and (possibly) less obvious or severe impairments in visual-perceptual and visuospatial abilities. The principal reasons for these findings may be that "reading" at ages 5–7 is largely single-word reading, whereas more advanced "reading" requires higher-order conceptual skills for the achievement of rapid scanning with comprehension.

(5) Even taking into consideration the developmental parameters emphasized in (4), it remains probable that a child at any age will have difficulty in learning to read if he or she has a marked deficiency in those skills ordinarily thought to be subserved by the left or the right or both cerebral hemispheres.

(6) Two retarded readers at a given age may exhibit the same impaired level of reading as a result of different neuropsychological deficits.

(7) In view of (4), (5), and (6), it is clear that a research strategy which seeks to determine *the* deficit or even *the set* of deficits which is "responsible" for reading retardation is doomed to failure.

(8) Investigations dealing with pathognomonic signs, clinical symptoms, and clinical tests have yielded data which must be

evaluated within the context of socioeconomic factors, methodological considerations, and clinical imperatives. That is, although the general "thrust" of this data would support a neuropsychological interpretation of reading retardation, such a conclusion must be tempered by consideration of the limitations imposed by specific sampling practices, the composition of control groups, and the many issues regarding cross-validation and the reliabilities of the measuring techniques employed. Of possibly greater importance is the relatively small amount of variance in the criterion measure (i.e., reading retardation) which can be accounted for in terms of these signs, symptoms, tests, or examinations.

(9) Investigators who conduct studies which involve cross-sectional designs to assess age-difference trends in the ability deficiencies of retarded readers should be aware of the potential pitfalls which can be encountered when phenomena such as "spurts" and "plateaus" in development are overlooked.

(10) In any area of scientific study, failure to pay sufficient attention to the achievement of consistency in the interpretation of research results can lead investigators to espouse positions which are logically inconsistent. This has occurred in many studies which have addressed issues relating to cerebral dominance.

(11) One issue which emerges with unmistakable clarity and irresistible necessity is the need for generating sufficiently complex theoretical models of the reading process and of types of reading retardation if advances in the neuropsychology of reading disorders are to take place (see Doehring, 1976b for a more extended discussion of this issue). It is also clear that a nosological category of "reading retardation" which is characterized solely by a "level of performance" approach is no longer adequate for either research or clinical purposes.

Chapter 8
THE DYSLEXIAS: A DISCUSSION OF NEUROBEHAVIORAL RESEARCH

OTFRIED SPREEN

Rourke has presented an excellent overall review of the state of art in this field. The discussant of such a review has two choices: (1) to add comments point by point to the topics outlined in the main paper, or (2) to select areas of research which deserve special attention and discuss them in some depth. I have chosen the latter course.

At the beginning, some points of research strategy will be stressed. This emphasis will continue throughout the discussion of the question of etiology and types of dyslexia in relation to a neurobehavioral model, and—through the subsequent discussion—of research on cerebral dominance, integration and sequencing, attentional factors, and neurolinguistic aspects.

RESEARCH STRATEGIES

Rourke has outlined three principal strategies, which not only apply to neuro-behavior but also to other areas of research with dyslexics and other groups of behavioral problems as well, (1) the single-variable approach, (2) the broad battery multiple-variable approach, and the (3) group or type approach with or without predictive hypotheses. As for the first approach, the probabilities of finding yet another difference between dyslexics and normal readers are ominously high, unless strict control over a large number of other variables on which such groups may also differ, is exercised. Meehl (1967) once pointed out that in a sample of 55,000 high school seniors, the pairwise comparison of two groups may yield as much as 91 percent significant differences in 45 variables. Thus the chances that two groups differing in one variable (reading) also differ on any number of additional variables are extremely high regardless of what variable is investigated. This confirms Thorndike's old dictum that "in general, desirable human characteristics are slightly, but positively correlated." Single-variable studies without adequate control over other possibly significant covariates are, for this reason, not likely to contribute to our knowledge in the field.

The second approach, i.e., batteries of tests, is subject to similar considerations unless differential directional predictions ("this variable is expected to be higher in group A, this is expected to be lower") on the basis of sound theoretical considerations are made and adequate group matching or covariance analyses are carried out. The third approach, also emphasized by Rourke, is more promising whether based on theoretical grouping or on Q-factor analysis and similar techniques.

All three approaches are subject to the frequently raised criticism that these investigators conduct correlational rather than experimental research; the argument was once again voiced after Cohen's (1976) criticisms of correlational research (1976) in the *Journal of Special Education*. Cohen argued that most of the research in the learning-disability area merely investigates labels, etiologies, verbal constructs, and *ex post facto* designs. An experimental design requires that we actively manipulate treatment or other environmental variables before the change in the dependent variable is measured again. However, this argument, which would invalidate a large portion of our present data, is not applicable to the group-prognostic approach, nor is it necessarily valid for the investigation of group differences without prediction and follow-up. The argument does alert us, however, to the necessity for sound reasoning before groups are established, for meaningful predictions about group differences, and for the need to create groups that are meaningful in terms of the structure of outcome or in terms of distinct differences in precursors (if retrospective), since little can be gained by the creation of yet another classification system without meaning for the life of the individual. On the other hand, the single-minded manipulation of an ill-chosen variable in the "experimental" design as practiced in some behavior modification research, does not necessarily make such a study more respectable or "scientific." I agree that replication and cross-validation are probably the most needed approach to test the meaningfulness of the numerous, and at times contradictory, findings in our field.

A final problem, which has been touched upon by Benton (1962) and Shankweiler (1964), is still haunting research in the field. It is basically a subject selection problem, although it can also be seen as a problem of the definition, or of assessing the severity of the reading problem. Results from reading clinics often cannot be replicated with classroom populations. It would appear that, even when severity is held constant, the two population sources differ considerably, since the problem reader in the classroom has not yet been singled out for referral, whereas the clinic subject has been singled out and referred for any number of reasons. This is an example of how seemingly irrelevant variables in subject selection may affect results rather dramatically.

A last comment on research strategy, particularly applicable to neuro-behavioral research, comes from Bronfenbrenner (1974) who complains that "much of American developmental psychology is the science of the behavior of children in strange situations with strange adults." Looking at a dyslexic child subjected to a dichotic listening apparatus with little preparation or explanation, lined up for the experimenter or fetched one-by-one from the classroom, makes it clear that the test and laboratory experiment approach is indeed "strange" and far removed from the daily living of the child. It reminds us that we should perhaps review our research with a view toward approximating some of the child's actual experiences, although I confess that I do not see any immediate solutions to this problem for the neuropsychologist entrenched in experimental or testing procedures pursuing a highly specific problem.

Somewhat related to the last point, another criticism has been raised by educators and has been strongly voiced by the proponents of behavior modification: that neurobehavioral research and testing is usually a single "probe" into an individual's behavior, possibly followed up a year or more later. Such test results at a single point in time cannot reflect the capacity of the individual for learning and should be supplemented by a test-teach-test approach, which may not only result in additional insights into the capacity to learn but into the most appropriate training for that individual as well. As far as I am aware, this approach has so far been neglected in neurobehavioral research.

ETIOLOGY AND THE NEUROBEHAVIORAL MODEL

Rourke emphasized the need for neurobehavioral models of the reading process and of types of dyslexia. From the discussion of research strategies above, it is evident that "fishing expeditions" are useless unless backed by solid theory which can be tested and confirmed or laid to rest. Even though many researchers still treat dyslexia as an entity, multiple-etiology models have been advocated for some time. Quadfasel and Goodglass (1968) advocated at least three forms (a "symptomatic" form resulting from early cerebral damage, a "primary" form without brain damage, possibly based on genetic mechanisms, and a "secondary" form resulting from environmental, emotional, and health factors). A similar system was proposed by Rabinovitch (1968) and Keeney and Keeney (1968). Bannatyne's (1971) hierarchical model of classifications and causes (Table 8-1) used a similar grouping and goes into many details outlining the factors involved in poor reading. Other authors have concentrated on specific areas of deficit, e.g., Johnson and Myklebust (1967) distinguished between visual and auditory dyslexia and list other abilities essential for the reading process (e.g., memory, sequence memory, right–left discrimination, time orientation, body image, locomotor coordination, topographic orientation), suggesting that perhaps a further breakdown into types of specific deficit may be necessary.

For a discussion of neurobehavioral correlates, our primary focus is on those specific deficits which accompany the symptomatic (or brain-damage) form of dyslexia. For example, in her color-naming study with severely dyslexic boys, Denckla (1972a) proposed what she called a "rare subgroup" which resembles a pure alexia of the aphasic type, once again using the analogy with acquired alexia. She explains this type as a "patchy immaturity" of the cerebral language areas which can be differentiated in highly specific fashion and which may suffer discrete malfunction. In fact, many authors reserve the term dyslexia for this form of reading deficit only. However, our discussion should also include the primary (or genetic) form, since many authors have proposed that subtle maturational changes of brain function occur in primary dyslexia even though they may not be detectable as neurological symptoms—on gross brain examination or even on histological studies after autopsy.

It is unfortunate that in spite of these major subdivisions of reading problems, few studies have investigated possible differences between such groups. Such hypothetical groupings should be testable by discriminant function analysis, studying quite literally those variables which the authors themselves have proposed to be responsible for crucial group differences. Predictions of performance on each variable for each group can be made, so that not only multivariate group differences should emerge, but specific predictions can be tested. Such procedures may settle some of the controversies.

TABLE 8-1 A hierarchical classification of the causes and types of dyslexia* (from Bannatyne, 1971)

Universe of Study	All Language and Reading Disabilities						
Major Groupings	Low IQ (intellectually retarded)	Maladjustment (emotionally disturbed)	Dyslexia				
Groups		Social, Cultural or Educational Deprivation	Primary Emotional Communicative Causes	Minimal Neurological Dysfunction (MND)	Aphasia	Autism	Other
Subgroups			Disinterested Mothers, Depressed Mothers, Angry Mothers, Other Possible Causes (e.g., institutionalized children, twins, living in a foreign country)	Visuo-spatial, Auditory, Integrational Disorders, Conceptualizing and Thought Disorders, Motor, Tactile and Kinesthetic Disorders			Genetic Dyslexia
Sub-subgroups (in some categories)				Integration of Limbs, Hands, Fingers; Eye Muscles; Speech Articulation			

Major Characteristics (not all need be present):

1. Often poor auditory discrimination of vowels.
2. Inadequate phonemegrapheme sequencing memory (for matching).
3. Poor sound blending and auditory closure on experience.
4. Mildly deficient speech development and feedback which may persist.
5. Maturational lag in most language functions.
6. Reasonably efficient visuo-spatial ability.
7. Unlateralized gaze (when reading).
8. Mirror imaging and writing of letters (hemispheric in origin?).
9. Directional configuration inconstancy also causing mirror imaging of letters.
10. Difficulty in associating verbal labels to directional concepts but no visuo-spatial disorientation of any kind.
11. Residual spelling disability.
12. Poor self-concept.

* These categories are not mutually exclusive. Characteristics are classified, not children.

For example, it is quite possible that the difference between the outcome of classroom population and clinical-referral population studies can be explained by the fact that they not only differ in severity of the disorder, but that the clinic-referral population has a large number of brain-damaged dyslexics as well as some reading problems secondary to behavior and emotional problems, whereas the primary dyslexic is less noticeable (at least up to a certain age) and hence more frequently found in classroom studies.

Other authors have deliberately taken the position that dyslexia is only part of a general learning disability (Hartstein, 1971; Kephart, 1968), which includes those conditions resulting from brain damage. On the opposite side is the view that only primary dyslexia (also called specific developmental dyslexia, congenital word blindness, etc.) deserves special attention and is, in fact, present in the majority of cases. This position is taken by such researchers as Critchley (1966), Hagger (1968), and Satz and Sparrow (1970). Again, the hypothesis is testable as outlined in the previous paragraph.

BRAIN DAMAGE AND OTHER CAUSES

Whether or not brain damage is present remains another issue to be resolved. Positions taken in the literature range from one extreme to the other: i.e., that "minimal" brain damage should be present in most cases of dyslexia (frequently taken by Russian researchers) to the position that most cases cannot be ascribed to brain damage (cf. Davidenkov and Dotsenko, 1956; Lebendinskaia and Poliakova, 1967; Erhard and Lempe, 1968; Ingram et al., 1970; Luria, 1970; Becker, 1974). Intermediate to this is the view that brain function is abnormal with no structural pathology. Yet another position is the maturational lag hypothesis which may or may not promise a happy outcome, depending on whether or not the concept of critical periods is considered decisive. Those who advocate disordered brain functioning most frequently single out the parietal area as a possible locus, although other authors (e.g., Silver, 1971) talk about a "neurohumoral imbalance affecting the reticular and the limbic system" or about cerebellar-vestibular dysfunction (e.g., Frank and Levinson, 1973). The outcome of most studies attempting to determine the presence or absence of brain damage remains equivocal. For example, Bowley (1969) concludes for her highly selected group of dyslexics that the disorders found "appear to be due to specific immaturities in these areas, sometimes neurological disorders, and sometimes a combination of both." If dyslexia is treated as an entity, the outcome of such studies is likely to remain fuzzy. Whether or not neurological impairment will be a useful distinction of *one* group of the dyslexias or not, remains to be seen. The inclusion of brain-damaged control groups without dyslexia, as stressed by Mattis, would seem to be crucial in future studies of this kind. Another view is the hypothesis of lack of cerebral dominance, to which I will return later.

Among those who look for etiologies other than the brain, the hypothesis of visual disorders is still the most popular (Beinart, 1974). While this notion has been carefully reviewed and rejected by Rourke in his chapter and by Vellutino and collaborators (1972, 1973, 1975), individual findings of subtle disorders of eye movements (Dunlop et al., 1973) or "vision laterality" (Rubino and Minden, 1973), and of other orthoptic measures continue to be reported. Indirectly, this hypothesis is also maintained by Satz et al. (1971) even though the deficit is seen as a passing stage in younger children which later disappears. Satz and several other authors see such a deficit as related to cerebral maturation and emphasize that the whole problem of neurobehavioral correlates has to be seen in the context of an age-related hierarchical development of the individual. I deliberately omit a discussion of the many factors invoked for the secondary dyslexias, e.g., language conflicts, home environment, cultural conflicts, and attitudes.

I can see no immediate solution to these conflicting views on etiology. It should be emphasized that most authors tend to allow for etiologies other than the ones described here as central to their thinking. However, if we consider the earlier discussion of forms of dyslexia, it is obvious that the two topics overlap to a certain extent, i.e., that some etiologies are the direct hypothetical basis for the proposed groupings. If this is the case, then the study of forms of dyslexia will provide at least an indirect proof of the usefulness (if not the validity) of the etiological viewpoint on which the grouping is based. More pragmatically, one might also question the usefulness of etiological differentiations if they do not show up in actual differences between the groups proposed.

It is possible that groups do not differ at a single point in time, but that they differ in the eventual outcome. Some of the later chapters present information on this question. At this point, I would like to refer to some results of our own follow-up study of dyslexics and those with similar learning problems identified between the ages of 8 to 12 years, who on follow-up four or more years later (mean age at follow-up = 18 years) showed some distinct differences in adjustment, which corresponded to whether there was definite, minor, or no indication of brain damage at the time of first examination (Table 8-2). These preliminary results on the first 140 subjects of our study are presented without detailed discussion merely as a demonstration of one possible way of grouping dyslexics, with emphasis on outcome variables.

As will be seen, the table shows little difference between groups on criminal and other offenses, general health, etc. But subjects in the brain-damaged group appear to be susceptible to more seizures and accidents, take more prescription drugs, drink less alcohol, have more need for affection, and be more sensitive to criticism; subjects in the dyslexic group without demonstrated brain damage tend to show more negativistic tendencies, daydream more, and show and need less affection than the brain-damaged subjects. Such a pattern of differences will have to be confirmed by discriminant function analysis and reviewed in relation to a number of covariates, especially in relation to the initial presenting problem and the test results on first referral. On an adjustment rating scale these same groups differed significantly on the factors of tenseness and insomnia (vs. relaxedness) and of disorganized, impulsive, and incautious behavior (vs. carefulness and cautiousness).

Another study by McKeever and VanDeventer (1975) dealt with chronic dyslexia in adolescence and found, in contrast with other studies, that visual and auditory processing of simple language stimuli and auditory memory for verbal material was impaired. The authors postulate a "left-hemisphere visual association area functional deficit." This finding would suggest that a highly selected group of dyslexics at a later age may still show deficits which are not found in the slow readers investigated in many studies of younger children (see also Frisk et al., 1967).

AREAS OF NEUROBEHAVIORAL DISORDER

Numerous specific deficits or disorders have been proposed as concomitant with dyslexia. On reviewing the literature, I could not see a distinction, in the enumeration of such disorders, between primary (congenital) and symptomatic (brain-damaged) forms of dyslexia and hence will discuss the disorders without reference to these different etiologies. It should be obvious, however, that if the distinction between primary and symptomatic dyslexia is valid, then consistent findings in neurobehavioral variables should not be ex-

TABLE 8-2

Results of structured interview questions regarding adjustment of 140 children earlier referred as learning problems between the age of 8 and 12 (elapsed time between referral and follow-up: minimum 4 years, median 6 years) according to presence or absence of brain damage (in percent of "Yes" response).

QUESTION	1 DEFINITE BRAIN DAMAGE	2 PROBABLE BRAIN DAMAGE	3 NO BRAIN DAMAGE	4 CONTROLS WITHOUT LEARNING PROBLEMS
Is his/her general health good?	70	72	80	75
Any seizures or related problems?	29	13	13	12
Any accidents in the interim?	53	40	40	38
Any behavior problems in the interim?	67	69	64	0
Any problems which parents or teachers could not understand?	73	72	36	16
Taking of prescribed drugs	58	47	29	38
Offenses with or without sentence by police	37	33	47	38
Regular drinking of alcohol	67	79	86	87
Not satisfied with his/her friends	24	16	20	0
Can he/she find friends when needed?	62	78	70	100
Getting along poorly with others	26	34	35	0
Family is getting along poorly	18	16	26	0
Does he/she have reasonable judgment?	80	80	67	100
Does he/she view herself as different from others?	68	52	43	0
Do others see him/her as different?	56	46	50	0
Is he/she satisfied with the way his/her life is now?	21	65	65	100
Very sensitive to criticism	87	78	48	47
Tendency to be impulsive	67	65	42	24
Tendency to daydream a lot	43	63	65	6
Stubborn and set in his ways	31	23	25	35
Disobedient and "nonconformist"	22	41	41	12
Negativistic or "contrary"	31	42	52	12
Increased need for affection	51	57	26	6
Shows a lot of affection	57	45	31	41

pected. In fact, the distinction of subgroups may resolve some of the controversies regarding neurobehavioral findings.

The disorders of central origin include all of the areas listed by Rourke: (1) finger agnosia, (2) right–left discrimination difficulties, (3) oculomotor, visuomotor, visuoperceptual disorders, (4) visual-spatial difficulties, (5) serial and time sequencing disorders, (6) abnormal intersensory integration, (7) neurolinguistic disorders, as well as (8) variation in the cerebral dominance function. In addition (9) eyedness, handedness, and footedness have often been treated as separate from cerebral dominance. And numerous other disorders including (10) locomotor disorders, (11) memory disorders, as well as (12) related disorders of writing, spelling, arithmetic, and foreign language ability (Myklebust and Johnson, 1962) have been proposed and investigated. (Neurophysiological correlates are omitted and findings of the clinical neurological examination as well as of antecedent conditions at birth are viewed here as independent variables, not as correlates.) It is obvious that such lists are heavily influenced by the earlier clinical studies of acquired dyslexia in adults and may not necessarily be appropriate for the dyslexic child. Another position taken by Satz and Sparrow (1970) is that not all these disorders may be apparent simultaneously; the development of abilities basic to reading in specific stages according to age may explain some discrepancies in the results of different investigators. As mentioned by Rourke, some findings of recent cross-sectional and longitudinal studies tend to support this notion, although such studies may account for only a portion of the variance.

Regarding precursors of reading disability, numerous perceptual and language-related indicators have been used, together with measures of laterality, fitting a hierarchical model of development of skills basic to reading. It is in the nature of such studies that at earlier ages more and more reliance has to be placed on simple motor tests, but so far little evidence has been presented which can be used to determine whether a very young child is at risk and what the pertinent area of motor performance is in particular. A study by Schirm, Bahl, and Randolph (1972) investigates this topic and describes six areas of motor performance in children from three to seven years which are suitable for the investigation of "minimal movement disorders" which are not accessible with the better known techniques of Ozeretzki and Sloan or Gollnitz.

Finally, Rourke has emphasized that brain damage or even developmental, congenital functional disorder of central origin cannot be expected to result in identical deficits in every child. This position, taken to the extreme, would lead us to expect a multitude of individual subforms without any consistency at all (cf. Applebee, 1971; Doehring, 1976a, Wiener and Cromer, 1967).

In spite of these three sources of variance, namely (1) distinction between symptomatic and congenital forms (as well as other nonneurological forms), (2) developmental progression, and (3) nonuniform effect of central damage or disorder, studies in each of these areas have usually started out with the assumption that we are dealing with a homogeneous group. It is not surprising that some studies have found little support for this assumption and that the findings of other studies are probably meaningless once the across-the-board differences between normal and retarded readers mentioned at the beginning of this discussion are taken into account. Rourke's review of the various areas reflects the frustration of searching through numerous studies for consistencies where none can really be expected.

CEREBRAL DOMINANCE AND LATERALITY

This field is a typical example of confusion resulting from a neurobehavioral approach without solid theorizing. The field was already satiated with inconsistent results on the eye, hand, foot, and smell right-or-left preference studies in normal and disabled readers (cf. Carmon, Nachshon, and Starinsky, 1976) and the right- or left-turning hair whorl had been considered as a last resort (Tjossem et al., 1961) before Kimura (1961, 1966) adapted Broadbent's (1957) dichotic stimulation technique to the study of cerebral dominance for hearing and vision. In addition, a flood of studies of what essentially would seem to be another version of the extinction with bilateral stimulation technique (Bender, 1952) was supplemented by studies of differential finger and gestural movements and other methods—e.g., Dirk's (1964) filtered dichotic hearing, Katz' (1962) staggered spondaic word test (cf. Brunt and Goetzinger, 1968), Perl's (1970) verbal transformation effect, and dichotomous tactual stimulation (Witelson, 1976a).

The initial assumption that such techniques would provide reliable indications of cerebral dominance without the necessity for surgical and similar procedures has not been sustained. One wonders whether we have gained much advantage over the original hand-eye-foot preference techniques both in terms of validity and in terms of fruitfulness in dominance research. Two simple assumptions are often made in the field of dyslexia: (1) that the technique constitutes a valid indicator of cerebral dominance, either in right vs. left or in a quantitative fashion, and (2) that reversal or lack of strong lateralization is an indicator of brain dysfunction. While the first assumption is open to serious doubt, the second one deserves critical exploration. The logic of this assumption, as applied to dyslexia, appears to be that reversal of cerebral dominance or failure to develop strong cerebral dominance is the result of early brain lesions or, alternatively, is *the* congenital defect for dyslexia. This notion competes with Critchley's assumption that the congenital problem is in the parietal area and with Silver's notion that the limbic and/or reticular systems are affected. What makes the cerebral-dominance explanation more attractive is the reasoning by Orton and others that poor development of cerebral dominance leads to late development or failure in the development of hand preference, which makes right–left discrimination more difficult, which in turn leads to mirror-image and reversal errors—interfering with the learning-to-read process (see Bond and Tinker, 1967).

This lengthy string of syllogisms may seem farfetched, yet it has generated far more detailed study than any other neuropsychological hypothesis in the area of dyslexia. Rourke has taken issue with one point in this string of deductions, namely that such dominance problems are the result of brain dysfunction. Yet brain dysfunction is not even a necessary part of this line of reasoning. Considering the poor support of the cerebral-dominance hypothesis in most studies, one should perhaps raise the question whether the whole argument breaks down at an earlier point and is therefore altogether misleading. Zangwill (1962) has suggested the alternative that poorly developed cerebral dominance may result in vulnerability for learning disorders and that we are dealing with a (possibly quite small) subgroup of dyslexics. Benton (1975) finds support for the cerebral-dominance hypothesis in the findings of Cameron, Currier, and Haerer (1971) that aphasia in illiterates is rare and argues that illiteracy may be the result of an interaction between poorly established dominance and cultural deprivation. However, Damasio et al. (1976) have not found such a link between illiteracy, lack of cerebral dominance, and relative rarity of aphasia.

This notion of Zangwill's, together with other explanatory concepts, should lead to empirical tests of alternative or coexisting forms of dyslexia: Clearly the behavioral deficits in a dyslexic resulting from incomplete or reversed dominance should result in a predictable pattern of deficits involving right–left orientation, directional sense, mirror tracing, rod-and-frame tasks, abnormal patterns of extinction on bilateral simultaneous stimulation, and typical reading–writing errors, etc., whereas other etiologies should result in different patterns, to be discussed later.

Before leaving the area of cerebral dominance and laterality, a study by Kornmann et al. (1974) on handedness should be mentioned. This study did not produce convincing evidence for the deviant laterality hpothesis, but it did show that a useful distinction between preference for unilateral activities and performance dominance for activities carried out by either hand can be made. The significantly higher amount of variance for hand preference in dyslexics as compared to normal elementary school children and to slow learners again suggests that the possibility of a specific subform of dyslexia with divergent laterality patterns cannot be ruled out. Silver and Hagin (1960) claimed that side differences on Schilder's arm extension test hold promise in the identification of such groups, a finding that has not found replication so far. The investigation of eye dominance perhaps has fared worst, as shown in the review by Porac and Coren (1976); even agreement among the different measures of eye dominance is extremely poor (Palmer, 1976).

Hence we are left with a confusing array of findings on laterality preference in many different areas. Yet, Corballis and Beale (1970) have cogently argued that "a perfectly bilateral machine could not perform" such tasks as right-left discrimination, mirror-image stimulus discrimination, and left-right response differentiation. It is understandable that the relationship between these abilities, lateral preference, and reading failure should be postulated. Corballis and Beale (1976) further point out the relative rarity of dyslexia among Japanese children (Makita, 1968) where symbol reversal appears to be impossible both in Kana and in Kanji script, which is read vertically, and the fact that reversal errors and left-right scanning problems have been typically found only for the worst readers in dyslexic groups. They propose that severe dyslexia may be found more frequently among persons lacking asymmetry of lateralization. This position should add at least one testable prediction to the model, i.e., that children with deviant dominance should be more severely dyslexic than others. Finally, another variation on the theme of lateralization and cerebral dominance was recently introduced by Shankweiler and Studdert-Kennedy (1975), who propose that we are dealing with a continuum of lateralization rather than a straight dichotomy. The varying degrees of cerebral equipotentiality for dichotic tasks were successfully predicted by these authors on the basis of a multiple regression analysis of the results of four manual performance dominance (dexterity) tasks. Such a proposal certainly complicates the analysis of models of dyslexia, but it adds a welcome refinement to the cerebral-dominance model which still remains testable.

AUDITORY-VISUAL-MOTOR INTEGRATION
AND TEMPORAL SEQUENCING

These areas have already been considered by Rourke as well as in the review by Benton (1975). The reason for looking at them again is that they pose another line of reasoning about the nature and the origin of dyslexia distinctly different from the laterality-dominance hypothesis. The system of reading and writing is developed relatively late in life, after the establishment of language as a second signal system. Such a system can be seen as superimposed on a functional language system; yet it requires new cortical or subcortical connections with the visual areas and new auditory discriminations as well as connections to the motor system. From a connectionist viewpoint, one can argue that full intersensory and motor integration is a *sine qua non* for reading and writing. Temporal sequencing is an essential component of such integration, not an independent ability, since in its relationship to the reading and writing process, temporal discrimination and temporal as well as spatial sequences are demanded if intersensory integration operates well. The logical place for such integration to take place is the occipital-parietal region of the language-dominant hemisphere, central to the participating regions of the brain. Clinical studies of acquired dyslexia in adults point out the importance of this area (Geschwind, 1970; Benson, 1976). Hence, this line of reasoning proposes what Benton called the "parietal theory" of dyslexia, assuming a congenital or early traumatic etiology leading to dysfunction.

Again, as pointed out by Rourke, the evidence for neurobehavioral correlates of dyslexia in the area of integration and sequencing is not compelling. A long series of rather ingenious tasks have been developed for the examination of these abilities. The short-term memory factor has effectively been excluded in some of these studies. Yet it is clear that no unitary explanation for the mechanism or the etiology of dyslexia can be found in this domain. However, it is obvious that a "parietal theory" would make an entirely different set of predictions for the behavioral deficiencies of dyslexic children and hence cannot be ruled out as a model which could account for a certain proportion of dyslexics. A recent variation of the topic is the distinction between simultaneous and successive processing. In this view, simultaneous processing is frequently seen as spatial-temporal, possibly related more to right-hemisphere function; and successive processing is seen as more analytic-synthetic, related to left-hemisphere function (Levy, 1974; Das, Kirby, and Jarman, 1975; Leong, 1976). Hence we find a combination of the lateralization of function with another version of the intersensory integration and processing model. This model has so far been insufficiently tested. Each model should generate the prediction of a highly specific form or several subforms (dependent on which part or form of the integration is most affected). It should be tested in competition with other models, confirmed by discriminant function analysis, or put to rest.

ATTENTIONAL DEFICIT

Insofar as lack of attention is not seen as a result of the frustration of a child experiencing repeated failures or showing lack of interest in the subject, it has been interpreted as a neurological deficit model and occasionally been invoked for the explanation of dyslexia. Silver's limbic and/or reticular dysfunction model suggests that deficits in arousal, general activity level, and focused attention may be the line of reasoning to follow for the dyslexic child. A recent study (Levine, 1976) suggests that the attention mechanisms involved in intrasensory and intersensory integration are affected by the level of oxygen supply. Little information is available to substantiate such a theory. In fact, it is difficult to see why dyslexia specifically should result rather than a general learning disability; even Silver admits this. Yet the model leads to a treatment approach with drugs, highly popular at present, and deserves consideration (Douglas, 1975; Doyle, Anderson, and Halcomb, 1976).

The model has also assumed much more complexity than originally suggested. Proceeding from the "preattentive processes" proposed by information processing theory (Neisser, 1967), Kinsbourne and Smith (1974) propose an attentional model for functional roles of the cerebral hemispheres. Whereas most theories on cerebral dominance appear to assume a differentiation between hemisphere functioning which is structural and fixed by nature in the development of the individual, Kinsbourne argues that though lateralization of function exists, this lateralization is only an evolutionary "division of labor" and that attentional processes tend to shift from one hemisphere to the other dependent on the preattentional processes demanded by the task at hand. Attentional processes tend to inhibit the activity of the other hemisphere through transcallosal interaction. Lateralization of function may not be a specificity present in newborn or even in older children; it may result from a tendency to unilaterally focus attention dependent on the set and the preattentive state of the individual. Unilateral neglect and extinction can be readily explained in such terms of attention. Kinsbourne does not specify what structures are involved in attentional focusing but suggests that they are subcortical. He implies that "anomalous lateralization" may be a "drawback for survival" and may lead also to "less grave difficulties, such as slowness in learning to read" and that "difficulty in selective looking and listening or a disorganized overview of the printed page" may be present.

This theory appears to be a major reformulation of the cerebral-dominance model, couched in terms of attentional processes, and hence makes a different assumption in terms of underlying pathology. The major weakness of the attention-deficit hypothesis, however, is still apparent when it is applied to dyslexia: it is difficult to see why anomalous lateralization resulting from failure to focus attention, proper interaction, and mutual inhibition/disinhibition of the two hemispheres should result in a highly specific deficit such as dyslexia. Rather, one would expect a general learning problem as a result.

Since this model has not been thoroughly studied, one would like to include it as an alternate model in the investigation of types of dyslexia. The proposed concomitant deficits could readily be defined from the model with the assistance of already existing methodology in the field of signal detection and vigilance and information processing.

NEUROPSYCHOLINGUISTICS

Rourke has turned to neuropsycholinguistic studies as another area contributing to the study of correlates of dyslexia, but he has confined himself mainly to studies of verbal-performance IQ differences in dyslexic readers. His conclusion is that dyslexia is frequently associated with general language deficit (even though specific clusters of such deficits may emerge). Such studies and studies of the factor structure of intelligence and language tests (e.g., the WISC and ITPA) frequently appear in the literature (e.g., Knabe, 1969; Wallbrown et al., 1974), but they contribute little beyond the obvious conclusion that children with poor language development also have difficulty in acquiring reading skills.

The acceptance of such results is somewhat defeatist in itself. If broad deficits in language development exist, why single out reading and what purpose is there in speaking about a *specific* developmental dyslexia? If we were to accept the position that general language impairment or delay accompanies the dyslexias, we would also open the door to another source of confusion. Is it justifiable to speak so casually about accompanying language retardation as if language disorders in childhood were a single unit? Numerous forms of language disorders have been described. Are all of them involved in the dyslexias, or, if not, which of them are?

There is little doubt that poorly developed language often leads to poor reading achievement, since reading is built upon the cornerstone of a sufficiently developed second signal system. It would be more reasonable to reject cases of broad impairment in language skills for the purpose of studying dyslexia. However, many authors have seen dyslexia as "an integral part of total language development" (Myklebust and Johnson, 1962), and there is little argument with that point of view. In this sense, delayed language development may be the forerunner of dyslexia. One must insist, however, that in order to speak of specific dyslexia, language development must be reasonably complete. Broad tests of language development should be used as control variables in establishing groups of dyslexic children instead of being left to vary at random. That such highly specific dyslexias exist has been demonstrated in a study of gifted children with reading/spelling difficulties (Knabe, Missberger, and Schjmiedeberg, 1970), the study of chronic dyslexics in adolescence (McKeever and VanDeventer, 1975), and in the occasional descriptions of bright adult dyslexics with excellent language abilities (Perlo and Rak, 1971).

If we insist on this degree of control over the general language development, a psycholinguistic approach has considerable promise for the description of the dyslexic problem itself. With the exception of the studies and considerations of Bierwisch (1972) and Weigl (1972, 1975) on grapheme-phoneme correspondence in the acquisition of written language, neuropsychology in general has spent little time on describing the dyslexic problem; usually a coarse yardstick is used for definition and then efforts are concentrated on neurobehavioral correlates. Psycholinguists and teachers tend to look more at the details of the presenting problem but care little about the other variables discussed in this session. Rarely do we find the two approaches combined. At best, as in the Ingram et al. (1970) study, distinctions were made between "audiophonic" errors (poor phonic knowledge, confusion of vowel sounds, incorrectly synthesized letters) and "visuospatial" errors (visual discrimination, directional reading errors, shape confusion for letters), but this hardly constitutes a full psycholinguistic analysis. Liberman et al. (1971) analyzed four types of errors, but found only the reversal of letter sequences and the reversal of letter orientation in sufficient quantity for their analysis. Interestingly, they found that the two types of errors were not correlated in their population of dyslexics, suggesting that perhaps two different forms of dyslexia were involved.

It is my intent to point out the potential fruitfulness of such a combined approach. We may start with a full-scale error analysis of the writing or, even better, of the oral reading of the dyslexic child. Numerous measures, including an analysis of hesitations, repetitions, repeated attempts at words, pauses, mispronunciations; also phoneme, syllable, and word substitutions; and additionally omissions and idiosyncratic productions could be used. Analyses of errors at the beginning, middle, and end of a word and of a sentence, errors in syntactical structure, errors in inflectional endings, and many others are readily available from the field of psycholinguistics (Le Jeune, 1974; Spreen and Wachal, 1973) but have rarely been applied to the performances of dyslexic readers or writers (e.g., Naidoo, 1972; Nelson and Warrington, 1974, 1976).

Other studies have attempted to vary the meaningfulness of sequentially presented material (Bakker, 1967) and found differences between good and poor readers in their handling of reproduction of meaningful material, but not of nonsense figures. In another study Bakker, Teunissen, and Bosch (1976) showed that reading strategies at age eight have implications for the future development of reading ability: their slow but accurate young readers remained slow, while the fast but sloppy young reader developed into a competent fast reader in a four-year follow-up. Downing (1973) pointed out that the comprehension of relatively abstract concepts (i.e., "letters are words, words are made up of units of letters, spaces are used as boundaries," etc.) are necessary before a child can meaningfully approach reading instruction. After a careful analysis of the acquisition of phonology in relation to reading, Menyuk (1976) concludes that "we have yet to discover the strategies used by successful readers." The benefits of such studies and detailed analyses for remediation are obvious (cf. Hartlage, Lucas, and Main, 1972).

Necessary as careful comprehensive psycholinguistic analyses of reading and studies of special problems are, in the context of this discussion, the immediate link to the preceding suggestions for the analysis of models should be stressed. Each of the models discussed is likely to generate distinct predictions for the type of errors dyslexic children make. An integration- and sequencing-deficit model would suggest phonetic errors, whereas a deficiency-in-asymmetry model would suggest scanning and mirror image errors as well as up-down reversal errors as prominent features.

Marshall and Newcombe (1973) attempted an analysis of error patterns in acquired dyslexia and suggested that three types of dyslexia could be distinguished: (1) "visual dyslexia" with occipital lesion, (2) "surface" dyslexia with predominantly grapheme-phoneme difficulties (temporal-parietal lesions) and (3) "deep" dyslexia with syntacto-semantic problems (deeply penetrating lesions, probably parietal). These researchers (Holmes, Marshall, and Newcomb, 1971) also investigated the relative difficulty of different syntactic classes for normal readers and for subjects with acquired dyslexia. Richardson (1975) investigated the effect of word imageability. If the model of acquired dyslexias is to be used as a guide to the search for subforms of developmental dyslexia, psycholinguistic studies of acquired dyslexia such as these could profitably be replicated.

Boder (1970) suggested the possibility of three types of dyslexia based on diagnostic reading/spelling patterns (i.e., the "dysphonetic," the "dyseidetic" or gestalt-blind, and the "mixed dysphonetic-dyseidetic" or alexic child, and assumes a "neurogenic" etiology for all three types. Another attempt to differentiate dyslexics on the basis of their ability to use syntactic and lexical cues (Guthrie, 1973) failed and showed only quantitative differences between good and poor readers; however, this study takes a limited approach to psycholinguistic analysis and is based on the findings in 12 "poor readers" rather than on selected dyslexics.

One could go on predicting what other specific psycholinguistic features are likely to be found, purely speculatively at this point. What is important is that a psycholinguistic approach could be very useful in testing hypothetical models and, if such models are confirmed, could be of direct diagnostic value.

CONCLUDING REMARKS

If we are to move to a testing of models, a look at existing studies approaching such a goal may be appropriate. The approach of Doehring and Hoshko (1977) uses a Q-type factor analysis without preconceived groupings, although models for grouping may be used as predictors for the outcome of a Q analysis. Mattis, French, and Rapin (1975) make an attempt to delineate three syndromes (language disorder, articulatory and graphomotor dyscoordination, visuospatial disorder syndrome). This was a post-hoc effort after their initial attempt to find a difference between brain-damaged dyslexics and non-brain-damaged dyslexics failed (as it did largely in the studies of Black (1973, 1976). Attempts by Rugel (1974) and Fuller and Friedrich (1975) to differentiate the three-subgroup system developed by Bannatyne resulted in the suggestion that symptomatic dyslexics show more conceptual and spatial deficits, primary (congenital) dyslexics show more conceptual and sequential deficits, and secondary dyslexics as a group perform better than the other two. However, these studies were based on WISC results only and the placement of children into subgroups on the basis of the Minnesota Percepto-Diagnostic Test appears questionable. Other studies have approached the problem in the context of follow-up analyses with subsequent breakdown into groups with good and poor prognosis. Lyle (1970) used multiple-regression equations to evaluate the antenatal, perinatal, and early developmental variables as predictors of his two-factor analysis of reading retardation. All these approaches and those outlined by Rourke have merit, but it should be stressed that the systematic testing of predictions generated by the proposed models has yet to be carried out. A different, though equally important, question is the empirical testing of models proposed for the cognitive structure in dyslexia and the differences in comparison with the cognitive structure in normal readers. That in such a test the age-related hierarchy of developing skills (as outlined earlier) has to be observed, and that matching for variables irrelevant to the model tested has to be carried out, should be restated.

The neurobehavioral approach to dyslexia is an ambitious one, since it implies that we are not only searching for correlates, accompanying deficits, and early signs for identification, but also that models for the underlying brain mechanism of reading failure are proposed. Such models need not imply etiology, but should be sufficiently far-reaching to have explanatory power for at least one of the major forms of dyslexia.

Chapter 9

DIRECTIONS OF NEUROBEHAVIORAL RESEARCH

ROBERT M. KNIGHTS

Rourke's review of the neurobehavioral literature related to reading disorders indicates the importance of using all the methods and technologies available for evaluating the relationship between the neurological characteristics of children with reading disabilities and observable behavior. The research cited in his survey is primarily of the type which examines the level of performance of good and poor readers on a wide variety of tasks. With the development of new and advanced technologies such as computerized tomography, biofeedback, electromyography, and galvanic skin response, it is likely that many future studies will be based on this paradigm.

In the conclusion of his chapter Rourke comments that research which compares the level of performance of good and poor readers on these various tasks has really contributed little to the understanding of reading retardation. In fact, he calls it a "dead issue." Rourke is reacting to the nature of research in this area by questioning the extent to which research findings contribute to our understanding of the basic reading process. This author agrees. The neurobehavioral research in reading really has told us little about the development of reading or how to treat or prevent reading problems. In order to illustrate this point, several topics in his chapter may be considered. For example, in the studies of perinatal factors it is known that there is a significant positive correlation between the severity of reading retardation and the severity of impairment on a large number of variables. The question still remains—what is the exact nature of the relationship between specific events in the development of the newborn and the types of reading problems later encountered?

A second illustration of this point can be made by reviewing the survey of EEG studies in retarded readers. It is well known that many retarded readers have unusual EEG patterns, but not all retarded readers show this pattern. This literature illustrates more about problems in the nature of the EEG than it does about reading impairment or dyslexia. The results of the past ten years of research have indicated that reading difficulties are not caused by deficiencies in EEG but that they are, in some way, related to them.

A final example of this point is the group of studies relating cerebral dominance to reading retardation. This work reveals more about the brain and its functioning than about reading disabilities. Dichiric haptic processing tells us about perception in children but fails to provide information about dyslexia. Studies of temporal sequencing abilities show that there are marked individual differences in performance even among normal readers. Comparison of normal and poor readers in this skill may produce differences, however, in light of the large variation in normal readers' performance, the results are tenuous. As Rourke points out, in some studies poor readers appear to be deficient in the ability to integrate auditory and visual stimuli but the importance of these integration skills for reading is unknown. Again, the laboratory studies have succeeded in informing us about integration in children but tell us little about the reading process, and provide no clues directed at the prevention or treatment of reading problems.

A CHANGE IN PARADIGM

If, as Rourke states, studies comparing normal and poor readers do not provide the information we need, where do we go from here? It seems apparent that the model used is inadequate for unlocking the necessary information about reading. A change in paradigm is necessary. The primary reason that reading retardation is not understood is that the nature of this problem itself has not been carefully observed and documented. Instead we have been too concerned with the correlates of reading retardation. It is suggested that careful observation of the child and of the reading process is necessary in order to understand reading retardation and/or dyslexia. The ontogeny of the reading process must be thoroughly examined. If one moves toward this paradigm there are three areas of study necessary for understanding the factors related to the process. First, the development and acquisition of reading skills must be observed individually in normal children. Second, experiential factors must be examined. Third, the constitutional factors which influence the nature of acquisition of reading skills must be considered. It is only after detailed studies have been completed that Bronfenbrenner's (1974) admonition can be followed. He has emphasized the point that if one is to understand a process, one must try to change it. The nature of the attempt to change something depends, of course, on the factors that one believes are important for influencing the change. We can only change the nature or rate of reading acquisition if a point of view based on observational studies is acquired. That is, if one attempts to change the rate of reading acquisition or the reading ability of the disabled reader, factors used to effect the change are necessarily a function of whether the reading retardation is considered to be primarily experiential, primarily constitutional, or both. Bronfenbrenner's point is a significant one. It is important to note however, that it cannot be satisfied until careful observational studies identify the important factors involved.

OBSERVATIONAL STUDIES

Observational studies must be conducted with children as they grow from preschoolers, unable to translate symbols, to children who, during the next two years, acquire an enormous amount of sophistication in interpreting standardized symbols in both a phonetic and a meaningful manner. We need not look at how a child becomes a problem reader, but instead, at how a child normally acquires this sophisticated skill. An interesting beginning on this work is the research conducted by Hardy (1973) and her associates in which some of the skills that were considered basic to reading were surveyed. They administered approximately 30 tests of basic skills to children in kindergarten and grades one and two. These tests included simple discrimination of shapes and letters, auditory discrimination skills, visual discrimination skills, integration skills and others. They examined the pattern of performance on these various tests related to later success in reading. On the basis of this survey the most important predictors were selected for a more detailed examination. These five tests have since been made into a screening battery (Knights and Hardy, 1976) and are helpful in the assessment of children in the early grades for future remedial planning.

Aside from the importance of determining the most basic skills for reading, Hardy observed hundreds of children during the early stages of the acquisition of their reading skills. The most striking finding was the variety of methods that children used to decode words. Although they had been taught by the phonetic method and/or by sight word recognition, they used a wide variety of analytic techniques to determine the sound and meaning of words. All types of associative cues were used in addition to the phonetic and spatial aspects. Although there was great individual variability, there was some similarity in the methods which children used to decode words. The study of the child's own methods suggests that assessment and remediation techniques be based on observational procedures.

It is argued that this type of longitudinal observational study on an individual basis will add much to our knowledge of reading retardation. In addition to observational studies, two other variables, experiential and constitutional factors, deserve more attention than they are currently receiving.

EXPERIENTIAL FACTORS

It is well known that children from disadvantaged homes are delayed in reading acquisition as compared to children from normal, middle class backgrounds. Previous studies of reading skills have not carefully delineated the socioeconomic status or environmental background of the children involved in the usual studies of good and poor readers. This point was evident to the present author when an attempt was made to locate children who were retarded readers in the suburbs of Ottawa, Ontario. Although fifth-grade children were examined in an elementary school population of approximately 24,000 it was exceedingly difficult to find youngsters who were two years behind in reading. That is, very few of the fifth-grade children were reading at a third-grade level. In contrast, Vellutino (1975c) in Albany, New York found that a number of middle-class children were two years below grade level in reading and thus were easily accessible for his studies on auditory-visual integration. It seems likely that the environmental background of children in the primary grades, as they begin to acquire reading skills, is more important than any other single factor in their academic life. Certainly the importance of early stimulation in verbal training for later development in a wide variety of areas is well documented for disadvantaged children (Ryan, 1973). Therefore it is deemed essential in this study of the nature of retarded reading to take into account the child's environmental and socioeconomic background.

Another experiential factor which is of concern is the influence of the teaching process. The most effective methods of teaching reading are not known, although a variety of methods are available. Some research has been concerned with the comparison of teaching techniques (for example, Chall, 1967). However, exactly which type of teaching or training is best for children with specific skill deficits is unknown because comparative studies have not been made. It seems reasonable to suggest that there must be differences in the sensitivity of teachers to the progress of children during critical reading acquisition stages. Teachers often do not receive training that would enable them to recognize the pattern of a child's deficits and provide appropriate teaching of specific skills as a result of this analysis. A child-computer-teacher assessment and remedial program for children with poor reading skills has been developed to assist teachers with the problem of diagnosing and teaching their retarded readers (Knights and Hardy, 1976). It may well be that the teacher variable is one of the more important experiential factors in learning to read.

There are so many variables related to the experiential factors in learning to read that it is very difficult to separate them. They do not act independently, but rather one factor may hinder another. The type of research proposed in this chapter should assist in evaluating the interaction of these experiential factors.

CONSTITUTIONAL FACTORS

A further need in the study of children with problems in acquiring reading skills is a variation on the pedigree studies. It is reasonable to assume that poor reading ability can be defined on the basis of some type of inheritance pattern and that there are children who inherit a disability with respect to reading skills. Most pedigree studies are concerned with prevalence and/or the pattern by which reading problems are inherited. Perhaps a more useful pedigree study would be oriented toward the detailed observation of all members of families who show reading retardation as an inherited disorder. This type of study would be concerned with determining the exact nature of the abilities and the development and change of abilities over time for the good readers and the poor readers in the family. An interesting observation of our own clinical experience in assessing children with reading problems is that many parents who are truck drivers or firemen are also dyslexic or have poor reading skills. An observational pedigree study concerned with collecting detailed data about all individuals of a family would yield more information about such patterns and clinical observations.

Such a study of specific families over many generations would differentiate between those individuals who are good and those who are poor readers and provide a basis for interesting variations in the method of acquisition of basic reading skills as well.

CONCLUSIONS

The normal procedure in observational studies is first to observe all classifiable behaviors that are believed to be relevant. The second phase is to isolate factors related to, or basic to, the predictor variable. In the present example this is reading skill. The third phase is to assess the child on these selected factors and demonstrate that training in these areas does, in fact, change reading skill or facilitate the more rapid acquisition of reading ability. This summarizes the position taken in this discussion of neurobehavioral research in reading retardation and indicates the nature of the shift in paradigm that is required.

Part IV

ELECTROENCEPHALOGRAPHIC AND NEUROPHYSIOLOGICAL STUDIES

Chapter 10

ELECTROENCEPHALOGRAPHIC AND NEUROPHYSIOLOGICAL STUDIES IN DYSLEXIA

JOHN R. HUGHES

I. PROBLEMS IN CORRELATING EEG AND DYSLEXIA

The usefulness of the electroencephalogram in studying children with dyslexia and other learning disabilities has been controversial. The reasons for the controversy include: (1) the imprecise definitions of the groups under study and the overlapping of these groups, (2) the presence of *questionable* EEG findings in many of these children, and (3) the relatively high incidence of "abnormal" EEG findings in control groups of similar age. Regarding the different kinds of groups studied, an attempt will be made in this presentation to collate the data from patients with dyslexia in particular, but studies dealing with unspecified learning disabilities will also be included. The presence of questionable and controversial EEG findings is a reflection of the need for further research in a field that otherwise makes a strong contribution in today's clinical setting. The relatively high incidence of "abnormal" EEG findings in control groups is also a reflection of the latter point, but statistically significant differences between the control and dyslexic groups are clearly evident in a number of studies.

II. GENERAL CLINICAL ENTITIES AND EEG RESULTS

Although considerable overlap exists among various broad clinical entities, the main conclusion in dealing with different cognitive and behavioral disorders is that the EEG tends to be more abnormal with more clinical disturbance. Table 10-1 summarizes the findings from many different studies and demonstrates this point. Thus, most children classified as hyperkinetic have a higher incidence of EEG disturbance (89%) than those considered to have a behavior disorder (59%). Also, patients with definite mental retardation more often have an EEG abnormality (63%) than those with a learning disability (46%) or with a specific dyslexia (45%), the latter two groups with a similar incidence. Tables 10-2 to 10-5 show the studies that contribute to the generalization noted in Table 10-1. Also consistent with the general point that the greater clinical disability is associated with a higher incidence of EEG abnormality, a study by Ingram et al. (1970) shows differences not evident by the similarly weighted means of dyslexics and learning disorders seen in Table 10-1. These investigators reported that 34 percent of children with a

TABLE 10-1
Incidence EEG Abnormality Behavioral Cognitive Disorders

CLINICAL ENTITY	NO. OF PATIENTS	% ABNORMAL
Hyperkinetic	383	89
Behavior disorder	208	59
Mental retardation	1592	63
Learning disability	924	46
Dyslexia	530	45

TABLE 10-2
Incidence EEG Abnormality Hyperkinetic Behavior Disorders

NO. OF PATIENTS	% ABNORMAL	INVESTIGATORS
Hyperkinetic		
353	90	Klinkerfuss et al., 1965
30	87	Anderson, 1963
383 (total)	89 (wt. mean)	
Behavior disorder		
70	71	Jasper et al., 1938
40	63	Knobel et al., 1959
97	47	Stevens et al., 1968
207 (total)	59 (wt. mean)	

TABLE 10-3
Incidence EEG Abnormality Mental Defectives

NO. OF PATIENTS	% ABNORMAL	INVESTIGATORS
200	43.0	Brandt, 1957
84 (without seizures)	54.0	Walter et al., 1956
401	58.9	Fuglsang-Frederiksen, 1961
74	59.9	Beckett et al., 1956
578	65.9	LaVeck and De la Cruz, 1963
40	70.0	Posey, 1951
55 (mongolian idiots)	78.2	Fuglsang-Frederiksen, 1961
85	78.6	Landucci and Piantoni, 1961
75 (with seizures)	90.7	Walter et al., 1956
1592 (total)	62.7% (wt. mean)	

TABLE 10-4
Incidence EEG Abnormality Learning Disabilities

NO. OF PATIENTS	% ABNORMAL	INVESTIGATORS
21	95	Gubbay et al., 1965
41	88	Paine, 1962
35	80	Murdoch, 1974
82	63	Chiofalo et al., 1971
63	62	Hughes, 1967
106	50	Capute et al., 1968
214	41	Hughes, 1971
128	37	Gerson et al., 1972
57	32	Satterfield et al., 1973
177	25	Koppitz, 1971
924 (total)	46 (wt. mean)	

specific disorder of reading and spelling had an abnormal record, contrasted to 84 percent with a general learning disorder, in addition to a reading and spelling deficit.

The reviewer is aware that these studies show a range of (1) variability in the time when the investigation was performed, (2) criteria used to designate an EEG abnormal, and (3) criteria used to define the clinical entity under investigation. In addition, the other reasons that make collated data from different studies on cognitive and behavioral disorders inconclu-

TABLE 10-5
Incidence EEG Abnormality Dyslexics

NO. OF PATIENTS	% AB- NORMAL	(% CONTROLS)	COMMENT	INVESTIGATORS
33	27	(%)	mainly delta waves and focal	Fenelon et al., 1972
62	34		more abnormality (84%) in general "learning disability"	Ingram et al., 1970
60	35	(7%)	50% abnormality if inadequate visual perception	Black, 1972
157	36		21% with positive spikes, 10% with occipital slowing	Hughes and Park, 1968
46	50	(10%)	slowing, especially occipital, & generalized paroxysms	Cohn, 1961
31	55	(29%)	most common abnormality was temporal spike	Torres and Ayres, 1968
41	59		also with speech retardation, 27% focal abnormality	Webb and Lawson, 1956
50	62		41% with positive spike, 50% occipital slowing	Knott et al., 1965
34	71		all with behavior disorders also	Kennard et al., 1952
16	88		slow alpha and pathological features	R. Roudinesco et al., 1950
530 (total)	45%			

sive may not allow for precise inferences. However, a trend does seem to be indicated.

III. INCIDENCE OF EEG ABNORMALITY IN DYSLEXIA

Table 10-5 shows the different studies on the incidence of EEG abnormality in dyslexic children and demonstrates that a range of 27 to 88 percent can be found in these various investigations. The weighted mean of the total group of 530 patients is a 45 percent incidence of abnormal EEGs. In those studies that have specifically included normal control groups, statistically significant differences between the control and dyslexic groups are found. In most of the remaining studies, other specific questions were asked of the data so that normal groups, at times, were not utilized. However, the overall incidence of EEG abnormality at 45 percent is so very high compared to any control group that there seems to be no question that there is a significantly increased number of abnormal EEGs in patients with a specific dyslexia. The incidence of EEG abnormality in the normal control groups (Table 10-5) varies considerably from 0 to 29 percent, and thus different criteria were used by the different investigators to determine positive EEG findings. It seems fair to conclude, however, that the same criteria were used to judge the records of the dyslexics, which included a significantly higher incidence of these positive EEG findings.

Benton (1975) acknowledges this increased incidence but concludes that "a specific association between EEG and reading disability has not been unequivocally demonstrated." This statement may be justified only by the use of the terms, *specific* and *unequivocally,* as our foregoing discussion will likely suggest.

IV. TYPES OF EEG ABNORMALITY IN DYSLEXIA

Schain (1972) has emphasized that some of the abnormalities frequently reported in children with learning disabilities or dyslexia are controversial or questionable. Into that group Schain has placed the 6–7 and 14/sec positive spikes, occipital or posterior temporal slow waves, nonfocal sporadic sharp waves, excessive slowing, increase in slowing with hyperventilation, and mild diffuse dysrhythmias. The reviewer is in agreement that some of these patterns are clearly questionable, e.g., increase in the slowing during hyperventilation, and that some of the other patterns are very controversial, e.g., 6–7 and 14/ sec positive spikes. However, in dealing with clinical entities like dyslexia or learning disabilities, disorders unrecognized by the professional psychologist or neurologist until only very recently, the predicted EEG patterns would not likely be gross abnormalities, like a focus of delta slow waves. Instead, the more subtle patterns would be expected, like excessive posterior slow waves or possibly positive spikes.

A. POSITIVE SPIKES

The most controversial pattern is likely the 6–7 and the 14/sec positive spike pattern (Gibbs and Gibbs, 1952). This pattern has aroused the greatest debate, but 10 years ago nearly 100 papers had been written about its probable clinical significance (Henry, 1963; Hughes, 1965). However, certain studies, especially those of Lombroso et al. (1966), have reported such a high incidence in asymptomatic children that many electroencephalographers now have considered this pattern to be within normal limits. The great difference in the incidence of positive spikes in "normals" reported by Lombroso and his colleagues in 1966, namely 58 percent, and that of 35 percent, based on data from the *same* patients but presented at a different time by the *same* group of investigators (Schwartz et al., 1966) raises some question about these studies. Also, the studies involving the largest number of asymptomatic children thus far investigated were those of Eeg-Olofsson (1971) and Hughes (1971). Each of these latter studies involved approximately 600 children. They show a similar incidence, namely 16–17 percent, and the great difference between the latter percentage and 58 percent is difficult to reconcile, but the sample size, EEG criteria used, or the clinical setting may prove to be important.

It seems possible that positive spikes in the adolescent may prove to be similar in significance to temporal slow waves in the aged. The latter slow waves appear so commonly in the aged that they may be noted even in the majority of certain older age groups. On the basis of one definition of "normal"—namely a condition found in the majority of a given population—these slow waves could then be called "normal." However, some aged subjects do *not* have these slow waves and careful study of various clinical subtleties, utilizing tests measuring cognitive function, has revealed that the temporal slow waves do, in fact, significantly correlate with a general cognitive disorder in aged subjects, who are considered otherwise well and remain active in the community (Drachman and Hughes, 1971). A similar situation may pertain to positive spikes which are not uncommon in adolescents. Like almost all other EEG waveforms, positive spikes are found in some subjects who are asymptomatic but, as a relatively "benign" waveform, they are found with a higher incidence than most other EEG abnormalities. Like temporal slow waves in the aged, these spikes may be found in the majority of certain special clinical groups, but labeling them all "normal" ignores the huge number of papers which argue strongly for a correlation with neurovegetative or behavioral disorders (Hughes, 1965). A recent review by the present author of the studies done on positive spikes within the past ten years has revealed that over 40 more papers have been published that argue further for their possible clinical significance. However, a number of other authors have drawn negative conclusions regarding their possible significance (e.g., Long and Johnson, 1968). One relevant philosophical question here is whether negative evidence ever provides the ultimate "truth" about a given phenomenon in the face of a large number of investigations with positive results. In the opinion of the reviewer positive spikes are neither *always* nor are they *never* of clinical significance and the exact determination of this significance awaits further investigation.

A considerable range of incidence has been found for positive spikes in dyslexics. Hughes and Park (1968) reported a 21 percent incidence of those who had sleep records, Knott et al. (1965) 30 percent, Bryant and Friedlander (1965) 35 percent, and Muehl et al. (1965) 55 percent. Torres and Ayers (1968) found no significant difference in the positive spikes found in dyslexics and those in the controls; nor did Bryant and Friedlander who reported a 28 percent incidence in their control group of 18 subjects. Clearly, the number of subjects in the latter study was far too small to draw any definite conclusions. In a study by Hughes on learning disorders (1971) a 1 percent incidence was found in the control group of 214 subjects, compared to a 20 percent incidence of 214 underachievers; the p value of 0.099 showed that statistical significance (0.05) was not quite achieved but a clear trend was indicated. Although the latter study was performed on learning disorders in general, a similar trend seems possible for dyslexia in particular.

B. OCCIPITAL SLOW WAVES

Excessive occipital slowing is one other abnormality commonly mentioned in EEG studies on learning disabilities or dyslexia. Knobel et al. (1959) reported a 47 percent incidence in hyperkinetic children, but a lower incidence has been found in various types of learning disorders. Hughes (1971) found a statistically significant difference ($p = 0.008$) for all slow waves regardless of location in underachievers compared with their controls, but it was the slowing on the temporal areas that was significantly different ($p = 0.003$), not that on the occipital areas (10% in all underachievers). However, when the underachievers were divided into two different groups that were clinically determined, the one group that showed the greatest difference from their controls had significantly more slow waves in general and nearly half of these were on the occipital regions. In dyslexics the incidence of increased occipital slowing seems similar to that found in learning disorders in general and Hughes and Park (1968) reported a 10 percent incidence constituting 27 percent of those with some type of EEG abnormality. Knott et al. (1965) and Murdoch (1974) obtained higher values (50% and 54%) for posterior slowing among dyslexics with abnormal EEGs. In addition, Cohn (1961) has emphasized the presence of 4–5/sec slow waves on the occipital areas of the same type of children. Other studies that may be related because of a reported increased slowing, but without designating a specific location, include those of Ingram et al. (1970) and Satterfield et al. (1973) who indicated that 12 percent and 32 percent (respectively) of their dyslexic patients had increased slow waves. Finally, Roudinesco et al. (1950) have emphasized the pathological features of the EEG records in their dyslexics, especially 3/sec waves on the right side and Statten (1953) has also stressed that delta waves are sometimes seen on the occipital areas of these individuals. The emphasis in this section on slow waves on the occipital (and temporal) areas may find support in studies of patients who have clear organic defects localized within those same regions and who have also developed a dyslexia. One example is a case report (Denckla and Bowen, 1973) of a patient with a (left) occipital-temporal lobectomy whose worst impairment was a dyslexia. However, it should be made clear that excessive occipital slowing in children with learning disabilities is usually bilateral, but the temporal slowing is often more on the left (Hughes, 1971).

C. DIFFUSE ABNORMALITIES

Another type of abnormality sometimes mentioned in these dyslexic children is a diffuse or generalized disorder. Studying hyperkinetic children, Anderson (1963) reported that two-thirds of these subjects showed a diffuse abnormality constituting three-fourths of all abnormality found and in the study by Gubbay (1965) on apraxia and agnosia, diffuse slowing was also the major abnormality found. Capute et al. (1968) reported on children with minimal brain dysfunction or learning disability and found that half of these children had abnormal slowing which was considered nonfocal or diffuse. However, in studies specifically dealing with dyslexia, similar diffuse abnormalities have not been prominently mentioned. For example, Hughes and Park (1968) found that only three of 157 dyslexics had diffuse slow waves. On the other hand Roudinesco et al. (1950) did mention the slowing of the alpha rhythm in dyslexics and this finding could be considered a nonfocal or diffuse abnormality. Also, Webb and Lawson (1956) reported that 11 of 24 patients with dyslexia and an abnormal EEG had a focal abnormality, leaving 13 with nonfocal findings.

D. EPILEPTIFORM ACTIVITY

The last abnormal pattern mentioned here is the sharp wave, spike, or spike-and-wave complexes, usually considered an epileptiform discharge. Here great discrepancies are found by various investigators in the incidence of some type of EEG discharge. Some studies on dyslexics report very few of these abnormalities, and others prominently mention them. For example, in Hughes's study (1971) fewer than 6 percent of underachievers showed this type of waveform, and in dyslexics in particular fewer than 4 percent did (Hughes and Park, 1968), accounting for only 11 percent of all the EEG abnormalities noted in these children. On the other hand, Torres and Ayers (1968) claimed that focal spikes or sharp waves on the temporal areas were the most common abnormality found. But Ingram et al. (1970) found that only 7 percent of dyslexics showed a focal spike or spike-and-wave complex, but, on the other hand, Murdoch (1974) reported that there were more epileptic abnormalities in their patients with minimal cerebral dysfunction than in the control group. Also, Fenelon et al. (1972) reported that, of the nine patients with reading disability who showed abnormality in the EEG, two of them showed nonfocal epileptiform discharges and six of them showed focal spikes or sharp-wave discharges. Cohn in 1961 reported that the abnormal records in his patients having reading disability at times showed general paroxysmal activity, without specifying the exact type of abnormality.

Drew in 1956 reported on two half-brothers with reading disability, both of whom shared some type of discharge, including one with a generalized spike-and-wave complex. Other studies that place emphasis on the epileptiform discharge include the one case reported by Baro (1968) involving a patient with reading disability who was said to have epileptic discharges on the EEG and to show an improvement in reading when given anticonvulsant Dilantin. Oettinger et al. (1967) reported on 19 patients with reading disability, five of whom had an "induced dysrhythmia," especially during reading. However, the examples of these sharp complexes leave some serious question in the mind of the reviewer as to whether or not they are truly epileptiform discharges. Volterra and Giordani (1966) reported on 193 cases having occipital spikes, some of whom clinically appeared as dyslexics. In a collection of 102 patients with some type of spike or sharp-wave discharge, Lairy and Harrison (1968) reported that those with occipital foci often showed visual or oculomotor types of disorders, but did not designate these children specifically as dyslexics.

E. GENERAL CONCLUSIONS

The general conclusions that can be drawn from this section are that positive spikes seem to be more frequently mentioned in the studies on dyslexia than other waveforms, but a definite conclusion regarding their incidence (and significance) in these patients seems impossible at this time in view of the variability (and controversy) mentioned. It is unfortunate that this waveform has become so controversial that further studies to resolve some of these questions may not ever be done. The data from the dyslexic studies, however, are very suggestive and the incidence of positive spikes ranges from 20 to 50 percent of the children tested. Excessive occipital slowing is another waveform that is commonly mentioned. The same general conclusion can be drawn for this EEG pattern as for positive spikes, and these latter two waveforms do have a relationship to each other (Kellaway et al., 1959). The data on posterior slowing suggest at least a 10 percent incidence in learning disabilities or dyslexia, but further studies are clearly needed. The other two waveforms mentioned have in common that they may be found with a relatively high incidence by some investigators but not by others. Thus, a diffuse abnormality or epileptiform activity may be emphasized in some studies but may not even be mentioned in others. It seems that the selection of the population studied may be crucial in explaining the great variability in the incidence of these latter two patterns.

V. CORRELATION OF EEG ABNORMALITY WITH CLINICAL CONDITIONS

A. EEG ABNORMALITY IN GENERAL

A number of authors have associated the presence of an abnormal EEG in general with specific clinical conditions. For example, Black (1972) found a significantly increased incidence of EEG abnormality in dyslexics, if there was also evidence of either inadequate visual perception or some type of birth defect. Likewise, Gerson et al. (1972) found more abnormal EEGs in learning-disabled children who had an abnormality found on neurological examination and in those with histories of birth complications. In the study by Ingram et al. (1970), those with a greater incidence of EEG abnormality were patients who also demonstrated evidence of brain damage assessed by birth history, developmental history, or clinical examination. A significant relationship between EEG abnormality and dyslexia was found by Tuller and Eames (1966) and by Ayers and Torres (1967). The latter investigators found that, even in the control group ranked for reading ability, 55 percent of those in the bottom quartile had an abnormal EEG, while the remaining three-fourths had only a 20 percent incidence of abnormal records—not significantly different from other control populations (Gibbs and Gibbs, 1964). In the study by Burks in 1957 on 137 patients with behavior disorders, an abnormal EEG was associated with lower verbal than performance IQ subtests and also with greater difficulty in perceptual or general academic function; patients with social or emotional disorders tended to have normal records. However, Kennard et al. (1952) found that in a population having behavior disorders there was no significant difference in the incidence of EEG abnormality between the normal and abnormal readers. Also, Muehl et al. (1965) reported a disappointing lack of relationship between severity of reading disability and degree of EEG abnormality.

A few investigators have associated the effectiveness of certain medications with the presence or absence of abnormal EEGs. For example, Satterfield et al. (1973) found that those with an abnormal EEG had a better clinical response to methylphenidate than those with normal records, and Fenelon et al. (1972) reported that nitrazepam improved abnormal EEGs and also improved the performance of patients with reading disabilities.

B. POSITIVE SPIKES

Certain correlations have been found between specific EEG waveforms and various clinical conditions. For example, Smith et al. (1968) found that, in patients with positive spikes, ethosuximide improved the verbal and full-scale IQ, but did not change the personality and motor performance test scores in these patients. However, in the investigation by Muehl et al. (1965) positive spikes did not correlate with any psychological test score. On the other hand in their study on dyslexics, Hughes and Park (1968) found that those with positive spikes were the brightest children among four different EEG groups, but with the greatest difference between their potential and their actual achievement in reading. Also, these same dyslexics with positive spikes scored high on different tests measuring tension and metabolic rate. These latter findings may be consistent with a finding that positive spikes are often found in behavior disorders with impulsivity (Schwade and Geiger, 1956; Hughes, 1965).

C. OCCIPITAL SLOW WAVES

Correlation between excessive occipital slowing and different clinical conditions can be found in various studies. For example, this type of slow-wave abnormality was found more frequently in deaf children than in patients with learning disabilities, and the same deaf children also tended to have diminished photic responses (Hughes, 1971). This latter study tied together the relationship between excessive occipital slowing and some type of visual response. In the study on speech disorders by Pavy and Metcalfe (1965) occipital slowing was associated with abnormal results on a visuomotor performance test. Hughes and Park (1968) found that dyslexic children with this same EEG abnormality were the poorest readers, having poor potential and decreased visual responsivity, especially in the form of poor visual duction. These latter studies do emphasize that occipital slowing may, at times, be associated with visual disabilities, as might be predicted by neuroanatomical considerations. The only correlation that Chiofalo et al. (1971) found with excessive occipital slowing was that these children had a less impaired learning disability than the other children studied and also usually had normal IQs.

It should also be made clear that the same waveform may be seen in patients whose primary clinical disorder seems to be more behavioral than scholastic or visual (Cohn and Nardini, 1958).

D. DIFFUSE ABNORMALITIES

Specific clinical correlations with diffuse or generalized abnormalities have rarely been made. In a study by Stevens et al. (1968) on behavior disorders, these investigators reported that diffuse EEG abnormalities were sometimes associated with antisocial activities, aggressiveness, low tolerance, clumsiness, and variability of behavior. Chiofalo et al. (1971) studied children with learning disabilities and found that such diffuse slow-wave abnormalities were often associated with a low IQ and visuomotor deficits. In a study on dyslexics, in particular, such generalized abnormalities were associated with retarded speech and motor development (Roudinesco et al., 1950).

E. EPILEPTIFORM ACTIVITY

Correlations with epileptiform activity have been reported by many investigators. Although they studied primarily behavior disorders, Stevens and her colleagues found that children with sharp waves or spikes had defects in attention and ideation. Some of the patients showing discharges studied by Green (1961) showed short attention span, especially those with spikes on the temporal or occipital areas. Hughes and Park found that in a group of dyslexics, the small group with such discharges showed evidence of organicity in the form of high thyroid (PBI) values and also abnormal neutrophil counts. (Park and Schneider (1975) have confirmed that dyslexics in general have high thyroxine levels.) Perhaps the most suggestive organic aspects of the dyslexics showing discharges were the visual deficiencies in the form of abnormal duction tests; nearly half of these children had weak or absent stereopsis. However, Flax (1968) has stressed that the impairment of visual skills, such as fusion, can contribute to dyslexia but is not likely a primary factor in extreme cases. His view was that other functions, like form perception, were more closely associated with dyslexia. Corcelle et al. (1968) found that dyslexics who were also clinically epileptic had a high incidence of spatial disorders and also disorders of verbal communication; disorders of written language were less frequently noted.

Other investigators reporting correlations with EEG discharges include Stores (1973) who found that patients with these abnormalities had a special problem with impaired attention; however, both subclinical discharges and the effect of anticonvulsant drug medication might contribute to this impaired attention. In addition, impaired attention might be found in these patients because mental subnormality may coexist with a seizure disorder without one causing the other. The conclusion of Woodruff (1974) on the effect of the seizure discharge on memory and learning was that such a discharge impairs retrieval, rather than storage. The same type of conclusion was found by Geller and Geller (1970) who studied five patients with generalized spike-and-wave discharges. These latter investigators found that there was an impaired recall even up to 4 sec before the presentation of the stimulus and Hutt et al. (1963) found a similar effect up to 2 sec. In patients with learning disabilities, Chiofalo et al. (1971) found that those with occipital discharges had relatively normal IQs (and at times higher than normal) and only minor visuomotor deficits. The studies by Lairy and Netchine (1963) on partially sighted patients have placed emphasis on the relatively high incidence (25%) of occipital and temporal discharges, especially on the left occipital area, in these patients. Later, Lairy and Harrison in 1968 reported that the occipital spikes were found primarily in patients with visual and oculomotor disorders, predominantly the former, especially in those with left occipital foci. Thus, the presence of a spike and sharp-wave discharge seems clearly associated at times with visual disorders and also with defects of attention among children with dyslexia or general learning disabilities.

VI. SPECIAL FEATURES OF THE EEG

A. FAST ACTIVITY (40/SEC)

Considerable evidence exists that one of the major problems in dyslexics is a lack of focused attention (Knights and Bakker, 1976); electrophysiological studies dealing with arousal and attention thus seem pertinent. An example of such a study dealing with arousal and attention is that of Sheer (1976), who found that a significant increase in 40/sec activity was noted on both parietal areas during problem solving in normal children, but not in children with a learning disability. These studies are difficult to control since the possibility exists that during mental effort some low-amplitude muscle activity may masquerade as 40/sec cerebral rhythms from the parietal regions. In 1970 Sheer and Grandstaff found bursts of 40/sec activity in the visual and motor cortex of animals; this activity was noted for 0.5 sec and also remained continuous for about 1.5 sec after a correct bar press from these animals. The same type of rhythm, namely 40/sec activity, was noted by Das and Gastaut (1955) in trained yogis during the most concentration stage of their meditation. Also, Banquet (1973) had reported 40/sec activity in subjects said to be in the third stage of transcendental meditation. Thus, some evidence exists that 40/sec activity may be related to states of attention in man, but it is also interesting that the same kind of activity has been associated with violent behavior (Gibbs et al., 1950).

B. ALPHA REACTIVITY

It is well known that the alpha rhythm usually decreases in amplitude with arousal stimuli, especially visual. Grunewald-Zuberbier et al. (1975) found that hyperactive children had higher amplitudes of alpha and beta waves than nonhyperactive children, but their more pertinent findings were that the amplitude reduction to a conditioning tone developed more slowly in the hyperactive children who showed shorter arousal responses to light stimuli and a faster regeneration of alpha amplitude. Also, there was a longer latency for the reaction time in the hyperactive. To the authors these findings indicated a lower state of EEG arousal in the hyperactive group.

C. ALPHA AND SACCADIC EYE MOVEMENTS

Attention and perception have also been studied by relating alpha activity to saccadic eye movements. Leisman and Schwartz (1976) concluded that the alpha activity of man was related to saccadic eye movements and that the difference in the duration and velocity of such movements in subjects with attentional deficits was related to the ability to perceive and integrate visual information in the cortex. Visual perception was viewed as a discontinuous process with a discontinuity temporally and phase-linked with the saccadic eye movements. It was during the saccade that the visual information was considered to be transmitted to the visual cortex. Further studies on the saccadic eye movements and their relation to perception were performed by Gaarder et al. (1964). These investigators found electrical responses to saccadic eye movements and concluded that an evoked response produced by a retinal image displacement accompanied saccadic eye movements, so that these movements did help to maintain vision. Two years later Gaarder and his colleagues showed that alpha-like activity in the evoked response was phase locked to saccadic eye movements. Since the alpha-like component was phase locked before as well as after the saccade, this fact argued against the possibility that the saccade was causing the locking and pointed to the alpha component pacing the saccade or to both the saccades and the alpha component being paced by something else. These authors developed a model of visual information processing in which the saccade generated discontinuous packets of edge-information which were cycled as a short-term template at a rate reflected by the alpha-component frequency. The latter studies argue that saccades are important in the processing of visual information.

D. ALPHA AND STABILIZED RETINAL IMAGES

Other reports seem to indicate that the *stabilization* of the retinal image rather than its displacement by a saccade may augment the processing of visual information. For example, Leisman (1973) studied patients with attention problems and found a significant increase in the duration of the alpha blocking during a conditioning stimulus by the use of such stabilized retinal images. The alpha blocking response was considered to be representative of the patients' attention to the stimulus, and the increase in such a response by the stabilized retinal image technique argued that the technique increased the attention of the patients. In 1974 the same author studied the duration of the saccadic eye movements in normal and in brain-damaged patients and found that differences in the duration were related to the ability of these different individuals to perceive and integrate visual information. If the brain-damaged patients were able to use the stabilized-image technique to eliminate saccadic eye movements, then the alpha changed and there was an increased ability on the part of the patients to recall visual information. Thus, one group of studies would seem to indicate that the movement or displacement on the retina of a stimulus enhances visual processing and, on the other hand, other data would indicate that the stabilization of such a retinal response enhances such processing.

Kris (1969) briefly reported on the combined use of binocular electro-oculograms (EOG) and EEG monitoring during perceptual tests in order to investigate ocular-cerebral interaction and alertness level, in addition to ocular fusion and deviation. Later in 1970, the same author briefly reported on the simultaneous monitoring of the EOG and EEG in determining whether visual, auditory, or a combined method of reading practice helped to improve a child's working efficiency and performance score in reading. No clear results are given in these two brief reports, but the technique seems to offer some promise for dyslexics.

E. ALPHA SYNCHRONIZATION

The synchronization of the alpha activity was the subject of study by Martinius and Hoovey (1972). These investigators studied three groups of children from 8 to 11 years of age: (1) a group that had special difficulty with attention or concentration, (2) a group of dyslexics, and also (3) normal control group. These authors found that most children increased the synchronization of their alpha between the two occipital regions when attending to an auditory discrimination problem. However, the dyslexic children actually showed a decrease in such synchronization and the latter group performed less well in terms of alpha enhancement than even the group with short attention span. The conclusion of the authors was the alpha synchronization was an expression of a general activation process and improved alpha synchrony was related to the function of attention. If one assumes the latter relationship, these data provide neurophysiological evidence for the suggestion that the factor of attention is crucial in patients with dyslexia.

F. ORGANIZATION OF ALPHA

The latter studies on the synchronization of the alpha rhythms are reminiscent of the results of a study by Hughes (1971) who showed that the organization or rhythmicity and the development or amplitude of the background (alpha) rhythm proved to be significant variables in a study on learning-disabled children. Not only was the incidence of poorly organized or non-rhythmic alpha activity shown to be significantly higher in the learning-disability groups compared to the normal controls, but this latter factor best separated underachievers from their controls when the prediction of who would be an underachiever was made on the basis of EEG. Murdoch (1974) has also reported that children with minimal cerebral dysfunction tend to have poorly organized alpha activity. The term "organization" has also been used by Lairy and associates but they gave a slightly different meaning to it (Lairy and Netchine, 1960, 1963; Lairy and Harrison, 1968). In Lairy's work the term refers to a judgment or measurement of the topographic differentiation of the alpha activity as it appears from different areas. Poor organization referred to a lack of individualization of the posterior regions compared to the more anterior regions. Although this latter definition of organization was based on spatial grounds and Hughes's dealt with the rhythmicity regardless of spatial differentiation, examples from each of the two different studies seem to indicate that the two definitions may have a common denominator. Rhythms considered well organized in one study would tend to be similarly considered in the other.

Lairy and Netchine (1963) reported that, among sighted children and adolescents seen in a neuropsychiatric practice, records of poor organization were obtained among those showing psychomotor disturbances. Among the partially sighted group of children studies by Lairy and colleagues, a positive relationship was also noted between the degrees of organization of the background rhythm and the quantity of residual vision; those with poor organization tended to have poor visual acuity. Lairy and Harrison (1968) compared the incidence of poor organization (that is, with poor spatial differentiation) in three different groups of children. The poorly organized alpha rhythms were seen especially in children from a neuropsychiatric clinic who had epileptiform foci—more than in those without such foci and more than in normal children. These data and also our own indicate that the spatial and temporal aspects of the background alpha rhythm are important in attempting to correlate the EEG with emotional or learning disorders. Fenelon et al. (1972) attempted to confirm the usefulness of the spatial index of Lairy and found that it was lower in children with a reading disability than in other groups studied, including those with behavior disorders; but a statistically significant difference could not be found. One interesting finding was that Mogadon (Nitrazepan) seemed to improve the dyslexics not only with regard to specific and nonspecific features of the EEG, but also in terms of better spatial organization of their background rhythms. This finding suggests the need for further investigation into the usefulness of various medications like anticonvulsants among dyslexics and the possibility that such drugs could effect various aspects of their alpha rhythms in such a way as to correlate with improved reading performance.

G. FREQUENCY ANALYSIS

Sklar et al. (1972, 1973) have performed an interesting study on dyslexics and normal children with the use of the digital computer. These authors provided spectral estimates of different bands of EEG activity, monitored during certain tasks and also during rest. The dyslexics demonstrated more energy in the band between 3–7/sec and 16–32/sec, while the normals showed more energy within the 9–14/sec band. However, during reading the autospectral disparity between these two groups reversed and now the faster activity between 16–32/sec was found more in the normal group than in the dyslexics. This increase in fast activity during reading is reminiscent of the studies by Sheer, who showed an increase in fast activity at 40/sec during problem solving requiring attention in normals but not in dyslexics. The coherence of all activity was also assessed by Sklar and colleagues. These results provided the most discriminating feature of all during the reading task; within the *same* hemisphere the coherence of the activity between leads was higher in dyslexic than in the normal children, but between *symmetrical* regions across the midline of the head the coherence tended to be higher in the normal children. Thus, there seems to be more of a synchronization within one hemisphere, rather than between the two hemispheres, in dyslexics during reading. These investigators presented many tables of different F ratios involving discrimination analysis and indicated that differences exist between the dyslexics and normal groups with regard to many different frequency bands and also different test conditions. In a later report (Hanley and Sklar, 1976) these discrimination analyses and the general findings were made clearer. The authors emphasized that it was activity from the left parieto-occipital area that represented the most discriminating feature between the dyslexics and controls. The dyslexic children showed peaks at 6, 17, 20, and 24/sec but without a well-developed alpha band (reminiscent of the poorly organized alpha mentioned in the previous section). The normal controls showed a peak at 9–12/sec. The difference at rest in the autospectral pattern from the parieto-occipital area was sufficient to classify children with

87 percent accuracy. The second feature was the coherence function between O_1-T_3 and T_3-F_3, which increased the accuracy to 93 percent. During reading the best discriminating feature was the coherence between O_2-T_4 and T_4-F_4 in the 16–22/sec band, which allowed for 76 percent accuracy in classifying the children. The second feature, the autospectral density between T_3-F_3 in the 3–7/sec band added another 6 percent. During reading a 6/sec peak was added and an 18/sec peak was removed from the dyslexics. One suggestion regarding treatment made by Hanley and Sklar was to train the dyslexic child to generate a more normal EEG frequency spectrum by training trials. This suggestion assumes that the latter differences in the computer analyses were related to the cause of the dyslexia, rather than the effect and this assumption may not be warranted (see Section VII following).

VII. SPECIAL INTERPRETATION
OF POSITIVE EEG FINDINGS

The results of a number of studies on children with various types of learning or behavioral disorders have led to conclusions opposite to what might be expected based on traditional concepts in electroencephalography. For example, Morin (1965) found that stutterers who *failed* to show improvement with training had *normal* EEGs while those who *improved* usually had *abnormal* records. Bergés, Harrison, and Lairy (1965) found that there was a *favorable* prognosis in children with a speech disorder who had an *abnormal* EEG and an *unfavorable* prognosis for those with normal records. In the study by Knobel et al. some of the most *severely involved* hyperkinetic children had *normal* EEGs. In two different articles Tymchuk, Knights, and Hinton (1970a,b) have shown in the comparison between the normal and abnormal EEG groups that the subjects with a *normal* EEG performed at a *lower level* than the abnormal subjects in 7 out of 9 tests that showed a significant difference. In a second report the poorest of the subjects with normal recordings was shown to be on tests measuring motor function. Chiofalo et al. (1971) reported that clinical *progress* in learning disorders was more satisfactory for the children with *abnormal* EEGs than in those with electrical stability. Finally, Hughes (1971) found that, when underachievers were clinically divided into the less and the more abnormal group, the *less abnormal* group, called borderline, had a greater incidence of EEG *abnormality*.

These latter findings indicate that we may need to look upon some positive EEG findings in ways other than what is traditional. For example, in the case of spike-and-wave complexes of petit mal epilepsy, this discharge is considered to be related to the cause of the epilepsy, not the effect. However, in the case of learning disabilities, positive EEG findings could represent the effect, not the cause, of the disorder. Following the suggestion of Lairy and Harrison (1968), one may assume that the dyslexic child becomes maladjusted to the scholastic environment, that the CNS (central nervous system) has reacted to this maladjustment, and that the positive EEG findings may represent the electrical manifestation of this reactivity or compensation. Thus, improvement in the scholastic situation is possible because the CNS is reacting or compensating. However, in other children with dyslexia, the CNS may not react to correct the maladjustment and, therefore, there are fewer positive EEG findings, as the manifestation of the brain's poor reactivity, and little improvement therefore occurs. In Hughes's study on learning disorders the borderline group may have shown more positive EEG findings because of the greater reactivity of the CNS to the scholastic maladjustment and, accordingly, these individuals demonstrated only a minimal academic deficit. On the other hand, the more severely involved learning-disordered subjects in that study may have been a group with less reactivity of the CNS to the scholastic difficulties; therefore those subjects would have greater clinical deficits, and fewer EEG findings would appear as a manifestation of this diminished reactivity. Thus normal EEGs are found not only in individuals with normal function, but also may be found in abnormal subjects in whom there is no more reactivity of the CNS to a maladjusted environment. It seems, therefore, the positive or abnormal EEG findings may, at times, represent the reaction of the brain to stress.

Lairy and Netchine (1963) found, consistent with this latter interpretation, poorly organized EEGs in their partially sighted children, but such an organization was considered by these authors to represent a normal adaptation to the visual defect. To Lairy and colleagues, normal records with better organization in these poorly sighted children would have carried a pessimistic prognosis, connoting a permanent mental retardation. Also, these investigators found that these same children tended to have spikes or sharp waves on the left occipital regions; however, to these authors these discharges did not represent necessarily an "abnormality," but only a certain type of EEG signal representing an adaptation to the visual defect. This type of mechanism of adaptation was considered to be favorable to the individual and the discharges were viewed as a functional expression of the "oversolicitation" of the occipital region. The disappearance of the left-occipital spike foci with increasing age and with further training or learning usually accompanied an improvement in the perceptual motor performance. In a later study, Lairy and Harrison (1968) studied 102 school-age children who had spikes or sharp waves, but not clinical epilepsy, compared to a group without such discharges. In children with Rolandic or central foci, there was a significant inferiority of motor ability, especially with regard to manual skill of the dominant hand; in those with occipital foci there were visual or oculomotor disorders especially involving a perceptual motor disturbance. However, the EEG evolution never was toward a clinical epilepsy, and the disappearance or decrease in the activity within the focus usually accompanied clinical improvement of the motor or psychomotor disturbance. The persistence or the exacerbation of the focus was associated with persistence of the clinical problem; and the speed of the evolution of the focus when it did disappear was considered a measure of cerebral plasticity. Thus, the quicker the EEG returned to normal without such a focus, the more rapid the clinical recovery. To these authors the existence of such EEG foci therefore encouraged, rather than contraindicated, re-educative or psychotherapeutic actions. In children with such clinical disorders, but with a perfectly normal EEG, this particular finding would indicate a stable biological equilibrium and the absence of the necessary plasticity to allow for scholastic improvement. Lairy has mentioned that the evolution of the EEG discharges in these latter children was not toward a clinical epilepsy, but there is little doubt that there are other children with similar discharges which are associated with the *cause* of a learning disorder (Stores, 1973; Woodruff, 1974). In these patients anticonvulsant medication is advised. Further research is needed to determine which discharges may be associated with the cause and which may be related to the effect of a learning disorder.

VIII. OTHER ELECTROPHYSIOLOGICAL STUDIES

A. CONTINGENT NEGATIVE VARIATION (CNV)

The contingent negative variation is an electrical waveform found primarily on the vertex region in individuals who have an expectancy that a given event is about to occur. Dykman et al. (1971) have indicated that the CNV is reduced in children with a learning disability or dyslexia. Although Low and

Stoilen (1973) were not able to establish the CNV as a graded phenomenon related to the learning function in children with "minimal cerebral disabilities," Cohen (1976) has reported that the CNV was reduced or absent in 60 percent of 41 children with learning disorders. Age was considered to be a significant factor in that the mean age with an *absent* CNV was 8.5 years, while for a *reduced* amplitude it was 10 years. Some EEG abnormality was found in 11 of these 41 learning disorders and 8 of those 11 had an absent CNV. Cohen speculated that one difference between his study and that of Low and Stoilen was that he made corrections for baseline shifts if the computer determination seemed inappropriate. Cohen's conclusion that the presence of a CNV was a favorable prognostic indicator in children with a learning disability was not based on follow-up data but likely on the fact that all the children in the control group without any learning disability had a CNV. Fenelon (1968) had earlier reported a difficulty in establishing the "expectancy wave" (CNV) in young dyslexics, but only three subjects were tested with somewhat ambiguous results.

B. VISUAL EVOKED RESPONSE (VER)

In a study on learning disabilities with double-blind controls (Hughes, 1971) one effective way to separate the underachievers from the controls was on the basis of the organization and development of the background rhythm (see Section VI.F), but one other important factor was the presence of asymmetrical photic driving responses with depression of amplitude on the left side. The depressed photic responses on the left side were found to be significantly different between the underachiever and control groups. This finding introduces the interesting question of the way in which evoked responses may correlate with dyslexia. Conners (1971) studied a family of poor readers and found a decreased amplitude in the late components of the VER on the left parietal area, a region near the angular gyrus where Geschwind (1965) postulated the locus of auditory-visual integration. Also, in children with learning disabilities Conners found a significant relationship on the left parietal area with the late wave VI. It was the amplitude of wave VI from the left parietal area that showed the highest correlation with reading achievement. However, Kooi (1972) has criticized these studies of Conners by pointing out that the electrical reference of the activity from the left parietal area was to the central vertex region, a very active region at times in the VER. Kooi claimed that nothing could be stated with exactness about the response as a whole or of any of its components if such a reference was used. Since all electrical recordings represent the difference between the activity from two different sites, the utilization of such an active reference region left serious question as to the validity of the results, according to Kooi. However, Conners (1973) in his response, has pointed out that there is certainly no cancellation of the activity between the parietal regions and the central vertex and, in addition, differences between the left and right sides were found. O'Malley and Conners (1972) reported on an attempt to increase the amplitude of the VER by alpha feedback training and claimed success. The subjects were given a feedback response when they produced 0.5 sec of alpha on the left side and concurrently 0.5 sec of beta or theta on the right! The authors reported an increase in alpha time on the left, in beta and theta on the right, and also in the VER. All of these conclusions seem suspect, especially in view of the unlikelihood of alpha on one side and theta appearing on the other.

Preston et al. (1974) attempted to confirm Conners's results and mentioned in his methods section that a reference electrode was used on the left mastoid and also on the central vertex; but he did not make clear what his special electrode arrangements were. In the Conners study, comparisons were made between relatively good and relatively poor readers, but all the children studied were from a school for children with learning disabilities. In the study by Preston and colleagues, there was an attempt to investigate the difference between normal children and those with a reading disability. Two control groups were used, one matched for age and IQ and one matched for reading level and IQ. One distinct criticism of this study is that activity was checked only at 180 millisec and at 600 millisec after the visual stimulus, apparently without checking the entire waveform, but only recording the amplitude of activity at those particular points in time. Therefore, peaks may have existed just before or just after such windows, and the results could therefore be misleading. Preston's group did find, however, that the dyslexia group showed a lower amplitude at 180 millisec than either of the control groups. Their conclusion was that there was a relationship between the VER and reading disability and that this was a reliable, detectable relationship, but one only marginal in strength. It seems important, however, to point out that it was the late components which Conners found that were especially significant in his study. No significant difference was found by Preston with regard to the late activity at 600 millisec.

C. AUDITORY EVOKED RESPONSE (AER)

Satterfield et al. (1973) have studied children with minimal brain dysfunction with regard to auditory evoked responses. They found a significantly lower amplitude for the average AER in the children with minimal brain disorder, compared to normal controls; the best differentiating feature was a late positive component seen during the fast stimulus rate of 2/sec, rather than at the slow rate of one stimulus per 2.5 sec. In particular, 59 percent of the children with a learning disability had a lower amplitude than the normal children. Also, a lower amplitude was found in the measurement between the first negative and second positive component and also between the second positive and the second negative component. Finally, a significantly longer latency was noted in the children with minimal brain dysfunction for the first negative and second positive wavelets.

D. PHYSIOLOGICAL SIGNIFICANCE OF EVOKED RESPONSES

1. General comments

These latter studies have emphasized the difference in the amplitude of various components of certain evoked potentials. The possible meaning or significance of changes in such evoked activity, especially of the late components, has been summarized by Buser (1970). He indicated that these evoked responses in man (1) decrease when stimuli are monotonous leading to a decrease in attentiveness, (2) decrease when the subject is presented other kinds of stimuli so that attention shifts to those other sensory modalities, (3) correlate with reaction times in that faster reactions are associated with larger responses, and (4) increase when the subject is attentive to the particular stimulus used. Buser further points out that the most conspicuous change in these responses involves the *late* components between 160 and 330 millisec, those which seem to originate from or depend for their amplitude on the nonspecific projection system. Results from many different authors seem to emphasize the essential role of the nonspecific system in the higher elaboration and cognition of visual information at subcortical or possibly at cortical stations within the primary visual system.

Consistent with Buser's summary, Faure et al. (1968) emphasized the importance of the correlation of level of vigilance with the late components of evoked responses. Also, Spong and colleagues (1965) have shown that responses to light flashes recorded from the occipital area were larger when the individual attended to such a visual stimulus and the responses to clicks recorded from the temporal areas were larger when attention was directed to such an auditory stimulus. Also consistent with Buser's generalizations, Lindsley (1970) pointed out that the average evoked response to a somatosensory stimulus showed a reduced amplitude for the short-latency components but an *increased* amplitude for the *longer latency* components, if the individual attended to such a stimulus. Thus, the short latency or primary components of the response appeared to represent one system and the longer latency components another, in view of the differential reaction to the same stimulus under the same attentive set or conditions. Lindsley also found that the degree of any enhancement of the late potential during selective attention was a function of the general arousal or activation level. The specific selective attention factor seemed to stem from what just occurred in the past, especially because such factors may serve as a guide or anticipation or even an *expectancy* of what is to come in the future. This result introduces again a concept of the contingent negative variation, a waveform that seems to be associated with expectancy. As mentioned previously, the CNV and also the late components of evoked responses tend to be reduced in children with learning disorders.

2. *Informational content of stimulus*

Many other investigators have been concerned about the meaning or exact significance of the waveforms representing various types of evoked responses. Sutton and colleagues (1967) studied the AER and concluded that the waveform of such a response was not only determined by the physical aspects of the stimulus, but also varied as a function of the effective information provided by such a stimulus. The latency of the positive component was determined by a point in time at which ambiguity was reduced, and the shape and amplitude of this component seemed to be influenced by external events which delivered information to the subjects. The authors concluded that these findings may reflect general fluctuations of *attention* and that the fluctuations of the *late positive components* in this evoked response could be a reflection of the informational content of the stimulus.

Consistent with the conclusions of Sutton et al., Cohen and Walter (1966) have also concluded that the amplitude of the response to a visual stimulus relates to the *informational content* and to subjective factors, rather than to the physical strength of the stimulus. These investigators found that the response to symbolic and meaningful semantic stimuli was more elaborate than the response to a click or flash of light. A higher amplitude of response was recorded when *different* pictures were presented than with repeated exposures to the *same* picture; also, a slow *late* positive swing was seen after the recognition of the visual stimulus.

Two other studies have reached similar conclusions regarding the psychological features that correlate with changes in the evoked response. Black and Walter (1965) found a reduced *late* response when two stimuli were associated in time, but the response to the second stimulus increased in amplitude when an *un*associated stimulus was used. The authors concluded that the response of the (anterior) nonspecific cortex to associated sensory stimuli was a function of the *probability of association* between them. Finally, Begleiter and Platz (1969) found that the *late* components of the VER were significantly related to both stimulus and response conditions. The amplitude was larger when taboo words were used than with neutral words or blank flashes. The response effect was considered to be the result of *increased attention* required under the response conditions.

3. Decision-making process

Shelburne has studied the VER in both adults (1972) and children (1973). His conclusion was that the *late* positive components of the evoked response to word stimuli were related to decision-making. He presented three-letter words to the subjects and asked them to determine if the words were nonsense syllables or familiar words. This task required attention to the third positional stimulus and under these circumstances the amplitude to that particular stimulus increased at the central vertex, especially the components at 450–550 millisec, and such an increase thus seemed related to the decision-making process.

4. IQ studies

Evoked potentials have also been associated with IQ in general and Chalke and Ertl (1965) have reported that high psychometric intelligence was associated with the late components of the response, namely those from 140 to 370 millisec. Four years later Ertl and Schafer (1969) confirmed the earlier findings and showed that the latency of the sequential components of the VER bore a highly significant inverse correlation with IQ scores. The *later* components correlated better than the earlier ones. To these authors the evoked response reflected the time course of informational processing by the brain.

During the same year Rhodes et al. (1969) published results consistent with this latter study. These investigators showed that the *late* (100–250 millisec) components of the VER from the central and occipital regions were larger in bright than in dull children. The dull children showed no hemispheral difference in the amplitude on the central regions, but the bright ones showed *late* responses on the right central area consistently larger than on the left central area. This difference was not a function of maturation, since the amplitudes from the bright children were similar to those of children 3–4 yrs older, and the dull children showed amplitudes smaller than either normal or younger children of their own age. The higher amplitude on the right and lower amplitude on the left central regions, seen only in the *bright* children, seems inconsistent with Conners's findings of a decreased amplitude on the left parietal area found in *poor* readers.

To summarize Section VIII, the late components of evoked potentials seem related to both the informational content of the stimulus and the attentiveness of the subjects, and these components tend to be reduced in amplitude when learning disorders are present.

IX. QUESTION OF CEREBRAL DOMINANCE

Satz (1976) has summarized the data relating cerebral dominance and dyslexia and has claimed that information is still lacking on this crucial issue. Also, Michaels (1974) has concluded that cerebral dominance is not related in any simple way to field dominance and that crossed dominance is seen in good as well as bad readers. This author concluded that there was no known scientific evidence to support the claim for an improvement in performance of dyslexic children by visual exercises or laterality training. Helveston and colleagues (1970) found no correlation between laterality and reading ability in either normal controls or dyslexics. Therefore, treatment aimed at changing the laterality pattern was not justified, and such patterns were not considered by these investigators to be reliable predictor of reading ability. During that same year Helveston reported that changing the controlling eye in dyslexics could not be credited with improving reading ability. Also this author found that the determination of laterality by comparing the controlling eye and dominant hand had no value in predicting reading ability.

On the other hand, Hagger (1968) has reported that there is a high correlation between the presence of dyslexia and disorders of cerebral dominance. Yeni-Komshian et al. (1975) found that poor readers were more lateralized than good readers with regard to visual half-field presentations, with deficits especially with left-field presentations. These results suggested to the authors that poor readers either suffer from some form of "degraded processing" within the right hemisphere or that transmission from the right to the left hemisphere may be abnormal. In his general summary on dyslexia, Ritchie (1971) concluded that there are two syndromes among dyslexic children and one deals with a mixed-hemisphere dominance as shown by left-right confusion. Critchley (1967), in summarizing his views on dyslexia, stated that few dyslexics have well-established hemispheral dominance, as shown by the high incidence of crossed laterality in this group. To Critchley the quest for some reliable index for cerebral dominance offered a worthwhile field of research and most of the suggested clues were unconvincing to this author. It was somewhat surprising to this reviewer to read that Critchley considered as the most promising index the location of a hair whorl which usually lies over the more dominant hemisphere and also with a midline hair whorl possibly equated with ambivalent dominance. Only a few attempts have been made to correlate electrophysiological data with this question of cerebral dominance. For example, Eason and colleagues (1967) found a higher amplitude in the VER in left-handers when the stimulus was on the left rather than right field. The magnitude of the response from the right lobe seemed greater for the left-handers, and there was no consistent difference seen for the right-handers. Thus, there does seem to be some evidence of a difference of amplitude of the VER of the two sides, possibly related to handedness.

Data from studies comparing the amplitude of the alpha rhythm on the right and left sides are of greater interest. Since alpha is the expression of the resting brain and usually desynchronizes when activated, the *lower* amplitude of alpha activity may be considered to arise from the more active (dominant) hemisphere with the higher amplitude of alpha from the nondominant side. Oller-Daurella and Masó-Subirana (1965) have made a careful study of this problem after categorizing subjects' laterality into exclusively right (R), more right (r), ambidextrous but more right (rl), ambidextrous but more left (lr), more left (l), and exclusively left (L). The percentage of subjects with alpha rhythms higher on the right side was (respectively) 58, 52, 33, 20, 15, and 0. The percentage with alpha higher on the left was 19, 25, 33, 50, 55, and 0. Thus, Subirana (1969) states, "It can be concluded that alpha asymmetry is undoubtedly related to hemispheral dominance but has no absolute value for each individual case." In 1959 Subirana et al. had approached the problem by assessing the organization of the alpha rhythm which was found best in right-handers and worst in poorly lateralized children. Also, a greater percentage of theta rhythms was found in left-handers and poorly lateralized subjects. However, the most promising data in EEG relevant to the problem of cerebral dominance are from studies dealing with amplitude asymmetry of the alpha rhythm.

X. QUESTION OF HEREDITY

In 1949 Chalfant and Scheffelin concluded that future research in dyslexia should examine the neurophysiological conditions which seem to interfere with reading and which may also be transmitted genetically. They pointed to the need for family studies including siblings or fraternal and identical twins reared together and apart. One of the major questions to them was the role of genetic transmission in dyslexia, later discussed as "congenital word-blindness" by Hallgren (1950). Unfortunately, very few studies in neurophysiology or electroencephalography can be brought to bear on this important question. Drew (1956) reported on three cases of developmental dyslexia and concluded that the common defect was a disturbance in the Gestalt function which was considered by this author to be inherited as the dominant trait. Drew believed that there was a delayed development of the parietal lobes as the anatomical substrate for this disturbance of Gestalt. The EEGs that were reported in these three cases were said to show "borderline" disturbances of various types of discharges, but these findings do not seem to be of great significance to this investigator.

XI. SUMMARY AND RECOMMENDATIONS

This review has dealt with the electrophysiological findings in dyslexia and has shown that the results from most of the studies are sufficiently encouraging to justify further investigation in nearly all areas that have been previously explored. However, there are priorities. First of all, more EEG studies are needed, especially to determine if those with abnormal tracings have a better or worse prognosis. EEG abnormalities found in *preschool* children before a dyslexia becomes evident and before the CNS may begin to react or compensate for the anticipated stress should then be related to the cause, not the effect, of any dyslexia that may later develop. Questions relevant to dyslexia and pertaining to specific EEG findings include the relationship between positive spikes and levels of tension, between excessive occipital slowing and oculomotor deficits, and between epileptiform discharges and inattention. The usefulness of various medications (especially anticonvulsants) for dyslexic children with positive spikes, but mainly with epileptiform discharges, is relatively unknown. High in priority are electrophysiological studies dealing with attentiveness, especially follow-up investigations on the usefulness of alpha synchronization to judge this elusive variable of attention. Other studies related to this variable are those dealing with very fast activity, mainly from the parietal areas, to be determined by digital computer analysis, which could also provide data on the spatial and temporal aspects of alpha organization, including determinations of coherence functions within each and between both hemispheres. Also high in priority would be studies on the late components of the evoked potentials, especially the VER, and the differences in these responses between the two sides. Finally, further investigation is needed into the question of the CNV.

The latter questions could be answered by the following all-encompassing investigation. Two large groups would be studied, both preschool and school-aged children. The tests performed would include the EEG during rest, reading, and sleep (the latter for the detection of epileptiform discharges); also the CNV, VER, and AER; tests measuring tension and attentiveness; and finally an ophthalmological examination. During the resting EEG and during reading, the activity would be tape-recorded for later computer analysis, including the fast fourier transform and coherence functions. Follow-up data in three years would provide the means of judging the usefulness of various EEG or evoked potential parameters to predict prognosis and the usefulness of different types of medication to attempt to alter the usual course of dyslexia.

As an example of a specific project which, if carried out, could generate needed data, the following study outline on "EEG Correlates of Dyslexia" was designed jointly by Martha Bridge Denckla (whose own chapter follows this one) and the present writer.

I. *Population to be Studied:* Selection would be made, for subjects (dyslexic) and controls alike, from *one* middle-class average

IQ community, of white, right-handed boys age 9 years ± 9 months (range 8 years 3 months, through 9 years 9 months), for whom the following data would be collected and made available to the investigators:

A. Medical, family, and social history
B. Rating scales (Conners, 1973 —parent and teacher
C. WISC-R
D. Gilmore Oral Reading Test (accuracy or "decoding" measure)
E. Neurological examination—performed "blind" after initial selection criteria and group subdivisions have been made—see below.
F. IQ and reading achievement data

II. *Selection of Subjects*
A. Exclusion of those with sensory (vision, hearing) handicap, major documented neurological condition (seizures also grounds for exclusion), or emotional/psychiatric disturbance revealed on *history* and/or *rating scale* items designed to reveal such deviations.
B. WISC-R Full Scale at least 90 but (especially important for controls) no higher than 119. Controls will be more stringently screened such that verbal IQ versus performance IQ differences could not exceed ± 10 points.*

III. *Definition of Dyslexic:* reading (Gilmore Oral Reading Test) at or more than 2 SDs below level expected on basis of a multiple regression equation in which the constants are derived from the *community's* existing intercorrelations of reading, age, and IQ and the individual's age and IQ therefore are the predictor variables *for him* in that community. (This is Rutter's definition of "specific reading disability," an alternative to the RQ or MA-RA criteria.)

IV. *Two Subgroups in III, Namely, "Dyslexia" and "Dyslexia-Plus":* Conners' rating scales for parents and teachers, scored for 9 of the 10 items used in "hyperactive syndrome" resource

* At this point a pool of subjects and controls is available for inclusion and characterization as in Part III.

(excluding the "learning-disabled" item) would be used as a "cutting point." Where parent and teacher ratings are both 16 or more, the individual will be characterized as "dyslexia-plus"; where parent and teacher ratings are discordant in that one or the other falls below 16, then a rating of at least 10 on one and of at least 20 on the other will also be sufficient for classification as "dyslexia-plus." At least 15 subjects of each type ("dyslexia-pure," "dyslexia-plus") will be selected.

V. *Neurological Examination:* at this point will not further exclude subjects but categorize them in terms of the presence or absence of traditional neurological signs (deviations from normal qualitatively off the developmental continuum, e.g., reflex asymmetries, involuntary movements) as compared to development only (Kinsbourne, 1963a: "had the child been younger, the finding would have been normal"). All subjects and controls will be thus examined and signs listed under "N" and "D" per child by an examiner who is "blind" to the reading or behavior-rating status of the child. (Developmental "infrabehavioral" expectations for the 9 year ± 9-month-old boy may be found in Denckla, 1973; and Denckla and Rudel, 1974.) Retrospectively, data will be available for correlational analysis of EEG and "infrabehavioral" examination findings. Similarly, perinatal, acquired, and family history items will be be kept as part of data analysis but not used for further breakdown of experimental subject groupings. Each child (15 "dyslexia pure," 15 "dyslexia-plus," and 30 controls) would have EEG studies.

VI. *Resting EEG:* Criteria for abnormality as listed below, read "blind" and 50 percent of records reread for reliability:
   A. "Occipital slowing"—require rhythmic delta (<4/sec)
   B. Frontal theta (4.5–7.5) higher in amplitude and more prominently represented than alpha
   C. Diffuse slowing-delta frequencies scattered on both sides
   D. Positive spikes: at 6–7/sec and 14/sec separately handled, as either plus or minus finding
   E. Only clear focal slowing or diffuse spike/wave complexes, called "positive" during hyperventilation
   F. All sharp waves, spikes, slow waves reported

VII. *Additional Special Studies*

A. Tape record parietal, temporal, and occipital areas bilaterally, under different task conditions (see below) and check for 13–75/sec activity, spectral analysis, and coherence functions (Sklar, Hanley, and Simmons, 1973; Hanley and Sklar, 1976).

B. Visual evoked responses—tape record; place leads on frontal, parietal, and occipital areas, referred to ipsilateral ear; and measure amplitude and latency, wavelets I, II, III, IV V.

C. *Tasks* for A and B to be varied along stimulus material dimension:

   1. Diffuse light flashes

   2. Words

   3. Nonverbal unfamiliar configurations (Fedio and Buchsbaum) and response dimension

     a. Oculomotor scan

     b. Oculomotor track

       (EOM monitoring required)

     c. Discriminative finger-on-key release

     d. Nondiscriminative finger-on-key release

Chapter 11

CRITICAL REVIEW OF "ELECTROENCEPHALOGRAPHIC AND NEUROPHYSIOLOGICAL STUDIES IN DYSLEXIA"

MARTHA BRIDGE DENCKLA

I. THE PROBLEM OF DEFINING
CLINICAL ENTITIES

Hughes has opened his state-of-the-art review with an honest *caveat* about the "imprecise definitions of the groups under study" and the "overlapping of these groups." Since the present chapter is written by a clinician and clinical researcher who is acutely aware of the major problems posed by confused nosology/terminology, the bulk of it will be devoted to the question, "EEG correlates of *what?*"

It is indeed difficult to make sense out of the different and/or apparently conflicting reports of any correlate (not only an EEG correlate) of "dyslexia" unless the reports address the issue of definition of "dyslexia." The term may be used to describe a symptom or it may be used with the implication that a specific neurologically based syndrome is being diagnosed. By analogy, therefore, it appears in the literature in the status of "headache" and in the status of "migraine." The same can be said of "reading disability" or "learning disability" as terms found both in "chief complaint" and "diagnosis" sections of clinic notes. The studies reported by Hughes might have been divided into those reporting "EEG correlates of dyslexia as a symptom" (for example, "dyslexics who are also clinically epileptic") and those studies reporting "EEG correlates of a syndrome, dyslexia, defined by characteristics A, B, C . . . ." It will be argued that there is utility in reporting findings associated with dyslexic-epileptic children if these cases are matched not only with "normal controls" but with nondyslexic-epileptic children. There is additional or complementary utility in reporting correlates of the *syndrome* "dyslexia," but one does not necessarily have to wait forever in puristic zeal in order to focus more specifically on the neuropsychological issue of "dyslexia" (Denckla, 1977a and b). However, this strategy has been ignored by all but a few of the researchers whose EEG studies have been reported (the exceptions notably being Ingram, 1970 and Gerson et al., 1972, in Hughes's review cited, pp. 208–10). Despite the fact that overlap exists between and among groups described as "dyslexic" (Peters, Romine, and Dyckman, 1975; Rutter and Yule, 1975) a multifactorial description of the population studied, specifying boundaries of type, history, examination findings (neurological and psychometric), and criteria for academic underachievement (Benton, 1975) may *also* have many of the defining characteristics of "the hyperkinetic syndrome"—a situation for which the broader term "minimal brain dysfunction" was originally intended (Peters et al., 1975). Such a child might be thought of as "dyslexia-plus," since the focus of the chief complaint *is* the reading retardation (Denckla, 1977b); but this category is differentiated from the behaviorally delightful group characterized by "unexpected reading failure" (Symmes and Rapoport, 1972). Furthermore, either "dyslexia-plus" or "dyslexia-pure" can be associated with (1) suspect perinatal events and/or (2) classic, as opposed to developmental, neurological signs (Denckla, 1977a). One cannot improve upon Rutter and Yule's eloquent statement of the case for the multifactorial definition of syndromes (1975), as it is only under such conditions of definition that syndromes emerge; then one may argue about terminology to distinguish one syndrome from another.

Could the EEG itself become one of the syndrome-defining factors, and, if so, how? As suggested before, a model for how a correlate becomes a defining characteristic appears to be available if one inspects the research of the last decade (reviewed in detail in Chaps. 4 and 7 by Vellutino and Rourke, respectively). The model involves the use of "dyslexia" as a symptom, frequently generating hypotheses from cases of adult-acquired symptomatic dyslexia and then the testing these hypotheses in several populations, each matched in a variety of ways, rather like rotating population factors about the axis of "dyslexia" as opposed to trying to match with a *single* control group *every* factor but reading competence. Reading the literature in this way, one finds that speech, language, and sequencing deficits have become positive defining correlates of "dyslexia." It remains to be seen whether, if researchers patiently stalk the rare "pure" variety, these same deficits will define a single syndrome toward which genetic research could then be directed (Rutter and Yule, 1975; Preston et al., 1977).

EEG studies, particularly those which include anlysis of expectancy waves (e.g., CNV) or those components of evoked responses which reflect attentional variables (see Hughes's discussion), may be particularly helpful in furthering our understanding of "dyslexia plus." This is because clinical and experimental behavioral measures of attention are the weakest parts of our observational armamentarium (see Chap. 4) even though we suspect that varieties of attentional deficit are important, if not overriding, determinants of educational outcome. Satz (Chap. 16) reports that between the second and fifth grade the percentage of severely disabled readers rises from 12 to 20%. Satz's predictive measures, largely complex perceptual-motor items, predict fewer of the fifth-grade failures than the second grade "severe" ones. As a clinician, one suspects that this is not only because in older groups there emerges the importance of linguistic deficits (discussed in this volume by Satz, Jansky, Rutter, and Vellutino) but also more prominent effects of attentional deficits, as higher grades demand more independent and organized work habits. It is possible that electroencephalography could fill the gap in our ability to examine attentional processes and provide us with a physiologically meaningful, operationally defined nosology of "attention" as measured during specified tonic and phasic states and tasks.

EEG correlates could be approached in the same manner as speech and language correlates, as long as the awareness of the need for control groups other than "normals" is part of the design. Thus, an EEG variable in "dyslexia plus" should be controlled for in "nondyslexic hyperkinetic" as well as "pure dyslexic" groups. From this point of view, the Conners (1971) study reporting EEGs of good and poor readers *within* a learning-disabled population, should receive special commendation. Otherwise, reports on "minimal brain dysfunction" or "learning disabled" populations include in lumped fashion all three groups and run the risk either of internal cancellation or extreme variance of results, in much the same manner as would a study of heterogeneous "epileptics." Considerations relevant to etiology can then be introduced, as in the study of Gerson et al. (1972). As has been the case with "the epilepsies," similar clinical syndromes of differing etiology may well turn out to have similar—but not identical—EEG abnormalities/deviation (by analogy to the instances, "true" *petit mal* vs. *petit mal variant*).

II. THE PROBLEM OF DEFINING "NORMAL"

When dealing with nonprogressive, nonlethal chronic conditions such as dyslexia or other learning disabilities, the establishment of norms and the very concept of a "condition" represent substantial challenges to those of us

245

trained in traditional medical models. Hughes has touched upon these issues in writing about positive spikes in the adolescent and temporal slow waves in the aged, but the case should be stated even more strongly with respect to dyslexia and other closely related developmental disabilities. These conditions are not necessarily to be thought of as "abnormal," i.e., "off the bell-shaped curve of the normal distribution," but rather often as extreme-position variants, clustered toward one end of the normal distribution for the characteristic(s) clinically attended to (e.g., poor reading), while well toward the middle of the curve for other characteristics (e.g., intelligence). Thus, a continuous-spectrum rather than a dichotomous-threshold approach to EEG correlates of any relatively circumscribed clinical variation might, as Hughes suggests with respect to positive spikes and "neurovegetative or behavioral disorders," yield more meaningful syndrome-specific information. An example of this continuous-spectrum approach, not with the EEG but with one neurological sign, is the research on choreiform movements in "normal" school children (Wolff and Hurwitz, 1973). To echo Rutter and Yule (1975) again, the conditions encompassed by the terms "learning disabilities" are expressed clinically as a result of multiple additive factors, the intrinsic ones (presumably reflected on neurological or EEG examination) being risk factors—extreme positions on the normal curve which, depending upon how an individual fits on other curves (both intrinsic and extrinsic aspects of his situation) may or may not lead to an overt clinical "condition" labeled, e.g., "dyslexia."

This view of "dyslexia" makes imperative the painstaking accumulation of normative data for each and every EEG variable utilized in any study of subtle clinical "conditions." Presentation of data on "matched" controls is not as satisfactory as presentation of normal developmental curves which, like height and weight charts, serve as background information against which an individual's position, *per variable,* on a normal distribution may be plotted. "Matched controls" are always suspect, for there is a high probability that the "normals" harbor individuals with risk factors overlapping those of the "clinical" symptoms or alternatively, that careful matching diminishes sample sizes to biologically unacceptable "n's." This reviewer is persuaded that collection of normal developmental EEG data is a prerequisite for optimal research in the field of dyslexia. For example, such data would clarify the apparent contradiction cited by Hughes of similar amplitude asymmetry in studies of "bright children" and "poor readers." In fact, many "bright children *are* indeed "poor readers," as would become apparent if the separate distribution curves for each characteristic were considered. Without normative data for each clinical and EEG variable, however, one is stuck back at the unsatisfactory global level of Hughes's statement that "the EEG tends to be more abnormal with more clinical disturbance," or one remains naively disappointed by the "lack of relationship between severity of reading disability and degree of EEG abnormality." The position toward which research should be moving is that of searching for EEG variants as risk factors within "normal" populations.

Viewing EEG correlates in this status of "risk factors," alternative explanations of the data summarized in Hughes's section entitled "Special Interpretation of Positive EEG Findings" seem warranted. When a "less normal" group, in terms of favorable prognosis, has a "more abnormal" EEG, one might conclude that a medical therapy has more to offer when the physical factor reflected in the EEG "abnormality" is a relatively greater "risk factor" in the multifactorial equation determining clinical expression. One example is that of the virtually mute child with a temporal-lobe focus, for whom anticonvulsant therapy offers great improvement. By contrast, the speech-impaired child with a normal EEG, a positive family history of speech delay, and a language-deprived environment may, because of combined factors of nature and nurture, prove to have a more dismal prognosis. Another example is that of the hyperactive child with an abnormal EEG, but a disorganized environment, who often responds poorly to pharmacological intervention. In summary, the good prognosis of clinically expressed multifactorial disorders in which the "abnormal EEG" factor looms large may be interpreted as the result of the greater ease with which pharmacological, as contrasted with environmental, treatment programs may be achieved and bring about short-term changes.

The discussion of EEG abnormality as reflecting central nervous system plasticity or adaptive reactivity may be characterized as highly speculative.

III. METHODOLOGICAL CONSIDERATIONS

    a. Test conditions
    b. Statistical analyses

a. Deserving of further emphasis is the lack of caution with which some of the studies cited report EEG correlates of such factors as "arousal" or "attention," without adequate description of test conditions. For example, alpha reactivity in hyperactive children cannot be discussed without reference to ambient lighting and eye movement activity in these children (this connection being implicit in, but not explicitly related to cited clinical studies in the section on alpha and saccadic eye movements). Focusing of the eyes may be the critical factor in alpha blocking; and although nobody would deny that ocular focus upon a visual stimulus and selective focus of attention upon the same stimulus are frequently parallel, it cannot be similarly assumed (when presenting a conditioning auditory signal, or tone) that where the subject's eyes are roving or fixating is not an even more powerful determinant of what happens to subject's alpha than is presumed auditory attention. Similarly, before drawing conclusions as to the importance of (or operational definition of) "attentional deficit" in dyslexic children, a variety of tasks, tapping nonverbal and particularly spatial discriminations, should be contrasted with auditory discrimination or reading tasks.

b. A brief comment about statistics may be useful as a "consumer's guide" to critical evaluation of many EEG studies; i.e., an array of components of waveforms sampled from many electrode placements, are sometimes subjected to multiple individual *post hoc* comparisons such that one or more "significant levels" of differences between groups may emerge by chance alone. When the mathematically significant difference between subjects and controls appears to have "face validity" by virtue of the electrode placement being in anatomic proximity to a part of the brain presumed to be of importance in the clinical situation being studied, such a result is often accepted less critically than would be the case for a similarly derived neurobehavioral result, bereft of anatomical associations.

IV. DATA ON ISSUES OF CEREBRAL DOMINANCE AND HEREDITY

If one approaches the issue of cerebral dominance as follows, i.e., "what portion of a given function is subserved primarily by which hemisphere and how is interhemispheric integration achieved?", then Dr. Hughes has understated the contribution to this dynamic issue of studies cited in previous sections of his review. For example, degree of interhemispheric synchronization of alpha during auditory discrimination may be viewed as an index of interhemispheric integration. The work of Sklar, Hanley, and Simmons (1972, 1973), suggesting a relative lack of coherence between symmetrical regions of the two hemispheres in dyslexic children during a reading task, is a strong contribution to the concept of "poorly established cerebral dominance" as a factor in dyslexia. Studies relating EEG correlates to hand or eye preferences and studies of the resting (as opposed to working, task-specific) state are less likely to illuminate the meaning of cerebral dominance.

The issue of heredity has been addressed in an EEG study (VERs) in adults who had participated in a family study (Finucci et al., 1976) by virtue of each adult subject having at least one child with reading disability (Preston et al., 1976). In this study, adult familial "dyslexic" subjects showed diminished word-minus-flash differences at P3 (left parietal electrode) but equalled controls with their 100 percent word recognition accuracy. Because this result was obtained in adults performing the task in question *without* difficulty, it is of interest with respect to the issue of cerebral dominance, in the sense of demonstrating a lesser linguistic-processing specialization on the left in this particular group.

SUMMARY

Thus far, as reflected in the "state-of-the-art" paper of Hughes, the EEG has been used to attempt intergroup discrimination. Unfortunately, inadequate clinical description and definition of groups have characterized most studies. Even the EEG data contribution toward definition of groups has been limited by (1) choice of recording and/or reporting restricted or even selected single-lead placements; (2) single or ill-defined psychophysical condition(s) of EEG recording; and (3) naive statistical analysis—all of which reflect commitments to a *priori* "intuitively reasonable" hypothesis-making with respect to the physiological meaningfulness of the EEG. A laudable exception to this commentary is the study of Sklar, Hanley, and Simmons (1972). As yet there have been no studies addressed to the issue of EEG in individual/group membership discrimination, i.e., diagnosis. With the availability of computers, statistical designs, and complex pattern recognition techniques, it is not unreasonable to expect that spectral analysis of multiple spatial/temporal EEG components may become a useful diagnostic instrument for the subtle, multifactorial disorders now know collectively as "learning disabilities."

Chapter 12

CRITICAL REVIEW OF "ELECTROENCEPHALOGRAPHIC AND NEUROPHYSIOLOGICAL STUDIES IN DYSLEXIA"

C. KEITH CONNERS

I. INTRODUCTION

The EEG has been a valuable clinical tool for the detection of brain abnormalities and by now has achieved a firm place in scientific studies of brain function. Hughes, as one of the investigators most responsible for rigorous applications of the EEG in investigatory work, tries to establish the link between dyslexia and the EEG by first arguing that there is a general association between clinical EEG findings and the degree of clinical severity of a variety of behavioral and cognitive disorders. Although each of these clinical entities has their own problems of definition, there can be little doubt that, as a broad proposition, the more severe the impairment of the cognitive or other brain function, the more likely the EEG will have been shown to detect abnormality.

This finding makes it natural to assume that the EEG should show abnormality for a condition such as dyslexia which, although subtle diagnostically, almost certainly represents some form of alteration of brain development, function, or structure. However, problems in verifying this proposition are encountered on both sides of the equation: the definition of what constitutes a clinical "abnormality"; and what constitutes dyslexia. My own conclusion after reading the detailed supporting evidence, is that the clinical EEG has *not* been established as a correlate of dyslexia, although certain more recent computerized analyses of the EEG tracing do show promise of important association.

II. THE EVIDENCE FOR CLINICAL
EEG-DYSLEXIA ASSOCIATION

Hughes cites 10 papers which give a percentage of abnormality ranging from 27 to 88 percent, in which four studies containing controls each show significantly more abnormality among the dyslexics. The first things that strikes one's attention about these data is the wide range of estimates of abnormality—so wide, in fact, as to call into question the validity of the basic conclusion or at least to raise the question of whether "abnormality" and "dyslexia" can have the same meaning across these studies. In statistical terms, the variance *between* studies is larger than the variance within studies which compare controls and dyslexics.

It is entertaining to note that if one computes the Spearman rank-order correlation between the percent abnormality in a study and the year in which the study was completed, we get a *rho* equal to −0.91. That is, the more recent the study, the smaller the degree of abnormality reported in the EEGs of dyslexics. Such a finding might be interpreted as showing that definitions of dylexia have changed over time in such a way as to progressively eliminate those forms of the disorder involving disturbed brain physiology; or alternatively, that more rigorous modern investigations have eliminated sources of artifact in the correlations. Another feature of these studies apparent from Hughes's Table 10-5, is that the types of abnormality have varied from study to study. The finding of so many different types of abnormality either leads to a conclusion that dyslexia is associated with multifaceted derangements of brain physiology, or that different types of dyslexia were being investigated, or that the measures are unreliable. The many types are an embarrassment of riches as far as any conclusions are concerned regarding sources of brain dysfunction which can be inferred from the clinical EEG.

Let us examine the individual pieces of evidence upon which the overall conclusion is drawn, examining those reports available which Hughes has cited in support of an EEG-dyslexia relationship. Webb and Lawson (1956) reported on 41 children "with severe speech retardation or severe reading disabilities" selected from a group of "6 to 700 children, on the basis that although the disabilities were severe and despite careful investigation, no other neurological, organic, emotional or intellectual impairment was uncovered." This sample thus includes a group with a *dual* handicap, including severe speech disorders, and any generalizations regarding dyslexia alone are impossible. The EEG readings were nonblind and criteria for dyslexia are not indicated.

Cohn (1961) studied 46 children between 7 and 10 years who were "considered to show 'specific' reading and writing difficulties by the school authorities. An associated phenomenon in nearly all of these subjects was aggressive, inappropriate, antisocial behavior." Two control groups were used; one was a group of 130 randomly chosen children in normal schoolroom classes between the ages of 6 and 12 years; the other a group of 7½ to 14 year-old children with reading difficulties who had been retained in normal classrooms and were working under normal pedagogical discipline. It is notable that neither the patients nor the controls are described with respect to SES or other demographic background variables. EEG analyses were non-blind, nonquantitative, and reported in general terms. The groups were clearly not matched for age. It seems safe to assume that referrals from school authorities of children with both learning problems and aggres-sive, antisocial behavior include a very heterogeneous mixture of problems, many of which might cause learning backwardness, and some of which would be secondary to learning defects, or related to social class or school op-portunity factors. This study would have had to include a control group of aggressive, antisocial subjects without reading disability for the EEG to have meaning for dyslexics per se.

Knott et al. (1965) reported on a series of 50 children "with a mean reading retardation of 2.5 years." There is some confusion in the report be-cause the authors refer to 19 of 50 EEGs being normal (62% abnormal), but later say that, "Thus, it appears that reading disability is associated with ab-normal EEGs (total abnormal 84%)." The study employed no controls and nonblind EEG analyses.

In a different report in the same year, the same authors (Muehl, Knott, and Benton, 1964–5) report on a sample of 59 patients, with chrono-logical ages between 7–6 and 15–9, and reading retardation levels ranging from 0.6 to 7.2 grades. Eleven of the subjects also had behavior problems (using as a criterion previous referral to a psychiatric clinic). These problem children did not differ from the nonproblem children in presence of EEG abnormality. No relationship was found between the degree of reading re-tardation and type of EEG abnormality or severity. This latter finding is peculiar, given the very wide range of "reading retardation." There was also no relationship between WISC profiles and EEG abnormality.

In a follow-up study of 43 of these children five years later, the same group (Muehl and Forell, 1973–74) found that "(a) poor readers in elementary and junior high school, as a group, continued to be poor readers in high school five years after diagnosis; (b) there was no relationship among EEG classifications at diagnosis and high school reading, although a consistent trend favoring the reading performance of the abnormal-other EEG group compared to the abnormal positive-spike and normal EEG groups was observed at both testing periods." Hughes has commented on the paradoxical finding that the outcome of the abnormal EEG group is more favorable than that for poor readers with normal EEGs; but even if the present finding was statistically significant, the meaning would be hard to interpret. In contrast to the EEG, the WISC Verbal IQ and age at diagnosis were related to later outcome, a fact which makes the earlier report of nonassociation between EEG and WISC pattern more pointed.

Ayres and Torres (1967) performed a more sophisticated study than those previously described. They restricted their sample to third-grade students from a large metropolitan school system, thus making their sample groups homogeneous for age and school experience. Group 1 consisted of 129 subjects with reading difficulties who were referred for comprehensive diagnosis of their special learning disabilities, but also included hyperactive and inattentive children. Group 2 was 31 subjects randomly selected from a list of children awaiting placement in remedial reading classes (IQ 90, 2 years retarded in reading, teacher referral). Group 3 was a control group of 53 children selected through a stratified random sampling procedure, of whom 47 were admitted for study. They found that the two clinical groups did not differ from each other (47% and 55% abnormality for clinical and reading groups), and both differed from the controls (29% abnormality). They further showed that 55 percent of children in the bottom quartile of reading achievement among the normals had abnormal EEGs, while the remaining $3/4$ of the control group had a 20 percent rate.

Since all subjects were referred to the encephalographer as "learning problems," the readings were in effect done blindly with respect to knowledge of diagnosis. No breakdown of type of abnormality is provided in the report, and the criteria for abnormality are unspecified. There is no way of knowing whether children waiting for remedial reading are comparable to dyslexics and whether either group suffers from associated clinical problems or neurological involvement, though a later abstract of the same study (Torres and Ayer, 1968) mentions that the clinical groups had "only minor neurological abnormalities." One other comment not reported in the earlier paper was that there was 76 percent concordance between interpretations when the records were read a second time after an interval of 15–36 months. It is rare that attempts are made at specifying reliability of clinical EEG readings, either as test-retest as in this case, or in terms of interobserver agreement.

Hughes and Park (1968) conducted an extensive investigation of the correlates of normal-abnormal EEG readings in 157 subjects referred to the Dyslexia Memorial Institute of Chicago "because of reading disability detected in school." The subjects varied in age from 7 to 18 years. The criteria for determining dyslexia are described as follows: "Children were usually accepted by the Institute for intensive study if the Full-Scale IQ . . . was at least 85 and if the reading retardation was considered at least 1½ years as determined by the California Reading Test." However, the *average* for the sample was only 1.5 grades retardation in reading, with a standard deviation of about 1.6 grades, suggesting that the sample would include a number of children (over 6%, assuming a symmetrical normal distribution) with *no* reading difficulty. In any case the overall rate of abnormality for the sample was 36 percent (which is only slightly different from the incidence found in the normal controls of the Torres and Ayres study of 29%) and there were no differences in reading levels between the normal and abnormal EEG groups.

Myklebust et al. (1969) reported one of the most carefully controlled and extensive investigations. The initial report describes a study done on 99 learning-disability subjects, 99 matched controls, 101 borderline learning disabilities, and 101 matched controls for the latter group. Subject selection and matching were done with careful attention to many relevant variables, and learning disability was specified in terms of objective criteria. The reliability of EEG interpretations was extremely high and clearly documented.

Despite these ideal conditions of study, *no difference in any EEG variable was found between controls and learning-disabled subjects.* This applied to an overall index of abnormality as well as to 14 subtypes of abnormality. One small .05 level difference appeared between the borderline subjects and their controls in the frequency of focal slow waves. The same negative findings were reported for a rank-ordering by learning quotients for reading, nonverbal, and mixed types of learning disability. Again, the only effect was a single finding of greater abnormality in the borderline group (of the nonverbal type) compared with their controls. Discriminant analysis once again confirmed that *it was the less severe disabilities, particularly the nonverbal types, where differences between those with and without abnormal EEGs were discerned.* The authors state that the findings indicate that "An implication might be that when the brain involvement is on the right hemisphere, the

257

EEG more often reveals dysfunctioning." In any case, this study would seem to virtually eliminate any conclusion of greater abnormality of the EEG among poor readers, when such subjects are defined in the manner employed in this study. By virtue of its greater methodological sophistication, the Myklebust study would appear to carry more weight than the many less rigorous investigations in the literature.

In a more complete report of the same study, Hughes (1971) found that there was a 41.2 percent abnormality in the underachiever group vs. 29.8 percent in the matched controls, a difference which is highly significant. However, this difference is entirely accounted for by the borderline, rather than the severe, underachievers. Further analyses reveal that *combinations* of disabilities (e.g. reading *and* arithmetic) were significantly associated with EEG abnormality compared with the control groups. Analyses also reveal that much of the variance is contributed by those subjects with deficiencies in perceptual-motor (nonverbal) functions. But the fact still remains that reading disability *per se* is not significantly associated with EEG abnormality, and the statement that "No single test (nonacademic or academic) given during the screening procedure or during the intensive examinations was found to correlate significantly with abnormality in the EEG . . ." must surely put to rest any likelihood that the clinical EEG can detect reading disorder *in the absence of other disabilities.*

Ingram, Mason, and Blackburn (1970) reported a study of 82 highly selected reading-disabled children, on whom 38 EEGs were obtained. The study is not clear in indicating how those given EEGs were selected. The authors note that 62 of the 82 subjects met an operational criterion for dyslexia: "children who, in the absence of low intelligence, emotional disturbance or adverse environmental (especially educational) factors, experience difficulty in learning to read and spell, although they perform satisfactorily in school subjects independent of reading—particularly in mechanical arithmetic."

These "specifics" as they are called were found to have significantly *less* EEG abnormality than the "generals" (66% normal vs. 16% normal, respectively). The authors state their conclusion that, "In spite of the fact that evidence of brain damage was more often, though not exclusively, associated with general learning difficulties, it was not associated with a greater degree of difficulty in learning to read. In fact the reverse was the case. . . . All these findings show that the assumption that specific dyslexia must be associated with organic brain defect is unfounded." This study is the only one besides the Hughes's studies that carefully delineates reading disability from other types of learning disability; it clearly weighs against any findings of an association between EEG abnormality and dyslexia once associated neurological or general learning defects are separated out.

In a rather complex drug-treatment study, Fenelon et al. (1972) compared reading disability ($N = 33$), behavior problems ($N = 14$), and normal controls ($N = 12$). EEGs were read blind. The authors claim to find approximately 27 percent abnormality in the reading-disabled group which is less than that reported in some studies for normal controls. Most importantly, however, the reading-disabled group age range is 25 months lower at one end and 15 months higher at the other end of the distribution compared with the normals. The latter were also clearly unmatched for SES, and, as the authors state, "In social and intellectual status, this group was strongly biased, containing mainly children of professional colleagues." The obtained EEG differences were mainly "dysrhythmias" (7 cases) and focal spikes and sharp waves (6 cases). The authors define a dysrhythmic record as one with "brief episodes, usually of less than one second duration, of higher voltage 2–4 Hz activity seen over both hemispheres synchronously, maximal frontally or posteriorly. These often occur immediately following eye closure, without associated spike activity, which, if it occurred, would type them definitely as epileptic episodes." It is not clear but entirely possible that these abnormalities might be related to age characteristics of the sample. The blind reading of the EEG is somewhat vitiated by the imbalance in the number of cases since, if the encephalographer was aware of the proportion of poor readers, a simple bias in base rate of seeing abnormality would give a greater chance for representation in the larger group.

III. SUMMARY AND CONCLUSIONS

In summary, we find the following issues revealed by detailed examination of the supporting data for the general conclusion of an association between EEG abnormality and dyslexia:

1. Most studies employ nonblind readings of unknown reliability;

2. Studies vary in the definition of the dyslexic group;

3. Studies frequently do not rule out associated condtions such as behavior problems or neurological abnormalities;

4. Matching of experimental and control samples is usually poor, and where it is good there is no EEG-reading association;

5. More recent and well-controlled studies show significantly less abnormality than is reported for earlier studies;

6. The range of degree-of-abnormality reported is too large to inspire confidence in the reliability of the findings;

7. No consistent findings have appeared with respect to either the locus or type of abnormality associated with dyslexia;

8. In the cases where follow-up evaluations of EEG-studied dyslexics were performed, the EEG contributes nothing to prediction of outcome;

9. There are several instances where the greater degree of abnormality of the EEG is associated with the milder conditions of the reading disorder;

10. There are several instances where the greater degree of abnormality among the dyslexics is less than that found in other studies among controls.

Our own interpretation of these studies cited by Hughes is that they lend little support to the main conclusion, and in fact can be just as easily interpreted as showing the *absence* of EEG abnormalities among dyslexics. The better controlled studies in particular lead to this interpretation. Whether this latter "hardline" interpretation is accepted or not, we would argue that at least the positive association cannot be accepted as proven. The most plausible interpretation, in our opinion, is that the various studies find EEG abnormality in proportion to the extent to which various associated conditions, such as behavior or neurological abnormalities, are included in the samples.

IV. RELATIONSHIP OF DYSLEXIA TO OTHER ELECTROCORTICAL MEASURES

A number of studies have established that the evoked potential can be used to measure differential processing of verbal and nonverbal information, and that such differences are related to hemispheric specialization for language (Begleiter and Platz, 1969; Buchsbaum and Fedio, 1969; Brown et al., 1973; Buchsbaum and Fedio, 1970; Calloway, 1975, pp. 96–111; Cohn, 1971; Conners, 1971; Crowell et al., 1973; Davis and Wada, 1974; Friedman et al., 1975; Galambos et al., 1975; Haaland, 1974; Harmony et al., 1973; Matsumiya et al., 1972; Morrell and Salamy, 1971; Preston et al., 1974; Wood et al., 1971). Not all of these studies are consistent in the nature and direction of their findings, but they appear to have one important element in common which differentiates the results from the previous studies on the EEG; namely, that an active challenge to the brain is investigated. Where that challenge involves verbal or semantic stimuli, effects are likely to show clearer localization of function, especially over the angular gyrus (Preston et al., 1974; Conners, 1971). Other studies, which use power spectral analyses and coherence measures, also find differences between dyslexics and normals (Sklar et al., 1972, 1973) and some work with the CNV also finds reliable differences among dyslexics and controls when semantic stimuli are employed (Fenelon, 1968).

Thus it would appear that electrocortical measures are capable of isolating processes involved in reading when specific processing demands made and recorded by appropriate averaging techniques. It can be anticipated that these methods will provide greater insight into the pathophysiology of dyslexia as further studies are continued.

Part V

GENETIC FACTORS

Chapter 13

DYSLEXIA– GENETIC ASPECTS

FREYA W. OWEN

BACKGROUND INFORMATION

In 1900 James Hinshelwood was preparing his paper on congenital work blindness. In the earlier papers he had described four "distinct varieties" of letter and word blindness. In this paper he was detailing yet another variety and at that point he ventured to state that the subject was not yet exhausted. Hinshelwood was surgeon to the Glasgow Eye Infirmary and Assistant to the Professor of Clinical Medicine at the University of Glascow. With this professional background it is not surprising that his major interest in congenital word blindness focused on his patient's visual disabilities.

He observed that the trouble the patient experienced in learning to read arose from the fact that his visual memory for words and letters was congenitally defective. He stated "I have shown that there is a definite cerebral area within which these visual memories of words and letters are registered— the angular and supramarginal gyri. If there be any abnormality within this area due either to injury at birth or to defective development, it is easily conceivable how such an individual should experience great difficulty in learning to read." As he continued to study individual clinical cases he observed the familial incidence of the problem.

An earlier writer in the field was Pringle Morgan who in 1896 published a case study of congenital word blindness. He observed that it was most probably due to "defective development of that region of the brain, disease in which in adults produces practically the same symptoms, that is the left angular gyrus." Thus we see that two of the early papers on the topic were very specific about the anatomical location of this dysfunction.

A number of investigators in the field credit Thomas (1905) with the first speculations about the possibility of hereditary causes for congenital word blindness. Thomas was a school physician affiliated with the London County Counsel Education Authority. In 1905 he stated "It is to be noted that it frequently assumes a family type. There are a number of incidents of more than one member of the family being affected and the mother often volunteers the statement that she herself was unable to read, although she had every opportunity." He followed this by observing that congenital word blindness occurred considerably more frequently in boys than girls. So much so, that among those initial cases recorded in England, all were boys. In fact, he indicated that some investigators had stated that it was a disability only occurring in the male sex. Thomas himself, had recorded some cases in females and suggested that approximately 25 percent of those suffering from word blindness were girls. He made an additional observation of considerable importance; namely, that the condition was associated with extremely good visual memory for things other than words. Many of the children were what psychologists term strong in visual capabilities, and yet had no visual memory for "ideographs."

In the United States in 1930, Samuel Orton pointed out that two or more cases of various language disorders, such as reading and writing disabilities and speech defects, as well as left-handedness, were often found in the same family. Orton suggested that there was a genetic association among these disorders. He stressed that one of the disorders may occur as an isolated phenomenon in several generations of one family, but that in the majority of families, there are also left-handed individuals who have none of the disorders. Orton gave an account of nine selected families in which one or more language disorder and/or left-handedness occurred in different members of the same family in three or four successive generations. In two families he reported direct inheritance of specific reading disability in two generations. He emphasized, however, that the histories were too incomplete to permit any unequivocal conclusions. Orton observed that language disorders were more common among boys than girls. He postulated a sex-influenced inheritance but rejected the possibility of a sex-linked mode of inheritance.

Eustis (1947a, b) considered that specific language disabilities including left-handedness or ambidexterity, unusual body clumsiness, late development of speech, speech defects, and reading disability must develop from some common and underlying cause. He based his conclusions on a study of a family complex comprising 33 members, all of whom were over the age of two. He had known every member of the family personally and had studied most of the members of the fourth and some of the third generation. In these families, he reported 14 out of the 33 or 42 percent of the members over the age of two and 25 or 48 percent over the age of six showed one or more of the disabilities. He concluded that these conditions were inherited.

Norrie reported that she had observed specific dyslexia in "practically all" the parents of those children with specific dyslexia whom she had examined. Kagen (1943) stated that he had found a familial occurrence of specific dyslexia in 30 percent of his cases, and Ramer (1947) reported that he obtained a history of the familial occurrence of this disorder in 50–60 percent of his cases.

TWIN STUDIES

Comparisons between monozygotic and dizygotic twins have often been used to study the possible contributions of environmental and genetic factors in childhood disorders. If a disease occurs with far greater frequency in monozygotic than in dizygotic twins, the genetic influence would seem to outweigh environmental factors. The Danish investigator Knud Hermann (1959) summarized the results of twin studies in the area of congenital word blindness. He reported that Hallgren had six sets of twins: three monozygotic, all of whom were concordant, and three dizygotic, one concordant and two discordant. In 1954, Edith Norrie supplied additional cases—a total of 7 monozygotic and 21 dizygotic sets of twins. When data from these two sources were summed up and when four sets of twins—one monozygotic and three dizygotic—from the Word Blind Institute in Copenhagen were added, Hermann reported that 11 monozygotic sets of twins were 100 percent concordant and 27 dizygotic sets of twins were 33 percent concordant (i.e., only in 9 sets of dizygotic twins were both persons word-blind). Hermann stated that these figures show with "all desirable clarity" that congenital word blindness is hereditarily conditioned.

Hermann went on to observe that the fundamental disturbance in congenital word blindness was the same as that of Gerstmann's syndrome. The major symptoms of Gerstmann's syndrome include right-left confusion, finger agnosia, dyscalculia, and agraphia. He suggested that there was a fundamental disorder of the patient's idea of direction in space and that word-blind persons more frequently than normal readers showed uncertainty in the discrimination between right and left and in the naming of the fingers, a factor

269

which he felt further supported the theory that the functional disturbance in Gerstmann's syndrome and in congenital word blindness was the same. He further concluded that the underdevelopment of the patient's idea of direction in space was transmitted by dominant genes.

BERTIL HALLGREN'S WORK

Among the most notable studies relating congenital word blindness to hereditary factors was the work of Bertil Hallgren (1950). Hallgren's study was carried out in the Psychiatric Clinic of the Karolinska Institute in Stockholm, Sweden during the years 1947–1950. Hallgren used the term "specific dyslexia" to denote the disorder which earlier had been referred to in the medical literature as "congenital word blindness." He preferred the term dyslexia because the reading difficulty was the main symptom of the disorder. He qualified the term "specific" since his definition was based on symptoms alone, and he did not wish to include the etiology of the disorder in his definition. In Hallgren's investigation, the following criteria were laid down for a positive diagnosis of specific dyslexia:

1. Difficulties in learning to read and write;
2. Reading and writing proficiency during the first years at school definitely below the average of the class the child attended (before a possible assignment to a reading class or failure to obtain a pass to a higher class);
3. A definite discrepancy between proficiency in reading and writing and in other school subjects;
4. A definite discrepancy between proficiency in reading and writing and the child's general intelligence.

Hallgren stated that he did not find it possible to define the syndrome of specific dyslexia more exactly. Therefore, there was no sharp borderline between the cases of specific dyslexia and other cases of reading disorder.

The goals of Hallgren's study were as follows:

1. To determine the possible existence of one or more hereditary form of specific dyslexia;

2. In the event that the disorder proved to be hereditary, to make a genetic statistical analysis and to determine the mode of inheritance;
3. To make a clinical analysis of specific dyslexia with special regard to certain physical, mental, and environmental factors.

He selected his sample from two different sources. The first of these was the clinic at the Karolinska Institute. He studied the card indexes of the clinic and then selected those cases that were registered under the diagnoses of speech defects and reading and writing disabilities. He further screened the list and excluded children who suffered from speech defects, but had no reading problems. In addition, it was necessary to exclude children with no siblings of school age. After talking to teachers and parents, he found 81 cases belonging to 77 families in the clinic population. His second subject pool was the middle school (junior high school) located in Stockholm. All pupils registered on a medical certificate as word-blind were included in the sample. Thus 22 additional cases were added to the basic clinic sample. In order to collect his control cases, every third boy and every second girl in the three lowest classes were selected for investigation, regardless of whether they were registered as dyslexics. He later discovered that nine of these subjects were registered as dyslexics. He, therefore, included them in the experimental sample.

Hallgren himself interviewed the families. Included in his case history were the delivery and circumstances surrounding the birth of the child, development during childhood and adolescence, the development of motor functions and speech, nervous symptoms, behavior problems, handedness, auditory and visual defects, head injuries, mental disorders, social adaptability, age at which school was started, attitude to school and school work, school reports, difficulties at school, and the repetition of classes or assignment to special classes. The children were given visual tests, hearing tests, and individual tests for side dominance. A neurological examination was made on 72 out of the 79 experimental subjects and 34 of their siblings. Individual intelligence tests were available for the clinic population. The children from the school sample were tested for the study. Hallgren reports that the children's reading, writing, and spelling abilities were carefully evaluated. He does not, however, provide standardized test information on these abilities for his sample.

His series, then, consisted altogether of 112 families. In order to carry out a Mendelian genetic analysis, he divided his sample into three separate groups—(1) the parent mating affected × affected, which was present in 3 percent of his cases (Group 1); (2) the parent mating affected × unaffected (Group 2) was found in 80 percent of the families; and (3) the parent mating unaffected × unaffected (Group 3) which accounted for 17 percent of the sample. He concluded that the occurrence of a large percentage of affected parents spoke in favor of a dominant mode of inheritance. The occurrence of a heredity disorder in three or more successive generations also argued in favor of a dominant mode. He did admit that difficulties might be encountered in making an analysis of dyslexia over several generations. Obviously, it would be virtually impossible to carry out direct studies on the grandparents of a significant number of the affected children in the sample. Hallgren, however, concluded that his interview data were sufficiently strong to allow him to decide that direct inheritance could be demonstrated in three generations in a large number of the families in his sample. Thus he felt that these data spoke in favor of a dominant mode of inheritance.

When Hallgren carried out the Mendelian analysis on his three groups, he reported that the number of families in the affected × affected parent mating group was so small (three families) that it would not permit a calculation of the Mendelian ratio. In the overwhelming majority of his families, in 90 out of 112, the parent mating was affected × unaffected. With that group Hallgren stated the theoretical expectation for the Mendelian ratio would be 50 percent, provided that the affected parent was heterozygous for the dominant gene. Expecting 50 percent, he reported that the clinic population analyses yielded 47.7 percent and the school population 39 percent. When he combined the clinic and the school, the reported ratio was 45.7 percent. A study of these figures shows that the Mendelian ratios were somewhat lower in the school sample than in the clinic sample. Hallgren suggested that this might be attributable to the fact that he was unable to diagnose all the cases of specific dyslexia in this sample. Moreover, he reported that the children from the school sample came from affluent families and were of high intelligence. He therefore speculated that the children's problems might have been ameliorated at an early age and that they would not have been identified as dyslexic by the time they reached the middle school. The difference between observed Mendelian ratios for the clinic sample and the school sample, however, was not significant.

Hallgren concluded that the genetic statistical analyses showed that specific dyslexia with a high degree of probability followed a dominant mode of inheritance. He believed that dyslexia is determined by an alternate form of a gene, which is placed on a chromosome other than a sex chromosome, with the character being dominant.

RECENT STUDIES

Sladen (1971), on the other hand, utilizing Hallgren's familial data, speculated that the character has variable dominance in males and that it is largely recessive in females. She further made the interesting observation that matings among dyslexics may not be random since her work suggested that dyslexics tend to group together.

While Hallgren found little inequality in the sex distribution in his sample, Sladen disagreed with his interpretations of the data. Although there were 89 boys and 27 girls in his original sample of dyslexics, when he examined the children's parents and siblings, there was only a small, though significant, excess of males. Hallgren attributed the 3 to 1 ratio of males to females in his original sample as being due to greater parental concern for their sons with school problems.

Finucci et al. (1976) have recently completed a familial study of specific reading disability. Twenty disabled readers, including 15 boys and 5 girls ranging from 8 to 11 years of age, were identified for the study. Among the families of the probands there were 86 first-degree relatives. Seventy-five of these family members were examined to determine the prevalence of reading disability within the families. Forty-five percent of the first-degree relatives were affected and there was a significantly greater number of affected male than female relatives. After inspecting the pedigrees of the families, the investigators concluded that no single mode of genetic transmission was evident. They suggested that the disorder is genetically heterogeneous and that various subgroups of disabled readers should be more fully investigated.

LEARNING DISORDERS IN CHILDREN: SIBLING STUDIES

In 1971 Owen et al. published the results of their familial studies of learning disabilities. The studies had two major purposes: (1) to discover whether the characteristics of academically handicapped children could be more precisely identified and described; (2) to clarify further the causes and the familial patterns of learning disabilities. These authors did not specifically utilize the term "dyslexia." The learning-handicapped children were referred to as educationally handicapped (EH). As used in the study, the term referred to children with a significant discrepancy between ability and school achievement (1.5–2 years below grade-level expectancy in spelling and/or reading and with an IQ of 90 or above on the WISC Full Scale. The problems related to developing a good operational definition for learning disability have been discussed by many investigators. The decision to select a sample on the basis of reading and spelling disability has the advantage of being relatively unambiguous. On the other hand, it has the disadvantage related to the different meanings of "below grade level" functioning at different age levels. In the Palo Alto Unified School District in California, where the children in this study were enrolled, there is a special remedial program for educationally handicapped (EH) pupils. At the time of the study approximately 2 percent of the school district population were being selected for this remedial help. Hence, the children represented a rather severely impaired group academically.

The remedial population in the school district was screened to locate EH students with same-sex siblings of school age. After written permission was obtained from the parents for their children to participate, the EH children were given individual intelligence tests to see whether they would meet the criterion of a WISC Full Scale IQ of 90 or above.

Once having selected an appropriate EH-HS pair we located a successful academic (SA) child with an appropriate sibling to match the EH pair. We tested 184 children in order to locate the 76 matched sets of EH and SA children included in the study. Of the 76 EH subjects, 64 were located from within the population of remedial children. Twelve subjects were recommended by school principals and guidance consultants.

Some of the siblings of the EH and SA children were older and some were younger. There were, however, no significant differences in the distribution of older and younger siblings between the EH and control groups, nor was ordinal position within the family significantly related to learning disability. Data obtained from parent interviews and school records indicated that the EH and control groups did not significantly differ in socioeconomic level, ethnic background, or fathers' educational level.

All the children in the study were given psychological and educational evaluations and a pediatric neurologist examined all EH, EHS, and SA children. Following the medical examinations, the children's mothers were interviewed by a physician to obtain the family medical history and signed releases for hospital birth records on the children. Twenty-five quartets (EH-EHS, SA-SAS) were given EEG evaluations.

School behavior ratings of the children were obtained on all children. The mothers and fathers were interviewed separately and a reading test was administered to them. In addition, their high school transcripts were secured.

As indicated, the relative academic performance in reading and spelling and the intellectual level was determined at the time of selection for the EH and the successful academic (SA) control. On the other hand, the academic capabilities and ability levels of the siblings, by design, were unknown at the time they were selected for the study. A number of comparisons between EH and SA and EHS and SAS were related to our speculation that there would be significant similarities between the educationally handicapped children and their siblings.

When we examined the reading and spelling performance of the EH siblings, we discovered that they were indeed significantly lower in both reading and spelling when compared with the SA controls. The EH siblings were slightly below grade-level expectancy in reading, while the SA children and their siblings were almost a year above grade-level expectancy. In the spelling area, the educationally handicapped children's siblings were almost a year below grade-level expectancy. It has been repeatedly noted (Walker and Cole, 1965) that spelling is a more sensitive indicator of language disability than reading in an adult population, possibly because fewer and apparently less effective methods for compensation are available.

Longitudinal studies of the intellectual development of related individuals (Honzik, 1957; McCall, 1970; Wilson, 1972) would lead us to expect high positive relationships with respect to both the levels and patterns of intellectual development among our sibling groups. Examination of our data indicates that the subtest scores of the EH children and their siblings were highly correlated on tests that involve verbal ability requiring conceptualization and verbal expression, namely comprehension and similarities, while for the SA children and their siblings, the correlations on these subtests were not significant. The SA children and their siblings, however, had a high correlation on the information subtest.

On the WISC Performance Scale, scores on the object assembly and coding subtests for the EH children and their siblings were more highly correlated than were these scores for the SA children and their siblings. These two tests are thought to measure perceptual-motor functioning and eye-hand coordination. Although the correlation between both pairs of siblings on IQ scores were significant, they were slightly higher for the EH pairs.

If specific reading disabilities are familial and/or genetic, we would anticipate that the language or learning disabilities would be present in the parents during adult life. It was therefore predicted that the fathers and mothers of the EH children would perform more poorly on the reading tests and that their high school English grades would be significantly poorer than those of the parents of the SA children. Examination of our data on the parents indicates that the fathers of the SA children had the most superior reading scores. The mothers of the SA children were the second highest. The fathers of the EH children were third and the mothers of the EH children obtained the lowest scores. The differences between the EH and SA fathers were significant. The difference between the mothers approached significance. The grades in English courses at the high school level also differentiated the parents, the SA children's parents having significantly higher grades. In mathematics, there were no significant differences between the fathers. The EH mothers, however, were significantly poorer than the SA mothers. Thus there is little doubt that the parents of the EH children had academic problems in the language areas when they were in school, which persisted in adulthood to some degree.

These findings for the mothers in our sample are both provocative and intriguing. Critchley (1964) has documented studies from 1927 to 1950 carried out in different parts of the Western World, comparing the percentages of boys and girls diagnosed as suffering from specific learning or language disabilities. The percentages of males he reports range from a low of 66 percent through a high of 100 percent. The percentage for females is the reciprocal, i.e., 0–34%. The combined data of these studies would suggest that about four males to one female may be accepted as a reasonable figure. Our data, on the other hand, would suggest the presence of a significant reading and learning disability among the *mothers* as well as the fathers in our learning handicapped sample.

A number of investigators, including Vernon (1957), have questioned the higher incidence of language and reading disabilities among males. She believed that the preponderance of boys was due to the fact that nonreading boys create more trouble at school than do nonreading girls, or at least bring their disability more forcibly to the teacher's notice. Further, it has been suggested that parents are more alarmed by inability to read in a boy than in a girl. Pilot studies by Owen and Adams (1964) suggested that girls identified for remedial reading programs were less able intellectually than boys. Owen speculated that in order to come to the attention of a remedial program, a disabled girl needed to be both disabled in her reading ability and less able intellectually. At any rate, the results of our studies of the parents of the learning-disordered children plainly suggest that the mothers of these children suffered from reading and learning disabilities of at least the same degree of severity that the fathers experienced.

These findings were confirmed independently during the medical interviews with the mothers of the EH children: 22 of the mothers reported having learning disabilities during their own school years; 18 of the mothers reported that their husbands had had learning difficulties at school. Only four mothers in the SA family stated that they had school difficulties, and nine identified their husbands as having learning problems. Thus, the results of the adult reading tests, the high school transcripts, and the medical interview data provide strong learning-disorder histories among the mothers of the educationally handicapped children in our sample.

A comprehensive neurological examination was administered to all of the subjects by the same pediatric neurologist and we were able to compare our educationally handicapped subjects and their siblings. We predicted that some of the neurological immaturities or "soft" neurological signs would be common to both EH and his or her sibling. These speculations were supported by our data, since the children were remarkably similar in their performance across a wide range of tasks that were presented to them by the neurologist. Their similarity of impairment was apparent on auditory tapped patterns, on right-left discrimination, on extinction to double simultaneous tactile stimulation, and on fast alternating finger and hand movement tests.

Forty-seven percent of the EH children were identified as having significant speech and language variations. The physician talked to the mothers about the amount of time that they read to their children and how well their children attended. The mothers of 20 EH families reported poor attention in one or both of their children. Only five SA mothers stated that their children could not sit and listen. Mothers were also asked which child they found easier to talk to. Twenty-eight mothers reported a difference between the EH child and the sibling. In 26 cases the EH child was more difficult to talk to than the sibling. Only six SA mothers noted that one sibling was easier to talk to than the other. These reports by mothers of high distractability and poor attention for stories in preschool EH children may well be precursors of later language disabilities.

We examined medical histories obtained from the parents as well as the hospital birth records of the children. These records were obtained in over 75 percent of our population. Of the 264 subjects examined, only four children were found to have definitive signs of neurological abnormality. Three

277

were EH children and one was an SA child. We did not find that possible prenatal, neonatal, or postnatal insults were significantly more frequent in the EH population. Our population had very few premature births and no relationship to birth weight was found. In individual cases, however, the direct relationship of such complications to neurological abnormality was apparent.

SUBGROUPS

In an attempt to improve our understanding of the variables related to learning disabilities, we examined the children on the basis of their possible membership in one or more of the following subcategories: Relatively high incidence of medical neurological findings; relatively large WISC Verbal vs. Performance discrepancy; social deviancy; relatively high WISC Full Scale IQ; and relatively low WISC Full Scale IQ. The reason for selecting these particular subgroups for analysis was related to the diverse characteristics of the total learning-disability population included in this project. Since the children were selected on the basis of a simple discrepancy between reading and spelling ability and normal intellectual capability, it was assumed that this sample would include children with learning and/or behavior disorders. It was hoped that analyses of these subcategories would help to clarify some of the relationships among biological and psychological factors. Applebee (1971) has reviewed earlier unsuccessful attempts to investigate the possibility of stable subgroups within such a sample. As might be expected, we discovered that there was considerable overlap among these subcategories. Only 32 of the children fell exclusively into one category. Twenty children did not fall into any of the categories. At present, this group can only be described by statements about what their characteristics did not include.

The children in each subgroup were compared statistically with their siblings and with their SA controls. Subgroups were not statistically compared with other subgroups because of the overlap. One subgroup is of particular interest in relation to the familial aspects of reading disorders. This is the group identified as the relatively high Verbal vs. Performance IQ discrepancy group. Twenty children in our sample had a positive Performance discrepancy of fifteen or more points on the WISC. These were children with outstanding abilities in dealing with spatial relationships. Of this group, 80 percent were male. Their mean Full Scale WISC IQ was 108.5 and that of their siblings 106.2. Forty-five percent of the children in this group and 35 percent of their siblings had speech problems and received therapy in school. Their speech difficulties seemed to be related to an inability to reproduce groups of patterns of auditory stimuli in correct order. The siblings of the children with high WISC Performance gave evidence of the same inability to sequence sounds within words. In addition, their mothers gave evidence of language disability, since they were significantly poorer readers as adults. These combined findings emphasize the familial language disabilities within this group. It may be recalled that, when we compared the total sample of EH mothers' adult reading capabilities with those of the SA children's mothers, no significant difference was found. However, in this smaller subgroup we found that the mothers are significantly poorer readers during adult life.

There were some interesting sibling similarities on the WISC. For example, information, arithmetic, and digit span did not differentiate the EH and his sibling. In other words both groups were impaired in these three areas of performance. On the other hand, for picture completion, picture arrangement, and block design, the EH children were significantly superior to their controls. They did not differ significantly from their siblings on picture completion and picture arrangement but were superior on block designs.

The medical neurological findings indicated that the children differed from their controls on a number of items such as prenatal complications, digestive disturbances, temper tantrums, left-hand preference, ease in being talked to, listening in school, and educational problems. They did not, however, differ from their siblings on any of these items with the exception of the ease with which the mother could talk to the child during early life.

A tantalizing item which emerged from the medical examination was related to the neurologist's blind evaluation of morphological abnormalities of the external ear. Earlier studies of neurologically impaired children have sometimes suggested variations in size, form, and symmetry of the external ear as a common minor anomaly in this population. The pediatric neurologist, therefore, completed a checklist for each child that he examined. This examination was, of course, carried out visually by the physician, but since he did not know to which population each child belonged, the significant difference which was found in the direction of a higher frequency of abnormality in the EH children as compared to the controls is intriguing. Again, the abnormalities of the external ear that differentiated the EH from his control did not differentiate the EH from his siblings; that is to say the siblings of the educationally handicapped children had as many signs of deviations in the formation of the external ear as did the EH children themselves.

The learning-disabled children that participated in this study were from a privileged suburban community. They did not differ from their successful controls with respect to parental level of education or social, economic, or ethnic background. Their learning problems in general presumably were not related to a lack of early stimulation, to deprivation, or to inadequate language exposure. When we began the study, we speculated that there were many types and degrees of learning handicap. We had reason to believe, on the basis of earlier studies, that there would be children with subtle signs of neurological impairment, children with maladjusted personalities, and children with specific language disabilities or familial learning problems. We found these groups not as clearly differentiated as is often supposed and we concluded that in reality there is a great deal of overlapping among these three areas.

We did, however, theorize that the children with high performance discrepancies on the WISC (i.e., 15 or more points higher on performance than verbal IQ) would represent the most pure group of familial-specific language-disabled children in our sample. Our data supported this speculation in that the siblings of these children showed many similarities. Between these sibling pairs we observed the concordance of neurological differences, speech problems, and WISC Subscale patterns, both strengths and weaknesses. The poor adult reading skill of their mothers also emphasized the familial aspect of the language learning handicap in this group. Whether or not this familial aggregation is genetically determined was a question that we did not attempt to answer; but that there is a marked familial incidence among certain learning-handicapped groups is unequivocal.

IMPLICATIONS

While Hallgren's work must be viewed with admiration, his final conclusions must be challenged. In order to employ the techniques of Mendelian analysis, one must be able to define clearly distinguishing characteristics from which the relevant genetic constitution can be inferred. Hallgren (like many other investigators) was unable to produce an unambiguous definition that would firmly establish the existence of a homogeneous group of dyslexic children. Vernon (1976) has argued that objections of this sort can be answered, since almost all research and theory in psychology is based on constructs, which are justified insofar as they enable us to make testable predictions.

In addition, it is necessary to raise questions about Hallgren's conclusion that the occurrence of learning disorders in two or three generations of the same family necessarily leads to the conclusion that the disability is genetically determined. Many characteristics or behaviors continue through generations within families on a cultural basis. Is it not possible that a bright parent who did poorly in school could, through deviant social learning patterns, inadvertently teach his or her bright children to perform poorly in school? Are there patterns of learning and behavior that are so deeply ingrained and so carefully learned that they are transmitted from one generation of the family to the next through social learning rather than through hereditary means?

How do our studies differ from Hallgren's work? First, of course, no attempt was made to carry out a genetic study and to utilize the techniques of Mendelian analysis. As Scarr-Salapatek (1975) has stated "explaining gene behavior relations entails knowing every aspect of the developmental pattern; its inception, its relation to the environment, its biochemical individuality and its adaptiveness. When these things are known it is possible to enter an experimental wedge at any level and to adjust gene expression anywhere within the limits of modification." A goal such as this is still in the future in the study of developmental dyslexia.

Under these circumstances, what kind of inferences or speculations can we make about the familial similarities that we have documented in our learning-disabled population? Certainly we would have expected similarities among our sibling pairs either from the affected or nonaffected families on their performance on an intelligence test. Earlier research has suggested that the level of IQ is moderately heritable and that pattern of intellectual development is more variable than level within families. If we look at the relative strengths and weaknesses of our learning-disabled children in the high WISC Performance discrepancy subgroup which has already been theoretically identified as our strongest familial subsample, we find that they are as a group significantly poor on the information, arithmetic, and digit span subscales of the WISC. We also discovered that they were significantly superior on picture completion and picture arrangement subtests on the WISC. It is possible that there is a familial genetic predisposition for these children that has influenced this pattern of intellectual development.

Perhaps of greater interest are the neurological immaturities that were documented. If these are not familial genetic patterns of development, how can we explain the similar disabilities that these children showed in reproducing auditory tapped patterns, in distinguishing double simultaneous touch, in carrying out fast alternating finger and hand movements, and in making right-left discriminations? These were sibling patterns of disability and they

suggest familial genetic differences between these children and their successful academic controls. These neurological immaturities would not seem to be
accessible to social learning.

The writer would theorize that multifactorial genetic predisposition
is the source of at least one type of learning disability. In some cases the genetic contribution may be of such strength that later environmental experiences cannot significantly alter the inexorable expression of the disordered
learning and behavior. In other cases we might theorize that the genetic
makeup of the individual would allow for alternate forms of development.
That is to say, adequate or inadequate environmental experiences could modify the phenotype; and alternative patterns of learning and behavior could
develop.

The concept or theory of canalization developed by Waddington
(1957) is particularly relevant to this theoretical position. Scarr-Salapatek
(1975) has provided a brief discussion of this concept. She states "the concept of canalization in development accounts for many phenotypic phenomena. Canalization is the restriction of alternative phenotypes to one or few
outcomes. The developing phenotype is represented as more or less difficult
to deflect from a growth path *depending upon the degree of genotypic control, the force of the deflection, and the timing of the deflection.*"

Waddington's epigenetic landscape, as shown in Figure 13-1, is a
model of the varying canalization in the development of different aspects of
the organism (Waddington, 1957). The ball is the developing phenotype
which rolls through valleys of varying widths and depths. At some points a
minor deflection can send the phenotype into a different channel of development; at other points, a major deflection would be required to change the
course of development because genetic canalization (represented by a narrow,
deep valley) is very strong. Lesser canalization means greater modifiability.
Greater canalization means that a large array of environmental events may
have little or no effect on the development of the phenotype.

These speculations are based on research studies that have utilized the
familial incidence of dyslexia. Since familial incidence, however, will never
provide the information we seek regarding the genetic contribution to dyslexia, we must look elsewhere. Other approaches to the study of human genetics are on the horizon. Tools are emerging that will make it possible to
further unravel the mysteries of DNA and to map human genes. Early studies
suggest that there are distinctive patterns of "banding" on chromosomes. Possibly the chromosomes contributed by each parent will "band" differently. In

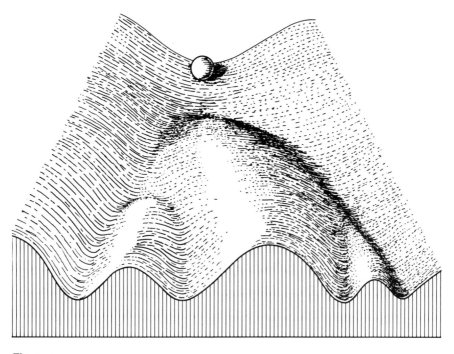

Figure 13-1
    Waddington's epigenetic landscape: a model of genetic canalization in development. (From Waddington 1957.)

this way we may be able to study the relationships between parents and children.

Current knowledge suggests that certain types of dyslexia may be transmitted through multifactorial inheritance. Thus, the disability might be determined by a large number of genes, each contributing a small amount to the trait. The expression and severity of the disability, then, would be a function of the interaction between this genetic predisposition, environmental experiences, and changes in the effectiveness of methods of treatment. It is therefore well worth searching for the environmental components. In those cases where there is a strong genetic liability, it may be possible to soften the impact by protecting the child from the environmental component and providing the best treatment. When the genetic contribution is weak, the expression of the trait may be prevented altogether by altering the environmental factors.

This review points up the fact that we do not yet have the means to reach a decisive answer regarding the relationship between genetics and specific dyslexia. Indeed, given our current level of knowledge, we cannot yet absolutely define specific dyslexia. Nevertheless, we have come a long way since the early papers of Morgan and Hinshelwood. But, as Hinshelwood prophetically stated, the subject is indeed not yet exhausted.

Chapter 14

REVIEW OF "DYSLEXIA–GENETIC ASPECTS"

G. E. McCLEARN

Owen's review of research on the genetic aspects of dyslexia provides an accurate picture of the current state of the field. There are bountiful data attesting to the familial nature of the disorder and strong presumptive evidence that this familial distribution is due at least in part to genetic factors, although assessment of specific hypotheses concerning modes of inheritance has been confusing and inconclusive.

The work by Owen and her colleagues, as described in Chapter 13, provides valuable information on sibling resemblance. One aspect of her results that is quite puzzling is the lack of a sibling correlation in the control population for tests of verbal ability. This finding is contrary to the results of a large body of research on twin and parent-offspring resemblance (see De-Fries, Vandenberg, and McClearn, 1976).

It should be noted that the discovery of reading disability in mothers in Owen's study does not contradict the nearly ubiquitous finding of a higher incidence in males than in females. If reading disability is influenced by genetic factors, one would expect a much higher incidence of phenotypic expression among mothers of probands than among women in general.

Owen's discussion of the possibility that familial distribution could be due to environmental transmission is very pertinent. Familial distribution of any trait is not definitive evidence of *either* genetic *or* environmental influence. There has been a tendency in behavioral science, however, to regard environmental hypotheses as *a priori* more acceptable than genetic ones. Vague and implausible environmental hypotheses are very often accepted until such time as they may be shown to be incorrect. A genetic role is very often rejected *a priori* until such time as undeniable and incontrovertible evidence of its importance is provided. Surely, good scientific practice requires a more even-handed approach. It is gratifying that, in the case of reading disability, there is a history of consideration of both hereditary and environmental causation.

Owen quite correctly points to the promise of newer biochemical and cytological techniques for analyzing genetic influences. These are only just now being brought to bear upon problems of reading disability, and they offer prospects for real advances in our understanding of the etiology of the condition. It is important, however, to call attention to the increasingly powerful techniques of segregation analysis and linkage analysis that may be applied to data on resemblance among relatives. The peculiar power of modern adoption designs in providing unambiguous evidence of hereditary influence is also worthy of note. In spite of the very great difficulties that would be entailed, a large-scale adoption study of reading disability could provide landmark data.

Owen appears to justify the lack of a Mendelian analysis in her own work by a quotation from Scarr-Salapatek (1975). In this context, the quotation might appear to be a counsel of despair, suggesting that one must wait until "every aspect of the developmental pattern; its inception, its relation to the environment, its biochemical individuality and its adaptiveness" is understood before attempts can be initiated to understand gene-behavior relations. Surely, the quotation must be taken to mean that complete genetic understanding will depend upon knowledge of these other matters and vice versa. In order to advance knowledge in the area of reading disabilities, I believe a strong argument can be made in favor of proceeding on behavioral, genetic, and physiological fronts simultaneously in closely coordinated, interdisciplinary studies.

The brief discussion by Owen of gene-environment interactions in development is germane to the topic of reading disability. Understanding of this basic concept is a much needed antidote to antiquated conceptions of the nature vs. nurture variety. Individual differences in most attributes must be conceived as determined by both genetic and environmental factors, and these must be regarded as potentially co-acting and interacting in development. Conceptual advances in quantitative genetics, such as path analysis, are helpful both in revealing the complexities of such interactions and in determining their magnitude. However, Owen's notion that "adequate or inadequate environmental experiences could modify the genotype . . ." would be more accurate if rephrased to say that environmental factors could modify the *phenotypic* expression of the *genotype*. Alterations of the *genotype* are mutations; they are rare and caused by a limited array of environmental factors such as radiation and certain chemical agents. It is also worth emphasizing that it is not only in the case of multifactorial inheritance that environmental components should be sought. The condition of phenylketonuria comes to mind as an example of a classical Mendelian condition in which alterations of nutritional environment can modify the phenotypic expression of the genotype.

There is a persistent and recurrent suggestion, which Owen reminds us had its origin with Hinshelwood, that reading disability is a heterogeneous complex of etiologically distinct entities. Many behavioral phenotypes have yielded slowly and incompletely to analysis because traits with different causal mechanisms have been considered together in a single generic category. Both theoretical considerations and the empirical literature suggest that such may be the case with respect to reading disabilities. There may be a number of subtypes of reading disability, each with its own unique etiology.

A MULTIPLE-FACTOR MODEL

A perspective that is useful in approaching this problem incorporates environmental and genetic factors. It emphasizes the possibilities of co-action and interaction of heredity and environment in influencing behavioral processes in general and, specifically, those processes involved in reading ability.

Gene pairs (loci) are represented by the paired circles on the left in Figure 14-1. Only seven paired circles are shown in this illustration, but it should be kept in mind that perhaps as many as 100,000 such loci contain the genetic code of a human being. From each gene pair, a short arrow connects with an asterisk or star-like symbol. These symbols represent enzymes, and the representation indicates that the primary action of each gene pair is the production of unique enzymes. The enzymes promote biochemical reactions that determine the development of the organ systems of the body and influence the function of these organ systems, represented by squares identified by numerals 1 through 10. These squares are to be understood to be those aspects of the endocrine systems, the receptor systems, the motor systems, and the autonomic and central nervous systems that have any degree of influence on the phenotype of interest. In the present case, of course, this phenotype is reading ability.

Thus, square 1 might represent the level of a particular neurotransmitter, square 2 might be dendritic density, square 3 might pertain to hemispheric lateralization, square 5 to ocular musculature, and so on. These organ

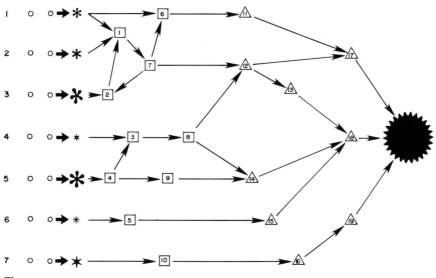

Figure 14-1
   Schematic illustration of the effects of genes (paired circles) upon the reading ability phenotype (large multifaceted endpoint), as conveyed by the production of enzymes (asterisks or star-like symbols) which influence a network of organ systems (squares) and behavioral processes (triangles).

systems may interact with each other and, singly or jointly, exert influence on behavioral systems proximal to the reading ability phenotype. The behavioral processes are shown by triangles (numbered 11–19) which may be taken to represent such "behavioral" phenomena as memory and coding capacity, temporal serialization, semantic processing, pattern perception, emotionality, and other behavioral processes. Reading ability itself in the diagram is displayed as a large multi-faceted endpoint upon which the various routes of influence converge.

   Several particularly pertinent aspects of this schema may be noted. For example, it is apparent that a given pathway can be influenced by more than one gene. Consider the route culminating △14 → △18 → Reading Ability. Behavioral process △14 has input from locus 4 through organ systems 3 and 8. It also has input from locus 5 through organ systems 4 and 9. Further complexities may arise from feedback systems (for example, the simple 1 → 7 → 2 → 1 circuit illustrated here) that can tie together the effects of a variety of genes. As a consequence of this particular feedback loop, loci 1, 2, and 3 all feed into a common pathway. When several loci contribute to a phenotype, it becomes difficult or impossible to trace the effects of each individual locus by classical Mendelian methods. The methods of quantitative genetics, concerned with variance partitioning, regression and correlational analyses, and related procedures, must be employed.

A given gene pair can also influence more than one causal pathway. Locus 5 for example, influences behavioral process △18 through pathway [4] → [9] → △14, through [4] → [3] → [8] → △14, and through [4] → [3] → [8] → △12 → △13. Furthermore, this gene pair has an effect on the final phenotype through pathway [4] → [3] → [8] → △12 → △17.

The genes are shown here simply as open circles. However, they are capable of existing in alternate states, called "alleles," which are characterized by different functional properties. We can represent the alleles at a locus as closed or open circles. Thus, a given pair of genes can exist in one of three states: ● ●, ● ○, or ○ ○. The term *homozygous* is applicable to the first and third states, while the term *heterozygous* describes the second.

The mode of gene action may differ from locus to locus. Assume, for example, that locus 1 acts in an additive fashion. In this case, some phenotype, say △11, will be small if the allelic state is ○ ○, intermediate if it is ● ○, and large if it is ● ●. Another mode of gene action is that of dominance-recessiveness. In such a case, the phenotypic expression of heterozygote, ● ○, will be the same as that of one of the homozygotes (say, ● ●), while the other homozygote (○ ○) may exhibit essentially none of the trait in question. The consequences of such a situation may be much more important in some pathways than in others. For example, suppose a homozygous state of locus 7 led to complete absence of [10]. This would eliminate the contribution of △19 to reading ability. If the influence of △19 is large, locus 7 will be identifiable by classical Mendelian analysis. On the other hand, consider the possible sequelae of a similar condition at locus 2. The primary influence of this locus is on [1], which also has input from locus 1 and from locus 3 through [2]. Thus, because of the other pathways of influence, it is possible that the absence of influence from locus 2 would be less noticeable than a similar situation at locus 7. In any case, the influence of [1] on reading ability runs through the complex pathways that converge on △17, which is subject to all the influences shown in Figure 14-2. It is obvious that the identification of single loci is more difficult in such a system of polygenic inheritance than in the classical Mendelian single-gene case.

Given that the allelic state at any locus is independent of the allelic state at another, it is apparent that the potential exists for an enormous range of variability in the genetic substrate of reading ability. In other words, there may be many "genetic" variables which lead to a particular degree of reading ability or reading disability.

To complete the schema, it is necessary to add another realm of influence, that of the environment. These influences are represented in Figure 14-3 by the outline arrows, which are shown to be influencing every organ system and every behavioral process. The fact that the extent of variation inducible by a particular environmental agency can vary from organ system to organ system and from behavior to behavior is represented by the different sizes of the arrows. Environmental influence in this context must be conceived very broadly. For example, we can imagine the environmental arrow at $\boxed{8}$ to represent an influence of maternal nutrition and that at $\boxed{2}$ to represent an effect of placental efficiency. The large arrow at $\triangle$ may represent a major influence of the formal environmental manipulation we term "education." Again, feedback loops may exist. For example, a reading disability may give rise to failure experiences, confrontation with parents and teachers, and other problems that generate stress which can be conceived of as an arrow impinging upon the adrenal system (one of the squares in the causal nexus). These environmental effects contribute to variability and to the variety of reasons for attainment of a particular degree of reading ability. Their existence adds

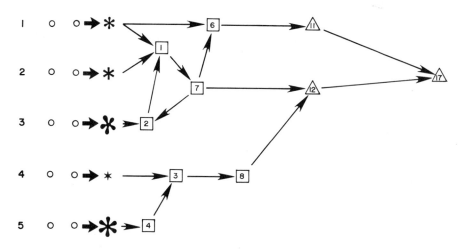

Figure 14-2

Portion of Figure 14-1 shown separately to illustrate a system of polygenic inheritance in which several genes influence the same behavioral process.

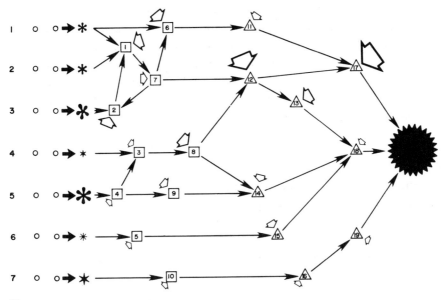

Figure 14-3
    Arrows of different sizes are added to the schematic illustration of genetic effects in order to indicate variation in the effects of the environment upon organ systems and behavioral processes.

to the necessity for a polygenic or multiple-factor approach in the study of this complex phenotypic domain.

    These schematic representations aid in understanding the variety of data with respect to correlational structure found in reading disability studies. Those characteristics that are part of a particular pathway will covary due to both common genetic influence and common environmental influence. However, by virtue of the existence of multiple routes, we cannot expect *all* individuals with reading disability to have the *same* constellation of attributes. The importance of sampling bias in the exploration of correlated characteristics in reading disability is also made clear. For example, if one investigator were to select subjects so that all or most of them had the behavioral attribute represented by △18, then the degree of disability would be related to the systems and processes causally related to △13 and △14, but only marginally to △11 and not at all to ⬜10 → △16 → △19 (unless, of course, there are common environmental effects shared by the various pathways). Another investigator whose criteria for selection were biased in favor of reading-disabled individuals with attribute 🔺 would obtain quite contradictory results. The import of these observations is that, insofar as this model represents the complexity of mechanisms in reading disability, there is an urgent need for differential diagnosis that will enable us to distinguish individuals whose condition is due to polygenic, single-gene, or environmental conditions. At least the beginnings of insights into different causal pathways must be achieved before rational therapeutic and intervention measures may be undertaken.

DIFFERENTIAL DIAGNOSIS IN MENTAL RETARDATION

Many of the specific points of the foregoing model can be exemplified by an examination of progress in differential diagnosis of subtypes of mental retardation.

In 1914, Goddard published a book presenting extensive information on the roles of nature and nurture in what was then called "feeblemindedness." It was contended that some cases had environmental origins and that others were hereditary. With respect to the latter group, Goddard made a pioneering effort to apply the recently rediscovered Mendelian laws of inheritance and concluded, in a somewhat inverted way, that "normal-mindedness" is transmitted as a dominant Mendelian character (i.e., that feeblemindedness is recessive). By present standards, we would regard this conclusion as going rather beyond the data; however, recurrent though marginal evidence of recessive transmission in subsequent research kept the hypothesis alive. In a review of the literature in the 1930s, Gates (1933) interpreted the published data as suggesting that the inheritance of feeblemindedness is "generally recessive," although he cautioned that "occasionally the inheritance is of a different type." A particularly strong challenge to the notion of Mendelian transmission of feeblemindedness was provided by those in the Pearsonian group, who argued vigorously that mental attributes are continuously distributed characters and are not amenable to Mendelian analysis.

A real breakthrough occurred when Folling (1934) found that there was a special characteristic unique to a particular subtype of feeblemindedness. This exotic indicator (urine of the subjects changed the color of a ferric chloride solution) was discovered to be due to the presence of abnormal amounts of phenylpyruvic acid. Almost immediately, strong presumptive evidence was presented that this particular variety of mental retardation is transmitted in a Mendelian recessive manner. Once this condition of phenylketonuria (PKU) was identified as an etiologically distinct subtype of mental retardation, studies focusing on that type alone were able to illuminate the nature of the metabolic defect, describe the neurological sequelae, and achieve the level of understanding necessary for early diagnosis and the development of rational therapy. Subsequent research has revealed that the initial genetic interpretation was in fact oversimplified. The phenotype of excessive phenylpyruvic acid in the urine is now known to arise from at least two different genetic conditions. The therapy that is useful for phenylketonuria is harmful to patients with hyperphenylalanemia. Thus, the need for differential diagnosis has been made even more clear by these recent advances.

Another example of differential diagnosis within mental retardation can be taken from the history of mongolism (now referred to as "Down's syndrome"). Although this type of mental retardation had long been recognized as presenting distinctive facial anomalies and other symptoms, Down's syndrome cases were frequently lumped with all others in studies directed at understanding the causes of retardation. Lejeune, Gautier, and Turpin (1959) found Down's syndrome to be due to the presence of a third chromosome added to the normal pair identified in the nomenclature of human cytogenetics as number 21. In addition to the situation in which affected individuals have three of these chromosomes, an individual with Down's syndrome will occasionally be found to have the normal pair plus a part of an extra chromosome 21 attached to some other chromosome. These translocation cases have been described as having significantly higher IQ scores than patients with the classical "trisomy" (Johnson and Abelson, 1969).

These examples have inspired research leading to descriptions of many single-gene conditions in which other chromosomal anomalies or defects of amino acid, lipid, or carbohydrate metabolism are accompanied by some degree of mental retardation. We now see "mental retardation" as a complex class of phenotypes, consisting of many different disorders with distinct etiologies—some due to single recessive genes, some due to dominant genes, some due to chromosomal anomalies, some (multifactorial or polygenic) due to segregation of many genes each having a small effect on intellectual functioning, and some due to environmental factors ranging from birth trauma to social disadvantage. *The paramount point is that, given the different mechanisms culminating in the conditions of retardation, attempts at prevention or remediation which may be successful for one subgroup might be totally ineffective or possibly even detrimental to another.*

It must be emphasized that successful differential diagnosis does not guarantee immediately improved remediation. To continue with our examples from the field of mental retardation, rational therapy in the case of PKU was a consequence of research aimed at explicating the principal diagnostic symptom—the metabolic disturbance. However, in the case of Down's syndrome, none of the associated distinctive symptoms has yet suggested effective modes of intervention (although they have led to antenatal diagnosis and improvements in genetic counseling). It would appear that the early development of successful remediation for a particular disorder will depend a great deal upon whether the distinguishing symptoms are prior to the principal symptom (mental retardation, reading disability) in the causal nexus or whether they are at about the same level and are thus merely correlated characters.

THE SITUATION IN READING DISABILITY

In many ways, today's research on the genetics of reading disability presents a picture similar to studies in the area of mental retardation in the 1920s and 1930s. There is persistent evidence of familial distribution and tantalizing near-misses in identifying specific Mendelian modes of inheritance. Furthermore, there is great confusion as to the exact definition of the phenotype. This situation is exactly what one would expect if there are many different types of reading disability. Let us suppose, for purposes of argument, that there does indeed exist a form of reading disability characterized by atypical lateralization. Let us then suppose a second type, in which disorders interfering with integration of audiovisual information are an essential feature, and a third type strongly associated with a reduction in contingent negative variation. Furthermore, let us make the assumption that some of these types of reading disability are due to single recessive genes, some to dominant genes, others to sex-linked genes, still others to polygenic segregation, and some to environmental accidents or experiential background. Lumping them all together would result in lack of replicability due to sampling fluctuations or differences in criteria for selecting subjects, disappointing near-significant results, the finding of general trends with glaring individual exceptions, and overall small differences in means or in incidence of one or another attribute between the reading-disabled population and the population of normal readers.

If this scenario is even remotely correct, then expectations of finding uniform causation, correlation, or effective remediation for all reading disabilities are unrealistic. The geneticist will make slow or no progress until phenotypically distinct entities are available for analysis. The behavioral or educational scientist who seeks to understand mechanisms as a prelude to prevention or therapy may find this to be impossible if many different mechanisms are involved and if specific mechanisms underlying particular cases cannot be identified. An attempt at differential diagnosis in the field of reading disability is therefore not just another good type of research to be encouraged. It must be seen to be logically prior to other research efforts, and it must become our first urgent order of business.

Chapter 15

A MEDICAL
GENETICS APPROACH TO
THE STUDY OF
READING DISABILITY

BARTON CHILDS
JOAN M. FINUCCI
MALCOLM S. PRESTON

In her chapter, Owen alludes to some of the ways in which specific reading disability (SRD) is an awkward phenotype for genetic study. These include the question of discrimination between persons who should be called affected and those who should not and the uncertainty in assigning the cause of familial aggregations of cases to genetic influences as opposed to such nongenetic explanations as the unconscious assimilation of familial antagonism to learning. Although she admires the scope of Hallgren's study and the energy with which he pursued it, she doubts that specific reading disability is likely to prove to be a Mendelian character; she suggests instead a multifactorial alternative. She accepts the idea of subtypes and points out that neurological signs support the genetic hypothesis for some. Her own approach to the question of genetic influences appears to be a modification of the conventional behavior genetics method which tests the degree to which some quality is genetically determined, but is not concerned with the properties of each individual in the population.

A MEDICAL GENETICS APPROACH

An alternative method for such a study is that of medical genetics, which is primarily interested in the individual rather than in statistical differences between groups. In addition, the medical geneticist is not interested in the origins of the variance for the normal range of measurements of skills whose biological basis is unknown and unmeasurable. Thus, for the medical geneticist, the genetic contribution to variation in measurements in reading skill would not be an appropriate object of study. But specific reading *disability* is a different matter. There we are interested in identifying biological qualities which compromise the capacity to learn to read and such qualities could be discrete and precisely measured. In this regard, specific reading disability may be analogous to mental retardation or dwarfism. Frequency distributions which include many measurements of IQ or height are skewed to the left, revealing a shoulder or hump suggesting scores not accommodated under a perfectly normal curve. When one looks at the individuals whose measurements lie in this part of such distributions, one finds people who are mentally retarded or are dwarfed for a variety of reasons, both genetic and nongenetic. There is a tendency for the most peripheral genetic causes to be Mendelizing characters; those closer to the rapidly ascending part of the distribution are less likely to segregate according to any Mendelian mode, although they may be familial. To understand the single-gene causes of the former, one needs no knowledge at all of the biological basis for performance in IQ tests or for the achievement of height, but only the details of the factors which have prevented the normal development of those characteristics.

We may apply the same approach to the understanding of severe reading disability, limiting our analysis to persons whose measurements of reading skills fall in the lower reaches of the distribution, while ignoring the normal part of the curve. However, it is important to understand the steps in developing reading skill and to dissect the mechanisms involved. To do so is to discover directions in which to look for properties to measure and analyze in the disabled readers and to expose evidences of heterogeneity of expression and of cause.

DISCRIMINATION OF DISABLED READERS FROM NORMAL READERS

As it turns out, distributions of scores of reading skill are similar to those for IQ and height, showing the same skew on the left (Yule et al., 1974). This does not help, however, in deciding in every case who is reading retarded and who is not. Obviously there are no problems at the opposite ends of the distribution but, since it is a continuous one, the question arises as to where to cut it. There is no answer to this question. If the skewness represents distortion due to the inclusion of scores derived from a distribution of a different population; namely, readers whose disabilities are associated with some interference with normal processes, then readers from both populations will appear on both sides of most points within the skewed part of the curve. Thus, although an arbitrary cut in the distribution is necessary to begin with, some independent classification of the individuals will be necessary.

THE USE OF TOLERANCE TESTS

The tolerance test is a conventional genetic maneuver which aims at enhancing discrimination of contrasting genotypes. When successful, it may divide a continuous distribution into two separate populations. Such tests consist of stressing the system under scrutiny, thereby bringing out inherent weaknesses. We have used such tests in our study of SRD (Finucci et al., 1976), asking subjects to read passages from reading tests in which the words or letters have been rearranged in various ways; for example, upside-down, in mirror image, or with the letters normally oriented but the words spelled backward. In addition, we use paragraphs containing many neologisms in which the syntax appears to be intact; and finally, there is a test of oral reading speed. These tests are intended to rob the subject of reading cues he may have devised for himself, exposing his underlying incompetence. Using several such tests, together with conventional ones, and comparing scores with suitable controls, we classified the adult relatives of children ascertained as disabled readers as normal or disabled readers. Then, a linear combination of test scores obtained from these relatives was shown to discriminate them into two nonoverlapping populations of "normal" and "disabled" readers.

Problems of discrimination are confounded by the nonbiological nature of reading. It is not a physiological property with any natural measure like blood pressure or blood glucose or serum phenylalanine. Thus, the measurements of the tests are arbitrary and may not be testing directly the unknown property in which we are interested, namely, the biological attributes of SRD. In addition, a point of discrimination suitable for purposes of deciding whether or not a child needs remedial reading in some school system may not be ideal for a biological study. That is, the diagnosis of reading disability depends upon the expectations of educators who set the standards for students. If the expectations are low, as perhaps they were a generation or two ago, there will be fewer disabled readers; if high, there will be more. It is possible, for example, to set standards which allow all but a small fraction to pass or other standards which bar all but a few. As these standards bear only incidental relation to the biological capacity of the species, it is difficult to know where the biological limits of "normality" are. In a society that sets great store by reading, these are probably tested better by the low standard than the high. At the least, the most severe and obvious cases, due perhaps to the greatest diversity of cause, would be exposed by the low standard. The high standard would expose others, too, but they would be diluted by those who fail for such nonbiological reasons as poor teaching or lack of interest. Still, one must work with the methods which come to hand while searching for biological measures more suitable for a genetic analysis.

MENDELIAN ANALYSIS OF SPECIFIC READING DISABILITY

Is it possible to do a Mendelian genetic analysis of severe specific reading disability? The Mendelian method involves study of the distribution of a discrete quality among members of families. It aims at assignment of the origin of the trait to alleles at particular loci in specific chromosomes. It also aims to classify variants of the traits as originating in any one of several alleles, or as stemming from mutants occupying different loci. This method is one which is used to test hypotheses, and hypotheses are only tested by it, not proved. Thus, there must be doubts about the strength of the association of a gene with a trait until several tests of the hypothesis fail to disprove it. For example, to find familial aggregation of affected individuals may be compatible with one or other of several genetic hypotheses, but proves none. Accordingly, the discovery of familial aggregation of disabled readers is only a preliminary to other tests; if one stops there, one has said very little about genetics, even if the distribution fits the Mendelian pattern.

SUBTYPES AND GENETIC HETEROGENEITY

The intent of the investigator in using the Mendelian method is seldom to discover something abstract about the species, as, for example, whether some quality is heritable or to what degree. It is rather to discover variant individuals who can be helped as a result of the knowledge. It is, ultimately, to discover where the measurements of a property of a given individual fit in distributions and why they fit there. This gives information about him personally, which can lead to therapeutic maneuvers which may restore measurements of this function to the normal parts of the distributions or make such measurements nugatory. The necessity to look carefully at each individual in each family is underlined by the requirement to make the therapeutic approach appropriate, not to some general class of the phenotype, but to each affected person whose expression designates some subtype. The genetic method is a particularly apposite one for this kind of classification, since rigor is introduced into the analysis by the strong probability that if a condition is associated with a single gene, all affected members of the family will have the same gene. Thus, heterogeneity is suggested by within-family phenotypic likeness and between-family differences.

Subtypes have been mentioned by many investigators of specific reading disability, but none has been tested genetically. If there are types of reading disability in which defects in auditory or visual perception or memory represent the biological reason for the reading deficit, then the discovery that all affected persons in a family have the same deficit is at once compatible with the genetic hypothesis and a confirmation of the existence of the subtype. Boder (1973) has suggested three types of specific reading disability based on the quality of spelling errors. The validity of these subtypes could be tested in the family context.

LINKAGE STUDIES

This approach is appealing because the discovery of a tight linkage between some marker and specific reading disability in one or more families would be good evidence for the genetic origin of at least one kind of specific reading disability, but it is unlikely to be very productive just now for two reasons. The first is the conventional one of an insufficient number of useful markers; and the second, that of heterogeneity, is even more discouraging. That is, to do a linkage study of SRD in our present state of diagnostic imprecision would be like doing such a test on "mental retardation" or "dwarfism" without regard for the known genetic and phenotypic variation. On the other hand, when some subtypes have been clearly defined, linkage studies could be very useful.

PHYSIOLOGICAL ATTRIBUTES

Any genetic hypothesis is given firmer footing if a phenotype can be shown to be closely associated with some measurable physiological or biochemical quality. It is not immediately clear what biochemical attributes should be searched for in a population of persons with SRD. It might be more fruitful to do reading tests on persons with inborn errors which do not produce early death and whose intellect is not impaired. Alternatively, reading tests might be done on persons known to be heterozygous for genes which in homozygotes produce marked developmental retardation. Such genes might produce sufficient neurological abnormalities in some of the heterozygotes to be expressed as SRD. It should be noted that while such diseases are usually rare, the heterozygotes are relatively common, reaching frequencies of 0.2–2.0 percent.

A neurophysiological approach perhaps offers more promise. Vaguely described EEG differences between retarded readers and normal readers have appeared in the literature. Conners (1970) was the first to use the visual evoked responses (VER) technique in a family with specific reading disability, and Preston has since studied additional subjects. Using flashes of light and words as stimuli, Preston et al. (1977) measured the amplitude of the P200 and the late positive component (LPC) in adult normal and disabled readers at parietal and occipital placements of both hemispheres. For normal readers, the mean LPC amplitudes are higher in response to words than light flashes primarily on the parietal leads, with the greatest difference between stimuli evident on the left parietal electrode. The disabled readers as a group showed a significantly smaller word-minus-flash difference on the left parietal placement. A similar significant difference between groups was noted on the same lead for P200. In an earlier study, Preston et al. (1974) also showed significant mean differences between a population of reading-disabled children and two sets of controls, the latter consisting of normal readers of the same chronological age as the disabled readers and younger children who were reading at about the same grade level as the disabled readers. This study suggested that the difference between these populations is not associated simply with the inability to read. Preston has also shown some differences between members of the families studied recently by Finucci who were designated as disabled readers and those who were normal readers. These are all mean differences, and the VER procedure is not yet sufficiently refined to apply to individuals. It is to be hoped that a more refined test will prove to be useful as an independent discriminant of reading disability as well as a means of designating subtypes.

Cerebral lateralization
It has been suggested that reading disability is associated with incomplete cerebral lateralization or with maturational delay in achieving that degree of organization of the brain. Dichotic listening studies have shown differences between populations of disabled readers and normal controls in the degree of right-ear advantage for memory of digits (Bryden, 1970; Thompson, 1976; Witelson and Rabinovitch, 1972). Recently Witelson (1975) has shown a difference between such populations in hand asymmetry-of-object recognition using a test in which the subject palpates objects of slightly different configuration with both hands at once. In none of these tests have individual differences been considered. These, together with tests involving the independent presentation of stimuli to the visual hemifields, should be extended with special attention to individual differences and within- and between-family likeness. It should be stated, however, that these tests, as they are currently performed, may turn out to be suitable only for the detection of mean differences between groups and not for discrimination between individuals.

THE MULTIFACTORIAL HYPOTHESIS

The analogy with mental retardation and dwarfism suggests that some sizeable proportion of specific reading disability may be multifactorial in origin; that is, associated with several or many genes which require particular environments to produce the phenotype. This is an unsatisfying designation in which neither the number and quality of the putative genes nor the presumed environmental requirements can be understood. The assumption of genetic origin of such traits rests usually on mathematical analysis of non-Mendelian familial aggregations and heritability studies, neither of which is of much use to individuals, even assuming the validity of the methods or of their conclusions, assumptions which are being questioned of late. In any case, such a diagnosis is of limited predictive value to individuals, since such predictions are based on empiric risk figures derived from observations of the frequency with which relatives share the phenotype with the index case. In general the frequency of affected persons within the families is some multiple of that of the general population, and it drops off rapidly as the degree of affinity of the relationships drops. In this connection, it is worth pointing out that an important test of the Mendelian hypothesis consists of studying collaterals; if the phenotype is an autosomal dominant, for example, the concentration of affected first cousins will be less than that of the sibs, but much more than it would be if the character were multigenic in origin (Edwards, 1960).

Since there is no genetic analysis which can be of much use to individuals with multifactorial conditions, one must look for other approaches. Something is needed which can rescue definable subtypes from the undifferentiated mass. Medical experience reveals that this has been done; for example, there are many forms of diabetes and of hypertension which are mendelizing characters and which have been distinguished from the remaining "multifactorial" forms. The appropriate method for such studies is epidemiology, a discipline which has been too little employed in past studies of SRD and one which is explicitly devoted to the discovery of causes. Such a method is not limited to the elucidation of genetic factors, but applies equally to those special environmental conditions which are required for expression of phenotypes. Obviously the latter are of greater practical importance than the former, since environmental manipulation is our only therapeutic recourse. Short of characterization of the heterogeneity of SRD in which evidence of genes and special experiences are sorted out, we are left with metaphorical descriptions of developmental alternatives and the vapidity of the multifactorial diagnosis.

CULTURAL TRANSMISSION

Owen has raised the question of the transmission (or unconscious teaching) of antipathy to learning. An intelligent parent who failed in school for social reasons passes on his or her deviant learning pattern to the offspring. This hypothesis should be tested by the same rigorous, quantitative epidemiological analysis as others. Social, psychological, and biological variables should be sorted out and contrasted in an effort to find some consistent qualities which distinguish the families in which this antagonism to learning appears. The psychological qualities which account for such destructive behavior might be discernible, given the right conditions of inquiry, and it might be possible to show that such parents differ in those attributes from others.

CONCLUSION

In summary, it is not possible at the moment to state unequivocally whether specific reading disability is genetically determined or not, or whether some cases are and others are associated with something else, or whether if there is some genetic element in some cases it consists of genes at one locus or at many. Rather, the position at the moment is one of designing the appropriate conditions to test these hypotheses. These tests must be rigorous, quantitative, and directed to the distinction of the characteristics of individuals.

Part VI

EARLY DETECTION AND PREVENTIVE INTERVENTION

Chapter 16

SOME DEVELOPMENTAL AND PREDICTIVE PRECURSORS OF READING DISABILITIES: A SIX YEAR FOLLOW-UP

PAUL SATZ
H. GERRY TAYLOR
JANETTE FRIEL
JACK M. FLETCHER

The present chapter is addressed to the current status of research on the early identification of children destined to become disabled readers in our schools. These children, most of whom are boys, represent a staggering proportion of our school population. Prevalence estimates suggest that approximately 15 percent of the children in our schools have severe reading disabilities. This represents an incidence of approximately 8 million children in the United States (Kline, 1972; Myklebust and Boshes, 1969). Similar estimates have also been reported for Canada (CELDIC Report, 1 Million Children, 1970), Great Britain (Kellmer-Pringle, Butler and Davie, 1966), France (Gaddes, 1976), and Denmark (Gaddes, 1976). The empirical basis for these estimates, however, has come under serious criticism. "Definitions differ and classifications differ, depending upon whether they are based upon a medical or educational model; or whether they are based primarily on cause, symptoms or treatment" (CELDIC Report, 1970, p. 51). Many of these prevalence studies are based on highly selected samples that fail to differentiate backward readers from children who have specific reading handicaps (Yule and Rutter, 1976). Despite these definitional problems, the consistency of estimates in recent years is more prominent than the variability (CELDIC Report, 1970).

The high incidence of reading disorders represents only part of the problem confronting our educational system. More ominous are the results of follow-up studies. It has been reported that reading disorders which persist into late childhood often lead to secondary emotional and behavioral disturbances (Gates, 1968; Kline, 1972; Eisenberg, 1966). Four recent studies have also reported that reading disorders persist when followed into early adolescence (Muehl and Forell, 1973; Yule and Rutter, 1976). Reading disorders represent the major single cause of school drop-outs in our educational system (Silberman, 1964). In addition, they are a major problem observed in referrals to clinics and juvenile courts (Meerlo, 1962; Schmideberg, 1949; Critchley, 1968; Mendelson, Johnson, and Stewert, 1971; Wright, 1974). Life history studies suggest that reading and learning problems in elementary school may represent developmental precursors of more serious emotional disturbances in late adolescence and early adulthood (Robins, 1966; Watt and Lubensky, 1976; Albee, Lane, and Reuter, 1964; Lane and Albee, 1970). Equally striking is the relationship between reading failure and criminal behavior (Wright, 1974).

Viewed in this light, the problem of reading disabilities encompasses not only the educational system but our social, economic, and legal institutions as well. The price is therefore high for a society which promotes educational opportunity but is confronted with such a significant loss of human potential.

THE NEED FOR EARLY DETECTION

The purpose of this chapter is to review some recent findings that involve early identification of high-risk children at the beginning of formal schooling. The research springs from the need for a valid early detection system that could be administered before the child begins formal reading, at a time when the central nervous system may be more plastic and responsive to change and when the child is less subject to the shattering effects of repeated academic failure. The need for early detection research has long been recognized but has been marked by a paucity of well-controlled long-term longitudinal studies (Critchley, 1968; Money, 1962; Eisenberg, 1966; Gallagher and Bradley, 1972; Kline, 1972; Ames, 1966; Satz, 1973). The advantages of an early identification and remediation program are highlighted by the survey by Keeney and Keeney (1968). Similarly, Strag (1972) showed that ". . . when the diagnosis of dyslexia was made in the first two grades of school nearly 82 percent of the students could be brought up to their normal classroom work, while only 46 percent of the dyslexic problems identified in the third grade were remediated and only 10 to 15 percent of those observed in grades 5–7 could be helped when the diagnosis of learning problems was made at those grade levels (p. 52)." This report is compatible with the more recent study by Muehl and Forell (1973). Results indicated that early diagnosis, regardless of amount of subsequent remediation, was associated with better reading performance at follow-up five years later. The tragedy, however, is that most of the children with reading and learning problems are not referred for diagnostic evaluation until the ages of 9–11—at which time the child may be maturationally less ready and already exposed to years of reading failure.

Experimental studies with humans and infrahumans suggest that the child may be more responsive to environmental stimulation (e.g., remediation) during that period in which the brain is maturing and when behavior is less differentiated (Caldwell, 1968). Bloom (1964) has shown that variations in the environment have their greatest quantitative effect on a characteristic (e.g., speech) at its most rapid period of change (i.e., ages 2–10) and the least effect at the least rapid period of change (i.e., ages 11–15). Infrahuman studies also suggest that organization can be strongly modified only when active processes of organization are underway, and the facilitation of these processes progressively inhibits their attempts at reorganization (Scott, 1968).

SOME PROBLEMS AND RISKS
IN EARLY DETECTION RESEARCH

Despite the obvious advantages of early intervention, it must be based on a valid and efficient detection program, especially when the detection measures are applied before formal reading instruction is commenced. Within such a prevention context, certain types of prediction errors are crucial to the utility of an "early warning" system—e.g., the false positive and negative signs. To initiate an intervention program for test-classified high-risk children in kindergarten may be fruitless if the majority of true high-risk children are missed by the tests. Equally serious and perhaps more risky is the case in which an intervention program is based on erroneously test-classified positives (high risk) who in three years would have become average to superior readers without remediation. These prediction errors can occur despite an apparent demonstration of test validity by simplified descriptive univariate tests of significance. The experimental validation of an early detection battery is greatly enhanced by the incorporation of a multivariate design in which multiple measurements are made on the same subjects over time. Another requirement is sufficient temporal separation between the initial test probe and the criterion reading assessment in later years. This type of design should utilize a longitudinal framework preferably based on a total population, rather than smaller samples of children, to offset the potential attrition effects over time and to provide more reliable base-rate estimates of reading disability in the designated population. Further, the selection of a more homogeneous population provides an opportunity to obtain a group at higher risk for later reading disability without confounding sex, race, or cultural variables (Bentzen, 1963; Satz, 1973). A final methodological requirement, essential to the evaluation of an early detection battery, is the use of a separate group of children upon which to cross-validate the predictive validity of the tests administered to the standardization population. Failure to incorporate these methodological factors into an early detection study would surely limit, if not invalidate, the results. A review of the current early detection literature reveals disregard of these problems and a scathing indictment of the area (Gallagher and Bradley, 1972).

An equally serious problem in the early detection literature is the lack of a theoretical framework in which to conceptualize the nature of reading disorders and their antecedents, and by which to generate testable hypotheses. Without a testable theory one lacks guidelines for the selection of a test battery which purports to identify the potentially high-risk child. Although a theory represents a framework in which to organize diverse sets of data, its ultimate validation must rest on empirical verification. In the present context, a theory which postulates the precursors of reading disabilities before the child begins formal reading can be evaluated empirically only within a longitudinal framework. If empirical support for the theory can be replicated and cross-validated in later years, information is then available for application and for further understanding of the etiology and mechanism underlying this complex disorder of childhood.

OBJECTIVES

In view of the preceding methodological and theoretical comments, a critical review of the literature on early detection is unnecessary, particularly in view of two recent reviews on the subject (Gallagher and Bradley, 1972; Satz, 1978a). More relevant, however, is the fact that virtually none of the early identification studies has fulfilled the outlined requirements.

Only one project to date has fulfilled some of these minimal methodological requirements. It will be presented in this chapter. In deciding upon this exclusionary focus, the authors recognize the implicit, if not self-serving, bias involved. It is also recognized that much of the conceptualization underlying the current project evolved from the landmark contributions of two earlier longitudinal predictive studies, namely, de Hirsch, Jansky, and Langford (1966), Jansky and de Hirsch (1972), and Silver and Hagin (1975). Their respective contributions will be discussed within the context of the present findings.

The chapter is divided into three sections. The first is addressed to the standardization and validation of an early detection battery and reviews the current predictive status of the standard and abbreviated batteries administered in grade K (1970) against criterion reading outcomes in follow-up years 3 (grade 2) and 6 (grade 5). Two additional subsections, one dealing with the relationship of predictive utility and early intervention, and the second with the problem of cross-validation, follow. Sections II and III are addressed to problems concerning the nature of the developmental precursors of specific reading disability and its long-term prognosis. Section II deals with the problem of teasing out the contribution of psycholinguistic and related cognitive factors as antecedents or predictors of reading disability. Section III addresses the problem of incidence and prognosis of reading disturbances in follow-up years.

THEORY

The theory which provides the methodological and conceptual framework for the current longitudinal research has been discussed in previous papers (Satz and Sparrow, 1970; Satz, Rardin, and Ross, 1971; Satz and Van Nostrand, 1973). It postulates that reading disabilities reflect a lag in the maturation of the brain which differentially delays those skills which are in primary ascendancy at different chronological ages. Consequently, those skills which develop ontogenetically earlier during childhood (e.g., visual-perceptual and cross-modal sensory integration) are more likely to be delayed in younger children who are maturationally immature. Conversely, those skills which have a slower rate of development during childhood (e.g., language and formal operations) are more likely to be delayed in older children who are maturationally immature.

The theory is compatible with developmental positions which hypothesize consecutive stages of thought during child development, each of which incorporates the processes of the preceding stage into a more complex and hierarchically integrated form of adaptation (Hunt, 1961; Piaget, 1926; Bruner, 1968). Thus it is predicted that those preschool children who are delayed developmentally in skills which are in primary ascendancy at this stage will eventually fail in acquiring reading proficiency. It is also predicted that these children will eventually "catch up" on these earlier developing skills but will subsequently lag on conceptual-linguistic skills which have a slower and later ontogenetic development (Thurstone, 1955; Bloom, 1964). If the lag in these later-developing linguistic skills persists beyond puberty, at which time maturation of the central nervous system is complete, then a more permanent delay or defect is expected. This formulation thus predicts that the nature of the disorder will vary in part as a function of the chronological age of the child.

More specifically, the lag in brain maturation is postulated to delay the acquisition of those developmental skills which have been shown to be crucial to the early phases of reading—for example, learning to differentiate graphic symbols (Gibson, 1968) or the perceptual discrimination of letters (Luria, 1966). Both authors recognize an orderly developmental sequence in which the early phases of reading are characterized by processes of perceptual discrimination and analysis. In this early phase the child must discriminate the distinctive features of letters (e.g., break vs. close, line vs. curve, rotation and reversal) before he can proceed to *later* phases which require the use of more complex linguistic strategies. Smith (1971) also recognizes the importance of learning the distinctive features of written language in the beginning phases of reading, but cautions that fixation at this level will retard acquisition of the syntactic strategies underlying fluent reading.

The theory conceptualizes developmental reading disorders as more than a unitary phenomenon. Reading disorders are explained as delays in those crucial early sensory-perceptual and later conceptual-linguistic skills that are intrinsic to the acquisition of reading. Underlying these delays is a lag in the maturation of the cerebral cortex. Developmental reading disabilities are seen as disorders in central processing, the nature of which varies with the chronological age of the child. These disorders of central processing are not meant to imply damage, loss of function, or impairment. Such terms are more compatible with a disease model which often implies a static developmental-acquisition course. At present the theory is unclear as to whether the lag in cognitive-linguistic functions which is postulated to develop in older reading-disabled children (ages 11–14) reflects a transitory or more permanent defect in cognitive functioning. It is hypothesized that if the language disorder persists after maturation of the central nervous system is completed, then a permanent defect in function may occur. If true, it would suggest that the lag is associated primarily with earlier stages in development.

With respect to the early detection of high-risk children, the theory predicts that delays in those developmental skills which are in primary ascendancy during preschool (grade K) are most likely to forecast later problems in reading (grades 3–6). If a battery of tests sensitive to the development of these early skills can predict reading disability, then this constitutes one source of support for the theory.

I. STANDARDIZATION AND VALIDATION OF AN EARLY DETECTION BATTERY

A. REVIEW STUDY: A THREE YEAR PREDICTIVE FOLLOW-UP (1970–1973)

Subjects
The original sample consisted of white male kindergarten pupils in the Aiachua County, Florida school system and the University of Florida Laboratory school. This sample represented virtually all of the white male population enrolled in the schools at the time of testing. Subjects were tested individually under uniform conditions.

Predictor variables and factor analysis
The standardization battery consisted of 16 variables described in detail elsewhere (Satz and Friel, 1973). Factor analytic methods were employed in an effort to define the underlying performance dimensions measures by the battery (cf. Fletcher and Satz, 1977). Fourteen measures obtained in kindergarten (age and day of testing were excluded) were subjected to an initial common factor analysis. An iterated principal axes solution (communalities in the diagonal) was used in which ten principal axes emerged. Eight principal factors were rotated to orthogonal (Varimax) and oblique (Simple Loadings) solutions. In both analyses three major factors were obtained. However, because of a correlation of about .70 between Factors I and III, the oblique solution produced a better resolution of factor structure. Factor II correlated about .45 with Factors I and III.

Of the three which were interpretable after rotation, Factor I seemed to compose a general sensorimotor-perceptual factor. Factor II composed measures of verbal-conceptual function, and Factor III was labeled a verbal-cultural factor. It may be noted that factor analyses of several prereading readiness batteries (e.g., Metropolitan Readiness Tests, Monroe Readiness Battery) reveal two factors: a perceptual-motor factor and a language factor (Lindgren, 1975). Additionally, the emergence of Factor III is important, especially in view of the influence of preschool cultural deprivation on reading disorders (Eisenberg, 1966).

Criterion variables

Reading measures were obtained three years later on this population of boys when they reached the end of grade 2. The first reading criterion was based on Classroom Reading Level as indicated by individual teachers. Subjects whose reading was assessed at levels "No Readiness through Primer" were designated as the Severely Disabled readers. Those assigned at First Reader comprised the Mildly Disabled reading group. Subjects reading at Second Reader levels were designated as Average readers, and those reading above that level comprised the Superior reading group.

The second reading criterion was based on a combination of Classroom Reading Level and the IOTA, affording the advantage of incorporating both the teacher's assessment of reading, based on nearly a year's interaction with the child, and an independent, individually administered, objective reading test. The scores on each of the two measures were averaged and the resulting distribution divided into four reading groups (Severe, Mild, Average, and Superior).

Classroom reading level

The first four-group discriminant function analysis was computed on Classroom Reading Level in order to compare the predictive validity of the tests against the reading criterion at the end of grade 2. The results of this analysis can be seen in Table 16-1 by comparing the test predictions (rows) against the criterion outcomes (columns). The distribution of reading groups was as follows: Severe ($N = 54$), Mild ($N = 66$), Average ($N = 270$), Superior ($N = 68$). This distribution reveals a 26 percent overall incidence of reading disability (Severe + Mild) and an incidence of 12 percent in the Severe group.

To further assess the validity of this criterion measure, vocabulary recognition scores on the Gates-McGinitie were examined. Averaged differences between attained grade equivalency levels and actual grade level (dis-

TABLE 16-1

Predictive Classification of Children into Classroom Reading Level Groups (Grade 2) Based on Discriminant Function Composite Scores (Grade K)

PREDICTIONS		CRITERION GROUPS			
		SEVERE	MILD	AVERAGE	SUPERIOR
(+)	N	48	47	74	4
	%	(89)	(71)	(27)	(6)
(−)	N	6	19	196	64
	%	(11)	(29)	(73)	(94)
Total		54	66	270	68

crepancy scores) on this test were compatible with the results of Classroom Reading Level for each of the reading groups (Severe, −12.3 mos.; Mild, −6.5 mos.; Average, +7.9 mos.; and Superior, +18.8 mos.), and the correlation between the two reading measures was high ($r = .78$).

Table 16-1 also reveals that the predictive accuracy of the tests was largely confined to the extreme reading groups (valid positives = 89% of Severes; valid negatives = 94% of Superiors) with overlap error largely confined to the Mildly Disabled and Average reading groups. In terms of overall hit rate, the tests correctly predicted 78 percent of the population.

Predictive ranking of tests

A stepwise procedure was then computed to determine the ranking of the predictor variables in terms of their criterion discrimination. The Finger Localization Test ranked highest (71%) followed cumulatively by the Alphabet Recitation Test (76%), Recognition-Discrimination Test (77%), and Day-of-Testing (77%).[1] The remaining tests contributed an additional increment of less than one percent to the total hit rate of 78 percent. These preliminary findings were felt to strengthen the validity of sensorimotor-perceptual abilities in forecasting subsequent reading achievement levels.[2]

1. A new study by Fletcher and Satz (1977) has shown that the inclusion of Day-of-Testing represents an artifact of stepwise selection procedures. The contribution of Day-of-Testing to group discrimination is negligible.

2. Caution should be employed in interpreting the results of these different stepwise analyses. Many factors could be involved in producing different rankings (Fletcher and Satz, 1977).

TABLE 16-2

Predictive Classification of Children into Combined Criterion Reading Groups (Grade 2) Based on Discriminant Function Composite Scores (Grade K)

PREDICTIONS	CRITERION GROUPS			
	SEVERE	MILD	AVERAGE	SUPERIOR
(+) N	61	51	68	2
%	(91)	(66)	(32)	(3)
(−) N	6	26	146	59
%	(9)	(34)	(68)	(97)
Total	67	77	214	61

Combined criterion

This analysis was based on the predictive accuracy of the kindergarten tests to the combined grade-2 criterion of Classroom Reading Level plus IOTA Word Recognition. These results can be seen in Table 16-2 by comparing the test predictions (rows) against the criterion outcomes (columns). The criterion distribution reveals an increased incidence of reading disability: Severe ($N = 67$), Mild ($N = 77$), Average ($N = 214$), and Superior ($N = 61$). These values yield a 34 percent incidence of overall reading disability and a 16 percent incidence in the Severe group.

Vocabulary recognition scores on the Gates McGinitie were in essential agreement with the reading groups based on this combined reading criterion (Severe, −12.1 mos.; Mild, −10.7 mos.; Average, +3.3 mos.; and Superior, +16.3 mos.), and the two measures were highly correlated ($r = .76$).

In terms of predictive hits, the valid positive rate was 91% for the Severes and 66% for the Mild cases. The tests correctly predicted 68% of the Average readers and 97% of the Superior readers (valid negatives). Once again, accuracy was largely confined to the extreme reading groups.

The stepwise procedure revealed the same discriminative ranking of tests that was found using Classroom Reading Level as the criterion (Finger Localization, Alphabet Recitation, Recognition-Discrimination, and Day-of-Testing).

An additional finding from this third-year follow-up was that an abbreviated sample of the 16 tests yielded virtually the same predictive accuracy as the full battery. Selection of this abbreviated battery was based on empirical evaluation of the highest ranking tests in each of the stepwise discriminant function analyses across the follow-up years. The eight tests selected detected almost all of those children destined to extremes in the combined reading criterion distribution at the end of grade 2 (i.e., Severe and Superior groups). The same three tests again ranked highest (Finger Localization, Alphabet Recitation, and Recognition-Discrimination).

B. NEW STUDY: A SIX YEAR PREDICTIVE FOLLOW-UP (1970–1976)

In view of the high predictive accuracy of the developmental tests against the grade-2 reading criteria, the question remained as to whether predictive accuracy would attenuate as the test-criterion interval increased to six years. An interval of this magnitude would seemingly increase the number of uncontrolled environmental, growth, learning, and experiential factors which could produce changes in criterion group membership, and thus lower the predictive accuracy of the early tests. The vast majority of children in the Severe group were, in fact, receiving remedial help either in the schools or privately by the end of grade 3. It therefore became necessary to determine whether the incidence of reading problems decreased between grades 2 and 5, and, if not, to determine whether the same children again fell in the same outcome groups. This question will be addressed in the section on prognosis (Section III).

Criterion variable
Classroom Reading Level was again used to assign children into the four reading criterion groups at the end of Grade 5. The criterion groups and their corresponding reading levels were Severe (Third Reader or below), Mild (Fourth Reader), Average (Fifth Reader), and Superior (Sixth Reader or above). The resulting distribution of 442 Ss included 90 Severe, 94 Mild, 168 Average, and 90 Superior, revealing a major increase in the incidence of Severes between grades 2 and 5 (12% vs. 20%) using the same subjects!

Predictive analyses
The next question was whether this reassignment of children into new criterion groups, plus the uncontrolled sources of variation between grades 2 and

325

TABLE 16-3
Predictive Classification of Children into Classroom Reading Level
Criterion Reading Groups (Grade 5) Based on Discriminant
Function Composite Scores (Grade K)

	CRITERION GROUPS			
PREDICTIONS	SEVERE	MILD	AVERAGE	SUPERIOR
(+) N	77	56	50	13
%	(86)	(60)	(36)	(14)
(−) N	13	38	108	77
%	(14)	(40)	(64)	(86)
Total	90	94	168	90

5, would lower the predictive accuracy of the kindergarten tests. A four-group discriminant function analysis was therefore computed, using only those tests which in recent years have been employed as an experimental five-variable abbreviated battery (FL, R-D, VMI, Alph., and PPVT).

Table 16-3 presents a comparison of the 1970 test predictions (rows) against the grade-5 outcomes (columns). The valid positive rate was 86 percent for Severe cases, but only 20 percent for the Milds. The tests correctly predicted 64 percent of the Average readers and 86 percent of the Superior readers (valid negatives). One striking feature in this table is that the predictive outcomes were virtually identical to the third-year follow-up (Table 16-3). Again, predictive accuracy was largely confined to the extremes of the reading distribution. Also, the overall hit rate in this six-year follow-up was only slightly lower than the third-year follow-up (72% and 76%, respectively). Despite the overlap error in the Mild and Average reading groups in both follow-up years, the developmental test battery nevertheless managed to forecast the vast majority of children destined to become disabled readers in later grades (2–5). The stability of results between follow-up years three and six is particularly striking by virtue of the number of uncontrolled sources of variation (e.g., environmental, growth, treatment) that could have produced changes in reading achievement during these years.

Predictive ranking of tests

A stepwise discriminant function analysis was then computed on the *total* 16-variable test battery to determine the ranking of the predictor variables in terms of their criterion discrimination. Results showed that the Finger Localization Test ranked highest, followed cumulatively by the *Peabody, Beery,* and Alphabet Recitation tests. Two tests again loaded on Factor 1 which was postulated to tap those sensorimotor-perceptual skills felt to develop early in childhood.

Related achievement criteria
Because of the marked increase in reading disorders in the population in the last three years, more careful independent evaluation of classroom performance seemed warranted. Individual handwriting and math scores were therefore obtained on each of the children from the classroom teachers at the end of grade 5. WRAT scores for reading, spelling, and math were also obtained on a smaller number of children in each criterion group who were residing in Florida and Georgia at the end of that grade.

Handwriting skills
Each child's handwriting skills were rated by his teacher on a 5-point scale ranging from unsatisfactory through excellent. An ANOVA revealed significant differences between Classroom Reading Level groups, with the Severe and Mild reading disability groups both rated as deficient in handwriting skills.

Math skills
Ratings of math skills were obtained via teacher questionnaire for all of the children using a 10-point grade-level scale. An ANOVA revealed a robust difference between reading groups, with the Severe group exhibiting an almost 2.5-year lag in math skills.

WRAT reading, spelling, and math skills
Significant differences between Classroom Reading criterion groups were revealed by ANOVA's computed on the grade-month equivalency scores for each of these subtests. In the areas of reading and math, the grade levels skills obtained on this objective test were virtually identical to those obtained from the teacher ratings of classroom performance.

The results of these additional criterion analyses provide additional support for the validity of the Classroom Reading Level measure used throughout years 3–6 of this project. The results also indicate that the achievement disability in the Severe group involves more than a reading handicap per se in that substantial lags were also noted in related skills such as *math, spelling,* and *handwriting.*

C. AN EARLY INTERVENTION MODEL:
AN EXAMPLE OF PREDICTIVE UTILITY

This section is addressed to a theoretical application of the predictive test signs derived from the abbreviated test battery administered in grade K. In view of the reduced time for administration of this battery and its apparent stability as a predictor in follow-up years, its potential relevance increases for educational application. If one assumes that preliminary validation of the battery is demonstrated, then one might proceed to issues of cost, risk, and utility (e.g., statistical decision theory). In the present context, the question might be raised as to the utility of this test battery in providing a decisional basis upon which to initiate or withhold treatment for an individual child at the beginning of kindergarten. This decisional process, which was prompted by the consistently high predictive accuracy in the extreme reading groups across years, is determined by computing the conditional probability of the differential test signs $(+, -)$. These conditional probability values are based on the inverse probabilities of the test signs (valid and false positives, and valid and false negatives) and the base rates of reading competency in this population (Meehl and Rosen, 1955; Satz, Fennell, and Reilly, 1970). To compute the conditional probabilities for each of the test signs, the $(+)$ and $(-)$ rows in Table 16-4 were subdivided (on the basis of the original four-group discriminant function analysis) to generate four levels of test decisions $(++), (+), (-), (--)$. Table 16-4 presents this 4×4 contingency table in which test signs (and decisions) are represented by rows and the outcomes are represented by columns. This table allows the educator to determine the probability that a given child is destined to reading disability or competence in six years, given that his test scores fall in the $(++), (+), (-), (--)$ range. As such, it also provides him with grounds for deciding whether intervention should be instituted or withheld.

The results of this analysis indicate that, given a severe high-risk sign $(++)$, the decision to initiate treatment in grade K would have been correct in 78 percent of the cases and would have included the majority (67%) of the potential Severe cases; only 4 percent of the potential Superior readers would have been identified for the prevention program. If, on the other

TABLE 16-4

Probability of Decision Risk (Treatment/No Treatment) Associated
With Differential Composite Test Score Predictions to Grade 5 Classroom
Reading Level

				CRITERION GROUPS			
PREDIC- TIONS	DECI- SION	SEVERE	MILD	AVERAGE	SUPERIOR	RATIO CORRECT	p
(++)	T	60	28	21	4	88/113	.78
(+)	T	17	28	39	9	45/93	.48
(−)	NT	4	29	48	21	69/102	.68
(− −)	NT	9	9	60	56	116/134	.87
	Total	90	94	168	90		

hand, a more liberal intervention policy was adopted, i.e., to also initiate treatment for children who showed less severe high-risk signs (+), this decision
would have produced too many false positive errors. For example, while it
would have yielded an additional number of high-risk children into the treatment program, it would have been compromised by the excessive number of
low-risk children. The probability of being correct with this test sign (+)
would therefore have been low (35/93 = .32).

The decision outcomes for low-risk test signs were respectable for
both liberal (−) and conservative (− −) treatment strategies. Given a low-
risk test sign (−), the decision to *withhold treatment* in grade K would
have been correct in 68 percent of the cases (69/102); however, it would
have screened out 33 high-risk children, four of whom would have become
Severe reading casualties in six years. If, on the other hand, a more conservative decision policy was adopted, i.e., to withhold treatment only for children
who showed extremely low risk test signs (− −), then this decision would
have been correct in 87 percent of the cases. Long-term treatment decisions
made during kindergarten, using these test signs, would have therefore been
correct decisions in the majority of cases for three of the test signs. This decision matrix would have provided some protection against treating a misclassified high-risk child, particularly a potential Superior reader, while at the same
time assuring valid early detection of at least 67 percent of the children destined to become severely disabled readers in later years.

These findings illustrate the potential usefulness of a brief and economical detection procedure which generates the conditional outcome probabilities for an individual child during kindergarten. Within this framework, educators could base treatment strategies on a number of factors including the incidence of severe high-risk children in the school, available resources, and the risks associated with intervention vs. nonintervention.

It should be apparent that the final decision to initiate or withhold treatment should be made by the educator who considers a multiplicity of factors. The utility table presented in this section simplifies this decisional task by generating the likelihood probabilities and risks for either decision (T or NT) in each individual case.

D. CROSS-VALIDATION ON INDEPENDENT SAMPLES

1. Review study: a three-year predictive follow-up
This section summarizes the first major cross-validation of the predictive test battery given to the original kindergarten population. Despite the high predictive accuracy and internal consistency (predictive ranking) which was demonstrated across follow-up years for both the full and abbreviated test batteries, the results may be interpreted as only preliminary until replicated on an independent group of children evaluated within the same time framework. A review of the early detection literature reveals virtually no attempt to address this crucial validation problem.

In this study (Satz, Friel, and Rudegair, 1976), it was decided to cross-validate the discriminant function composites derived from the third-year follow-up of the standardization population (grade 2) against a new sample of children who were tested at the beginning of kindergarten in 1971 and whose criterion reading scores were obtained three years later at the end of grade 2. This cross-validation sample included 181 white boys who were individually tested under conditions identical to the standardization population in 1970. The same two types of reading assessment which were utilized with the standardization group were obtained at the end of grade 2: Classroom Reading Level and Classroom Reading Level plus IOTA Word Recognition.

Classroom Reading Level: Prediction was based on test scores of the cross-validation group during kindergarten and the grade 2 standardization discriminant functions against the criterion of Classroom Reading Level assessed at the end of grade 2 for the cross-validation group. Reading measures were obtained for 96 percent of the original 181 Ss. The resulting distribution of reading groups can be seen in the column totals of Table 16-5: 18 Severe, 25 Mild, 92 Average, and 40 Superior. This distribution reveals a 25 percent overall incidence of reading disability and an incidence of 10.3% in the Severe group. These percentages are almost identical to the figures obtained in grade 2 for the standardization population (cf. Table 16-1).

The predictive hits of the abbreviated test battery can also be seen in Table 16-5. The tests correctly predicted 89 percent of the Severe cases but only 36 percent of the Mild cases (valid positives). They correctly predicted 70 percent of the Average readers and 93 percent of the Superior readers (valid negatives). These detection outcomes are virtually the same as with the standardization population for the third and sixth year follow-up (grades 2 and 5), in that predictive accuracy was greatest for the extreme reading groups (Severe and Superior). The overall hit rate was 72 percent of the sample. This predictive accuracy, based on discriminant functions derived from a different sample and with a test-criterion interval of nearly three years, lends convincing support for the intrinsic validity of the tests.

Predictive ranking of tests
A stepwise discriminant function analysis was computed on the full battery to see if the discriminative ranking of the tests remained essentially the same for this cross-validation sample of children. The results were as follows: Fin-

TABLE 16-5
Predictive Classification of Cross-Validation Sample into Classroom Reading Level Criterion Reading Groups (Grade 2) Based on Discriminant Function Weights of Standardization Population

	CRITERION GROUPS			
PREDICTIONS	SEVERE	MILD	AVERAGE	SUPERIOR
(+) N	16	9	28	3
%	(89)	(36)	(30)	(7)
(−) N	2	16	64	37
%	(11)	(64)	(70)	(93)
Total	18	25	92	40

ger Localization Test ranked highest, followed cumulatively by the Embedded Figures Test and the WISC Similarities Subtest. It is interesting to note that the Finger Localization Test again ranked highest in terms of criterion discrimination, but that the rankings varied from the standardization studies in terms of tests and factor loadings. Although the two top ranking tests were again associated with Factor I, the next was associated with Factor II (Similarities). This change in discriminative ranking reflects subtle differences in the composition of the cross-validation group as compared to the standardization population, one difference stemming from a selection bias in favor of urban schools. A second difference might relate to the expected discrepancy between a sample ($N = 181$) and a population ($N = 497$). Regardless of the reason for this difference, the overall hit rate remained essentially unchanged.

2. Review study. A one year predictive follow-up
The purpose of this study (Satz and Friel, 1978) was to determine whether the eight-variable abbreviated test battery, given in September, could predict achievement ratings at the end of kindergarten on a new group of kindergarten children (boys, girls, blacks, whites) in an entire elementary school. An additional purpose was to institute a prevention program on a random sample of predicted high-risk (++) children in this group and to evaluate the test outcomes despite the possible ameliorative effects of treatment. This design was felt to provide a more powerful test of the predictive efficiency of the abbreviated battery.

The sample consisted of all the children who entered kindergarten in September 1974 at Stephen Foster Elementary School. The 132 Ss consisted of 28 black Ss (13 boys, 15 girls) and 104 white Ss (54 boys, 50 girls). At the conclusion of the individual test administrations, the data were analyzed utilizing the lambda weights derived from the pooled standardization and cross validation groups of white boys ($N = 633$). Based on this analysis, 44 children were identified as severe high risk, 28 of whom were randomly assigned to two treatment groups for the duration of the school year. The remaining 16 Ss were placed into a nontreatment group ($N = 16$). This random assignment yielded approximately equal numbers of children (by race and sex) in each of the three groups. To prevent individual labeling of children, all test information was withheld from the teachers during the school year. As a further control, selected children from the other predicted groups (low risk) were periodically brought to the intervention site during the year for additional research study.

Achievement Criterion Ratings. An overall achievement rating made by the kindergarten teachers at the end of the year was used to provide four different achievement groups. Criterion information yielded 12 Severe, 33 Mild, 63 Average, and 20 Superior. This criterion evaluation, while tentative, has nevertheless been shown to hold up in later years after more objective reading measures became available (Satz, Friel, and Rudegeair, 1976).

Classification Results. A comparison of the predicted achievement group based on the tests given in September with the end-of-year achievement groups is presented in Table 16-6. The composite test predictions, reduced to high risk and low risk, are represented by rows; the four achievement outcomes are represented by columns. Inspection of this table reveals that the tests correctly predicted 100 percent of the Severe and Superior groups, while misclassifying 21 percent of the Mild group and 41 percent of the Average group. The overall hit rate was 74 percent for this cross-validation sample.

The outcomes for the severe high-risk predictions (++) which formed the decisional basis for the treatment programs in September were determined. These indicators (++) detected 100 percent of the children who at the end of kindergarten fell in the Severe group and 58 percent of those who fell in the Mild group. Although it misclassified 13 children (20%) who fell in the Average group at the end of kindergarten, it did not misclassify any children who later fell in the Superior group.

TABLE 16-6
Predictive Classification of Cross-Validation Sample II into Achievement Groups (End of Grade K) Based on Discriminant Function Weights from Standardization Population and Cross-Validation Group I

		CRITERION ACHIEVEMENT GROUPS			
PREDICTIONS		SEVERE	MILD	AVERAGE	SUPERIOR
(+)	N	12	26	26	0
	%	(100)	(80)	(41)	(0)
(−)	N	0	7	37	20
	%	(0)	(20)	(59)	(100)
	Total	12	33	63	20

When these children with severe risk signs were examined for treatment-group assignment it was found that eight of the 13 misclassified children were in treatment groups, which potentially reduces the predictive error to only five children.

3. New study: a two year predictive follow-up

This study was addressed to the second-year follow-up of those children discussed in the preceding subsection. At the end of grade 1, criterion rating forms were obtained on 114 of the original population of 132 children.

Criterion rating forms were completed by the individual classroom teachers based on the actual Classroom Reading Level of each child. Children were then classified into one of four different criterion groups as follows: Severe ($N = 4$), Mild ($N = 17$), Average ($N = 57$), and Superior ($N = 36$). This distribution reveals an incidence of only 4 percent for children with severe reading problems. Although this incidence is somewhat lower than that obtained for the standardization sample at the end of year 3, it is comparable to the percentage of predicted Severes in the same sample for the two-year follow-up (Satz and Friel, 1974). Because of the low number of Ss in the Severe group, it was decided to combine the Severe and Mild groups into a High Risk ($N = 21$) group and the Average and Superior Ss into a Low Risk ($N = 93$) group. Combining groups ensures the appropriateness of the multivariate statistical procedures employed and enhances the prospects for cross-validation of results with the present sample in future years. It should be noted that this time interval (2-year follow-up) represents only a preliminary assessment of Reading Level. At the end of grade 2 (3-year follow-up) a more valid assessment can be obtained, which should also assign enough Ss to the Severe group for the standard four-group analyses.

A stepwise linear discriminant function was then computed using the test scores from the eight-variable kindergarten battery and the grade-1 Classroom Reading Level criterion. The tests correctly identified 86 percent of the High Risk children (valid positives), and 88 percent of the Low Risk children (valid negatives). This latter finding reveals a lower false positive rate (12%), as the interval between test and criterion evaluation increased to two years. In terms of overall hit rate, the tests correctly identified 100 of the 114 children (88%).

A stepwise discriminant function analysis was computed to determine the predictive ranking of the variables. Socioeconomic Status ranked the highest, followed by Alphabet Recitation, Finger Localization, and PPVT. This particular ranking undoubtedly reflects the more heterogeneous nature of the present sample.

II. SOME DEVELOPMENTAL PRECURSORS OF READING DISABILITY: THE PROBLEM OF LANGUAGE READINESS

The purpose of this section is to review briefly the nature of those variables which have consistently been shown to forecast subsequent problems in reading and other achievement areas in this project and to examine the predictive discriminability of these variables when compared with a new battery of language tests. The reason for this latter comparison is due largely to the absence of psycholinguistic measures in the original standardization battery.

Although three measures of verbal-conceptual function were included (PPVT, WPPSI Similarities subtest, and Verbal Fluency), each of which loaded on Factor II, they comprised only a small part of the test battery and provided no assessment of morphology or syntax. Consequently, any conclusions concerning the unique contribution of "earlier developing" sensori-motor-perceptual skills (Factor I) would be unwarranted within the context of the present theory. This is particularly true in view of the contention within the area of developmental psycholinguistics that certain components of language, especially syntax, develop very rapidly and are in primary ascendancy during preschool years (cf. Dale, 1976).

Before discussing this recent comparison study, it might be helpful to review the results of the separate stepwise discriminant function analyses for the original standardization population in follow-up years three to six, respectively. Inspection of the predictive rankings for each of these criterion follow-up years shows that Finger Localization was selected first in each of the years despite the administration of independent reading measures at each criterion probe. Similar results were observed for the cross-validation samples across years. The most striking finding is the frequency of Factor I tests in the top discriminative ranks. One might also note that the verbal-conceptual factor (II) was selected only once across the four follow-up years (3–6). Furthermore, despite the instability often characteristic of stepwise procedures (Fletcher and Satz, 1977), the triad of Finger Localization (I), Alphabet

Recitation (III), and Recognition-Discrimination (1) ranked high in each of follow-up years. In year six, Recognition-Discrimination was replaced by the Beery (VMI), another Factor I measure of perceptual-cognitive processing.

While these results are compatible with the theory that those skills which primarily assess the maturational and developmental readiness of the child during preschool are most likely to forecast later progress in reading, they do not permit any conclusions regarding the role of language and conceptual processes as developmental precursors of reading disability. To repeat, the battery comprised only a small number of language tests, none of which assessed morphological or syntactic competence. Each of these language measures, however, though seldom emerging in the top predictive rankings, has nevertheless continued to discriminate between reading groups (univariate tests) across follow-up years (Satz, Friel, and Rudegeair, 1976).

For this reason, it was decided to conduct a separate longitudinal-predictive study which comprised tests from the standard eight variable abbreviated test battery and a battery of five psycholinguistic measures. The sample selected comprised children who began kindergarten in 1974. Comparisons of predictions based on the battery and criterion follow-ups at the end of grade K (cross-validation) and grade 1 (validation) were presented in the last section. The present study is addressed to the question of improving prediction with the inclusion of additional psycholinguistic measures.

CRITERION VARIABLE

Criterion rating forms were completed by the individual classroom teachers based on actual Classroom Reading Level at the end of grade 1. Children ($N = 114$) were then classified into two groups: High Risk ($N = 21$) and Low Risk ($N = 93$). This assessment represents only a preliminary attempt at criterion evaluation in a very heterogeneous and small sample. Consequently, the results must be interpreted with caution until more adequate reading measures are obtained on the children at the end of grade 2.

LANGUAGE MEASURES

The following five language tests were individually administered during kindergarten over a period of two months after the abbreviated battery:

Verbal Fluency, ITPA Grammatic Closure subtest (Kirk, McCarthy, and Kirk, 1968), Berry-Talbot Comprehension of Grammar Test (Berry, 1969) and Syntax Test (Scholes, Tanis, and Turner, 1977). The Peabody Picture Vocabulary Test, which was administered in September, was also included in this language battery.

The *Verbal Fluency* test is identical to the one used on the standard unabbreviated battery and requires the child to name (orally) as many words as he can denoting objects belonging in various household rooms (e.g., kitchen) under timed conditions. The ITPA Grammatic Closure subtest requires oral inflections to a variety of real words, thereby assessing the child's ability to form plurals, possessives, and other grammatic inflections. The Berry-Talbot assesses the child's knowledge of English morphology by requiring him to inflect and derive nonsense words from various stimuli. Thus, for pluralization, the child is shown a picture of a bird-like creature and told it is a "wug." Then two of the pictured creatures are presented and the child is asked how many of the creatures there are (e.g., two "wugs"). This particular test has been shown to tap skills developing primarily between the ages of 5 and 8 (Berko, 1961) and has been administered to older (second grade) reading-disabled children (Vogel, 1974). The Syntax Test (Scholes, Tanis, and Turner, 1977) purports to assess syntactic comprehension based on the location and presence of the article "the" in the resolution of direct/indirect object ambiguity. The ambiguity is presented by reading different sentence types (varying in linguistic complexity) to the child, who is required to point to the picture which correctly matches the sentence. The preceding auditory and/or visual tests are appropriate for use with five-year-old children and do not require any reading ability.

PREDICTIVE RESULTS: LANGUAGE BATTERY

A stepwise linear discriminant function was computed on the language scores and the Classroom Reading Level criterion at the end of grade 1. Socioeconomic Status was included as a predictor variable to equate the comparative analyses and help account for the relative heterogeneity of this sample in terms of SES and Race. The results of this analysis can be seen in Table 16-7. The tests correctly identified 71 percent of the High Risk children and 84% of the Low Risk children. Overall, the tests correctly identified 93 of the 114 children (82%). Despite the preliminary status of the criterion measure, these

TABLE 16-7

Predictive Classification of Cross-Validation Sample II into Grade 1
Achievement Groups Based on Language Battery (Grade K)

		CRITERION GROUPS	
PREDICTIONS		HIGH RISK	LOW RISK
(+)	N	15	15
	%	(71)	(16)
(−)	N	6	78
	%	(29)	(84)
	Total	21	93

predictive findings are almost as high as the abbreviated test battery for the same children and two-year test-criterion interval.

The stepwise procedure revealed the following ranking of tests in the language battery: SES ranked highest followed by the Grammatic Closure, PPVT, World Fluency, Berry-Talbot, and Syntax tests. It is interesting to note that two of the best three predictors in this language battery are also included in the standard battery which was administered to the original population.

PREDICTIVE RESULTS: NONLANGUAGE BATTERY

A second stepwise discriminant function analysis was computed using tests from the abbreviated battery against grade 1 Classroom Reading Level, but which excluded PPVT in order to remove the effects of the Verbal Factor (II) on predictive classification. The tests correctly identified 90 percent of the High Risk children and 87 percent of the Low Risk children. The overall hit rate (88%) was slightly higher than the 82 percent classification rate obtained with the language battery, while both false positive and false negative decision errors were slightly lower for the nonlanguage battery. Stepwise ranking was as follows: *Socioeconomic Status, Alphabet Recitation,* and *Finger Localization.*

In order to make a more direct comparison between the two batteries, a final linear stepwise discriminant function was computed using the 12 tests from both batteries. No increase in predictive power was found with the inclusion of the additional language measures. The stepwise procedure revealed that Socioeconomic Status again ranked highest, followed by Alphabet Recitation and Finger Localization.

The results provide additional information on the developmental precursors of reading disability. It must be emphasized, however, that the results are based on a preliminary criterion derived from a small sample, which, due to the inclusion of blacks, was probably more heterogeneous with respect to SES. Hence the emergence of SES and Alphabet Recitation, both Factor-III measures, as the best predictors in all the comparative analyses.

The results suggest that cultural, linguistic, conceptual, and perceptual skills all play an important role in forecasting later reading achievement. In terms of predictive power, however, the contribution of psycholinguistic variables may be secondary to those preconceptual sensory-motor and perceptual skills which have been shown to develop earlier during the ages of five to seven. Such a finding is consistent with those of White (1965), who has focused on the transitional shift in mental activity that is presumed to occur during this developmental period in which juvenile mental processes give way to higher mental processes. He has suggested that an unfolding developmental process occurs during this transition period, particularly for preconceptual activity, whereas conceptual processes (e.g., verbal mediation) are just beginning to develop. This latter process, which White refers to as the "cognitive layer" has two distinctive features: (1) it inhibits lower-level associates responses, and (2) it develops relatively slower and later. This position is therefore quite compatible with the developmental studies of Bloom (1964) and Thurstone (1955) that were reviewed briefly under the section dealing with theory.

More direct evidence for the concept of developmental shifts in language acquisition (phonology, syntax, and semantics) are reviewed in a recent paper by Palermo and Molfese (1972). They point out that these shifts (between 5 and 8 years and between 10 and 15 years) are marked by instability in linguistic development and are followed by growth to new levels and more stable linguistic performance. "It may not be coincidental," they state, "that these are precisely the periods in cognitive development marked by Piaget (1970) as transition points from preoperational thought to concrete operations in the first case and from concrete operations to formal operations in the second case."

Palermo and Molfese's position is heuristic in that it advocates that a theory of language development must be embedded within the larger context of a theory of cognitive development. "While cognitive development may precede its expression in language, it is obvious that the reverse is unlikely. Thus, for example, the use of plural inflections must be preceded by a concept of number, and the full comprehension of the logical connective 'or' must be preceded by the concept of set union." In a similar vein, Slobin (1971) wrote that "cognitive and linguistic development do not run off in unison." He also contended, however, that cognitive development must precede linguistic development because a child expresses and comprehends only those "meanings consistent with the child's level of development." Such a contention may be important even for the very early acquisition of language. In describing the earliest stage of childhood speech (Stage I), Brown (1973) suggested that "the meanings of Stage I derive from sensorimotor intelligence. . . ."

Hagen, Jongeward, and Kail (1975) have proposed that such concepts in cognitive development be employed to understand how children later develop more efficient strategies in memory processing. The role of age differences in the types of strategies used for remembering (and learning) in children is highlighted in their review. They cite, for example, Underwood's (1969) theory of a developmental sequence of attribute dominance, such that the use of different stimulus attributes is apparent at different ages. Hagen and colleagues suggest that when a child's ability to immediately acquire and recall information is exceeded, higher-order linguistic strategies are required. Because such semantically based strategies emerge over a period of years, their implementation in active memorizing (and learning) is consistently seen only at 10–11 years of age (and later). "The child's increased knowledge of linguistic properties and conceptual relations can and will be used if appropriate to the task at hand" (p. 95). The ability to use this knowledge occurs primarily in older children because of the complexity and slower developmental acquisition of these strategies.

The preceding comments on language acquisition must be treated as speculative when applied to the relationship between *language readiness* and later *reading competence*. Of course, many of the linguistically based strategies involved in memory are clearly important for older fluent readers. For beginning readers, the role of language readiness is unclear. Some research with relatively older reading-disabled children has demonstrated the presence of linguistic deficits (e.g., Blank and Bridger, 1966; Vellutino et al., 1975b; Vogel, 1974). Other research has shown, in contrast, no difference between younger normal and reading-disabled children in the attainment of an important 5–7 developmental change, the syntagmatic-paradigmatic shift (Bartel, Grill, and Bartel, 1973). From a predictive point of view, the present study, which is tentative and rests on a preliminary two-year follow-up of a small heterogeneous sample, is among the few providing empirical assessment of the relative importance of early language readiness.

A more parsimonious approach to the question of which early skills are most important would be to conceptualize the problem in terms of developmental or maturational readiness and to dismiss reference to specific precursor skills (e.g., linguistic or perceptual). This latter position is reflected in the work of de Hirsch, Jansky, and Langford (1966) who found that later achievement in reading and writing was predicted significantly better by developmental tests that were maturation-sensitive. They reported that 76 percent of the maturation-sensitive tests were significantly correlated with second-grade achievement, compared to only 17 percent of the nonmaturation-sensitive tests. It is interesting to note, however, that a majority of their maturation-sensitive tests comprised measures of sensorimotor and perceptual skills that have been postulated to develop earlier (Satz and Van Nostrand, 1973). Tests of language comprehension, word finding, and grammatical form were reflected in the nonmaturation-sensitive tests.

The primary role of early-developing skills (particularly in sensorimotor and perceptual-motor integration) as developmental precursors in reading disability has already been suggested. Visual perception, for example, has long been known to play a part during the early stages of reading ". . . but becomes far less important at higher grades when cognitive and, above all, linguistic competences move more and more into the foreground" (Jansky and de Hirsch, 1972, p. 14). Visual-perceptual processes have been shown to be crucial in the early stages of reading when irrelevant perceptual information must be reduced and nondistinctive features of configurations must be filtered out (Gibson, 1968).

The theory advanced in this chapter (Satz and Van Nostrand, 1973) postulates that a lag in the maturation of the brain delays the acquisition of those developmental skills which are in primary ascendance between five and six years of age. Consequently, this lag will be expressed behaviorally as a general developmental unreadiness in the child which will produce subsequent delays in the acquisition of reading skills. The theory predicts, however, that these high-risk children will eventually "catch up" on these earlier-developing skills but will then lag on those more cognitive-linguistic skills which are presumed to have a slower and later ontogenetic development (Palermo and Molfese, 1972; Hagen et al., 1975). Preliminary support for this hypothesis was found in a recent three-year follow-up of the children in the original standardization population (Satz, Friel, and Rudegeair, 1974).

When retested at the end of grade 2 (at which time criterion reading measures were obtained), it was shown that the disabled readers caught up to their matched controls only on those measures which, during grade K, represented the best predictive estimates of later reading disability (i.e., Finger Localization, Alphabet Recitation, and Recognition-Discrimination). (In the case of two of these measures [FL and Alph], a possible ceiling effect may have obscured group differences at the end of grade 2.) Despite this delayed recovery or acquisition, the children continued to lag in reading and writing skills. Had these developmental measures been employed initially at eight years of age, no group differences would have been observed, nor would any information have been available on the status of these measures *before* the child began to read. Additional support for the *predictive* accuracy of visual-discrimination and sensory-perceptual tasks during early grades is evident in the results of five recent longitudinal studies. The most recent study (Rourke and Orr, 1976) was addressed specifically to the relative accuracy of a number of reading and spelling tests, two measures of psychometric intelligence (WISC and PPVT), and a speeded visual discrimination task (Underlining Test) in predicting four-year follow-up reading achievement from grades 1–2 to grades 4–5. The power of this study is that it compared the discriminative ranking of both nonverbal-perceptual and verbal-cognitive measures, the latter of which were virtually identical to the subsequent criterion measures (i.e., reading and spelling). According to the authors, "The visual discrimination measure utilized in the present study, a paper-and-pencil test originally developed by Doehring (1968), was selected in light of the Satz et al. findings and because performance on this test had consistently yielded rather marked discrepancies between normal and retarded readers over the first three evaluation periods" (pp. 6–7).

The results of the stepwise regression analysis showed that performance on the Underlining Test was ". . . a far more potent means of identifying retarded readers who are 'at risk' (at ages 7–8) with respect to eventual reading and spelling achievement (at ages 11–12) than are the measures of psychometric intelligence, reading, or spelling which were used" (p. 18). Those subtests of the Underlining Test which appeared in the best regression models most often involved target and distractor items which were nonverbal: sequences of geometric forms (#8) and gestalt figures (#4).

An earlier study by Gruen (1972) compared the predictive accuracy of a battery of perceptual-motor and cognitive-intellectual tasks administered to a large group of first-grade ($N = 204$) and third-grade Ss ($N = 202$) against the end-of-year reading achievement. The multiple regression analyses showed that the perceptual-motor tests accounted for more of the explained variation in reading achievement scores (vocabulary and comprehension) than did cognitive-intellectual tests for *first-grade* boys and girls. In contrast, the cognitive-intellectual tests accounted for more of the explained variation in reading achievement scores (vocabulary and comprehension) than did perceptual-motor tests for *third-grade* boys and girls.

Somewhat similar findings were reported in a recent study of children who were tested at the *end* of grade K and whose reading scores were assessed at the end of grade 1 (Lindgren, 1975). This study is of particular interest because it employed many of the tests used in the Satz abbreviated battery, although initial testing occurred when the children were approximately nine months older. The predictive hits, based on a stepwise discriminant function analysis, resulted in an overall accuracy of 91 percent (valid positives = 79%, false positives = 4%). The discriminative ranking was as follows: Letter Naming, PPVT(IQ), Finger Localization, and Beery (VMI). Lower rankings were found for SES, family history of reading problems, speech difficulties, and Behavior Checklist scores. The lower ranking for Finger Localization, while still additive, may have been due to the older ages of the children when tested.

Jansky and de Hirsch (1972), in a predictive follow-up of 508 children tested at the end of grade K, found that their Screening Index correctly identified 76 percent of the remaining 355 children at the end of grade 2. The tests identified 79 percent of the failing readers (valid positives), but misclassified 25 percent of the good readers (false positives). In terms of predictive ranking, Letter Naming ranked highest followed by Picture Naming, Word Matching (Gates Reading Readiness subtest), and copying of the Bender Gestalten. According to the authors (p. 57): "Three of these activities, letter naming, copying the Bender designs, and word matching, can be considered hardy perennials, and it is thus not surprising that they rose to the top of the ranks of potential predictors again in the present study."

The predictive SEARCH battery of Silver and Hagin (1975) has consistently found that tests of visual perception (discrimination, recall, and visuomotor control) contribute significantly in forecasting later reading and learning problems. Although only one year follow-ups have been conducted, the authors have followed this screening with early intervention and have found that remediation of these lags in early grades leads to improved reading and learning in school (Silver, Hagin, and Hersh, 1967).

The preceding discussion suggests that the search for the developmental precursors of specific reading disability may profit from the use of a longitudinal developmental perspective. There are two immediate advantages in this approach. First, it provides the opportunity to uncover those behavioral-developmental antecedents that precede the onset of the reading disorder which in turn could bring us one step closer to etiology. Second, through early identification, based on these developmental precursors, attempts could be made to implement prevention programs when the child is younger, more plastic, and free from the shattering effects of repeated academic failure.

The nature of these developmental precursors, however, still remains unclear. Some evidence was presented which suggests that they are not necessarily closely associated with general language readiness at age five; however, terminological problems continue to retard progress in this theoretical area. The need for basic studies with younger normal readers is certainly indicated to help isolate the potential effects of cultural experience, perceptual learning, cognitive strategies, and language development on reading. Finally, future research should incorporate the methodological guidelines outlined in Section I: large, homogeneous populations should be employed which provide better control over factors such as cultural deprivation and early preschool experience. Such control was not achieved in the present study, which may limit the generalization of the results of this Section (II).

III. INCIDENCE AND PROGNOSIS:
A THREE- AND SIX-YEAR FOLLOW-UP

The purpose of this section is to return to the original standardization population discussed in Section I and to examine some preliminary findings on the yearly incidence and prognosis of reading disability in this population of white boys who began kindergarten in 1970.

The selection of a total population of children, particularly boys who are at higher risk for reading disability, plus the use of yearly criterion probes coupled with a negligible attrition rate in this population over the last six years (10%), provides a rare opportunity to address these problems. The need for epidemiological research in this area has been emphasized by Yule and Rutter (1976). For this reason it was decided to compute the yearly incidence rates in this population of boys starting from the end of grade 1 at which time reading measures were first employed. The results can be seen in Figure 16-1.

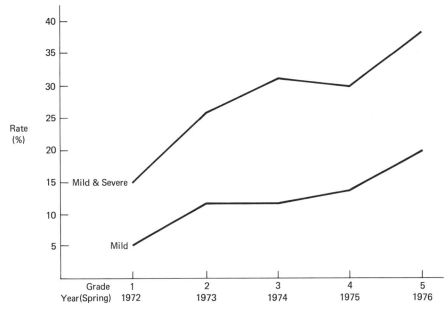

Figure 16-1
    Yearly incidence rates of severe and mild reading disability in population of white boys who began grade K in 1970: a six-year follow-up.

Inspection of this figure reveals that the incidence of Severe and Mild reading disorders increased after grade 1 when more objective reading measures were available, and remained essentially the same (grades 2–4) until the last year, at which time a significant increase in both Severe and Mild cases again occurred.

    The percentage of Severe cases is more illustrative because it refers to those children at each grade level who were at least 1–2.5 years behind in reading. It is largely these children to whom prevalence studies have referred (Gaddes, 1976). Until grade 5 it appeared as if the incidence of Severe cases had plateaued at approximately 12 percent; this estimate increased dramatically to 20 percent, however, between grades 4 and 5. It was shown earlier (Section I) that this increase was not an artifact of the criterion measure (i.e., Classroom Reading Level) because similar lags were found on the WRAT, which revealed significant delays in reading, math and spelling. Although seemingly high, this estimate (i.e., 20%) is approximately what would be expected for a male population. If the national incidence is approximately 15 percent (Gaddes, 1976) with a sex ratio of 4 : 1 in favor of boys, then the incidence should increase to 24 percent in a male population. It was also learned that this upward shift in reading disorders may have been related to the decreased emphasis on basic reading skills during grade 5. Consequently, many of those high-risk children who for years had been classified within the Mild reading-disability group became increasingly vulnerable over time, particularly to external changes in the teaching curriculum. In fact, of the 32 additional children who entered the Severe group at the end of grade 5, 78 percent came from the grade 4 Mild reading-disability group. Unfortunately, 95 percent of those children who were in the severely disabled reading group at the end of grade 4 remained problem readers at the end of grade 5. Only one child improved significantly and became Average, while six were reclassified as Mild.

PROGNOSIS

In view of the increasing incidence of Severe reading cases in this population during grade 5 it was decided to examine the prognosis for the entire population of children between grades 2 and 5 for whom independent criterion reading measures were available in both years ($N = 426$, or 86% of the original population). The results can be seen in Table 16-8.

TABLE 16-8

Prognostic Changes in Reading Level Groups Between Grades 2 and 5
A Three-Year Follow-up

READING GROUPS (Yr. 3)	READING GROUPS (Yr. 6)				
	SEVERE	MILD	AVERAGE	SUPERIOR	TOTAL
Severe	40	6	3	0	49
Mild	24	27	8	3	62
Average	20	55	123	54	252
Superior	0	2	30	31	63
Total	84	90	164	88	426

Note: $\chi^2 = 237.79$, $df = p < .001$

346

Inspection of this table shows that only 3 of the 49 Severe cases in grade 2 improved by the end of grade 5 (6.1%), whereas 11 of the 62 Mild cases showed improvement during this same follow-up interval (17.7%). By contrast, 75 of the 252 Average readers had become problem readers by the end of grade 5 (30%), whereas only 2 of the 63 Superior readers shared a similar fate during this same follow-up interval (3.2%). The results, if replicable in the cross-validation sample in year six, are sobering. There is virtually no improvement in the problem readers (Severe and Mild) between grades 2 and 5, with some likelihood (30%) of delayed reading problems in grade 5 for Average readers in Grade 2. The most optimistic prognosis occurred for those children who were classified as Superior readers at the end of grade 2. Approximately 97 percent of them continued to be reading at grade level or above at the end of grade 5. The results of a Chi-square test for independence computed on this table were highly significant ($\chi^2 = 237.79$, $p < .001$), revealing a strong relationship between grades 2 and 5 in terms of criterion group membership.

These findings, while generally discouraging for children having reading problems in early grades, are compatible with four recent longitudinal follow-up studies (Muehl and Forell, 1973; Trites and Fiedorowicz, 1976; Yule and Rutter, 1976; Rourke and Orr, 1977). Reading problems identified during childhood continue to persist during adolescence. It is unclear as to whether the persistence of the reading disorder in these children is due to secondary emotional problems or merely to a failure of our educational system to help them sooner.

Chapter 17

PREVENTION

ARCHIE A. SILVER

In Chapter 16, Satz and his associates summarize their longitudinal research in identifying predictive antecedents of reading disability, present the theoretical model upon which this work is based, and compare their "abbreviated" test battery with selected psycholinguistic tests as predictors of reading achievement at the end of grade one. They present three different population samples: The first consists of white boys tested with a battery of 16 variables in October through March of their kindergarten year and followed to the end of their fifth grade. The second sample, a group of children representing the total population of white boys enrolled in five urban elementary schools in a county in Florida, were tested by means of an eight-item "abbreviated" battery and followed to the end of grade two. The third sample consists of all children (boys, girls, black, white) entering a Florida elementary school in September and followed to the end of their first grade. The criterion for reading achievement was teacher rating, and in some cases, teacher rating combined with the IOTA Word Recognition Test. The test battery comprised those items that fit the authors' theoretical construct that reading disability "reflects a lag in the maturation of the brain, which delays differentially those skills which are in primary ascendency at different chronological ages." At the kindergarten age, these skills are described as "sensory-perceptual-motor-mnemonic" abilities.

Satz and his associates state that their treatment is admittedly a biased one with "an exclusionary focus." My own contribution will be an attempt to balance this exclusionary focus and to put Satz's work in clearer perspective, particularly in light of the work which preceded his own and that which is proceeding concurrently. In doing so, I may be guilty of some measure of bias of my own.

Five major questions are considered: (1) What efforts have been made toward the primary prevention of reading failure? (2) What are the ideal characteristics of a scanning instrument for secondary prevention? (3) What should be included in a predictive battery? (4) What do readiness and scanning tests measure? (5) Can children at risk for reading failure be detected earlier than in kindergarten?

WHAT EFFORTS HAVE BEEN MADE FOR PRIMARY PREVENTION OF READING FAILURE?

Reading failure is but a symptom, a final common pathway stemming from a multitude of factors, singly or in combination. As in any complex behavior, reading involves the interaction of factors: biological (genetic, maturational, pathological) (Witsell and Silver, 1971), psychological (motivation, attention, inhibition), social (appropriate stimulation at critical ages) (Brody and Axelrad, 1970), "maternal style" (Hess and Baer, 1968), educational opportunity (Stodolsky and Lesser, 1967), appropriateness and adequacy of teaching (Hall, Keogh, and Becker, 1975). It is reasonable to assume that when the causes of reading failure become clearly understood and definable, primary preventive measures can be applied.

The *primary prevention* of reading failure therefore involves an evaluation of the contribution of each of these factors and subsequent specific intervention procedures. Such intervention may require broad social and educational planning; the control of prenatal, paranatal and neonatal defects; and modification of the environment of the first three years of life. These goals, overwhelming as they appear, should not be dismissed as unrealistic. Modest attempts to alter the effects of poverty and inappropriate stimulation upon the child have already been made in Head Start (Cicirelli, 1969, 1970; Datta, 1969; Smith and Bissell, 1970), in Early Education Programs such as those of Bereiter and Engelmann (1966, 1972), The Perry Preschool Project (Weikart, 1967, 70, 72), the Early Training Project (Klaus and Gray, 1968, 1970), The Comparative Urbana Illinois Study (M. Karnes, 1969), and those of M. Deutsch (1965). Critical review of these programs appears in Meier (1973). Their long-range effect has yet to be evaluated.

To reduce perinatal casualties, programs have been funded to the extent of $20 million over a period of five years, enabling eight medical centers to provide a full range of services for high-risk pregnancies and high-risk newborns (AMA News, August 4, 1975).

Full-scale implementation of primary prevention, however, awaits greater understanding of the process of learning to read and why children fail in reading. Given the present state of knowledge, we are for the most part limited to secondary prevention—to detect, independently of cause, those children *likely* to fail in reading and to intervene before failure occurs. Such a program ideally consists of three stages: scanning, diagnosis, and intervention.

This review will concern itself primarily with attempts at secondary prevention, the detection of the precursors of reading failure *before* actual failure has occurred.

WHAT ARE THE IDEAL CHARACTERISTICS OF A SCANNING INSTRUMENT?

Scanning is the first step of secondary prevention. By *scanning* we mean the survey of entire populations to detect those children who will fail in reading in their elementary school years. Effective detection implies that the instrument can predict future reading failure; that the incidence of false positives is negligible and of false negatives minimal; that it can be given to large numbers of children quickly and economically; that the administration of the test and the interpretation of results can be done skillfully by school personnel after brief training; that the predictive instrument is able to locate those children who need more detailed and expensive diagnostic procedures; that it is statistically acceptable from standardization through interpretation; that it is appropriate for the population studied; and that it provides a basis for intervention.

There are a number of caveats associated with scanning for early detection:

(a) Scanning does not imply diagnosis. All that scanning hopes to do is to identify those children who will fail in reading, regardless of the cause or causes of their reading failure. A scanning instrument thus is not confined to the prediction of "dyslexia," or of "specific reading disability" as currently defined. Diagnosis implies an evaluation of the neuropediatric, psychiatric, psychological, social, and educational status of each individual child to determine those factors or interaction of factors affecting the child's ability to learn. Scanning is designed only to detect a heterogeneous group whose members have but one factor in common: their function in those parameters assessed by the scanning instrument is immature when compared to their peers.

(b) It would follow that because reading failure may result from so many forces, it would be overly optimistic to expect even a multivariate scanning instrument, designed to tap all those skills thought to be important in beginning reading, to predict all children who will fail in reading and all those who will not fail. A rapid screening instrument cannot detect all the variables involved. False negatives, therefore, are to be expected. The real danger to the child comes from the false positive, i.e., the test predicts failure when the child will not fail. This raises the specter of "labeling" and of creating a "self-fulfilling prophecy."

WHAT SHOULD BE TESTED
IN A PREDICTIVE BATTERY?

There is no generally accepted unified theory as to the nature of the reading process and thus no general agreement as to what should be tested in a predictive instrument. Research here has attempted to find, by factor analysis or by discriminant function techniques, which factor or factors tested at Time$_1$ will predict success or failure on selected criteria of reading at Time$_2$.

As far back as in 1928, Nila Banton Smith found that letter matching tested in the first week of first grade yielded a correlation of .87 with the Detroit Word Recognition Test 2 weeks later. Barrett (1965a,b), reviewing the literature on the relationship between measures of prereading visual discrimination and first-grade reading achievement, found that visual discrimination and knowledge of letter names were of some value as a predictor of reading. In a second paper Barrett (1965c), quoting a 1962 doctoral dissertation of Dykstra, indicated the additional importance of auditory discrimination of beginning sounds as a predictor of later reading ability. Auditory skills have also been emphasized by some researchers. In contrast, Hammill and Larsen (1974) found that auditory discrimination, auditory memory, blending, and audiovisual integration were not useful in predicting reading ability. Bond and Dykstra (1967), in a review of the Cooperative Research Program in First Grade Reading Instruction concluded that "such pupil capabilities as auditory or visual discrimination, pre-first-grade familiarity with print, and intelligence are all substantially related to success in learning to read." In their study knowledge of letter names accounted for 25 to 36 percent of the variance in reading ability found at the end of the first grade. This predictive relationship persisted at the end of second grade (Dykstra, 1968). In a more recent review of sense modality research, Silverstone and Deichman (1975) found visual discrimination of letter size and shape to be cues necessary for beginning word discrimination. Surveys of the literature on prediction covering (singly or in combination) such predictive variables as age, sex, socioeconomic status, neurological status, laterality, visual perception, body image, auditory perception, oral language, intersensory integration, and emotional state, concluded that there is no general agreement that any one skill or combination of skills is central to reading, although each contributes to prediction (cf. de Hirsch, 1971; Jansky and de Hirsch, 1972).

It has been suggested that functioning on higher integrative levels differentiates retarded readers from normal readers. Blank and Bridger (1967), for example, found that symbolic mediation was a necessary condition for children to solve problems involving temporally presented stimuli regardless of modality. The difficulty, they state, is not simply in cross-modality transfer, but rather in applying relevant verbal labels to stimuli even in the same modality. These findings are in agreement with the views of Vellutino, as expressed in Chapter 4 of this volume. In the last chapter Satz et al. cited studies relating psycholinguistic variables to reading. In Chapter 7 Rourke has reviewed the neuropsychological studies attempting to differentiate the good reader from the poor one.

One of the problems inherent in all these studies is that they tend to view the symptom of reading retardation as a unitary condition. Even controlling for age, sex, intelligence, socioeconomic status, and educational experience, these studies assume that the defects associated with reading failure in one child are the same in any other child who fails in reading. In reality, within the group of children designated as disabled in reading, there are marked individual differences in function and a wide range in distribution of assets and deficits. These may appear in all aspects of perceptual, associative, and emissive language function; in all aspects of dysgnosias, dyspraxias, and dysphasias (Silver and Hagin, 1960, 1972).

The importance of these variations is that in any statistical survey of large numbers of children, not only will etiological factors vary, but also individual differences in distribution of functions may well cancel each other out. The investigator may dismiss as insignificant some variables which may have crucial importance to some children in the sample. Thus conclusions about the predictive antecedents of reading may be misleading. What is needed is a unifying concept of the reading process itself in order to reveal the common denominator behind the many different symptom pictures in children who fail to learn to read.

Satz and co-authors postulate that, in kindergarten children who will fail to learn to read, there is a lag in the development of those skills presumed to be crucial to early phases of reading, namely perceptual discrimination and analysis. They subsume these skills under the term *sensory-perceptual-motor-mnemonic* ability. In the factor analysis of their sixteen-test standardization battery, these variables clustered into a single factor to account for 31 percent of the total variance. This factor together with three additional factors (socioeconomic status 16%, conceptual-verbal 13%, motor dominance and laterality 8%) accounted for 68 percent of the variance in this analysis. Their theory further postulates that the kindergarten children who will fail in reading "will eventually catch up on those earlier developing skills but will subsequently lag in conceptual-linguistic skills which have a slower and later ontogenetic development."

The concept of developmental lag, in contrast to "brain damage," was developed in 1938 by Arnold Gesell and Helen Thompson. Its application to psychiatric problems in nursery-school children was first seen by Bender and Yarnell (1941), and related specifically to the concept of "brain damaged" children and to reading disability by Bender (1942). It will be noted that the group of children designated in the early 1940s by Strauss as "brain damaged," is now largely characterized by showing "minimal cerebral dysfunction."

The concept of developmental lag, however, does not insure that children will "outgrow" that lag. Satz refers to studies which imply the continuation of reading problems into adolescence. Silver and Hagin (1964) in a 10- to 12-year follow-up of children with the symptom of reading disability seen in the children's mental hygiene clinic at Bellevue Hospital found that not only did the reading problems persist into adulthood, but that the same types of perceptual and neurological deficit found when the children were 8 to 10 years old were also seen when they were 20 to 22. This was particularly true in those children in whom "soft" neurological signs were found. The importance of "soft" neurological signs in prediction was emphasized. Conversely, in a retrospective study of adults coming for psychiatric treatment with a variety of symptoms, routine perceptual, neurological, and educational study revealed the presence of neurological and/or perceptual deficits in those who had difficulty reading; we had previously associated such symptoms with children with reading disability (Hagin and Silver, 1977). It appears clear that perceptual dysfunction does not necessarily mature spontaneously and that reading disability is a long-term problem in the life of any individual.

In further attempts to understand the meaning of the diverse perceptual deficits found in children with reading disability, Silver and Hagin (1960) postulated that these deficits may be understood in relation to orientation in space and time. Immaturities, therefore, may be seen in the visual discrimination and recall of asymmetric figures, in specific angulation and verticalization problems in visuomotor function, in the temporal sequencing of auditory stimuli, and in the orientation of the body in space—as seen in finger gnosis, praxis, right–left discrimination, and in those postural responses relating to orientation in space. The perceptual deficits seen, regardless of modality, have a common denominator, namely spatial and temporal organization.

The predictive value of this theory was seen in an intensive examination of all children in the first grade of a school in the Kips Bay area of New York City during the years 1969–70 and 1970–71 (Silver and Hagin, 1972). This examination was an intensive, individual study involving neurological, psychiatric, psychological, social, and educational examinations. Not only did this study provide epidemiological information (*vide infra*) but it also yielded predictive data which detected (with only 1% false positives) those children who would fail in reading two years later, by the end of second grade (Hagin and Silver, 1977).

Factor analysis of the variables in this study identified five factors accounting for 61 percent of the total variance. These factors were: (1) an auditory associative factor (18.9% of variance), (2) visual-neurological (17.6%), (3) psychiatric impairment (6.9%), (4) chronological age (6.3%), and (5) general intelligence as measured by the WPPSI (11.4%). The auditory-associative and the visual-neurological factors were combined into a predictive measure to include ten subtests (visual discrimination and recall of asymmetric figures; visuomotor function; auditory discrimination and rote sequencing; articulation and an intermodal dictation test; tests of finger gnosis, praxis, and right-left discrimination). Directions for administration, scoring, and interpretation of these tests are found in SEARCH (Silver and Hagin, 1975, 1976).

Comparison of these ten measures with predictive indices found in

357

other studies reveals both similarities and differences. Satz and co-workers find that finger localization, alphabet recitation, and recognition-discrimination, together correctly classified 77 percent of the children into adequate and inadequate readers. Finger localization accounted for 70.5 percent of the correct classification. Hainsworth and Siqueland in their Meeting Street School Screening Test (1969) not only examined visual-perceptive-motor skills, but also evaluated gross and fine motor skills and such language functions as listening, testing, sequences, and formulating language. The Meeting Street School Screening Test has the psycholinguistic information processing model of Osgood (1963) as its theoretical base.

Jansky and de Hirsch (1972) found that the five kindergarten tests which predicted reading success best in second grade were, in order: letter naming, picture naming, Gates Word Matching, Bender Motor Gestalt, and Binet Sentence Memory. The importance of the ability to retrieve stored verbal symbols in reading is stressed by Jansky and deHirsch. This battery, administered at preschool years, predicts 75 percent of failing readers in second grade.

A more general approach to prediction is represented in the reading readiness tests which have addressed themselves to practical decisions in school placement for many years. Austin and Morrison (1974) found that 85 percent of schools in a national survey routinely used readiness tests in the first grade. Efforts to identify the cognitive, perceptual, experiental, and emotional characteristics necessary for successful learning in first grade became focused in the 1920s when the concept of "reading readiness" (i.e., the maturational level at which a child could be expected to read and be ready for formal reading instruction), was introduced.

In 1935, Marion Monroe published a test of prereading skills which attempted to assess maturation in "memory of orientation of forms, oculomotor control and attention, drawing from memory, motor speed and steadiness, word discrimination, sound blending, and vocabulary." Her test was the prototype of succeeding readiness tests which have proliferated in the past ten years. In 1966, Buros listed 8 readiness tests, as compared to 29 in his 1972 edition. Content analysis of these tests, as shown in Table 17-1 (Beecher and Goldfluss, 1975) reveals a striking similarity to the components Monroe used in 1935. The skills tapped by tests are analyzed in 20 different areas: visual letter and word discrimination and knowledge, visuomotor, auditory discrimination, recall (visual and auditory), sequencing and comprehension, ability to follow directions, vocabulary, sound blending, articulation, emissive speech and language content, intermodal integration, concept development, gross and fine motor abilities. Review of readiness tests reveals that the areas most frequently tapped are visual discrimination, auditory discrimination of initial sounds, and visuomotor skills. Many of the tests thus overlap in content, yet may differ in detail of testing.

Table 17-2, compiled by Beecher and Goldfluss (1975), analyzes technical aspects of the tests whose content was reviewed in Table 17-1. Such aspects as nature of standardization sample, evidence of reliability and validity, nature of norms, provision for local and/or age norms, and nature of the predictions are considered. As we review the content of Readiness-Scanning Batteries, we are impressed with their redundancy and complexity. Most deal with skills which practical judgement indicates are related to early reading (Farr, 1969). There is a trend now, however, as seen in the work of Satz, Friel, and Fletcher and of Silver and Hagin, to look for the precursors of even those skills.

Summary: The content of readiness tests in current use covers a broad range of skills involving visual and auditory perception, language comprehension and use, intermodal integration, and gross and fine motor abilities. Such tests overlap in content, are replete with redundancy, and in general deal with skills which practical judgment suggests are related to early reading. Scanning instruments are designed to predict reading ability before such skills are developed. Such precursors are termed by Satz et al. as sensory-perceptual-motor-mnemonic skills and tests sampling these abilities comprise their predictive battery. Silver and Hagin believe that the common precursor to reading is the development of spatial orientation and temporal organization and their predictive battery taps these attributes in visual, auditory, and body image perception. The Meeting Street School Screening Test (1969), springing from a psycholinguistic processing model, adds such functions as listening and formulating language. Jansky and de Hirsch (1972) stress the retrieval of stored verbal symbols in letter and picture naming, word matching, and sentence memory.

WHAT DO READINESS AND SCANNING TESTS MEASURE?

Even when the content of a readiness battery has been determined and statistical constraints have been satisfied, there are problems in understanding just

TABLE 17-1
Areas of Functioning Tapped by Representative Readiness Tests (Beecher and Goldfluss, 1975)

TEST	Conceptual	Following directions	Vocabulary	Letter & word knowledge	AUDITORY Discrimination	AUDITORY Sequential memory	AUDITORY Blending	AUDITORY Comprehension	Tactile	VISUAL Discrimination	VISUAL Sequencing	VISUAL Memory	VISUAL Tracking	Visumotor	Gross motor	Articulation	Intermodal	Expressive language	Neurological	Social-affective
Readiness																				
Boehm Test of Basic Concepts (Boehm, 1969)	X																			
Gates-MacGinitie Reading Readiness (Gates & MacGinitie, 1968)		X		X	X		X	X		X				X						
Lippincott Reading Readiness Test (McLeod, 1965)			X	X		X	X	X		X				X	X		X	X		X
Metropolitan Readiness Test (Hildreth, Griffiths & McGauvran, 1965)	X		X	X				X		X				X						
Reading Aptitude Test (Monroe, 1935)			X		X	X	X			X		X		X	X	X		X	X	
Screening																				
Diagnostic Intervention for the Four-Year-Old Kindergarten (Milwaukee	X		X		X				X	X		X		X	X			X		X

Test	1	2	3	4	5	6	7	8	9	10	11	12	13	14	15	16	17	18
First Grade Screening Test (Pate & Webb, 1969)	x	x	x															
Meeting Street School Screening Test (Hainsworth & Siqueland, 1969)	x	x				x			x	x	x		x	x			x	
Pre-Reading Expectancy Screening Scales (Hartlage & Lucas, 1973)	x			x		x			x									
Pre-Reading Screening Procedures (Slingerland, 1968)				x	x	x			x			x		x			x	
Pre-School Screening Instrument (Fort Worth Public Schools, 1973)	x	x	x			x	x		x	x	x	x	x	x				
Psychoeducational Inventory of Basic Learning Experiences (Valett, 1968)	x	x	x	x		x		x	x	x	x	x	x	x		x	x	x
Screening Index (Jansky & de Hirsch, 1972)			x	x		x			x			x						
Screening Method for Early Identification of Learning Disabilities (Corey & Nessa, 1973)	x		x	x	x		x		x			x						
Screening Test for Identifying Children with Specific Language Disability (Slingerland, 1961)			x	x		x			x		x		x			x	x	
Search (Silver & Hagin, 1974)				x	x				x		x		x		x	x		x

TABLE 17-2
Technical Aspects of Tests Reviewed (Beecher and Goldfluss, 1975)

TEST	DATE OF STANDARD-IZATION	STANDARD-IZATION SAMPLE	RELIABILITY MEASURES	VALIDITY MEASURES	NATURE OF NORMS	PROVISION FOR LOCAL AND/OR AGE NORMS	NATURE OF PREDICTIONS AND CAUTIONS
Boehm Test of Basic Concepts (Boehm, 1969)	1968–69	2204 children K–2 representing low, middle, & high SES	Split half using Spearman-Brown formula Range .81–.91 SE_M range: 1.7–2.7	Content	Percentile by grade and SES level	Percent passing analysis can be done for each classroom; separate norms for grades K–2	Identify children with poor conceptual knowledge. Performance should be viewed in relation to rest of class.
Gates-MacGinitie Reading Readiness (Gates & MacGinitie, 1968)	1966–68	4500 children grades K & 1–35 communities selected by census data which were not given	Kuder-Richardson for each subtest Range .63–87	Prediction of 1st grade reading achievement $r = .59–.60$ with Gates-MacGinitie, Primary A	Weighted scores Stanines Percentiles	Separate norms for kindergarten and 1st grade	Used to find deficit areas of individual children. Use caution in interpreting differences between subtest scores. Relate child's deficits to method of reading instruction.
Lippincott Reading Readiness Test (McLeod, 1965)					Readiness categories based on local percentiles	Local percentiles	Used for grouping and identifying child for further evaluation
Metropolitan Readiness Test (Hildreth, Grif-fiths & McGauv	1964	12,231 children grade 1 through-out U.S. Geo-graphically hal	Odd-even for total score; above .90	Content based on research and professional	Percentiles Stanines Readiness		Readiness for 1st grade, forming reading groups. Do not interpret indi-

Test	Sample	Reliability	Validity	Norms	Comments
			Letter Ratings		given.
			with Murphy Durrell Readiness $r = .76$ with Pintner-Cunningham Primary Predictive Range $r = .58-.73$ with Metropolitan Achievement Test Subtests Range $r = .52-.75$ with Stanford Achievement Test; Primary Subtests		Used for reading readiness and diagnosis.
Reading Aptitude Test (Monroe, 1935)	437 children age 5½–8½ years	Spearman-Brown (odd-even) $r = .87$	Predictive correlation of entering 1st grade scores with end of 1st grade reading achievement. (Gray Oral or Iota) $r = .75$	Percentile	
Diagnostic Intervention for the Four-Year-Old	Experimental version; technical data not yet available.		Ages at which items should be passed	Ages at which items to be passed	Assess child's present functioning; plan school program matched to his

TABLE 17-2 (*continued*)
Technical Aspects of Tests Reviewed (Beecher and Goldfluss, 1975)

TEST	DATE OF STANDARDIZATION	STANDARDIZATION SAMPLE	RELIABILITY MEASURES	VALIDITY MEASURES	NATURE OF NORMS	PROVISION FOR LOCAL AND/OR AGE NORMS	NATURE OF PREDICTIONS AND CAUTIONS
Kindergarten (Milwaukee Public Schools, undated)							developmental needs; assess growth by means of pre- and post-testing.
First Grade Screening Test (Pate & Webb, 1969)	1965	8792 children K–1st nationwide sample described in detail.	Test-retest 2 weeks $r = .84$ $SE_M = 1.68$–1.88 8 weeks $r = .82$ Intra-scorer $r = .98$ Inter-scorer $r = .98$ for 1st grade only	Predictive cross-validation study with teacher ratings of readiness for next grade: 68–76% of "not ready" groups identified range of $r = .59$–$.79$ with California SRA and Stanford Achievement Tests	Percentile	Separate norms for kindergarten and 1st grade. Suggested development of local "cutting scores."	Used for identifying possible deficits and grouping for instruction. Test does not make definitive diagnosis of mental retardation, brain dysfunction, emotional disturbance, or other conditions.
Meeting Street School Screening Test (Hainsworth & Siquel-		494 children in grades K–1st in East Providence schools	Test-retest (2–4 weeks): for total score $r = .85$, subtest	Concurrent: with ITPA $r = .77$ with Frostig Predictive:	Scaled scores	Separate cutoffs for grades K, 1	Identify children likely to have learning disability. In diagnosis use with psychological and

Test	Sample	Reliability	Validity	Scores	Comments
Pre-reading Expectancy Screening Scales (Hartlage & Lucas, 1973)	1384 1st graders. Washington Township Schools, Indianapolis	Inter-rater above .95 Split-half (odd-even) by subtest range of $r = .78$ to $.91$	score $= .66$; r with achievement at end of 1st grade $= .63$ MSST in 1st grade, r with 1st grade achievement $= .53$; with 2nd grade achievement $= .46$ Concurrent: range of $r = .15–.64$. Subtests correlated with WRAT Oral Reading range of $r = .24–.70$, subtests correlated with Teacher Ranks of Reading	Percentiles by sex and by total group	Readiness for reading
Pre-reading Screening Procedures (Slingerland, 1969)	400 children age 5.7–7.5 years in Northwest and in Texas with IQ $= 90$			Scores converted to one of five ratings ranging from high to low.	Used with Metropolitan Readiness & Pintner-Cunningham to identify children w/potential reading, writing, and spelling difficulty. Note quality of errors.

TABLE 17-2 (*continued*)
Technical Aspects of Tests Reviewed (Beecher and Goldfluss, 1975)

TEST	DATE OF STANDARD- IZATION	STANDARD- IZATION SAMPLE	RELIABILITY MEASURES	VALIDITY MEASURES	NATURE OF NORMS	PROVISION FOR LOCAL AND/OR AGE NORMS	NATURE OF PREDICTIONS AND CAUTIONS
Pre-School	Spring 1972	947 children in grades K–1 described by sex and ethnicity	Test-retest 2–3 weeks r = .83, SE_M 1.3 Intra-rater r = 8.9, Inter-rater r = .71	Content: items written by educational specialists. Concurrent: significant chi-square with teacher rating of readiness. Predictive: study in progress	Quartiles with 1st quartile the cutoff for further evaluation and special services	Separate quartiles for grades K and 1.	Identify children in need of further evaluation and special services. Other components of screening should include: screening by school nurse; speech and language evaluation; psychological evaluation.
Psycho-educational Inventory of Basic Learning Experiences (Valett, 1968)					5-point rating scale to indicate strengths and weaknesses		Identify areas of disability which necessitate programming.
Screening Index (Jansky & de Hirsch, 1972)		401 children drawn from 5 public schools of		Given in K, the Index identified 75% of children	Converted scores based on multiple regression	Children are ranked by score. Local cutting	Used to identify high risk for reading failure. Intervention, based on

Sample described in terms of sex and ethnicity.	reading at end of 2nd grade. (2.2 or lower on Gates Advanced Primary or Gates-MacGinitie Paragraph Reading Test)		cen or 2nd grade reading failure plus 10%.	(Diagnostic Battery) should follow.
Screening Test for Identifying Children with Specific Language Disability (Slingerland, 1969)		12–15 errors indicate difficulty		Used to screen those with potnial or existing language difficulties; prevention.

what these tests measure. The Metropolitan Readiness Test, used by 36 percent of 93 school districts sampled by Maitland, Nadeau, and Nadeau (1974), is an example of the complex items found in many readiness tests. The Metropolitan (Hildreth, Griffiths, and McGauvran, 1965) consists of six sections in which the child records his responses by circling the correct answer on a record blank. Section 1 is called "Word Meaning." In it, the examiner names an object which the child must circle in a three-picture array. Is this a test of word meaning, of picture recognition, of figure-ground perception, of attention? Section 2, called "Listening" is even more complex. The examiner tells a two-sentence story about a picture; the response is made by circling the correct picture in an array. Is this a test of auditory memory or comprehension or attention or combinations of all three? Section 3 requires the child to match words and abstract forms although the perceptual skills required for the two matching tasks appear to be different. Section 4 is alphabet recognition. Is it a socioeconomic index or is it a test of previous educational experiences? The responses elicited by these tests are complex and difficult to interpret. All are intermodal, involving auditory, visual, and praxic components. What is measured is not necessarily what the label on the test says it is.

Factor analytic studies of readiness tests, such as has been done by Stott and Ball (1955) for infant and toddler "intelligence" tests (Cattell, Bayley, Gesell, Merrill-Palmer, and Stanford-Binet) have yet to be done. Such studies might help to clarify the question of what is being measured and interpreted. For example, in a factor analysis of the ITPA (Kirk et al., 1968), Burns (1972) identified five factors. The findings did not support the claim that the ITPA tapped separate language processes of reception and association, and separate levels of organization (automatic or representational).

The functions studied in the readiness tests may not really be discrete functions at all but, in fact, segments of the same basic function. Redundancy within the instrument, and obscurity of what is really being measured characterize most of the first-grade readiness tests.

However, while readiness tests give little information as to the basic processes involved in reading, they do accomplish some measure of what they set out to do. These tests are designed to be given in kindergarten or early in first grade. They are cross-sectional and determine the child's status with respect to a normative group. While they are not designed to evaluate the predictive antecedents of reading, they do have some predictive value. The relationship of .87 between tests and criterion at the end of first grade, found by Smith in 1928, has not been equalled. However, as is seen in Table 17-2, the Metropolitan Readiness Test, for example, has at the end of first grade, a product-moment correlation of .52–.73 with subtests of the Metropolitan Achievement Test, and of .52–.75 with the Primary Subtests of the Stanford Achievement Tests. Barrett (1965–6) pointed out that readiness tests do measure factors which have a relationship with first-grade reading and that the more closely these factors resemble reading, the higher the relationship between the readiness test and later reading achievement.

Turning now to the scanning instruments, do they predict reading failure? The Meeting Street School Screening Test correlates .63 with reading achievement at the end of first grade. The Jansky and de Hirsch Screening Index, given in kindergarten, identifies 75 percent of children who failed in reading at the end of second grade. Satz and co-workers also report overall correct predictions in the 75 percent range at end of first and second grades, but the "hit rate" falls to 57 percent in fifth grade.

Equally important, however, are the failures of the test, i.e., test positives who have learned to read, and test negatives who have failed. In Satz's original group followed to fifth grade, the percentage of false positives is 17 percent at end of grade one, 20 percent at end of grade three, and 5 percent at the end of grade five. The false negatives run from 5 percent at grade one and 8 percent at three to 25.6 percent at end of grade five. The total percentage of misclassifications ranges from 22 to 32; approximately 1 child in 4 is misclassified. If only those children who become severely retarded readers are considered, then 42 percent errors on the scanning test are found in fifth grade. The authors mentioned that they have successfully identified 58 percent of the severely retarded readers, but there are 42 percent not successfully identified in that group. One begins to wonder if such judgments could have occurred by chance. A glass half full is still half empty.

One would also wonder about the effectiveness of the educational program in the schools under study when there is such a dramatic increase in incidence of retarded readers in grade five. Of those children who become mildly retarded readers at grade five, the test battery correctly predicts 19 of 94 children and incorrectly predicts 75 of 94 (approximately 80%). Better success is achieved in predicting those who will succeed in reading: 157 correct predictions of 168 average readers and 89 correct predictions of 90 superior readers.

Their cross-validation group one at the end of grade two, and cross-validation group two at the end of grade one, also have a high percentage of false positives (18% and 25%). In cross-validation group two there are 13 misclassifications (30%) of the 44 children who earned the most severely aberrant scores on their predictive battery, i.e., 30 percent false positives. Of those children who were the most disabled readers 16 of 18 (89%) are correctly identified; but of the mildly retarded readers, only 36 percent were correctly identified.

As indicated earlier in the chapter, because of the many factors entering into learning to read, a brief scanning instrument may be expected to have false negatives. As Hall, Keogh, and Becker state (1975) "Risk is not simply the status or condition of the child . . . (it is), also a function of the school, the classroom atmosphere, the teacher, and the nature of the instructional program." The child who scores just above the vulnerable cut-off point on the battery may in later years be unable to cope with the school variables or with the vicissitudes of his own life and may fail (false negatives).

The percentages of false positives found by Satz et al. are excessive and the inability to detect the mildly retarded reader suggests that the test could not be used in educational decision-making in its present form. It is particularly unfortunate for the mildly retarded readers, because it is in this group that educational intervention can be most effective.

In fact, the number of false positives can be reduced by lowering the vulnerable cut-off point on the battery. This is not discussed by Satz but is mentioned by Jansky. With the lowering of the cut-off point, the false positives will decrease but it must be realized in doing so the false negatives will increase. To my mind, this is certainly more acceptable than a high percentage of false positives.

Silver and Hagin have attempted to solve this dilemma by first establishing the incidence of reading retardation within the schools of the Lower East Side of New York City. To do this they examined the data of their intensive study of intact first grades (1972). The incidence of children with evidence of immaturity in spatial and temporal organization was 25 to 30 percent. This finding of one-third to one-quarter of the entire first grade having specific perceptual immaturity was substantiated in a similar examination conducted by different examiners of the intact first grades of two different schools in the academic year 1973–74. The cut-off point on each component test of the scanning instrument was therefore set at the lowest one-third of the distribution scores. The predictive value of this cut-off score is seen in control schools (i.e., those in which our intervention program was not introduced) where no false positives were found in the severely retarded readers and less than 1 percent in the mildly retarded, while 10 percent false negatives was obtained (Silver, Hagin, and Beecher, 1976).

It does appear that scanning instruments which do not utilize factors resembling reading but which are attempting to reach out into the antecedents of reading, can be modestly successful in predicting at age five which children will fail and which will succeed in reading.

At this point, it may be asked what the criteria are for deciding the relationship between the scanning tests and reading. What criteria for evaluating reading ability are used? Satz and his associates have used teacher ratings as one criterion, teacher ratings plus the IOTA Word Recognition Test as another. Their mainstay, however, is teacher ratings. There is much argument about this criterion. Keogh and Becker (1973) and Shardone and Keogh (1975) suggest that while "teachers' perceptions are useful for screening high-risk pupils, other measures and indices are also needed to monitor aspects of children's performance and competence." Guidelines for use of achievement tests as criterion measures are discussed in Farr (1969) and in *A Practical Guide to Measuring Project Impact on Student Achievement* (1975).

There is, however, an additional criterion against which predictive instruments may be tested; namely, individual neurological and psychiatric and psychological examinations. This criterion was chosen by Silver and Hagin (1976), relating scores on SEARCH earned by 171 children tested in the fall of their kindergarten year with intensive individual interdisciplinary study of the same children in the spring of first grade. The children with SEARCH scores of 0 to 3 (comprising about 10% of the total group) had, in addition to evidence of immaturity in measures of temporal or spatial orientation, neurological signs. particularly problems with fine motor coordination and motor impulse control. Their intellectual levels as measured by the full scale WIPPSI were generally below 80. The children earning scores of 4 to 5 (comprising approximately 15% of the total) did not have neurological signs other than immaturity in praxis, finger gnosis, and right–left discrimination, and evidence that clear-cut cerebral dominance for language was not yet established. Those earning 8 to 10 were clinically without impairment. The 6 to 7 group was the most heterogeneous. Many had emotional and/or family problems; many were just above the cut-off points on several SEARCH components. It is from this group that most of the false negatives were drawn. The children for whom reading failure is predicted are those scoring 0 to 5.

Clinical criteria are important in evaluating the meaning of scores obtained on the scanning instrument. It will be recalled that scanning is no substitute for diagnosis. Many scanning tests (e.g., Jansky and deHirsch Battery, SEARCH, MSSST) recommend that following their identification, vulnerable children be given more intensive diagnosis to attempt to establish etiological factors and to aid in intervention.

Scanning, with its companion diagnosis, also requires intervention to complete a program of secondary prevention. Ideally, the scanning instrument itself should provide cues for intervention. If we accept the concept that word recognition and beginning reading require skills of spatial and temporal orientation, and if we agree that immaturities in these behaviors are found in children who have difficulty learning to read, then it follows that intervention methods should be based upon the neuropsychological deficits. This formulation has been adopted by Silver, Hagin, and Hersh (1967); Silver and Hagin (1972); and Hagin, Silver, and Kreeger (1976) in developing the SEARCH and TEACH program. SEARCH, the scanning instrument, profiles the distribution of spatial and temporal function in visual, auditory, body image, and intermodal modalities; TEACH provides teaching tasks to train out the defects found. The program is reported to be successful in forming a basis for word recognition (Silver, Hagin, and Beecher, 1976).

Validation of the SEARCH and TEACH approach was obtained by Arnold and coworkers in an independent study involving a different population from that of Silver and Hagin. They found that in a pre-test vs. post-test design with two matched control groups and involving 86 first graders screened as vulnerable to learning failure by SEARCH and assigned to one of three groups ("intervention" i.e., perceptual stimulation via TEACH, "contact control" i.e., academic tutoring, and "no contact control"), gains in the intervention group on "most measures including perceptual and achievement test and behavior ratings by teachers" were significantly greater than in the other two groups. This gain was maintained one year later.

Scanning instruments provide further data. From an epidemiological point of view, there is general agreement that approximately one-third of the total number of children in the kindergarten and first grades studied are vulnerable to reading failure. Of these, approximately 10 percent of the total will become severe learning failures. These data are seen in diverse populations: in the Florida study, in that from urban and suburban New York City (The NYU-Bellevue Medical Center Study), and in the Rocky Mountain State survey of John Meier (1971). The problem transcends the urban ghetto.

Summary: While what readiness tests and scanning instruments measure in neurophysiological and neuropsychological terms is unknown, and while the test label is a poor indication of the presumed underlying process which the test measures, readiness tests and scanning instruments do have modest predictive value. Reading tests measure factors which have a relationship to first-grade reading and the more closely these factors resemble reading, the higher the relationship. Scanning instruments are designed to predict reading achievement before the child develops skills resembling reading. The correct overall prediction of such tests, in the first two grades, is in the 75 percent range. By the fifith grade, correct predictions in the Florida study fell to 57 percent, and only 58 percent of the severely retarded readers were successfully identified. It is suggested that the false positive rate may be adjusted by lowering the cut-off point on the test battery. One study has set its cut-off point to conform to the incidence of spatial and temporal immaturity found in study of intact first graders. A prediction of reading failure for 25 percent of the entire kindergarten class is found in several studies.

Ideally, the scanning instrument should provide cues for intervention. A program of perceptual stimulation to conform to the deficits found by the scanning instrument is reported to be successful in forming a basis for word recognition.

CAN CHILDREN AT RISK FOR READING FAILURE BE DETECTED EARLIER THAN AT AGE FIVE?

We can certainly identify as high risk those children who have suffered prenatal or perinatal insult. A review of the literature (Balow, Rubin, and Rosen, 1975) on perinatal events as precursors of reading disability suggests a causal chain from perinatal anomaly to neurological insult to reading disability. Balow et al. state that "within each group of studies—retrospective, retrospective follow-up, and prospective—more studies support than fail to support the hypothesis that perinatal stress is related to reading disability: the correlations are significant, (they are) however, always low and the absolute amount of difference between means rarely large, making predictions and decisions nearly impossible from such findings alone."

As an example, the classic study of Kawi and Pasamanick (1958) found that while 45 percent of children with reading disability had a history of prematurity or of complications of pregnancy and labor, 25 percent of the controls did also. Masland (1968) pointed out that the association of organic defect of the central nervous system with learning disability is not necessarily a direct one. A variety of dysfunctions, only one of which may relate to delay in reading, may result from brain injury. Pre- or perinatal stress or low birth weight, however, are danger signals.

Three other high-risk groups may be mentioned: (1) Within the broad group of children with organic dysfunction of the central nervous system is a smaller group characterized by the presence of subtle static signs (Quinn et al., 1976). These may be epicanthal folds inconsistent with family appearance, dermatoglyphic abnormality, small head circumference, and/or external ear abnormality. These signs suggest deviations in fetal development which may render a child vulnerable to delay in acquisition of language. (2) Because of the possibility of genetic predisposition, siblings of children known to have reading problems may be considered high risk for language problems of their own. (3) Children exhibiting delay in the acquisition of spoken language may be at risk for later reading disability.

Comprehensive inventories designed to detect developmental anomalies in the preschool years have been based upon pediatric-neurological evaluations (Ford, 1951; Paine and Oppe, 1966; Prechtl and Beintema, 1965; Eagan, 1969; Drillen, 1964; Illingsworth, 1974; and Peiper, 1963); upon psychological testing (Binet, 1916; Cattell, 1960; Bayley, 1933; Griffiths, 1954; Haeussermann, 1958; Wechsler, 1949, 1963, 1974); and upon the Gesell Developmental Schedules (1941). They assume quantitatively different levels of function at varying ages for a broad range of abilities, each of which is developing at a rate dependent upon biological resources and environmental interaction. Reviews of these comprehensive schedules revealing their overlapping content and statistical characteristics appear in Meier (1973) and in Thorpe and Weiner (1974). These inventories have proliferated since the mid-1960s with the passage of the 1967 amendment to Title XIX of the Social Security Act which mandates early and periodic screening, diagnosis, and treatment (EPSDT) of all eligible individuals under the age of 21.

In general, the inventories also suffer from serious problems: internal problems of standardization, reliability, and validity as well as questions they raise about the cultural bias, the "labeling" of vulnerable children on unproven evidence, the maintenance of confidentiality, and the lack of follow-up and of intervention programs when developmental defects have been uncovered.

SUMMARY

Although broad-scale programs of social, educational, and medical intervention for the primary prevention of reading and learning failure have been attempted, their success has been equivocal because of the complex etiological factors resulting in the symptom of reading failure. Similarly, the diversity of etiologies together with the marked differences in function and the wide range of assets and defects seen in children with reading disability have also made the secondary prevention of reading disability difficult.

A multivariate battery designed for rapid, economical, large-scale scanning of kindergarten children cannot be expected to detect all those kindergarten children cannot be expected to detect all those kindergartners who will fail as well as all those who will succeed. Modest success, however, at early identification in first grade already has been achieved by readiness tests, and in kindergarten, by scanning surveys. The former tests have as their prototype the 1935 program of Marion Monroe and retain as their content those skills which "practical judgment" indicates are related to early reading. Most frequently tapped are visual discrimination, auditory discrimination of initial sounds, and visuomotor skills. A review of readiness tests in use depicts 17 additional variables, all demanding complex responses. The meaning of these responses in neuropsychological or neurophysiological terms is difficult to interpret.

By contrast, the scanning tests attempt to reach beyond "practical judgment" and attempt to find the "predictive antecedents" to reading. The content of these tests is usually based upon clinical experience and/or statistical study of many variables. From these are derived theoretical models of beginning reading. Satz et al. thus stress sensory-perceptual-motor-mnemonic skills; Silver and Hagin see temporal and spatial disorganization as unifying the diverse defects of poor readers; Hainsworth and Siqueland use the psycholinguistic processing model of Osgood; Jansky and de Hirsch consider the retrieval of stored verbal symbols as basic. Silver and Hagin further postulate that underlying the spatial and temporal distortions in poor readers is a problem in the establishment of clear-cut cerebral dominance for language and/or problems in interhemispheric transfer of information.

The scanning instruments must, however, be tested by validity studies over a long time interval, and must also be subjected to repeated study to understand just what the component tests really measure and how they relate to the total process of language. The data, so far, raise serious doubts about the applicability of some of these as predictive instruments. A 75 percent "hit rate" really means that one child in four is misclassified. More important is the incidence of false negatives and of false positives. It is recognized that a small percentage of misclassification cannot be avoided. It is suggested, however, that a false positive rate of 15 to 20 percent is excessive. A test which

375

does not identify 42 percent of severely retarded readers and misses 80 percent of the mildly retarded readers cannot be used as a basis for educational decisions. The cut-off point, i.e., that point on the test above which success is predicted and at or below which failure is predicted, thus becomes an important issue. A clear presentation of rationale in the selection of cut-off points is much needed.

Prediction has further pitfalls. It has been pointed out that reading success or failure depends upon experiential as well as biological factors. An instrument designed to find the biological antecedents of reading disability may well fail because of inadequate and/or inappropriate educational experience. What happens in the schools between the initial evaluation and the criterion measure of achievement is therefore an important variable which must be put into the equation to understand the significance of the initial testing.

Scanning alone is only one-third of a problem of secondary prevention. Diagnosis of vulnerable children and intervention are the other components of the triad. Ideally, the scanning instrument should point toward the educational intervention needed. One approach has been to train out the neuropsychological immaturities revealed by the scanning instrument. Paradoxically, of course, the greater the success of intervention for a group of vulnerable children, the less valid will be predictions made when the group was initially scanned.

The scanning of kindergarten children by different groups of investigators in different settings has yielded general agreement that the incidence of potential reading failure is high, with 8 to 10 percent severe failures, and with perhaps 25 percent of entire kindergarten classes classified as vulnerable to later reading failure. Scanning can offer educational administrators a profile of the entire kindergarten grade and, when combined with diagnosis and appropriate intervention, can make educational planning less intuitive and more responsive to reality.

Chapter 18

A CRITICAL REVIEW
OF "SOME DEVELOPMENTAL AND
PREDICTIVE PRECURSORS
OF READING DISABILITIES"

JEANNETTE JEFFERSON JANSKY

This review will focus on two aspects of Chapter 16 by Satz: the prediction of reading disabilities and the significance of the results for theory. The Satz chapter will serve as the point of departure for illustration of general issues in the area under discussion. This, rather than a survey of literature, is the subject of the comments that follow. Because the studies of early intervention have raised complex questions and have advanced diverse conclusions, that topic probably warrants an entirely separate review. However, I shall comment briefly on the implications of prediction research for early intervention.

The research of Satz was stimulated by the desire to develop a sound and valid predictive battery within a theoretical framework that would permit the testing of hypotheses and replication of results.

Satz maintains that an adequate design would include a multivariate orientation in which the same subjects would be measured longitudinally, with ample time between prediction and outcome; there should be a homogeneous sample to avoid the confounding effects of race, sex, and cultural variations; and finally, a second group for cross-validation should be included.

According to his theoretical formulation, reading failure stems from a lag in maturation of the brain which differentially delays those skills that are in primary ascendancy at different chronological ages. Those skills that develop ontogenetically earlier (visuomotor and cross-modal sensory integration) are more likely to be delayed in younger children who are immature. Again, according to Satz, those skills that have a later or slower rate of development (language and formal operations) are more likely to be delayed in older children who are immature. His theory predicts that those preschool children who are delayed in skills that are in primary ascendancy at this stage will fail to acquire reading proficiency. The children will then catch up on these earlier developing skills but lag subsequently on conceptual linguistic skills that have a slower, later ontogenetic development. If a battery of tests sensitive to the development of these early skills could predict reading disabilities, it would constitute support for the theory.

PREDICTION

To develop his predictive battery Satz undertook a number of measurements including a determination of:

(1) the predictive efficiency of 16 variables, from the kindergarten vantage point, to forecast end of second-grade reading for a sample of white boys;

(2) the predictive efficiency of the tests for the same group of subjects at end of fifth grade;

(3) the predictive efficiency, for purposes of cross-validation, of the same kindergarten tests for a *new* sample of white boys for end-of-second-grade reading;

(4) the predictive efficiency of the kindergarten tests (abbreviated battery), administered *early* in the fall, for *end* of kindergarten achievement ratings for an additional sample of black and white boys and girls;

(5) the predictive effectiveness of the abbreviated kindergarten battery for the same black and white boys and girls at the end of first grade.

There were, then, three different samples under study over the years: the group of white boys, tested at kindergarten, end of second, and end of fifth grades; the group of white boys tested at kindergarten and end of second grade; and, finally, the group of white and black boys and girls tested at beginning and end of kindergarten and at end of first grade.

The kindergarten battery consisted of 14 tests and two additional items, Day of Testing and SES. A factor analysis of the battery showed that it was heavily loaded (31% of the common variance) with measures of sensory motor and mnemonic ability (Factor 1), moderately weighted (16%) with socioeconomic status (Factor II) and conceptual ability (13%, Factor III), and, to a much lesser extent, with motor dominance and laterality (8%, Factor IV).

Criterion measures were Classroom Reading Level, a rating assigned by the teacher based on the textbook the child was using, and, in some cases, the IOTA.

The principal statistical procedures used, in addition to factor analysis, were four-group discriminant function analysis to compare the predictive validity of the kindergarten tests against the reading criteria, and stepwise discriminant function analysis to determine the ranking of the predictor variables in terms of their criterion determinants. For purposes of cross-validation, the kindergarten test scores of the "new" groups were multiplied by the lambda weights forming the standardization group discriminant function against the reading criterion.

It was found that, in general, the tests adequately predicted the children at the extremes of ability. Certain kindergarten predictors (and they tended to be the same ones for the three samples) identified most children who later read very poorly and those who read very well. The kindergarten predictors were less precise for children in the "gray" area, that is, for those who were characterized as mild reading failures and those who were average in ability. This has been the weakness of most predictive batteries. Monroe discussed the problem in 1935. This accuracy-of-hit pattern differed somewhat in the case of the long-term prediction, initiated at kindergarten level for *fifth* grade. In this instance, the kindergarten predictors continued to isolate the average and superior readers, but precision dropped to about chance for the failing and mildly lagging boys. When the two failing groups are combined, the kindergarten predictors pick up fewer fifth graders who were poor readers. Thus the long-range efficiency of the kindergarten predictors in identifying poor readers remains to be established.

Satz rightly notes that the uses to which kindergarten predictors are put will depend on the needs of the setting. It is possible that it would serve some schools to single out the children who are going to excel; selecting participants for accelerated programs would be an example. The Satz battery would be very useful to this end. One would conclude, however, from the comments about the alarmingly high incidence of national reading failure and about the desirability of instituting intervention at an early age, when the central nervous system may be more plastic and responsive to changes, that he is primarily concerned with kindergarten children who are at risk.

Therefore, results that refer to the accuracy of the predictors in identifying children who eventually failed should be scrutinized closely. Satz reports an increase in severe reading disorder from second to fifth grade, in which most of the additional severe cases came from the group originally characterized as "mild." The results confirm the observation that, when left untreated, the marginally failing child, far from catching up, slips farther behind. In looking at predictive accuracy for the failing group, therefore, it would seem reasonable to combine the results for the mild and severe cases. The determination of what constitutes a reasonable "miss" level is, of course, essential. It seems to me that "miss" proportions in excess of 25 to 30 percent go beyond the tolerable limit. For Satz's initial measure (kindergarten to grade 2) the miss rate was 22%, or acceptable, for the combined group of failing readers. For the second (kindergarten to grade 5) the proportion (61%) well exceeded this limit; in the case of the third measure (new sample, kindergarten to grade 2) the miss livel (42%) was also high; for the fourth assessment (kindergarten Fall–kindergarten Spring, $N = 128$) the miss rate (16%) was low; for the final measure (kindergarten to grade 1) the miss level (29%) approached the limits of tolerance. In sum, the predictors were adequately effective in singling out poor readers in two (or, if one stretches a point, three) out of five of the substudies; in the best of cases, the tests would probably fail to identify 15 to 25 percent of the high-risk children.

The predictive misses raise intriguing questions. The homogeneity of the subjects in the original group and in the "new" sample affords an opportunity to identify, on a case-by-case basis, the children in the group of failing readers who were mispredicted. Is there some pattern in their early test performance that sets them apart from the group for whom predictions were accurate? An analysis of the group of misses might be fruitful, not only for our understanding of prediction, but also of development. One would also like to investigate the implications for development of the finding that the best readers were consistently well predicted. A thorough study of the fate of long-range predictions, above all the fascinating finding that the hit rate for failing readers dropped from 78 percent at second grade to 39 percent at fifth grade, while that for passing readers rose from 75 percent at second grade to a remarkable 95 percent at fifth grade, would contribute to our understanding of changes during this critical developmental period.

It is theoretically meaningful to study a homogeneous group that is especially vulnerable to developing the characteristic being investigated. However, practical considerations dictate that the usefulness of the measure so developed be demonstrated for the various subgroups of the general population. The results show that SES was the top ranking discriminator between outcome groups in the heterogeneous sample. One would like to know whether the tests are equally predictive for boys and for girls, and for children who differ in intelligence. In a quite different study (Jansky, 1970), the results suggested that white girls constituted a different group predictively and the question was raised whether the same predictors were effective for both boys and girls. It is not known whether this effect was an artifact of conditions of that specific sample and the kindergarten tests used, or whether it picked up a maturational characteristic of white girls. Be that as it may, the Satz SES findings, as well as those referring to white girls in my study, suggest that variables external to the theoretical framework set out by Satz really do, in our heterogeneous world, affect predictive effectiveness. These effects deserve intensive and careful study.

I believe that no kindergarten test battery, regardless of its makeup, is going to predict *failing* readers in prospective samples at better than the 75 percent level. Obviously, variables that intervene between prediction and outcome account for some predictive failures. The skill of the teacher, the approach to reading she uses, the frequency of school changes, the child's attendance record, his health, the vicissitudes of his home life, cultural differences in the attitudes toward learning, experiential background and SES factors, not to mention the dramatic physiological changes characteristic of the ages five to seven, are variables that cannot be controlled and that operate in ways that vary from child to child to affect prediction.

I believe that even if the ideal kindergarten predictors were assembled, even if the child's performance on them reflected his status faithfully, and even if the above variables could be controlled, it would still be impossible to predict with perfect accuracy on the basis of kindergarten tests. The reason, in part, that reading seems to be a complex, developmentally "new" accomplishment that is more than and different from the learning that precedes it (Jansky, 1973). Various factor analytic studies, in which reading tests have been pooled with other measures that have been shown to be related to reading, reveal that reading tests tend to cluster together and separately from other measures. This holds whether the other measures are assessed years before or at the same time reading is tested (Chall and Feldmann, 1966). These findings only confirm common sense observation. And because there is not a one-to-one correspondence between the readiness performances and reading, readiness tests cannot be expected to identify all failing readers.

It does not follow that the researcher should not persist in his efforts to develop predictive instruments that are as accurate as possible. Satz has clearly contributed to our body of information. He has been more conscientious than some other researchers about cross-validating his tests and his initiation of a series of prospective studies on new groups of children is commendable.

Nor does the unlikelihood of developing a perfectly predictive kindergarten test battery mean that predictions for high-risk groups cannot be improved. The outstanding accuracy over the years of the predictions of experienced kindergarten teachers is a case in point. Dykstra (1967) noted that teachers, after spending a few weeks with a group of kindergarten children, can predict quite well how successful each child will be. The data of Satz point in the same direction. He found that Classroom Reading Level correlated closely with IOTA scores; the textbook level assigned to the child is very much a matter of teacher judgment. It is not really necessary for teachers to know why they forecast as they do in a given case. Their intuition may take into account some of the uncontrolled variables not reflected directly in the children's test performance. In any case, it seems wasteful not to take advantage of their more intimate working knowledge of the children in their classes. Because it would be inadvisable to rely solely on the subjective judgments of teachers, since some are less able and less experienced than others, ranking systems have been devised for combining test scores with teachers' judgments and these have been found to do much to cut down errors in prediction (Jansky and de Hirsch, 1972).

In addressing the problem of generalizing results for an experimental sample to new groups, I have utilized such a combined score (based on teacher ratings and test data) to devise a system for adjusting predictive battery score cutting levels to the failure rate expected at individual schools. This is accomplished by arriving at a staff consensus as to what constitutes a reading failure score for end-of-second-grade performance. The percentage of children attaining that score and below for the current and immediately preceding years constitutes the expected failure rate. The same proportion of low kindergarten performers, as reflected by the combined teacher ranking-predictive index score, will make up the kindergarten high-risk group (Jansky and de Hirsch, 1972, pp. 61–66). Silver and Hagin (1975) have adopted a similar strategy.

Predictive programs serve a purpose only in the context of carefully devised and far-reaching strategies for intervention. If the school system has made provisions for teaching high-risk children, it will matter less that 25 percent of those likely to fail are not identified. When the difficulties of such children come to light the appropriate placement can be made.

THEORY

Satz conceptualizes developmental reading disorders as more than a unitary phenomenon. Reading problems are explained as delays in those crucial early sensory perceptual and later conceptual linguistic skills that are intrinsic to the acquisition of reading. Developmental reading disorders are seen as disorders in central processing, the nature of which varies with the chronological age of the child. With respect to the early detection of high-risk children, the theory predicts that delays in those developmental skills which are in primary ascendance during kindergarten are most likely to forecast later problems in reading. If a battery of tests sensitive to the development of these early skills (visual perceptual and cross-modal sensory integration) were to predict reading disability at higher grades, then it would constitute one type of support for the theory.

The theory first suggests that tests of visual perceptual and cross-modal sensory integration should be more powerful predictors than are language factors when predictions are being made from kindergarten vantage point, and poorer predictors when the children are in third grade or higher. Support for the theory would require that the visual-perceptual and cross-modal sensory integration and the language measures be adequately representative of the respective abilities at each age, and also have equal weight in the battery as a whole.

Satz describes his results as preliminary. He acknowledges that language tests were not adequately represented in his early battery. It will be recalled that when the battery was factor analyzed, Factor I, Sensory Motor Mnemonic Ability accounted for 31 percent of the common variance, with SES at 16 percent, and Conceptual Ability at 13 percent. It is interesting that the test Alphabet Recitation, seemingly a language measure, clustered with Factor I tests, such as the Berry Visuo-Motor Integration Test, Right-Left Discrimination, and Finger Localization, rather than with other language items, such as the PPVT, Verbal Fluency, and Similarities, that made up Factor III, Conceptual Ability.

In any case, he found that after SES, the tests that were consistently the best predictors were Factor I tests, namely, Finger Localization, Alphabet Recitation, and Recognition-Discrimination. While he considered the results compatible with the theory, Satz recognized that they did not permit conclusions regarding the role of language and conceptual processes as precursors of reading, because the battery was overloaded with tests favoring the hypothesis. Therefore, he administered additional language tests to his third group of children, the heterogeneous sample he had followed from kindergarten through end of grade 1 ($N = 114$). These were Verbal Fluency, which required that the child produce as many words as he could denoting objects belonging to various household rooms, and three tests assessing various aspects of grammatical maturity. The PPVT was also included in this language battery.

It was found that the language battery was about as predictive of subsequent reading status as was the abbreviated battery made up of Factor I tests. To make a more direct comparison between the two batteries, a linear stepwise discriminant function was computed using tests from both batteries. The hit rate for the combined tests was the same as that obtained for the batteries separately. The measures that accounted for most of the predictive hits were SES, Alphabet Recitation, and Finger Localization. Satz feels that results show that the contribution of psycholinguistic variables may be secondary to the preconceptual sensory-motor and perceptual skills, but he acknowledges that cultural, linguistic, conceptual, and perceptual skills play an important role in forecasting later achievement.

I believe that the language battery failed to include a measure of an important aspect of language functioning. While it adequately tapped comprehension of single words and of sentences and, on the expressive side, facility in categorizing objects and in performing grammatical operations, it did not include any measure of the naming function which has been shown to be highly predictive of reading status (Jansky and de Hirsch, 1972).

I also feel that it would have been desirable to factor analyze the combined batteries, i.e., the tests of sensory-motor mnemonic factor and the language tests. The analysis would have revealed the balance of the battery in terms of contributing abilities and it would also have shed light on the factorial composition of the tests administered. One wonders if, in the new configuration, alphabet recitation would have remained in its original cluster or would have shifted to the side of the language sets. If it were to do so, the implications of Satz's results for the theory would change dramatically.

Finally, it would have been desirable to administer both sensory-perceptual and linguistic tests to older children to explore the hypothesis that the lagging children catch up on the sensory-motor skills but fall down on the linguistic-conceptual side. Satz cites the results of an earlier study that pointed to the phasing out of the contribution of perceptual and motor variables when such tests were administered to groups of older elementary school children (Satz, Friel, and Rudegeair, 1974). On the other hand, Silver and Hagin (1964) found that both the reading and the perceptual problems of children seen first at about age 8 were also demonstrated when the subjects were re-evaluated at about age 20. (The results cannot, however, be interpreted to mean either that the perceptual problems exerted a causal effect or that they were the only correlates of poor reading.)

386

Administration of oral language tests to second and third graders would have shown the extent of the contribution of language to reading performance. It would be interesting to determine whether there would have been changes with age in the closeness of association with reading and in the type of language variable associated with reading. The presence of oral language deficits in children demonstrating difficulty with mastery of written language would have underscored the significance of a generalized language involvement.

ANOTHER POINT OF VIEW

I admit to a theoretical predisposition on the other side of the question as to the nature of early predictor variables. With de Hirsch, I became familiar with difficulties with written language through contact with children who had difficulties with spoken language. In following four- and five-year-olds who had been treated for their language disabilities, we observed that many had trouble learning to read after they had entered school (de Hirsch, 1957).

Aware that we were not seeing a normal sample, we undertook the task of prediction for a small group of public school children. The battery administered was heavily loaded with language tests (de Hirsch, Jansky, and Langford, 1966). Encouraged by the results of the pilot study, I undertook prediction for a second group of children from kindergarten to end of second grade. While the major goal of the investigation was to develop an adequate predictive battery, a secondary aim was to determine the relative contribution of various kindergarten abilities to achievement (Jansky, 1970). Because this aim, formulated in 1965, is very much related to the question raised by Satz, and because there has been, as he has pointed out, little empirical study of the matter, the results will be summarized.

To determine the abilities tapped by the 19 kindergarten tests, a factor analysis was performed. The procedure showed a five-factor organization. The first three factors, I Visuo-Motor Ability, II Oral Language A, and Factor III Pattern Matching, contributed comparable proportions of the common variance. Factor IV (Pattern Memory) contributed somewhat less, and Factor V (Oral Language B) least of all to the common variance.

The preschool abilities involved were quite similar to those found by other investigators who had studied children of about the same age (Meyers et al., 1964; Spache et al., 1966). Therefore, it seems safe to assume that the factors represented real abilities and were not simply artifacts of the particular test battery used. There seems little doubt about the existence of a specific oral language ability in kindergarten children. A number of the oral language measures were repeated at the time the children's reading comprehension abilities were tested. Changes in test means showed the tests to be maturation sensitive. Thus, the kindergarten oral language factor clearly included measures that reflected the child's maturing oral language status. Satz, in his review of the literature, stresses that the kind of language abilities associated with higher-level logical operations do not emerge until the child is eight or so. This is a debatable point. The question is whether the language ability of kindergarten children is really static in terms of maturation (a prospect that would seem most unlikely) or whether there are aspects that are maturing and whether these will predict later reading achievement.

To determine the relative contribution of the kindergarten abilities to reading, the kindergarten factors were related to end-of-second-grade reading and spelling by stepwise regression analysis. It was found that Oral Language contributed most to reading (with Pattern Matching and Visuomotor Organization second and third); Visuomotor Ability contributed most to spelling (with Oral Language and Pattern Matching second and third).

Two additional findings from the 1970 study seem pertinent in the light of questions raised by Satz. The first relates to the nature of the two factors called Pattern Matching and Pattern Memory. It was found that neither was modality-specific; tests defining the abilities cut across sensory-modality boundaries. Because nearly all the tests defining the two factors involved verbal activities, it might be assumed that the characteristic common to both are different aspects of symbolic or cognitive functioning. The second refers to the makeup of the oral language factor. Many of the tests reflected the ability to assign names. The picture naming test, categories, story telling about a cartoon sequence, the Boston Speech Sound Discrimination Test (which employs pictures), and the letter naming activity fall into that classification. An additional contributor to the oral language factor was Binet Sentence Repetition, which may reflect awareness of deep linguistic structure. This measure was also a strong predictor of end-of-second-grade reading. It is suggested, then, that the Satz language battery did not adequately tap certain critical linguistic functions that were emerging during the time in question and which appear to forecast reading very well. In our research, for example, the correlation between picture naming and reading when both were assessed at the end of second grade continued to be high ($r = .53$).

Seen in this light, the findings of both the Satz and the Jansky-de

Hirsch studies, and those of other investigators, suggest that at kindergarten age it is delayed or irregular functioning in a variety of areas, including the sensory-motor and the verbal, that makes the difference for reading later on. The several test batteries used to date are not refined enough to indicate which of the various contributors are most heavily implicated in later reading. A test of the question would require a representative sample (for age) of tests in each area and a matching of test characteristics on each side to insure that the measures of each aspect are of equal potency.

The above results suggest that the nature of the interrelationships during the critical years of five to eight may be more complex than the Satz model indicates. The position being reviewed implies that dysmaturation is global as far as correlates critical to reading are concerned, that first visuo-motor cross-modal sensory integration, and later, language variables are involved. In other words, the Satz position appears to suggest that all reading-delayed children will show both early perceptual difficulties and later language problems. According to the theory, then, the dysmaturity would be all-embracing, and not selective, in terms of skills critical for reading. The argument would speak against a relatively isolated perceptual or an isolated language lag in poor readers. But every clinician can cite instances of otherwise normal five year olds who present severe isolated perceptual disturbances and others who demonstrate a variety of isolated oral language dysfunctions; in both groups there are children who develop reading problems. (By the same token, many children with isolated perceptual or language deficits *have* learned to read.)

It seems very likely that neither reading nor the critical early abilities—perceptual-motor and oral language—are unitary competencies. What may determine the child's ultimate success or failure in reading are the subtle interactions of areas of immaturity and compensatory strengths wherever these occur. Thus, a child may have considerable difficulty with pencil management, yet succeed in joining two geometric figures as shown in a model. The same youngster may speak clearly and volubly and with rather mature grammar, yet show marked word finding problems. Whether or not he learns to read would depend on the interplay of particular constellations of strengths and weaknesses in many areas and, to no small extent, on when he was introduced to reading, how competently he was taught, and his cultural and experiential background. An additional possibility is the one alluded to earlier, namely, that the maturation of critical abilities may vary and may have different meanings as a function of sex and race.

Finally, it seems unlikely that the poor readers, even the group of white boys in the Satz study, and certainly the samples of other investigators, constitute a really homogeneous group. There is no evidence that the Satz children were investigated neurologically or psychologically. Therefore, it is in no way certain that reading failure was related to maturational lag in all children. A child might have performed poorly on a test for any number of reasons. Putting aside for the moment the children who failed because they did not attend school, were poorly taught, showed marked neurological damage, were too disturbed emotionally, or too burdened by the effects of economic deprivation to be available for learning, it is possible that some were simply achieving at the level of their innate propensity (whatever the term implies) for language. It is possible, moreover, that this propensity, like others, varies in degree from individual to individual. Proficiency may increase as a function of maturation but, without intervention, may not ever equal that of peers of comparable intelligence.

If an individual is inept athletically or musically, he may choose to avail himself of specialized assistance in order to achieve passable proficiency, or he may simply turn to another activity. Clumsiness in coping with printed language, however, cannot be dealt with so lightly, inasmuch as it is a sine qua non for learning in our culture. Poor reading constitutes a handicap that, unlike some others, cannot be ignored. While some children who are late in learning to read do catch up, if left to themselves, the literature and clinical evidence indicate that many do not "grow out of it." In some cases it may be more a function of their individual constellation of strengths and weaknesses than of maturational lag. This is not to say that delayed or erratic maturational styles do not also account for many reading disorders. The point is that, in advancing conclusions about the maturational nature of the disorder, the hypothesized association between reading dysfunction and developmental lag must be tested *before* the association is assumed.

PREDICTION AND THEORY: A SUMMARY

Prediction. The Satz study demonstrated the value of an extended, longitudinal approach to the identification of good predictor variables. His design provided for the use of results of early analyses to modify later procedures. The dynamic interchange between theory and practice is essential in all aspects of applied study and no more so than in the area of prediction, where the need for accurate early identification is so urgent that the investigator's theoretical predisposition must not be allowed to close the way to promising but different possibilities.

One of Satz's best predictors of reading success or failure was SES. This variable alone forecasts reading status with considerable efficiency.

The Satz battery will predict quite accurately the children who subsequently read very well. However, the Satz instrument, like most predictive measures, is less effective in sorting out children in the "gray" area, those who are average or a bit below or above in reading performance. Moreover, the efficiency of the battery was not strong when put to the test of identifying failing readers over a five-year-span.

Theory. The results of the study discussed do not, to this reviewer, constitute substantial support for Satz's initial hypothesis. It was found that linguistic variables, as well as measures of visuomotor and cross-modal sensory integration ability, contribute to later mastery of reading. In a previous study, Satz produced evidence consistent with the section of his hypothesis regarding the declining significance of visual-perceptual factors as children advance through the grades. He did not, however, test his hypothesis concerning the primary importance of linguistic and cognitive factors for success in reading in the upper grades.

RECOMMENDATIONS FOR FUTURE RESEARCH

Prediction

1. The results of previous research indicate that the same predictive battery may not be equally efficient for all subgroups of a sample. Cross-validation studies should include analysis of the accuracy of identification for boys and for girls, and for children of different levels of intelligence.

2. An exploration of the characteristics of the children who were misidentified and of those who were accurately identified would be worthwhile. The results might lead to refinements of the battery.

3. An attempt should be made to account for some intervening variables, at least for a representative subgroup.

4. Some system by which teachers' predictions are combined with test scores should be adopted, because previous research indicates that such procedures increase predictive accuracy.

5. Predictive screening should be anchored in a long-range educational strategy that includes intervention for children who need it. The long

view will insure that prediction does not become an end in itself. Fixation upon prediction could divert attention from taking the responsibility for making crucial adjustments in educational planning. Moreover, if programs are available for teaching children whose educational styles differ, corrections can be made for inaccurate predictions, once it becomes evident that children are not in the program that is best suited to them.

Theory

1. The testing plan should include the administration of a variety of oral language tests believed to tap representative aspects of learning, in addition to reading and spelling performance over a period of years. Factor or cluster analysis might study the results horizontally (tests administered at the same time only) and vertically (all tests administered to date). Because such studies would provide evidence of which abilities, if any, belong to the reading cluster, the findings might further elucidate the nature of reading at early and later ages. The analysis would also indicate the internal stability of the various ability clusters over the years.

2. An assessment by means of regression analysis of the relationship between the abilities at different ages and reading would indicate the relative contribution to reading of various abilities, both as predictors and concurrently.

3. The degree of sensitivity of the tests to changes in chronological age should be determined so that statements can be made regarding changes in abilities as a function of maturation.

4. The division of the sample, for the above analysis, into various subgroups would permit the study of the degree to which relationships characteristic of the whole heterogeneous group would apply to various subgroups. For example, such a procedure might investigate whether the relationship of ability to reading is the same for boys as for girls and whether or not the changes that occur with age are similar for both groups.

5. Case studies of the test results and classroom observation of individual children in various categories should be accumulated for a period of years. Studying such individual records, against the background of results for the sample as a whole, would be illuminating and might provide hypotheses for further study. For example, it may be that one or two determining characteristics for prediction is the child's maturational status or his inherent propensity in the several critical readiness areas. It is possible, since the various readiness abilities seem not to be unitary, that it is the subtle interaction of strengths and weaknesses across areas that makes the difference for later suc-

cess. Careful analysis of various individual performance profiles should shed light on this possibility.

A COMMENT ABOUT INTERVENTION

The framework of the present discussion has left little opportunity to consider early intervention. Given the very incomplete and tentative state of our knowledge of what contributes to later success in reading, a conservative final statement appears to be in order.

Because it seems unlikely that reading is simply an advanced form of reading readiness, it might be best to think of intervention at the two levels as having different aims. At the readiness level, one would strive to foster the child's mastery of skills representing the several critical precursor abilities for reading. This would include graphomotor activities, language stimulation work, and the introduction of the letters and phonemes of the language. The Liberman-Shankweiler program (1976) represents a very structured device for accomplishing the last objective. Very brief and carefully crafted experience stories might help to illustrate the correspondence between spoken and printed linguistic units.

As soon as the child seems ready to respond to printed words, the focus would shift specifically to techniques for reading and writing words and sentences, with an immediate eye to the communication of meaning via the printed word (as opposed to an emphasis on the manipulation, in isolation, of graphemes and phonemes, though analytic techniques will clearly have to be taught).

Readiness training is of value in its own right because it seems to enrich the matrix or foundation that is the base for the "new" accomplishment, reading. However, one probably cannot expect that readiness work will be all that is necessary in order to teach many high-risk children to learn to read. Intervention initiated at kindergarten level should be continued until the child has demonstrated mastery of reading and writing.

Several important questions arise from these observations based on clinical experience and the consideration of research results. Is reading, characterized by a degree of mastery of a complex linguistic process, actually a "new" accomplishment? If it is, does it reflect a corresponding advance in neurophysiological development? If both are the case, then a careful analysis of what occurs during the shift from reading readiness to real reading might provide valuable leads about the parallel mechanisms that govern the transition between developmental levels. Research in prediction and intervention is particularly well suited to the exploration of this extremely complex aspect of development. The painstaking, extended study of the functioning of individuals, against the background of findings for groups, would appear to be a fruitful avenue of inquiry.

Satz's theory has opened the way for the exploration of a variety of possibilities. His longitudinal orientation and his investigation of large samples are strategies that should be followed by others who wish to study a problem that clearly has different shapes as the child matures and interacts with his environment. It seems to me that relevant data from longitudinal investigations would increase immeasurably not only our skill in predicting but also our knowledge of the development of abilities that are central for academic learning.

Part VII

REMEDIATION

Chapter 19

REMEDIAL APPROACHES
TO DYSLEXIA

DORIS J JOHNSON

Children with reading difficulties have concerned educators, psychologists, physicians, and parents for many years. Most children enter school eager to learn, and their teachers are equally eager to instruct them. When they fail to read, frustrations are inevitable. The child may feel he is slow or mentally incapable; the teacher may feel inadequate or guilty; the parents wonder about their effectiveness. The search for counsel and advice often produces more frustrations. Some parents are told to wait and see—"he will read when he is ready" or "he'll grow out of it." Others are told to retain the child in the same grade or hire a tutor. Still others are told to have a visual, psychological, or neurological examination. Thus many professionals have been involved in the study of reading disorders, each viewing the child from a different background of training and experience. Subsequently many labels have been ascribed to the problems and many approaches to assessment and management have been developed.

Most professionals agree that there are many reasons for reading problems including sensory impairments, mental retardation, emotional disturbance, lack of opportunity or instruction, poor motivation, and specific reading disability or dyslexia (Eisenberg, 1966). Therefore, a comprehensive study by a multidisciplinary team is often needed. Many also agree that there are children who have many assets and ample opportunity for conventional instruction but who find reading very difficult. There is little agreement, however, regarding nomenclature or criteria for diagnosis. However, the need for remedial instruction is evident. These children, who are the focus of this discussion, have been the concern of many professionals since Morgan's first description in 1896. Only in recent decades have major efforts been made to provide for the needs of exceptional children. With the advent of mandatory education and changes in society it became apparent that reading competence is crucial for vocational mobility. The individual who cannot read often is unable to pursue an academic career and is restricted in his choice of occupations even though he may have superior mental ability. The subsequent effects on self-concept and mental health often are great.

The identification of children with specific reading disabilities led to the development of remedial procedures. Hollingworth (1923) described her experiments from 1918 to 1922 with an 11-year-old nonreader and was an early proponent of scientifically differentiated instruction. She felt that our schools should be more responsive to individual needs in order to avoid the despair of chronic failure experienced by many children. Hollingworth concluded, as we must conclude today, that no single method was the only successful approach. This is due, at least in part, to the fact that the dyslexic population, while homogeneous in certain respects, also is heterogeneous. Not all exhibit the same symptoms. Some have disturbances in auditory learning, whereas others have more difficulty with visual learning. Some have problems comprehending; others do not. Thus we need to analyze the characteristics of those children for whom a particular approach is successful or unsuccessful. Such information is rarely available (at least the unsuccessful attempts) but it would be valuable for research purposes.

The ultimate goal is to match the child's overall pattern of strengths and weaknesses with a particular method, to select a method by choice rather than by chance (Johnson and Myklebust, 1967). In order to meet that goal, future studies will need to provide more data pertaining to the characteristics of the population and significant details related to methods and procedures. In addition, we should avoid overgeneralizations when describing methods. There are many subtle but important differences in procedures that need to be considered when teaching dyslexic children. For example, both Gillingham and Stillman (1960) and Fernald (1943) employed multisensory stimulation, but the vocabulary and sequence of instruction in their methods were very different. Similarly, some phonic methods are taught analytically, whereas others are taught synthetically. Some approaches utilize color to highlight new phonemes, whereas others require a higher level of abstraction. Some reading methods require the learning of explicit syllabication rules, while others are designed to help the child acquire rules implicitly. These differences can be masked if we attempt to classify methods according to a single feature.

This review will contain brief descriptions of methods that have been used with dyslexics. These will be followed by suggestions for delineating populations and procedures in the future. Finally, factors related to progress and prognosis will be summarized.

A review of this type is complex and difficult because of the varied terminology and lack of carefully planned, longitudinal studies. Few methods have been subjected to rigorous controls over long periods of time. Often the experimental procedures were developed in clinics or university settings where children came for brief periods of instruction. Nevertheless, clinical studies can form the basis for future research hypotheses and investigations.

THE ORTON-GILLINGHAM APPROACH

One of the earliest programs of remediation for dyslexic children was developed by Gillingham who worked closely with the neurologist, Orton. The method was designed for children with normal or superior intelligence who had difficulty learning to read by the sight method (Orton, 1937). The children often came from families in which there was left-handedness or language difficulty. When learning to read they showed marked confusions with the orientation and order of letters in words. Usually they evidenced delay or incomplete establishment of one-sided motor preference; many tended to be left-handed or ambidextrous. In addition to problems in reading, some also had speech and language defects.

Orton approached reading as "one stage of the child's language development preceded by spoken language (hearing and speaking) and expressed in writing which includes spelling" (J. Orton, 1966, p. 122). He viewed language as an "evolutionary human function associated with the development of a hierarchy of complex interactions in the nervous system and culminating in unilateral control by one of the two brain hemispheres (cerebral dominance)" (1966, p. 122). In explaining the nature of specific reading disability Orton hypothesized an "intermixture of control in the two hemispheres of the brain in those areas which subserve the visual or reading part of the language function and are normally active only in the dominant hemisphere. He postulated that "the mirrored images of the two hemispheres might then conflict when the child attempted to build associations between letters and spoken words, producing confusions and orientation errors and a general delay in learning to read" (1966, p. 123).

Because of the complexity of language disabilities, Orton recommended a comprehensive assessment which included family and educational history and an evaluation of hearing, vision, intelligence, achievement, and neurological status. Several language measures were given to study auditory processes, vocabulary, and grammar. Reading tests were designed to elicit reversals, sequencing errors, and mirror reading. Throughout the evaluation, the examiner noted that nature of the stimulus and responses to various tasks.

Orton emphasized two basic principles for remediation (J. Orton, 1966). The first was simultaneous association of visual, auditory, and kinesthetic language stimuli—tracing and sounding the visually presented words and maintaining left–right direction by following the letters with the fingers during the synthesis of syllables and words. The second major principle involved the fusing of small units into more complex wholes. Thus, the method might be classified as a multisensory, synthetic, alphabetic approach. The child begins by learning individual letters and phonemes and by establishing linkages between the auditory, visual, and motor aspects of speech and writing. Consonants and vowels are printed on different color flash cards. Simple words with consistent phoneme-grapheme correspondence are introduced after the child has learned letter sounds. Careful attention is given to blending since many students have problems with auditory synthesis and sequencing. When the child has learned to read and write three-letter words he combines them into sentences and stories. Syllabication principles for longer words are taught later. Throughout the program emphasis is given to the mastery of skills so the child can attack words independently.

Reports of progress made by dyslexics who were taught by this method are included in Orton's own work and in the Bulletin of The Orton Society. Orton (1946) said, "Whether or not our theory is right, I do not know, but I do know that the methods of retraining which we have derived from that viewpoint have worked. I do not claim them to be a panacea for reading troubles of all sorts but I do feel that we understand the blockade which occurs so frequently in children with good minds and which results in the characteristic reading of the strephosymbolic type in childhood." June Orton (1966) states that hundreds if not thousands of disabled readers have been helped to overcome their handicaps.

Childs (1965) documents progress made by several students who were taught by the Gillingham approach. In one study she reports the improvement of 14-year-old male twins who were severe dyslexics but in different schools. One of the boys who was in a public school progressed in reading from a grade level of 4.1 to 4.5 within a six-month period. The other was taught by the Gillingham method in a special school and progressed from grade 3.3 to 4.3 within the same time period. In another instance she reported that two teenage girls progressed from the eighteenth and twenty-second percentile in reading to the seventieth and the ninety-first percentile within a period of seven months. Childs also reports group progress made by children who were taught by these procedures. Other case studies are presented by remedial specialists in the Bulletin of the Orton Society (Cox, 1967; McClelland, 1973; Robinson, 1969).

In a follow-up study of 216 children, Kline and Kline (1975) reported that children with severe dyslexia who were taught by the Orton-Gillingham method made impressive gains in relatively short periods of time in nearly 96 percent of the cases. Of those who were not taught by these procedures, 49 percent failed to make progress. The Klines felt that this latter finding reflected the failure of schools or parents to follow recommendations or to use a program of effective remediation. Most children required at least two years of therapy for good results and some required even more time. Continued support, consultation, and on-going training are recommended to insure success.

A longitudinal study of dyslexic boys in a private, independent school was reported by Rawson (1968). The students tended to be above average intellectually, but several had specific language and reading disabilities. Those with problems were taught with the Gillingham approach. Rawson states that by the time they left the school "twenty-five percent of the boys in the Low Language Facility group were reading at a superior level, forty percent at a level close to their grade placement, and thirty-five percent were still rated as inadequate by half a year or more, although most of them eventually learned to read more satisfactorily. In spelling, however, only five percent of the boys in the Low Language Facility group had reached the superior level, five percent the average level, while ninety percent were still below grade." Despite the continued problems Rawson presents an optimistic picture for overall prognosis. She states that ". . . the boys who were early diagnosed as having severe to moderate specific language disabilities (dyslexia) have achieved at least as high levels of education and socioeconomic status as their more linguistically facile schoolmates. On the other hand, several individuals still find that some of the residuals of their language problems are sources of difficulty in their current lives. They have not been stopped in their careers." She concludes that dyslexics need not be considered poor risks for academic and occupational pursuits.

Critics of the Gillingham approach contend that too little emphasis is given to comprehension and concern has been expressed about the lack of meaningful material. Rawson and others, however, indicate that the good teacher always checks word meanings. It is quite possible that these procedures are most effective for those children whose primary problems are in decoding rather than in comprehending. Gates (1947) has criticized the method because it is rigid and forfeits interest in the initial stages of reading. He feels that it may produce slow, labored reading with excessive lip movements.

Some educators are concerned with the high emphasis on auditory perception and blending, particularly for young children and for those with specific auditory deficits (Wepman, 1960). Thus, different approaches are advocated for children with auditory disorders (Johnson and Myklebust, 1967; Boder, 1971).

Despite these criticisms, Harris (1970) believes that there are positive aspects including interest and motivation that are created by success. When the child is introduced to reading he has a sound basis for attacking words. The method appears to be beneficial when visual methods fail. In the future it would be helpful to study more specifically the characteristics of children who do or do not profit from particular procedures. It is important to note the students who make limited progress as well as those who improve markedly.

THE FERNALD APPROACH

Another approach to instruction for disabled readers was developed in the 1920s by Fernald in the Clinic School at the University of California (Fernald, 1943). The program was designed to meet the needs of children with many types of learning problems, but it included those with normal intelligence who had severe reading disabilities. Although Fernald is known primarily for her kinesthetic procedures, it is important to review her basic philosophy. She believed that children needed successful experiences in school if they were to make a satisfactory adjustment. Many negative emotional reactions are exhibited when children are kept in situations where they cannot achieve. Therefore, she advocated a "reconditioning method" which directed the child's attention away from experiences that provoked unpleasant emotional reactions. Her goal was to start the child in the Clinic School with successful experiences on the first day. No one was expected to return to the regular class until he could succeed in this environment.

The disabled reader, taught by the Fernald method, begins by selecting any words he wants to learn. This is in contrast to the highly controlled vocabulary recommended by Gillingham. Words are written with rather large script or print on separate cards. The child traces over the word with his finger tip saying each part as he traces. Fernald felt that the direct finger tracing provided more input than that which could be achieved by copying with a pencil or a stylus. The child continues tracing over the word until he can write it from memory. Then the words are alphabetized and placed in a file box. Words are always learned as wholes and are used in meaningful contexts.

As the child improves, the tracing procedures are discontinued; he looks at a word, says it simultaneously and writes it from memory. Fernald felt that the child must establish associations between the printed, spoken, and written forms as did Gillingham. Finally the child is encouraged to look at the word without saying it and to write it. In the final stage the child is expected to generalize from known to unknown words. No emphasis is given to sounding out individual phonemes or syllables. Rather, phonic principles are acquired from reading a variety of materials in context.

Marjorie Johnson (1966), a proponent of VAKT (visual-auditory-kinesthetic-tactile) methods, states that for tracing and kinesthetic techniques to be really effective, they should be used within an experience approach, that is, in accord with the child's language and interests. She recommends the procedures for severe dyslexics because the child is maximally engaged in the learning process. In addition, many opportunities for reinforcement are available since short-terms goals are always met. Johnson emphasizes that only highly trained teachers should use these procedures and that they should be used within the entire framework in order to be successful.

Advocates of this approach frequently respond to two major points. The first pertains to motivation and success, whereas the second relates more to neurophysiological concepts. With regard to the latter issue Myers and Hammill (1969) report that "the act of tracing a word several times prepares the mental coordinates for an important message and then follows through on a selective avenue of approach. Thus the auditory and visual pathways are being activated in the same manner as the child sees and says the word as he is tracing it."

Myers and Hammill state that children with visual-perceptual and memory disorders probably profit more from the approach than do those with auditory disorders. However, some authors attribute the success of the method to the auditory feedback the child receives while saying and tracing the word. Others suggest that the slow tracing helps the child attend to the visual sequence of letters.

Harris (1970) says that although the procedures are designed to use motor imagery to reinforce audiovisual associations, the kinesthetic elements may be of minor importance and that writing helps the child remember the word because he must attend to all of the auditory and visual features. He believes that remediation with a typewriter works as well as with tracing.

Desirable features of the method are summarized by Harris (1970). It forces careful and systematic observation and study of words. It makes necessary a consistent left-to-right direction in reading and provides opportunity for repetition. Errors are immediately noted and progress can be noted by the child during each lesson. He feels that the sensory impressions from tracing, writing, and saying the words reinforce the visual impressions and are of definite value to children whose visual memory is poor.

Harris also reviews certain objections. He notes that the teacher has to direct and check each step in the child's work and must teach every new word. Thus the child is unable to do any independent reading in the early stages of instruction. He feels that most nonreaders can learn to recognize words by methods which are faster than tracing. In addition, the procedures are more adapted to clinical settings than to the public school.

The effectiveness of the VAKT approach was tested by Talmadge, Davids, and Laufer (1963) with a group of dyslexic children with cortical dysfunction caused by minimal brain damage and a group of dyslexics without brain damage. During a three-month period the former group gained 1.04 years on a reading test, whereas the latter gained only .62 years. Similar children, with and without brain damage, improved by only .45 years when taught by traditional methods.

Ofman and Schaevitz (1963) compared a look–say method with tracing methods for learning nonsense syllables. They found that tracing with the eye was as effective as tracing with the finger and that both methods produced better results than the look–say procedures. They indicated, however, that the improvement may result from attention to details of the visual sequence rather than to the kinesthetic input. Roberts and Coleman (1958) found that poor readers who had good visual perception were not aided by kinesthetic cues, but those who were inefficient in utilizing visual cues were helped by tracing.

Johnson and Myklebust (1967) report that some learning-disabled children appear to be overloaded by multisensory stimulation. They cannot look, listen, and trace simultaneously. This is in keeping with the hypothesis of Blau and Blau (1968) who suggested a method which initially involved tracing with the eyes closed. The purpose is to avoid interference from poor or distorted visual perception. These authors suggest that after the "feel" has been properly established the child will then need to build kinesthetic and visual associations. Johnson (1969) states that it is necessary to "balance the input stimulation" in order to facilitate learning.

This reviewer also found when using the Fernald method that some dyslexic children did not acquire phonic principles. Therefore a more structured vocabulary was needed. As indicated previously, it is important to define clearly the nature of the population with whom the procedures are most and least effective.

COLOR PHONICS METHODS

Several educators have explored the use of color coding as a means of helping children learn to read. One of the earliest methods was developed by Edith Norrie, a dyslexic who devised a method to teach herself when she was in her twenties and who later founded the Ordblinde Institute in Copenhagen (Bannatyne, 1966). Essentially her method involves synthetic phonic training with color cues to help the child recall certain sounds. Emphasis is given to the motor patterns necessary for producing phonemes. Initially the children are introduced to the Norrie Letter Case or Composing Box which contains letters that are arranged phonetically. Vowels are printed in red and the child learns that there cannot be a syllable or word without a red letter. Consonants are coded according to lip sounds or labials, palatals, and gutterals, and also according to whether the sounds are voiced or voiceless. The initial vocabulary consists of phonetically regular words which the child spells from the letters in his box. A mirror is used to show the child the placement of the tongue, lips and jaws when producing various phonemes. Additional training is provided on listening for the number of syllables in words, on grammar, and on left–right scanning. Apparently the approach has been successful with dyslexics in Denmark.

Bannatyne (1966) also developed a color phonics system which he recommends for several reasons. He states that the only methods that have been successful with dyslexics are those that are founded on a firm phonetic basic. He feels that color coding facilitates the learning of sound–symbol associations and that the technique allows for sound–symbol associations to be developed through a variety of pathways. He believes that the basic neuropsychological deficit of the pure dyslexic is an inability to sequence properly. Therefore, the method allows for arrangement and rearrangement of sounds into words. However, the sequencing problems are primarily auditory and any deficit in visual performance is secondary. Burns (1975) found that dyslexic children had significantly more difficulty sequencing digits than normal children; however, the problems were present independently of mode of input or output. It would appear that phonics methods, especially those with color cuing, may help stabilize the audiovisual sequence in words. Although Bannatyne's color system was not designed for children with visuospatial and motor deficits, he indicates that the procedures have been effective with a wide variety of children.

Gattegno and Hinman (1966) also advocate the use of color, particularly to alleviate problems of spatial orientation and sequencing encountered by many young readers. Over 50 colors are used to represent each of the sounds in Gattegno's "Words in Color" system. Letters such as p, e, and b are printed in different colors, and vowel confusions are also reduced. The child learns that the sound "a" in "came" will be represented in the same color whether it contains the ay, ai, or a-e spelling. Through a process of dictation the child associates a spatial sequence of letters with a temporal sequence of sounds. According to Gattegno and Hinman, the system has been tested and used in several regular as well as special education classes. Once the child learns the patterns, he can read and write whatever he can say, reversals disappear, and he becomes more aware of sounds in words.

As with other methods, there is no evidence to suggest these procedures will be effective with all children. Harris (1970) states that the substantial cost of multicolor printing is a disadvantage and that some materials may need to be made by the teacher. In the opinion of Bernstein (1967), the method is too complex and the transition from color to black and white may be somewhat difficult. Dean (1966) also criticizes the method because he feels children may become proficient in word calling without comprehension. The same criticism has been made of other synthetic phonic methods.

This reviewer is more concerned with the added element of representation which is required with color coding. Our current research indicates that some children with verbal disorders have problems with many forms of representation including gesture, pantomime, pretended behavior, and other nonverbal symbols. Therefore, when color is used to stand for something else, the child has multiple translation tasks. He must understand that letters stand for sounds and that particular colors represent particular groups of phonemes such as those which are voiced or voiceless.

Color coding sometimes has been used on a simpler level with learning-disabled children. Strauss and Lehtinen (1947) found it beneficial to assign a color to each vowel and to develop an association between color and sound. Cruikshank et al. (1961) also recommended the use of color, since color perception frequently is intact when other dimensions of visual perception are impaired.

MODIFIED ALPHABETS

Some theories have hypothesized that reading problems may result from the irregular spelling patterns of our language, and several systems have been devised to provide more uniform patterns (Harris, 1970). One of the best known, the Initial Teaching Alphabet, was designed by Sir James Pitman. The alphabet consists of 44 characters; each grapheme represents a particular phoneme, so the child does not have to deal with many irregularities. Once the child learns the letter-sound relationships he should be able to decode and spell the words he can say. Although there is controversy about the value of ITA, Vernon (1971) states that children do learn to read more easily than with the traditional alphabet. Transfer to English does, however, present some problems (Chall, 1967).

No conclusive studies have been done using ITA with dyslexics. As with other synthetic phonic methods, this alphabet might help the child perceive and integrate the temporal-spatial pattern of words. Myers and Hammill (1969) state that children who rely solely upon the visual characteristics of words printed in ITA may have difficulty transferring to the traditional system.

LEARNING PROCESSES AND LEARNING DISABILITIES

During recent years considerable emphasis has been given to individual cognitive styles and learning patterns. This is due, in part, to developments within the field of learning disabilities. Concern for these children stimulated research and development of instruments designed to investigate learning through a particular sensory modality (Birch and Belmont, 1964; Frostig, 1964; Kirk, 1961). Attempts were made to classify children as auditory or visual learners (Wepman, 1964) and to note strengths and weaknesses (Zigmond, 1966; Kirk, 1961). If a child demonstrated a particular problem, activities were recommended to overcome the deficit (Frostig, 1964).

Several attempts have been made to place children in remedial groups according to their preferred modalities (Jones, 1972), but in some instances the stimuli were not related to the printed word. In our experience, a child may be poor in visual nonverbal learning and yet do well in reading. The converse also has been observed. Another problem arose when children were to be taught by an auditory or visual method. Jones (1972, p. 36) says "one would be hard pressed to locate a method of learning to read which limits the role of the auditory or the visual mode to a significant degree." There probably is no discrete auditory or visual approach that can be used to help children decode words.

One of the oversimplifications in the field is this tendency to classify the child as an auditory or a visual learner without considering the nature of the information to be processed, that is, whether it is verbal or nonverbal. Thus the research that has been done on reading methods by modality groupings is not conclusive. Research on learning processes, however, continues. In the field of learning disabilities and remedial reading, many professionals object to the use of the term "dyslexia." The following section is devoted to programs of remediation by those who use the term.

REMEDIATION OF DYSLEXIA

Myklebust and Johnson (1962) view dyslexia as a symbolic deficit within the broad category of learning disabilities. Learning to read is an integral part of total language development and, therefore, the study of this process must be related to all other aspects. Reading is a visual symbol system superimposed on auditory language and followed by written expression. Failure to read may result from a variety of auditory, visual, or integrative disorders. Thus it is necessary to do a comprehensive study and a "systems analysis" in order to determine the child's pattern of strengths and weaknesses. No single method will be successful with all children.

Several frames of reference are incorporated into the diagnostic study. The first is the input-integration-output schema. This suggests that the child might be considered as an information processor with multiple systems for input and output and with the potential for complex networks of integration. Since disturbances may occur at any point, the diagnostician tries to determine which systems for input and output are intact and whether the child is able to associate meaning with experience. Some dyslexics have difficulty with auditory processing; others have difficulty with visual learning; still others are skilled in transducing graphemes to phonemes but fail to comprehend.

A third frame of reference pertains to verbal and nonverbal behavior. Johnson and Myklebust (1967) suggest that it is necessary to determine whether a child has difficulty processing verbal or nonverbal information. Although some children have difficulty with both types, others have difficulty with only one form. For example, some dyslexics have excellent visual-nonverbal skills as demonstrated in graphic arts. By contrast, certain learning-disabled children have no difficulty learning to read but do have severe problems in visuospatial learning which interfere with writing or arithmetic. Because of these differences Johnson (1975) feels that one must not overgeneralize and label a child as an auditory or visual learner without considering the nature of the information to be processed. In addition, one must be cautious in making predictions about reading performance from various visual-nonverbal tasks. Some of the studies which have attempted to group children by sensory modality fail to consider this aspect of learning.

A fourth frame of reference used is the hierarchy of experience. Myklebust (1960) proposed that it is necessary to determine the level at which learning may be impaired, that is, whether the disturbance occurs at the level of sensation, perception, imagery, symbolization, or conceptualization. Although some reading disturbances may result from problems in auditory or visual perception, others are related to problems of memory or comprehension. All these frames of reference are used when selecting diagnostic instruments and interpreting results.

Even though there is variability among problems of learning-disabled children, Johnson and Myklebust identified two relatively broad groups of dyslexics. One group is designated as having visual dyslexia. These children are similar to the strephosymbolics described by Orton (1937). Many have problems with the orientation of letters, visual perception, or memory. Thus whole-word or sight methods are difficult for them. A synthetic phonic method is recommended. Little or no emphasis is given to learning letter names. Words with perfect letter–sound correspondence are introduced so that the children can systematically attack them. Sounds are carefully blended together and words are combined into sentences. Sight words are introduced in context. The instructor frequently asks the children to give the meaning of the word or use it in a sentence to insure comprehension. In addition to this major focus, work is done to improve underlying deficits in visual processing. Johnson and Myklebust (1967) recommend a two-pronged approach fo: the remediation of dyslexia. The basic method capitalizes on the child's strengths, whereas minor emphasis is given to the deficit. Therefore, the major approach for the visual dyslexic is a synthetic, phonic method, but exercises for visual perception or memory are included. Work on the deficit is not done with geometric designs or other types of nonverbal material, but with the printed word. The objective is to help the child learn to read and to facilitate learning through the impaired modalities.

Another group of children are designated as auditory dyslexics. They may acquire a small sight vocabulary, but they have difficulty with phonics and auditory processes and so cannot generalize from known to unknown words. Many are deficient in the ability to rhyme, to sequence sounds, and to analyze or synthesize words. Some have retrieval problems and are slow to call up letter names, sounds, or words. This characteristic was observed by Mattis, French, and Rapin (1975) in a group of dyslexic children and young adults. Johnson and Myklebust (1967) recommend that the auditory dyslexic be taught by a whole-word or story method. Since they have difficulty retaining nonmeaningful units such as letter sounds, they are taught whole words, particularly nouns and verbs so they can match objects or pictures with the printed word. Functor words, prepositions, and articles are taught in context. The minor prong of this method involves considerable work on auditory analysis and synthesis. After the child has learned a basic sight vocabulary of nouns and verbs, the instructor begins to identify words that begin or end with the same sounds. Thus, the initial vocabulary should have the potential for this type of analysis. When the child first learns a new word little emphasis is given to auditory analysis and synthesis. Only after he has associated the printed word with a meaningful experience does the work on auditory processing begin. Phonics principles are taught implicitly, since many children with auditory language disorders are confused by verbal rules for syllabication.

Because not all children fall easily into these categories, reading methods need to be analyzed and modified along several parameters in order to select appropriate procedures (Johnson, 1969). Critical questions pertaining to methods include the following:

1. What is the nature of the input stimulation? Is it primarily visual; does it combine auditory and visual stimulation; are all sensory channels used simultaneously?

2. What is the expected response from the child? Is he required to match figures or to mark something? Is he required to give an oral or written response?

3. What is the nature of the vocabulary? On what basis were the words selected? How controlled is the vocabulary? Do the words have a consistent phoneme-grapheme relationship? How many meaningful words are used (specifically nouns and verbs)?

4. What is the nature of the sentence structure? Is it similar to the child's language?

5. What is the nature of the content of the stories? Is the material in keeping with the child's level of experience and interest?

6. Does the method require deductive or inductive thought processes? Does the child work from the whole word to the part or from the part to the whole?

These and other variables including length of story, the nature of pictures or illustrations, and size of print are important to consider when planning remediation.

Johnson (1969) states that the dyslexic child might be likened to a special type of computer. The computer has a potential capacity for processing information. However, it will not function properly unless it is fed a particular program. A program that fits one computer will not necessarily work for one of a different type. These subtle variations of methods make instruction more difficult for the teacher—we agree with Gillingham who suggested that each child be considered as an experiment.

Although no data are available which utilize these approaches on groups of dyslexics, Behrens (1963) completed a follow-up study on a group of learning-disabled children who had been seen by Myklebust and Johnson. The population included children with writing, mathematics, and nonverbal disorders as well as those with reading difficulty. Results of the investigation indicated that for 41 percent of the psychological measures employed, the improvement between the means of the initial and second study was significant at least at the .10 level of confidence. Behrens found that there was an overall tendency toward a more substantial improvement in verbal than in nonverbal abilities. Significant changes were observed on similarities, auditory attention span, visual attention span, auditory blending of letter sounds, phrase perception in reading, and in written language. Behrens did not study dyslexics as a single group, nor did he investigate the changes that occurred in any subgroup of reading disorders.

Naidoo (1970) appears to agree with the basic philosophy that training should begin with processes in which the child is adept and provide supplementary training to overcome weaknesses. Vernon (1971) however, states that no firm evidence is available to support this contention.

Some investigators suggest that phonic methods are necessary for all dyslexics. Bryant (1968) states that dyslexics are unable to extract and recognize details within wholes, whether they be auditory or visual. Therefore, remediation should emphasize discrimination, blending, and sequencing.

Spache (1976) raises some questions with regard to the perceptual-deficit and sensory modalities issues in reading disabilities. He feels that we need to establish the validity of various methods and their relative dependence upon different channels as well as responses of learners to the procedures.

BODER

Boder (1971) proposed a plan for the evaluation of dyslexic children which is based primarily on a direct analysis of reading and spelling errors rather than indirect studies of learning processes from intelligence tests, neuropsychological examinations, and other procedures designed to explore modality strengths and weaknesses. Her analysis, which was intended to qualitatively evaluate the child's reading and spelling ability, yielded three subtypes of dyslexics.

The first was dysphonetic dyslexic. The reading–spelling pattern in these cases reflects a deficit in symbol–sound integration and in phonetic word analysis. The second group was dyseidetic or gestalt blind. In these cases the reading–spelling pattern reflects a deficit in the ability to perceive letters and whole words. The third was a group of mixed dysphonetic-dyseidetic dyslexics in which the reading–spelling pattern reflects basic deficits in both phonetic analysis skills and whole-word perception. The remediation for Boder's first group is similar to that for the auditory dyslexic described by Johnson and Myklebust (1967), whereas the second is similar to that for the visual dyslexic and therefore is taught by a synthetic phonic method. The third group, those with the most severe problems, are neither visile or audile and require tactile-kinesthetic techniques.

Boder did not present data pertaining to progress, but she did indicate the prognosis for the three groups. She states that the prognosis for groups one and two is better since the deficit occurs primarily in one channel.

According to her observations, the child in group one approaches normal proficiency in contextual reading since he acquires a sight vocabulary at grade level or above. However, word-analysis skills often do not become automatic and spelling tends to remain poor. Boder says the children in group two tend to remain slow readers and usually do not achieve a sight vocabulary commensurate with grade level. Although data were not available, Boder's observations suggest that the prognosis for reading is better in group one and the prognosis for spelling is better in group two. The outlook for the children in her third group is less favorable. Boder states that without intensive long-term remediation the prosnosis must be guarded. None of the group-three children in her study had achieved proficiency in reading or spelling at the high school level.

PROGRESS AND FACTORS RELATED TO PROGNOSIS

Vernon's (1971) review of research indicates that severe reading disability is often highly resistant to instruction. Although some cases improve rapidly, others make very slow progress. Some acquire basic reading skills but they do not read fluently. Many continue to have spelling problems. Despite the importance of clinical progress records, one must agree with Botel (1968) that there is no reliable evidence regarding the success of various procedures. We do not know for certain which methods are most effective for the many subgroups of children in classroom or clinical settings.

It is difficult to know how much progress can be expected with dyslexics at different age levels because success depends upon many factors. Spache (1976) reports the gains made by students in several different remedial reading programs. However, the populations were rather heterogeneous. He found that the median ratio of remedial gain per period of instruction was 1.2 in 21 studies. The range is large, varying from 0. to 7.4, but, in general, the gains from remedial reading are about double the amount that might be expected in any given period of time. This ratio is a helpful guide in setting certain goals, but it is clear that progress will vary. Future studies should be designed to determine more about the characteristics of the children, the program, and other variables discussed below.

It is doubtful that simple solutions are forthcoming because the subject of our investigation is a very complex organism. The developing child, with his enormous capacity for receiving and transmitting information, is the subject of scientific investigations by psychologists, neurologists, educators, linguists, and others. The atypical child requires even more careful study in order to determine the nature of his learning patterns. Moreover, it is clear that the child cannot be studied in isolation. Whatever complex intraorganismic analyses we design to study learning must be related to the environment and society in which the child exists. The interaction of the child with his family, his peers, and instructors will influence the outcome of instruction.

Some of the variables that are related to prognosis for dyslexics are rather intangible and difficult to quantify. One of these is *expectancy,* a quality that is known to every teacher and student, if not consciously, at least unconsciously. The importance of this factor was emphasized by Gardner (1961) when he stated, "more and more we are coming to see that high performance, particularly where children are concerned, takes place in a framework of expectations. If it is expected it will often occur. If there are no expectations, there will be little high performance." Rawson conveys this attitude with regard to the population she studied. She says ". . . we knew they (the dyslexics) were intelligent and we *believed* they could come through though we were sometimes hard put to convince *them!"* She adds, "it may easily be true that one of our most valuable contributions was to the boys' self concepts. . . . Let us not do anything to close doors in advance for them by unrealistically pessimistic prognosis" (Rawson, 1966).

Unfortunately expectancy for dyslexics is not always this high. Sometimes it is reduced too early. Frequently teenagers are placed in vocational programs or in alternative schools where the curriculum is all auditory. While these plans may be appropriate for some students, others are eager to learn to read. Each time we reduce reading instruction the student may feel he is incapable of learning. In a series of interviews with teenagers Johnson (1970) explored the dyslexics' reaction to school and remediation. One 14-year-old stated his feelings about expectancy clearly. He said, "when nobody expects anything of you any more . . . when they don't call on you or give you any homework then you really know you're hopeless." Clearly the dyslexic will not learn to read if we do not teach him and if we do not believe he is capable of making gains. Even the slightest progress can make a difference in academic and vocational pursuits.

Among the variables more easily quantified is age at identification and initiation of remedial instruction. Harris (1970) quoted Schiffman who found that the chances of satisfactory progress were related to the age at which remediation was begun. Schiffman (cited by Goldberg, 1968) reported that 82 percent of the dyslexics who were diagnosed during the first two grades in school learned to read normally. In contrast, only 46 percent of those diagnosed in third grade, 42 percent in fourth grade, and 10 to 15 percent in fifth through seventh grades learned to read adequately. Vernon (1971) says this suggests that dyslexics do not outgrow their disability without assistance and that the problems are more ingrained at the upper levels. Older students frequently have reduced motivation because of repeated failure and frustration.

Jansky (1975) feels that special attention should be given to the "marginally ready child." This is one who may enter school with minor problems in oral language, sequencing, and spatial relationships. If help is not offered early, by the time the child is nine or ten years old his problems are as severe as those of youngsters whose early deficits were more obvious. She says, "Ironically, many children in this group are just beginning to fall apart when their fundamentally more disabled peers who have been intensively tutored are emerging and moving toward solid academic competency. Thus, this group in which deficits at the time of school entrance are marginal has about the same potential for maladaptation as does the other with inherently more severe problems. The major difference is that for the marginal group the yield in terms of quick remediability is far higher. Therefore, I believe their need for early identification and treatment is just as pressing and the returns are far greater."

Spache (1976) cites Balow's research which indicated that children who have reading problems in the primary grades can make considerable gains with special instruction. He states, however, that older students and secondary students respond more quickly to treatment and show greater long-term progress. These findings must be related to the nature of the disability and type of instruction. These generalizations, according to Spache, do not apply in cases which show severe general retardation in reading.

Another major variable which influences the ultimate prognosis is duration of remedial training. Often services are available only in the elementary grades. The studies of Rawson (1968) and Kline and Kline (1975) indicate that remediation may need to be continued through high school and even college. Our own experience suggests that dyslexics can make progress during adulthood and hence that special instruction should be available as long as the student is motivated and making gains.

Although we would agree that early identification and treatment is important, this should not deter us from initiating remediation with older students who seek help. We have worked with adolescents and young adults for several years and have found that many can make marked progress. One student who did not begin remedial instruction until the age of 17 progressed from the second to the tenth grade reading level within a period of three years (Johnson and Myklebust, 1965).

Some experimenters have compared the relative merits of individual instruction and small-group remediation. Vernon (1971) states that it is generally agreed that severely dyslexic children profit more from individual instruction. This is in contrast to the findings of Steirnagle who found poorer results in one-to-one or one-to-two tutoring than in remediation with groups of five children. Spache (1976) says that small-group therapy with five or six children three or four times a week may be the most economical and profitable arrangement. Our clinical experience indicates that this factor, along with others, is individually determined. Children with similar problems do, indeed, profit from small-group instruction and appear to be more motivated. On the other hand, children with unique patterns of strengths and weaknesses often need individualized instruction. We have found that groups are most effective when the children are working on decoding skills, whereas individual instruction is often necessary when training on word meanings and comprehension is required.

Personality and motivation are other variables that must be considered when evaluating the progress and prognosis for dyslexics. Spache (1976) states that the personality adjustment of the retarded reader is a significant element of his problem. Eisenberg (1975) feels that students with specific language disabilities will have some emotional or adjustment problems. Thus, additional counseling may be necessary. Rabinovitch (1962, p. 78) says "it is evident that children with marked incompetence in an area so vital to their ego-attitude, and sometimes to their survival in today's world, will suffer inordinately. Often bright, perceptive, and sensitive, they tend to react successively with anger, guilt feelings, depression, and finally, resignation, and compromise with their hopes and aspirations. . . . The fact that he appears normal, and is so except in the one area of his deficiency compounds his problem."

The support systems provided by the home, school, and community are very important for dyslexics. While there is much concern over the emotional and behavioral disorders that result from failure, we are continually impressed with the ego strength of many adolescents and young adults in our clinical population. A study of the family, the school, and ancillary services may provide more insight into the student's self-concept. Some members of our group indicated that the greatest problem was that remediation was not available long enough, particularly in high school. An inspection of several records indicates that some dyslexics continued to make good progress as long as they were receiving help, but they were unable to make independent gains without additional instruction.

FUTURE STUDIES

Although the findings regarding instruction and prognosis for dyslexics are inconclusive, further studies and programs are justified. Many students have made significant progress, but the successes as well as the failures of the past should guide us in future research.

One need for future research is a detailed description of the population. Results of many studies are difficult to interpret because of the vague terminology and description of the subjects. While the term "dyslexia" is used by some investigators, it is avoided by others. Thus, there are undoubtedly children with similar characteristics in remedial reading programs, in learning-disability programs, and in classes or schools for dyslexics.

We agree with Vernon (1971) who says it is difficult to differentiate dyslexics from other poor readers. However, she suggests that one might classify as dyslexic only those who have a defect in reading ability resulting from deficiencies in the capacity to associate visual and linguistic sequences. The deficiency would be noted in persistent reversals in reading and writing, poor directionality and left–right discrimination, sequential ordering, and reconstruction of complex forms. Vernon feels that the problems resulting from linguistic deficits would be more difficult to classify because of cultural factors. Whether one agrees with Vernon's position or not, it is essential to have a clear clinical image of the range, type, and degree of disturbances in order to replicate studies.

Secondly, a model for describing the nature, scope, and sequence of the remedial plan should be developed. It should include a system for recording both successes and failures. Although some methods are highly structured, other approaches allow for individualized instruction. The latter are more difficult to incorporate into rigorous research projects. In these instances it may be more profitable to keep detailed dairies of the type described by Calfee (1975). It is suggested that the clinical teacher and researcher develop programs for "N of 1" studies. Procedures advocated by behavioral psychologists can be used to measure the effects of remediation.

Improved plans for pre- and post-testing also should be defined and disseminated to investigators. Spache (1976) outlines many weaknesses in current testing programs. He feels that the evaluation of short-term remedial programs cannot be done accurately by comparing pre- and post-tests, by comparing gains with "normal" growth, or by noting the decrease in the gap between achievement and mental age. He suggests the use of a formula to find "true" gain by allowing for the initial status in the pre-test and the reliability of the measures used.

Spache (1976) is concerned with the narrowness of a reading test as a significant criterion. Equally important are motivation, improvement of attention, and positive effects upon self-concept. If the remedial program has permanent value for the student we should try to measure other results. Johnson and Myklebust (1967) suggest that measures of social maturity can be used to demonstrate the impact of a disability on the individual's ability to care for himself and others. The same measures can be used to demonstrate progress.

Improved programs of teacher preparation also are needed, both in general and special education. An awareness of specific reading disabilities could facilitate early referrals and identification of problems. It seems logical that all states would require at least one course in reading for all teachers. However, a recent survey by the International Reading Association (1976) indicates that many states certify teachers in learning disabilities without this requirement. Unless teachers have adequate preparation in reading and reading disabilities, many children will not make progress even though they are in special programs.

Many more services are needed at the junior high school and secondary levels. Although some programs have been initiated, the instruction is often tutoring in school subjects. Others offer vocational programs or an auditory curriculum. While such modifications may be needed, it is equally important to provide opportunities for reading instruction.

More research on remedial procedures also is needed but we agree with Torgeson (1975, p. 47) who says, "the greatest usefulness of research may not be in the construction of specific remedial techniques, but in the contribution which it makes to the cataloging and proper description of the variety of human abilities. Once clinicians and educators are aware of the relevant dimensions along which children's abilities may vary, they can begin to construct programs that make allowances for the unique problems of each child with learning difficulties." Often the study of pathology adds to the body of knowledge pertaining to normal learning. Our tasks for the future are difficult but not insurmountable.

A wise physician once said that clinical diagnosis involves great sifting and sorting of information but clinical medicine involves the manipulation of multiple variables. So also clinical teaching for dyslexic children requires the manipulation of many variables. This is a part of all good teaching, but because the dyslexic presents such unique learning patterns the instructional task becomes a challenging experiment.

Chapter 20

PRINCIPLES OF INSTRUCTION: A CRITIQUE OF JOHNSON'S "REMEDIAL APPROACHES TO DYSLEXIA"

JOHN T. GUTHRIE

APPROACHES TO REMEDIATION

Several approaches to remediation have been presented by Johnson. They include: the Orton-Gillingham method, the Fernald technique, color phonics, modified alphabets (particularly the initial teaching alphabet), and the Johnson and Myklebust approach, consisting of synthetic phonics for visual dyslexics and the whole word or story method for auditory dyslexics.

There are many others not mentioned by Johnson. Spache (1976) recommends instructional strategies based on counseling, operant conditioning, perceptual deficits, peer tutoring, skill deficits, language deficits, learning styles, and audiovisual equipment. More may be found in *The Reading Teacher*, a journal for reading specialists and teachers. Authors have proposed teaching disabled readers with: a combination of language experience and cloze (Lopardo, 1975); the intersensory reading method (Pollack, 1969); development of interpersonal relationships (Hirt, 1970); programmed instruction (Burkott and Clegg, 1968; directed-reading-thinking activities (Schwartz and Scheff, 1975); and the synthesis of about seven available techniques (Morsink, 1971).

THE ALPHABETIC METHOD

Of the few outlined by Johnson, one of the more popular methods is the Orton-Gillingham. As Johnson explains, "A child begins by learning individual letters and phonemes by establishing linkages between the audiovisual and motor aspects of speech and writing. . . . Simple words with consistent phoneme-grapheme correspondences are introduced for which the child has learned letter sounds. When the child has learned to read and write three-letter words, he combines them into sentences and stories" (p. 402). This approach is more widely known as the alphabetic method. It is used for normally developing children in public schools. It was used by the Greeks in the time of Plato, the Puritans in the time of the Hornbook, contemporary Israelis, and others dedicated to literacy. The appellation of Orton-Gillingham to this approach is unfortunate, since it implies that the method is unique. The implication is that dyslexics require qualitatively different instruction from other children with subnormal reading, which is probably not the case. Had Samuel Orton read books in education, as well as neurology, in preparation for teaching dyslexics, he might have named his method after any of a score of teachers who used it before him. Teaching reading according to the sequence of letter recognition, letter-sound correspondences, simple words, short sentences, and brief stories has a substantial amount of intuitive appeal for many teachers working with many types of children.

CLINICAL EVIDENCE OF EFFECTIVENESS

The alphabetic method has been promulgated on intuitive grounds. But the other methods listed previously have been promoted with equal fervor. How shall we choose among them? Johnson would choose on the basis of case studies. She attributes effectiveness to the Orton-Gillingham approach on the basis of improvement by two children. This information does not constitute evidence of effectiveness since we do not know what would have happened to these children if they were tutored by a different approach. They might have made equal progress. Counter examples of children who were taught by the Orton-Gillingham method and who made negligible progress are also available (Kline and Kline, 1975). There is a host of reasons why one child under a particular method at a particular time should learn very well or very poorly. Information from these cases is almost totally useless for deciding whether an educational activity or teaching technique has worked in the past. It is equally useless for predicting the effectiveness of a method in the future.

Reports of clinicians who have used a certain method are also regarded by Johnson as evidence about effectiveness of teaching. For example, Kline and Kline (1975) followed 216 children who they had taught with the Orton-Gillingham method. A vast majority of the children were reported to have improved in reading. Kline and Kline (1975) also reported that, "A survey of the Orton-Gillingham treated cases who did not do well revealed that success with the method is closely related to the skillful application of the method" (p. 139). It seems that the Orton-Gillingham method cannot fail. If children who have supposedly been taught with the method do not learn, the method could not have been properly applied and implemented. Independent observers would probably draw different conclusions from the evaluations of the 216 children in this study. Clinical opinions on the impact of teaching are devoid of the scientific criterion of public agreement. No information about replicability or concurrence among disinterested observers is available. As a result, these opinions are not admissible as evidence regarding the effectiveness of remediation.

Useful knowledge about remediation of dyslexics consists of principles of instruction. These principles relate educational activities, characteristics of teachers, and characteristics of materials to the reading achievement of children. By definition, principles are generalizable across particular instances of classrooms, teachers, or workbooks, and are based on evidence that is gathered scientifically. To the extent that we know principles of instruction, each child does not have to be an educational experiment, and each teacher does not have to rediscover quite everything about teaching.

To be aimed precisely toward reading achievement, principles of instruction must include teaching conditions that will improve different cognitive components of the reading process. A component of reading is a cognitive process that is necessary for reading and that can be taught. For instance, learning to read requires processing the set of grapheme/phoneme correspondences between the written form of consonants in the initial word position and their sounds. In the word "tap" the letter "t" is associated with the sound /t/. A nonexemplar of a cognitive component of reading is the processing required in the Birch and Belmont (1964) task, in which a serial pattern of dots printed on a page must be associated with a serial set of tones presented aurally. Neither set of stimuli (the dot patterns and tones) bear any resemblance to the letters and speech sounds that are processed in reading. Improvements on the task are not likely to improve reading performance. Consequently, this task cannot be said to measure a cognitive component of reading.

COGNITIVE COMPONENTS OF READING

Four major cognitive components of reading have been identified for which disabled readers are inferior to normal readers and to which instruction may be directed.

1. Decoding Accuracy. This process refers to the precision with which children render written, printed language into oral language. At the first-grade level, Biemiller (1970) and Weber (1970) have shown that extremely good and extremely poor readers differ primarily in decoding accuracy. During oral reading the graphic similarity of the word in the text and the erroneous attempt by the child to pronounce the word is very low among disabled readers. The extent to which the errors preserve the grammatical and semantic constraints of the sentence does not differentiate the groups. Shankweiler and Liberman (1972) confirm that disabled readers at the primary level do not decode simple words in isolation proficiently. Disabled readers at higher levels of proficiency (grades 4, 5, 6) are also inferior in decoding accuracy in terms of real words or nonsense words that are governed by common orthographic rules (Calfee, Venezky, and Chapman, 1969; Guthrie, 1973). This decoding process is similar to the visual-verbal learning process on which Vellutino et al. (1975d) have found disabled readers to be markedly deficient.

2. Decoding Speed. The time required to render printed words into their spoken counterparts correlates with reading achievement, particularly at the intermediate levels of proficiency (Perfetti and Hogaboam, 1975; LaBerge and Samuels, 1974).

3. Semantic Segmentation. Identification of specific aspects of meaning in a word or sentence is important for reading. Disabled readers are weaker than normal readers in locating target words of a semantic category (animals) within written paragraphs (Steinheiser and Guthrie, 1974), and making fine discriminations between words in oral vocabulary (Belmont and Birch, 1966).

4. Semantic Construction. Combining information from words and clauses in the text and from long-term memory are clearly needed for reading comprehension. There is some evidence that disabled readers are inferior on this component. The processes of drawing inferences during reading (Waller, 1976) and recalling information from multi-clause sentences (Perfetti and

Goldman, 1976) seem to be weaker in disabled readers than normal readers. Since memory and inferencing are useful for constructing meaning from discourse, disabled readers appear to be at a disadvantage in comprehending written text. However, provision of elaborate semantic cues to relationships among concepts in discourse increases comprehension for both normal and disabled readers (Peters, 1975–76). Addition of semantic and syntactic properties to word strings to create anomalous or meaningful sentences benefits both groups equally (Guthrie and Tyler, 1976). The ability of disabled readers to use cues in the text for semantic construction is not clear and this important component requires more research.

SUBTYPES OF READERS

Principles of instruction in reading must accommodate any distinctions among subtypes of readers that can be legitimately drawn. From a teaching viewpoint, there is a justifiable distinction between: (1) children who are achieving normally in reading, and (2) children whose reading is poorer than others of the same age and who are not intellectually deficient (IQ below about 80). These two groups are distinct in terms of: the cognitive processes that are used in reading; and the characteristics of instruction that will facilitate improvement in reading. The first group might be called normal readers, and the second, disabled readers.

Many investigators have suggested that there are different types of disabled readers. However, in Chapter 1, Rutter argues that there is no evidence to support these hypothetical distinctions. Little convincing support has been adduced for subgroups of disabled readers based on brain damage, psychiatric disorders, socioeconomic status, genetic and/or familial history. The distinctions made by Yule (1973) between backward readers and retarded readers should not be neglected, however. Backward readers have a smaller discrepancy between mental age and reading achievement and they develop higher reading achievement but lower mathematical achievement than retarded readers. While this distinction is useful for general educational programming, it does not have any specific implications for reading instruction.

There is at least one type of evidence about subgroups that would make a difference for instruction, if it were developed. Within the population of disabled readers a bimodal distribution on any given variable would be interesting. Consider the variable of word recognition speed as measured by the time required for a child to read a single isolated word aloud correctly. A bimodal distribution on this variable would occur if some disabled readers performed at a normal level and others performed at a markedly lower level. Instruction, then, might be directed to word recognition speed for the one group but not for the other. However, there do not appear to be cognitive variables that show this characteristic. Although patterns of subgroups may be delineated in the future, they are not evident at present. Consequently, principles of instruction will be appropriate for all disabled readers.

PRINCIPLES OF INSTRUCTION

1. Focus instruction on the deficient cognitive components of reading.

Children at different levels of proficiency may need remedial instruction in different components of reading. At the primary level (grades 1, 2, 3) a major problem in reading disability is decoding accuracy. At the intermediate grade levels of proficiency (4, 5, 6), there is evidence that the other components outlined in the previous paragraphs may also be deficient. Instruction that emphasizes decoding is particularly effective for children with reading difficulties at the primary level. One program of this type is Distar. In the Distar reading program, children are taught to say the sounds for letters and to sound out regular words. Irregular sounding, words and letter combinations are added. Finally, the children are taught to read for new information and to use that new information. A highly structured, programmed system is used to teach all of the skills. In a recent evaluation (Becker and Engelmann, 1976), children with reading difficulties were taught Distar from first through third grade. At the beginning of first grade, their entering percentile score on the WRAT Reading test was 18. By the end of third grade, they attained the 83rd percentile score on WRAT Reading test and the 40th percentile score on the total reading score of the Metropolitan Achievement Test. This is an increase of about one standard deviation unit in comparison to the national norms over the three-year period. Progress in reading made by children who received the Distar teaching method was about one-half a standard deviation higher than the average progress for children in 13 specially developed programs in Project Follow-Through. While the latter programs were heterogeneous, none of them contained as heavy a decoding emphasis as Distar.

Wallach and Wallach (1976) also developed a decoding program for first-grade children who were judged to have severe reading deficiencies. These children were tutored to recognize the shapes of letters and the sounds usually associated with them, to decode three-letter words, and to read simple stories with words that were learned previously. An experiment was conducted with this method. Matched pairs of children who were extremely low in reading readiness at the beginning of first grade were randomly assigned to normal first-grade instruction or to the same teaching supplemented by the Wallach treatment. On the Spache test of word recognition given at the end of first grade, children who were taught with the Wallach system were about ¾ of a standard deviation higher than the control children. The effect was highly significant statistically.

The evidence in the previous two paragraphs points to the conclusion that instructional emphasis on the decoding component seems to be useful for children with extreme difficulties in the initial stages of reading acquisition. Studies of children in first grade are not irrelevant to remediation of older children. Regardless of chronological or mental age, decoding is critical to success in the first phases of reading. Principles of instruction that are pertinent for younger ages are probably useful for older. Needless to say, this does not vitiate the need for instructional research with disabled readers.

2. Instruct children in all the components of reading.

While instruction should be focused on skills that need to be learned most urgently, instruction should also be given in other cognitive processes that are valuable for reading. At the intermediate grade levels (grades 4, 5, 6) of reading proficiency, children with specific reading disability show inferiority in a substantial number of cognitive operations including accuracy, decoding speed, semantic segmenting, and semantic constructing (Guthrie and Tyler, 1977). Doehring (1968) reported on 73 tests that discriminated between normal and disabled readers; the latter were inferior on 68 of them, or 93 percent. Since disabled readers are deficient in a large number of processes, it is sensible to provide instruction in all of them. We do not yet have much evidence about the interaction between these components. We do not know whether decoding accurately controls semantic constructing, or vice versa, or the nature of their reciprocity. Until that information is available, it is reasonable to provide instruction across all of the deficient areas.

3. Provide intensive interaction between the instructor and the student.

Brophy and Evertson (1976) studied 31 teachers who had been identified as unusually effective with primary-grade children whose reading achievement was extremely low. After examining 371 instructional process variables, one of their conclusions was that intensive interaction between teachers and learners was important. Children learned most readily when they experienced a large amount of supervised seat work, a high percentage of correct answers, immediate correction when mistakes were made, and a high frequency of leading questions (p. 366). One means of achieving a highly intense interaction is to have a low teacher–pupil ratio. A comparison of 15 remedial reading programs that differed on many dimensions showed that low teacher–pupil ratios of one-to-one to one-to-four produced consistently higher gains in reading than higher ratios. While teacher–pupil ratio distinguished the more successful from the less successful programs, there were no consistent effects observed from other variables including teaching personnel, ages of the children, location of remediation (in-school or clinic), and socioeconomic background of the children (Guthrie, Seifert, and Kline, 1977).

4. Maximize the amount of instructional time.

Harris and Serwer (1966) studied reading programs that were designed to improve reading for first-grade children who were expected to be disabled readers. Amount of time devoted to direct reading instruction correlated .5 to .6 with achievement in word recognition and .55 with achievement in comprehension. Instruction included work in basal readers, experience charts, sight word drill, and phonics activities. Supportive activities, such as writing, art, discussion, and dramatization, did not correlate significantly with achievement. In an independent investigation, time spent in reading activities in school correlated .4 with reading achievement in grade 1, and .32 with reading achievement in grade 3, for children with normal intelligence and low reading achievement (Stallings, 1975). Although instructional time is only a proxy for events which are likely to facilitate learning to read, it seems that the quantity, as well as the quality, of instruction is a critical ingredient for reading improvement among children who have not attained an expected level of proficiency.

Two major distinctions can be made between these principles of instruction and Johnson's teaching strategies. First, the principles are built on four cognitive components, all of which are necessary for learning to read. Johnson's teaching strategies, on the other hand, are based on the premise that auditory and visual processes are independent, and are equally viable, alternative channels for learning to read. Second, the principles state that all components must be taught with an emphasis on the most deficient, whereas

Johnson claims that the sensory channel on which the child is more proficient is the preferable avenue for instruction.

APPRAISAL OF PRINCIPLES

Are these instructional principles useful as a guide to the development of teaching for disabled readers? One test is whether the application of a principle can lead to accurate predictions about the effectiveness of a remedial reading program. The first principle is that instruction be focused on deficient cognitive components of reading. One teaching program that violates this principle is the Frostig curriculum which is designed to teach visual perception of geometric forms. We may predict that this program should not increase reading achievement. Confirmation of the prediction has been documented by Hammill (1972). A second prediction could be that psychomotor training will not improve reading achievement. Support may be found in an investigation by Painter (1966). Third, the duration and intensity of remediation should be important. It has been found that programs must be longer than 50 hours to have effects that are maintained for more than a few months and that daily instruction is needed to produce gains for disabled readers (Guthrie, Seifert, and Kline, 1977). Since four instructional principles can be used to assess different educational activities, they are valid generalizations about teaching.

These principles are suggested as an approach toward a representation of current instructional knowledge about reading disability. An exhaustive literature review and more studies are needed to elaborate, extend, and differentiate them. Not only can these principles, and their successors, be used as guidelines for teachers and administrators in the selection of materials and programs, they can also be employed by investigators in designing research that is relevant to remediation.

Beyond an explanation of dyslexia lies its solution and critical to this solution is a science of instruction.

Chapter 21

REMEDIATION OF DYSLEXIA: A DISCUSSION

NAOMI ZIGMOND

We are concerned with the surprisingly large number of children, estimated at 15 percent (NACD, 1969) who fail to learn to read. It seems even more surprising that a majority of children do profit from reading instruction which often consists of haphazardly selected materials, sequences, and practices. Methods advocated for elementary school children have ranged from the alphabetic methods used at the end of the eighteenth century to a wide spectrum of modern educational approaches, each of which has been labeled "best." With each approach there have been successes and failures. Successes are attributed to the fine quality of the instructional program. Failures are blamed on the student who is labeled "dyslexic." The popular view is that if *most* students learn to read using a particular method of instruction, and *some* students do not, then there must be something intrinsically wrong with the latter group. While this conclusion may be acceptable to the medical profession, for educators it is inexcusable. It obscures and avoids the conclusion that failure of the "dyslexic" to learn to read is the result of failure of teachers to teach.

Learning is an interactive process. Whatever learning occurs is a complex product of what the learner brings to the situation, and what the situation brings to the learner (see Adelman, 1970–71, 1971, 1976, for a thorough discussion of this view). In this context, failure to learn to read can be seen as the result of something being wrong with the person, *or* the result of something being wrong with the environment (teaching) *or* an interaction of both. While the preponderance of literature on reading disabilities attributes the problem to the person, we must not use the concept of dyslexia as an excuse to condone poor teaching. Teaching which disregards the significant differences among students in motivation, developmental levels, and rate and style of learning in planning instruction is poor teaching. We believe that it produces disabled learners. If "dyslexic" children are placed in educational environments which acknowledge individual differences and which provide for alternative teaching strategies related to these differences, then a significant number of "disabled" learners will begin to learn effectively. These learners could then no longer be viewed as having some "specific intrinsic disorders," leaving only a very small minority who continue to have problems to be labeled "dyslexic," i.e., unable to profit from reading instruction as we currently know how to deliver it.

While most discussions of remediation of reading disorders do not differentiate between these two groups, we believe that different approaches apply. In this paper we will review approaches to remediation which have been proposed for the large group of problem readers. Then we will suggest approaches which may be appropriate for the small minority of "very-hard-to-teach" students. Finally, we will describe some of the advantages in differentiating between these two populations of problem learners.

APPROACHES TO TEACHING PROBLEM READING

Intervention or remediation strategies for students with reading problems fall into three categories: those that root the reading problem in lack of prerequisite skills; those that focus on determining the one best method for teaching reading; and those that emphasize identifying individual differences and matching these to instructional treatments.

TEACHING PREREQUISITE SKILLS

The first category derives from the point of view that inherent dysfunctions must be remediated before any academic training is given. Treatments within this category focus on the need for providing opportunities to learn certain prerequisite or readiness skills that, for some reason, are not present. Advocates of this view hold that the disabled learners lack these prerequisite skills, but do not lack the capacity to learn to read. Kephart (1960) was a major theorist within this tradition. Frostig's approach (Frostig and Horne, 1964) is similar. The remedial strategies which they and others propose were not based on research findings, but rather on the reasonable (though untested) assumption that deficits exist and can be corrected or at least alleviated by the procedures advocated.

Empirical evidence to justify these remedial programs is not convincing. Hammill, Goodman, and Weiderholt (1974) reviewed 76 studies of the Frostig and Kephart programs and concluded that visual and motor perceptual training programs have not demonstrated an effect on academic achievement and that we must question the assumption that perceptual-motor inadequacy causes reading problems. Ysseldyke and Salvia (1975) severely criticize the "process training" approach for (a) using hypothetical constructs which go beyond observed behaviors and inferring that they are causes of the observed differences, (b) using diagnostic tests of questionable reliability, and (c) hypothesizing that "processes" are essential prerequisites to reading achievement when data show that reading skills can be taught directly to students deficient in "processes" (e.g., Bijou, 1970; Cohen, 1969; Abt Associates, 1976). In spite of the fact that the essential premises of this approach remain unsupported, programs based on the notion of training prerequisite or readiness skills continue to dominate the field. Harris (1976) suggests that this situation exists because research has not had sufficient impact to overcome the three forces he sees as controlling: the "bandwagon," the "pendulum," and the Zeitgeist effects.

APPLYING THE "ONE BEST METHOD"

Into the second category of approaches fall the strategies of Orton-Gillingham, Fernald, and treatments using Words in Color or Modified Alphabets reviewed by Dr. Johnson. One might also include: the Distar Reading System (Englemann and Bruner, 1969), the Peabody Rebus Reading Program (Woodcock, 1969), the Language-Experience method (Lee and Van Allen, 1963), the neurological impress method (Langford et al., 1974), and Individualized Reading (Veatch, 1959)—all of which have been suggested as cures for reading failure. Most of these approaches were not designed specifically to remediate dyslexia, but they have been used for that purpose. Authors and advocates of each program claim near zero failure rates in teaching problem readers when their procedures are conscientiously applied.

439

An examination of the research attempting to determine the relative usefulness of the various approaches indicates that some preference, particularly in the early grades, can be awarded to those approaches which stress decoding taught through synthetic phonics (Bleisner and Yarborough, 1965; Chall, 1967). However, there are several such approaches and very little research has focused on what Johnson calls "the subtle but important differences" among them. Moreover, the preference for synthetic phonics is built upon research which focuses on short-term results; the long-term effect of these approaches is yet to be adequately investigated (see Rawson, 1975). For example, Silberberg, Iverson, and Goins (1973) studied four groups of problem readers in third-grade remedial classes. Each group of children was taught using a different remedial method, including three "pure" methods (visual, auditory-phonic, and kinesthetic) and a fourth, multisensory, method. All methods improved children's reading dramatically, although the phonics method appeared to be a little stronger than the other three in terms of the immediate effects. But by the middle of fourth grade, much of this difference had "washed out."

Although attempts are being made to design appropriate research to determine the "best way" to teach reading, the prospects for a clear-cut answer are not good.

Any study which attempts to find the "best" system would certainly explode into a major undertaking. It would have to be limited to populations of hard-to-teach readers, and not include the vast majority of students who learn to read adequately regardless of the system employed. It would have to utilize approaches that were comparable in the aspects of reading with which each is dealing. The approaches compared would have to apply to the same grade and age levels, with the IQ measured in nonverbal terms. Other factors such as socioeconomics, cultural background, experimental background, health and physical fitness, motivation for reading, emotional adjustment, psychoneurological conditions, attitude toward self and significant others, teacher preparation, availability of time, amount and type of reinforcement and reward, knowledge of success, previous experience with reading and/or readiness skills, as well as many other variables would have to be controlled within reasonable limits to provide a sound basis for factorial analysis. Furthermore, comparisons would only be valid among studies of long-term results.

But even if the chances of a definitive answer were better, there is a real possibility that the problem has been viewed incorrectly. Perhaps researchers should not be asking "What is *the* optimum reading method?" but "What is the optimum reading method for *this* particular child?." If this latter question is asked, then the choice of an instructional method depends upon many additional variables not now being considered in most studies: the characteristics of the child's classroom; the environment in which the child lives; the availability of such supplementary aids as resource rooms, volunteers, and teaching machines; and, most important, the specific characteristics of the individual child.

MATCHING STUDENT CHARACTERISTICS
AND TEACHING METHOD

In the third category of approaches to remediation, the assumption is made that a relationship exists between certain characteristics of the child and certain variables in the instructional procedures and that to reduce failure, we should look for the right "match" between pupil type and instruction type. This concept is supported by an impressive list of authorities in reading disability (Johnson and Myklebust, 1976; Wepman, 1964, 1971; Lerner, 1971; Kirk, 1972; de Hirsch, Jansky, and Langford, 1966; Silver and Hagin, 1967). It is an appealing point of view for it is based on the notion of individualized instruction, in which the designers of educational experiences take into account unique qualities of the learner. Research designed to validate this approach must demonstrate that the effectiveness of instruction depends on the type of pupil being taught. Demonstrating this kind of disordinal interaction is not an easy task (Cronbach and Snow, 1969). Indeed, most early attempts to test the hypothesis have failed.

Bateman (1977) reviewed 15 reading studies which designed or used materials that stress various modalities and attempted to discover modality–instructional interactions. The findings are remarkably consistent in that 14 of the 15 found no interactions consistent with modality model predictions. Bateman concludes, as have other reviewers (e.g., Ysseldyke, 1973) that either the modality model is invalid or, given current limitations in educational assessment and programming techniques, it is merely not applicable.

Before abandoning this approach, we must consider the possibility that, in concentrating on modality strengths and weaknesses, we have been looking at the wrong variables. Stallings (1970), for example, found a significant interaction between performance on the sequencing subtests of the Illinois Test of Psycholinguistic Abilities and type of initial reading instruction. Low scorers were better with a whole-word method while high scorers were better with a linguistic (i.e., structured phonics) method. This finding suggests a relationship between sequencing ability and appropriate reading approach, and deserves to be investigated further.

A substantial amount of evidence (e.g., Weinstein and Rabinovitch, 1971) has been collected which indicates that reading-disabled children are poorer in many aspects of oral language than are normal readers. This is hardly surprising since, as Miller and Yoder (1972) have observed, reading skills must ultimately derive from linguistic skills. In both receptive and expressive speech, children with reading problems are found to be less fluent, know fewer words, and give less mature definitions (de Hirsch et al., 1966). Problem readers also do not perform as well in processing grammatical structure. Steiner, Weiner, and Cromer (1971), for example, found that given prior information about material they were to read, good readers could be led to make more anticipation errors than poor readers made. The poor readers appeared to respond word-by-word, ignoring prior context, and therefore made fewer anticipation errors.

Johnson offers additional child variables ("frames of reference") which she incorporates into the diagnostic study of a problem reader. They include (1) the input-integration-output schema, (2) auditory and visual processing, (3) verbal and nonverbal behavior, and (4) a hierarchy of experience. Only for the audiovisual dimension does Johnson provide a guide as to how knowledge of the competence of a student leads to decisions about differential approaches to teaching reading. She does not suggest ways in which diagnostic information about the other variables directs decisions about the materials, sequences, strategies, or content of reading instruction.

Other theorists are equally delinquent. For example, Estes (1970), Dykeman et al. (1971), Ross (1976), and Hallahan and Kaufmann (1976) all have suggested that attentional disorders characterize problem learners, but none have indicated the way in which knowledge of a student's competence in attending can be used in making *differential* decisions about reading instruction.

There appear to be no guidelines to help the practitioner determine what student variables (motivation, self concept; language, social, cognitive, or perceptual levels; rate or style of learning; attentiveness) are significant in learning to read or to assist him to use knowledge about individual differences in such variables in selecting a reading program.

The other side of the equation is just as confusing to the reading teacher. There is no answer to the question: What are the significant dimensions on which to vary reading instruction for a particular child? Woodcock (cf. Frierson, 1976) suggests that there are at least 45 ways to teach reading. His presentation involves a simple mathematical model.

He said that in certain reading approaches the symbols used were changed in some way (add color as in Words in Color; introduce new symbols for specific sounds as in The Initial Teaching Alphabet; modify the symbols by drawing objects or characteristic clues as in a snow-covered letter "I"—the icicle sound, or a candy cane letter "C"—the candy sound; substitute letter symbols with picture word symbols as in the Rebus Reading Program; and, of course, use a Traditional Orthography or common alphabet changed only in size and manner of presentation). Thus, one could identify at least five distinctive variations in symbol systems (orthography) which might be characteristic of a reading methodology.

Secondly, he pointed out that reading approaches tended to be either highly structured as in programmed reading systems (e.g., Michigan Successive Discrimination Reading Program) or quite unstructured as in certain language-experience approaches where the teacher follows the often unpredictable interests and expression of the children to provide content, sequence, and structure for the reading program. A third level of structure is that common to most basal reader programs. In these classic systems, the teacher is "programmed" to provide a clearly defined structure which does allow for some flexibility. One could identify, then, three distinctive degrees of structure, rigidity, or preordination which might be characteristic of a reading methodology.

Three distinctive points on the part–whole continuum were also identified by Woodcock. These were the traditional, highly synthetic (begin with isolated, meaningless signs and sounds), the controversial analytic (begin with whole ideas, expressions, and words which are inherently meaningful), and the mix-match approach where uncommitted teachers and systems consistently use a little bit of both.

Now the basis for the suggestion that any reading program would be classified as one of the "Forty-Five Ways to Teach Reading" is appreciated. Any program would use some symbol system (five choices), some degree of structure (three choices), and one type of strategy (three choices). The possible variations are simply 5 × 3 × 3 or 45 in number (Frierson, 1976, p. 19). Frierson adds:

> It would not be hard to identify other distinctive dimensions. Some would argue for five modes (visual, auditory, tactile, kinesthetic, combinations). Others would add environmental characteristics (stimuli-free, highly distract-

ing, normal). Still others would demonstrate convincingly that the means of presentation makes a distinctive contribution (slides projected at far point vision, computerized typwriter feedback, animated films, etc.). In short, the list of characteristics could become lengthened so that the ways to teach reading would become infinite (adding the elements suggested in this paragraph alone increases the possible "ways" to over two thousand). (Frierson, 1976, p. 20)

There is no evidence that each of these combinations would produce an effective means of teaching reading to a particular child with particular characteristics. In fact, we know very little about whether systematic variations in the materials, content, sequences, or strategies of reading programs would produce different learning outcomes in students. Johnson suggests a set of critical questions which might be used in analyzing any approach to reading instruction. But we must also know how to use the answers to those questions to facilitate the match between learner characteristics and teaching approach.

Adelman (1971) proposes a practical solution to this problem of individualizing instruction: he suggests a period of trial teaching. During this period, dimensions of the learning task and the environment are varied systematically, and the impact of these variations on student performance are noted. The need is for Adelman's approach to be expanded into a major research undertaking. Poor readers (adequately described in terms of a large number of child variables—including but not limited to motivation, developmental levels, rate and style of learning) would receive reading instruction varied systematically along various dimensions (including but not limited to the materials, content, sequence, and strategy of instruction). Careful documentation of the outcomes of the instruction in each case would help teachers to identify the optimal match. Only after the accumulation of a significant number of N of 1 studies will we be in a position to determine the validity of the position that "hard-to-teach" students can be helped most effectively when reading instruction is truly individualized.

NEED FOR RESEARCH IN TEACHING PROBLEM READERS

Current efforts in remedial education are not very successful. Bateman (1971) points out that in referring to remedial reading, one must be talking about a program to help youngsters to catch up. The only way children who are be-hind can catch up is if they are taught more and faster. The follow-up data reported by Johnson attest to the fact that very few programs actually accom-plish this. Long-term follow-up studies on the effects of remedial reading in-struction by Balow (1965) and Buerger (1968) lead both authors to con-clude that reading disability should probably be considered a chronic illness. This is an unacceptable conclusion to those of us who accept the premise that the failure of this group of students to learn to read is per se clear and con-vincing evidence that the instruction is inadequate (see also Cohen, 1973; Englemann, 1967, 1969; Bateman, 1977). If we are to change this situation, further research is needed.

APPROACHES TO TEACHING DYSLEXIC STUDENTS

We contend that most students currently labeled "dyslexic" are simply "hard-to-teach" and that they read poorly because our instruction has been inade-quate. But these students will learn to read if instruction were more person-alized and individualized. We would reserve the label "dyslexic" only for the much smaller group of students who do not respond favorably to highly in-dividualized trial teaching. This is a group of students to whom we are unable to teach the most fundamental reading skills and who remain functionally illiterate. For this "very-hard-to-teach" minority, remediation of dyslexia may be a contradiction in terms.

For these students, perhaps a more productive approach would be the design of school programs that allow for alternatives to reading and writing. "Bookless" curricula and other innovations have been introduced in a number of settings (Silberberg and Silberberg, 1969), but the key to their success often lies in the availability of someone who can help teachers to understand the illiterate but intelligent student. In a Child Service Demonstration Center for Urban Secondary Students with Learning Disabilities in Pittsburgh, we have introduced the role of the Resource Teacher whose responsibility it is to deal with the difficulties faced by nonreading high school students in the main-stream of education. These teachers work primarily on a one-to-one basis with content-area teachers who have nonreaders in their classes. The Resource Teacher helps the mainstream teacher to define instructional objectives and to develop alternative ways of teaching. Courses are not watered down, but al-

445

tered in terms of the methods of presentation or evaluation. The Resource Teacher assists in preparing materials appropriate to the needs of the disabled learners in each classroom, and in searching out supplementary film strips, tapes, and other media which might be useful. The Resource Teacher acts as a liaison between the student and the content-area teacher to help each student "make it" in the mainstream. Our experience has taught us that teachers can change and can accept and accommodate nonreaders if this kind of support is provided to them.

We have also learned that "making it" requires not only that we work in a new way with teachers, but also that we work in a new way with students. Most of our severely retarded readers need to be taught how to cope with the school environment, how to deal successfully with the social and emotional pressures they experience in school. They need "school survival skills."

We have developed a School Survival Skills curriculum as part of our prototype for comprehensive services for learning-disabled students. The emphasis of the School Survival Skills curriculum is on exploring and developing coping skills. Since the secondary school faculty is typically large and diverse, our learning-disabled students must acquire response patterns that are appropriate to many kinds of adults. Typically, students learn the positive value of "teacher-pleasing behaviors" without specific instruction; many learning-disabled youngsters do not, and for these students instruction may be essential to school survival. Once each week, in small groups of four to six students, the Resource Teacher explores with students the importance of getting to class on time, having a pencil and the right books, sitting straight and looking attentive, making eye contact with the teacher, responding to questions, etc. Students are helped to an awareness of what behaviors make classroom situations more positive. Students learn to recognize the impact of their behavior on teacher and student attitudes toward them and to control behaviors which lead to detention and suspension. Sessions also deal with the problems of how to study and how to prepare independently for tests. Some group meetings are used for values clarification activities and for group discussions of career and vocational goals. Others explore how to deal with a society that equates literacy with intelligence, and how to control the anger that comes from having been failed by the educational system yet having been blamed for that failure. The impact of the School Survival Skills curriculum is seen in improved attitudes of students toward mainstream classes and of mainstream teachers toward the handicapped learners, as well as reduced levels of student detentions and suspensions. Neither the consultation with mainstream teachers nor the School Survival Skills curriculum teach nonreaders to read, but they allow these students (and their teachers) to "make it" through the educational system in a positive and productive way.

SUMMARY AND CONCLUSIONS

In this chapter we have tried to point out that there are two groups of students with serious reading difficulties. We have suggested that there is a sizeable number of "problem readers" who *will* achieve competency in reading if only we improve our teaching. We have also suggested that there will remain a small minority of learners with whom we will be unsuccessful at achieving reading competence. We contend that only this latter group should be considered "dyslexic," or *disordered* in the basic processes required for learning to read. This is not simply a question of semantics. Taken together, the two groups represent an extremely heterogeneous set of poor learners. The medical, psychological, and educational characteristics of these two groups may be quite different. Thus, research which does not sort them out—and this includes most research to date—may be of little value.

In our review of remedial approaches used with "problem readers" we have identified three categories. Of these we believe individualized instruction to be the most promising and suggest it as the target for future research. We feel that through such research we should be able to refine our capacity to match individual learner characteristics to the strategies, materials, content, and sequence of reading instruction. At the same time, identification of a group of students who are very resistant to reading instruction will force us to develop alternative school programs to accommodate these youngsters within the educational system. We have proposed two components of these alternative programs: consultation for the mainstream teachers and a School Survival Skills curriculum for the learners. Research on this very small group of true dyslexics also may lead finally to a better understanding of what constitutes "not being able to read."

We believe that this overall philosophy toward the remediation of reading difficulties will help us to serve this group of special children more effectively. We also believe it will have an even broader impact. While the focus of this chapter has been on problem learners, individual differences

447

abound in every classroom. As teachers begin to provide more appropriate educational experiences to the few who are desperate, the whole class will benefit. When the nonachieving child becomes less so, the change cannot help but affect the classroom climate for the better. In this improved atmosphere the achieving learners are likely to find their educational tasks more relevant and more challenging as well.

Part VIII

INTEGRATIVE SUMMARY

Chapter 22

SOME CONCLUSIONS ABOUT DYSLEXIA

ARTHUR BENTON

The chapters of this book provide a penetrating analysis of current thinking about the condition known as "developmental dyslexia," "specific reading disability," or "specific reading retardation." The fact that estimates of the prevalence of this disability depend upon how it is defined has been made clear, as has the association between reading failure and social and cultural factors. The evidence that neither reading failure in general nor specific dyslexia is a unitary disability but rather a group of disabilities, each with its own distinctive constellation of characteristics, has been carefully examined. The meaning of the diverse behavioral and cognitive defects that are found in association with specific reading retardation has been probed. The rather scanty knowledge that exists about the neurological basis and genetic background of the disability has been assessed. On the basis of a critical evaluation of past research, new approaches that offer the promise of deeper understanding and more effective treatment have been presented. The prevailing tone of the volume is thoughtful and realistic. The fact that a satisfactory understanding of the nature of this disorder has not been achieved and that specific treatment and remediation methods of proven effectiveness have still to be developed has not been skirted.

Yet this book also makes it clear that investigative work during the past 15 years has resulted in significant advances in knowledge and understanding of the disorder. As compared to 15 years ago, we have more detailed information about the conditions under which the disability develops and the settings within which it occurs. We can now identify with considerable success the preschool child at risk for future reading failure, thus providing the opportunity for early intervention designed to prevent that failure. Progress in the development of effective remediation measures has been made. We are more keenly aware of the complexities of the problem, for example, of the necessity for a careful and maximally useful definition of the boundaries of the disorder, than we were 15 years ago. The methodology of investigation in the field has improved immeasurably. The newer research designs that have been outlined undoubtedly will generate more pertinent information than have earlier approaches, and it is reasonable to expect that they will resolve some persisting questions in the field.

THE PROBLEM OF DEFINITION

The serious concern with problems of definition, which is evident throughout the book, has a sound basis. Obviously there has to be agreement about the limiting characteristics of the condition if valid estimates of its prevalence are to be made and if teachers, physicians, researchers, and those responsible for establishing social and educational policy are to communicate meaningfully with each other. The successful search for causes, preventive measures, and effective methods of treatment also depends upon a reasonably clear specification of what it is that one is trying to investigate, prevent, or treat.

The earliest workers in the field understood that a more-or-less precise definition was a necessity and they carefully distinguished between specific reading disability and reading failure attributable to more general factors, such as subnormal intelligence or lack of educational opportunity. Their definitions emphasized the specificity of the syndrome, the "purity of the symptoms," as Hinshelwood phrased it, with deliberate exclusion of those extraneous factors, such as intellectual subnormality, educational deprivation, sensory defect, and emotional disturbance, that might in themselves be sufficient to cause reading failure.

In their concern to insure that specific reading disability was not confused with reading failure which was only one expression of a more pervasive condition such as mental retardation or cultural deprivation, professional and scientific workers have tended to formulate definitions of a restrictive nature such as that adopted some years ago by the Research Group on Developmental Dyslexia of the World Federation of Neurology (cf. Critchley, 1970, p. 11; Rutter, Chap. 1, this volume). These formulations have emphasized the unique character of dyslexia as a clinical entity and have defined the condition in negative terms (i.e., *not* due to subnormal intelligence, *not* due to inadequate instruction). In essence, they provide for a diagnosis by exclusion (cf. Benton, 1975; Denckla, 1977a). The shortcomings of this "exclusionary" type of definition and the problem of formulating a revised definition, which is more useful from both a pragmatic and a theoretical standpoint, have been the subject of much discussion at this conference.

One criticism of this type of definition is that terms which are an intrinsic part of it, such as "normal" or "adequate intelligence," "conventional instruction," and "normal motivation," are themselves not well defined and hence open to different interpretations. For example, the point has been made that, if normal intelligence is strictly interpreted as an IQ of 90 or above, then by definition children with IQs of less than 90 cannot be considered to be "dyslexic." But such exclusion contradicts common clinical experience that many psychometrically "dull" and "borderline" children in fact show a degree of reading failure that would not be predicted from their mental age. A criterion such as this also ignores the possibility that the relatively poor intellectual development of such a child may itself be the consequence of a primary reading disability. Finally, as Eisenberg (Chap. 2) points out, the effects of this and other exclusionary criteria on public educational policy need to be carefully considered.

Other terms in the restrictive type of definition are equally ambiguous. Does "adequate conventional instruction" mean attendance in any regular grade, regardless of the location, social character, teacher–pupil ratio, or class size of a school? Many, perhaps most, clinicians proceed on this interpretation. Other clinicians, more keenly aware of the extreme variability of schools and of the fact that some are in reality custodial (rather than educational) institutions, require assurance that a child who has failed to learn to read has had the benefit of consistent exposure over an extended period of time to competent and conscientious reading instruction before they will categorize him as dyslexic.

It is obvious that the meaning of the terms in these restrictive definitions needs to be clarified through more explicit specification. Such specification would make the definitions more useful without altering their essential character.

There are, however, more important reasons for dissatisfaction with the "classic" definitions. One is that they assume that specific reading disability is a homogeneous condition, a single syndrome. The experience of teachers, clinicians, and researchers over the past 15 years indicates that, apart from the finding of a level of reading achievement below expectations, there is little evidence of homogeneity among dyslexics with respect to the qualitative aspects of their reading performances, the status of other cognitive functions, their history, or their neurological condition. Thus a definition which is more in accord with the facts as known today would provide for the possible existence of different types of dyslexia, each with its own distinctive set of characteristics and conceivably also with its own distinctive antecedent conditions.

The search for these more precisely defined syndromes is now underway. One approach is exemplified by the differentiation made by Johnson and Myklebust (1967), Ingram, Mason, and Blackburn (1970), and Boder (1970, 1971, 1973) between an audiophonological and a visuospatial type of disability, as reflected in the kinds of errors made by dyslexic children in their reading. Performances predominantly characterized by audiophonological errors (e.g., confusion of vowel sounds, consonant substitution, mispronunciation of diphthongs) are more frequently encountered than are those characterized predominantly by visuospatial errors such as reversals and failure to discriminate between words that are similar in shape. Boder has reported that, although both types of error were evident in the reading of many dyslexic children, a majority of them could be placed in one or the other category. The classification has obvious implications for the direction that remedial teaching should take. Apart from this, the significance of the dichotomy remains to be investigated more thoroughly. There is some evidence that the neurological and psychological correlates of the two types of reading performance are different. Reversal errors, the cardinal feature of a visuospatial type of disability, have been found to be associated with right–left confusion in body schema performances, with lefthandedness and mixed laterality, with a more generalized learning disability extending beyond reading, and with signs of neurological abnormality (Shankweiler, 1963; Belmont and Birch, 1965; Ingram, Mason, and Blackburn, 1970). These concomitant disabilities are less frequently seen in children with audiophonological difficulties (Ingram, Mason, and Blackburn, 1970). In general, the outlook for improvement in reading level appears to be better for the child with audiophonological difficulties (Boder, 1971).

There are other qualitative features of the reading performances of dyslexics to which little attention has been paid probably because of the assumption that they merely reflect the severity of the reading disability. The phonological component, i.e., grapheme-phoneme matching, is often considered to be the primary ability upon which higher-level abilities such as sequential reading and semantic decoding are superimposed. However, this hierarchical arrangement is not universally valid. There are dyslexic children who, like many aphasic patients, show a significantly higher level of silent reading comprehension (as reflected in performance in word-picture matching and reading a text for meaning) than of phonological efficiency (as reflected in oral reading). There are also dyslexic children who, like another type of aphasic patient, read aloud with fair accuracy and fluency, but show a striking disability in apprehending the semantic aspects of the message. As Rutter comments, such a child, who often escapes identification as a dyslexic, "has not yet mastered what reading is all about." An extreme example of this state of affairs, in which phonological reading is actually in advance of semantic reading, is the so-called "hyperlexic" child who shows exceptionally good ability to read aloud in relation to his intelligence level—without, however, a comparably good understanding of the meaning of the material which he reads so fluently (cf. Silberberg and Silberberg, 1968; Mehegan and Dreifuss, 1972; Huttenlocher and Huttenlocher, 1973). I once called this condition "the opposite of dyslexia," since these children's oral reading is in advance of their mental age (Benton, 1975). I now would tend to view it as a particular form of dyslexia.

A number of important approaches to classification are described in this volume, such as the syndromes developed by Mattis, French, and Rapin and by Denckla and the multiple-syndrome paradigm of Doehring. In his chapter, Mattis has outlined the defining characteristics of three more-or-less homogeneous dyslexic syndromes: a *language disorder* syndrome with defects in both the understanding and expression of oral language; a *dyscoordination syndrome* with defects in speech articulation and design copying and normal understanding of oral language; and a *visuospatial–perceptual disorder* syndrome with defective visuoperceptive and visuoconstructive capacity and intact oral language abilities. To these can be added the *dysphonemic sequencing disorder* syndrome described by Denckla (1977a) and now found by Mattis and co-workers in their cross-validation study. There is also the syndrome of *verbal memorization disorder* with noteworthy impairment in sentence repetition and verbal paired-associates learning seen by Denckla (1977a) in older children and which may be, as Denckla and Mattis suspect, a milder form of the language disorder syndrome identified in younger dyslexics.

These classifications must be viewed as tentative and subject to such modification as may be indicated by future findings. One sees that there are two systems of classification, one based on the analysis of reading performance per se and the other on the occurrence of concomitant disabilities in oral language, motor skill, perceptual capacity, and short-term memory. Future investigative work no doubt will consider the two systems jointly in continuing the search for distinctive syndromes of dyslexia. It is possible that no meaningful connection between them will be found. But it is also possible that systematic relationships will be disclosed, for example, between the visuospatial type of defective reading and the *visuospatial–perceptual disorder* syndrome of Mattis, French, and Rapin or between the audiophonological type and Denckla's *dysphonemic sequencing disorder* syndrome.

An effort such as this implies a more refined assessment of reading performance than is usually made in neurological and neuropsychological studies of dyslexic children. Most researchers appear to be satisfied with a single test score or even teachers' ratings as a measure of reading level. Aside from the ambiguity of the concept of "reading level," to which Denckla has called attention, it is clear that a number of determinations including measures of letter and word recognition, oral reading, silent reading of text for meaning, sound blending, spelling, and the reading of reversible words, are required to obtain an adequate assessment of a child's reading skills.

CAUSATION AND PATHOGENESIS

The successful identification of more homogeneous dyslexic syndromes can be expected to result in significant improvement in our ability to predict outcome, to institute appropriate remedial measures, and perhaps also to focus our efforts in the areas of preventive intervention. But the fact remains that such a classification will still be on the surface level of behavior without any necessary reference to underlying causation and pathogenesis. Each component in the classification is a syndrome only in the sense that it represents a number of cognitive deficits that appear in combination. It is not a syndrome in the more basic sense that it represents a constellation of symptoms indicative of a distinctive underlying cause or disease process. It will therefore be necessary to relate these behavioral clusters to neurological status, as assessed by a variety of functional and structural criteria, to antecedent medical and social events, and to genetic variables in the search for basic pathogenetic mechanisms that may underlie at least some forms of dyslexia. In brief, our task is to penetrate beneath the surface level of behavior to discover the organismic processes which, under certain conditions, produce the behavioral disability that is the focus of concern. This is, of course, the same task that we face when we try to understand mental retardation or infantile autism and to help children suffering from these forms of behavioral disorder.

Eisenberg (Chap. 2) has emphasized this point and has provided a most instructive description of the chain of events that occurred when the pathological mechanisms underlying a particular condition which had been reasonably well defined on clinical grounds were identified. The example he used, thalassemia, comes from the field of hematology and, as he pointed out, a stepwise progression took place: (1) clinical identification of the disorder on the basis of observation; (2) identification of the basic or ultimate cause in the form of genetic abnormality; (3) description of a more proximate cause in the form of hematologic abnormality; (4) as a consequence of this newly acquired basic knowledge, a clinical redefinition of the disorder in the direction of a looser, more inclusive concept that recognizes variants and incomplete forms as expressions of the disorder as well as the "classic" form originally developed on clinical grounds.

Another example of the process which Eisenberg has described, one involving behavioral deficit, is general paresis. The condition was first identified as a distinctive symptom-complex on clinical grounds in 1822 by Bayle who insisted that it needed to be differentiated from other forms of psychotic disorder and that it had a distinctive neuropathological basis. During the ensuing decades, postmortem study established the correlation, and this led to a broadening of the diagnosis to allow for the inclusion of "atypical" forms of the disorder that did not show all the features of the classic type with the intellectual deterioration, delusional mentation, and motor disability described by Bayle. Later, when it was unequivocally established that general paresis was a form of neurosyphilis and that the diagnosis could be made on the serological level, the criteria for diagnosis changed radically. The behavioral criteria for the diagnosis lost much of their definitional validity and patients whose clinical pictures did not conform at all to the classic model, for example, those who presented with depression, hypochondriasis, or a schizophreniform disorder without intellectual impairment, delusions, or motor disability, were diagnosed as "general paresis" on the basis of serological findings.

In summary, it appears that the criteria utilized in arriving at a surface clinical diagnosis may lose much of their definitional significance (although not necessarily their clinical importance) as knowledge of underlying pathogenetic mechanisms is gained and the condition is redefined in terms of those mechanisms. Appreciation of this important point made by Eisenberg surely has implications for the problem of defining dyslexia in the most fruitful way, given our present state of ignorance. There can be no quarrel with the necessity for precise definition and the search for homogeneous subtypes. But it may not be wise to adopt too restrictive a definition that would exclude cases which may in fact represent the outcome of the same pathogenetic mechanisms as the "classic" cases and investigation of which might lead to swifter identification of these mechanisms.

There is still another reason for dissatisfaction with the "classic" definition of dyslexia. It not only assumes that dyslexia is a homogeneous condition, but specifies adequate intelligence, cultural background, and educational opportunity (however these may be defined) as essential background characteristics of the disability. But, as Rutter (Chap. 1) has pointed out, there is evidence that some factors, such as family size, socioeconomic status, the cultural values of the community, and temperamental characteristics, are systematically associated not only with general reading backwardness but also with specific reading disability. He has therefore argued that children whose clinical pictures include these features should not thereby be excluded from the diagnostic category if they satisfy other definitional criteria.

I am in complete agreement with Rutter's position. The danger in excluding socially disadvantaged and emotionally disturbed children from consideration is not only the possible adverse effects on educational policy to which Eisenberg has called attention, but also the hazard that the diagnostic category thereby may be limited to what may be an atypical subgroup with its own peculiar problems. Thus it may be desirable, given our present state of ignorance, to cast a wide net and study children with a wide variety of deficits including those whose clinical pictures do not meet strict criteria of specific reading disability. This sample would include not only children with neurological, intellectual, and social handicaps, but also those whose reading achievement is not so deviant by current norms that they would be considered disabled in reading.

One such group comprises children with specific spelling disability. In his chapter, Rutter mentioned Naidoo's (1972) study of children with spelling disability without comparably severe reading disability. She found that their neuropsychological profile was similar to that of children with reading disability who, to be sure, were also defective in spelling. Rutter concluded that the two types of disability are "different facets of the same group of disorders." If this is so, it is within the realm of possibility that intensive study of dysorthographic children would facilitate our progress in understanding the cognitive disabilities underlying dyslexia as well as spelling disability per se.

Reversal errors in reading have not proved to be as important a characteristic of the performances of reading-disabled children as once was thought. Yet they are a prominent feature of the reading of some dyslexics and some specific associations between reversal errors and other factors have been reported. Shankweiler (1963) and Stone (1976) found the occurrence of reversal errors to be related to both impairment in right–left discrimination and deviant lateral preference. Belmont and Birch (1965) reported that impairment in right–left discrimination was more closely related to performance on sequential reading tests (where the opportunity for reversal errors is greater) than on word recognition tests. Is it possible that a performance characteristic such as the tendency to read in reverse relates to cognitive and neurological variables more closely than does overall reading level which, as Rutter has so convincingly demonstrated, is subject to the influence of a variety of factors such as socioeconomic status and family size?

A related performance characteristic is reflected in measures of sequential perception and praxis. The reviews of Rourke and Vellutino indicate that a substantial number of studies have found an association between defective sequencing ability (as measured by digit repetition, temporal-order judgment, memory for auditory and visual sequences, and similar tasks) and reading ability. What are the neurological and cognitive correlates of this type of performance? Is spelling ability more or less closely related to it than is reading level?

Another approach is suggested by employment of the "stress tests" designed by Finucci and co-workers (1976) to disclose reading deficiency in adults or bright children whose performances on conventional tests prove to be adequate, possibly because they have developed a good sight vocabulary and have learned to rely on contextual cues in reading. These tasks require the subject to read passages reprinted in different geometric transformations (upsidedown, mirror-image, backwards), nonsense passages, and speeded-reading passages consisting of unrelated sentences and presented at a rate of 100 or more words a minute. Studying the parents and siblings of dyslexic children, Finucci found a few apparently normal readers who performed on a grossly defective level, as compared to control subjects, on these tasks. As Childs (Chap. 15) points out, the application of such "stress tests" may prove to be particularly useful in genetic studies.

Admittedly, if all the phenomena found to be associated with reading failure are included in the study of "dyslexia," there is the risk of creating a field of inquiry which is too diffuse to be optimally useful for clinical or theoretical purposes. This outcome perhaps can be avoided if terminology is reasonably precise, working assumptions are made explicit, and the aims of studies are clearly stated. But the broad approach does offer the promise of disclosing unsuspected relationships that may lead to a deeper understanding of the cause and nature of developmental dyslexia.

DEVELOPMENTAL DYSLEXIA
AND ACQUIRED ALEXIA

When James Hinshelwood (1900) undertook the study of specific reading retardation, he adopted what was then known about acquired word blindness in adult patients as a model for interpreting the neurological bases of the developmental disability. The region of the left angular gyrus was considered to be a "center" for the visual memory of letters and words (cf. Bastian, 1898) and it was natural to conclude that specific reading disability resulted from defective development of this center. Interestingly, Hinshelwood (1904) insisted that the developmental fault was not bilateral but only left-sided and that such reading as the dyslexic child was capable of was accomplished by his utilization of "a part of the brain which does not usually discharge that function." We now know that this neurological inference is not tenable. But his interpretation that the dyslexic child reads (or tries to read) with the wrong half of his brain does have a modern ring.

How useful is it to adopt the models provided by acquired alexia in adult patients to guide us in our understanding of developmental dyslexia? Mentioning four different varieties of acquired alexia, Mattis (Chap. 3) has shown that they are at least of service in bringing home the fact that it is not necessary to postulate a single underlying cause for the developmental disability, since the acquired disability appears in different neurological and behavioral contexts and takes a number of qualitatively different forms (Benton, 1962; Geschwind, 1962; Benson and Geschwind, 1969; Benson, 1977; Damasio, 1977). A closer look at these forms of alexia and their possible relationship to developmental dyslexia may be worthwhile.

There is alexia without agraphia, or so-called "pure" alexia, involving significant loss of reading ability without comparable impairment in writing or in oral language, including oral spelling. Letters of the alphabet are generally read correctly and, by a process of combining letters, the patient may achieve recognition of simple words. But configurational word recognition is defective and the reading of connected text is impossible. Focal disease that produces a disconnection between occipital areas involved with the processing of visual information and the left parietal region involved with the linguistic interpretation of that information provides the neurological component of this well-recognized neurobehavioral syndrome.

No exact analog of alexia without agraphia is found as a developmental disorder in children. However, it is possible that the purer cases of dyslexia represent the infantile counterpart of this syndrome, even though certain differences are obvious. In contrast to the adult patient with "pure" alexia, the child with "pure" developmental dyslexia can neither write nor spell. But these differences are understandable, assuming that the acquisition of writing and spelling skills requires a critical level of reading competence as a basis, which the dyslexic child lacks. But like the alexic patient, his oral language is essentially intact and he shows little in the nature of associated disabilities. A specific visual–verbal associational disability has often been postulated as the basis for developmental dyslexia. Little empirical support for such a specific associational impairment, as contrasted to more generalized associational defect, can be found in the literature (cf. Brewer, 1967). However, investigations of the question have not been very critical with respect to the selection of subjects, and it is possible that study of a more carefully defined sample of dyslexic children would generate more interesting results. One wonders, for example, whether those dyslexic children identified by Denckla (1972a) as having a noteworthy deficit in the naming of colors might show a specific visuoverbal associative disability.

A second fairly well-defined syndrome of acquired reading disability is *alexia with agraphia* with mild disturbances in oral speech expression in the form of anomia and occasional paraphasic speech. The patient with this type of alexia has difficulty in reading letters as well as words and oral spelling is also defective. Focal disease of the posterior parietal region, where visuoverbal and audioverbal information is presumably integrated, produces this syndrome which often includes the presence of concomitant defects such as impairment in calculation and in visuoconstructional ability. Is there a comparable syndrome within the cadre of dyslexia? The *language disorder syndrome* identified by Mattis, French, and Rapin seems to approximate it.

Another type of alexia, found in association with frontal lesions and a nonfluent type of aphasic disorder, has rather different qualitative characteristics. In contrast to the pattern of pure alexia, in this variation letters of the alphabet are less readily recognized than words, which are often grasped (or guessed at) as gestalts. Writing, oral spelling, and recognition of orally spelled words are defective. The context in which this form of alexia usually appears is a Broca type of aphasia distinguished by halting speech and misarticulation. The dyslexic *dyscoordination* syndrome of Mattis, French, and Rapin is similar in a number of respects to this form of acquired alexia.

Still another form of reading disability seen in patients with brain disease appears within the context of more pervasive visuoperceptual and visuospatial impairment. The reading failure in patients of this type is sometimes not considered to be a form of "alexia" because it seems to be merely an expression of higher-level perceptual or orientational impairment, and it lacks a linguistic character. But the disability is quite real, extends to writing as well as reading, and frequently involves the misreading of letters and simple words as well as connected text. If one looks for a developmental counterpart for it, the *visuospatial–perceptual disorder* syndrome isolated by Mattis, French, and Rapin naturally comes to mind.

Each of these forms of acquired alexia has specific neurological and behavioral correlates. This fact has been emphasized by recent authors who also point out some of its implications. Having described the anterior Broca type of alexia, Benson (1977, p. 331) writes: "Not only are the clinical-anatomical correlations of this disorder valid and useful for the clinician, but they should prove valuable for future research on reading, both as a normal phenomenon and as an abnormal function." Similarly, Damasio (1977, p. 326) discussing the "varieties and significance of the alexias" concludes: "The clinical variation of the alexias and the multiplicity of loci of brain dysfunction with which they associate provide a basis for the construction of neuropsychological models of reading, which take into account different components of behavior and attempt their correlation with functional structures of the brain. The heuristic value of such an integrated model for advancing knowledge of brain-behavior relationships and of specific problems, such as developmental reading disability, is clear."

On balance, it seems probable that what is known about acquired disorders of reading in patients with brain disease can serve as one (not necessarily the only) useful model for achieving further understanding of developmental reading disability. The great value of the model resides in the specific neurobehavioral correlations that have been established for the acquired alexias. At the same time, it must be recognized that information about the performance characteristics and behavioral correlates of the various types of acquired alexia is rather sparse. In fact more is known about these topics in the field of developmental dyslexia. Thus it is likely that utilization of the same models for the study of the developmental and acquired alexias will advance understanding in both areas.

NEUROBEHAVIORAL CORRELATIONS

Although there is no doubt that social factors, such as cultural background and values and quality of instruction, significantly affect the development of reading skills and particularly their final status as the adult years are reached, the opinion of most professional workers is that endogenous factors, reflected in anomalies of central nervous system function, constitute the primary basis for specific reading retardation. It is for this reason that identification of the neurological correlates of the disability is generally regarded as the major research task today.

The search for neurological correlates has taken two forms. The direct approach, exemplified by the contributions of Hughes, Denckla, and Conners, seeks to identify functional abnormalities of the brain that are associated with reading disability and that presumably are antecedent to it. In principle, structural abnormalities of the brain should be looked for, but current noninvasive methods of study have yielded negative findings. This is perhaps attributable to technical limitations and it may be that Mattis's hope— that further developments in computerized axial tomography will disclose structural correlates for dyslexia—will be realized. What does seem to be clear is that the current version of the CAT scan is not equal to the task. For the present, the direct approach consists of a search for abnormalities of cerebral function, primarily in terms of electrical indices.

Hughes's comprehensive review of the literature on this topic indicates that a global positive association between cerebral electrophysiological abnormality and behavioral abnormality has been demonstrated beyond doubt. On the other hand, few conclusions about the nature of the relationships between electroencephalographic abnormality and specific reading retardation can be drawn from this large body of data which includes a number of suggestive findings, but at the same time so many conflicting results. Denckla identifies what is probably the major source of confusion in this area when she asks the simple question, "EEG correlates of what"? It is too much to expect that the EEG and cognate measures of brain function will relate in an unambiguous way to deficiency in reading skills arising from diverse causes and appearing in diverse contexts. Hughes is in essential agreement for he gives "the imprecise definition of the groups under study and the overlapping of these groups" as a major reason for the discordant findings on "the usefulness of the electroencephalogram in studying children with dyslexia or learning disabilities."

The validity of the EEG as an index of diverse forms of brain pathology has been established for decades and its usefulness in this respect has increased steadily as new techniques of analysis have been developed. Given both this fact and the demonstrated positive association of a global nature between EEG abnormality and behavioral abnormality, it is *not* too much to expect that more refined correlational investigation will yield a clearer understanding of the role that the EEG and cognate phenomena can play in identifying the neurological basis of specific reading retardation. One direction that such refinement must take has been indicated by Hughes and Denckla. It is on the behavioral side of the brain–behavior equation. Clearly there is no point in continuing to estimate the frequency and type of EEG abnormality in children with unspecified reading failure or unspecified academic failure (sometimes labeled "general learning disability"). The outcome of such studies would only confirm the findings of previous studies that these children, like other types of deviant children, tend to show a somewhat higher frequency of EEG abnormality than do normal children. What is needed at this time is investigation focused on the EEG characteristics of clearly defined subgroups of dyslexic children with and without associated clinical signs of minimal brain dysfunction. A likely outcome of studies such as these is, as Denckla suggests, that the EEG abnormality will be found to be a defining factor in some syndromes and not in others. If this should prove to be the case, it would represent a significant forward step in progress toward understanding the neurological background of at least some subgroups in the dyslexia category.

Hughes has reported two rather curious findings that deserve attention. The first is the indication of an inverse relationship between severity of disability and frequency of EEG abnormality. In his own work, for example, he found that children with relatively mild learning disabilities showed a substantially higher frequency of EEG abnormality than did either those with more severe disabilities or control children (Hughes, 1971). In fact, children with severe learning disabilities did not differ from their controls in this respect. The second seemingly paradoxical finding is that in certain groups an abnormal EEG is associated with a better prognosis than a normal EEG. Lairy and Harrison (1968) interpreted this observation to suggest that the EEG abnormality found in some children may be a reflection of emotional disturbance resulting from stressful experience rather than a primary phenomenon. Hughes considers the interpretation to be tenable, but warns against too facile an application of it. In any case, these observations by Lairy and Harrison and others have added a new dimension to EEG interpretation that must be taken into account in considering the implications of research findings.

Hughes also describes the results that have come from employment of special types of analyses of the EEG, specifically, synchronization of alpha rhythms (Hughes, 1971), their spatial organization (Lairy and Netchine, 1960, 1963; Lairy and Harrison, 1968), and frequency analysis as reported by Sklar, Hanley, and Simmons (1972, 1973; Hanley and Sklar, 1976). These approaches have yielded evidence of differences between normal and handicapped readers and have generated hypotheses about the nature of the neurophysiological background of dyslexia that call for further investigation.

Another promising electrophysiologic approach is represented by the cortical visual-evoked response (VER). Following upon the initial study of Conners (1970), who found attenuation of the late negative component of the VER in the left parietal region in retarded readers, Preston, Guthrie, and Childs (1974) have compared the VER characteristics of dyslexic and normal children and confirmed Conners' finding. In a later study of adults with reading disability, the differences in response to words as compared to light flashes proved to be a discriminating characteristic (Preston et al., 1977).

The "pilot study" of the EEG correlates of dyslexia outlined by Hughes and Denckla (Chaps. 10 and 11) incorporates assessment of many of the variables that need to be investigated in future study of the question. As will be seen, their plan calls not only for analysis of the resting EEG, but also for EEG analysis during different task performances and VER determinations.

A less direct approach to the problem of identifying the neurological correlates of developmental dyslexia is represented in the studies reviewed by Rourke, Spreen, and Knights dealing with the behavioral correlates of reading disability. These studies differ from those concerned with psychological factors in reading disability, as reported by Vellutino, Doehring, and Blank, not in their essential nature but in their intent. The purpose of the latter group of studies is to identify those cognitive disabilities, such as defective visual processing, visuoperceptive weakness, and attentional deficit, which may underlie reading failure and which, if alleviated, may remove obstacles to normal progress in learning to read. The purpose of the "neurobehavioral" studies covered by Rourke, Spreen, and Knights, which often deal with the same cognitive variables, is to utilize discovered relationships as a basis for inferring the neurological status of dyslexic children. For example, the association between reading disability and right–left orientation has been investigated because of the previously established finding that both adults and children with confirmed brain disease may show right–left disorientation. The observation that some dyslexic children show defective right–left orientation is then utilized as one bit of evidence pointing to cerebral abnormality in these children. Depending upon one's beliefs about the localizing implications of right–left disorientation in adult patients, the observation may even be used to infer the presence of focal cerebral abnormality in dyslexic children.

The basic logic of this approach is sound. However, it is well to appreciate the fact that it is indirect in nature and that it proceeds on the basis of analogical reasoning. It is therefore necessary to be cautious in its application. The behavioral capacities selected for study, because of their association with brain disease, are sometimes labeled as "brain-dependent," "brain-related," or of "central origin" and hence particularly suitable for study. It is not altogether clear what terms such as these are intended to mean. Do they imply that the selected behavioral capacities differ from another class of behavioral capacities which are not "brain-dependent"? This is manifestly not the case. Do they mean that the selected behavioral capacities are relatively more sensitive to cerebral status and relatively less sensitive to the influence of social and cultural factors than other behavioral capacities? This may be true, but it has not been demonstrated.

The selection of certain behavioral capacities and not others such as, for example, abstract reasoning ability or temporal orientation, is based on the belief that the former are more promising for the purpose of neurological inference. Again, this may be true but it has not been demonstrated. Abstract reasoning ability and temporal orientation are just as "brain-dependent" and in fact are found to be impaired in patients with brain disease just as frequently as are the selected measures.

Rourke has presented a comprehensive survey and critical evaluation of the large body of behavioral studies which have been undertaken with the hope that their findings will disclose the neural mechanisms underlying specific failure to learn to read. Positive associations of a modest degree have been found between reading retardation and deviant performance on a variety of tasks making demands on perceptual, linguistic, sequencing, and intersensory integrative abilities. In truth, it would be difficult to find a task on which reading-disabled children have not been reported to be deficient (cf. Doehring, 1968). At the same time, failure to find differences between good and poor readers has also been reported with respect to these performances. Thus even the conclusion of a modest positive association between certain cognitive deficiencies and reading failure is weakened by empirical inconsistency. Nor does it appear that the results of these behavioral studies have led us any closer to their avowed goal of identifying the neural mechanisms underlying dyslexia. Rourke and Spreen indicate some reasons for this disappointing outcome. They point out that simple between-group comparisons of performance on one or another task or even a whole battery of diverse tasks without a theoretical model that yields differential predictions for empirical test cannot lead us beyond the superficial knowledge that we already possess. They also point out, as have other participants in the conference, that specific reading retardation globally considered is too amorphous an entity to serve as a useful behavioral variable for correlational studies. They therefore advocate investigations that are based on explicit models of the reading process and its deviations and that employ more refined definitions of dyslexia. To this may be added the recommendation that studies purporting to be neuropsychological in nature should include independent indices of the structure or functions of the brain as essential data for analysis. Dyslexic children have real, as well as conceptual, nervous systems.

PSYCHOLOGICAL FACTORS

The investigation of psychological factors in dyslexia aims to identify the more fundamental cognitive disabilities that are responsible for failure to learn to read and to provide guidelines for effective remediation. Vellutino's well-organized review offers a detailed description and critical analysis of studies in this area and the information which they have yielded. He has focused attention on four major approaches, each of which has generated a substantial amount of empirical investigation.

The first identifies *defective visual perception and memory* as a basic cognitive disability which is frequently associated with dyslexia. Vellutino's analysis indicates that there is little support for this hypothesis. If this type of disability is a significant determinant of reading failure, it is operative in only relatively few cases. But here it is well for us to recall Mattis's observation that a low frequency does not mean a lack of significance. Visual-perceptual disability *may* be a decisive interactive determinant of reading failure in a defined subgroup of cases. Moreover, Blank (Chap. 5) points out that not all dimensions of visual perception have been thoroughly investigated, particularly that mode which requires suppression of salient information in order to achieve swift and accurate recognition. From Vellutino's review, the visual-perceptual task that has been most consistently successful in discriminating between good and poor readers appears to be the Embedded Figures Test of Gottschaldt. The demands made by this task correspond well to Blank's formulation of a type of visual information processing involving inhibition of response to the most arresting features of a visual display. Parallel observations on the performances of adult patients with brain disease prove to be of interest in this respect. While performance on most visuoperceptual tasks is found to be more frequently and more severely impaired in patients with right-hemisphere lesion than in those with left-sided disease (including aphasics), the Gottschaldt test proves to be an exception (cf. Teuber and Weinstein, 1956; Weinstein, 1964; Russo and Vignolo, 1967; Orgass et al., 1972). As a group, aphasic patients perform defectively on this test, their performance level being comparable to that of the poorest subgroup of patients with right-hemisphere disease, namely, those with posterior parietal lesions.

A second approach, arising out of the pioneer studies of Birch and co-workers, identifies impairment in the capacity for *intersensory integration,* as a basic cognitive disability. As Blank indicates, empirical testing of this hypothesis has generated a number of related hypotheses for investigation. Thus it has been of considerable heuristic value. But the hypothesis, as stated in its original form, has not fared well. Some replications have confirmed the original finding of an excessive number of failing performances among dyslexics, but others have not. More importantly, closer analysis suggests that other mechanisms, such as attention, short-term memory, temporal sequencing, and temperospatial matching, may be the essential determinants of performance level on this task rather than its bisensory nature. The task itself remains a useful vehicle for investigating a number of cognitive capacities in dyslexic children.

Another approach identifies defects in the perception and retention of *temporally organized stimuli* as a central cognitive deficit in dyslexics. As with the intersensory matching task, performance on temporal sequence tasks involving recall of the serial order of stimuli or imitation of sequential movements has often been found to be deficient in retarded readers. Again, as in the case of intersensory matching, the postulated basis for failure on this type of task has been questioned and the point has been made that recall or imitation tasks simply may be providing a convenient process for assessing short-term memory capacity.

Finally, there is the concept that dyslexia is most fruitfully viewed as a specific or attenuated form of a more pervasive *developmental language dis-*

ability. Many (probably the majority of) dyslexic children can be shown to have relatively poor ability in one or another language area: in naming, in phonemic discrimination, in syntactic development, in short-term verbal memory, or in verbal reasoning capacity. The WISC pattern of a lower verbal scale than performance scale IQ, which is shown by so many reading-disabled children, is one rather gross and imperfect reflection of this more general language disability.

Of course, it is quite possible to view these verbal deficiencies as the consequence of a primary reading disability. And indeed it is difficult to see how a serious reading disability could fail to retard the growth of vocabulary, knowledge of syntax, and verbal-conceptual abilities to some degree. But it is clear that there is much more in the association than this. A history of delayed speech and language development is a frequent finding in the history of dyslexic children, particularly those with the characteristic WISC Verbal-Performance profile, and the status of oral language at kindergarten age is a potent predictor of subsequent reading achievement.

Thus it is highly probable that relative deficiency in oral language skills is the central factor in the genesis of dyslexia in a particular subgroup of failing readers. However, as Blank has pointed out, the particular facets of language development which are crucial in this respect remain a question for investigation. The diverse deficits found in the language disorder syndrome of Mattis, French, and Rapin suggest the possibility that any of a number of aspects of linguistic development may be crucial. Or, as Blank suggests, so-called "metalinguistic" abilities, that is, the capacity to manipulate language as an object, may prove to be particularly important.

GENETIC ASPECTS

The question of the role of genetic factors in dyslexia is not only important in its own right; it also carries interesting implications in that it suggests the existence of a specific type of cerebral organization which makes learning to read particularly difficult. The known facts in this field and new research designs to resolve unanswered questions are presented in the chapters by Owen, McLearn, and Childs.

There is no question that dyslexia can "run in families." On the other hand, estimates of the frequency of "familial" dyslexia, as defined by the presence of the disability in close relatives of the probands, vary considerably. Hallgren (1950) reported a familial incidence of 90 percent, but most other workers have found decidedly lower frequencies. For example, Ingram, Mason, and Blackburn (1970) studying a sample of 82 dyslexic children, found evidence of reading difficulty in one or more relatives (parents, siblings, aunts, and uncles) in 37 percent of the group. Indications of reading disability in the relatives of a control group of 30 normal readers of comparable intelligence and social status was found to be 10 percent. Bettman et al. (1967) found that 49 percent of a group of 47 dyslexic children had similarly affected parents or siblings, while the comparable figure in a group of normal readers was 6 percent. However, in agreement with Hallgren's early study, Finucci and co-workers (1976) found instances of reading disability in the families of 17 of 20 dyslexic children, i.e., a relative frequency of 85 percent. This variation in estimates is quite understandable in view of the lack of employment of a common criterion for defining "reading disability." In any case, even the lowest estimates are far higher than the most generous estimate (10 percent) in the total population.

A positive family history of dyslexia argues for a genetic determination of the disability but, of course, does not prove it. Familial cultural transmission is always a possibility. A more direct approach to the question is provided by the study of dyslexia in monozygotic and dizygotic twins. The data are sparse, but most impressive. Analyses of the literature by Hallgren (1950), Hermann (1959), and Zerbin-Rudin (1967) indicate that monozygotic twins show 100 percent concordance, while dizygotic twins show about 33 percent, i.e., a proportion within expectations for the siblings of probands.

It is important to appreciate that the proponents of the genetic approach to dyslexia do not contend that all cases of specific reading disability represent the expression of hereditary factors. Their point is rather that a significant proportion of these cases are genetically influenced. At the present time it is not possible to specify how high this proportion is. Moreover, the nature of the genetic mechanisms that are operating remains an open question. Owen, McLearn, and Childs have outlined the possibilities in this regard. More important, they have described specific research strategies that offer the promise of answering the question. The task is a difficult one, complicated as it is by definitional problems and the circumstance that one is dealing with a cultural product and not a biological characteristic.

PREDICTION AND REMEDIATION

The identification of the preschool child who is at risk for specific reading failure so that appropriate placement or remediation can be instituted before that failure occurs is a task that has occupied educators for decades. The numerous "reading readiness" test batteries that have been developed and are given to kindergarten children reflect this concern. The more carefully designed predictive batteries, e.g., those of de Hirsch, Jansky, and Langford (1966; Jansky and de Hirsch, 1972), Satz (Satz and Sparrow, 1970; Satz and Friel, 1973, 1974; Satz, Friel, and Rudegeair, 1974), and Silver and Hagin (1976) predict later reading success or failure with fair accuracy, the "hit rate" being about 80 percent. As Jansky (Chap. 18) points out, it is not likely that this level of predictive accuracy will be significantly increased, given all the uncontrolled factors (e.g., quality of instruction, illness, maturational changes) that intervene between prediction and outcome. Definitional vagueness, the lack of meaningful estimates of the prevalence of the disability, and the fact that specific reading disability probably consists of a number of distinctive syndromes also operate to limit the predictive accuracy of reading readiness batteries.

The theoretically oriented predictive batteries designed by Satz, Jansky and Silver and Hagin represent major advances in this field. They have provided the means for carefully executed longitudinal studies that take account of problems of sampling, criterion measures, long-term prediction, and statistical analysis. In turn, these longitudinal studies have generated important information about the cause and outcome of reading failure and the cognitive variables that underlie it. The pointed distinction made by Silver (Chap. 17) between "scanning," i.e., prediction of success or failure without regard to causation, and "diagnosis," i.e., evaluation of the factors underlying success or failure, is particularly relevant in this context.

The great variety of methods currently employed in the remedial instruction of dyslexic children and the conceptual bases of these methods are critically evaluated in the chapters of Johnson, Guthrie, and Zigmond. There is general agreement that, given the diverse nature of the deficits underlying reading failure, no single approach is appropriate for all cases. This assumption is quite plausible, but as yet there has been no convincing empirical dem-

473

onstration that one method is more effective than another method for a specific type of dyslexia and that the reverse is true for another type.

As is true for other forms of behavioral treatment such as psychotherapy and aphasia rehabilitation, professional opinion about the effectiveness of remedial instruction in dyslexia varies widely. The findings of empirical studies of the question are inconclusive, a not unexpected outcome when one considers the numerous uncontrolled variables outside of the instructional situation that influence the academic achievement and life adjustment of the dyslexic child. There is evidence that the younger the age at which remedial instruction is begun, the better the outcome. But, since some young children experience transient difficulty which yields to conventional instruction, the inference of a causal relationship does not necessarily follow from this finding. The significance of other instructional variables such as intensity and duration is also not clear. What is evident is that the approach to remediation via visuo-perceptual and visuomotor training has not been effective.

Progress in understanding the complex issues discussed by Johnson, Guthrie, and Zigmond and in adopting (or developing) remediation methods of proven effectiveness would seem to depend upon a number of factors. On the methodological side, comprehensive and broadly accepted tests of reading ability must be used as criterion measures in order to render the findings of different studies comparable. The procedures utilized in remediation must be operationally defined so that the critical components of different methods are clearly understood. The social, educational, psychological, and neurological characteristics of the children must be specified. Information such as this is a necessary basis for the meaningful assessment of the effectiveness of specific remediation methods, for the appropriate application of these methods to defined groups of dyslexic children, and for the validation of new procedures.

THE DIRECTIONS OF FUTURE RESEARCH

Not everyone will agree with this assessment of our current understanding of developmental dyslexia. Some will feel that our knowledge of the nature and causes of the disability is much more secure than has been suggested. Others will consider that the significance of such factors as EEG abnormality and genetic influences has been overrated. (See, for example, the critique of the EEG literature by Conners in Chap. 12.) Still others will take issue with its general orientation which places more emphasis on endogenous variables than on social and educational factors. But there is not likely to be disagreement about the necessity for further investigation of persisting problems or for the completion of unfinished tasks in the field.

The indications for future research on specific problems in the field have been discussed and new approaches suggested in each section of the book, as well as in this concluding chapter. With perhaps one exception, there is no need to repeat these ideas and recommendations. The exception is the problem of definition which, because of its central position in determining the relevance of studies of causation, pathogenesis, prevention, and remediation, deserves special emphasis. It is essential that genetic, neurological, cognitive, and epidemiological investigation proceed on the basis of a clear conception of what the subject of investigation is. This requirement will be met only when the problem of definition is satisfactorily resolved.

One important advance in this respect would be the formulation of specific guidelines for an adequate clinical description of the disability itself. It might be assumed that, after 70 years of scientific study of developmental dyslexia, a clinical description of the qualitative features of the reading performances of an individual child would provide the basis for investigations of dyslexic children. In fact, this is far from being the case. For the most part, even the better studies have utilized a single criterion, such as teacher's ratings or the score on a single test of word recognition or oral reading, as the basis for classifying a child as "dyslexic." Reading specialists are well aware that dyslexics are not a homogeneous group and they find it necessary to analyze the reading performance of a dyslexic child in considerable detail in order to plan an appropriate remedial program for him. But individual differences among dyslexics have been generally ignored by researchers who are content to rely on a single index of performance level. An empirical study of cognitive abilities or lesional localization in aphasia that did not include information about the qualitative nature of the patients' expressive speech disorder and the status of their oral comprehension, reading, and writing would be judged to be of very limited significance. Similar studies in the field of dyslexia are of equally limited significance. There can be little doubt that the mass of contradictory results to be found in research literature is due in large part to the diverse and inadequate criteria used in subject selection.

This is surely the time to formulate an adequate battery for the assessment of relevant dimensions of reading performance that could be utilized by researchers as a basis for subject selection and classification. The broad employment of a comprehensive assessment battery would be of immeasurable

475

value in facilitating meaningful communication and interaction among specialists in the field. The development of such a battery can best be accomplished through a formal cooperative effort by specialists from various disciplines.

A related problem of definition is associated with the growing realization that developmental dyslexia, even when it is narrowly defined as reading failure in spite of adequate intelligence and adequate instruction, probably represents not a single disorder but a number of syndromes, each with its own distinctive antecedent and concurrent correlates. The most impressive recent effort in the direction of identifying relatively homogeneous dyslexic syndromes (in this case defined in terms of cognitive correlates) is that of Mattis, French, and Rapin. It is encouraging that the existence of the three syndromes that were isolated on the basis of objective criteria in the initial study has been confirmed in an independent sample of cases (see Mattis, Chap. 3). Further replicative studies are indicated and these should include collection of diverse measures of reading performance as well as neurological data. The *sequencing disorder* syndrome of Denckla and the types of disability discussed by Doehring and Spreen should also be investigated through appropriate performance measures. Since a large number of cases is required to secure stable results in this type of investigation, only a well-organized collaborative project involving several clinical and educational research centers can be expected to achieve these purposes.

It is within this framework of a more adequate description of the disability itself, both in terms of the characteristics of reading performance and of syndromes defined by correlated cognitive performances, that the question of its genetic, neurological, cognitive, and social determinants can be most fruitfully attacked. Its adoption should lead to investigative work which is methodologically superior to past efforts and which should generate the basic information required for a satisfactory understanding of dyslexia.

References

A practical guide in measuring project impact on student achievement. Stock # 017-080-01460-2, U.S. Govt. Printing Office, Washington, D.C., 1975.

Abt Associates. *Education as experimentation: a planned variation model* (Vol. III). Boston: Abt Associates, 1976.

Ackerman, P. T., Peters, J. E., and Dykman, R. A. Children with specific learning disabilities: WISC profiles. *Journal of Learning Disabilities,* 1971, *4,* 150–166.

Ackerman, P. T., Dykman, R. A., and Peters, J. E. Hierarchical factor patterns on the WISC as related to areas of learning deficit. *Perceptual and Motor Skills,* 1976, *42,* 583–615.

Adelman, H. A. Learning problems: Part I. An interactional view of causality. *Academic Therapy,* 1970–71, *6,* 117–123.

Adelman, H. S. The not so specific learning disability population. *Exceptional Children,* 1971, *37,* 528–533.

Adelman, H. S. and Taylor, L. *Learning Problems and the Fernald Laboratory: Beyond the Fernald Technique,* mimeograph. 1976.

Ades, H. W. Central auditory mechanisms. In J. Field, H. W. Magoun, and V. E. Hall (Eds.), *Handbook of Physiology* (Vol. 1). Baltimore: Williams and Wilkins, 1959.

Albee, G. W., Lane, E. A., and Reuter, J. Childhood intelligence of future schizophrenics and neighborhood peers. *Journal of Psychology,* 1964, *58,* 141–144.

Alexander, D. and Money, J. Reading ability, object constancy and Turner's syndrome. *Perceptual Motor Skills,* 1965, *20,* 981–984.

Allen, T. W. Patterns of attention to temporal stimulus sequences and their relationship to reading achievement. *Child Development,* 1975, *46,* 1035–1038.

A.M.A. News. Infant mortality program funded, August 4, 1975, *12.*

Ames, L. B. Learning disabilities: the developmental point of view. In H. R. Myklebust (Ed.), *Progress in Learning Disabilities* (Vol. 1). New York: Harper and Row, 1966.

Anapolle, L. Visual training and reading performance. *Journal of Reading,* 1967, *10,* 373–382.

REFERENCES

Anderson, W. The hyperkinetic child: a neurological appraisal. *Neurology*, 1963, *13*, 968–973.

Applebee, A. N. Research in reading retardation: two critical problems. *Journal of Child Psychology & Psychiatry*, 1971, *12*, 91–113.

Austin, M. C. and Morrison, C. Early school screening practices. *Journal of Learning Disabilities*, 1974, 7, 55–59.

Ayers, F. W. and Torres, F. The incidence of EEG abnormalities in a dyslexic and a control group. *Journal of Clinical Psychology*, 1967, *23*, 334–336.

Bakker, D. J. Temporal order, meaningfulness, and reading ability. *Perceptual and Motor Skills*, 1967, 24, 1027–1030.

Bakker, D. J. *Temporal order in disturbed reading.* Rotterdam: University Press, 1972.

Bakker, D. J. *Perceptual asymmetries and reading proficiency.* Amsterdam, The Netherlands: Paedologisch Instituut Research Report, No. 2, 1976.

Bakker, D. J., Tuenissen, J., and Bosch, J. Development of laterality—reading patterns. In R. M. Knights and D. J. Bakker (Eds.), *Neuropsychology of learning disorders: theoretical approaches.* Baltimore: University Park Press, 1976.

Balow, B. The long-term effect of remedial reading instruction. *The Reading Teacher*, 1965, *18*, 581–586.

Balow, B. and Bloomquist, M. Young adults ten to fifteen years after severe reading disability. *Elementary School Journal*, 1965, 66, 44–48.

Balow, B., Rubin, R., and Rosen, M. S. Prenatal events as precursors of reading disability. *Reading Research Quarterly*, 1975–76, *11*, 36–71.

Bakwin, H. Reading disability in twins. *Developmental Medicine and Child Neurology*, 1973, *15*, 184–187.

Bannatyne, A. The color phonics system. In J. Money and G. Schiffman (Eds.), *The disabled reader.* Baltimore: The Johns Hopkins University Press, 1966.

Bannatyne, A. *Language, reading and learning disabilities.* Springfield, Ill.: Charles C. Thomas, 1971.

Bannatyne, A. Diagnosis: a note on recategorization of the WISC scaled scores. *Journal of Learning Disabilities*, 1974, 7, 13–14.

Banquet, J. P. Spectral analysis of the EEG in meditation. *Electroencephalography & Clinical Neurophysiology*, 1973, *35*, 143–151.

Barker, D. J. P. and Edwards, J. H. Obstetric complications and school performance. *British Medical Journal*, 1967, *3*, 695–699.

Baro, W. Z. Is there an EEG abnormality in reading difficulties. *Electroencephalography & Clinical Neurophysiology*, 1968, 24, 393–394.

Barrett, T. C. Visual discrimination tasks as predictors of first grade reading achievement. *The Reading Teacher*, 1965(a), *18*, 276–282.

Barrett, T. C. Predicting reading achievement through readiness tests in *Reading and Inquiry*, International Reading Association, 1965(b), *10*, 26–29.

Barrett, T. C. Relationship between measures of pre-reading visual discrimination and first grade reading achievement: review of the literature. *Reading Research Quarterly*, 1965(c), *1*, 51–76.

Bartel, N. R., Grill, J. J., and Bartel, H. W. The syntagmatic-paradigmatic shift in learning disabled and normal children. *Journal of Learning Disabilities,* 1973, *6,* 518–523.

Bastian, H. C. *A treatise on aphasia and other speech defects.* New York: Appleton, 1898.

Bateman, B. *The essentials of teaching.* Sioux Falls, S.D.: Adapt Press, 1971.

Bateman, B. Teaching reading to learning disabled children. In L. B. Resnick and P. A. Weaver (Eds.), *Theory and Practice of Early Reading* (4 vols.). Hillsdale, N.J.: Lawrence Erlbaum Associates, 1977.

Bayley, N. Mental growth during the first three years. *Genetic Psychological Monographs,* 1933, *14,* 1–89.

Bax, M. and Whitmore, K. Neurodevelopmental screening in the school-entrant medical examination. *Lancet,* 1973, *2,* 368–370.

Becker, R. D. Minimal cerebral (brain) dysfunction—a clinical fact or neurological fiction? The syndrome critically reexamined in the light of some hard neurological evidence. *Israel Annals of Psychiatry and Related Disciplines,* 1974, *12,* 87–106.

Becker, W. and Engelmann, S. *Analysis of achievement data on six cohorts of low income children from 20 school districts in the University of Oregon Direct Instruction Follow-Through Model* (Technical Report No. 76-1).

Beckett, P., Bickford, R., and Keith, H. The electroencephalogram in various aspects of mental deficiency. *American Journal of Diseases of Children,* 1956, *92,* 374–381.

Beecher, R. and Goldfluss, N. Personal communication, 1975.

Beer, S. *Platform for change.* New York: Wiley, 1975.

Beery, J. Matching of auditory and visual stimuli by average and retarded readers. *Child Development,* 1967, *38,* 827–833.

Begleiter, H. and Platz, A. Cortical evoked potentials to semantic stimuli. *Psychophysiology,* 1969, *6,* 91–100.

Behrens, T. A study of psychological and electroencephalographic changes in children with learning disorders. Unpublished doctoral dissertation. Northwestern University, 1963.

Beinart, G. A possible visual origin of writing difficulty. *Developmental Medicine and Child Neurology,* 1974, *16,* 766–772.

Belmont, L. and Birch, H. G. Lateral dominance, lateral awareness, and reading disability. *Child Development,* 1965, *36,* 59–71.

Belmont, L. and Birch, H. G. The intellectual profile of retarded readers. *Perceptual and Motor Skill,* 1966, *22,* 787–816.

Bender, L. A. *Psychopathology of children with organic brain disorders.* Springfield, Ill.: Charles C. Thomas, 1956.

Bender, L. A. Specific reading disability as a maturational lag. *Bulletin of the Orton Society,* 1957, *7,* 9–18.

Bender, L. A. The visual motor gestalt function in six and seven year old normal and schizophrenic children. In J. Zubin and G. Jervis (Eds.), *Psychopathology of Mental Development,* 544–563. New York: Grune & Stratton, 1966.

Bender, L. A. A fifty-year review of experiences with dyslexia. *Bulletin of the Orton Society,* 1975, *25,* 5–23.

REFERENCES

Bender, L. A. and Yarnell, H. An observation nursery. *American Journal of Psychiatry,* 1971, 97, 1158–1172.

Bender, M. B. *Disorders in Perception With Particular Reference to the Phenomena of Extinction and Displacement.* Springfield, Ill.: C. C. Thomas, 1952.

Benson, D. F. Alexia. In J. T. Guthrie (Ed.), *Aspects of Reading Acquisition.* Baltimore: Johns Hopkins Press, 1976.

Benson, D. F. The third alexia. *Archives of Neurology,* 1977, 34, 327–331.

Benson, D. F., Brown, J., and Tomlinson, E. G. Varieties of alexia. *Neurology,* 1971, 21, 951–957.

Benson, D. F. and Geschwind, N. The alexias. In P. J. Vinken and G. W. Bruyn (Eds.), *Handbook of Clinical Neurology* (Vol. 4, pp. 112–140). Amsterdam: North-Holland, 1969.

Benson, D. F. and Geschwind, N. Developmental Gerstmann syndrome. *Neurology,* 1970, 20, 293–298.

Benson, D. F. and Geschwind, N. The aphasias and related disturbances. In A. B. Baker and L. H. Baker (Eds.), *Clinical Neurology* (Vol. 1, Chap. 8). New York: Harper and Row, 1975.

Benton, A. L. Dyslexia in relation to form perception and directional sense. In J. Money (Ed.), *Reading Disability: Progress and Research Needs in Dyslexia* (pp. 81–102). Baltimore: Johns Hopkins Press, 1962.

Benton, A. L. Development dyslexia: neurological aspects. In W. J. Friedlander (Ed.), *Advances in Neurology* (Vol. 7, pp. 1–47). New York: Raven Press, 1975.

Benton, A. L. and Bird, J. W. The EEG and reading disability. *American Journal of Orthopsychiatry,* 1963, 33, 529–531.

Bentzen, F. Sex ratios in learning and behavior disorders. *American Journal of Orthopsychiatry,* 1963, 23, 92–98.

Bereiter, C. An academic preschool for disadvantaged children: conclusions from evaluation studies. In J. Stanley (Ed.), *Preschool Programs for the Disadvantaged* (pp. 1–21). Baltimore: Johns Hopkins Press, 1972.

Bereiter, C. and Engelmann, S. *Teaching disadvantaged children in the preschool.* Englewood Cliffs, N.J.: Prentice Hall, 1966.

Berger, M., Yule, W., and Rutter, M. (1975): Attainment and adjustment in two geographical areas: II. The prevalence of specific reading retardation. *British Journal of Psychiatry,* 1975, 126, 510–519.

Bergés, J., Harrison, A., and Lairy, G. EEG and speech disturbance in children. *Electroencephalography & Clinical Neurophysiology,* 1966, 18, 425.

Berko, J. The child's learning of English morphology. *Word,* 1958, 14, 150–177.

Berko, J. The child's learning of English morphology. In S. Saporta (Ed.), *Psycholinguistics: A Book of Readings.* New York: Holt, Rinehart and Winston, 1961, 339–375.

Berlin, C. I., Hughes, L. F., Low-Bell, S. S., and Berlin, H. L. Dichotic right ear advantage in children 5 to 13. *Cortex,* 1973, 9, 394–402.

Bernstein, M. Reading methods and materials based on linguistic principles for basic and remedial instruction. *Academic Therapy Quarterly,* 1967, 2, 149–154.

Berry, K. and Buktenica, N. A. *Developmental Test of Visual-Motor Integration.* Chicago: Follett Educational Corp. 1967.

Berry, M. F. *Language disorders of children: the basis and diagnoses.* New York: Appleton-Century-Crofts, 1969.

Bettman, J. W., Stern, E. L., Whitsell, L. J., and Gofman, H. F. Cerebral dominance in developmental dyslexia. *Archives of Ophthalmology,* 1967, *78,* 722–729.

Biemiller, A. The development of the use of graphic and contextual information as children learn to read. *Reading Research Quarterly,* 1970, *6,* 75–96.

Bierwisch, M. Schriftstruktur und Phonologie. *Probleme und Ergebnisse der Psychologie,* 1972, *43,* 21–44.

Bijou, S. W. What psychology has to offer education—now. *Journal of Applied Behavior Analysis.* 1970, *3,* 65–71.

Binet, A. *The development of intelligence in children* (p. 338). Baltimore: Williams and Wilkins, 1916.

Birch, H. G. Dyslexia and maturation of visual function. In J. Money (Ed.), *Reading Disability: Progress and Research Needs in Dyslexia.* Baltimore: Johns Hopkins Press, 1962.

Birch, H. G. and Belmont, L. Auditory-visual integration in normal and retarded readers. *American Journal of Orthopsychiatry,* 1964, *34,* 852–861.

Birch, H. G. and Belmont, L. Auditory-visual integration, intelligence, and reading ability in school children. *Perceptual and Motor Skills,* 1965, *20,* 295–305.

Birch, H. G. and Gussow, J. D. *Disadvantaged children: health, nutrition and school failure.* New York: Harcourt, Brace, Janaovitch, 1970.

Birch, H. G. and Lefford, A. Intersensory development in children. *Monographs of the Society for Research in Child Development,* 1963, *28,* 5 (No. 89).

Black, F. W. EEG and birth abnormalities in high and low-perceiving reading retarded children. *Journal of Genetic Psychology,* 1972, *121,* 327–32.

Black, F. W Neurological dysfunction and reading disorders. *Journal of Learning Disabilities,* 1973, *6,* 313–316.

Black, F. W. WISC Verbal-Performance discrepancies as indicators ot neurological dysfunction in pediatric patients. *Journal of Clinical Psychology,* 1974, *30,* 165–167.

Black, F. W. Cognitive, academic, and behavioral findings in children with suspected and documented neurological dysfunction. *Journal of Learning Disabilities,* 1976, *9,* 55–60.

Black, S. and Walter, W. G. Effects on anterior brain responses of variation in the probability of association between stimuli. *Journal of Psychosomatic Research,* 1965, *9,* 33–43.

Blank, M. Cognitive processes in auditory discrimination in normal and retarded readers. *Child Development,* 1968, *39,* 1091–1101.

Blank, M., Berenzweig, S. S., and Bridger, W. H. The effects of stimulus complexity and sensory modality on reaction time in normal and retarded readers. *Child Development,* 1975, *46,* 133–140.

Blank, M. and Bridger, W. Deficiencies in verbal labeling in retarded readers. *American Journal of Orthopsychiatry,* 1966, *36,* 840–847.

Blank, M. and Bridger, W. H. Perceptual abilities and conceptual deficiencies in retarded readers. In J. Zubin and G. A. Jervis (Eds.), *Psychopathology of Mental Development.* New York: Grune & Stratton, 1967.

Blank, M., Weider, S., and Bridger, W. Verbal deficiencies in abstract thinking in early reading retardation. *American Journal of Orthopsychiatry*, 1968, *38*, 823–834.

Blau, H. and Blau, H. A theory of learning to read. *Reading Teacher*, 1968, *22*, 126–129.

Bliesner, E. P. and Yarborough, B. H. A comparison of ten different beginning reading programs in first grade. *Phi Delta Kappan*, 1965, *June*, 500–504.

Bloom, S. *Stability and change in human characteristics*. New York: Wiley, 1964.

Boder, E. Developmental dyslexia: a new diagnostic approach based on the identification of three subtypes. *Journal of School Health*, 1970, 40, 289–290.

Boder, E. Developmental dyslexia: a diagnostic screening procedure based on three characteristic patterns of reading and spelling. In B. Bateman (Ed.), *Learning Disorders*. Seattle: Special Child Publications, 1971.

Boder, E. Developmental dyslexia: prevailing diagnostic concepts and a new diagnostic approach. In H. Myklebust (Ed.) *Progress in Learning Disabilities* (Vol. II, pp. 293–321). New York: Grune & Stratton, 1971.

Boder, E. Developmental dyslexia: a diagnostic approach based on three atypical reading patterns. *Developmental Medicine and Child Neurology*, 1973, *15*, 663–687.

Boehm, A. E. *Boehm test of basic concepts*. New York: Psychological Corporation, 1969.

Bond, G. L. and Dykstra, R. The cooperative research program in first grade reading instruction. *Reading Research Quarterly*, 1967, *2*, 1–142.

Bond, G. L. and Tinker, M. A. *Reading difficulties: their diagnosis and correction*. New York: Appleton-Century-Crofts, 1967.

Botel, M. Methods and systems for teaching dyslexic pupils. In A. Keeney and V. Keeney (Eds.), *Dyslexia: Diagnosis and Treatment of Reading Disorders* (pp. 120–130). St. Louis: C. V. Mosby, 1968.

Bowles, S. and Gintis, H. I.Q. in the U.S. class structure. *Social Policy*, 1973, *3*, 65–96.

Bowley, A. Reading difficulty with neurological dysfunction: a study of children in junior schools. *Developmental Medicine & Child Neurology*, 1969, *11*, 493–503.

Branch, C., Milner, B., and Rasmussen, J. Intracarotid sodium amytal for the lateralization of cerebral dominance. *Journal of Neurosurgery*, 1964, *21*, 399–405.

Brandt, S. EEG findings in 200 children with mental retardation. *Electroencephalography & Clinical Neurophysiology*, 1957, *9*, 735.

Brewer, W. F. Paired-associate learning of dyslexic children. Unpublished doctoral dissertation, University of Iowa, 1967.

Broadbent, D. E. Immediate memory and simultaneous stimuli. *Quarterly Journal of Experimental Psychology*, 1957, 9, 1–11.

Brody, S. and Axelrad, S. *Anxiety and ego-formation in infancy*. New York: International Universities Press, 1970.

Bronfenbrenner, U. Developmental research, public policy, and the ecology of childhood. *Child Development*, 1974, *45*, 1–5.

Brophy, J. and Evertson, C. Process product correlations, *From* B. Rosenshine, "Classroom Instruction." In *The Psychology of Teaching Methods*. The 75th

Yearbook of the National Society for the Study of Education, Chicago: University of Chicago Press, 1976.

Brown, J. Some tests of the decay theory of immediate memory. *Quarterly Journal of Experimental Psychology*, 1958, *10*, 12–21.

Brown, R. *A first language—the early stages*. Cambridge: Harvard University Press, 1973.

Brown, W., Marsh, J., and Smith, J. Contextual meaning effects on speech evoked potentials. *Behavioral Biology*, 1973, *9*, 711.

Bruner, J. S. The course of cognitive growth. In N. S. Endler, L. R. Boulter, and H. Osser (Eds.), *Contemporary Issues in Developmental Psychology* (pp. 476–494). New York: Holt, Rinehart and Winston, 1968.

Bryant, N. D. Characteristics of dyslexia and their remedial implication. *Exceptional Children*, 1965, *31*, 195–199.

Bryant, N. Some principles of remedial instruction for dyslexia. In G. Natchez (Ed.) *Children with Reading Problems*. New York: Basic Books, 1968.

Bryant, N. and Friedlander, W. J. "14 + 6" in boys with specific reading disability. *Electroencephalography & Clinical Neurophysiology*, 1965, *19*, 322.

Bryant, P. E. Comments on the design of developmental studies of cross-modal matching and cross-modal transfer. *Cortex*, 1968, *4*, 127–128.

Bryant, P. E. Cross-modal development and reading. In D. D. Duane and M. B. Rawson (Eds.), *Reading, Perception and Language*. Baltimore: York Press, 1975.

Bryden, M. P. Laterality effects in dichotic listening: relations with handedness and reading ability in children. *Neuropsychologia*, 1970, *8*, 443–450.

Bryden, M. P. Auditory-visual and sequential-spatial matching in relation to reading ability. *Child Development*, 1972, *43*, 824–832.

Buchsbaum, M. and Fedio, P. Visual information and evoked responses from the left and right hemispheres. *Electroencephalography & Clinical Neurophysiology*, 1969, *26*, 266.

Buchsbaum, M. and Fedio, P. Hemispheric differences in evoked potentials to verbal and nonverbal stimuli in the left and right visual fields. *Physiology & Behavior*, 1970, *5*, 207.

Buerger, T. A. A follow-up of remedial reading instruction. *The Reading Teacher*, 1968, *21*, 329–334.

Burkott, A. and Clegg, A. Programmed vs. basal readers in remedial reading. *The Reading Teacher*, 1968, *2*, 745–748.

Burks, H. F. The effect on learning of brain pathology. *Exceptional Children*, 1957, *24*, 169–174.

Burns, G. W. A factor analytic study of the revised edition of the Illinois test of psycholinguistic abilities with under-achieving children, *Dissertation Abstracts International*, 1972, *33* (4-A) #1548.

Burns, S. A study of sequential memory skills in reading disabled and normal children. Unpublished doctoral dissertation, Northwestern University, 1975.

Buros, O. K. (Ed.) *Mental Measurements Yearbook* (6th ed.). Highland Park, N.J.: Gryphon Press, 1966.

Buros, O. K. (Ed.) *Mental Measurements Yearbook* (7th ed.). Highland Park, N.J.: Gryphon Press, 1972.

Buser, P. Nonspecific visual projections. In F. A. Young and D. B. Lindsley (Eds.), *Early Experience and Visual Information Processing in Perceptual and Reading Disorders* (pp. 157–166). Washington: National Academy of Science Publication Office, 1970.

Butler, S. Predicting reading failure in the infant school. Unpublished Ph.D. thesis, University of London, 1971.

Caldwell, B. M. The usefulness of the critical period hypothesis in the study of filiative behavior. In N. S. Endler, L. R. Boulter, and H. Osser (Eds.), *Contemporary Issues in Developmental Psychology* (pp. 213–223). New York: Holt, Rinehart and Winston, 1968.

Calfee, R. C. Memory and cognitive skills in reading acquisition. In D. D. Duane and M. R. Rawson (Eds.), *Reading, Perception & Language*. Baltimore: York Press, 1975.

Calfee, R. C. Assessment of independent reading skills: basic research and practical applications. In A. S. Reber and D. L. Scarborough (Eds.), *Towards a Psychology of Reading*. Hillside, N.J.: Erlbaum Associates, 1977.

Calfee, R. C., Venezky, R., and Chapman, R. *Pronunciation of synthetic words with predictable and unpredictable letter-sound correspondences* (Tech. Rep. No. 71). Madison: Wisconsin Research and Development Center, 1969.

Calloway, E. *Brain electrical potentials and individual psychological differences.* New York: Grune & Stratton, 1975.

Cameron, R. F., Currier, R. D., and Haerer, A. F. Aphasia and literacy, *British Journal of Disordered Communication,* 1971, 6, 161–163.

Capute, A. J., Niedermeyer, E. F. L., and Richardson, F. The electroencephalogram in children with minimal cerebral dysfunction. *Pediatrics,* 1968, 41, 1104–1114.

Carmon, A., Nachshon, I., and Starinsky, R. Developmental aspects of visual hemifield differences in perception of verbal material. *Brain and Language,* 1976, 3, 463–469.

Cashdan, A. Backward readers—research on auditory visual integration. In N. I. C. Gardner (Ed.), *Reading Skills: Theory and Practice.* London: Ward Lock Educational, 1970.

Cattell, P. *The measurement of intelligence in infants & young children.* New York: Psychological Corp., 1960.

Cavalli-Sforza, L. L. and Bodmer, W. F. *The genetics of human populations.* San Francisco: Freeman, 1971.

Cazden, C. B. *Child language and education.* New York: Holt, Rinehart and Winston, 1972.

CELDIC Report, *One million children: a national study of Canadian children with emotional and learning disorders.* Toronto, L. Crainford, 1970.

Chalfant, J. D. and Scheffelin, M. A. *Central processing dysfunction in children: a review of research.* Bethesda, Maryland: National Institute of Neurological Diseases and Stroke, Monograph No. 9, U.S. Public Health Service, 1969.

Chalke, F. C. R. and Ertl, J. Evoked potentials and intelligence. *Life Sciences,* 1965, 4, 1319–1322.

Chall, J. *Learning to read—The great debate.* New York: McGraw Hill, 1967.

Chall, J. and Feldmann, S. *A study in depth of first grade reading: an analysis of the interactions of professed methods, teacher implementation and child back-ground.* Final Report, project No. 2728, Cooperative Research Program of the Office of Education, U.S. Department of Health, Education, and Welfare, 1966.

Childs, S. Teaching the dyslexic child: dyslexia in special education. Monograph Vol. I. Pomfret, Conn., The Orton Society, 1964.

Chiofalo, N., Bravo, L., Perez, M., and Villavicencio, C. El electroencefalograma en niños con trastornos del aprendizaje. *Acta Neurologica Latino Americana,* 1971, *17,* 164–171.

Cicirelli, V. Project head start; a national evaluation: summary of the study. In D. C. Hays (Ed.), *Britannica Review of American Education.* Chicago: Encyclopedia Britannica, 1970.

Cicirelli, V., et al. The impact of head start: an evaluation of the effects of head start on children's cognitive and affective development. *Westinghouse Learning Corporation,* Ohio University under Contract B89-4536 with Office of Economic Opportunity, Washington, D.C., 1969.

Clark, M. M. *Reading difficulties in school.* Harmondsworth, England: Penguin, 1970.

Cohen, J. Learning disabilities and conditional brain activity. In R. Karrer (Ed.), *Developmental Psychophysiology of Mental Retardation* (pp. 334–360). Springfield, Ill., Charles C. Thomas, 1976.

Cohen, J. and Walter, W. G. The interaction of responses in the brain to semantic stimuli. *Psychophysiology,* 1966, *2,* 187–196.

Cohen, S. A. Studies in visual perception and reading in disadvantaged children. *Journal of Learning Disabilities,* 1969, *2,* 498–507.

Cohen, S. A. Minimal brain dysfunction and practical matters such as teaching kids to read. In F. de la Cruz, B. ox, and R. Roberts (Eds.), *Minimal Brain Dysfunction.* New York: Annals of the New York Academy of Sciences, 1973.

Cohen, S. A. The fuzziness and the flab: some solutions to research problems in learning disability, *Journal of Special Education.* 1976, *10,* 129–136.

Cohn, R. Delayed acquisition of reading and writing abilities in children: a neurological study. *Archives of Neurology,* 1961, *4,* 153–164.

Cohn, R. Dyscalculia. *Archives of Neurology,* 1961, *4,* 301–307.

Cohn R. Differential cerebral processing of noise and verbal stimuli. *Science,* 1971, 172–599.

Cohn, R. and Nardini, J. The correlation of bilateral occipital slow activity in the human EEG with certain disorders of behavior. *American Journal of Psychiatry,* 1958, *115,* 44–54.

Coleman, R. I. and Deutsch, C. P. Lateral dominance and right-left discrimination: a comparison of normal and retarded readers. *Perceptual and Motor Skills,* 1964, *19,* 43–50.

Conners, C. K. Cortical visual evoked response in children with learning disorders. *Psychophysiology,* 1970, 7, 418–428.

Conners, C. K. Letter to the Editor. *Psychophysiology,* 1972, *9,* 473.

Conners, C. K. Rating scales for use in drug studies with children. *Psychopharmacology Bulletin Special Issue,* 1973, 24–29.

Conrad, R. Acoustic confusions in immediate memory. *British Journal of Psychology,* 1964, *55*, 75–84.

Conrad, R. Order error in immediate recall of sequence. *Journal of Verbal Learning and Verbal Behavior,* 1965, *4*, 161–169.

Corballis, M. C. and Beale, I. L. Bilateral symmetry and behavior, *Psychological Review,* 1970, *77*, 451–464.

Corballis, M. C. and Beale, I. L. *The psychology of left and right.* Hillsdale, N.J.: Lawrence Erlbaum, 1976.

Corcelle, L., Rozier, J., Dedieu, E., Vincent, J. D., and Faure, L. Variations of cortical evoked potentials according to the modality of sensory stimulation in dyslexic children. *Review of Laryngoscopy (Bordeaux),* 1968, *89,* 458–468.

Corkin, S. Serial-ordering deficits in inferior readers. *Neuropsychologia,* 1974, *12,* 347–354.

Coury, P. and Nessa, D. B. *Memphis City School Screening,* Board of Education, Memphis City Schools, 1973.

Cox, A. Final report on language training of "Stanley Brown." *Bulletin of the Orton Society,* 1967, *17,* 63–67.

Craik, F. I. M. and Lockhart, R. S. Levels of processing: a frameword for memory research. *Journal of Verbal Learning & Verbal Behavior,* 1972, *11,* 671–684.

Crinella, F. M., Beck, F. W., and Robinson, J. W. Unilateral dominance is not related to neuropsychological integrity. *Child Development,* 1971, *42,* 2033–2054.

Critchley, M. *Developmental dyslexia.* Springfield, Ill.: Charles C. Thomas, 1964.

Critchley, M. Is development dyslexia the expression of minor cerebral damage? *Clinical Proceedings,* 1966, *23,* 213–222.

Critchley, M. Some observations upon developmental dyslexia. *Modern Trends in Neurology,* 1967, *4,* 135–144.

Critchley, M. Dysgraphia and other anomalies of written speech. *Pediatric Clinics of North America,* 1968, *15,* 639–650.

Critchley, M. *The Dyslexic Child.* Springfield, Ill.: Charles C. Thomas, 1970.

Critchley, M. Some problems of the ex-dyslexic. *Bulletin of the Orton Society,* 1973, *23,* 7–14.

Cronbach, L. J. and Snow, R. E. *Individual differences in learning ability as a function of instructional variables.* Final Report, 1969, School of Education, Stanford University, Contract No. OEC-4-6-061269-1217, U.S. Office of Education.

Crossman, E. R. F. W. Information and serial order in human immediate memory. In C. Cherry (Ed.), *Proceedings of the 4th London conference on information theory.* London: Butterworth, 1960.

Crowell, D., Jones, R., Kapuniai, L., and Nakagawa, J. Unilateral cortical activity in newborn humans; an early index of cerebral dominance. *Science,* 1973, *180,* 205.

Croxen, M. E. and Lytton, H. Reading disability and difficulties in finger localization and right-left discrimination. *Developmental Psychology,* 1971, *5,* 256–262.

Cruickshank, W. M. The problems of delayed recognition and its correction. In A. H. Keeney and V. T. Keeney (Eds.), *Dyslexia: Diagnosis and Treatment of Reading Disorders.* St. Louis: C. V. Mosby, 1968.

Cruickshank, W. M., Bentzen, F., Ratzeburg, F., and Tannhauser, M. *A Teaching method for brain-injured and hyperactive children.* Syracuse, N.Y.: Syracuse University Press, 1961.

Dale, P. S. *Language development: structure and function* (2nd ed.). New York: Holt, Rinehart and Winston, 1976.

Damasio, A. R. Varieties and significance of the alexias. *Archives of Neurology,* 1977, *34,* 325–326.

Damasio, A. R., Castro-Caldas, A., Grosso, J. T., and Ferro, J. M. Brain specialization for language does not depend on literacy. *Archives of Neurology,* 1976, *33,* 300–301.

Darby, R. Ear asymmetry phenomenon in dyslexic and normal children. Unpublished Master's thesis, University of Florida, 1974.

Das, J. P., Kirby, J., and Jarman, R. F. Simultaneous and successive syntheses: an alternative model for cognitive abilities. *Psychological Bulletin,* 1975, *82,* 87–103.

Das, N. N. and Gastaut, H. Variations de l'activité électrique du cerveau, du coeur, et des muscles squellettiques au cours de la méditation et de l'extase yogique. *Electroencephalography & Clinical Neurophysiology,* 1955, *6,* 211–219.

Datta, L. A report on evaluation studies of project head start. Office of Child Development, U.S. Department of Health, Education, and Welfare, Washington, D.C., 1969.

David, R., Butler, N., and Goldstein, H. *From birth to seven: a report of the national child development study.* London: Longman, 1972.

Davidenkow, S. N. and Dotsenko, S. N. Is an isloated affliction of the visual analysis of the first and second signal system possible? (Russian) *Journal of Higher Nervous Activity,* 1956, *6,* 1–14.

Davis, A. and Wada, J. Hemispheric asymmetry: frequence analysis of visual and auditory evoked responses to non-verbal stimuli. *Electroencephalography & Clinical Neurophysiology,* 1974, *37,* 1.

Davis, R. S. and Cashdan, A. Specific dyslexia. *British Journal of Educational Psychology,* 1963, *33,* 80–82.

Dean, J. Words in color. In J. Downing (Ed.), *The First International Reading Symposium.* New York: Day, 1966.

DeFries, J. C., Vandenberg, S. G., and McClearn, G. E. Genetics of specific cognitive abilities. *Annual Review of Genetics,* 1976, *10,* 179–207.

de Hirsch, K. Tests designed to discover potential reading difficulty. *American Journal of Orthopsychiatry,* 1957, *27,* 566–576.

de Hirsch, K. Prediction in reading disability: a review of the literature. In A. Hayes and A. Silver (Eds.), *Report of the Interdisciplinary Committee on Reading Disability.* Washington, D.C.: Center for Applied Linguistics, 1971.

de Hirsch, K., Jansky, J., and Langford, W. *Predicting reading failure.* New York: Harper and Row, 1966.

Denckla, M. B. Color-naming defects in dyslexic boys. *Cortex,* 1972a, *8,* 164–176.

Denckla, M. B. Performance on color tasks in kindergarten children. *Cortex,* 1972b, *8,* 177–190.

Denckla, M. B. Research needs in learning disabilities: A neurologist's point of view. *Journal of Learning Disabilities,* 1973, *6,* 44–450.

Denckla, M. B. Minimal brain dysfunction and dyslexia: beyond diagnosis by exclusion. In M. E. Blaw, I. Rapin, and M. Kinsbourne (Eds.), *Topics in Child Neurology*. New York: Spectrum Publications, 1977a.

Denckla, M. B. The neurological basis of reading disability. In F. G. Roswell and G. Natchez (Eds.), *Reading Disability: A Human Approach to Learning*. New York: Basic Books, 1977b.

Denckla, M. B. and Bowen, E. P. Dyslexia after left occipitotemporal lobectomy—a case report. *Cortex*, 1973, *9*, 321–328.

Denckla, M. B. and Rudel, R. G. Rapid "automatized" naming of pictured objects, colors, letters, and numbers by normal children. *Cortex*, 1974, *10*, 186–202.

Denckla, M. B. and Rudel, R. Naming of object-drawings by dyslexia and other learning disabled children. *Brain and Language*, 1976a, *3*, 1–15.

Denckla, M. and Rudel, R. Rapid "automatized" naming (R.A.N.): Dyslexia differentiated from other learning disabilities. *Neuropsychologia*, 1976b, *14*, 471–479.

Department of Education and Science. *Children with Specific Reading Difficulties*. Report of the Advisory Committee on Handicapped Children. London: HMSO, 1972.

Department of Education and Science. *A language for life*. The Bullock Report. London: HMSO, 1975.

Deutsch, C. P. Auditory discrimination and learning: social factors. *Merrill-Palmer Quarterly*, 1964, *10*, 277–296.

Dillard, J. L. *Black English*. New York: Random House, 1972.

Dirks, D. Perception of dichotic and monaural verbal material and cerebral dominance for speech. *Acta Otolaryngologica*, 1964, *58*, 73–80.

Doehring, D. G. *Patterns of impairment in specific reading disability*. Bloomington: Indiana University Press, 1968.

Doehring, D. G. Evaluation of two models of reading disability. In R. M. Knights and D. J. Bakker (Eds.), *The Neuropsychology of Learning Disorders*. Baltimore: University Park Press, 1976, (a).

Doehring, D. G. and Hoshko, I. M. Classification of reading problems by the O-technique of factor analysis. *Cortex*, 1977, *13*, 281–294.

Douglas, J. W. B., Ross, J. M., and Cooper, J. E. The relationship between handedness, attainment and adjustment in a national sample of school children. *Educational Research*, 1967, *9*, 223–233.

Douglas, V. I. Effects of medication on learning efficiency. In R. P. Anderson and C. G. Halcomb (Eds.), *Learning Disability—Minimal Brain Dysfunction Syndrome*. Springfield, Ill.: Charles C. Thomas, 1975.

Downing, J. *Comparative reading*. New York: Macmillan, 1973.

Downing, J. Cognitive factors in dyslexia. *Child Psychiatry and Human Development*, 1973, *4*, 115–120.

Downing, J. and Brown, A. L. (Eds.), *The Second International Reading Symposium*. London: Cassell, 1967.

Doyle, R. B., Andersen, R. P., and Halcomb, C. G. Attention deficits and the effect of visual distraction. *Journal of Learning Disabilities*, 1976, *9*, 48–54.

Drachman, D. A. and Hughes, J. R. Memory and the hippocampal complexes, III. Aging and temporal EEG abnormalities. *Neurology,* 1971, *21,* 1–14.

Drew, A. L. A neurological appraisal of familial word-blindness. *Brain,* 1956, *79,* 440–460.

Drillien, C. M. *The growth and development of the prematurely born infant* (p. 376). London: E. S. Livingston, Edinburgh, 1964.

Dunlop, D. B., Dunlop, P., and Fenelon, B. Vision laterality analysis in children with reading disability: the results of a new technique of examination. *Cortex,* 1973, *9,* 277–236.

Dykman, R. A., Ackerman, P. T., Clements, S. D., and Peters, J. E. Specific learning disabilities: at attentional deficit syndrome. In H. R. Myklebust (Ed.), *Progress in Learning Disabilities* (Vol. II, pp. 56–93). New York: Grune & Stratton, 1971.

Dykstra, R. The use of readiness tests for prediction and diagnosis: a critique. *Perspectives in Reading,* 1967, *8,* 35–50.

Dykstra, R. Summary of the second-grade phase of the cooperative research program in primary reading instruction. *Reading Research Quarterly,* 1968, *2,* 49–70.

Eakin, S. and Douglas, V. I. "Automatization" and oral reading problems in children. *Journal of Learning Disabilities,* 1971, *4,* 31–38.

Eason, R. G., Groves, P., White, C. T., and Oden, D. Evoked cortical potentials: relation to visual field and handedness. *Science,* 1967, *156,* 1643–1646.

Edwards, J. H. The simulation of mendelism. *Acta Genetica,* 1960, *10,* 63–70.

Edwards, R. P., Alley, G. R., and Snider, W. Academic achievement and minimal brain dysfunction. *Journal of Learning Disabilities,* 1971, *4,* 134–138.

Eeg-Olofsson, O. The development of the electroencephalogram in normal children from the age of 1 through 15. 14 and 6 Hz positive spike phenomenon. *Neuropaediatrie,* 1971, *2,* 405–427.

Efron, R. Temporal perception, aphasia, and déjà vu. *Brain,* 1963, *86,* 403–424.

Egan, D. F. et al. Developmental screening 0–5 years. *Clinics in Developmental Medicine,* No. 30. London, Heinemann, 1969.

Egeland, B. Training impulsive children in the use of more efficient scanning techniques. *Child Development,* 1974, *45,* 165–171.

Eisenberg, L. The epidemiology of reading retardation and a program for preventive intervention. In J. Money (Ed.), *The disabled reader: education of the dyslexic child.* Baltimore: Johns Hopkins Press, 1966.

Eisenberg, L. Clinical considerations in the psychiatric evaluation of intelligence. In J. Zubin and G. A. Jervis (Eds.), *Psychopathology of Mental Development.* New York: Grune and Stratton, 1967, 502–513.

Eisenberg, L. Psychiatric aspects of language disability. In D. D. Duane and M. B. Rawson (Eds.), *Reading, Perception and Language.* Baltimore: York Press, 1975, 215–230.

Eisenberg, L. Development as a unifying concept in psychiatry. *British Journal of Psychiatry,* 1977, *131,* 225–237.

Eisenberg, L. and Earls, F. J. Poverty, social depreciation and child development. In D. A. Hamburg and H. K. M. Brodie (Eds.), *American Handbook of Psychiatry* (Vol. VI, pp. 275–291). New York: Basic Books, 1975.

Elkind, D. and Deblinger, J. Perceptual training and reading achievement in disadvantaged children. *Child Development,* 1969, *40,* 11–19.

Elkonin, D. E. "U.S.S.R." in J. Downing (Ed.), *Comparative Reading.* New York: Macmillan, 1973.

Engelmann, S. Relationship between psychological theories and the act of teaching. *Journal of School Psychology,* 1967, *5,* 93–100.

Engelmann, S. *Conceptual Learning.* Sioux Falls, S.D.: Adapt Press, 1969.

Engelmann, S. and Bruner, E. C. *Distar Reading I and II: An Instructional System.* Chicago: Science Research Associates, 1969.

Erenberg, G., Mattis, S., and French, J. H. Four hundred children referred to an urban ghetto developmental disabilities clinic: computer assisted analysis of demographic, social, psychological, and medical data. (Unpublished manuscript)

Erhard, C. H. and Lempp, K. Zur Aetiologie der Legasthenie, *Praxis der Kinderpsychologie und Kinderpsychiatrie,* 1968, *17,* 161–164.

Ertl, J. P. and Schafer, E. W. P. Brain response correlates of psychometric intelligence. *Nature,* 1969, *223,* 421–422.

Estes, W. K. *Learning theory and mental development.* New York: Academic Press, 1970.

Eustis, R. S. The primary etiology of the specific language disabilities. *Journal of Pediatrics,* 1947a, *31,* 448–455.

Eustis, R. S. Specific reading disability. *New England Journal of Medicine,* 1947b, *237,* 243–249.

Farr, R. Reading, what can be measured? *Eric/Crier Reading Review Series* (p. 10). Newark, Delaware: International Reading Association, 1969.

Faure, J. M. A., Rozier, J., Bensch, C., Vincent, J. D., Corcelle, L., and Portmann, M. Potentiels associatifs evoqués par des stimulations combinées auditives et visuelles chez l'enfant amblyope fonctionnel strabique et chez l'enfant dyslexique. *Revue Neurologique,* 1968, *118,* 502–512.

Fenelon, B. Expectancy waves and other complex cerebral events in dyslexic and normal subjects. *Psychonomic Science,* 1968, *13,* 253–254.

Fenelon, B., Holland, J. R., and Johnson, C. Spatial organization of the EEG in children with reading disabilities: a study using nitrazepam. *Cortex,* 1972, *8,* 444–464.

Fernald, G. *Remedial techniques in basic school subjects.* New York: McGraw Hill, 1943.

Feshbach, S., Adelman, H., and Fuller, W. W. Early identification of children with high risk of reading failure. Paper presented at the American Educational Research Association Meeting, New Orleans, 1973.

Finlayson, M. A. J. and Reitan, R. M. Tactile-perceptual functioning in relation to intellectual, cognitive and reading skills in younger and older normal children. *Developmental Medicine and Child Neurology,* 1976, *18,* 442–446.

Finucci, J. M., Guthrie, J. T., Childs, A. L., Abbey, H., and Childs, B. The genetics of specific reading disability. *Annals of Human Genetics,* 1976, *40,* 1–23.

Flavell, J., Beach, D., and Chinsky, J. Spontaneous verbal rehearsal in a memory task as a function of age. *Child Development,* 1966, *37,* 283–299.

Flax, N. Visual function in dyslexia. *American Journal of Optometry*, 1969, *45*, 574–586.

Flax, N. The contribution of visual problems to learning disability. *Journal of the American Optometric Association*, 1970, *41*, 10.

Fletcher, J. M. and Satz, P. Developmental changes associated with reading disability: a multivariate test of a theory. (Unpublished manuscript)

Folling, A. Ueber Ausscheidung von Phenylbrenztraubensäure in den Harn als Stoffwechselanomalie in Verbindung mit Imbezillität. *Zeitschrift fuer Physiologische Chemie*, 1934, *227*, 169–176.

Ford, F. *Diseases of the nervous system in infancy, childhood and adolescence* (3rd ed.). Springfield, Ill.: Charles C. Thomas, 1951.

Fort Worth Public Schools. *Pre-school screening instrument.* Fort Worth: Department of Curriculum, 1973.

Fox, F. J., Orr, R. R., and Rourke, B. P. Shortcomings of the standard optometric visual analysis for the diagnosis of reading problems. *Canadian Journal of Optometry*, 1975, *37*, 57–61.

Frank, J. and Levinson, H. Dysmetric dyslexia and dyspraxia. *Journal of Child Psychiatry*, 1973, *12*, 690–701.

Frank, S. M. and Osser, H. A psycholinguistic model of syntactic complexity. *Language and Speech*, 1970, *13*, 38–53.

Franklin, A. W. (Ed.) *Word Blindness or Specific Developmental Dyslexia.* London: Pitman, 1962.

Friedes, D. Human information processing and sensory modality: cross-modal functions, information complexity, memory and deficit. *Psychological Bulletin*, 1974, *81*, 284–310.

Friedman, D., Simson, R., Ritter, W., and Rapid, I. Cortical evoked potentials elicited by real speech words and human sounds. *Electroencephalography & Clinical Neurophysiology*, 1975, *38*, 13.

Frierson, E. The educator's dilemma in dyslexia and learning disability, *CEC DCLD Newsletter*, 1976, *1*, 15–21.

Frisk, M., Wegelius, E., Tenhunen, T., Widholm, O., and Hortling, H. The problem of dyslexia in teenage. *Acta Paediatrica Scandinavica*, 1967, *56*, 333–343.

Frostig, M. and Horne, D. *The Frostig Program for the Development of Visual Perception.* Chicago: Follett, 1964.

Frostig, M., Leferver, D., and Whittlesey, J. *The Marianne Frostig Developmental Test of Visual Perception.* Palo Alto, Cal.: Consulting Psychologists Press, 1964.

Frostig, M. and Maslow, P. *Learning problems in the classroom: prevention and remediation.* New York: Grune & Stratton, 1973.

Fry, M. A. A transformational analysis of the oral language structure used by two reading groups at the second grade level. Unpublished doctoral dissertation, University of Iowa, 1967.

Fry, M. A., Johnson, C. S., and Muehl, S. Oral language production in relation to reading achievement among select second graders. In D. J. Bakker and P. Satz (Eds.), *Specific Reading Disability: Advances in Theory and Method.* Rotterdam: Rotterdam University Press, 1970.

Fuglsang-Frederiksen, V. The EEG in mental deficiency. *Electroencephalography & Clinical Neurophysiology,* 1961, *13,* 481.

Fuller, G. B. and Friedrich, D. The diagnostic patterns of reading disabilities. *Academic Therapy,* 1975, *10,* 210–231.

Gaarder, K., Koreski, R., and Kropfl, W. The phasic relation of a component of alpha rhythm to fixation saccadic eye movements. *Electroencephalography & Clinical Neurophysiology,* 1966, *21,* 544–551.

Gaarder, K., Krauskopf, J., Graf, V., Kropfl, N., and Armington, I. Averaged brain activity following saccadic eye movements. *Science,* 1964, *146,* 1481–1483.

Gaddes, W. Learning disabilities: prevalence estimates and the need for definition. In R. Knights and D. J. Bakker (Eds.), *The Neuropsychology of Learning Disorders.* Baltimore: University Park Press, 1976.

Galambos, R., Benson, P., Smith, T., Schulman, Galambos, C., and Osier, H. On hemispheric differences in evoked potentials to speech stimuli. *Electroencephalography & Clinical Neurophysiology,* 1975, *39,* 379.

Galante, M. B., Flye, M. E., and Stephens, L. S. Cumulative minor deficits: a longitudinal study of the relation of physical factors to school achievement. *Journal of Learning Disabilities,* 1972, *5,* 75–80.

Gallagher, J. J. and Bradley, R. H. Early identification of developmental difficulties. In I. J. Gordon (Ed.), *Early Childhood Education.* Chicago: University of Chicago Press, 1972, 291–303.

Gardner, J. *Excellence.* New York: Harper and Row, 1961.

Garner, W. R., Hake, H. W., and Eriksen, C. W. Operationism and the concept of perception. *Psychological Review,* 1956, *63,* 149–159.

Gascon, G. and Goodglass, H. Reading retardation and the information content of stimuli in paired associate learning. *Cortex,* 1970, *8,* 417–429.

Gates, A. I. *The improvement of reading* (3rd ed.). New York: Macmillan, 1947.

Gates, A. I. The role of personality maladjustment in reading disability. In G. Natchez (Ed.), *Children with Reading Problems* (pp. 80–86). New York: Basic Books, 1968.

Gates, A. I. and MacGinitie, W. *Gates-MacGinitie Reading Readiness Tests.* New York: Teachers College Press, 1968.

Gates, R. R. The inheritance of mental defect. *British Journal of Medical Psychology,* 1933, *13,* 254–267.

Gattegno, C. and Hinman, D. Words in color. In J. Money and G. Schiffman (Eds.), *The Disabled Reader.* Baltimore: Johns Hopkins Press, 1966.

Gazzaniga, M. S. *The bisected brain.* New York: Appleton-Century-Crofts, 1970.

Geller, M. and Geller, A. Brief amnestic effects of spike-wave discharges. *Neurology (Minneapolis),* 1970, *20,* 1089–1095.

Gerson, I. M., Barnes, T. C., Mannino, A., Fanning, J. M., and Burns, J. J. EEG of children with various learning problems. I. Outpatient study. *Dis. Nerv. Syst.,* 1972, *33,* 170–177.

Geschwind, N. The anatomy of acquired disorders of reading. In J. Money (Ed.), *Reading Disability: Progress and Research Needs in Dyslexia* (pp. 115–129). Baltimore: Johns Hopkins Press, 1962.

Geschwind, N. The organization of language and the brain, *Science*, 1970, *170*, 940–944.

Gesell, A. *Infant development*. New York: Harper Brothers, 1952.

Gesell, A. and Amatruda, C. *Developmental diagnosis* (p. 496). New York: Paul Hoeber, 1941.

Gesell, A. and Thompson, H. *The psychology of early growth*. New York: Macmillan, 1938.

Getman, G. N. *How to develop your child's intelligence*. Luverne, Minn.: Announcer Press, 1962.

Gibbs, E. L., Lorimer, F. M., and Gibbs, F. A. Clinical correlates of exceedingly fast activity in the electroencephalogram. *Diseases Nervous System*, 1950, *11*, 323–326.

Gibbs, F. A. and Gibbs, E. L. Thalamic and hypothalamic epilepsy. In *Atlas of Electroencephalography* (Vol. 2, pp. 329–345). Cambridge, Mass.: Addison-Wesley, 1952.

Gibbs, F. A. and Gibbs, E. L. *Atlas of Electroencephalography* (Vol. 3). Cambridge, Mass.: Addison-Wesley, 1964.

Gibson, E. Learning to read. *Science*, 1965, *148*, 1066–1072.

Gibson, E. J. Learning to read. In N. S. Endler, L. R. Boulter, and H. Osser (Eds.), *Contemporary Issues in Developmental Psychology*. New York: Holt, Rinehart and Winston, 1968.

Gibson, E. J. *Principles of perceptual learning and development*. New York: Appleton-Century-Crofts, 1969.

Gibson, E. J. Perceptual learning and the theory of word perception. *Cognitive Psychology*, 1971, *2*, 351–368.

Gibson, E. J. and Levin, H. *The psychology of reading*. Cambridge, Mass.: MIT Press, 1975.

Gillingham, A. and Stillman, B. *Remedial training for children with specific disability in reading, spelling and penmanship*. Cambridge, Mass.: Educators Publishing Service, 1960.

Gilmore, J. V. *Gilmore Oral Reading Test*. New York: Harcourt, Brace and World, 1968.

Gleitman, L. and Rozin, P. Teaching reading by use of a syllabary. *Reading Research Quarterly*, 1973, *3*, 447–483.

Goddard, H. H. *Feeblemindedness: its causes and consequences*. New York: Macmillan, 1914.

Goetzinger, C. P., Dirks, D. D., and Baer, C. J. Auditory discrimination and visual perception in good and poor readers. *Annals of Otolaryngology, Rhinology, and Laryngology*, 1960, *69*, 121–136.

Goldberg, H. Vision, perception and related factors in dyslexia. In A. Keeney and V. Keeney (Eds.) *Dyslexia*. St. Louis: C. V. Mosby, 1968.

Goldberg, H. K. and Arnott, W. Ocular motility in learning disabilities. *Journal of Learning Disabilities*, 1970, *3*, 160–166.

Goodman, K. S. Dialect barriers to reading comprehension. *Elementary English*, 1965, *42*, 853–860.

Goodman, K. D. The psycholinguistic nature of the reading process. In K. S. Goodman (Ed.), *The Psycholinguistic Nature of the Reading Process.* Detroit: Wayne State University Press, 1968.

Gottesman, I. I. Severity/concordance and diagnostic refinement in the Maudsley-Bethlem schizophrenic twin study. In D. Rosenthal and S. S. Kety (Eds.), *The Transmission of Schizophrenia.* Oxford: Pergamon, 1968.

Gottesman, R., Belmont, I., and Kaminer, R. Admission and follow-up status of reading disabled children referred to a medical clinic. *Journal of Learning Disabilities,* 1975, *8,* 642–650.

Gottschalk, J., Bryden, M. P., and Rabinovitch, M. S. Spatial organization of children's responses to a pictorial display. *Child Development,* 1964, *35,* 811–815.

Goyen, J. D. and Lyle, J. Effect of incentives and age on the visual recognition of retarded readers. *Journal of Experimental Child Psychology,* 1971a, *11,* 266–273.

Goyen, J. D. and Lyle, J. Effect of incentives upon retarded and normal readers on a visual-associate learning task. *Journal of Experimental Child Psychology,* 1971b, *11,* 274–280.

Goyen, J. D. and Lyle, J. Short-term memory and visual discrimination in retarded readers. *Perceptual and Motor Skills,* 1973, *36,* 403–408.

Gray, S. W. and Klaus, R. A. *The early training project: a seventh year report.* Nashville, Tenn.: George Peabody College for Teachers, 1970.

Green, J. B. Association of behavior disorder with an EEG focus in children without seizures. *Neurology,* 1961, *11,* 337–344.

Griffiths, R. *The abilities of babies.* London: University of London Press, 1954.

Groenendall, H. A. and Bakker, D. J. The part played by mediation processes in the retention of temporal sequences by two reading groups. *Human Development,* 1971, *14,* 62–70.

Gruen, R. S. Prediction of end-of-year reading achievement for first and third grade pupils. *Proceedings of the American Psychological Association,* 1972, 563–564.

Grunewald-Zuberbier, E., Grunewald, G., and Rasche, A. Hyperactive behavior and EEG arousal reactions in children. *Electroencephalography and Clinical Neurophysiology,* 1975, *38,* 149–159.

Gubbay, S. S., Ellis, E., Walton, J. N., and Court, D. M. Clumsy children: a study of aproxic and agnosic defects in 21 children. *Brain,* 1965, *88,* 295–312.

Guyer, B. L. and Friedman, M. P. Hemispheric processing and cognitive styles in learning-disabled and normal children. *Child Development,* 1975, *46,* 658–668.

Guthrie, J. T. Reading comprehension and syntactic responses in good and poor readers. *Journal of Educational Psychology,* 1973a, *65,* 294–299.

Guthrie, J. T. Models of reading and reading disability. *Journal of Educational Psychology,* 1973b, *15,* 663–687.

Guthrie, J. T., Seifert, M., and Kline L. Clues from research on programs for poor readers. In S. J. Samuels (Ed.), *What Research Says to Classroom Teachers.* Newark, Del., International Reading Association, 1977.

Guthrie, J. T. and Tyler, S. Psycholinguistic processing in reading and listening among good and poor readers. *Journal of Reading Behavior,* 1976, *8,* 415–426.

Guthrie, J. T. and Tyler, S. *Cognition and instruction of poor readers.* (Unpublished manuscript)

Haaland, K. The effect of dichotic, monaural, and diotic verbal stimuli on auditory evoked potentials. *Neuropsychologia,* 1974, *12,* 339–345.

Haeussermann, E. *Developmental potential of pre-school children.* New York: Grune & Stratton, 1958.

Hagen, J. W., Jongeward, R. H., and Kail, R. V. Cognitive perspectives on the development of memory. In H. W. Reese (Ed.), *Advances in Child Development and Behavior* (Vol. 10), 57–101. New York: Academic Press, 1975.

Hagger, T. D. Congenital word blindness or specific developmental dyslexia: a review. *The Medical Journal of Australia,* 1968, *1,* 783–789.

Hagin, R. A. and Silver, A. A. Learning disability: definition, diagnosis and prevention. *New York University Education Quarterly,* 1977, *8,* 9–16.

Hagin, R. A., Silver, A. A., and Kreeger, H. *Teach.* New York: Walker Educational Book Corp., 1976.

Hainsworth, P. and Siqueland, M. *Meeting Street School Screening Test.* Providence, R.I.: Crippled Children and Adults of Rhode Island, 1969.

Hall, R. J., Keogh, B. K., and Becker, L. D. Follow up of kindergarten high risk pupils in the primary grades. *Technical Report* 1975–79. Graduate School of Education, University of California, Los Angeles, Dec. 1975.

Hallahan, D. P. and Kaufmann, J. M. *Introduction to learning disabilities: a psycho-behavioral approach.* Englewood Cliffs, N.J.: Prentice Hall, 1976.

Hallgren, B. Specific dyslexia ("congenital word blindness"): a clinical and genetic study. *Acta Psychiatrica et Neurologica Scandinavica,* 1950, Supplement No. 65.

Hammill, D. Training visual perceptual processes. *Journal of Learning Disabilities,* 1972, *5,* 552–560.

Hammill, D. D., Goodman, L., and Weiderholt, J. L. Visual-motor processes: Can we train them? *The Reading Teacher,* 1974, *27,* 469–478.

Hammill, D. D. and Larsen, S. C. Relationship of selected auditory perceptual skills and reading ability. *Journal of Learning Disability,* 1974, *7,* 429–435.

Hanley, J. and Sklar, B. Electroencephalic correlates of developmental reading dyslexics: computer analysis of recordings from normal and dyslexic children. In G. Leisman (Ed.), *Basic Visual Process and Learning Disability,* 212–243. Springfield, Ill.: Charles C. Thomas, 1976.

Hardy, M. Development of beginning reading skills: recent findings. In *Reading and Related Skills.* Proceedings of the 9th Annual Study Conference of UKRA. London: Ward Lock Publishers, 1973.

Harmony, T., Otero, R., Fernandez, G., Llorente, S., and Valdes, P.: Symmetry of visual evoked potential in normal subjects. *Electroencephalography and Clinical Neurophysiology,* 1973, *35,* 237.

Harris, A. *How to Increase Reading Ability* (5th ed.). New York: David McKay, 1970.

Harris, A. J. Practical applications of reading research. *The Reading Teacher*, 1976, *29*, 559–565.

Harris, A. and Serwer, B. The Craft Project: instructional time in reading research. *Reading Research Quarterly*, 1966, *2*, 27–57.

Hartlage, L. C. and Green, J. B. The EEG as a predictor of intellective and academic performance. *Journal of Learning Disabilities*, 1973, *6*, 239–242.

Hartlage, L. C., Lucas, D., and Main, W. Comparison of three approaches to teaching reading skills. *Perceptual and Motor Skills*, 1972, *34*, 231–232.

Hartlage, L. C. and Lucas, D. *Pre-reading expectancy scales*. Jacksonville, Ill.: Psychologists and Educators, 1973.

Hartstein, J. *Current concepts in dyslexia*. St. Louis: C. V. Mosby, 1971.

Hauser, S. L., DeLong, G. R., and Rosman, N. P. Pneumographic findings in the infantile autism syndrome: a correlation with temporal lobe disease. *Brain*, 1975, *98*, 667–688.

Hayes, C. J. A. Two types of reading failure: the role of temporal order perception and operant remediation. Unpublished Ph.D. thesis, University of London, 1975.

Healy, A. F. Separating item from order information in short-term memory. *Journal of Verbal Learning and Verbal Behavior*, 1974, *13*, 644–655.

Hebb, D. The semi-autonomous process: its nature and nurture. *American Psychologist*, 1963, *18*, 16–27.

Hécaen, H. and Kremin, H. Neurolinguistic research on reading disorders resulting from left hemisphere lesions: aphasic and "pure" alexias. In H. Whitaker and H. A. Whitaker (Eds.), *Studies in Neurolinguistics* (Vol. 2). New York: Academic Press, 1976.

Heiman, J. R. and Ross, A. O. Saccadic eye movements and reading difficulties. *Journal of Abnormal Child Psychology*, 1974, *2*, 53–62.

Helfgott, J. Phonemic segmentation and blending skills of kindergarten children: implications for beginning reading acquisition. *Contemporary Educational Psychology*, 1976, *1*, 157–169.

Helveston, E. M., Billips, W. C., and Weber, J. C. Controlling eye-dominant hemisphere relationships as a factor in reading ability. *American Journal of Ophthalmology*, 1970, *70*, 96–100.

Herjanic, B. and Penick, E. C. Adult outcome of disabled child readers. *Journal of Special Education*, 1972, *6*, 397–410.

Hermann, K. *Reading disability: a medical study of word-blindness and related handicaps*. Copenhagen: Munksgaard, 1959.

Heron, W. Perception as a function of retinal locus and attention. *American Journal of Psychology*, 1957, *70*, 38–48.

Hess, R. D. and Baer, R. M. (Eds.), *Early education*. Chicago: Aldine, 1968.

Hildreth, G., Griffiths, N., and McGauvran, N. *Metropolitan Readiness Tests*. New York: Harcourt, Brace and World, 1965.

Hinshelwood, J. Word blindness and visual memory. *Lancet*, 1895, *2*, 1564–1570.

Hinshelwood, J. *Letter-word and mind-blindness*. London: H. K. Lewis, 1900.

Hinshelwood, J. Congenital word-blindness. *Lancet*, 1900, *1*, 1506–1508.

Hinshelwood, J. Congenital word-blindness, with reports of to cases. *Ophthalmology Review*, 1902, *21*, 91–99.

Hinshelwood, J. A case of congenital word-blindness. *British Medical Journal,* 1904, *2,* 1303–1307.

Hinshelwood, J. *Congenital word-blindness.* London: H. K. Lewis, 1917.

Hirsh, I. J. Auditory perception of temporal order. *The Journal of the Acoustical Society of America,* 1959, *31,* 759–767.

Hirsh, I. J. and Sherrick, C. E. Perceived order in different sense modalities. *Journal of Experimental Psychology,* 1961, *64,* 1–19.

Hirt, D. Teaching children with severe learning disabilities. *The Reading Teacher,* 1970, *23,* 304–310.

Hochberg, J. Attention and perception in reading. In F. A. Young and D. B. Lindsley (Eds.), *Early Experience and Visual Information Processing in Perceptual and Reading Disorders.* Washington, D.C.: National Academy of Sciences, 1970.

Hollingworth, L. S. *Special talents and defects: their significance for education.* New York, Macmillan, 1923.

Holmes, J. M., Marshall, J. D., and Newcombe, F. Syntactic class as a determinant of word-retrieval in normal and dyslexic subjects. *Nature,* 1971, *234,* 418.

Honzik, M. P. Developmental studies of parent-child resemblance in intelligence. *Child Development,* 1957, *28,* 215–228.

Hook, P. A study of metalinguistic awareness and reading strategies in proficient and learning disabled readers. Unpublished doctoral dissertation, Northwestern University, 1976.

Huelsman, C. R. The WISC subtest syndrome for disabled readers. *Perceptual and Motor Skills,* 1970, *30,* 535–550.

Hughes, J. R. A review of the positive spike phenomenon. In W. E. Wilson (Ed.) *Applications of Electroencephalography in Psychiatry.* Durham, N.C., Duke University Press, 1965.

Hughes, J. R. Electronencephalography and learning. In H. R. Myklebust (Ed.), *Progress in Learning Disabilities* (Vol. 1). New York: Grune and Stratton, 1968.

Hughes, J. R. Electroencephalography and learning disabilities. In H. R. Myklebust (Ed.), *Progress in Learning Disabilities* (Vol. 2). New York: Grune and Stratton, 1971.

Hughes, J. R. Biochemical and electroencephalographic correlates of learning disabilities. In R. M. Knights and D. J. Bakker (Eds.), *Neuropsychology of Learning Disorders: Theoretical Approaches.* Baltimore: University Park Press, 1976.

Hughes, J. R. and Park, G. E. The EEG in dyslexia. In P. Kellaway and I. Petersen (Eds.), *Clinical Electroencephalography of Children* (pp. 307–327). Stockholm: Almquist and Wiksell, 1968.

Hunt, J. McV. *Intelligence and experience.* New York: Ronald Press, 1961.

Hutt, S. J., Lee, D., and Ounsted, D. Digit memory and evoked discharges in four right-sensitive epileptic children. *Developmental Medicine and Child Neurology,* 1963, *5,* 559–577.

Huttenlocher, P. R. and Huttenlocher, J. A study of children with hyperlexia. *Neurology,* 1973, *23,* 1107–1116.

Illingsworth, R. S. *The development of the infant and young child* (p. 377). London: Churchill Livingston, 1974.

Ingram, T. T. S. and Reid, J. F. Developmental aphasia observed in a department of child psychiatry. *Archives of Disorders of Childhood,* 1956, *31,* 161.

Ingram, T. T. S. Paediatric aspects of specific developmental dysphasia, dyslexia, and dysgraphia. *Cerebral Palsy Bulletin,* 1960, *2,* 254–277.

Ingram, T. T. S. The nature of dyslexia. In F. A. Young and D. B. Lindsley (Eds.), *Early Experience and Visual Information Processing in Perceptual and Reading Disorders.* Washington, D.C.: National Academy of Sciences, 1970.

Ingram, T. T. S., Mason, A. W., and Blackburn, I. A retrospective study of 82 children with reading disability. *Developmental Medicine and Child Neurology,* 1970, *12,* 271–281.

Ingram, D. Cerebral speech lateralization in young children. *Neuropsychologia,* 1975, *13,* 103–105.

International Reading Association, Report of Disabled Reader Committee. *The Reading Teacher,* 1972, 26, 341.

Jansky, J. The contribution of certain kindergarten abilities to second grade reading and spelling achievement. Unpublished Ph.D. thesis, Columbia University, 1970.

Jansky, J. Early prediction of reading problems. *Bulletin of the Orton Society,* 1973, *23.*

Jansky, J. The marginally ready child. *Bulletin of the Orton Society,* 1975, *25,* 69–85.

Jansky, J. and de Hirsch, K. *Preventing reading failure—prediction, diagnosis, intervention.* New York: Harper and Row, 1972.

Jasper, H. H., Bradley, C., and Soloman, P. EEG analysis of behavior problem children. *American Journal of Psychiatry,* 1938, *95,* 641–658.

Johnson, D. Treatment approaches to dyslexia. *International Reading Association: Conference Proceedings,* 1969, *13,* 95–102.

Johnson, D. Educational planning for children with learning disabilities. Paper presented at the 7th Annual Convention of the Association for Children with Learning Disabilities. Philadelphia, 1970.

Johnson, D. and Myklebust, H. Dyslexia in childhood. In J. Hellmuth (Ed.), *Learning Disorders* (Vol. 1, pp. 259–292). Seattle: Special Child Publications, 1965.

Johnson, D. J. and Myklebust, H. R. *Learning disabilities.* New York: Grune & Stratton, 1967.

Johnson, M. Tracing and kinesthetic techniques. In J. Money and G. Schiffman (Eds.), *The Disabled Reader.* Baltimore: The Johns Hopkins Press, 1966.

Johnson, R. C. and Abelson, R. B. Intellectual, behavioral, and physical characteristics associated with trisomy, translocation, and mosaic types of Down's syndrome. *American Journal of Mental Deficiency,* 1969, *73,* 852–855.

Jones, J. *Intersensory transfer, perceptual shifting, modal preference and reading.* Newark: ERIC/CRIER and the International Reading Association, 1972.

Kagan, J. Reflection—impulsivity and reading ability in primary grade children. *Child Development,* 1965, *36,* 609–628.

Kagen, B. Om ordblindhet. Pedagog. Skrifter 179–180:60 Stockholm, 1943.

Kahn, D. and Birch, H. G. Development of auditory-visual integration and reading achievement. *Percept. Mot. Skills,* 1968, *27,* 459–468.

Karnes, M. B., Hodgins, A. S., Testa, J. A., et al. *Research and Development Program on Preschool Disadvantaged Children* (Vol. 1). U.S. Office of Education, Washington, D.C., 1969.

Kastner, S. B. and Rickards, C. Mediated memory with novel and familiar stimuli in good and poor readers. *The Journal of Genetic Psychology,* 1974, *124,* 105–113.

Katz, J. The use of staggered spondaic words for assessing the integrity of the auditory system. *Journal of Auditory Research,* 1962, 2, 327–337.

Katz, L. and Wicklund, D. Word scanning rates for good and poor readers. *Journal of Educational Psychology,* 1971, *62,* 138–140.

Katz, L. and Wicklund, D. Letter scanning rate for good and poor readers in grades two and six. *Journal of Educational Psychology,* 1972, *63,* 363–367.

Katz, P. A. and Deutsch, M. The relationship of auditory and visual functioning to reading achievement in disadvantaged children. Paper presented at the Society for Research in Child Development, New York, March 1967.

Kawi, A. A. and Pasamanick, B. P. Association of factors of pregnancy with reading disorders in childhood. *Journal of the American Medical Association,* 1958, *166,* 1420–1423.

Kawi, A. A. and Pasamanick, B. Prennatal and perinatal factors in the development of childhood reading disorders. *Monographs of the Society for Research in Child Development,* 1959, *24.*

Keeney, A. H. and Keeney, V. T. *Dyslexia: diagnosis and treatment of reading disorders.* St. Louis: C. V. Mosby, 1968.

Kellaway, P., Crawley, J. W., and Kagawa, N. A specific electroencephalographic correlate of convulsive equivalent disorders in children. *Journal of Pediatrics,* 1959, *55,* 582–592.

Kellmer-Pringle, M. L., Butler, N. R., and Davie, R. *11,000 Seven-Year-Olds, Studies in Child Development.* London: Longmans, 1966.

Kennard, M. A., Rabinovitch, R., and Wexler, D. The abnormal electroencephalogram as related to reading disability in children with disorders of behavior. *Canadian Medical Association Journal,* 1952, *67,* 330–333.

Kenny, T. J., Clemmens, R. L., Cicci, R., Lentz, G. A., Nair, P., and Hudson, B. W. The medical evaluation of children with reading problems. *Pediatrics,* 1972, *49,* 438–442.

Keogh, B. and Becker, L. Early detection of learning problems, cautions and guidelines. *Exceptional Children,* 1973, *40,* 5–11.

Kephart, N. The slow learner in the classroom. Columbus, Ohio: Charles E. Merrill, 1960.

Kephart, N. C. Let's not misunderstand DYSLEXIA. *The Instructor,* 1968, *78,* 62–63.

Kershner, J. R. Cerebral dominance in disabled readers, good readers, and gifted children. *Child Development,* 1977, *48,* 61–67.

Kimura, D. Cerebral dominance and the perception of verbal stimuli. *Canadian Psychologist,* 1961, *15,* 166–171.

Kimura, D. Dual functional asymmetry of the brain in visual perception. *Neuropsychologia,* 1966, *4,* 275–285.

Kimura, D. Functional asymmetry of the brain in dichotic listening. *Cortex*, 1967, *3*, 163–178.

Kimura, D. Cerebral dominance for speech. In D. B. Tower (Ed.), *The Nervous System* (Vol. 3), Human communication and its disorders. New York: Raven Press, 1975.

Kinsbourne, M. Looking and listening strategies and beginning reading. In: J. T. Guthrie (Ed.), *Aspects of Reading Acquisition*, 141–161. Baltimore: Johns Hopkins University Press, 1976.

Kinsbourne, H. and Smith, W. L. *Hemispheric disconnection and cerebral function*. Springfield: C. C. Thomas, 1974.

Kinsbourne, M. and Warrington, E. K. Developmental factors in reading and writing backwardness. *British Journal of Psychology*, 1963a, *54*, 145–156.

Kinsbourne, M. and Warrington, E. K. The developmental Gerstmann syndrome. *Archives of Neurology*, 1963b, *8*, 490–501.

Kirk, S. A. *Educating exceptional children*. Boston: Houghton-Mifflin, 1972.

Kirk, S., McCarthy, J., and Kirk, W. *Illinois of psycholinguistic abilities, examiner's manual*. Urbana: University of Illinois Press, 1961a.

Kirk, S., McCarthy, J., and Kirk, W. The Illinois Test of Psycholinguistic Abilities—an approach to differential diagnosis. *American Journal of Mental Deficiency*, 1961b, *66*, 399–412.

Kirk, S., McCarthy, J., and Kirk, W. *The Illinois Test of Psycholinguistic Abilities*, Rev. Ed. Urbana, Ill.: University of Illinois Press, 1968.

Klaus, R. A. and Gray, S. W. The early training project for disadvantaged: A report after 5 years. *Monographs of the Society for Research in Child Development*, 1968, 120.

Kline, C. L. The adolescents with learning problems: How long must they wait? *Journal of Learning Disabilities*, 1972, *5*, 127–144.

Kline, C. and Kline, C. Follow-up study of 216 dyslexic children. *Bulletin of the Orton Society*, 1975, *25*, 127–144.

Klinkerfuss, G. H., Lang, P. H., Weinberg, W. A. and O'Leary, J. L. EEG abnormalities of children with hyperkinetic behavior. *Neurology* (Minneapolis), 1965, *15*, 883–896.

Knabe, G., Missberger, V., and Schmiedeberg, J. Die Arbeit mit einer Gruppe begabter lese-rechtschreib-schwacher Kinder in Koeln (Ein vorlaeufiges Modell zur Diskussion fortgeschrittenen Sondererziehungssystemen in den heutigen und zukuenftigen Schulen). *Praxis der Kinderpsychologie und Kinderpsychiatrie*, 1970, *19*, 170–184.

Knights, R. M. Problems of criteria in diagnosis: A profile similarity approach. *Annals of the New York Academy of Sciences*, 1973, *205*, 124–131.

Knights, R. M. and Bakker, D. J. (Eds.), *Neuropsychology of learning disorders: theoretical approaches*. Baltimore: University Park Press, 1976.

Knights, R. and Hardy, M. *A child-computer-teacher assessment and remedial program for children with poor reading skills: Phase 1*. Research Bulletin No. 14, Carleton University, Ottawa, Canada, 1976.

Knobel, M., Wolman, M. B., and Mason, C. Hyperkinesia and organicity in children. *Archives of General Psychiatry*, 1959, *1*, 310–321.

Knott, J. R., Muehl, S., and Benton, A. L. Electroencephalograms in children with reading disabilities. *Electroencephalography & Clinical Neurophysiology*, 1965, *18*, 513.

Knox, C. and Kimura, D. Cerebral processing of nonverbal sounds in boys and girls. *Neuropsychologia*, 1970, 8, 227–237.

Kooi, K. A. Letter to the editor. *Psychophysiology*, 1972, 9, 154.

Koppitz, E. M. *Children with learning disabilities: a five year follow-up study.* New York: Grune & Stratton, 1971.

Kornmann, R., Brauch, L., Hils, U., Riemer, C., and Schwender, V. Präferenzund Leistungs Dominanz der Hände bei Lernbehinderten Sonderschülern, Legasthenikern und Grundschülern, *Zeitschrift fur Heilpadagogik*, 1974, 25, 147–156.

Kris, C. Developmental and diagnostic EOG and EEG studies of binocular visual responsiveness and oculomotor control in children and adults with perceptual, reading and learning difficulties. *Electroencephalography & Clinical Neurophysiology*, 1969, 26, 633–634.

Kris, C. Simultaneous measurement of binocular EOG and bilateral EEG activation patterns in dyslexic children. *Electroencephalography & Clinical Neurophysiology*, 1970, 29, 413.

LaBerge, D. and Samuels, S. J. Toward a theory of automatic information processing in reading. *Cognitive Psychology*, 1974, 6, 293–323.

Lairy, G. C. and Harrison, A. Functional aspects of EEG foci in children: clinical data and longitudinal studies. In P. Kellaway and I. Petersen (Eds.), *Clinical Electroencephalography of Children* (197–212). New York: Grune & Stratton, 1968.

Lairy, G. C. and Netchine, S. Signification psychologique et clinique de l'organisation spatiale de l'E.E.G. chez l'enfant. *Revue Neurologique*, 1960, *102*, 380–388.

Lairy, G. and Netchine, S. The electroencephalogram in partially sighted children related to clinical and psychological data. Proceedings, First International Meeting on Technology and Blindness, 1963, 2, 267–284.

Landucci, L. and Piantossi, G. EEG and psychometric researches in children suffering from mental deficiency. *Acta Paedopsychiatrica*, 1961, 28, 161–171.

Lane, E. A. and Albee, G. W. Intellectual antecedents of schizophrenia. In M. Roff and D. F. Ricks (Eds.), *Life History Research in Schizophrenia* (Vol. 1). Minneapolis: University of Minnesota Press, 1970.

Langford, K., Slade, K., and Barnett, A. An explanation of impress techniques in remedial reading. *Academic Therapy*, 1974, 9, 309–319.

LaVeck, G. and De la Cruz, E. EEG and etiologic findings in mental retardation. *Pediatrics*, 1963, *31*, 478–485.

Lawson, L. Ophthalmological factors in learning disabilities. In H. R. Myklebust (Ed.), *Progress in Learning Disabilities* (Vol. 1). New York: Grune and Stratton, 1974.

Lebendinskaia, E. I. and Poliakova, A. G. Conflicts between the first and second signal systems. In Y. Brackbill and G. G. Thompson (Eds.), *Behavior In Infancy and Early Childhood.* New York: Free Press, 1967.

Lee, D. M. and Van Allen, R. *Learning to read through experience* (2nd ed.). New York: Appleton-Century-Crofts, 1963.

Lefford, A., Birch, H. G., and Green, G. The perceptual and cognitive bases for finger localization and selective finger movements in preschool children. *Child Development*, 1974, *45*, 335–343.

Leisman, G. Conditioning variables in attentional handicaps. *Neuropsychologia*, 1973, *11*, 199–205.

Leisman, G. The relationship between saccadic eye movements and the alpha rhythm in attentionally handicapped patients. *Neuropsychologia*, 1974, *12*, 209–218.

Leisman, G. The role of visual processes in attention and its disorders. In G. Leisman (Ed.), *Basic Visual Processes and Learning Disability*. Springfield, Ill.: Charles C. Thomas, 1975.

Leisman, G. and Schwartz, J. Ocular-motor variables in reading disorders. In R. M. Knights and D. J. Bakker (Eds.), *Neuropsychology of Learning Disorders: Theoretical Approaches*. Baltimore: University Park Press, 1976.

Lejeune, J., Gautier, M., and Turpin, R. Etude des chromosomes somatiques de neuf enfants mongoliens. *Comptes Rendue de l'Academie des Sciences, Paris*, 1959, *248*, 1721–1722.

Le Jeune, J. P. The vocabulary of aphasic speakers. Ph.D. Dissertation, University of Victoria, 1974.

Lenneberg, E. H. *Biological foundations of language*. New York: Wiley, 1967.

Leong, C. K. Lateralization in severely disabled readers in relation to functional cerebral development and synthesis of information. In R. M. Knights and D. J. Bakker (Eds.), *Neuropsychology of Learning Disorders: Theoretical Approaches*. Baltimore: University Park Press, 1976.

Lerner, J. W. *Children with learning disabilities*. Boston: Houghton-Mifflin, 1971.

Lerner, J. Two perspectives: reading and learning disabilities. In S. Kirk and J. McCarthy (Eds.), *Learning Disabilities: Selected ACLD Papers*. Boston: Houghton-Mifflin, 1975, 271–285.

Levine, M. J. Physiological responses in intrasensory and intersensory integration of auditory and visual signals by normal and deficit readers. In R. M. Knights and D. J. Bakker (Eds.), *The Neuropsychology of Learning Disorders, Theoretical Approaches*. Baltimore: University Park Press, 1976.

Levy, J. Psychobiological implication of bilateral asymmetry. In S. J. Dimond and J. Beaumont (Eds.), *Hemisphere Function in the Human Brain*. London: Elek, 1974.

Liberman, I. Segmentation of the spoken word and reading acquisition. Paper presented at the Symposium on Language and Perceptual Development in the Acquisition of Reading, Society for Research in Child Development, Philadelphia, March 1973.

Liberman, I. and Shankweiler, D. Speech, the alphabet, and teaching to read. Paper presented at the NIE conference on the theory and practice of beginning reading instruction, Learning Research and Development Center, University of Pittsburgh, May 21, 1976.

Liberman, I. Y. and Shankweiler, D. Speech, the alphabet and teaching to read. To appear in: L. Resnick and P. Weaver (Eds.), *Theory and Practice of Early Reading*. Hillside, N.J.: Erlbaum Associates, in press.

Liberman, I. Y., Shankweiler, D., Fischer, F. W., and Carter, B. Explicit syllable and phoneme segmentation in the young child. *Journal of Experimental Child Psychology*, 1974, *18*, 201–212.

Liberman, I. Y., Shankweiler, D., Liberman, A. M., Fowler, C., and Fischer, F. W. Phonetic segmentation and recoding in the beginning reader. In A. S. Reber and D. Scarborough (Eds.), *Reading: Theory and Practice*. Hillside, N.J.: Erlbaum Associates, 1976.

Liberman, I. Y., Shankweiler, D., Orlando, C., Harris, K. S., and Berti, F. B. Letter confusion and reversals of sequence in the beginning reader: implications for Orton's theory of developmental dyslexia. *Cortex*, 1971, *7*, 127–142.

Lindgren, H. C. and Bryne, D. *Psychology: an introduction to a behavioral science*. New York: Wiley, 1971.

Lindgren, S. D. The early identification of children at risk for reading disabilities: finger localization ability, verbal skills, and perceptual-motor performance in kindergarten children. Unpublished master's thesis, University of Iowa, 1975.

Lindsley, D. B. Discussion of attention in perception and reading. In F. A. Young and D. B. Lindsley (Eds.), *Early Experience and Visual Information Processing in Perceptual and Reading Disorders*. National Academy of Science, 1970.

Lombroso, C. T., Schwartz, I. H., Clark, D. M., Muench, H., and Barry, J. Ctenoids in healthy youths: controlled study on 14- and 6-per-second positive spiking. *Neurology (Minneapolis)*, 1966, *16*, 1152–1158.

Long, M. T. and Johnson, L. C. Fourteen and six-per-second positive spikes in a non-clinical male population. *Neurology (Minneapolis)*, 1968, *18*, 714–716.

Lopardo, G. LEA-cloze reading materials for the disabled reader. *The Reading Teacher*, 1975, *29*, 42–44.

Lovell, K., Gray, E. A., and Oliver, D. E. A further study of some cognitive and other disabilities in backward readers of average non-verbal reasoning scores. *British Journal of Educational Psychology*, 1964, *34*, 255–279.

Lovell, K., Shapton, D., and Warren, N. S. A study of some cognitive and other disabilities in backward readers of average intelligence as assessed by non-verbal test. *British Journal of Educational Psychology*, 1964, *34*, 58–64.

Low, M. D. and Stoilen, L. CNV and EEG in children: maturational characteristics and findings in the UCS syndrome. In W. C. McCallum and J. R. Knott (Eds.), Event Related Slow Potentials and Behavior. *Electroencephalography & Clinical Neurophysiology*, Suppl. 33, 1973.

Luria, A. R. *Higher cortical functions in man*. New York: Basic Books, 1966.

Luria, A. R. *Human brain and psychological processes*. New York: Harper & Row, 1966.

Luria, A. R. *Traumatic aphasia: its syndromes, psychology and treatment*. The Hague: Mouton, 1970.

Luria, A. R. *The working brain*. New York: Basic Books, 1973.

Lyle, J. G. Performance of retarded readers on the memory-for-designs test. *Perceptual and Motor Skills*, 1968, *26*, 851–854.

Lyle, J. G. Reading retardation and reversal tendency: a factorial study. *Child Development,* 1969, *40,* 833–843.

Lyle, J. G. Certain antenatal, perinatal, and developmental variables and reading retardation in middle class boys. *Child Development,* 1970, *41,* 481–491.

Lyle, J. G. and Goyen, J. Performance of retarded readers on the WISC and educational tests. *Journal of Abnormal Psychology,* 1969, *74,* 105–112.

Lyle, J. G. and Goyen, J. D. Effect of speed of exposure and difficulty of discrimination on visual recognition of retarded readers. *Journal of Abnormal Psychology,* 1975, *8, 6,* 673–676.

Maitland, S., Nadeau, J. B. E., and Nadeau, G. Early school screening practices. *Journal of Learning Disability,* 1974, *7,* 55–59.

Makita, K. The rarity of reading disability in Japanese children. *American Journal of Orthopsychiatry,* 1968, *38,* 599–614.

Maliphant, R., Supramaniam, S., and Saraga, E. Acquiring skill in reading: a review of experimental research. *Journal of Child Psychology & Psychiatry,* 1974, *15,* 175–185.

Malmquist, E. *Factors related to reading disabilities in the first grade of elementary school.* Stockholm: Almquist, 1958.

Marcel, T., Katz, K., and Smith, M. Laterality and reading proficiency. *Neuropsychologia,* 1974, *12,* 131–139.

Marcel, T. and Rajan, P. Lateral specialization for recognition of words and faces in good and poor readers. *Neuropsychologia,* 1975, *13,* 489–497.

Marshall, J. C. and Newcombe, F. Patterns of paralexia: a psycholinguistic approach. *Developmental Medicine and Child Neurology,* 1973, *2,* 175–199.

Martinius, J. W. and Hoovey, Z. B. Bilateral synchrony of occipital alpha waves, oculomotor activity and "attention" in children. *Electroencephalography & Clinical Neurophysiology,* 1972, *32,* 349–356.

Masland, R. L. Some neurological processes underlying language. *Annals of Otology, Rhinology and Laryngology,* 1968, *77,* 787–804.

Mason, A. W. Specific (developmental) dyslexia. *Developmental Medicine and Child Neurology,* 1976, *9,* 183–190.

Mason, M. Reading ability and letter research time: effects of orthographic structure defined by single-letter positional frequency. *Journal of Experimental Psychology: General,* 1975, *104,* 146–166.

Mason, M. and Katz, L. Visual processing of non-linguistic strings: redundancy effects and reading ability. *Journal of Experimental Psychology: General,* 1976, *105,* 338–348.

Matsumiya, Y., Tagliasco, V., Lombrosa, C., and Goodglass, H. Auditory evoked responses: meaningfulness of stimuli and interhemispheric asymmetry. *Science,* 1972, 175–190.

Mattingly, I. G. Reading, the linguistic provess, and linguistic awareness. In J. F. Kavanagh and I. G. Mattingly (Eds.), *Language by Fear and by Eye: The Relationship Between Speech and Reading.* Cambridge: M.I.T. Press, 1972.

Mattis, S., French, J. H., and Rapin, I. Dyslexia in children and young adults: three independent neuropsychological syndromes. *Developmental Medicine and Child Neurology,* 1975, *17,* 150–163.

Maxwell, A. E. The W.P.P.S.I.: a marked discrepancy in the correlations of the subtests for good and poor readers. *British Journal of Mathematical and Statistical Psychology,* 1972, *25,* 283–291.

Maxwell, A. E., Fenwick, P. B. C., Fenton, G. W., and Dollimore, J. Reading ability and brain function: a simple statistical model. *Psychological Medicine,* 1974, *4,* 274–280.

Mazurkiewicz, A. The initial teaching alphabet. In J. Money and G. Schiffman (Eds.), *The Disabled Reader.* Baltimore: The Johns Hopkins Press, 1966.

McCall, R. Intelligence quotient patterns over age: comparisons among siblings and parent-child pairs. *Science,* 1970, *170,* 644–648.

McClelland, J. Shadow and substance of specific language disability: a longitudinal study. *Bulletin of the Orton Society,* 1973, *23,* 169–181.

McKeever, W. F. and Huling, M. D. Lateral dominance in tachistoscopic word recognition of children at two levels of ability. *Quarterly Journal of Experimental Psychology,* 1970, *22,* 600–604.

McKeever, W. F. and VanDeventer, A. D. Dyslexic adolescents: evidence of impaired visual and auditory language processing associated with normal lateralization and visual responsivity. *Cortex,* 1975, *11,* 361–378.

McLeod, P. *Lippincott Reading Readiness Tests.* Philadelphia: J. P. Lippincott, 1965.

McLeod, J. A comparison of WISC sub-test scores of pre-adolescent successful and unsuccessful readers. *Australian Journal of Psychology,* 1965, *17,* 220–228.

Meehl, P. Theory-testing in psychology and physics: a methodological paradox. *Philosophy of Science,* 1967, *34,* 103–115.

Meehl, P. E. and Rosen, A. Antecedent probability and the efficiency of psychometric signs, patterns or cutting scores. *Psychological Bulletin,* 1955, *52,* 194–216.

Meerlo, J. A. Reading block and television apathy: an alarm for parents. *Mental Hygiene,* October, 1962.

Mehegan, C. C. and Dreifuss, F. E. Hyperlexia: exceptional reading ability in brain-damaged children. *Neurology,* 1972, *22,* 1105–1111.

Meier, J. H. Prevalence and characteristics of learning disabilities in 2nd grade children. *Journal of Learning Disabilities,* 1971, *4,* 1–16.

Meier, J. H. Screening and assessments of young children at developmental risk. Dept. of HEW, Pub. #(OS)73-90. Washington, D.C., 1973, 187.

Meier, J. H. *Developmental and learning disabilities.* Baltimore: University Park Press, 1976.

Mendelson, W., Johnson, N., and Stewart, M. A. Hyperactive children as teenagers: a follow-up study. *Journal of Nervous and Mental Disease,* 1971, *153,* 273–279.

Menyuk, P. Relations between acquisition of phonology and reading. In J. T. Guthrie (Ed.), *Aspects of Reading Acquisition.* Baltimore: Johns Hopkins Press, 1976.

Meyers, D., Dingman, H., Orpet, R., Sitkei, E., and Watts, C. Four ability-factor hypothesis at three preliterate levels in normal and retarded children. *Monographs of the Society for Research in Child Development,* 1964, *29,* 5.

Michaels, D. D. Ocular dominance. *Survey of Ophthalmology,* 1974, *17,* 151–163.

Miller, G. The magical number seven, plus or minus two: some limits on our capacity for processing information. *Psychological Review,* 1956, *63,* 81–97.

REFERENCES

Miller, J. F. and Yoder, D. E. A syntax teaching program. In J. E. McLean, D. E. Yoder and R. L. Schiefelbush (Eds.), *Language Intervention with the Retarded: Developing Strategies.* Baltimore: University Park Press, 1972.

Milner, B. Laterality effects in audition. In V. B. Mountcastle (Ed.), *Interhemispheric Relations and Cerebral Dominance.* Baltimore: Johns Hopkins Press, 1962.

Milner, B. Brain mechanisms suggested by studies of temporal obes. In C. H. Millikan and F. L. Darley (Eds.), *Brain Mechanisms Underlying Speech and Language.* New York: Grune and Stratton, 1967.

Milner, B. Hemispheric specialization: scope and limits. In F. O. Schmitt and F. G. Worden (Eds.), *The Neurosciences, Third Study Program.* Cambridge: M.I.T. Press, 1974.

Milwaukee Public Schools. *Four Year Kindergarten Screening Procedure.* Milwaukee: Division of Curriculum and Instruction (no date).

Mohan, P. J. Acoustic encoding in normal and retarded readers. *Child Development,* 1975, *46, 593–597.*

Money, J. (Ed.). *Reading disability: progress and research needs in dyslexia.* Baltimore: Johns Hopkins Press, 1962.

Money, J. Turner's syndrome and parietal lobe functions. *Cortex,* 1973, *9, 387–393.*

Money, J. and Schiffman, G. *The disabled reader.* Baltimore: The Johns Hopkins Press, 1966.

Monroe, M. *Children who cannot read.* Chicago: The University of Chicago Press, 1932.

Monroe, M. *Children who cannot read.* University of Chicago Press, Chicago, 1935.

Monroe, M. Reading aptitude tests for prediction and analysis of reading abilities and disabilities: primary form. *Education,* 1935, *56.*

Morgan, W. P. A case of congenital word-blindness. *British Medical Journal,* 1896, *2,* 1378.

Morin, S. EEG correlates of stuttering. *Electroencephalography & Clinical Neurology,* 1968, *18, 425.*

Morrell, L. and Salamy, J. Hemispheric asymmetry of electrocortical responses to speech stimuli. *Science,* 1971, *174, 164.*

Morsink, C. Teaching early elementary children with reading disability. *The Reading Teacher,* 1971, *24, 550–555.*

Muehl, S. and Forell, E. R. A follow-up study of disabled readers: variables related to high school reading performance. *Reading Research Quarterly,* 1973, *9,* 110–123.

Muehl, S., Knott, J. R., and Benton, A. L. EEG abnormality and psychological test performance in reading disability. *Cortex,* 1965, *1, 434–440.*

Muehl, S. and Kremenak, S. Ability to match information within and between auditory and visual sense modalities and subsequent reading achievement. *Journal of Educational Psychology,* 1966, *57, 230–239.*

Murdoch, B. D. Changes in the electroencephalogram in minimal cerebral dysfunction. Controlled study over 8 months. *South African Medical Journal,* 1974, *48,* 606–610.

Myers, P. and Hammill, D. *Methods of learning disorders.* New York: Wiley, 1969.

Myklebust, H. *Psychology of deafness.* New York: Grune and Stratton, 1960.

Myklebust, H. R. (Ed.) *Progress in learning disabilities* (Vol. 1). New York and London: Grune and Stratton, 1968.

Myklebust, H. R. and Boshes, B. *Final Report: Minimal Brain Damage in Children.* Washington, D.C.: Department of Health, Education, and Welfare, 1969.

Myklebust, H. R., Boshes, B., Olson, D. A., and Cole, C. H. *Minimal Brain Damage in Children.* Final report of USPHS Contract 108-65-142. DHEW, June 1969.

Myklebust, H. R. and Johnson, D. J. Dyslexia in children. *Exceptional Children,* 1962, *29,* 14–25.

NACD (National Advisory Committee on Dyslexia and Related Reading Disorders). "Reading Disorders in the United States," *National Institute of Health, Dept. of HEW.* Chicago: Developmental Learning Materials, 1969.

Naidoo, S. The assessment of dyslexic children. In A. Franklin and S. Naidoo (Eds.), *Assessment and Teaching of Dyslexic Children.* London: Invalid Children's Aid Association, 1970.

Naidoo, S. *Specific dyslexia.* New York: Wiley, 1972.

Naidoo, S. *Specific dyslexia.* London: Pitman, 1972.

Neisser, U. *Cognitive psychology.* New York: Appleton-Century-Crofts, 1967.

Nelson, H. E. and Warrington, E. K. Developmental spelling retardation and its relation to other cognitive abilities. *British Journal of Psychology,* 1974, *65,* 265–274.

Nelson, H. E. and Warrington, E. K. Developmental spelling retardation. In R. M. Knights and D. J. Bakker (Eds.), *The Neuropsychology of Learning Disorders—Theoretical Approaches.* Baltimore: University Park Press, 1976.

Nielsen, H. H. and Ringe, K. Visuo-perceptive and visuo-motor performance of children with reading disabilities. *Scandinavian Journal of Psychology,* 1969, *10,* 225–231.

Norrie, E. Ordblindheden. Cited by L. J. Thompson, *Reading Disability.* Springfield, Ill.: Charles C. Thomas, 1959.

Oettinger, L. Jr., Nekonishi, H., and Gill, I. G. Cerebral dysrhythmia induced by reading (subclinical reading epilepsy). *Developmental Medicine & Child Neurology,* 1967, *9,* 191–201.

Office of Education (1976): Assistance to states for education of handicapped children, notice of proposed rulemaking. Federal Register, Vol. 41 (No. 230): 52404–52407, November 29, 1976.

Ofman, W. and Shaevitz, M. The kinesthetic method in remedial reading. *Journal of Experimental Education,* 1963, *31,* 317–320.

Oller-Daurella, L. and Masó-Subirana, E. Semiologia clinica y EEG de la lateralidad preferencial. Madrid, Libro de ponencias, *VIII Congreso Nacional de Neuro-Psiquiatra,* 1965, 165–207.

Olson, W. C. *Child development.* Boston: Heath, 1949.

O'Malley, J. E. and Conners, C. K. The effect of unilateral alpha training on visual evoked response in a dyslexic adolescent. *Psychophysiology,* 1972, *9,* 467–470.

Orgass, B., Poeck, K., Kerschensteiner, M., and Hartje, W. Visuocognitive performances in patients with unilateral hemispheric lesions. *Zeitschrift für Neurologie,* 1972, *202,* 177–195.

REFERENCES

Orton, J. The Orton-Gillingham approach. In J. Money and G. Schiffman (Eds.), *The Disabled Reader*. Baltimore: The Johns Hopkins Press, 1966.

Orton, S. T. "Word-blindness" in school children. *Archives of Neurology and Psychiatry*, 1925, *14*, 581–615.

Orton, S. T. Reading disability. *Genetic Psychology Monographs*, 1926, *14*, 335–453.

Orton, S. T. Specific reading disability—strephosymbolia. *Journal of the American Medical Association*, 1928, *90*, 1095–1099.

Orton, S. T. Familial occurrence of disorders in the acquisition of language. *Eugenics*, 1930, *3*, 140–147.

Orton, S. T. *Reading, writing and speech problems in children*. New York: Norton, 1937.

Orton, S. T. Some disorders in the language development of children. In *Language in Relation to Psycho-Motor Development*. Langhorne, Pa.: Child Research Clinic of the Woods Schools, 1946.

Osgood, C. E. and Miron, M. S. (Eds.) *Approaches to the study of aphasia*. Urbana, Ill.: University of Illinois Press, 1963.

Osser, H., Frank, S. M., and Wang, M. The communicative abilities of preschool children. 1967 (unpublished manuscript).

Owen, F. W. and Adams, P. A. Pilot studies of educationally handicapped children in the Palo Alto Unified School District, Palo Alto, California. Unpublished report, 1964.

Owen, F. W., Adams, P. A., Forrest, T., Stolz, L. M., and Fisher, S. Learning disorders in children: sibling studies. *Monographs of the Society for Research in Child Development* (Vol. 36). Chicago: University of Chicago Press, 1971.

Paine, R. S. Minimal chronic brain syndromes in children. *Developmental Medicine & Child Neurology*, 1962, *4*, 21–27.

Paine, R. and Oppe, T. *Neurological examination of children* (p. 279). London: Spastics Society, Heinemann, 1966.

Painter, G. Effect of a rhythmic and sensory motor activity program on perceptual motor spatial activities of kindergarten children. *Exceptional Children*, 1966, *33*, 113–116.

Palermo, D. S. and Molfese, D. L. Language acquisition from age five onward. *Psychological Bulletin*, 1972, *78*, 409–428.

Palmer, L. L. Eye dominance in a reading clinic population. *Perceptual and Motor Skills*, 1976, *42*, 712–714.

Paris, S. and Carter, A. Semantic and constructive aspects of sentence memory in children. *Developmental Psychology*, 1973, *9*, 109–113.

Park, G. E. and Schneider, K. A. Thyroid function in relation to dyslexia (reading failures). *Journal of Reading Behavior*, 1975, *7*, 197–199.

Pate, E. and Webb, W. *First grade screening test*. Circle Pines, Minn.: American Guidance Service, 1969.

Pavy, R., and Metcalfe, J. The abnormal EEG in childhood communication and behavior abnormalities. *Electroencephalography and Clinical Neurophysiology*, 1965, *19*, 414.

Pearson, G. H. J. A survey of learning difficulties in children. *Psychoanalytic Study of the Child*, 1952, *7*, 322–386.

Peiper, A. *Cerebral function in infancy and childhood.* Consultant Bureau Enterprises, New York, 1963.

Pennington, H., Galliani, C. A., and Voegele G. E. Unilateral electroencephalographic dysrhythmia and children's intelligence. *Child Development,* 1965, *36,* 539–546.

Perfetti, C. A. and Goldman, S. R. Discourse memory and reading comprehension skill. *Journal of Verbal Learning and Verbal Behavior,* 1976, *14,* 33–42.

Perfetti, C. A. and Hogaboam, T. The relationship between single word decoding and reading comprehension skill. *Journal of Educational Psychology,* 1975, *67,* 461–469.

Perl, N. T. The application of the verbal transformation effect to the study of cerebral dominance. *Neuropsychologia,* 1970, *8,* 259–261.

Perlo, P. and Rak, T. Developmental dyslexia in adults. *Neurology,* 1971, *21,* 1233–1235.

Peters, C. The effect of systematic restructuring of material upon the comprehension process. *Reading Research Quarterly,* 1975–1976, *11,* 87–112.

Peters, J. E., Romine, J. S., and Dyckman, R. A. A special neurological examination of children with learning disabilities. *Developmental Medicine and Child Neurology,* 1975, *17,* 63–78.

Piaget, J. *Judgment and reasoning in the child.* New York: Harcourt Brace, 1926.

Piaget, J. Piaget's theory. In P. H. Mussen (Ed.), *Carmichael's Manual of Child Psychology.* New York: Wiley, 1970.

Pick, H. L. Systems of perceptual and perceptual motor development. In J. P. Hill (Ed.), *Minnesota Symposia on Child Development* (Vol. 4). Minneapolis: University of Minnesota Press, 1970.

Piggott, L. R., Kempler, H. L., Perez-Borja, C., Tigary, B. I., and Cutler, C. Stressful school work: an agent of EEG deterioration. *Journal of Learning Disabilities,* 1972, *5,* 61–67.

Pollack, C. Mass remediation of children's reading problems. *The Reading Teacher,* 1969, *22,* 714–719.

Porac, C. and Coren, S. The dominant eye. *Psychological Bulletin,* 1976, *83,* 880–897.

Posey, H. The EEG in mental deficiency. *American Journal of Mental Deficiency,* 1951, *55,* 515–520.

Prechtl, H. and Beintema, D. Neurological examination of the full term newborn infant. *Little Club Clinics in Developmental Medicine.* Heinemann, London, 1965, 74.

Preston, M., Guthrie, J. T., and Childs, B. Visual evoked response in normal and disabled readers. *Psychophysiology,* 1974, *11,* 452–457.

Preston, M. S., Guthrie, J. T., Kirsch, I., Gertman, D., and Childs, B. VERs in normal and disabled readers. *Psychophysiology,* 1977, *14,* 8–14.

Quadfasel, F. A. and Goodglass, H. Specific reading disability and other specific disabilities. *Journal of Learning Disabilities,* 1968, *1* 590–600.

Quinn, P. Q., Renfield, M., Burg, C., and Rapoport, J. L. Minor physical anomalies: a newborn screening and one year follow-up. Paper presented at meeting of American Academy of Child Psychiatry, 1976.

Rabinovitch, R. D. Reading and learning disabilities. In S. Arieti (Ed.), *American Handbook of Psychiatry*. New York: Basic Books, 1959.

Rabinovitch, R. Dyslexia: psychiatric considerations. In J. Money (Ed.), *Reading Disability: Progress and Research Needs in Dyslexia*. Baltimore: Johns Hopkins Press, 1962.

Rabinovitch, R. D. Reading problems in children: definitions and classification. In A. Keeney and V. Keeney (Eds.), *Dyslexia: Diagnosis and Treatment of Reading Disorders*. St. Louis: C. V. Mosby, 1968.

Rabinovitch, R. D., Drew, A. L., DeJong, R. N., Ingram, W., and Withey, L. A research approach to reading retardation. *Proceedings Association Nervous & Mental Diseases*, 1954, *34*, 363–396.

Rawson, M. Prognosis in dyslexia. *Academic Therapy Quarterly*, 1966, *1*, 164–173.

Rawson, M. *Developmental Language Disability: Adult Accomplishments of Dyslexic Boys*. Baltimore: Johns Hopkins Press, 1968.

Rawson, M. B. Developmental dyslexia: educational treatment and results. In M. B. Rawson and D. D. Duane (Eds.), *Reading Perception and Language: Papers from the World Congress on Dyslexia*. Baltimore: York Press, 1975.

Reed, J. C. Lateralized finger agnosia and reading achievement at ages 6 and 10. *Child Development*, 1967a, *38*, 213–220.

Reed, J. C. Reading achievement as related to differences between WISC verbal and performance IQ's. *Child Development*, 1967b, *38*, 835–840.

Reed, J. C. The ability deficits of good and poor readers. *Journal of Learning Disabilities*, 1968, *2*, 134–139.

Reed, H. B. C. and Reitan, R. M. Intelligence test performances of brain damaged subjects with lateralized motor deficits. *Journal of Consulting Psychology*, 1963, *27*, 102–106.

Reid, J. F. Dyslexia: a problem in communication. *Educational Research*, 1969, *10*, 126–133.

Reitan, R. M. Certain differential effects of left and right cerebral lesions in human adults. *Journal of Comparative and Physiological Pathology*, 1955, *48*, 474–477.

Reitan, R. M. A research program on the psychological effects of brain lesions in human beings. In N. R. Ellis (Ed.), *International Review of Research in Mental Retardation* (Vol. 1). New York: Academic Press, 1966.

Reitan, R. M. and Davison, L. A. *Clinical neuropsychology: current status and applications*. Washington, D.C.: V. H. Winston & Sons, 1974.

Rhodes, L. E., Dustman, R. E., and Beck, E. C. The visual evoked response: a comparison of bright and dull children. *Electroencephalography & Clinical Neurophysiology*, 1969, *27*, 364–372.

Richardson, J. T. E. Further evidence on the effect of word imageability in dyslexia. *Quarterly Journal of Experimental Psychology*, 1975, *27*, 445–449.

Ritchie, H. M. Dyslexic. *Lancet*, 1971, *1*, 755–756.

Roberts, R. and Coleman, J. An investigation of the role of visual and kinesthetic factors in reading failures. *Journal of Educational Research*, 1958, *58*, 445–451.

Robins, L. *Deviant children grown up*. Baltimore: Williams and Wilkins, 1966.

Robinson, H. M. and Smith, H. K. Reading clinic clients—ten years after. *Elementary School Journal*, 1962, *63*, 22–27.

Robinson, M. "Kenneth Johnson": A progress report on a search for literacy. *Bulletin of the Orton Society*, 1969, *19*, 134–140.

Robinson, M. E. and Schwartz, L. B. Visuo-motor skills and reading ability: a longitudinal study. *Developmental Medicine and Child Neurology*, 1973, *15*, 281–286.

Rosner, J. The development and validation of an individualized perceptual skills curriculum. Learning Research and Development Center, University of Pittsburgh, 1972.

Rosenzweig, M. R. Cortical correlates of auditory localization and of related perceptual phenomena. *Journal of Comparative and Physiological Psychology*, 1954, *47*, 269–276.

Ross, A. O. *Psychological aspects of learning disabilities and reading disorders.* New York: McGraw-Hill, 1976.

Roudinesco, J., Trélat, J., and Trélat, M. Etude de quarante cas de dyslexie d'évolution. *Enfance*, 1950, *3*, 1–32.

Rourke, B. P. Brain-behavior relationships in children with learning disabilities: a research program. *American Psychologist*, 1975, *30*, 911–920.

Rourke, B. P. Interactions between research and assessment. *Journal of Pediatric Psychology*, 1976a, *1*, 7–11.

Rourke, B. P. Issues in the neuropsychological assessment of children with learning disabilities. *Canadian Psychological Review*, 1976b, *17*, 89–102.

Rourke, B. P. Reading retardation in children: developmental lag or deficit? In R. M. Knights and D. J. Bakker (Eds.), *Neuropsychology of Learning Disorders: Theoretical Approaches.* Baltimore: University Park Press, 1976c.

Rourke, B. P. Minimal brain dysfunction: is diagnosis necessary? *Journal of Learning Disabilities*, 1978, in press.

Rourke, B. P., Dietrich, D. M., and Young, G. C. Significance of WISC verbal-performance discrepancies for younger children with learning disabilities. *Perceptual and Motor Skills*, 1973a, *36*, 275–282.

Rourke B. P. and Finlayson, M. A. J. Neuropsychological significance of variations in patterns of performance on the Trail Making Test for older children with reading disabilities. *Journal of Abnormal Psychology*, 1975, *84*, 412–421.

Rourke, B. P. and Orr, R. R. Prediction of the reading and spelling performances of normal and retarded readers: a four-year follow-up. *Journal of Abnormal Child Psychology*, 1977, *5*, 9–20.

Rourke, B. P., Yanni, D. W., MacDonald, G. W., and Young, G. C. Neuropsychological significance of lateralized deficits on the Grooved Pegboard Test for older children with learning disabilities. *Journal of Consulting and Clinical Psychology*, 1973b, *41*, 128–134.

Rourke, B. P., Young, G. C., and Flewelling, R. W. The relationships between WISC verbal-performance discrepancies and selected verbal, auditory-perceptual, visual-perceptual, and problem-solving abilities in children with learning disabilities. *Journal of Clinical Psychology*, 1971, *27*, 475–479.

Royce, J. R. and Buss, A. R. The role of general systems and information theory in multi-factor individuality theory. *Canadian Psychological Review,* 1976, *17,* 1–28.

Rubins, C. A. and Minden, H. A. An analysis of eye-movements in children with a reading disability. *Cortex,* 1973, *9,* 217–220.

Rudel, R. G., Denckla, M. B., and Spalten, E. Paired associate learning of Morse code and braille letter names by dyslexic and normal children. *Cortex,* 1976, *12,* 61–70.

Rugel, R. WISC subtest scores of disabled readers: a review with respect to Bannatyne's recategorization. *Journal of Learning Disabilities,* 1974, 7, 48–54.

Russo, M. and Vignolo, L. A. Visual figure-ground discrimination in patients with unilateral cerebral disease. *Cortex,* 1967, *3,* 113–127.

Rutter, M. The concept of "dyslexia." In P. Wolff and R. C. MacKeith (Eds.), *Planning for Better Learning.* Clinics in Develop. Med., No. 33. London: SIMP/ Heinemann, 1969.

Rutter, M. Emotional disorder and educational under-achievement. *Archives of Diseases in Childhood,* 1974, *49,* 249–256.

Rutter, M. Brain damage syndromes in childhood: concepts and findings. *Journal of Child Psychology & Psychiatry,* 1977, *18,* 1–22.

Rutter, M., Graham, P., and Birch, H. G. Inter-relations between the choreiform syndrome, reading disability and psychiatric disorder in children of 8–11 years. *Developmental Medicine and Child Neurology,* 1966, 8, 149–159.

Rutter, M., Graham, P., and Yule, W. *A neuropsychiatric study in childhood.* Clinics in Develop. Med., Nos. 35/36. London: SIMP/Heinemann, 1970.

Rutter, M. and Madge, N. *Cycles of disadvantage: a review of research.* London: Heinemann Educational, 1976.

Rutter, M., Tizard, J., and Whitmore, K. *Education, health and behaviour.* London: Longman, 1970.

Rutter, M., Tizard, J., Yule, W., Graham, P., and Whitmore, K. Research report: Isle of Wight Studies 1964–1974. *Psychological Medicine,* 1976, 6, 313–332.

Rutter, M. and Yule, W. Specific reading retardation. In L. Mann and D. Sabatino (Eds.), *The First Review of Special Education.* Philadelphia: Buttonwood Farms, 1973.

Rutter, M. and Yule, W. The concept of specific reading retardation. *Journal of Child Psychiatry,* 1975, *16,* 181–197.

Rutter, M. and Yule, W. Reading difficulties. In M. Rutter and L. Hersov (Eds.), *Child Psychiatry: Modern Approaches.* London: Blackwell Scientific, 1976.

Rutter, M., Yule, B., Quinton, D., Rowlands, O., Yule, W., and Berger, M. Attainment and adjustment in two geographical areas. III. Some factors accounting for area differences. *British Journal of Psychiatry,* 1975, *126,* 520–533.

Ryan, T. J. *Poverty and the child: a Canadian study.* Toronto: McGraw-Hill, 1973.

Sabatino, D. A. and Becker, J. T. Relationship between lateral preference and selected behavioural variables for children failing academically. *Child Development,* 1971, *42,* 2055–2060.

Sampson, O. C. Fifty years of dyslexia, a review of the literature, 1925–75. 1. Theory. *Research in Education (Manchester),* 1975 (Nov.), No. 14.

Satterfield, J. H., Lesser, L. I., Saul, R. E., and Cantwell, D. P. EEG aspects in the diagnosis and treatment of minimal brain dysfunction. In F. F. de la Cruz, B. H. Fox, and R. H. Robert (Eds.), *Annals of the New York Academy of Sciences* (*Minimal Brain Dysfunction*), 1973, *205,* 274–282.

Satz, P. *Learning disorders and remediation of learning disorders.* Research Task Force, National Institute of Mental Health, Section on Child Mental Illness and Behavior Disorders, 1973.

Satz, P. Cerebral dominance and reading disability: an old problem revisited. In R. Knights and D. J. Bakker (Eds.), *The Neuropsychology of Learning Disorders: Theoretical Approaches.* Proceedings of NATO Conference, Baltimore: University Park Press, 1976.

Satz, P. Laterality tests: An inferential problem. *Cortex,* 1977, *13,* 208–212.

Satz, P. Early screening tests: some uses and abuses. *Journal of Learning Disabilities,* 1978 (in press).

Satz, P., Achenbach, K., and Fennell, E. Correlations between assessed manual laterality and predicted speech laterality in a normal population. *Neuropsychologia,* 1967, *5,* 295–310.

Satz, P., Bakker, D. J., Teunissen, J., Goebel, R., and Van der Vlugt, H. Developmental parameters of the ear asymmetry: a multivariate approach. *Brain and Language,* 1975, *2,* 171–185.

Satz, P., Fennell, E., and Reilly, C. The predictive validity of six neurodiagnostic tests: a decision theory analysis. *Journal of Consulting and Clinical Psychology,* 1970, *34,* 375–381.

Satz, P., Friel, J., and Rudegeair, F. Differential changes in the acquisition of developmental skills in children who later became dyslexic. In D. G. Stein, J. J. Rosen, and N. Butters (Eds.), *Plasticity and Recovery of Function in the Central Nervous System* (pp. 175–202). New York: Academic Press, 1974.

Satz, P. and Friel, J. Some predictive antecedents of specific reading disability: a preliminary one-year follow-up. In P. Satz and J. J. Ross (Eds.), *The Disabled Learner: Early Detection and Intervention* (pp. 79–98). Rotterdam: University Press, 1973.

Satz, P. and Friel, J. Some predictive antecedents of specific reading disability: a preliminary two-year follow-up. *Journal of Learning Disabilities,* 1974, *7,* 437–444.

Satz, P. and Friel, J. The predictive validity of an abbreviated screening battery: a three-year cross validation follow-up. *Journal of Learning Disabilities,* 1978 (in press).

Satz, P., Friel, J., and Goebel, R. A. Some predictive antecedents of specific reading disability: a three-year follow-up. *Bulletin of the Orton Society,* 1975, *25,* 91–110.

Satz, P., Friel, J., and Rudegeair, F. Some predictive antecedents of specific reading disability: a two-, three-, and four-year follow-up. In *The Hyman Blumberg Symposium on Research in Early Childhood Education.* Baltimore: Johns Hopkins Press, 1974.

Satz, P., Friel, J., and Rudegeair, F. Some predictive antecedents of specific reading disability: a two-, three-, and four-year follow-up. In J. T. Guthrie (Ed.), *Aspects of Reading Acquisition.* Baltimore: Johns Hopkins Press, 1976.

Satz, P., Rardin, D., and Ross, J. An evaluation of a theory of specific developmental dyslexia. *Child Development,* 1971, *42,* 2009–2021.

Satz, P. and Sparrow, S. S. Specific developmental dyslexia: a theoretical formulation. In D. J. Bakker and P. Satz (Eds.), *Specific Reading Disability: Advances in Theory and Method.* Rotterdam: Rotterdam University Press, 1970.

Satz, P. and Van Nostrand, G. K. Developmental dyslexia: an evaluation of a theory. In P. Satz and J. Ross (Eds.), *The Disabled Learner: Early Detection and Intervention.* Rotterdam: Rotterdam University Press, 1973.

Savin, A. B. What the child knows about speech when he starts to learn to read. In J. F. Kavanagh and I. G. Mattingly (Eds.), *Language by Ear and by Eye— The Relationships between Speech and Reading.* Cambridge: MIT Press, 1972.

Scarr-Salapatek, S. Genetics and the development of intelligence. In *Review of Child Development Research* (Vol. 4). Chicago: University of Chicago Press, 1975.

Schaar, K. Differing views snag HEW regs on learning disabilities. *APA Monitor,* 1977, *8,* 10.

Schain, R. J. *Neurology of childhood learning disorders.* Baltimore: 1972, Williams and Wilkins, 1972.

Schiffman, G. Dyslexia as an educational phenomenon: its recognition and treatment. In J. Money (Ed.), *Reading Disability: Progress and Research Needs in Dyslexia.* Baltimore: Johns Hopkins Press, 1962.

Schiffman, G. Mature content for immature skills. In J. Money and G. Schiffman (Eds.), *The Disabled Reader: Education of the Dyslexic Child.* Baltimore: Johns Hopkins Press, 1966.

Schilder, P. Congenital alexia and its relation to optic perception. *Journal of Genetic Psychology,* 1944, *65,* 67–88.

Schirm, N., Bahl, R., and Randolph, R. Minimale zerebrale Bewegungsstörung. Eine faktorenanalytische Auswertung von Untersuchungen an Kindergartenkindern. *Fortschritte der Medizin,* 1972, *90,* 985–988.

Schmideberg, M. *Searchlights on delinquency.* New York: International University Press, 1949, 174–189.

Scholes, R. S., Tanis, D., and Turner, A. Syntactic and strategic aspects of the comprehension of indirect and direct object construction of children. *Language and Speech,* 1976, *19,* 212–223.

Schonell, F. E. *Educating spastic children.* Edinburgh: Oliver and Boyd, 1956.

Schulte, C. A study of the relationship between oral language and reading achievement in second graders. Unpublished doctoral dissertation, University of Iowa, 1967.

Schwade, E. D. and Geiger, S. G. Abnormal electroencephalographic findings in severe behavior disorders. *Diseases of the Nervous System,* 1956, *11,* 307–317.

Schwartz, E. and Scheff, A. Student involvement in questioning for comprehension. *The Reading Teacher,* 1975, *29,* 150–154.

Schwartz, I. H. and Lombroso, C. T. A controlled study of the incidence of 14 and 6/sec positive spikes (ctenoids). *Electroencephalography & Clinical Neurophysiology,* 1966, *21,* 410.

Scott, J. P. Critical periods in behavioral development. In N. S. Endler, L. R. Boulter, and H. Osser (Eds.), *Contemporary Tissues in Developmental Psychology.* New York: Holt, Rinehart, and Winston, 1968.

Seidel, U. P., Chadwick, O., and Rutter, M. Psychological disorders in crippled children: a comparative study of children with and without brain damage. *Developmental Medicine & Child Neurology,* 1975, *17,* 563–573.

Seidel, U. P., Chadwick, O. F. D., and Rutter, M. Psychological disturbances in physically disabled children. *Developmental Medicine & Child Neurology,* 1975, *17,* 563–573.

Semel, E. M. and Wiig, E. H. Comprehension of syntactic structures and critical verbal elements by children with learning disabilities. *Journal of Learning Disabilities,* 1975, *8,* 53–58.

Senf, G. M. Development of immediate memory for bisensory stimuli in normal children and children with learning disorders. *Developmental Psychology,* 1969, *6,* 28, Pt. 2.

Senf, G. M. and Feshbach, S. Development of bisensory memory in culturally deprived, dyslexic, and normal readers. *Journal of Educational Psychology,* 1970, *61,* 461–470.

Senf, G. M. and Freundl, P. C. Memory and attention factors in specific learning disabilities. *Journal of Learning Disabilities,* 1971, *4,* 94–106.

Senf, G. M. and Freundl, P. C. Sequential auditory and visual memory in learning disabled children. *Proceedings of the Annual Convention of the American Psychological Association,* 1972, *7,* 511–512.

Shaffer, D., Chadwick, O., and Rutter, M. Psychiatric outcome of localized head injury in children. In R. Porter and D. FitzSimons (Eds.), *Outcome of Severe Damage to the Central Nervous System.* Ciba Foundation Symposium 34 (new series). Amsterdam: Elsevier-Excerpta Medica-North Holland, 1975.

Shankweiler, D. A study of developmental dyslexia. *Neuropsychologia,* 1963, *1,* 267–286.

Shankweiler, D. Developmental dyslexia: a critique and review of recent evidence. *Cortex,* 1964, *1,* 53–62.

Shankweiler, D. and Liberman, I. Misreading: a search for courses. In J. Kavanagh and I. Mattingly (Eds.), *Language by Ear and by Eye.* Cambridge, Mass.: MIT Press, 1972.

Shankweiler, D. and Studdert-Kennedy, M. A continuum of lateralization for speech perception? *Brain and Language,* 1975, *2,* 212–225.

Shardone, J. and Keogh, B. Early identification of educationally high risk and high potential first grade children. *Technical Report.* University of California, Los Angeles, 1975.

Sheer, D. E. Electrophysiological correlates of memory consolidation. In G. Ungar (Ed.), *Molecular Mechanisms in Memory and Learning.* New York: Plenum Press, 1970.

Sheer, D. E. Focused arousal and 40-Hz EEG. In R. M. Knights and D. J. Bakker (Eds.), *The Neuropsychology of Learning Disorders.* Baltimore: University Park Press, 1976.

Sheer, D. E. and Grandstaff, N. W. Computer-analysis of electrical activity in the brain and its relation to behavior. In H. T. Wycis (Ed.), *Topical Problems in Psychiatry and Neurology.* Basel/New York: Karger Press, 1970.

Shelburne, S. A. Jr. Visual evoked responses to word and nonsense syllable stimuli. *Electroencephalography & Clinical Neurophysiology,* 1972, *32,* 17–25.

Shelburne, S. A. Jr. Visual evoked responses to language stimuli in normal children. *Electroencephalography & Clinical Neurophysiology,* 1973, *34,* 135–143.

Shields, D. T. Brain responses to stimuli in disorders of information processing. *Journal of Learning Disabilities,* 1973, *6,* 501–505.

Shipley, T. and Jones, R. W. Initial observations on sensory interaction and the theory of dyslexia. *Journal of Communication Disorders,* 1969, *2,* 295–311.

Silberberg, N. and Silberberg, M. The bookless curriculum. An educational alternative. *Journal of Learning Disabilities,* 1969, *2,* 302–307.

Silberberg, N. E. and Silberberg, M. C. Case studies in hyperplexia. *Journal of School Psychology,* 1972, *7,* 3–7.

Silberberg, N. E., Iverson, M. S., and Goins, J. T. Which remedial reading method works best? *Journal of Learning Disabilities,* 1973, *6,* 547–555.

Silberberg, N. E., Iverson, I. A., and Silberberg, M. C. A model for classifying children according to reading level. *Journal of Learning Disabilities,* 1969, *2,* 634–643.

Silberman, C. *Crisis in Black and White.* New York: Random House, 1964.

Silver, A. A. and Hagin, R. Specific reading disability: delineation of the syndrome and relationship to cerebral dominance. *Comparative Psychiatry,* 1960, *1,* 126–134.

Silver, A. A. and Hagin, R. A. Specific reading disability: follow-up studies. *American Journal of Orthopsychiatry,* 1964, *34,* 95–102.

Silver, A. A. and Hagin, R. A. Specific reading disability: reaching by stimulation of perceptual areas. *American Journal of Orthopsychiatry,* 1967a, *37,* 744–752; reprinted in *Annual Progress in Child Psychiatry and Child Development,* S. Chess and A. Thomas (Eds.). New York: Brunner, 1968.

Silver, A. A. and Hagin, R. A. Strategies of intervention in the spectrums of defects in specific reading disability. *Bulletin of the Orton Society,* 1967, *17,* 39–46.

Silver, A. and Hagin, R. Visual perception in children with reading disabilities. In F. A. Young and D. B. Lindsay (Eds.), *Early Experience and Visual Information Processing in Perceptual and Reading Disorders.* Washington: National Academy of Sciences, 1971.

Silver, A. A. and Hagin, R. A. Effects of perceptual stimulation on perception, on reading ability and on the establishment of cerebral dominance for language. *Final Report to Carnegie Corporation,* 1972a.

Silver, A. A. and Hagin, R. A. Profile of a first grade: a basis for preventive psychiatry. *Journal of American Academy of Child Psychiatry,* 1972b, *11,* 645–674.

Silver, A. and Hagin R. *Search: a scanning instrument for the identification of potential learning disability: experimental edition.* New York: New York University Medical Center, 1975.

Silver, A. A. and Hagin, R. A. *Search.* New York: Walker Educational Book Corp., 1976.

Silver, A. A., Hagin, R. A., and Beecher, R. Scanning: diagnosis and intervention in the prevention of reading disability. *Journal of Learning Disabilities,* 1976, in press.

Silver, A. A., Hagin, R. A., and Hersch, M. F. Reading disability: teaching through stimulation of deficit perceptual areas. *American Journal of Orthopsychiatry,* 1967, *37,* 744–752.

Silver, L. B. A proposed view on the etiology of the neurological learning disability syndrome. *Journal of Learning Disabilities,* 1971, *4,* 123–132.

Silverstone, R. A. and Deichman, J. W. Sense modality research and the acquisition of reading skills. *Review of Educational Research,* 1975, *45,* 149–172.

Simon, H. On the development of the processor. In S. Farnham-Diggory (Ed.), *Information Processing in Children.* New York: Academic Press, 1972.

Singer, J. E., Westphal, M., and Niswander, K. R. Sex differences in the incidence of neonatal abnormalities and abnormal performance in early childhood. *Child Development,* 1968, *39,* 103–112.

Singerland, B. H. *Screening tests for identifying children with specific language disability.* Cambridge, Mass.: Educators Publishing Service, 1969.

Sklar, B., Hanley, J., and Simmons, W. W. An EEG experiment aimed toward identifying dyslexic children. *Nature (London),* 1972, *241,* 414–416.

Sklar, B., Hanley, J., and Simmons, W. W. A computer analysis of EEG spectral signatures from normal and dyslexic children. *Institute of Electronics and Electrical Engineering Transactions of Biomedical Engineering,* 1973, *20,* 20–26.

Slade, P. D. and Russell, G. F. M. Developmental dyscalculia: a brief report on four cases. *Psychological Medicine,* 1971, *1,* 292–298.

Sladen, B. K. Inheritance of dyslexia. *Bulletin of the Orton Society,* 1971, *31,* 30–39.

Slobin, D. I. Soviet psycholinguistics. in N. O'Connor (Ed.), *Present Day Russian Psychology.* London: Pergamon Press, 1966.

Slobin, D. I. Developmental psycholinguistics. In W. O. Dingwall (Ed.), *A Survey of Linguistic Science.* College Park, Md.: University of Maryland Press, 1971.

Smith, A. C., Flick, G. L., Ferriss, G. S., and Sellmann, A. H. Prediction of developmental outcome at seven years from prenatal, perinatal, and postnatal events. *Child Development,* 1972, *43,* 495–507.

Smith, F. *Understanding reading: a psycholinguistic analysis of reading and learning to read.* New York: Holt, Rinehart and Winston, 1971.

Smith, M. S. and Bissell, J. Report analysis: the impact of head start. *Harvard Educational Review,* 1970, *40,* 51–104.

Smith, M. and Ramunas, S. Elimination of visual field effect by use of a single report technique: evidence for order of report artifact. *Journal of Experimental Psychology,* 1971, *87,* 23–28.

Smith, N. B. Matching ability as a factor in first grade reading. *Journal of Educational Psychology,* 1928, *19,* 560–571.

Smith, W. L., Philippus, M. J., and Guard, H. L. Psychometric study of children with learning problems and 14-6 positive spike EEG patterns, treated with ethosuximide (Zarontin) and placebo. *Archives of Diseases in Childhood,* 1968, *43,* 616–619.

Spache, G. *Diagnosing and correcting reading disabilities.* Boston: Allyn and Bacon, 1976.

Spache, G., Andrew, M., Curtis, H., Rowland, M., and Fields, M. A longitudinal first grade reading readiness program. *The Reading Teacher,* 1966, *19.*

Spalding, R. and Spalding, W. *The writing road to reading.* New York: Morrow, 1957.

Sparrow, S. and Satz, P. Dyslexia, laterality, and neuropsychological development. In D. F. Bakker and P. Satz (Eds.), *Specific Reading Disability: Advances in Theory and Method.* Rotterdam: Rotterdam University Press, 1970.

Sperling, G. The information available in brief visual presentations. *Psychological Monographs,* 1960, *74,* 20 (Whole No. 498).

Sperry, R. W. Lateral specialization in the surgically separated hemispheres. In F. O. Schmitt and F. G. Worden (Eds.), *The Neurosciences, Third Study Program.* Cambridge, Mass.: MIT Press, 1974.

Spong, P., Haider, M., and Lindsley, D. B. Selective attentiveness and cortical evoked responses to visual and auditory stimuli. *Science,* 1965, *148,* 395–397.

Spreen, O. and Wachal, R. S. Psycholinguistic analysis of aphasic language: theoretical formulations and procedures. *Language and Speech,* 1973, *16,* 130–146.

Spring, C. and Capps, C. Encoding speed, rehearsal, and probed recall of dyslexic boys. *Journal of Educational Psychology,* 1974, *66,* 780–786.

Spring, C. Encoding speed and memory span in dyslexic children. *The Journal of Special Education,* 1976, *10,* 35–40.

Stallings, J. Implementation and child effects of teaching practices in Follow-Through classrooms. *Monographs of Society for Research in Child Development,* 1975, *40,* Serial No. 163.

Stallings, J. A. and Keepes, B. D. *Student aptitudes and methods of teaching beginning reading: A predictive instrument for determining interaction patterns.* Final Report, Contract No. OEG-9-70-0005, Project No. 9-1-099, 1970. U.S. Office of Education, 1970.

State reading requirements for learning disabilities certification in the U.S. *The Reading Teacher,* 1976, *30,* 306–309.

Statten, T. Behavior patterns, reading disabilities and EEG findings. *American Journal of Psychiatry,* 1953, *110,* 205–206.

Steger, J. A., Vellutino, F. R., and Meshoulam, U. Visual-tactile and tactile-tactile paired associate learning in normal and poor readers. *Perceptual and Motor Skills,* 1972, *35,* 263–266.

Steiner, R., Wiener, M., and Cromer, W. Comprehension training and identification for poor and good readers. *Journal of Educational Psychology,* 1971, *62,* 506–513.

Steinheiser, F. and Guthrie, J. T. Scanning times through prose and word strings for various targets by normal and disabled readers. *Perceptual and Motor Skills,* 1974, *39,* 931–938.

Steirnagle, E. A five-year summary of a remedial reading program. *Reading Teacher,* 1971, *24,* 537–543.

Sterritt, G. M. and Rudnick, M. Auditory and visual rhythm perception in relation to reading ability in fourth-grade boys. *Perceptual and Motor Skills,* 1966, *22,* 859–864.

Stevens, J. R., Sachdev, K., and Milstein, V. Behavior disorders of childhood and the electroencephalogram. *Archives of Neurology,* 1968, *18,* 160–177.

Stodolsky, S. and Lesser, G. Learning patterns in the disadvantaged. *Harvard Educational Review,* 1967, *37,* 546–593.

Stone, N. M. Reversal errors in reading: their diagnostic significance and implications for neuropsychological theories of reading disability. Ph.D. Dissertation, University of Iowa, 1976.

Stores, G. Studies of attention and seizure disorders. *Developmental Medicine & Child Neurology,* 1973, *15,* 376–382.

Stott, L. H. and Ball, R. S. Infant and preschool mental tests: review and evaluation. *Monograph of the Society for Research in Child Development,* 1965, *30,* No. 3.

Strag, G. A. Comparative behavioral ratings of parents with severe mentally retarded, special learning disability and normal children. *Journal of Learning Disabilities,* 1972, *5,* 52–56.

Strauss, A. and Lehtinen, L. *Psychopathology and education of the brain-injured child.* New York: Grune & Stratton, 1947.

Sturge, C. Reading retardation and antisocial behavior. M. Phil. Thesis, University of London, 1972.

Subirana, A. Handedness and cerebral dominance. In P. J. Vinken and G. W. Bruyn (Eds.), *Handbook of Clinical Neurology* (Vol. 4). Amsterdam: North Holland, 1969.

Subirana, A., Corominas, J., Oller-Daurella, L., Masó-Subirana, E., and Hernandez, A. Données EEG apportées par l'influence de la maturation sur la dominance hemisphérique. *C.R. 17 ième Congr. Ass. Pediat. Langue Franc,* 1959, 149–204.

Sutton, S., Tueting, P., Zubin, J., and John, E. R. Information delivery and the sensory evoked potential. *Science,* 1967, *155,* 1436–1439.

Symmes, J. S. and Rapoport, J. L. Unexpected reading failure. *American Journal of Orthopsychiatry,* 1972, *42,* 82–91.

Talmadge, M., Davids, A., and Laufer, M. A study of experimental methods for teaching emotionally disturbed, brain damaged, retarded readers. *Journal of Educational Research,* 1963, *56,* 11.

Taylor, L. B. Perception of digits presented to right and left ears in children with learning difficulties. Paper presented at the meeting of the Canadian Psychological Association, Hamilton, Canada, 1962.

Teuber, H. L. Why two brains? In F. O. Schmitt and F. G. Worden (Eds.), *The Neurosciences,* Third Study Program. Cambridge, Mass.: MIT Press, 1974.

Teuber, H. L. and Weinstein, S. Ability to discover hidden figures after cerebral lesions. *Archives of Neurology & Psychiatry,* 1956, *76,* 369–379.

Thoday, J. M. Location of polygenes. *Nature,* 1961, *191,* 368–370.

Thomas, C. J. Congenital "word-blindness" and its treatment. *Ophthalmoscope,* 1905, *3,* 380–385.

Thompson, L. *Reading disability: developmental dyslexia.* Springfield, Ill.: Charles C. Thomas, 1966.

Thompson, M. E. A comparison of laterality effects in dyslexics and controls using verbal dichotic listening tasks. *Neuropsychologia,* 1976, *14,* 243–246.

Thorndike, R. L. *The concepts of over- and under-achievement.* New York: Bureau of Publications, Teachers College, Columbia University, 1963.

Thorpe, H. A. and Werner, E. Developmental screening of preschool children: a critical review of inventories used in Health and Education programs. *Pediatrics,* 1974, *53,* 362–370.

Thurstone, L. L. *The differential growth of mental abilities.* Chapel Hill, N.C.: University of North Carolina Psychometric Laboratory, No. 14, 1955.

Tjossem, T. D., Hansen, T. J., and Ripley, H. S. An investigation of reading difficulty in young children. Read at the 117th annual meeting of the American Psychiatric Association, Chicago, Ill., 1961.

Torgeson, J. *Problems and prospects in the study of learning problems.* Chicago: University of Chicago Press, 1975.

Torres, F. and Ayers, F. W. Evaluation of the electroencephalogram of dyslexic children. *Electroencephalography & Clinical Neurophysiology,* 1968, *24,* 281–294.

Treiman, R. A. Children's ability to segment speech into syllables and phonemes as related to their reading ability. Unpublished manuscript, Department of Psychology, Yale University, 1976.

Trites, R. and Fiedorowicz, C. Follow-up study of children with specific (or primary) reading disability. In R. Knights and D. J. Bakker (Eds.), *The Neuropsychology of Learning Disorders: Theoretical Approaches.* Proceedings of NATO Conference. Baltimore: University Park Press, 1976.

Tuller, D. and Eames, T. H. Electroencephalograms of children who fail in reading. *Exceptional Child,* 1966, *32,* 637.

Tversky, A. and Kahneman, D. Belief in the law of small numbers. *Psychological Bulletin,* 1971, *76,* 105–110.

Tymchuk, A. J., Knights, R. M., and Hinton, G. C. Neuropsychological test results of children with brain lesions, abnormal EEGs, and normal EEGs. *Canadian Journal of Behavioural Science,* 1970a, *2,* 322–329.

Tymchuk, A. J., Knights, R. M., and Hinton, G. C. The behavioral significance of differing EEG abnormalities in children with learning and/or behavior problems. *Journal of Learning Disabilities,* 1970b, *3,* 547–551.

Underwood, B. J. Attributes of memory. *Psychological Review,* 1969, *76,* 559–577.

Usprich, C. The study of dyslexia: two nascent trends and a neuropsychological model. *The Bulletin of the Orton Society,* 1976, *26,* 34–48.

Valett, R. E. *Psychoeducational inventory of basic learning abilities.* Palo Alto, Calif.: Fearon Publishers, 1968.

Van Duyne, H. J. and Bakker, D. J. The development of ear asymmetry related to coding processes in memory in children. Paper presented at the meeting of the International Neuropsychological Society, Toronto, 1976.

Vande Voort, L. and Senf, G. M. Audiovisual integration in retarded readers. *Journal of Learning Disabilities,* 1973, *6,* 170–179.

Vande Voort, L., Senf, G. M., and Benton, A. L. Development of audiovisual integration in normal and retarded readers. *Child Development,* 1972, *43,* 1260–1272.

Varlaam, A. Educational attainment and behaviour at school. *Greater London Council Intelligence Quarterly*, 1974, *29*, 29–37.

Veatch, J. *Individualize your reading program.* New York: Putnam, 1959.

Vellutino, F. R. *Dyslexia: theory and research.* Cambridge, Mass.: MIT Press. In press.

Vellutino, F. R., DeSetto, L., and Steger, J. A. Categorical judgment and the Wepman test of auditory discrimination. *Journal of Speech and Hearing Disorders*, 1972, *37*, 252–257.

Vellutino, F. R., Pruzek, R., Steger, J. A., and Meshoulam, U. Immediate visual recall in poor and normal readers as a function of orthographic-linguistic familiarity. *Cortex*, 1973, *9*, 368–384.

Vellutino, F. R., Harding, C. J., Phillips, F., and Steger, J. A. Differential transfer in poor and normal readers. *Journal of Genetic Psychology*, 1975a, *126*, 3–18.

Vellutino, F. R., Smith, H., Steger, J. A., and Kamin, M. Reading disability: age differences and the perceptual-deficit hypothesis. *Child Development*, 1975b, *46*, 487–493.

Vellutino, F. R., Steger, J. A., DeSetto, L., and Phillips, F. Immediate and delayed recognition of visual stimuli in poor and normal readers. *Journal of Experimental Child Psychology*, 1975c, *19*, 223–232.

Vellutino, F. R., Steger, J. A., Harding, C. J., and Phillips, F. Verbal vs. non-verbal paired-associates learning in poor and normal readers. *Neuropsychologia*, 1975d, *13*, 75–82.

Vellutino, F. R., Steger, J. A., Kaman, M., and DeSetto, L. Visual form perception in deficient and normal readers as a function of age and orthographic linguistic familiarity. *Cortex*, 1975e, *11*, 22–30.

Vellutino, F. R., Steger, J. A., and Kandel, G. Reading disability: an investigation of the perceptual deficit hypothesis. *Cortex*, 1972, *8*, 106–118.

Vellutino, F. F., Steger, J. A., and Pruzek, R. Inter- vs. intrasensory deficit in paired associate learning in poor and normal readers. *Canadian Journal of Behavioral Science*, 1973, *5*, 111–123.

Vernon, M. D. *Backwardness in reading, a study of its nature and origin.* Cambridge, England: Cambridge University Press, 1957.

Vernon, M. D. *Reading and its difficulties.* Cambridge, England: Cambridge University Press, 1971.

Vernon, P. E. Heredity and environment: present position of the problem. XXI International Congress of Psychology. Paris, France, July 1976.

Virkkunen, M. and Nuutila, A. Specific reading retardation, hyperactive child syndrome, and juvenile delinquency. *Acta Psychiatrica Scandinavia*, 1976, *54*, 25–28.

Vogel, S. A. Syntactic abilities in normal and dyslexic children. *Journal of Learning Disabilities*, 1974, *7*, 103–109.

Volterra, V. and Giordani, L. Considerazioni electrocliniche su 193 soggetti con EEG caratterizzato da punte e punte-onda in regione occipitale. *G. Psichiat. Neuropat.*, 1966, *94*, 337–373.

Waddington, C. H. *The Strategy of Genes.* London: George Allen & Unwin, Ltd., 1957.

Wallach, M. and Wallach, L. *Teaching all children to read.* Chicago: University of Chicago Press, 1976.

Walker, L. and Cole, E. M. Familial patterns of expression of specific reading disability in a population sample. *Bulletin of the Orton Society,* 1965, *15.*

Waller, T. G. Children's recognition memory for written sentences: a comparison of good and poor readers. *Child Development,* 1976, 47, 90–95.

Walter, R., Yeager, C., and Rubin, H. An EEG survey with activation techniques of "undifferentiated" mental deficiency. *American Journal of Mental Deficiency,* 1956, 60, 785–791.

Warren, D. H., Andoshian, L. J., and Widawski, M. H. Measures of visual-auditory integration and their relations to reading achievement in early grades. *Perceptual and Motor Skills,* 1975, *41,* 615–630.

Warren, R. M. Auditory temporal discrimination by trained listeners. *Cognitive Psychology,* 1974, *6,* 237–256.

Warrington, E. K. The incidence of verbal disability associated with retardation reading. *Neuropsychologia,* 1967, *5,* 175–179.

Watt, N. F. and Lubensky, A. W. Childhood roots of schizophrenia. *Journal of Consulting and Clinical Psychology,* 1976, 44, 363–375.

Waugh, N. C. and Norman, D. A. Primary memory. *Psychological Review,* 1965, *72,* 89–104.

Weatherall, D. J. Thalassemia: historical introduction. *Johns Hopkins Medical Journal,* 1976a, *139,* 194–195.

Weatherall, D. J. The molecular basis of thalassemia. *Johns Hopkins Medical Journal,* 1976b, *139,* 205–210.

Webb, E. M. and Lawson, L. The EEG in severe speech and reading disabilities of childhood. *Electroencephalography & Clinical Neurophysiology,* 1956, 8, 168.

Weber, R. M. First-graders' use of grammatical context in reading. In H. Levin and J. P. Williams (Eds.), *Basic Studies on Reading.* New York: Basic Books, 1970.

Wechsler, D. *Wechsler Intelligence Scale for Children.* New York: Psychological Corporation, 1949.

Wedell, K. and Horne, I. E. Some aspects of perceptual-motor disability in 5½ year-old children. *British Journal of Educational Psychology,* 1969, *39,* 174–182.

Weigl, E. Zur Schriftsprache und ihren Erwerb: Neuropsychologische und psycholinguistische Betrachtungen. Probleme und Ergebnisse der Psychologie, 1972, *43,* 45–105.

Weigl, E. Written language: acquisition and disturbances. In E. H. Lenneberg and E. Lenneberg (Eds.), *Foundations of Language Development: A Multidisciplinary Approach* (Vol. 2). New York: Academic Press, 1975.

Weikart, D. P. (Ed.) *Preschool intervention: a preliminary report of the Perry Preschool Project.* Ann Arbor, Mich.: Campus Publishers, 1967.

Weikart, D. P. Relationship of curriculum, teaching and learning in preschool education. In J. Stanley (Ed.), *Preschool Programs for the Disadvantaged.* Baltimore: Johns Hopkins Press, 1972.

Weikert, D. P., DeLoria, D., Lawsen, S. et al. *Longitudinal Results of the Ypsilanti*

Perry Preschool Project. Ypsilanti, Mich.: High/Scope Educational Research Foundation, 1970.

Weinberg, W. A., Dieta, S. G., Penic, E. C., and McAlister, W. H. Intelligence, reading achievement, physical size and social class. *Journal of Paediatrics,* 1974, *85,* 482–489.

Weinstein, R. and Rabinovitch, M. S. Sentence structure and retention in good and poor readers. *Journal of Educational Psychology,* 1971, *62,* 1, 25–30.

Weinstein, S. Deficits concomitant with aphasia or lesions of either cerebral hemisphere. *Cortex,* 1964, *1,* 154–169.

Wepman, J. M. *Auditory discrimination test.* Chicago: Language Research Associates, 1958.

Wepman, J. M. Auditory discrimination, speech, and reading. *The Elementary School Journal,* 1960, *9,* 325–333.

Wepman, J. M. The interrelationships of hearing, speech and reading. *The Reading Teacher,* 1961, *14,* 245–247.

Wepman, J. The perceptual basis for learning. In H. M. Robinson (Ed.), *Meeting Individual Differences in Reading.* Suppl. Educ. Monogr. 94, 25–33. Chicago: The University of Chicago Press, 1964.

Wepman, J. M. Modalities and learning. In H. M. Robinson (Ed.), *Coordinating Reading Instruction.* Glenview, Ill.: Scott, Foresman, 1971.

Wesman, A. G. Intelligent testing. *American Psychologist,* 1968, *23,* 267–274.

White, M. Does cerebral dominance offer a sufficient explanation for laterality differences in tachistoscopic recognition? *Perceptual and Motor Skills,* 1973, *36,* 479–485.

White, S. H. Evidence for a hierarchical arrangement of learning processes. *Advances in Child Development and Behavior.* New York: Academic Press, 1965, *2,* 187–220.

Wiener, M. and Cromer, W. Reading and reading difficulty: a conceptual analysis. *Harvard Educational Review,* 1967, *37,* 620–643.

Wiig, E. H., Semel, M. S., and Crouse, M. B. The use of English morphology by high-risk and learning disabled children. *Journal of Learning Disabilities,* 1973, *6,* 7, 457–465.

Willows, D. M. Reading between the lines: selective attention in good and poor readers. *Child Development,* 1974, *45,* 408–415.

Wilson, R. S. Twins: early mental development. *Science,* 1972, *175,* 914–917.

Winters, J. J., Gerjuoy, I. R., Crown, P., and Gorrell, R. Eye movements and verbal reports in tachistoscopic recognition by normals and retardates. *Child Development,* 1967, *38,* 1193–1199.

Wintrobe, M. M. *Clinical hematology* (p. 507). Philadelphia: Lea & Febiger, 1942.

Wintrobe, M. M., Lee, G. R., Boggs, D. R., Bithell, T. C., Athens, J. W., and Foerster, J. *Clinical Hematology.* Philadelphia: Lea & Febiger, 1974, 855–856.

Witelson, S. F. Brain lateralization in children: normal and dyslexic. 1975 (unpublished manuscript).

Witelson, S. F. Abnormal right hemisphere functional specialization in developmental dyslexia. In R. M. Knights and D. J. Bakker (Eds.), *Neuropsychology of*

Learning Disorders: Theoretical Approaches. Baltimore: University Park Press, 1976a.

Witelson, S. F. Sex and the single hemisphere: right hemisphere specialization for spatial processing. *Science,* 1976b, *193,* 425–427.

Witelson, S. Developmental dyslexia: two right hemispheres and none left. *Science,* 1977, *195,* 309–311.

Witelson, S. F. and Rabinovitch, M. S. Hemispheric speech lateralization in children with auditory-linguistic deficits. *Cortex,* 1972, *8,* 412–426.

Witsell, L. and Silver, A. A. Etiology and classification of reading problems. In A. A. Silver and A. Hayes (Eds.), *Report of the Interdisciplinary Committee on Reading Problems.* Washington, D.C.: Center for Applied Linguistics, 1971.

Wolff, P. H. and Hurwitz, I. Functional implications of the minimal brain damage syndrome. In S. Walzer and P. H. Wolff (Eds.), *Minimal Cerebral Dysfunction in Children.* New York and London: Grune and Stratton, 1973.

Wood, C., Goff, W., and Day, R. Auditory evoked potentials during speech perception. *Science,* 1971, *173,* 1248.

Woodcock, R. W. and Clark, C. R. *Peabody Rebus Reading Program.* Circle Pines, Minn.: American Guidance Service, 1969.

Woodruff, M. L. Subconvulsive epileptiform discharge and behavior impairment. *Behavioral Biology,* 1974, *11,* 431–458.

Worthen, B. and Sanders, J. *Educational evaluation: theory and practice.* Worthington, Ohio: Charles Jones, 1973.

Wright, P. W. Reading problems and delinquency. Paper presented at World Congress on Dyslexia, Mayo Clinic, 1974.

Yeni-Komshian, G. H., Isenberg, P., and Goldberg, H. Cerebral dominance and reading disability: left visual-field deficit in poor readers. *Neuropsychologia,* 1975, *13,* 83–94.

Young, F. A. and Lindsley, D. B. *Early experience and visual information processing in perceptual and reading disorders.* Washington, D.C.: National Academy of Sciences, 1971.

Young, G. C. and Rourke, B. P. A comparison of visual and auditory sequencing in good and poor readers in grades two and six. Paper presented at the meeting of the Canadian Psychological Association, Quebec, June 1975.

Ysseldyke, J. E. Diagnostic-prescriptive teaching: the search for aptitude-treatment interactions. In L. Mann and D. Sabatino (Eds.), *The First Review of Special Education* (Vol. 1). Philadelphia: Buttonwood Farms, 1973.

Ysseldyke, J. E. and Salvia, J. Methodological problems in aptitude treatment interaction research with intact groups. University Park, Pa.: mimeograph, 1975.

Yule, B. and Rutter, M. Unpublished data, 1976.

Yule, W. Predicting reading ages on Neale's analysis of reading ability. *British Journal of Educational Psychology,* 1967, *37,* 252–255.

Yule, W. Differential prognosis of reading backwardness and specific reading retardation. *British Journal of Educational Psychology,* 1973, *43,* 244–248.

Yule, W. and Rutter, M. The epidemiology and social implications of specific reading retardation. In R. Knights and D. J. Bakker (Eds.), *The Neuropsychology of Learning Disorders: Theoretical Approaches.* Proceedings of NATO Conference, Baltimore: University Park Press, 1976.

Yule, W., Rutter, M., Berger, M., and Thompson, J. Over- and under-achievement in reading: distribution in the general population. *British Journal of Educational Psychology,* 1974, *44,* 1–12.

Zangwill, O. L. *Cerebral dominance and its relation to psychological function.* Edinburgh: Oliver & Boyd, 1960.

Zangwill, O. L. Dyslexia in relation to cerebral dominance. In J. Money (Ed.), *Reading Disability: Progress and Research Needs in Dyslexia.* Baltimore: Johns Hopkins Press, 1962.

Zerbin-Rudin, E. Congenital word blindness. *Bulletin of the Orton Society,* 1967, *17,* 47–54.

Zifcak, M. Phonological awareness and reading acquisition in first grade children. Unpublished doctoral dissertation, University of Connecticut, 1976.

Zigmond, N. Intrasensory and intersensory processes in normal and dyslexic children. Unpublished doctoral dissertation, Northwestern University, 1966.

Zurif, E. B. and Carson, G. Dyslexia in relation to cerebral dominant temporal analysis. *Neuropsychologia,* 1970, *8,* 351–361.

INDEX